Family Maps
of
Jasper County, Illinois
Deluxe Edition

With Homesteads, Roads, Waterways, Towns, Cemeteries, Railroads, and More

Family Maps
of
Jasper County, Illinois
Deluxe Edition

With Homesteads, Roads, Waterways, Towns, Cemeteries, Railroads, and More

3 *Maps Per Township...*

Rivers, Creeks & Railroads

Roads

Homesteads & Other Land Patents

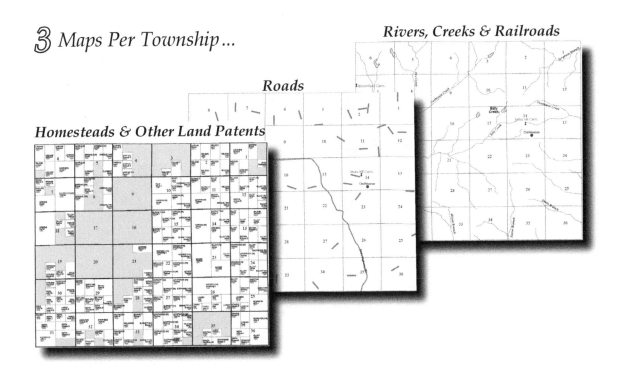

by Gregory A. Boyd, J.D.

Arphax Publishing Co.
www.arphax.com

Family Maps of Jasper County, Illinois, Deluxe Edition: With Homesteads, Roads, Waterways, Towns, Cemeteries, Railroads, and More.
by Gregory A. Boyd, J.D.

ISBN 1-4203-2027-0

Published by Arphax Publishing Co., 2210 Research Park Blvd., Norman, Oklahoma, USA 73069
www.arphax.com
1-800-681-5298

First Edition

ATTENTION HISTORICAL & GENEALOGICAL SOCIETIES, UNIVERSITIES, COLLEGES, CORPORATIONS, FAMILY REUNION COORDINATORS, AND PROFESSIONAL ORGANIZATIONS: Quantity discounts are available on bulk purchases of this book. For information, please contact Arphax Publishing Co., at the address listed above, or at (405) 366-6181, or visit our web-site at www.arphax.com and contact us through the "Bulk Sales" link.

—LEGAL—

The contents of this book rely on data published by the United States Government and its various agencies and departments, including but not limited to the General Land Office–Bureau of Land Management, the Department of the Interior, and the U.S. Census Bureau. The author has relied on said government agencies or re-sellers of its data, but makes no guarantee of the data's accuracy or of its representation herein, neither in its text nor maps. Said maps have been proportioned and scaled in a manner reflecting the author's primary goal—to make patentee names readable. This book will assist in the discovery of possible relationships between people, places, locales, rivers, streams, cemeteries, etc., but "proving" those relationships or exact geographic locations of any of the elements contained in the maps will require the use of other source material, which could include, but not be limited to: land patents, surveys, the patentees' applications, professionally drawn road-maps, etc.

Neither the author nor publisher makes any claim that the contents herein represent a complete or accurate record of the data it presents and disclaims any liability for reader's use of the book's contents. Many circumstances exist where human, computer, or data delivery errors could cause records to have been missed or to be inaccurately represented herein. Neither the author nor publisher shall assume any liability whatsoever for errors, inaccuracies, omissions or other inconsistencies herein.

Many thanks to the Illinois State Archives for permission to use its "Tract Sales" database index in the preparation of this book. All parcel/patent data presented here were derived from records in the Archive's web-pages available through:
http://www.cyberdriveillinois.com/departments/archives/data_lan.html

Editor: Vicki Boyd
Map Editor: Raine Boyd

This book is dedicated to my wonderful family:

Vicki, Jordan, & Amy Boyd

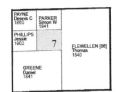

Contents

- Part I -

The Big Picture

- Part II -

Township Map Groups

(each Map Group contains a Patent Index, Patent Map, Road Map, & Historical Map)

Appendices

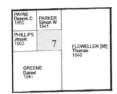

Preface

The quest for the discovery of my ancestors' origins, migrations, beliefs, and life-ways has brought me rewards that I could never have imagined. The *Family Maps* series of books is my first effort to share with historical and genealogical researchers, some of the tools that I have developed to achieve my research goals. I firmly believe that this effort will allow many people to reap the same sorts of treasures that I have.

The Illinois State Archives (much like the Federal Government's Bureau of Land Management) has given genealogists and historians an incredible gift by virtue of its enormous database housed on its web-site at www.cyberdriveillinois.com. There, you can search for and find over half-a-million descriptions of original land-purchases in Illinois.

This Illinois Archives site is in a small class of truly unique web-sites that present such a vast collection of records for FREE. But, the site is not for the faint of heart, nor is it for those unwilling or unable to to sift through and analyze the thousands of records that exist for most counties.

My immediate goal with this series is to spare you the hundreds of hours of work that it would take you to map the Land Patents for this county. Every Jasper County homestead or land patent that I have gleaned from the Illinos State Archives database is mapped here (at least ones that can be). Consequently, I can usually show you in an instant, where your ancestor's land is located, as well as the names of nearby land-owners.

Originally, that was my primary goal. But after speaking to other genealogists, it became clear that there was much more that they wanted. Taking their advice set me back almost a full year, but I think you will agree it was worth the wait. Because now, you can learn so much more.

Now, this book answers these sorts of questions:

- Are there any variant spellings for surnames that I have missed in searching Illinois land-records?
- Where is my family's traditional home-place?
- What cemeteries are near Grandma's house?
- My Granddad used to swim in such-and-such-Creek—where is that?
- How close is this little community to that one?
- Are there any other people with the same surname who bought land in the county?
- How about cousins and in-laws—did they buy land in the area?

And these are just for starters!

The rules for using the *Family Maps* books are simple, but the strategies for success are many. Some techniques are apparent on first use, but many are gained with time and experience. Please take the time to notice the roads, cemeteries, creek-names, family names, and unique first-names throughout the whole county. You cannot imagine what YOU might be the first to discover.

I hope to learn that many of you have answered age-old research questions within these pages or that you have discovered relationships previously not even considered. When these sorts of things happen to you, will you please let me hear about it? I would like nothing better. My contact information can always be found at www.arphax.com.

One more thing: please read the "How To Use This Book" chapter; it starts on the next page. This will give you the very best chance to find the treasures that lie within these pages.

My family and I wish you the very best of luck, both in life, and in your research.   Greg Boyd

How to Use This Book - A Graphical Summary

Part I
"The Big Picture"

Map A ▸ Counties in the State
Map B ▸ Surrounding Counties
Map C ▸ Congressional Townships (Map Groups) in the County
Map D ▸ Cities & Towns in the County
Map E ▸ Cemeteries in the County
Surnames in the County ▸ Number of Land-Parcels for Each Surname
Surname/Township Index ▸ Directs you to Township Map Groups in Part II

The <u>Surname/Township Index</u> can direct you to any number of **Township Map Groups**

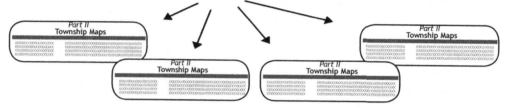

Part II
Township Map Groups
(1 for each Township in the County)

Each Township Map Group contains all four of of the following tools . . .

Land Patent Index ▸ Every-name Index of Patents Mapped in this Township
Land Patent Map ▸ Map of Patents as listed in above Index
Road Map ▸ Map of Roads, City-centers, and Cemeteries in the Township
Historical Map ▸ Map of Railroads, Lakes, Rivers, Creeks, City-Centers, and Cemeteries

Appendices

Appendix A ▸ Illinois State Archives Abbreviations
Appendix B ▸ Section-Parts / Aliquot Parts (a comprehensive list)
Appendix C ▸ Multi-patentee Groups (Individuals within Buying Groups)

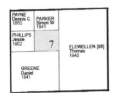

How to Use This Book

The two "Parts" of this *Family Maps* volume seek to answer two different types of questions. Part I deals with broad questions like: what counties surround Jasper County, are there any ASHCRAFTs in Jasper County, and if so, in which Townships or Maps can I find them? Ultimately, though, Part I should point you to a particular Township Map Group in Part II.

Part II concerns itself with details like: where exactly is this family's land, who else bought land in the area, and what roads and streams run through the land, or are located nearby. The Chart on the opposite page, and the remainder of this chapter attempt to convey to you the particulars of these two "parts", as well as how best to use them to achieve your research goals.

Part I
"The Big Picture"

Within Part I, you will find five "Big Picture" maps and two county-wide surname tools.

These include:

• Map A - Where Jasper County lies within the state
• Map B - Counties that surround Jasper County
• Map C - Congressional Townships of Jasper County (+ Map Group Numbers)
• Map D - Cities & Towns of Jasper County (with Index)
• Map E - Cemeteries of Jasper County (with Index)
• Surnames in Jasper County Patents (with Parcel-counts for each surname)
• Surname/Township Index (with Parcel-counts for each surname by Township)

The five "Big-Picture" Maps are fairly self-explanatory, yet should not be overlooked. This is particularly true of Maps "C", "D", and "E", all of which show Jasper County and its Congressional Townships (and their assigned Map Group Numbers).

Let me briefly explain this concept of Map Group Numbers. These are a device completely of our own invention. They were created to help you quickly locate maps without having to remember the full legal name of the various Congressional Townships. It is simply easier to remember "Map Group 1" than a legal name like: "Township 9-North Range 6-West, 5th Principal Meridian." But the fact is that the TRUE legal name for these Townships IS terribly important. These are the designations that others will be familiar with and you will need to accurately record them in your notes. This is why both Map Group numbers AND legal descriptions of Townships are almost always displayed together.

Map "C" will be your first intoduction to "Map Group Numbers", and that is all it contains: legal Township descriptions and their assigned Map Group Numbers. Once you get further into your research, and more immersed in the details, you will likely want to refer back to Map "C" from time to time, in order to regain your bearings on just where in the county you are researching.

Remember, township boundaries are a completely artificial device, created to standardize land descriptions. But do not let them become a boundary in your mind when choosing which townships to research. Your relative's in-laws, children, cousins, siblings, and mamas and papas, might just as easily have lived in the township next to the one your grandfather lived in—rather than in the one where he actually lived. So Map "C" can be your guide to which other Townships/ Map Groups you likewise ought to analyze.

Of course, the same holds true for County lines; this is the purpose behind Map "B". It shows you surrounding counties that you may want to consider for further reserarch.

Map "D", the Cities and Towns map, is the first map with an index. Map "E" is the second (Cemeteries). Both, Maps "D" and "E" give you broad views of City (or Cemetery) locations in the County. But they go much further by pointing you toward pertinent Township Map Groups so you can locate the patents, roads, and waterways located near a particular city or cemetery.

Once you are familiar with these *Family Maps* volumes and the county you are researching, the "Surnames In Jasper County" chapter (or its sister chapter in other volumes) is where you'll likely start your future research sessions. Here, you can quickly scan its few pages and see if anyone in the county possesses the surnames you are researching. The "Surnames in Jasper County" list shows only two things: surnames and the number of parcels of land we have located for that surname in Jasper County. But whether or not you immediately locate the surnames you are researching, please do not go any further without taking a few moments to scan ALL the surnames in these very few pages.

You cannot imagine how many lost ancestors are waiting to be found by someone willing to take just a little longer to scan the "Surnames In Jasper County" list. Misspellings and typographical errors abound in most any index of this sort. Don't miss out on finding your Kinard that was written Rynard or Cox that was written Lox. If it looks funny or wrong, it very often is. And one of those little errors may well be your relative.

Now, armed with a surname and the knowledge that it has one or more entries in this book, you are ready for the "Surname/Township Index." Unlike the "Surnames In Jasper County", which has only one line per Surname, the "Surname/Township Index" contains one line-item for each Township Map Group in which each surname is found. In other words, each line represents a different Township Map Group that you will need to review.

Specifically, each line of the Surname/Township

Index contains the following four columns of information:

1. Surname
2. Township Map Group Number (these Map Groups are found in Part II)
3. Parcels of Land (number of them with the given Surname within the Township)
4. Meridian/Township/Range (the legal description for this Township Map Group)

The key column here is that of the Township Map Group Number. While you should definitely record the Meridian, Township, and Range, you can do that later. Right now, you need to dig a little deeper. That Map Group Number tells you where in Part II that you need to start digging.

But before you leave the "Surname/Township Index", do the same thing that you did with the "Surnames in Jasper County" list: take a moment to scan the pages of the Index and see if there are similarly spelled or misspelled surnames that deserve your attention. Here again, is an easy opportunity to discover grossly misspelled family names with very little effort. Now you are ready to turn to . . .

Part II
"Township Map Groups"

You will normally arrive here in Part II after being directed to do so by one or more "Map Group Numbers" in the Surname/Township Index of Part I.

Each Map Group represents a set of four tools dedicated to a single Congressional Township that is either wholly or partially within the county. If you are trying to learn all that you can about a particular family or their land, then these tools should usually be viewed in the order they are presented.

These four tools include:

1. a Land Patent Index
2. a Land Patent Map
3. a Road Map, and
4. an Historical Map

As I mentioned earlier, each grouping of this sort is assigned a Map Group Number. So, let's now move on to a discussion of the four tools that make up one of these Township Map Groups.

Land Patent Index

Each Township Map Group's Index begins with a title, something along these lines:

MAP GROUP 1: Index to Land Patents
Township 16-North Range 5-West (2ⁿᵈ PM)

The Index contains eight (8) columns. They are:

1. ID (a unique ID number for this Individual and a corresponding Parcel of land in this Township)
2. Individual in Patent (name)
3. Sec. (Section), and
4. Sec. Part (Section Part, or Aliquot Part)
5. Purchase Date (Patent)
6. Sale Type (IL Archives Abbreviation).
7. IL Aliquot Part (more on this, below).
8. For More Info: varying information which often requires you to turn to Appendices A or C for clarification..

While most of these eight columns are self-explanatory, I will take a few moments to explain the "Sec. Part," "Purchase Date," "Sale Type, "IL Aliquot Part," and "For More Info" columns.

The "Sec. Part" column refers to what surveryors and other land professionals refer to as an Aliquot Part. The origins and use of such a term mean little to a non-surveyor, and I have chosen to simply call these sub-sections of land what they are: a "Section Part". No matter what we call them, what we are referring to are things like a quarter-section or half-section or quarter-quarter-section. See Appendix "B" for most of the "Section Parts" you will come across (and many you will not) and what size land-parcel they represent.

In the volumes in this series which rely on Illinois Archives data rather than on that of the Bureau of Land Management, this value is our translation

of that Aliquot Part as recorded by the Illinois Archives. Because the Archives chose to add much additional information to that value (more on this, below), sometimes the underlying Section Part is not ascertainable with complete certainty.

In short, the Sec. Part column will tell you where we mapped the parcel, whether or not that is where it actually lies. In the vast majority of cases, we feel like we will hit the spot.

The "Purchase Date" column displays just that: the date on which the patentee signed the necessary documents in the relevant Land Office, in order to seek his or her land-claim. This value differs from that stored in the BLM databases (and in our books based on them) where the "Issue date" is given---the "issue-date" is a later date on which the Federal Government effectively finalized the transaction.

The "Sale Type" column offers an abbreviation which you can locate in Appendix A. The vast majority of the patents here will be noted as an "FD" (Federal) sale-type.

The "IL Aliquot Part" column is one which we include as a response to the problem we identified above: sometimes we cannot ascertain the true location of the land based on the the Illinois Archive's stated "Aliquot Part." We do not state this as any sort of criticism: I challenge anyone to read a few hundred of these patents (particularly in urban areas or along rivers or canals) and try to come up with a standard way to describe the legal descriptions they contain---frankly, such a chore is beyond that which most of us would choose to entertain.

The Archives had a hard-time decyphering these legal descriptions, as did we. And because of this confession, we repeat, verbatim, the "IL Aliquot Part" in each Patent-Index so you may see what source information we used in our decision-making. We acknowledge that you may come to a different conclusion as to where some of these parcels actually lie.

A couple of final points need be made with regard to this "IL Aliquot Part" column.

First, if the meaning of its contents are not readily apparent, then it is likely you have come across one of the numerous examples wherein the Archives tacked on information not technically belonging to a standard legal description (and yet existed in the underlying patent). For instance, you may find a value like "NWNANDWRR." I hate to tell you, but this could mean several things: the northwest-quarter section, north and west of Rock River, being one reasonable intepretation, but there could be others. See Appendix "A" for the numerous abbreviations used in these descriptions.

Next, if the "IL Aliquot Part" entry contains the words "Lot" or "Block" or begins with either "L" or "B" and is then followed by a number (and sometimes an alphabetic character), then this is a lot. Its whereabouts within a section cannot be ascertained with the legal description alone, and so we cannot map them with the resources we possess. This does not thwart the uses for which we contemplate this series will be used, but we want you to be aware that you will need to locate plat-maps from the individual counties if you need to more precisely locate land within lots. We do list the lots out for you in the map, so you can know which section they fall within.

The "For More Info" column of the Index is variable in its content from one patent to another, as is the case with the underlying data provided by the Illinois Archives. There are three primary possible items you may find here, as evinced by looking at a sample of the Legend which accompanies each Patent-Map Index:

LEGEND
"For More Info . . . " column

G = Group (Multi-Patentee Patent, see Appendix "C")
R = Residence
S = Social Status

Below, I will explain what each of these items means to you as a researcher.

G = Group

(Multi-Patentee Patent, see Appendix "C")
A "G" designation means that the Patent was is-sued to a GROUP of people (Multi-patentees). The "G" will always be followed by a number. Some such groups were quite large and it was impractical if not impossible to display each individual in our maps without unduly affecting readability. EACH person in the group is named in the Index, but they won't all be found on the Map. You will find the name of only person listed in such a Group on the map with the Group number next to it, enclosed in [square brackets]. That square bracket [   ] is your key to locating patents on the patent map.

To find all the members of the Group you can either scan the Index for all people with the same Group Number or you can simply refer to Appendix "C" where all members of the Group are listed next to their number.

R = Residence

Though only a fraction of the patents here contain this wonderful bit of data, those which do, offer up a nice windfall to many researchers. This value comes from the language in patents which often includes words like "John Smith of Franklin County" or some similiar verbiage. There are people identified as having been "from" numerous states. If the location is within Illinois, usually we are given simply the county name.

S = Social Status

Again, most patents are not accompanied by this information, but those which do, will contain a value that can be looked-up in the Abbreviations found in Appendix "C."

Land Patent Map

On the first two-page spread following each Township's Index to Land Patents, you'll find the corresponding Land Patent Map. And here lies the real heart of our work. For the first time anywhere, researchers will be able to observe and analyze, on a grand scale, most of the original land-owners for an area AND see them mapped in proximity to each one another.

We encourage you to make vigorous use of the accompanying Index described above, but then later, to abandon it, and just stare at these maps for a while. This is a great way to catch misspellings or to find collateral kin you'd not known were in the area.

Each Land Patent Map represents one Congressional Township containing approximately 36-square miles. Each of these square miles is labeled by an accompanying Section Number (1 through 36, in most cases). Keep in mind, that this book concerns itself solely with Jasper County's patents. Townships which creep into one or more other counties will not be shown in their entirety in any one book. You will need to consult other books, as they become available, in order to view other countys' patents, cities, cemeteries, etc.

But getting back to Jasper County: each Land Patent Map contains a Statistical Chart that looks like the following:

Township Statistics

Parcels Mapped	:	173
Number of Patents	:	163
Number of Individuals	:	152
Patentees Identified	:	151
Number of Surnames	:	137
Multi-Patentee Parcels	:	4
Oldest Patent Date	:	11/27/1820
Most Recent Patent	:	9/28/1917
Block/Lot Parcels	:	0
Cities and Towns	:	6
Cemeteries	:	6

This information may be of more use to a social statistician or historian than a genealogist, but I think all three will find it interesting.

Most of the statistics are self-explanatory, and what is not, was described in the above discussion of the Index's Legend, but I do want to mention a few of them that may affect your understanding of the Land Patent Maps.

First of all, Patents often contain more than one

Parcel of land, so it is common for there to be more Parcels than Patents. Also, the Number of Individuals will more often than not, not match the number of Patentees. A Patentee is literally the person or PERSONS named in a patent. So, a Patent may have a multi-person Patentee or a single-person patentee. Nonetheless, we account for all these individuals in our indexes.

On the lower-righthand side of the Patent Map is a Legend which describes various features in the map, including Section Boundaries, Patent (land) Boundaries, Lots (numbered), and Multi-Patentee Group Numbers. You'll also find a "Helpful Hints" Box that will assist you.

One important note: though the vast majority of Patents mapped in this series will prove to be reasonably accurate representations of their actual locations, we cannot claim this for patents lying along state and county lines, or waterways, or that have been platted (lots). Shifting boundaries and sparse legal descriptions in the Illinois Archives data make this a reality that we have nonetheless tried to overcome by estimating these patents' locations the best that we can.

Road Map

On the two-page spread following each Patent Map you will find a Road Map covering the exact same area (the same Congressional Township).

For me, fully exploring the past means that every once in a while I must leave the library and travel to the actual locations where my ancestors once walked and worked the land. Our Township Road Maps are a great place to begin such a quest.

Keep in mind that the scaling and proportion of these maps was chosen in order to squeeze hundreds of people-names, road-names, and place-names into tinier spaces than you would traditionally see. These are not professional road-maps, and like any secondary genealogical source, should be looked upon as an entry-way to original sources—in this case, original patents and applications, professionally produced maps and surveys, etc.

Both our Road Maps and Historical Maps contain cemeteries and city-centers, along with a listing of these on the left-hand side of the map. I should note that I am showing you city center-points, rather than city-limit boundaries, because in many instances, this will represent a place where settlement began. This may be a good time to mention that many cemeteries are located on private property, Always check with a local historical or genealogical society to see if a particular cemetery is publicly accessible (if it is not obviously so). As a final point, look for your surnames among the road-names. You will often be surprised by what you find.

Historical Map

The third and final map in each Map Group is our attempt to display what each Township might have looked like before the advent of modern roads. In frontier times, people were usually more determined to settle near rivers and creeks than they were near roads, which were often few and far between. As was the case with the Road Map, we've included the same cemeteries and city-centers. We've also included railroads, many of which came along before most roads.

While some may claim "Historical Map" to be a bit of a misnomer for this tool, we settled for this label simply because it was almost as accurate as saying "Railroads, Lakes, Rivers, Cities, and Cemeteries," and it is much easier to remember.

In Closing . . .

By way of example, here is *A Really Good Way to Use a Township Map Group*. First, find the person you are researching in the Township's Index to Land Patents, which will direct you to the proper Section and parcel on the Patent Map. But before leaving the Index, scan all the patents within it, looking for other names of interest. Now, turn to the Patent Map and locate your parcels of land. Pay special attention to the names of patent-holders who own land surrounding your person of interest. Next,

turn the page and look at the same Section(s) on the Road Map. Note which roads are closest to your parcels and also the names of nearby towns and cemeteries. Using other resources, you may be able to learn of kin who have been buried here, plus, you may choose to visit these cemeteries the next time you are in the area.

Finally, turn to the Historical Map. Look once more at the same Sections where you found your research subject's land. Note the nearby streams, creeks, and other geographical features. You may be surprised to find family names were used to name them, or you may see a name you haven't heard mentioned in years and years—and a new research possibility is born.

Many more techniques for using these *Family Maps* volumes will no doubt be discovered. If from time to time, you will navigate to Jasper County's web-page at www.arphax.com (use the "Research" link), you can learn new tricks as they become known (or you can share ones you have employed). But for now, you are ready to get started. So, go, and good luck.

Postscript: these "Illinois Archives" editions, though substantially similar to their "GLO" (General Land Office) counterparts, do have a few important differences. First, Illinois has indexed far more patents (for Illinois, of course) than has the GLO and second, the Illinois data contains the residences for numerous patentees. In order to make room for this latter benefit, we have, by necessity, had to remove some features that are present in the GLO indexes: for example the noting of cancellations, overlaps, re-issues, and the like. We think the trade-off is a minor one and that on balance, the increased research value is enormous.

– Part I –

The Big Picture

Map A - Where Jasper County, Illinois Lies Within the State

——— Legend ———

State Boundary

County Boundaries

Jasper County, Illinois

——— Helpful Hints ———

1   We start with Map "A" which simply shows us where within the State this county lies.

2   Map "B" zooms in further to help us more easily identify surrounding Counties.

3   Map "C" zooms in even further to reveal the Congressional Townships that either lie within or intersect Jasper County.

Map B - Jasper County, Illinois and Surrounding Counties

Shelby

Cumberland

Clark

Effingham

Jasper

Illinois

Crawford

Clay

Lawrence

Richland

——— Legend ———

—— State Boundaries (when applicable)

—— County Boundaries

——— Helpful Hints ———

1 Many Patent-holders and their families settled across county lines. It is always a good idea to check nearby counties for your families.

2 Refer to Map "A" to see a broader view of where this County lies within the State, and Map "C" to see which Congressional Townships lie within Jasper County.

Map C - Congressional Townships of Jasper County, Illinois

Map Group 1 Township 8-N Range 8-E	Map Group 2 Township 8-N Range 9-E	Map Group 3 Township 8-N Range 10-E	Map Group 4 Township 8-N Range 11-E	Map Group 5 Township 8-N Range 14-W
Map Group 6 Township 7-N Range 8-E	Map Group 7 Township 7-N Range 9-E	Map Group 8 Township 7-N Range 10-E	Map Group 9 Township 7-N Range 11-E	Map Group 10 Township 7-N Range 14-W
Map Group 11 Township 6-N Range 8-E	Map Group 12 Township 6-N Range 9-E	Map Group 13 Township 6-N Range 10-E	Map Group 14 Township 6-N Range 11-E	Map Group 15 Township 6-N Range 14-W
Map Group 16 Township 5-N Range 8-E	Map Group 17 Township 5-N Range 9-E	Map Group 18 Township 5-N Range 10-E	Map Group 19 Township 5-N Range 11-E	Map Group 20 Township 5-N Range 14-W

——— Legend ———

Jasper County, Illinois

Congressional Townships

——— Helpful Hints ———

1 Many Patent-holders and their families settled across county lines. It is always a good idea to check nearby counties for your families (See Map "B").

2 Refer to Map "A" to see a broader view of where this county lies within the State, and Map "B" for a view of the counties surrounding Jasper County.

Map D Index: Cities & Towns of Jasper County, Illinois

The following represents the Cities and Towns of Jasper County (along with the corresponding Map Group in which each is found). Cities and Towns are displayed in both the Road and Historical maps in the Group.

City/Town	Map Group No.
Advance	4
Bogota	12
Boos	13
Brookville	8
Falmouth	8
Gila	2
Hidalgo	3
Hunt City	9
Island Grove	1
Latona	11
Lis	7
Newton	12
Plainfield	3
Point Pleasant	3
Raeftown	20
Rafetown	20
Rose Hill	3
Sainte Marie	14
Shamrock	17
West Liberty	18
Wheeler	6
Willow Hill	9
Yale	5

Map D - Cities & Towns of Jasper County, Illinois

Map Group 1 Township 8-N Range 8-E ● Island Grove	Map Group 2 Township 8-N Range 9-E ● Gila	Map Group 3 Township 8-N Range 10-E ● Hidalgo ● Point Pleasant ● ● Plainfield Rose Hill	Map Group 4 Township 8-N Range 11-E Advance ● ● Yale	Map Group 5 Township 8-N Range 14-W
Map Group 6 Township 7-N Range 8-E ● Wheeler ● Lis	Map Group 7 Township 7-N Range 9-E	Map Group 8 Township 7-N Range 10-E ● Falmouth ● Brookville	Map Group 9 Township 7-N Range 11-E Hunt City ● Willow Hill	Map Group 10 Township 7-N Range 14-W
Map Group 11 Township 6-N Range 8-E ● Latona	Map Group 12 Township 6-N Range 9-E Newton ● ● Bogota	Map Group 13 Township 6-N Range 10-E ● Boos	Map Group 14 Township 6-N Range 11-E Sainte Marie ●	Map Group 15 Township 6-N Range 14-W
Map Group 16 Township 5-N Range 8-E	Map Group 17 Township 5-N Range 9-E ● Shamrock	Map Group 18 Township 5-N Range 10-E ● West Liberty	Map Group 19 Township 5-N Range 11-E	Map Group 20 Township 5-N Range 14-W ● Raeftown

──── Legend ────

☐ Jasper County, Illinois

☐ Congressional Townships

──── Helpful Hints ────

1 Cities and towns are marked only at their center-points as published by the USGS and/or NationalAtlas.gov. This often enables us to more closely approximate where these might have existed when first settled.

2 To see more specifically where these Cities & Towns are located within the county, refer to both the Road and Historical maps in the Map-Group referred to above. See also, the Map "D" Index on the opposite page.

Map E Index: Cemeteries of Jasper County, Illinois

The following represents many of the Cemeteries of Jasper County, along with the corresponding Township Map Group in which each is found. Cemeteries are displayed in both the Road and Historical maps in the Map Groups referred to below.

Cemetery	Map Group No.
Abbott Cem.	16
Andrews Cem.	3
Assumption Cem.	14
Aten Cem.	3
Backbone Cem.	5
Bailey Cem.	11
Baily Cem.	10
Bethel Cem.	5
Bethel Cem.	18
Bowers Cem.	7
Brewer Cem.	1
Brick Cem.	7
Brockville Cem.	8
Brooks Cem.	8
Brown Cem.	3
Chaple Cem.	7
Coburn Cem.	7
Cummins Cem.	12
Dark Bend Cem.	20
Debord Cem.	5
Devore Cem.	16
Diel Cem.	2
Edison Cem.	9
Fairfield Cem.	2
Foster Cem.	11
Freeman Cem.	11
Fulks Cem.	16
Gila Lutheran Cem.	2
Hankins Cem.	17
Hayes Cem.	2
Headyville Cem.	11
Hicks Cem.	2
Hidalgo Cem.	3
Honey Cem.	12
Island Creek Cem.	1
Jones Cem.	7
Kedron Cem.	11
Kibler Cem.	7
Kilgore Cem.	3
Lancaster Cem.	17
Leamon Cem.	5
Madison Cem.	8
McFadden Cem.	5
Miller Cem.	15
Mound Cem.	10
Myer Cem.	2
New Saint Peters Cem.	8
Old Saint Peters Cem.	8
Plainfield Cem.	3
Pleasant Ridge Cem.	12
Pleasant Valley Cem.	16
Redford Cem.	7
Riverside Cem.	12
Ross Cem.	3
Sainte Marie City Cem.	14
Sainte Valentine Cem.	15
Sand Rock Cem.	10
Shiloh Cem.	13
Songer Cem.	2

Cemetery	Map Group No.
South Muddy Cem.	16
Swick Cem.	3
Swick Family Cem.	3
Tate Cem.	12
Texler Cem.	11
Todd Cem.	10
Vanderhoof Cem.	13
Ward Cem.	2
West Lawn Cem.	12
Wheeler Cem.	6
Woods Cem.	17
Worthey Cem.	11
Worthy Cem.	11
Yager Cem.	15
Yale Cem.	4

Map E - Cemeteries of Jasper County, Illinois

Island Creek Cem.	Diel Cem. Hayes Cem.	Hidalgo Cem.	Debord Cem. Leamon Cem.
Map Group 1 Township 8-N Range 8-E	Myer Cem. Map Group 2 Township 8-N Range 9-E Ward Cem.	Swick Family Cem. Swick Cem. Map Group 3 Township 8-N Range 10-E Aten Cem. Andrews Cem.	Map Group 4 Township 8-N Range 11-E McFadden Cem. Map Group 5 Township 8-N Range 14-W Backbone Cem.
Brewer Cem.	Hicks Cem. Fairfield Cem. Gila Lutheran Cem. Songer Cem.	Plainfield Cem. Kilgore Cem. Brown Cem. Ross Cem.	Yale Cem. Bethel Cem.
Map Group 6 Township 7-N Range 8-E Wheeler Cem.	Redford Cem. Coburn Cem. Chaple Cem. Map Group 7 Township 7-N Range 9-E Bowers Cem. Kibler Cem. Jones Cem.	Brooks Cem. Madison Cem. Brockville Cem. Map Group 8 Township 7-N Range 10-E	Map Group 9 Township 7-N Range 11-E Baily Cem. Sand Rock Cem. Map Group 10 Township 7-N Range 14-W Mound Cem.
	Brick Cem.	New Saint Peters Cem. Old Saint Peters Cem.	Edison Cem. Todd Cem.
Bailey Cem. Texler Cem. Kedron Cem.	West Lawn Cem. Riverside Cem.	Shiloh Cem. Vanderhoof Cem.	Map Group 14 Township 6-N Range 11-E Miller Cem.
Map Group 11 Township 6-N Range 8-E Worthey Cem. Foster Cem. Freeman Cem. Worthy Cem. Headyville Cem.	Map Group 12 Township 6-N Range 9-E Tate Cem. Pleasant Cummins Cem. Honey Ridge Cem. Cem.	Map Group 13 Township 6-N Range 10-E	Sainte Marie City Cem. Map Group 15 Township 6-N Range 14-W Assumption Cem. Sainte Valentine Cem. Yager Cem.
South Muddy Cem. Abbott Cem. Fulks Cem. Pleasant Valley Cem. Devore Cem. Map Group 16 Township 5-N Range 8-E	Lancaster Cem. Woods Cem. Map Group 17 Township 5-N Range 9-E Hankins Cem.	Map Group 18 Township 5-N Range 10-E Bethel Cem.	Map Group 19 Township 5-N Range 11-E Map Group 20 Township 5-N Range 14-W Dark Bend Cem.

——— Helpful Hints ———

1 Cemeteries are marked at locations as published by the USGS and/or NationalAtlas.gov.

2 To see more specifically where these Cemeteries are located, refer to the Road & Historical maps in the Map-Group referred to above. See also, the Map "E" Index on the opposite page to make sure you don't miss any of the Cemeteries located within this Congressional township.

Surnames in Jasper County, Illinois Patents

The following list represents the surnames that we have located in Jasper County, Illinois Patents and the number of parcels that we have mapped for each one. Here is a quick way to determine the existence (or not) of Patents to be found in the subsequent indexes and maps of this volume.

Surname	# of Land Parcels	Surname	# of Land Parcels	Surname	# of Land Parcels	Surname	# of Land Parcels
ABELL	3	BECKWITH	4	BRODERICK	6	CHOATE	2
ABELS	1	BEELES	2	BROOK	1	CHRISMAN	3
ADAMI	2	BEESON	4	BROOKS	34	CHRISS	9
ADAMS	36	BEMUSDOFFER	3	BROWN	18	CHURCH	1
ADAMSON	14	BENEFIELD	3	BROWNFIELD	3	CLARK	25
ADKINS	2	BENFORD	1	BROWNING	1	CLAWSON	3
ADKINSON	3	BENNETT	3	BRUCE	3	CLEMANS	3
ADKISSON	1	BENSON	1	BRUMFIED	1	CLEMENS	2
AKIN	3	BERCASTLE	1	BRUMFIELD	1	CLEMENTS	3
ALEXANDER	37	BERLIN	1	BRYAN	7	CLEMMONS	3
ALLEN	6	BERRY	46	BRYANT	3	CLEMONS	6
ALLENTHARP	2	BEUSDOFFER	1	BRYER	1	CLUBB	2
ALLISON	16	BICKERS	2	BUCHANAN	1	COALE	2
ALMAN	1	BICKUS	2	BUCKINGHAM	1	COAN	1
AMES	7	BIDEL	1	BUEL	3	COCHRAN	1
ANDERSON	7	BIRD	1	BUFFINGTON	2	CODD	1
ANDREWS	9	BIRT	4	BUHLER	2	CODER	1
ANSPACK	1	BISHOP	1	BULEY	1	COGGESHALL	4
ANTHOFER	1	BLACK	18	BUNTAIN	1	COHOON	4
ANTON	2	BLACKBURN	5	BURCHAM	6	COLBORN	2
ARBUCKELL	1	BLAIR	3	BURCHARD	1	COLBOURN	2
ARBUCKLE	4	BLAKE	8	BURFORD	3	COLBURN	2
ARCHER	6	BLANKENSHIP	1	BURNES	4	COLEMAN	5
ARDERY	1	BLASDEL	5	BURNHAM	1	COLLINS	13
ARMSTRONG	1	BLIDE	1	BURT	1	COMER	1
ARNOLD	8	BLISS	1	BUSH	7	COMSTOCK	1
ASHCRAFT	1	BODLE	1	BUSSELL	3	CONDE	2
ASHCROFT	10	BOGARD	7	BUTLER	13	COOK	1
ASHER	2	BOHAMAN	8	BYERS	3	COOLEY	1
ATKINS	1	BOHANNAN	9	BYRD	3	COOPER	3
AUSTIN	1	BOLANDER	1	BYRN	3	CORBIN	3
AVERY	30	BOLDNEY	1	BYRNE	3	CORRIGAM	1
BACHMAN	1	BOLENDER	1	CALDWELL	15	CORRIGAN	2
BADGER	2	BONE	3	CAMPBELL	1	COTTINGHAM	1
BAILEY	22	BONER	1	CAREY	1	COURE	1
BAIN	9	BONHAM	8	CARMEAN	1	COWGER	2
BAKER	12	BOOLE	2	CAROTHERS	1	COX	18
BALDREY	1	BOOS	8	CARPENTER	2	COZARD	1
BALEY	4	BOOTH	2	CARR	5	CRAIG	13
BALL	7	BORING	1	CARRELL	1	CRAMER	12
BANTA	1	BOSS	1	CARSON	4	CRAVENS	10
BARBER	2	BOSTER	1	CARTER	23	CREASON	1
BARKER	1	BOTOFF	2	CASEY	2	CREWS	23
BARKLEY	2	BOWEN	1	CASJENS	1	CRITTENDEN	3
BARLOW	2	BOWERS	3	CASSITY	1	CRONER	2
BARNES	2	BOWMAN	12	CATERS	1	CROSS	2
BARNS	2	BOYD	3	CATHEN	1	CROUSE	1
BARRASIER	1	BRACKET	1	CATHER	8	CROWLEY	12
BARRATT	2	BRACKNEY	3	CATLIN	1	CROWS	5
BARRET	2	BRADBERRY	2	CATT	3	CRUME	2
BARRETT	18	BRADSHAW	16	CHABLE	1	CRUSE	3
BARTEE	2	BRASSIER	1	CHAMBERLAIN	3	CRUZAN	2
BARTELLS	1	BRAZIER	1	CHANEY	3	CULNANE	1
BARTLETT	3	BREES	2	CHAPAN	2	CUMMANS	3
BARTLEY	10	BREWER	9	CHAPMAN	45	CUMMING	1
BARTON	3	BRICKENRIDGE	1	CHASTAIN	1	CUMMINS	14
BASORE	1	BRIDGES	11	CHEEK	6	CUMMONS	1
BATES	1	BRIGES	1	CHERRY	2	CURRIE	5
BATMAN	3	BRIGHT	1	CHESMETT	1	CURTIS	13
BAUMAN	1	BRINDLEY	2	CHESNUT	4	CURTISS	2
BAXTER	1	BRISTOL	5	CHESTNUT	3	DABBINS	1
BEACH	2	BROCK	8	CHITTENDAN	2	DAILEY	1

Surname	# of Land Parcels	Surname	# of Land Parcels	Surname	# of Land Parcels	Surname	# of Land Parcels
DALE	2	EPPERSON	5	GARDWAIN	1	HAMPSTEN	2
DASHLER	1	ERVIN	3	GAREE	3	HAMPSTON	1
DAVIS	18	ESSEX	5	GARRET	1	HANDELY	1
DAVISSON	2	EUBANK	3	GARRETSON	2	HANDER	4
DAY	1	EVANS	24	GARRISON	3	HANDLEY	1
DE GAEGER	2	EVERMAN	5	GARS	1	HANKINS	3
DE YAEGER	1	EYER	1	GARWOOD	8	HANNA	1
DEBORD	1	FAGG	2	GASS	1	HANNAH	1
DEBOW	2	FARIS	1	GAULLOFF	1	HANNEMANN	2
DECKER	3	FARLEY	4	GAYER	3	HARBERT	1
DELOTT	1	FARRIS	1	GEDDES	4	HARDING	14
DENMAN	3	FASSETT	2	GHAIST	1	HARGIS	1
DENNIS	8	FATOOT	1	GHARST	2	HARLAND	1
DERLER	1	FAWCETT	2	GHURST	1	HARLEN	5
DHOM	2	FAWSETT	1	GIBSON	4	HARMON	11
DICKMAN	1	FEAR	2	GIFFORD	7	HARPER	1
DILLMAN	1	FEARS	6	GILBRETH	1	HARRAH	7
DILLMON	2	FEESER	7	GILLESPIE	1	HARRINGTON	2
DITTEMOORE	3	FELDKAMP	2	GILLHAM	3	HARRIS	84
DITTEMORE	5	FENTONSPREAD	1	GILLMORE	1	HARRISON	7
DIXON	6	FERGUSON	13	GILMORE	1	HARTING	2
DOBBINS	2	FERREE	4	GLOUR	1	HARTMAN	1
DODD	1	FICKLIN	3	GLOVER	1	HARTRICH	2
DOERR	1	FIELD	4	GOEPPNER	1	HARTRICK	8
DOGGETT	2	FIELDS	1	GOLDSBY	1	HASKET	4
DONNELL	2	FINCH	1	GOOD	3	HASTINGS	3
DORN	3	FINEY	1	GOODWIN	5	HAWKINS	1
DOTY	3	FISHER	8	GORE	2	HAWKS	2
DOUTHIT	2	FITCH	2	GORNELL	2	HAWLEY	1
DOVEL	4	FITHIAN	15	GORRELL	1	HAWS	3
DOWELL	3	FLEANER	2	GORSLINE	1	HAY	5
DOWNER	1	FLEENER	2	GOSNELL	22	HAYDEN	1
DOWNEY	1	FLETCHER	3	GOSS	2	HAYES	6
DOWNS	1	FLINT	1	GOULD	6	HAYS	22
DOYLE	1	FOGLE	2	GRAVES	2	HAZELTON	2
DRAKE	6	FOGLER	2	GRAY	3	HEADY	7
DRYSDALE	3	FOLTZ	14	GREELY	7	HEARD	1
DUGAN	4	FOOR	1	GREEN	5	HEFFERNAN	1
DULGOR	1	FOOT	6	GREGORY	7	HEFNER	1
DUNCAN	1	FORCE	1	GRIFFING	3	HELMICK	2
DUNEGAN	1	FORD	1	GRIFFITH	3	HELVET	1
DUNGAN	2	FORE	3	GRIFFY	3	HENDERSON	4
DURHAM	1	FOREMAN	3	GRIMES	1	HENDRICKSON	1
DURKEY	1	FORESMAN	10	GROOTHINS	1	HENRICK	1
DUTELL	3	FOSTER	21	GROVE	14	HENSLEY	8
DUVAL	1	FOUST	5	GROVES	2	HEPNER	2
DUVALL	1	FOWLER	3	GRRELY	1	HERRON	14
EAGLETON	4	FOX	6	GRUB	3	HESLER	3
EAMES	1	FRAKES	1	GRUBB	1	HESS	1
EARLY	2	FRANCIS	1	GRUBBS	4	HETON	1
EARNEST	1	FRANKE	2	GUERIN	1	HICKS	2
EASTON	1	FRAZIER	3	GUGUMUS	1	HIGGINS	10
EATON	15	FREEMAN	8	GULLION	1	HILDERBRAND	1
EBALING	2	FRENCH	3	GUTHNICK	1	HILL	6
EBELING	1	FRIEDLEY	2	GUYNN	1	HILLBRANT	1
EBLEN	2	FRIEDLIEN	1	HACKNEY	1	HILLS	2
ECKARDT	1	FROST	2	HAGEMAN	3	HILLYER	2
EDERER	1	FRUCHTEL	1	HAGIMAN	4	HINDS	4
EDGERTON	2	FRUICHTEL	1	HAGY	1	HINES	1
EDWARDS	9	FRY	1	HALE	1	HINMAN	14
EICHER	2	FULLER	16	HALEY	3	HINTON	3
EILERS	1	FULTON	4	HALFHILL	1	HOARE	2
ELDER	21	GAINES	1	HALL	3	HODGE	1
ELIOT	1	GAINS	1	HALLENBECK	4	HOFFMAN	2
ELLIOTT	5	GALBREATH	2	HALSEY	11	HOFMAN	2
ELSON	4	GAMBRIEL	1	HALSTED	1	HOGUE	3
ELSTON	1	GARDENWINE	1	HAMIL	1	HOKE	1
ELY	1	GARDEWAIN	3	HAMILTON	8	HOLINGER	1
EMBODY	1	GARDINER	1	HAMMER	13	HOLLINGSWORTH	1
EMERSON	4	GARDNER	5	HAMPELMAN	2	HOLLOM	1

Surname	# of Land Parcels	Surname	# of Land Parcels	Surname	# of Land Parcels	Surname	# of Land Parcels
HOLLOPETERS	4	KELLY	29	LIDEY	9	MCCLELLAND	1
HOLM	7	KENEIPP	1	LIGHTNER	2	MCCLURE	3
HOLMES	1	KENNEDY	1	LILLY	5	MCCOLLUM	4
HOLSCHER	2	KENNERLY	1	LINDER	1	MCCOMAS	5
HOLT	1	KEPLER	1	LINDLEY	1	MCCOMMIS	1
HONEY	2	KEPLEY	1	LINK	1	MCCOOMAS	1
HOOVER	5	KERN	2	LINN	7	MCCORMICK	2
HOUGE	1	KESSLER	5	LINTHIEUM	2	MCCORNAS	1
HOUSE	4	KESTER	1	LIPTRAP	1	MCCOY	5
HOUSTON	8	KESTERSON	1	LISTER	1	MCCRACKEN	2
HOWARD	6	KETTLE	5	LITTLE	2	MCCRILLIS	1
HOWE	3	KIBLER	66	LITTON	1	MCCUBBIN	1
HOWELL	1	KIBLINGER	1	LITZELMANN	1	MCCUBBINS	9
HUDDLESTON	2	KILBOURN	2	LITZERMAN	1	MCCULLOUGH	11
HUDDLESTUN	3	KILGORE	1	LLOYD	1	MCDANIEL	17
HUDSON	1	KILLGORE	2	LOBMAIER	1	MCDONALD	2
HUFF	2	KING	14	LOGAN	1	MCDONNEL	1
HUFFARD	1	KINSLOW	2	LOLLAR	1	MCGAHEY	8
HUFFMAN	1	KINTZEL	2	LONG	9	MCGARNEY	1
HUGGINS	1	KIRKWOOD	3	LORANCE	2	MCGINNESS	2
HUGHES	4	KITCHELL	4	LOUGH	1	MCILVOY	8
HUGHS	2	KITTLE	1	LOVE	1	MCILWAIN	4
HUME	11	KLEIN	1	LOY	1	MCKAY	2
HUMES	1	KNIGHT	1	LUERSEN	1	MCKEARBY	1
HUMFREY	1	KOEBELE	1	LUSTIG	1	MCKEE	5
HUNT	27	KOONS	2	LUX	4	MCKINLEY	9
HUNTER	3	KOONTZ	3	LYONS	4	MCKINLY	2
HURD	1	KRAASS	1	MACHER	2	MCKINNEY	9
HURING	2	KRAUS	2	MACY	1	MCKINSTER	2
HURST	5	KRITOSER	2	MADDEN	3	MCKNIGHT	2
HUSHAW	3	KROUS	1	MAGILL	1	MCMANAMY	1
HUSSONG	2	KROUSE	1	MAHAN	1	MCNAIR	10
HUTSON	13	KRUZAN	2	MAIER	3	MCNIGHT	1
HYATT	1	KUYKENDALL	1	MALLORY	1	MCNUTT	1
INGLE	5	LAGOW	2	MALONE	2	MCPEAK	1
IRELAND	6	LAKE	2	MAMMOPER	1	MCQUAID	4
IRVIN	1	LAMASTERS	2	MAMMOSER	2	MCQUEEN	4
ISLEY	7	LAMB	1	MANDLOVE	1	MCQUISTON	3
JACK	1	LAMBERT	6	MANLEY	1	MCRENLEY	4
JACKSON	20	LAMM	1	MANNING	3	MEAKER	1
JAMES	10	LANCASTER	3	MARK	1	MEANS	1
JARED	6	LANCE	3	MARKLAND	2	MEDKIFF	1
JARRED	2	LAND	2	MARKS	3	MEEK	12
JASPER	2	LANGLE	1	MARKWELL	1	MEEKER	1
JAYCON	1	LARIMER	2	MARRS	2	MEERE	2
JAYCOX	4	LAUGHLIN	1	MARSH	3	MEESE	4
JEFFERS	8	LAUGHTER	1	MARSHALL	2	MEINHART	5
JENKINS	11	LAWALL	1	MARTIN	16	MEISLAHN	2
JOHNSON	21	LAWRENCE	7	MASCHER	5	MERCERET	3
JOHNSTON	3	LAWS	2	MASON	5	MERITT	2
JONES	35	LAY	1	MATHENY	2	MERRITT	1
JORDAN	2	LEACH	11	MATHEW	2	METHENY	4
JORDON	3	LEAMON	13	MATHEWS	2	METSKER	1
JOSEPH	1	LEATH	2	MATLOCK	2	METZ	2
JOURDAN	2	LEE	13	MATTHEWS	1	MICHAEL	3
JOURDEN	4	LEEMON	1	MATTINGLEY	6	MICHELL	2
KARR	2	LEFLER	1	MATTINGLY	9	MICKENBERGER	1
KAUFFMAN	2	LEGGITT	1	MAURER	3	MIDKIFF	15
KAUFFMANN	1	LEINHART	4	MAXWELL	7	MIKWORTH	1
KAUFMANN	1	LEISURE	4	MAY	14	MILLER	47
KEAN	3	LEMASTERS	4	MAYSEY	5	MILLIN	2
KEBLER	1	LEMAY	9	MAZE	2	MILLIS	2
KECK	1	LEMON	2	MCALLISTER	2	MINGS	2
KEENE	2	LENEX	1	MCBATH	5	MINOR	3
KEIF	1	LEONARD	2	MCCABE	4	MINTON	1
KEIFF	3	LETURRO	1	MCCAIN	3	MIRES	6
KEIFFE	1	LEVI	1	MCCALL	4	MISNER	1
KELLAM	2	LEVINGSTON	4	MCCARTHY	1	MITCHELL	13
KELLER	2	LEWELLYN	2	MCCARTY	13	MOCK	12
KELLEY	3	LEWIS	20	MCCLAIN	1	MONAHAN	1

Surname	# of Land Parcels	Surname	# of Land Parcels	Surname	# of Land Parcels	Surname	# of Land Parcels
MONDON	1	PATRICK	14	RHOADES	5	SEGELER	1
MONELL	1	PATTERSON	2	RHOADS	1	SEITH	1
MONROE	6	PAUGH	3	RIBLER	1	SELBY	21
MONRONEY	3	PAULUS	5	RICE	2	SELF	1
MOORE	14	PAYNE	8	RICENER	1	SELLERS	2
MOORMAN	1	PEARPOINT	2	RICHARD	1	SERIGHT	2
MORELAND	1	PECKLE	1	RICHARDS	10	SEXTON	1
MORGAN	9	PENHORWOOD	1	RICHEY	1	SHACKLEE	1
MORONEY	1	PENNINGTON	1	RICK	1	SHAFER	1
MORRIS	7	PERISHO	8	RICKMAN	4	SHAMHART	5
MOSCHENROSS	3	PETERSON	22	RIDENHOUR	4	SHAMHEART	2
MULGUEEN	1	PEYTON	1	RIDENOUR	7	SHARICK	12
MULLENS	1	PHELPS	1	RIDLEN	10	SHARP	2
MULLINS	1	PHILIPS	1	RIDLON	3	SHAW	1
MULVANY	1	PHILLIPS	1	RIFE	9	SHEALY	1
MURPHEY	3	PICQUET	90	RIFFETT	1	SHEARS	1
MURPHY	1	PIECUIT	2	RIGDON	2	SHELL	1
MURVIN	1	PIEQUET	4	RIGGLE	1	SHEPHERD	1
MUSER	1	PIKE	2	RIGHT	2	SHERER	1
MUSGRAVE	5	PINDELL	2	RILEY	9	SHERMAN	1
MUSGROVE	4	PING	23	RINJWALD	1	SHERWOOD	4
MYERS	22	PIQUET	2	RIPPETO	2	SHIPLEY	2
MYRES	1	PLANK	3	ROACH	2	SHIRDEN	1
NAGELY	4	POLLIS	1	ROBBINS	4	SHIRLEY	1
NATION	1	POMEROT	1	ROBE	1	SHOOK	1
NEAL	6	POMEROY	5	ROBERSON	2	SHORT	4
NEALE	1	POOR	2	ROBERTS	31	SHOWALTER	2
NEEDHAM	4	POWELL	17	ROBERTSON	3	SHUE	1
NEIBARGER	3	PRENTISS	2	ROBINSON	6	SHUH	1
NESSLEY	2	PRESTON	22	ROCH	1	SHY	2
NEWBOULD	5	PRICE	11	RODGERS	4	SICKMEN	1
NEWLIN	2	PRINCE	1	ROGERS	2	SIDDINS	1
NEWTON	1	PRINTZ	2	ROONEY	1	SIEFKEN	1
NICELY	3	PROSE	1	ROPER	2	SIGLER	1
NICHOLAS	8	PRUET	2	ROSS	13	SILLS	3
NICHOLS	20	PULLIAM	1	ROW	3	SIMMS	1
NIGHT	1	PULLIS	1	ROWLAND	1	SIMONS	1
NOEL	2	PURSELL	1	ROYAL	2	SIMPSON	9
NORRIS	3	PUTTROFF	1	RUDDELL	1	SIMS	3
NORTON	1	RAEF	12	RUSING	2	SINCLAIR	3
NOTINGHAM	2	RAFE	11	RUSSEL	1	SINK	6
NUTT	1	RAINES	2	RUTHERFORD	2	SKELTON	4
OBRIEN	2	RAMSEY	1	RYA	1	SKIDMORE	2
OCHELTREE	2	RANDOLPH	1	RYAN	6	SKINNER	2
OCONNOR	1	RANOLPH	1	RYON	1	SLAVEN	1
ODELL	2	RAPER	2	SAIGER	1	SMALL	5
ODLE	2	RAWLINGS	3	SAMPSON	7	SMALLWOOD	5
ODONNELL	1	RAY	3	SANDERS	1	SMART	4
ODOR	1	RAYLE	3	SANDS	1	SMITH	31
OGDEN	4	REA	2	SCHACKMAN	10	SNEARLEY	2
OKEAN	9	REDFORD	8	SCHACKMANN	2	SNEARLY	1
OKEEN	4	REDMAN	1	SCHAMHART	1	SNIDER	6
OLDAKER	1	REED	9	SCHATTMAN	1	SNODGRASS	1
ORR	1	REEDS	1	SCHEALDBANER	1	SNYDER	2
OSBORN	2	REEGLE	3	SCHEDLBANER	3	SOHEDLBANER	1
OSBURN	1	REEGLESBARGER	1	SCHELDBANER	5	SONG	2
OST	2	REELHORN	4	SCHIFFERSTEIN	6	SONGER	1
OURY	3	REEVES	1	SCHOTTMANN	5	SOURS	6
OWEN	2	REFFIT	3	SCHROADER	2	SOWERS	1
OWRY	1	REIGELSBERGER	4	SCHUFFENSTUN	6	SPEARS	5
PAGE	3	REIGLE	3	SCHUHK	1	SPIESL	1
PAIN	3	REILEY	1	SCHUMACHER	1	SPITZER	1
PAINE	1	REILLEY	1	SCHWAGER	1	SPIVEY	1
PARENT	1	REILLY	1	SCIFRES	1	SPOON	3
PARKER	7	REINS	4	SCOTT	11	STAELCUP	1
PARR	6	REISNER	3	SCRADER	1	STAFFORD	2
PARRENT	4	RENICK	2	SCREWS	1	STALLCUP	2
PARSHALL	2	REPETTO	2	SCRIVEN	1	STANDISH	1
PARSONS	5	REYNOLDS	6	SEAMON	3	STAPP	3
PATEE	2	RHEA	1	SEARSE	1	STARLING	3

Surname	# of Land Parcels	Surname	# of Land Parcels	Surname	# of Land Parcels
STARNIS	1	TOWNSEND	1	WHEELER	12
STATER	1	TRACY	1	WHIGHT	2
STEEL	23	TRAINER	5	WHITE	14
STEPHENS	1	TRAVIS	1	WHITECHURCH	1
STEPHENSON	1	TREXLER	16	WHITEHURST	5
STERCHY	1	TRIMBLE	2	WHITENACK	1
STEVENS	21	TROBAUGH	1	WHITLOCK	1
STEWARD	1	TROUTMAN	2	WHORTON	2
STEWART	16	TROWBRIDGE	4	WICHARD	1
STIENER	1	TRUITT	1	WICOFF	2
STILWELL	2	TUCKER	8	WILDAM	1
STINE	1	TURNER	5	WILES	1
STIPP	3	TUSING	1	WILFONG	1
STIVERS	2	UHL	5	WILKERSON	2
STOCKWELL	5	UNDERHILL	3	WILKINSON	1
STONEBARGER	3	VAN LUE	2	WILLIAM	1
STOUGHTON	1	VANATTA	2	WILLIAMS	7
STOVER	1	VANCE	4	WILLIAMSON	2
STRATTON	14	VANDERHOFF	2	WILLOUGHBY	3
STROLE	4	VANDERHOOF	4	WILSON	14
STRONG	1	VANLIEU	1	WINDSOR	2
STRUBING	1	VANLUE	6	WINES	2
STUBNER	1	VANMETER	8	WINTERS	3
STUMP	9	VANNATA	6	WISELEY	2
STURNS	1	VANNATTAR	1	WISEMORE	3
SUDDUTH	2	VANNETTA	2	WISHARD	16
SUTER	7	VANOLMAN	1	WISNER	2
SUTTON	25	VANRANT	2	WITSMAN	4
SWAIN	2	VANSANDT	2	WOHLTMANN	1
SWAK	1	VANSANT	2	WOLF	4
SWANEY	1	VANWINKLE	1	WOLFE	7
SWANK	1	VAROLE	1	WOLLACE	1
SWARTZ	1	VARVIL	3	WOOD	10
SWEET	1	VARVILLE	1	WOODARD	2
SWICK	7	VAUGHAN	5	WOODFORD	2
SWIM	1	VAUGHEN	1	WOODS	12
SWINEHEART	1	VAUGHN	1	WOODWORTH	2
SWOPE	11	VAUN	2	WOOLLEY	2
TARR	3	VICKREY	1	WORKS	2
TATE	6	VIXLER	2	WORMAN	2
TAYLOR	3	VOGEL	3	WORTHEY	5
TEDFORD	1	VON OLMAN	1	WRIGHT	15
TEMPLE	1	WADDLE	5	WYANT	3
TENNERY	5	WADE	3	YAEGER	1
TERREL	6	WAGLE	6	YAKELEY	1
TERWILLIGER	1	WAGNER	1	YAW	8
THADDAUS	2	WAGONER	2	YOUNG	7
THARP	1	WAITE	2	ZELL	5
THINOS	1	WAKEFIELD	1	ZIEGLER	2
THOM	1	WALKER	18	ZIMMERLEE	2
THOMAS	12	WALL	4		
THOMPSON	12	WALLACE	2		
THORNBURY	1	WAPLES	2		
THORNTON	3	WARD	12		
THROCKMORTON	2	WARNER	1		
TICHENOR	1	WARREN	6		
TICHNER	1	WATSON	1		
TIMMONS	1	WAYLE	2		
TINDAL	1	WAYMAN	2		
TINDALL	4	WEATHERINGTON	1		
TINGLEY	1	WEAVER	4		
TIPPIT	5	WEBB	2		
TOBIN	1	WEBSTER	4		
TODD	11	WEIMERT	2		
TOELLNER	1	WEISCOPF	1		
TOLES	3	WELDAM	5		
TOLIVER	1	WELLS	3		
TOMPKINS	2	WELTY	1		
TOTTEN	1	WEST	1		
TOWNSAND	3	WHEELELER	1		

Surname/Township Index

This Index allows you to determine which *Township Map Group(s)* contain individuals with the following surnames. Each *Map Group* has a corresponding full-name index of all individuals who obtained patents for land within its Congressional township's borders. After each index you will find the Patent Map to which it refers, and just thereafter, you can view the township's Road Map and Historical Map, with the latter map displaying streams, railroads, and more.

So, once you find your Surname here, proceed to the Index at the beginning of the **Map Group** indicated below.

Surname	Map Group	Parcels of Land	Meridian/Township/Range		
ABELL	**18**	3	3rd PM	5-N	10-E
ABELS	**6**	1	3rd PM	7-N	8-E
ADAMI	**13**	2	3rd PM	6-N	10-E
ADAMS	**12**	13	3rd PM	6-N	9-E
" "	**3**	7	3rd PM	8-N	10-E
" "	**5**	6	2nd PM	8-N	14-W
" "	**13**	5	3rd PM	6-N	10-E
" "	**7**	2	3rd PM	7-N	9-E
" "	**20**	1	2nd PM	5-N	14-W
" "	**8**	1	3rd PM	7-N	10-E
" "	**4**	1	3rd PM	8-N	11-E
ADAMSON	**11**	7	3rd PM	6-N	8-E
" "	**5**	3	2nd PM	8-N	14-W
" "	**4**	3	3rd PM	8-N	11-E
" "	**16**	1	3rd PM	5-N	8-E
ADKINS	**2**	2	3rd PM	8-N	9-E
ADKINSON	**5**	2	2nd PM	8-N	14-W
" "	**4**	1	3rd PM	8-N	11-E
ADKISSON	**3**	1	3rd PM	8-N	10-E
AKIN	**11**	3	3rd PM	6-N	8-E
ALEXANDER	**6**	32	3rd PM	7-N	8-E
" "	**1**	5	3rd PM	8-N	8-E
ALLEN	**7**	3	3rd PM	7-N	9-E
" "	**18**	1	3rd PM	5-N	10-E
" "	**12**	1	3rd PM	6-N	9-E
" "	**4**	1	3rd PM	8-N	11-E
ALLENTHARP	**5**	1	2nd PM	8-N	14-W
" "	**13**	1	3rd PM	6-N	10-E
ALLISON	**15**	9	2nd PM	6-N	14-W
" "	**5**	6	2nd PM	8-N	14-W
" "	**14**	1	3rd PM	6-N	11-E
ALMAN	**20**	1	2nd PM	5-N	14-W
AMES	**12**	4	3rd PM	6-N	9-E
" "	**17**	2	3rd PM	5-N	9-E
" "	**5**	1	2nd PM	8-N	14-W
ANDERSON	**1**	5	3rd PM	8-N	8-E
" "	**6**	2	3rd PM	7-N	8-E
ANDREWS	**3**	6	3rd PM	8-N	10-E
" "	**20**	2	2nd PM	5-N	14-W
" "	**2**	1	3rd PM	8-N	9-E
ANSPACK	**12**	1	3rd PM	6-N	9-E
ANTHOFER	**20**	1	2nd PM	5-N	14-W
ANTON	**12**	2	3rd PM	6-N	9-E
ARBUCKELL	**7**	1	3rd PM	7-N	9-E

Surname	Map Group	Parcels of Land	Meridian/Township/Range
ARBUCKLE	**7**	4	3rd PM 7-N 9-E
ARCHER	**5**	5	2nd PM 8-N 14-W
" "	**11**	1	3rd PM 6-N 8-E
ARDERY	**10**	1	2nd PM 7-N 14-W
ARMSTRONG	**6**	1	3rd PM 7-N 8-E
ARNOLD	**1**	7	3rd PM 8-N 8-E
" "	**6**	1	3rd PM 7-N 8-E
ASHCRAFT	**12**	1	3rd PM 6-N 9-E
ASHCROFT	**12**	10	3rd PM 6-N 9-E
ASHER	**1**	2	3rd PM 8-N 8-E
ATKINS	**1**	1	3rd PM 8-N 8-E
AUSTIN	**1**	1	3rd PM 8-N 8-E
AVERY	**6**	25	3rd PM 7-N 8-E
" "	**8**	4	3rd PM 7-N 10-E
" "	**3**	1	3rd PM 8-N 10-E
BACHMAN	**15**	1	2nd PM 6-N 14-W
BADGER	**7**	1	3rd PM 7-N 9-E
" "	**1**	1	3rd PM 8-N 8-E
BAILEY	**10**	14	2nd PM 7-N 14-W
" "	**5**	3	2nd PM 8-N 14-W
" "	**2**	2	3rd PM 8-N 9-E
" "	**13**	1	3rd PM 6-N 10-E
" "	**14**	1	3rd PM 6-N 11-E
" "	**8**	1	3rd PM 7-N 10-E
BAIN	**2**	9	3rd PM 8-N 9-E
BAKER	**16**	4	3rd PM 5-N 8-E
" "	**7**	3	3rd PM 7-N 9-E
" "	**11**	2	3rd PM 6-N 8-E
" "	**8**	2	3rd PM 7-N 10-E
" "	**12**	1	3rd PM 6-N 9-E
BALDREY	**17**	1	3rd PM 5-N 9-E
BALEY	**11**	3	3rd PM 6-N 8-E
" "	**10**	1	2nd PM 7-N 14-W
BALL	**16**	5	3rd PM 5-N 8-E
" "	**7**	2	3rd PM 7-N 9-E
BANTA	**13**	1	3rd PM 6-N 10-E
BARBER	**6**	1	3rd PM 7-N 8-E
" "	**1**	1	3rd PM 8-N 8-E
BARKER	**16**	1	3rd PM 5-N 8-E
BARKLEY	**7**	2	3rd PM 7-N 9-E
BARLOW	**5**	1	2nd PM 8-N 14-W
" "	**6**	1	3rd PM 7-N 8-E
BARNES	**12**	1	3rd PM 6-N 9-E
" "	**8**	1	3rd PM 7-N 10-E
BARNS	**13**	2	3rd PM 6-N 10-E
BARRASIER	**19**	1	3rd PM 5-N 11-E
BARRATT	**15**	2	2nd PM 6-N 14-W
BARRET	**15**	1	2nd PM 6-N 14-W
" "	**7**	1	3rd PM 7-N 9-E
BARRETT	**7**	9	3rd PM 7-N 9-E
" "	**2**	5	3rd PM 8-N 9-E
" "	**12**	4	3rd PM 6-N 9-E
BARTEE	**11**	2	3rd PM 6-N 8-E
BARTELLS	**6**	1	3rd PM 7-N 8-E
BARTLETT	**2**	2	3rd PM 8-N 9-E
" "	**1**	1	3rd PM 8-N 8-E
BARTLEY	**8**	10	3rd PM 7-N 10-E
BARTON	**18**	3	3rd PM 5-N 10-E
BASORE	**12**	1	3rd PM 6-N 9-E
BATES	**5**	1	2nd PM 8-N 14-W

Surname	Map Group	Parcels of Land	Meridian/Township/Range		
BATMAN	**8**	1	3rd PM	7-N	10-E
" "	**6**	1	3rd PM	7-N	8-E
" "	**7**	1	3rd PM	7-N	9-E
BAUMAN	**20**	1	2nd PM	5-N	14-W
BAXTER	**2**	1	3rd PM	8-N	9-E
BEACH	**17**	2	3rd PM	5-N	9-E
BECKWITH	**8**	4	3rd PM	7-N	10-E
BEELES	**3**	2	3rd PM	8-N	10-E
BEESON	**10**	4	2nd PM	7-N	14-W
BEMUSDOFFER	**8**	3	3rd PM	7-N	10-E
BENEFIELD	**8**	3	3rd PM	7-N	10-E
BENFORD	**6**	1	3rd PM	7-N	8-E
BENNETT	**20**	2	2nd PM	5-N	14-W
" "	**17**	1	3rd PM	5-N	9-E
BENSON	**4**	1	3rd PM	8-N	11-E
BERCASTLE	**8**	1	3rd PM	7-N	10-E
BERLIN	**20**	1	2nd PM	5-N	14-W
BERRY	**11**	25	3rd PM	6-N	8-E
" "	**16**	8	3rd PM	5-N	8-E
" "	**6**	7	3rd PM	7-N	8-E
" "	**1**	5	3rd PM	8-N	8-E
" "	**20**	1	2nd PM	5-N	14-W
BEUSDOFFER	**8**	1	3rd PM	7-N	10-E
BICKERS	**16**	2	3rd PM	5-N	8-E
BICKUS	**17**	2	3rd PM	5-N	9-E
BIDEL	**11**	1	3rd PM	6-N	8-E
BIRD	**9**	1	3rd PM	7-N	11-E
BIRT	**8**	3	3rd PM	7-N	10-E
" "	**3**	1	3rd PM	8-N	10-E
BISHOP	**20**	1	2nd PM	5-N	14-W
BLACK	**17**	9	3rd PM	5-N	9-E
" "	**7**	3	3rd PM	7-N	9-E
" "	**13**	2	3rd PM	6-N	10-E
" "	**3**	2	3rd PM	8-N	10-E
" "	**16**	1	3rd PM	5-N	8-E
" "	**12**	1	3rd PM	6-N	9-E
BLACKBURN	**13**	5	3rd PM	6-N	10-E
BLAIR	**17**	3	3rd PM	5-N	9-E
BLAKE	**3**	2	3rd PM	8-N	10-E
" "	**20**	1	2nd PM	5-N	14-W
" "	**15**	1	2nd PM	6-N	14-W
" "	**11**	1	3rd PM	6-N	8-E
" "	**8**	1	3rd PM	7-N	10-E
" "	**6**	1	3rd PM	7-N	8-E
" "	**1**	1	3rd PM	8-N	8-E
BLANKENSHIP	**17**	1	3rd PM	5-N	9-E
BLASDEL	**15**	5	2nd PM	6-N	14-W
BLIDE	**1**	1	3rd PM	8-N	8-E
BLISS	**8**	1	3rd PM	7-N	10-E
BODLE	**16**	1	3rd PM	5-N	8-E
BOGARD	**12**	4	3rd PM	6-N	9-E
" "	**15**	2	2nd PM	6-N	14-W
" "	**20**	1	2nd PM	5-N	14-W
BOHAMAN	**15**	8	2nd PM	6-N	14-W
BOHANNAN	**15**	9	2nd PM	6-N	14-W
BOLANDER	**15**	1	2nd PM	6-N	14-W
BOLDNEY	**16**	1	3rd PM	5-N	8-E
BOLENDER	**13**	1	3rd PM	6-N	10-E
BONE	**11**	2	3rd PM	6-N	8-E
" "	**16**	1	3rd PM	5-N	8-E

Surname	Map Group	Parcels of Land	Meridian/Township/Range		
BONER	8	1	3rd PM	7-N	10-E
BONHAM	3	8	3rd PM	8-N	10-E
BOOLE	17	2	3rd PM	5-N	9-E
BOOS	13	8	3rd PM	6-N	10-E
BOOTH	12	2	3rd PM	6-N	9-E
BORING	2	1	3rd PM	8-N	9-E
BOSS	13	1	3rd PM	6-N	10-E
BOSTER	6	1	3rd PM	7-N	8-E
BOTOFF	17	2	3rd PM	5-N	9-E
BOWEN	1	1	3rd PM	8-N	8-E
BOWERS	7	2	3rd PM	7-N	9-E
" "	8	1	3rd PM	7-N	10-E
BOWMAN	5	6	2nd PM	8-N	14-W
" "	12	6	3rd PM	6-N	9-E
BOYD	10	1	2nd PM	7-N	14-W
" "	16	1	3rd PM	5-N	8-E
" "	2	1	3rd PM	8-N	9-E
BRACKET	16	1	3rd PM	5-N	8-E
BRACKNEY	2	3	3rd PM	8-N	9-E
BRADBERRY	11	2	3rd PM	6-N	8-E
BRADSHAW	1	10	3rd PM	8-N	8-E
" "	2	6	3rd PM	8-N	9-E
BRASSIER	20	1	2nd PM	5-N	14-W
BRAZIER	19	1	3rd PM	5-N	11-E
BREES	3	2	3rd PM	8-N	10-E
BREWER	7	5	3rd PM	7-N	9-E
" "	1	3	3rd PM	8-N	8-E
" "	11	1	3rd PM	6-N	8-E
BRICKENRIDGE	18	1	3rd PM	5-N	10-E
BRIDGES	13	4	3rd PM	6-N	10-E
" "	12	3	3rd PM	6-N	9-E
" "	6	3	3rd PM	7-N	8-E
" "	7	1	3rd PM	7-N	9-E
BRIGES	11	1	3rd PM	6-N	8-E
BRIGHT	1	1	3rd PM	8-N	8-E
BRINDLEY	17	2	3rd PM	5-N	9-E
BRISTOL	12	2	3rd PM	6-N	9-E
" "	7	2	3rd PM	7-N	9-E
" "	17	1	3rd PM	5-N	9-E
BROCK	8	8	3rd PM	7-N	10-E
BRODERICK	8	6	3rd PM	7-N	10-E
BROOK	8	1	3rd PM	7-N	10-E
BROOKS	8	21	3rd PM	7-N	10-E
" "	13	5	3rd PM	6-N	10-E
" "	12	3	3rd PM	6-N	9-E
" "	3	3	3rd PM	8-N	10-E
" "	10	1	2nd PM	7-N	14-W
" "	9	1	3rd PM	7-N	11-E
BROWN	17	7	3rd PM	5-N	9-E
" "	16	5	3rd PM	5-N	8-E
" "	7	3	3rd PM	7-N	9-E
" "	6	2	3rd PM	7-N	8-E
" "	8	1	3rd PM	7-N	10-E
BROWNFIELD	20	2	2nd PM	5-N	14-W
" "	19	1	3rd PM	5-N	11-E
BROWNING	8	1	3rd PM	7-N	10-E
BRUCE	18	3	3rd PM	5-N	10-E
BRUMFIED	11	1	3rd PM	6-N	8-E
BRUMFIELD	11	1	3rd PM	6-N	8-E
BRYAN	12	3	3rd PM	6-N	9-E

Surname	Map Group	Parcels of Land	Meridian/Township/Range		
BRYAN (Cont'd)	**13**	2	3rd PM	6-N	10-E
" "	**11**	2	3rd PM	6-N	8-E
BRYANT	**12**	3	3rd PM	6-N	9-E
BRYER	**8**	1	3rd PM	7-N	10-E
BUCHANAN	**8**	1	3rd PM	7-N	10-E
BUCKINGHAM	**4**	1	3rd PM	8-N	11-E
BUEL	**7**	3	3rd PM	7-N	9-E
BUFFINGTON	**10**	2	2nd PM	7-N	14-W
BUHLER	**6**	2	3rd PM	7-N	8-E
BULEY	**12**	1	3rd PM	6-N	9-E
BUNTAIN	**11**	1	3rd PM	6-N	8-E
BURCHAM	**11**	3	3rd PM	6-N	8-E
" "	**10**	1	2nd PM	7-N	14-W
" "	**13**	1	3rd PM	6-N	10-E
" "	**8**	1	3rd PM	7-N	10-E
BURCHARD	**9**	1	3rd PM	7-N	11-E
BURFORD	**13**	1	3rd PM	6-N	10-E
" "	**8**	1	3rd PM	7-N	10-E
" "	**6**	1	3rd PM	7-N	8-E
BURNES	**20**	4	2nd PM	5-N	14-W
BURNHAM	**6**	1	3rd PM	7-N	8-E
BURT	**8**	1	3rd PM	7-N	10-E
BUSH	**12**	7	3rd PM	6-N	9-E
BUSSELL	**5**	2	2nd PM	8-N	14-W
" "	**4**	1	3rd PM	8-N	11-E
BUTLER	**10**	6	2nd PM	7-N	14-W
" "	**7**	4	3rd PM	7-N	9-E
" "	**2**	3	3rd PM	8-N	9-E
BYERS	**18**	2	3rd PM	5-N	10-E
" "	**17**	1	3rd PM	5-N	9-E
BYRD	**8**	2	3rd PM	7-N	10-E
" "	**2**	1	3rd PM	8-N	9-E
BYRN	**17**	3	3rd PM	5-N	9-E
BYRNE	**18**	2	3rd PM	5-N	10-E
" "	**10**	1	2nd PM	7-N	14-W
CALDWELL	**1**	10	3rd PM	8-N	8-E
" "	**6**	2	3rd PM	7-N	8-E
" "	**5**	1	2nd PM	8-N	14-W
" "	**13**	1	3rd PM	6-N	10-E
" "	**9**	1	3rd PM	7-N	11-E
CAMPBELL	**15**	1	2nd PM	6-N	14-W
CAREY	**2**	1	3rd PM	8-N	9-E
CARMEAN	**3**	1	3rd PM	8-N	10-E
CAROTHERS	**6**	1	3rd PM	7-N	8-E
CARPENTER	**16**	1	3rd PM	5-N	8-E
" "	**9**	1	3rd PM	7-N	11-E
CARR	**7**	2	3rd PM	7-N	9-E
" "	**12**	1	3rd PM	6-N	9-E
" "	**3**	1	3rd PM	8-N	10-E
" "	**2**	1	3rd PM	8-N	9-E
CARRELL	**11**	1	3rd PM	6-N	8-E
CARSON	**13**	2	3rd PM	6-N	10-E
" "	**15**	1	2nd PM	6-N	14-W
" "	**1**	1	3rd PM	8-N	8-E
CARTER	**12**	14	3rd PM	6-N	9-E
" "	**7**	4	3rd PM	7-N	9-E
" "	**15**	1	2nd PM	6-N	14-W
" "	**16**	1	3rd PM	5-N	8-E
" "	**17**	1	3rd PM	5-N	9-E
" "	**13**	1	3rd PM	6-N	10-E

Surname	Map Group	Parcels of Land	Meridian/Township/Range
CARTER (Cont'd)	**4**	1	3rd PM 8-N 11-E
CASEY	**15**	1	2nd PM 6-N 14-W
" "	**19**	1	3rd PM 5-N 11-E
CASJENS	**6**	1	3rd PM 7-N 8-E
CASSITY	**11**	1	3rd PM 6-N 8-E
CATERS	**11**	1	3rd PM 6-N 8-E
CATHEN	**11**	1	3rd PM 6-N 8-E
CATHER	**11**	8	3rd PM 6-N 8-E
CATLIN	**2**	1	3rd PM 8-N 9-E
CATT	**13**	3	3rd PM 6-N 10-E
CHABLE	**13**	1	3rd PM 6-N 10-E
CHAMBERLAIN	**17**	3	3rd PM 5-N 9-E
CHANEY	**2**	3	3rd PM 8-N 9-E
CHAPAN	**9**	1	3rd PM 7-N 11-E
" "	**4**	1	3rd PM 8-N 11-E
CHAPMAN	**3**	23	3rd PM 8-N 10-E
" "	**8**	9	3rd PM 7-N 10-E
" "	**4**	8	3rd PM 8-N 11-E
" "	**10**	2	2nd PM 7-N 14-W
" "	**9**	2	3rd PM 7-N 11-E
" "	**13**	1	3rd PM 6-N 10-E
CHASTAIN	**13**	1	3rd PM 6-N 10-E
CHEEK	**12**	4	3rd PM 6-N 9-E
" "	**11**	2	3rd PM 6-N 8-E
CHERRY	**20**	1	2nd PM 5-N 14-W
" "	**18**	1	3rd PM 5-N 10-E
CHESMETT	**11**	1	3rd PM 6-N 8-E
CHESNUT	**16**	2	3rd PM 5-N 8-E
" "	**11**	2	3rd PM 6-N 8-E
CHESTNUT	**16**	3	3rd PM 5-N 8-E
CHITTENDAN	**12**	2	3rd PM 6-N 9-E
CHOATE	**11**	2	3rd PM 6-N 8-E
CHRISMAN	**3**	3	3rd PM 8-N 10-E
CHRISS	**8**	9	3rd PM 7-N 10-E
CHURCH	**9**	1	3rd PM 7-N 11-E
CLARK	**3**	7	3rd PM 8-N 10-E
" "	**11**	4	3rd PM 6-N 8-E
" "	**10**	3	2nd PM 7-N 14-W
" "	**6**	3	3rd PM 7-N 8-E
" "	**18**	2	3rd PM 5-N 10-E
" "	**16**	2	3rd PM 5-N 8-E
" "	**4**	2	3rd PM 8-N 11-E
" "	**5**	1	2nd PM 8-N 14-W
" "	**7**	1	3rd PM 7-N 9-E
CLAWSON	**2**	3	3rd PM 8-N 9-E
CLEMANS	**10**	2	2nd PM 7-N 14-W
" "	**5**	1	2nd PM 8-N 14-W
CLEMENS	**10**	1	2nd PM 7-N 14-W
" "	**5**	1	2nd PM 8-N 14-W
CLEMENTS	**5**	3	2nd PM 8-N 14-W
CLEMMONS	**5**	3	2nd PM 8-N 14-W
CLEMONS	**5**	6	2nd PM 8-N 14-W
CLUBB	**18**	2	3rd PM 5-N 10-E
COALE	**3**	2	3rd PM 8-N 10-E
COAN	**1**	1	3rd PM 8-N 8-E
COCHRAN	**11**	1	3rd PM 6-N 8-E
CODD	**2**	1	3rd PM 8-N 9-E
CODER	**20**	1	2nd PM 5-N 14-W
COGGESHALL	**2**	4	3rd PM 8-N 9-E
COHOON	**4**	2	3rd PM 8-N 11-E

Surname	Map Group	Parcels of Land	Meridian/Township/Range		
COHOON (Cont'd)	5	1	2nd PM	8-N	14-W
" "	3	1	3rd PM	8-N	10-E
COLBORN	16	2	3rd PM	5-N	8-E
COLBOURN	16	2	3rd PM	5-N	8-E
COLBURN	16	2	3rd PM	5-N	8-E
COLEMAN	18	3	3rd PM	5-N	10-E
" "	20	1	2nd PM	5-N	14-W
" "	10	1	2nd PM	7-N	14-W
COLLINS	20	3	2nd PM	5-N	14-W
" "	18	3	3rd PM	5-N	10-E
" "	19	3	3rd PM	5-N	11-E
" "	17	2	3rd PM	5-N	9-E
" "	16	1	3rd PM	5-N	8-E
" "	1	1	3rd PM	8-N	8-E
COMER	7	1	3rd PM	7-N	9-E
COMSTOCK	5	1	2nd PM	8-N	14-W
CONDE	8	2	3rd PM	7-N	10-E
COOK	19	1	3rd PM	5-N	11-E
COOLEY	1	1	3rd PM	8-N	8-E
COOPER	5	3	2nd PM	8-N	14-W
CORBIN	11	3	3rd PM	6-N	8-E
CORRIGAM	6	1	3rd PM	7-N	8-E
CORRIGAN	6	2	3rd PM	7-N	8-E
COTTINGHAM	7	1	3rd PM	7-N	9-E
COURE	7	1	3rd PM	7-N	9-E
COWGER	11	2	3rd PM	6-N	8-E
COX	7	8	3rd PM	7-N	9-E
" "	10	6	2nd PM	7-N	14-W
" "	5	3	2nd PM	8-N	14-W
" "	8	1	3rd PM	7-N	10-E
COZARD	1	1	3rd PM	8-N	8-E
CRAIG	10	4	2nd PM	7-N	14-W
" "	16	4	3rd PM	5-N	8-E
" "	17	4	3rd PM	5-N	9-E
" "	13	1	3rd PM	6-N	10-E
CRAMER	5	12	2nd PM	8-N	14-W
CRAVENS	17	7	3rd PM	5-N	9-E
" "	16	3	3rd PM	5-N	8-E
CREASON	7	1	3rd PM	7-N	9-E
CREWS	1	19	3rd PM	8-N	8-E
" "	6	4	3rd PM	7-N	8-E
CRITTENDEN	1	3	3rd PM	8-N	8-E
CRONER	16	2	3rd PM	5-N	8-E
CROSS	20	2	2nd PM	5-N	14-W
CROUSE	16	1	3rd PM	5-N	8-E
CROWLEY	20	8	2nd PM	5-N	14-W
" "	18	3	3rd PM	5-N	10-E
" "	17	1	3rd PM	5-N	9-E
CROWS	16	3	3rd PM	5-N	8-E
" "	17	2	3rd PM	5-N	9-E
CRUME	13	2	3rd PM	6-N	10-E
CRUSE	1	3	3rd PM	8-N	8-E
CRUZAN	20	2	2nd PM	5-N	14-W
CULNANE	6	1	3rd PM	7-N	8-E
CUMMANS	3	3	3rd PM	8-N	10-E
CUMMING	6	1	3rd PM	7-N	8-E
CUMMINS	3	9	3rd PM	8-N	10-E
" "	8	3	3rd PM	7-N	10-E
" "	20	1	2nd PM	5-N	14-W
" "	18	1	3rd PM	5-N	10-E

Surname	Map Group	Parcels of Land	Meridian/Township/Range		
CUMMONS	**3**	1	3rd PM	8-N	10-E
CURRIE	**7**	5	3rd PM	7-N	9-E
CURTIS	**12**	6	3rd PM	6-N	9-E
" "	**10**	3	2nd PM	7-N	14-W
" "	**17**	2	3rd PM	5-N	9-E
" "	**7**	1	3rd PM	7-N	9-E
" "	**3**	1	3rd PM	8-N	10-E
CURTISS	**11**	1	3rd PM	6-N	8-E
" "	**2**	1	3rd PM	8-N	9-E
DABBINS	**6**	1	3rd PM	7-N	8-E
DAILEY	**3**	1	3rd PM	8-N	10-E
DALE	**11**	2	3rd PM	6-N	8-E
DASHLER	**19**	1	3rd PM	5-N	11-E
DAVIS	**2**	4	3rd PM	8-N	9-E
" "	**20**	3	2nd PM	5-N	14-W
" "	**5**	3	2nd PM	8-N	14-W
" "	**3**	3	3rd PM	8-N	10-E
" "	**15**	1	2nd PM	6-N	14-W
" "	**10**	1	2nd PM	7-N	14-W
" "	**13**	1	3rd PM	6-N	10-E
" "	**9**	1	3rd PM	7-N	11-E
" "	**4**	1	3rd PM	8-N	11-E
DAVISSON	**3**	2	3rd PM	8-N	10-E
DAY	**10**	1	2nd PM	7-N	14-W
DE GAEGER	**8**	2	3rd PM	7-N	10-E
DE YAEGER	**8**	1	3rd PM	7-N	10-E
DEBORD	**3**	1	3rd PM	8-N	10-E
DEBOW	**5**	2	2nd PM	8-N	14-W
DECKER	**6**	2	3rd PM	7-N	8-E
" "	**10**	1	2nd PM	7-N	14-W
DELOTT	**6**	1	3rd PM	7-N	8-E
DENMAN	**11**	1	3rd PM	6-N	8-E
" "	**12**	1	3rd PM	6-N	9-E
" "	**3**	1	3rd PM	8-N	10-E
DENNIS	**12**	8	3rd PM	6-N	9-E
DERLER	**20**	1	2nd PM	5-N	14-W
DHOM	**8**	2	3rd PM	7-N	10-E
DICKMAN	**11**	1	3rd PM	6-N	8-E
DILLMAN	**10**	1	2nd PM	7-N	14-W
DILLMON	**10**	1	2nd PM	7-N	14-W
" "	**5**	1	2nd PM	8-N	14-W
DITTEMOORE	**1**	3	3rd PM	8-N	8-E
DITTEMORE	**1**	5	3rd PM	8-N	8-E
DIXON	**8**	5	3rd PM	7-N	10-E
" "	**15**	1	2nd PM	6-N	14-W
DOBBINS	**11**	1	3rd PM	6-N	8-E
" "	**6**	1	3rd PM	7-N	8-E
DODD	**2**	1	3rd PM	8-N	9-E
DOERR	**6**	1	3rd PM	7-N	8-E
DOGGETT	**11**	2	3rd PM	6-N	8-E
DONNELL	**20**	2	2nd PM	5-N	14-W
DORN	**5**	2	2nd PM	8-N	14-W
" "	**8**	1	3rd PM	7-N	10-E
DOTY	**14**	2	3rd PM	6-N	11-E
" "	**15**	1	2nd PM	6-N	14-W
DOUTHIT	**11**	2	3rd PM	6-N	8-E
DOVEL	**11**	4	3rd PM	6-N	8-E
DOWELL	**5**	3	2nd PM	8-N	14-W
DOWNER	**16**	1	3rd PM	5-N	8-E
DOWNEY	**19**	1	3rd PM	5-N	11-E

Surname	Map Group	Parcels of Land	Meridian/Township/Range		
DOWNS	**2**	1	3rd PM	8-N	9-E
DOYLE	**18**	1	3rd PM	5-N	10-E
DRAKE	**16**	4	3rd PM	5-N	8-E
" "	**11**	2	3rd PM	6-N	8-E
DRYSDALE	**8**	3	3rd PM	7-N	10-E
DUGAN	**4**	2	3rd PM	8-N	11-E
" "	**7**	1	3rd PM	7-N	9-E
" "	**3**	1	3rd PM	8-N	10-E
DULGOR	**3**	1	3rd PM	8-N	10-E
DUNCAN	**11**	1	3rd PM	6-N	8-E
DUNEGAN	**1**	1	3rd PM	8-N	8-E
DUNGAN	**7**	2	3rd PM	7-N	9-E
DURHAM	**10**	1	2nd PM	7-N	14-W
DURKEY	**7**	1	3rd PM	7-N	9-E
DUTELL	**1**	3	3rd PM	8-N	8-E
DUVAL	**12**	1	3rd PM	6-N	9-E
DUVALL	**12**	1	3rd PM	6-N	9-E
EAGLETON	**2**	4	3rd PM	8-N	9-E
EAMES	**10**	1	2nd PM	7-N	14-W
EARLY	**18**	2	3rd PM	5-N	10-E
EARNEST	**8**	1	3rd PM	7-N	10-E
EASTON	**17**	1	3rd PM	5-N	9-E
EATON	**15**	10	2nd PM	6-N	14-W
" "	**5**	2	2nd PM	8-N	14-W
" "	**12**	2	3rd PM	6-N	9-E
" "	**10**	1	2nd PM	7-N	14-W
EBALING	**6**	2	3rd PM	7-N	8-E
EBELING	**6**	1	3rd PM	7-N	8-E
EBLEN	**17**	2	3rd PM	5-N	9-E
ECKARDT	**1**	1	3rd PM	8-N	8-E
EDERER	**8**	1	3rd PM	7-N	10-E
EDGERTON	**10**	2	2nd PM	7-N	14-W
EDWARDS	**2**	4	3rd PM	8-N	9-E
" "	**20**	2	2nd PM	5-N	14-W
" "	**10**	2	2nd PM	7-N	14-W
" "	**3**	1	3rd PM	8-N	10-E
EICHER	**13**	2	3rd PM	6-N	10-E
EILERS	**6**	1	3rd PM	7-N	8-E
ELDER	**17**	8	3rd PM	5-N	9-E
" "	**16**	4	3rd PM	5-N	8-E
" "	**12**	3	3rd PM	6-N	9-E
" "	**7**	3	3rd PM	7-N	9-E
" "	**11**	2	3rd PM	6-N	8-E
" "	**2**	1	3rd PM	8-N	9-E
ELIOT	**18**	1	3rd PM	5-N	10-E
ELLIOTT	**10**	4	2nd PM	7-N	14-W
" "	**1**	1	3rd PM	8-N	8-E
ELSON	**6**	4	3rd PM	7-N	8-E
ELSTON	**16**	1	3rd PM	5-N	8-E
ELY	**2**	1	3rd PM	8-N	9-E
EMBODY	**5**	1	2nd PM	8-N	14-W
EMERSON	**13**	4	3rd PM	6-N	10-E
EPPERSON	**1**	5	3rd PM	8-N	8-E
ERVIN	**3**	2	3rd PM	8-N	10-E
" "	**16**	1	3rd PM	5-N	8-E
ESSEX	**16**	5	3rd PM	5-N	8-E
EUBANK	**15**	3	2nd PM	6-N	14-W
EVANS	**16**	11	3rd PM	5-N	8-E
" "	**13**	8	3rd PM	6-N	10-E
" "	**11**	3	3rd PM	6-N	8-E

Surname	Map Group	Parcels of Land	Meridian/Township/Range
EVANS (Cont'd)	**12**	1	3rd PM 6-N 9-E
" "	**1**	1	3rd PM 8-N 8-E
EVERMAN	**10**	5	2nd PM 7-N 14-W
EYER	**18**	1	3rd PM 5-N 10-E
FAGG	**17**	2	3rd PM 5-N 9-E
FARIS	**2**	1	3rd PM 8-N 9-E
FARLEY	**5**	4	2nd PM 8-N 14-W
FARRIS	**2**	1	3rd PM 8-N 9-E
FASSETT	**12**	2	3rd PM 6-N 9-E
FATOOT	**1**	1	3rd PM 8-N 8-E
FAWCETT	**8**	1	3rd PM 7-N 10-E
" "	**3**	1	3rd PM 8-N 10-E
FAWSETT	**3**	1	3rd PM 8-N 10-E
FEAR	**8**	2	3rd PM 7-N 10-E
FEARS	**10**	3	2nd PM 7-N 14-W
" "	**5**	3	2nd PM 8-N 14-W
FEESER	**15**	3	2nd PM 6-N 14-W
" "	**10**	3	2nd PM 7-N 14-W
" "	**9**	1	3rd PM 7-N 11-E
FELDKAMP	**1**	2	3rd PM 8-N 8-E
FENTONSPREAD	**1**	1	3rd PM 8-N 8-E
FERGUSON	**8**	8	3rd PM 7-N 10-E
" "	**7**	3	3rd PM 7-N 9-E
" "	**9**	2	3rd PM 7-N 11-E
FERREE	**20**	2	2nd PM 5-N 14-W
" "	**18**	2	3rd PM 5-N 10-E
FICKLIN	**6**	3	3rd PM 7-N 8-E
FIELD	**11**	4	3rd PM 6-N 8-E
FIELDS	**11**	1	3rd PM 6-N 8-E
FINCH	**12**	1	3rd PM 6-N 9-E
FINEY	**3**	1	3rd PM 8-N 10-E
FISHER	**17**	4	3rd PM 5-N 9-E
" "	**7**	2	3rd PM 7-N 9-E
" "	**3**	2	3rd PM 8-N 10-E
FITCH	**12**	2	3rd PM 6-N 9-E
FITHIAN	**13**	8	3rd PM 6-N 10-E
" "	**6**	3	3rd PM 7-N 8-E
" "	**12**	1	3rd PM 6-N 9-E
" "	**8**	1	3rd PM 7-N 10-E
" "	**7**	1	3rd PM 7-N 9-E
" "	**1**	1	3rd PM 8-N 8-E
FLEANER	**17**	2	3rd PM 5-N 9-E
FLEENER	**17**	2	3rd PM 5-N 9-E
FLETCHER	**7**	3	3rd PM 7-N 9-E
FLINT	**3**	1	3rd PM 8-N 10-E
FOGLE	**8**	2	3rd PM 7-N 10-E
FOGLER	**6**	2	3rd PM 7-N 8-E
FOLTZ	**7**	11	3rd PM 7-N 9-E
" "	**12**	3	3rd PM 6-N 9-E
FOOR	**19**	1	3rd PM 5-N 11-E
FOOT	**7**	6	3rd PM 7-N 9-E
FORCE	**12**	1	3rd PM 6-N 9-E
FORD	**16**	1	3rd PM 5-N 8-E
FORE	**20**	1	2nd PM 5-N 14-W
" "	**15**	1	2nd PM 6-N 14-W
" "	**19**	1	3rd PM 5-N 11-E
FOREMAN	**2**	3	3rd PM 8-N 9-E
FORESMAN	**3**	10	3rd PM 8-N 10-E
FOSTER	**11**	17	3rd PM 6-N 8-E
" "	**1**	4	3rd PM 8-N 8-E

Surname	Map Group	Parcels of Land	Meridian/Township/Range		
FOUST	**6**	2	3rd PM	7-N	8-E
" "	**1**	2	3rd PM	8-N	8-E
" "	**2**	1	3rd PM	8-N	9-E
FOWLER	**15**	3	2nd PM	6-N	14-W
FOX	**18**	3	3rd PM	5-N	10-E
" "	**13**	2	3rd PM	6-N	10-E
" "	**10**	1	2nd PM	7-N	14-W
FRAKES	**7**	1	3rd PM	7-N	9-E
FRANCIS	**5**	1	2nd PM	8-N	14-W
FRANKE	**8**	2	3rd PM	7-N	10-E
FRAZIER	**2**	2	3rd PM	8-N	9-E
" "	**12**	1	3rd PM	6-N	9-E
FREEMAN	**11**	5	3rd PM	6-N	8-E
" "	**13**	2	3rd PM	6-N	10-E
" "	**8**	1	3rd PM	7-N	10-E
FRENCH	**3**	3	3rd PM	8-N	10-E
FRIEDLEY	**20**	2	2nd PM	5-N	14-W
FRIEDLIEN	**19**	1	3rd PM	5-N	11-E
FROST	**20**	2	2nd PM	5-N	14-W
FRUCHTEL	**8**	1	3rd PM	7-N	10-E
FRUICHTEL	**8**	1	3rd PM	7-N	10-E
FRY	**5**	1	2nd PM	8-N	14-W
FULLER	**7**	9	3rd PM	7-N	9-E
" "	**12**	5	3rd PM	6-N	9-E
" "	**15**	1	2nd PM	6-N	14-W
" "	**5**	1	2nd PM	8-N	14-W
FULTON	**16**	4	3rd PM	5-N	8-E
GAINES	**18**	1	3rd PM	5-N	10-E
GAINS	**18**	1	3rd PM	5-N	10-E
GALBREATH	**2**	2	3rd PM	8-N	9-E
GAMBRIEL	**11**	1	3rd PM	6-N	8-E
GARDENWINE	**8**	1	3rd PM	7-N	10-E
GARDEWAIN	**8**	3	3rd PM	7-N	10-E
GARDINER	**18**	1	3rd PM	5-N	10-E
GARDNER	**1**	4	3rd PM	8-N	8-E
" "	**16**	1	3rd PM	5-N	8-E
GARDWAIN	**3**	1	3rd PM	8-N	10-E
GAREE	**11**	3	3rd PM	6-N	8-E
GARRET	**5**	1	2nd PM	8-N	14-W
GARRETSON	**8**	2	3rd PM	7-N	10-E
GARRISON	**7**	2	3rd PM	7-N	9-E
" "	**8**	1	3rd PM	7-N	10-E
GARS	**11**	1	3rd PM	6-N	8-E
GARWOOD	**7**	4	3rd PM	7-N	9-E
" "	**13**	3	3rd PM	6-N	10-E
" "	**12**	1	3rd PM	6-N	9-E
GASS	**12**	1	3rd PM	6-N	9-E
GAULLOFF	**15**	1	2nd PM	6-N	14-W
GAYER	**15**	3	2nd PM	6-N	14-W
GEDDES	**5**	2	2nd PM	8-N	14-W
" "	**4**	2	3rd PM	8-N	11-E
GHAIST	**12**	1	3rd PM	6-N	9-E
GHARST	**12**	2	3rd PM	6-N	9-E
GHURST	**11**	1	3rd PM	6-N	8-E
GIBSON	**16**	2	3rd PM	5-N	8-E
" "	**18**	1	3rd PM	5-N	10-E
" "	**3**	1	3rd PM	8-N	10-E
GIFFORD	**8**	7	3rd PM	7-N	10-E
GILBRETH	**13**	1	3rd PM	6-N	10-E
GILLESPIE	**20**	1	2nd PM	5-N	14-W

Surname	Map Group	Parcels of Land	Meridian/Township/Range		
GILLHAM	**1**	3	3rd PM	8-N	8-E
GILLMORE	**2**	1	3rd PM	8-N	9-E
GILMORE	**2**	1	3rd PM	8-N	9-E
GLOUR	**1**	1	3rd PM	8-N	8-E
GLOVER	**1**	1	3rd PM	8-N	8-E
GOEPPNER	**14**	1	3rd PM	6-N	11-E
GOLDSBY	**2**	1	3rd PM	8-N	9-E
GOOD	**7**	3	3rd PM	7-N	9-E
GOODWIN	**17**	4	3rd PM	5-N	9-E
" "	**12**	1	3rd PM	6-N	9-E
GORE	**12**	2	3rd PM	6-N	9-E
GORNELL	**7**	2	3rd PM	7-N	9-E
GORRELL	**2**	1	3rd PM	8-N	9-E
GORSLINE	**3**	1	3rd PM	8-N	10-E
GOSNELL	**7**	10	3rd PM	7-N	9-E
" "	**5**	6	2nd PM	8-N	14-W
" "	**2**	4	3rd PM	8-N	9-E
" "	**4**	2	3rd PM	8-N	11-E
GOSS	**1**	2	3rd PM	8-N	8-E
GOULD	**16**	5	3rd PM	5-N	8-E
" "	**6**	1	3rd PM	7-N	8-E
GRAVES	**5**	1	2nd PM	8-N	14-W
" "	**4**	1	3rd PM	8-N	11-E
GRAY	**17**	2	3rd PM	5-N	9-E
" "	**2**	1	3rd PM	8-N	9-E
GREELY	**6**	7	3rd PM	7-N	8-E
GREEN	**3**	2	3rd PM	8-N	10-E
" "	**2**	2	3rd PM	8-N	9-E
" "	**7**	1	3rd PM	7-N	9-E
GREGORY	**16**	3	3rd PM	5-N	8-E
" "	**12**	3	3rd PM	6-N	9-E
" "	**11**	1	3rd PM	6-N	8-E
GRIFFING	**8**	3	3rd PM	7-N	10-E
GRIFFITH	**2**	3	3rd PM	8-N	9-E
GRIFFY	**10**	2	2nd PM	7-N	14-W
" "	**15**	1	2nd PM	6-N	14-W
GRIMES	**17**	1	3rd PM	5-N	9-E
GROOTHINS	**6**	1	3rd PM	7-N	8-E
GROVE	**16**	4	3rd PM	5-N	8-E
" "	**4**	4	3rd PM	8-N	11-E
" "	**17**	2	3rd PM	5-N	9-E
" "	**12**	2	3rd PM	6-N	9-E
" "	**6**	1	3rd PM	7-N	8-E
" "	**7**	1	3rd PM	7-N	9-E
GROVES	**3**	1	3rd PM	8-N	10-E
" "	**4**	1	3rd PM	8-N	11-E
GRRELY	**6**	1	3rd PM	7-N	8-E
GRUB	**13**	2	3rd PM	6-N	10-E
" "	**15**	1	2nd PM	6-N	14-W
GRUBB	**15**	1	2nd PM	6-N	14-W
GRUBBS	**17**	4	3rd PM	5-N	9-E
GUERIN	**13**	1	3rd PM	6-N	10-E
GUGUMUS	**15**	1	2nd PM	6-N	14-W
GULLION	**5**	1	2nd PM	8-N	14-W
GUTHNICK	**15**	1	2nd PM	6-N	14-W
GUYNN	**10**	1	2nd PM	7-N	14-W
HACKNEY	**3**	1	3rd PM	8-N	10-E
HAGEMAN	**11**	3	3rd PM	6-N	8-E
HAGIMAN	**11**	4	3rd PM	6-N	8-E
HAGY	**2**	1	3rd PM	8-N	9-E

Surname	Map Group	Parcels of Land	Meridian/Township/Range
HALE	**15**	1	2nd PM 6-N 14-W
HALEY	**18**	3	3rd PM 5-N 10-E
HALFHILL	**1**	1	3rd PM 8-N 8-E
HALL	**17**	2	3rd PM 5-N 9-E
" "	**11**	1	3rd PM 6-N 8-E
HALLENBECK	**7**	2	3rd PM 7-N 9-E
" "	**13**	1	3rd PM 6-N 10-E
" "	**8**	1	3rd PM 7-N 10-E
HALSEY	**18**	6	3rd PM 5-N 10-E
" "	**20**	3	2nd PM 5-N 14-W
" "	**13**	2	3rd PM 6-N 10-E
HALSTED	**15**	1	2nd PM 6-N 14-W
HAMIL	**15**	1	2nd PM 6-N 14-W
HAMILTON	**15**	3	2nd PM 6-N 14-W
" "	**18**	3	3rd PM 5-N 10-E
" "	**10**	2	2nd PM 7-N 14-W
HAMMER	**3**	13	3rd PM 8-N 10-E
HAMPELMAN	**13**	2	3rd PM 6-N 10-E
HAMPSTEN	**5**	2	2nd PM 8-N 14-W
HAMPSTON	**5**	1	2nd PM 8-N 14-W
HANDELY	**17**	1	3rd PM 5-N 9-E
HANDER	**12**	4	3rd PM 6-N 9-E
HANDLEY	**17**	1	3rd PM 5-N 9-E
HANKINS	**17**	2	3rd PM 5-N 9-E
" "	**2**	1	3rd PM 8-N 9-E
HANNA	**1**	1	3rd PM 8-N 8-E
HANNAH	**13**	1	3rd PM 6-N 10-E
HANNEMANN	**6**	2	3rd PM 7-N 8-E
HARBERT	**10**	1	2nd PM 7-N 14-W
HARDING	**2**	9	3rd PM 8-N 9-E
" "	**3**	5	3rd PM 8-N 10-E
HARGIS	**15**	1	2nd PM 6-N 14-W
HARLAND	**6**	1	3rd PM 7-N 8-E
HARLEN	**9**	3	3rd PM 7-N 11-E
" "	**14**	1	3rd PM 6-N 11-E
" "	**8**	1	3rd PM 7-N 10-E
HARMON	**10**	9	2nd PM 7-N 14-W
" "	**13**	1	3rd PM 6-N 10-E
" "	**7**	1	3rd PM 7-N 9-E
HARPER	**2**	1	3rd PM 8-N 9-E
HARRAH	**1**	7	3rd PM 8-N 8-E
HARRINGTON	**17**	1	3rd PM 5-N 9-E
" "	**12**	1	3rd PM 6-N 9-E
HARRIS	**2**	28	3rd PM 8-N 9-E
" "	**7**	23	3rd PM 7-N 9-E
" "	**12**	16	3rd PM 6-N 9-E
" "	**3**	7	3rd PM 8-N 10-E
" "	**13**	6	3rd PM 6-N 10-E
" "	**5**	4	2nd PM 8-N 14-W
HARRISON	**8**	5	3rd PM 7-N 10-E
" "	**3**	1	3rd PM 8-N 10-E
" "	**4**	1	3rd PM 8-N 11-E
HARTING	**6**	2	3rd PM 7-N 8-E
HARTMAN	**15**	1	2nd PM 6-N 14-W
HARTRICH	**13**	2	3rd PM 6-N 10-E
HARTRICK	**13**	7	3rd PM 6-N 10-E
" "	**15**	1	2nd PM 6-N 14-W
HASKET	**3**	4	3rd PM 8-N 10-E
HASTINGS	**16**	2	3rd PM 5-N 8-E
" "	**17**	1	3rd PM 5-N 9-E

Surname	Map Group	Parcels of Land	Meridian/Township/Range
HAWKINS	**10**	1	2nd PM 7-N 14-W
HAWKS	**11**	2	3rd PM 6-N 8-E
HAWLEY	**8**	1	3rd PM 7-N 10-E
HAWS	**8**	3	3rd PM 7-N 10-E
HAY	**20**	3	2nd PM 5-N 14-W
" "	**18**	2	3rd PM 5-N 10-E
HAYDEN	**13**	1	3rd PM 6-N 10-E
HAYES	**11**	3	3rd PM 6-N 8-E
" "	**6**	2	3rd PM 7-N 8-E
" "	**1**	1	3rd PM 8-N 8-E
HAYS	**1**	9	3rd PM 8-N 8-E
" "	**8**	5	3rd PM 7-N 10-E
" "	**2**	5	3rd PM 8-N 9-E
" "	**12**	2	3rd PM 6-N 9-E
" "	**13**	1	3rd PM 6-N 10-E
HAZELTON	**8**	2	3rd PM 7-N 10-E
HEADY	**17**	5	3rd PM 5-N 9-E
" "	**20**	1	2nd PM 5-N 14-W
" "	**12**	1	3rd PM 6-N 9-E
HEARD	**3**	1	3rd PM 8-N 10-E
HEFFERNAN	**1**	1	3rd PM 8-N 8-E
HEFNER	**8**	1	3rd PM 7-N 10-E
HELMICK	**5**	2	2nd PM 8-N 14-W
HELVET	**8**	1	3rd PM 7-N 10-E
HENDERSON	**6**	2	3rd PM 7-N 8-E
" "	**3**	2	3rd PM 8-N 10-E
HENDRICKSON	**10**	1	2nd PM 7-N 14-W
HENRICK	**8**	1	3rd PM 7-N 10-E
HENSLEY	**1**	6	3rd PM 8-N 8-E
" "	**7**	2	3rd PM 7-N 9-E
HEPNER	**10**	1	2nd PM 7-N 14-W
" "	**3**	1	3rd PM 8-N 10-E
HERRON	**13**	6	3rd PM 6-N 10-E
" "	**7**	5	3rd PM 7-N 9-E
" "	**12**	3	3rd PM 6-N 9-E
HESLER	**10**	2	2nd PM 7-N 14-W
" "	**9**	1	3rd PM 7-N 11-E
HESS	**1**	1	3rd PM 8-N 8-E
HETON	**5**	1	2nd PM 8-N 14-W
HICKS	**2**	2	3rd PM 8-N 9-E
HIGGINS	**17**	5	3rd PM 5-N 9-E
" "	**11**	3	3rd PM 6-N 8-E
" "	**15**	1	2nd PM 6-N 14-W
" "	**14**	1	3rd PM 6-N 11-E
HILDERBRAND	**6**	1	3rd PM 7-N 8-E
HILL	**11**	3	3rd PM 6-N 8-E
" "	**17**	2	3rd PM 5-N 9-E
" "	**10**	1	2nd PM 7-N 14-W
HILLBRANT	**16**	1	3rd PM 5-N 8-E
HILLS	**7**	1	3rd PM 7-N 9-E
" "	**2**	1	3rd PM 8-N 9-E
HILLYER	**2**	2	3rd PM 8-N 9-E
HINDS	**12**	3	3rd PM 6-N 9-E
" "	**11**	1	3rd PM 6-N 8-E
HINES	**18**	1	3rd PM 5-N 10-E
HINMAN	**20**	9	2nd PM 5-N 14-W
" "	**18**	4	3rd PM 5-N 10-E
" "	**10**	1	2nd PM 7-N 14-W
HINTON	**2**	3	3rd PM 8-N 9-E
HOARE	**6**	1	3rd PM 7-N 8-E

Surname	Map Group	Parcels of Land	Meridian/Township/Range
HOARE (Cont'd)	7	1	3rd PM 7-N 9-E
HODGE	16	1	3rd PM 5-N 8-E
HOFFMAN	18	2	3rd PM 5-N 10-E
HOFMAN	15	2	2nd PM 6-N 14-W
HOGUE	2	3	3rd PM 8-N 9-E
HOKE	17	1	3rd PM 5-N 9-E
HOLINGER	13	1	3rd PM 6-N 10-E
HOLLINGSWORTH	11	1	3rd PM 6-N 8-E
HOLLOM	6	1	3rd PM 7-N 8-E
HOLLOPETERS	8	3	3rd PM 7-N 10-E
" "	7	1	3rd PM 7-N 9-E
HOLM	6	6	3rd PM 7-N 8-E
" "	13	1	3rd PM 6-N 10-E
HOLMES	5	1	2nd PM 8-N 14-W
HOLSCHER	2	2	3rd PM 8-N 9-E
HOLT	5	1	2nd PM 8-N 14-W
HONEY	12	2	3rd PM 6-N 9-E
HOOVER	17	5	3rd PM 5-N 9-E
HOUGE	3	1	3rd PM 8-N 10-E
HOUSE	8	3	3rd PM 7-N 10-E
" "	5	1	2nd PM 8-N 14-W
HOUSTON	18	5	3rd PM 5-N 10-E
" "	20	2	2nd PM 5-N 14-W
" "	16	1	3rd PM 5-N 8-E
HOWARD	3	3	3rd PM 8-N 10-E
" "	5	2	2nd PM 8-N 14-W
" "	7	1	3rd PM 7-N 9-E
HOWE	7	3	3rd PM 7-N 9-E
HOWELL	13	1	3rd PM 6-N 10-E
HUDDLESTON	5	1	2nd PM 8-N 14-W
" "	4	1	3rd PM 8-N 11-E
HUDDLESTUN	4	3	3rd PM 8-N 11-E
HUDSON	3	1	3rd PM 8-N 10-E
HUFF	11	2	3rd PM 6-N 8-E
HUFFARD	20	1	2nd PM 5-N 14-W
HUFFMAN	14	1	3rd PM 6-N 11-E
HUGGINS	11	1	3rd PM 6-N 8-E
HUGHES	17	4	3rd PM 5-N 9-E
HUGHS	20	1	2nd PM 5-N 14-W
" "	18	1	3rd PM 5-N 10-E
HUME	8	8	3rd PM 7-N 10-E
" "	9	3	3rd PM 7-N 11-E
HUMES	8	1	3rd PM 7-N 10-E
HUMFREY	17	1	3rd PM 5-N 9-E
HUNT	3	16	3rd PM 8-N 10-E
" "	8	4	3rd PM 7-N 10-E
" "	7	3	3rd PM 7-N 9-E
" "	6	2	3rd PM 7-N 8-E
" "	4	1	3rd PM 8-N 11-E
" "	2	1	3rd PM 8-N 9-E
HUNTER	17	2	3rd PM 5-N 9-E
" "	3	1	3rd PM 8-N 10-E
HURD	4	1	3rd PM 8-N 11-E
HURING	2	2	3rd PM 8-N 9-E
HURST	16	2	3rd PM 5-N 8-E
" "	2	2	3rd PM 8-N 9-E
" "	17	1	3rd PM 5-N 9-E
HUSHAW	7	3	3rd PM 7-N 9-E
HUSSONG	5	1	2nd PM 8-N 14-W
" "	3	1	3rd PM 8-N 10-E

Surname	Map Group	Parcels of Land	Meridian/Township/Range
HUTSON	**2**	11	3rd PM 8-N 9-E
" "	**15**	1	2nd PM 6-N 14-W
" "	**3**	1	3rd PM 8-N 10-E
HYATT	**12**	1	3rd PM 6-N 9-E
INGLE	**8**	4	3rd PM 7-N 10-E
" "	**6**	1	3rd PM 7-N 8-E
IRELAND	**15**	4	2nd PM 6-N 14-W
" "	**10**	1	2nd PM 7-N 14-W
" "	**14**	1	3rd PM 6-N 11-E
IRVIN	**11**	1	3rd PM 6-N 8-E
ISLEY	**7**	4	3rd PM 7-N 9-E
" "	**2**	3	3rd PM 8-N 9-E
JACK	**2**	1	3rd PM 8-N 9-E
JACKSON	**6**	8	3rd PM 7-N 8-E
" "	**18**	6	3rd PM 5-N 10-E
" "	**17**	5	3rd PM 5-N 9-E
" "	**7**	1	3rd PM 7-N 9-E
JAMES	**15**	4	2nd PM 6-N 14-W
" "	**3**	3	3rd PM 8-N 10-E
" "	**20**	1	2nd PM 5-N 14-W
" "	**8**	1	3rd PM 7-N 10-E
" "	**7**	1	3rd PM 7-N 9-E
JARED	**5**	5	2nd PM 8-N 14-W
" "	**6**	1	3rd PM 7-N 8-E
JARRED	**5**	2	2nd PM 8-N 14-W
JASPER	**7**	2	3rd PM 7-N 9-E
JAYCON	**11**	1	3rd PM 6-N 8-E
JAYCOX	**11**	4	3rd PM 6-N 8-E
JEFFERS	**8**	5	3rd PM 7-N 10-E
" "	**10**	2	2nd PM 7-N 14-W
" "	**7**	1	3rd PM 7-N 9-E
JENKINS	**10**	8	2nd PM 7-N 14-W
" "	**20**	3	2nd PM 5-N 14-W
JOHNSON	**17**	6	3rd PM 5-N 9-E
" "	**12**	6	3rd PM 6-N 9-E
" "	**11**	4	3rd PM 6-N 8-E
" "	**8**	2	3rd PM 7-N 10-E
" "	**20**	1	2nd PM 5-N 14-W
" "	**15**	1	2nd PM 6-N 14-W
" "	**9**	1	3rd PM 7-N 11-E
JOHNSTON	**6**	2	3rd PM 7-N 8-E
" "	**15**	1	2nd PM 6-N 14-W
JONES	**11**	8	3rd PM 6-N 8-E
" "	**8**	8	3rd PM 7-N 10-E
" "	**7**	7	3rd PM 7-N 9-E
" "	**10**	4	2nd PM 7-N 14-W
" "	**2**	3	3rd PM 8-N 9-E
" "	**5**	2	2nd PM 8-N 14-W
" "	**15**	1	2nd PM 6-N 14-W
" "	**16**	1	3rd PM 5-N 8-E
" "	**12**	1	3rd PM 6-N 9-E
JORDAN	**13**	2	3rd PM 6-N 10-E
JORDON	**5**	2	2nd PM 8-N 14-W
" "	**7**	1	3rd PM 7-N 9-E
JOSEPH	**16**	1	3rd PM 5-N 8-E
JOURDAN	**6**	2	3rd PM 7-N 8-E
JOURDEN	**12**	2	3rd PM 6-N 9-E
" "	**7**	2	3rd PM 7-N 9-E
KARR	**15**	2	2nd PM 6-N 14-W
KAUFFMAN	**13**	2	3rd PM 6-N 10-E

Surname	Map Group	Parcels of Land	Meridian/Township/Range
KAUFFMANN	**18**	1	3rd PM 5-N 10-E
KAUFMANN	**13**	1	3rd PM 6-N 10-E
KEAN	**8**	2	3rd PM 7-N 10-E
" "	**7**	1	3rd PM 7-N 9-E
KEBLER	**7**	1	3rd PM 7-N 9-E
KECK	**6**	1	3rd PM 7-N 8-E
KEENE	**6**	2	3rd PM 7-N 8-E
KEIF	**10**	1	2nd PM 7-N 14-W
KEIFF	**10**	3	2nd PM 7-N 14-W
KEIFFE	**10**	1	2nd PM 7-N 14-W
KELLAM	**17**	2	3rd PM 5-N 9-E
KELLER	**20**	1	2nd PM 5-N 14-W
" "	**13**	1	3rd PM 6-N 10-E
KELLEY	**3**	3	3rd PM 8-N 10-E
KELLY	**3**	20	3rd PM 8-N 10-E
" "	**10**	7	2nd PM 7-N 14-W
" "	**8**	1	3rd PM 7-N 10-E
" "	**2**	1	3rd PM 8-N 9-E
KENEIPP	**6**	1	3rd PM 7-N 8-E
KENNEDY	**15**	1	2nd PM 6-N 14-W
KENNERLY	**18**	1	3rd PM 5-N 10-E
KEPLER	**13**	1	3rd PM 6-N 10-E
KEPLEY	**11**	1	3rd PM 6-N 8-E
KERN	**2**	2	3rd PM 8-N 9-E
KESSLER	**13**	5	3rd PM 6-N 10-E
KESTER	**11**	1	3rd PM 6-N 8-E
KESTERSON	**5**	1	2nd PM 8-N 14-W
KETTLE	**17**	5	3rd PM 5-N 9-E
KIBLER	**3**	27	3rd PM 8-N 10-E
" "	**7**	21	3rd PM 7-N 9-E
" "	**8**	7	3rd PM 7-N 10-E
" "	**2**	6	3rd PM 8-N 9-E
" "	**1**	5	3rd PM 8-N 8-E
KIBLINGER	**7**	1	3rd PM 7-N 9-E
KILBOURN	**3**	2	3rd PM 8-N 10-E
KILGORE	**3**	1	3rd PM 8-N 10-E
KILLGORE	**3**	1	3rd PM 8-N 10-E
" "	**2**	1	3rd PM 8-N 9-E
KING	**18**	9	3rd PM 5-N 10-E
" "	**17**	2	3rd PM 5-N 9-E
" "	**13**	2	3rd PM 6-N 10-E
" "	**16**	1	3rd PM 5-N 8-E
KINSLOW	**10**	2	2nd PM 7-N 14-W
KINTZEL	**8**	2	3rd PM 7-N 10-E
KIRKWOOD	**10**	2	2nd PM 7-N 14-W
" "	**3**	1	3rd PM 8-N 10-E
KITCHELL	**7**	3	3rd PM 7-N 9-E
" "	**17**	1	3rd PM 5-N 9-E
KITTLE	**17**	1	3rd PM 5-N 9-E
KLEIN	**16**	1	3rd PM 5-N 8-E
KNIGHT	**15**	1	2nd PM 6-N 14-W
KOEBELE	**1**	1	3rd PM 8-N 8-E
KOONS	**17**	2	3rd PM 5-N 9-E
KOONTZ	**6**	2	3rd PM 7-N 8-E
" "	**7**	1	3rd PM 7-N 9-E
KRAASS	**6**	1	3rd PM 7-N 8-E
KRAUS	**15**	2	2nd PM 6-N 14-W
KRITOSER	**13**	2	3rd PM 6-N 10-E
KROUS	**15**	1	2nd PM 6-N 14-W
KROUSE	**15**	1	2nd PM 6-N 14-W

Surname	Map Group	Parcels of Land	Meridian/Township/Range
KRUZAN	**11**	2	3rd PM 6-N 8-E
KUYKENDALL	**1**	1	3rd PM 8-N 8-E
LAGOW	**10**	1	2nd PM 7-N 14-W
" "	**18**	1	3rd PM 5-N 10-E
LAKE	**5**	1	2nd PM 8-N 14-W
" "	**1**	1	3rd PM 8-N 8-E
LAMASTERS	**5**	2	2nd PM 8-N 14-W
LAMB	**5**	1	2nd PM 8-N 14-W
LAMBERT	**11**	5	3rd PM 6-N 8-E
" "	**6**	1	3rd PM 7-N 8-E
LAMM	**12**	1	3rd PM 6-N 9-E
LANCASTER	**17**	2	3rd PM 5-N 9-E
" "	**16**	1	3rd PM 5-N 8-E
LANCE	**15**	3	2nd PM 6-N 14-W
LAND	**3**	2	3rd PM 8-N 10-E
LANGLE	**20**	1	2nd PM 5-N 14-W
LARIMER	**3**	1	3rd PM 8-N 10-E
" "	**2**	1	3rd PM 8-N 9-E
LAUGHLIN	**1**	1	3rd PM 8-N 8-E
LAUGHTER	**2**	1	3rd PM 8-N 9-E
LAWALL	**12**	1	3rd PM 6-N 9-E
LAWRENCE	**13**	3	3rd PM 6-N 10-E
" "	**18**	2	3rd PM 5-N 10-E
" "	**12**	2	3rd PM 6-N 9-E
LAWS	**12**	2	3rd PM 6-N 9-E
LAY	**16**	1	3rd PM 5-N 8-E
LEACH	**7**	4	3rd PM 7-N 9-E
" "	**10**	3	2nd PM 7-N 14-W
" "	**3**	3	3rd PM 8-N 10-E
" "	**2**	1	3rd PM 8-N 9-E
LEAMON	**5**	13	2nd PM 8-N 14-W
LEATH	**6**	2	3rd PM 7-N 8-E
LEE	**7**	7	3rd PM 7-N 9-E
" "	**13**	3	3rd PM 6-N 10-E
" "	**1**	2	3rd PM 8-N 8-E
" "	**15**	1	2nd PM 6-N 14-W
LEEMON	**20**	1	2nd PM 5-N 14-W
LEFLER	**14**	1	3rd PM 6-N 11-E
LEGGITT	**15**	1	2nd PM 6-N 14-W
LEINHART	**15**	3	2nd PM 6-N 14-W
" "	**13**	1	3rd PM 6-N 10-E
LEISURE	**8**	2	3rd PM 7-N 10-E
" "	**7**	2	3rd PM 7-N 9-E
LEMASTERS	**7**	2	3rd PM 7-N 9-E
" "	**20**	1	2nd PM 5-N 14-W
" "	**8**	1	3rd PM 7-N 10-E
LEMAY	**12**	8	3rd PM 6-N 9-E
" "	**7**	1	3rd PM 7-N 9-E
LEMON	**5**	2	2nd PM 8-N 14-W
LENEX	**10**	1	2nd PM 7-N 14-W
LEONARD	**11**	1	3rd PM 6-N 8-E
" "	**7**	1	3rd PM 7-N 9-E
LETURRO	**6**	1	3rd PM 7-N 8-E
LEVI	**12**	1	3rd PM 6-N 9-E
LEVINGSTON	**5**	4	2nd PM 8-N 14-W
LEWELLYN	**16**	2	3rd PM 5-N 8-E
LEWIS	**16**	10	3rd PM 5-N 8-E
" "	**6**	3	3rd PM 7-N 8-E
" "	**3**	3	3rd PM 8-N 10-E
" "	**12**	2	3rd PM 6-N 9-E

Surname	Map Group	Parcels of Land	Meridian/Township/Range		
LEWIS (Cont'd)	8	1	3rd PM	7-N	10-E
" "	4	1	3rd PM	8-N	11-E
LIDEY	2	8	3rd PM	8-N	9-E
" "	3	1	3rd PM	8-N	10-E
LIGHTNER	15	2	2nd PM	6-N	14-W
LILLY	12	4	3rd PM	6-N	9-E
" "	18	1	3rd PM	5-N	10-E
LINDER	20	1	2nd PM	5-N	14-W
LINDLEY	15	1	2nd PM	6-N	14-W
LINK	1	1	3rd PM	8-N	8-E
LINN	16	4	3rd PM	5-N	8-E
" "	17	3	3rd PM	5-N	9-E
LINTHIEUM	2	2	3rd PM	8-N	9-E
LIPTRAP	8	1	3rd PM	7-N	10-E
LISTER	16	1	3rd PM	5-N	8-E
LITTLE	2	2	3rd PM	8-N	9-E
LITTON	2	1	3rd PM	8-N	9-E
LITZELMANN	15	1	2nd PM	6-N	14-W
LITZERMAN	15	1	2nd PM	6-N	14-W
LLOYD	12	1	3rd PM	6-N	9-E
LOBMAIER	13	1	3rd PM	6-N	10-E
LOGAN	20	1	2nd PM	5-N	14-W
LOLLAR	16	1	3rd PM	5-N	8-E
LONG	2	5	3rd PM	8-N	9-E
" "	3	3	3rd PM	8-N	10-E
" "	18	1	3rd PM	5-N	10-E
LORANCE	15	1	2nd PM	6-N	14-W
" "	3	1	3rd PM	8-N	10-E
LOUGH	16	1	3rd PM	5-N	8-E
LOVE	6	1	3rd PM	7-N	8-E
LOY	7	1	3rd PM	7-N	9-E
LUERSEN	11	1	3rd PM	6-N	8-E
LUSTIG	6	1	3rd PM	7-N	8-E
LUX	6	4	3rd PM	7-N	8-E
LYONS	3	2	3rd PM	8-N	10-E
" "	2	2	3rd PM	8-N	9-E
MACHER	6	2	3rd PM	7-N	8-E
MACY	5	1	2nd PM	8-N	14-W
MADDEN	8	3	3rd PM	7-N	10-E
MAGILL	13	1	3rd PM	6-N	10-E
MAHAN	15	1	2nd PM	6-N	14-W
MAIER	6	3	3rd PM	7-N	8-E
MALLORY	3	1	3rd PM	8-N	10-E
MALONE	5	2	2nd PM	8-N	14-W
MAMMOPER	1	1	3rd PM	8-N	8-E
MAMMOSER	1	2	3rd PM	8-N	8-E
MANDLOVE	15	1	2nd PM	6-N	14-W
MANLEY	5	1	2nd PM	8-N	14-W
MANNING	11	1	3rd PM	6-N	8-E
" "	12	1	3rd PM	6-N	9-E
" "	3	1	3rd PM	8-N	10-E
MARK	1	1	3rd PM	8-N	8-E
MARKLAND	3	2	3rd PM	8-N	10-E
MARKS	6	3	3rd PM	7-N	8-E
MARKWELL	2	1	3rd PM	8-N	9-E
MARRS	1	2	3rd PM	8-N	8-E
MARSH	7	3	3rd PM	7-N	9-E
MARSHALL	8	2	3rd PM	7-N	10-E
MARTIN	3	7	3rd PM	8-N	10-E
" "	9	4	3rd PM	7-N	11-E

Surname	Map Group	Parcels of Land	Meridian/Township/Range		
MARTIN (Cont'd)	**8**	2	3rd PM	7-N	10-E
" "	**5**	1	2nd PM	8-N	14-W
" "	**12**	1	3rd PM	6-N	9-E
" "	**6**	1	3rd PM	7-N	8-E
MASCHER	**6**	5	3rd PM	7-N	8-E
MASON	**13**	3	3rd PM	6-N	10-E
" "	**16**	2	3rd PM	5-N	8-E
MATHENY	**5**	2	2nd PM	8-N	14-W
MATHEW	**2**	2	3rd PM	8-N	9-E
MATHEWS	**11**	1	3rd PM	6-N	8-E
" "	**9**	1	3rd PM	7-N	11-E
MATLOCK	**11**	2	3rd PM	6-N	8-E
MATTHEWS	**8**	1	3rd PM	7-N	10-E
MATTINGLEY	**18**	5	3rd PM	5-N	10-E
" "	**11**	1	3rd PM	6-N	8-E
MATTINGLY	**18**	6	3rd PM	5-N	10-E
" "	**12**	2	3rd PM	6-N	9-E
" "	**13**	1	3rd PM	6-N	10-E
MAURER	**1**	3	3rd PM	8-N	8-E
MAXWELL	**13**	6	3rd PM	6-N	10-E
" "	**12**	1	3rd PM	6-N	9-E
MAY	**19**	7	3rd PM	5-N	11-E
" "	**20**	5	2nd PM	5-N	14-W
" "	**18**	1	3rd PM	5-N	10-E
" "	**13**	1	3rd PM	6-N	10-E
MAYSEY	**5**	5	2nd PM	8-N	14-W
MAZE	**3**	2	3rd PM	8-N	10-E
MCALLISTER	**10**	2	2nd PM	7-N	14-W
MCBATH	**2**	5	3rd PM	8-N	9-E
MCCABE	**10**	2	2nd PM	7-N	14-W
" "	**5**	1	2nd PM	8-N	14-W
" "	**6**	1	3rd PM	7-N	8-E
MCCAIN	**3**	2	3rd PM	8-N	10-E
" "	**5**	1	2nd PM	8-N	14-W
MCCALL	**7**	4	3rd PM	7-N	9-E
MCCARTHY	**6**	1	3rd PM	7-N	8-E
MCCARTY	**17**	5	3rd PM	5-N	9-E
" "	**10**	3	2nd PM	7-N	14-W
" "	**15**	2	2nd PM	6-N	14-W
" "	**5**	2	2nd PM	8-N	14-W
" "	**7**	1	3rd PM	7-N	9-E
MCCLAIN	**5**	1	2nd PM	8-N	14-W
MCCLELLAND	**10**	1	2nd PM	7-N	14-W
MCCLURE	**20**	2	2nd PM	5-N	14-W
" "	**12**	1	3rd PM	6-N	9-E
MCCOLLUM	**16**	4	3rd PM	5-N	8-E
MCCOMAS	**3**	3	3rd PM	8-N	10-E
" "	**2**	2	3rd PM	8-N	9-E
MCCOMMIS	**3**	1	3rd PM	8-N	10-E
MCCOOMAS	**12**	1	3rd PM	6-N	9-E
MCCORMICK	**10**	2	2nd PM	7-N	14-W
MCCORNAS	**3**	1	3rd PM	8-N	10-E
MCCOY	**1**	3	3rd PM	8-N	8-E
" "	**5**	1	2nd PM	8-N	14-W
" "	**6**	1	3rd PM	7-N	8-E
MCCRACKEN	**3**	2	3rd PM	8-N	10-E
MCCRILLIS	**10**	1	2nd PM	7-N	14-W
MCCUBBIN	**5**	1	2nd PM	8-N	14-W
MCCUBBINS	**5**	6	2nd PM	8-N	14-W
" "	**4**	2	3rd PM	8-N	11-E

Surname	Map Group	Parcels of Land	Meridian/Township/Range
MCCUBBINS (Cont'd)	**6**	1	3rd PM 7-N 8-E
MCCULLOUGH	**12**	5	3rd PM 6-N 9-E
" "	**17**	3	3rd PM 5-N 9-E
" "	**18**	2	3rd PM 5-N 10-E
" "	**3**	1	3rd PM 8-N 10-E
MCDANIEL	**7**	13	3rd PM 7-N 9-E
" "	**2**	3	3rd PM 8-N 9-E
" "	**15**	1	2nd PM 6-N 14-W
MCDONALD	**12**	2	3rd PM 6-N 9-E
MCDONNEL	**13**	1	3rd PM 6-N 10-E
MCGAHEY	**18**	8	3rd PM 5-N 10-E
MCGARNEY	**3**	1	3rd PM 8-N 10-E
MCGINNESS	**10**	2	2nd PM 7-N 14-W
MCILVOY	**13**	8	3rd PM 6-N 10-E
MCILWAIN	**3**	4	3rd PM 8-N 10-E
MCKAY	**17**	2	3rd PM 5-N 9-E
MCKEARBY	**16**	1	3rd PM 5-N 8-E
MCKEE	**10**	3	2nd PM 7-N 14-W
" "	**5**	1	2nd PM 8-N 14-W
" "	**9**	1	3rd PM 7-N 11-E
MCKINLEY	**13**	8	3rd PM 6-N 10-E
" "	**8**	1	3rd PM 7-N 10-E
MCKINLY	**13**	2	3rd PM 6-N 10-E
MCKINNEY	**18**	5	3rd PM 5-N 10-E
" "	**20**	3	2nd PM 5-N 14-W
" "	**7**	1	3rd PM 7-N 9-E
MCKINSTER	**7**	2	3rd PM 7-N 9-E
MCKNIGHT	**18**	2	3rd PM 5-N 10-E
MCMANAMY	**6**	1	3rd PM 7-N 8-E
MCNAIR	**9**	7	3rd PM 7-N 11-E
" "	**8**	3	3rd PM 7-N 10-E
MCNIGHT	**18**	1	3rd PM 5-N 10-E
MCNUTT	**11**	1	3rd PM 6-N 8-E
MCPEAK	**16**	1	3rd PM 5-N 8-E
MCQUAID	**1**	3	3rd PM 8-N 8-E
" "	**6**	1	3rd PM 7-N 8-E
MCQUEEN	**16**	2	3rd PM 5-N 8-E
" "	**11**	2	3rd PM 6-N 8-E
MCQUISTON	**7**	3	3rd PM 7-N 9-E
MCRENLEY	**20**	4	2nd PM 5-N 14-W
MEAKER	**5**	1	2nd PM 8-N 14-W
MEANS	**10**	1	2nd PM 7-N 14-W
MEDKIFF	**18**	1	3rd PM 5-N 10-E
MEEK	**17**	9	3rd PM 5-N 9-E
" "	**12**	3	3rd PM 6-N 9-E
MEEKER	**5**	1	2nd PM 8-N 14-W
MEERE	**10**	2	2nd PM 7-N 14-W
MEESE	**15**	2	2nd PM 6-N 14-W
" "	**10**	2	2nd PM 7-N 14-W
MEINHART	**1**	5	3rd PM 8-N 8-E
MEISLAHN	**1**	2	3rd PM 8-N 8-E
MERCERET	**15**	2	2nd PM 6-N 14-W
" "	**20**	1	2nd PM 5-N 14-W
MERITT	**2**	2	3rd PM 8-N 9-E
MERRITT	**2**	1	3rd PM 8-N 9-E
METHENY	**5**	4	2nd PM 8-N 14-W
METSKER	**17**	1	3rd PM 5-N 9-E
METZ	**16**	2	3rd PM 5-N 8-E
MICHAEL	**8**	3	3rd PM 7-N 10-E
MICHELL	**11**	1	3rd PM 6-N 8-E

Surname	Map Group	Parcels of Land	Meridian/Township/Range		
MICHELL (Cont'd)	**6**	1	3rd PM	7-N	8-E
MICKENBERGER	**15**	1	2nd PM	6-N	14-W
MIDKIFF	**18**	8	3rd PM	5-N	10-E
" "	**20**	6	2nd PM	5-N	14-W
" "	**15**	1	2nd PM	6-N	14-W
MIKWORTH	**5**	1	2nd PM	8-N	14-W
MILLER	**10**	13	2nd PM	7-N	14-W
" "	**15**	9	2nd PM	6-N	14-W
" "	**5**	8	2nd PM	8-N	14-W
" "	**13**	8	3rd PM	6-N	10-E
" "	**6**	3	3rd PM	7-N	8-E
" "	**11**	2	3rd PM	6-N	8-E
" "	**1**	2	3rd PM	8-N	8-E
" "	**20**	1	2nd PM	5-N	14-W
" "	**12**	1	3rd PM	6-N	9-E
MILLIN	**11**	2	3rd PM	6-N	8-E
MILLIS	**3**	2	3rd PM	8-N	10-E
MINGS	**18**	2	3rd PM	5-N	10-E
MINOR	**6**	3	3rd PM	7-N	8-E
MINTON	**3**	1	3rd PM	8-N	10-E
MIRES	**8**	3	3rd PM	7-N	10-E
" "	**15**	2	2nd PM	6-N	14-W
" "	**14**	1	3rd PM	6-N	11-E
MISNER	**17**	1	3rd PM	5-N	9-E
MITCHELL	**8**	4	3rd PM	7-N	10-E
" "	**1**	3	3rd PM	8-N	8-E
" "	**11**	2	3rd PM	6-N	8-E
" "	**3**	2	3rd PM	8-N	10-E
" "	**6**	1	3rd PM	7-N	8-E
" "	**2**	1	3rd PM	8-N	9-E
MOCK	**3**	12	3rd PM	8-N	10-E
MONAHAN	**11**	1	3rd PM	6-N	8-E
MONDON	**2**	1	3rd PM	8-N	9-E
MONELL	**6**	1	3rd PM	7-N	8-E
MONROE	**17**	4	3rd PM	5-N	9-E
" "	**10**	2	2nd PM	7-N	14-W
MONRONEY	**4**	2	3rd PM	8-N	11-E
" "	**9**	1	3rd PM	7-N	11-E
MOORE	**2**	6	3rd PM	8-N	9-E
" "	**7**	5	3rd PM	7-N	9-E
" "	**3**	2	3rd PM	8-N	10-E
" "	**6**	1	3rd PM	7-N	8-E
MOORMAN	**5**	1	2nd PM	8-N	14-W
MORELAND	**3**	1	3rd PM	8-N	10-E
MORGAN	**18**	7	3rd PM	5-N	10-E
" "	**3**	2	3rd PM	8-N	10-E
MORONEY	**9**	1	3rd PM	7-N	11-E
MORRIS	**12**	4	3rd PM	6-N	9-E
" "	**11**	2	3rd PM	6-N	8-E
" "	**7**	1	3rd PM	7-N	9-E
MOSCHENROSS	**8**	3	3rd PM	7-N	10-E
MULGUEEN	**6**	1	3rd PM	7-N	8-E
MULLENS	**16**	1	3rd PM	5-N	8-E
MULLINS	**16**	1	3rd PM	5-N	8-E
MULVANY	**8**	1	3rd PM	7-N	10-E
MURPHEY	**12**	2	3rd PM	6-N	9-E
" "	**19**	1	3rd PM	5-N	11-E
MURPHY	**20**	1	2nd PM	5-N	14-W
MURVIN	**13**	1	3rd PM	6-N	10-E
MUSER	**17**	1	3rd PM	5-N	9-E

Surname	Map Group	Parcels of Land	Meridian/Township/Range		
MUSGRAVE	**3**	2	3rd PM	8-N	10-E
" "	**2**	2	3rd PM	8-N	9-E
" "	**6**	1	3rd PM	7-N	8-E
MUSGROVE	**2**	4	3rd PM	8-N	9-E
MYERS	**2**	12	3rd PM	8-N	9-E
" "	**1**	8	3rd PM	8-N	8-E
" "	**18**	2	3rd PM	5-N	10-E
MYRES	**6**	1	3rd PM	7-N	8-E
NAGELY	**13**	2	3rd PM	6-N	10-E
" "	**8**	1	3rd PM	7-N	10-E
" "	**7**	1	3rd PM	7-N	9-E
NATION	**12**	1	3rd PM	6-N	9-E
NEAL	**10**	3	2nd PM	7-N	14-W
" "	**15**	2	2nd PM	6-N	14-W
" "	**11**	1	3rd PM	6-N	8-E
NEALE	**11**	1	3rd PM	6-N	8-E
NEEDHAM	**17**	4	3rd PM	5-N	9-E
NEIBARGER	**5**	3	2nd PM	8-N	14-W
NESSLEY	**11**	2	3rd PM	6-N	8-E
NEWBOULD	**15**	5	2nd PM	6-N	14-W
NEWLIN	**1**	2	3rd PM	8-N	8-E
NEWTON	**1**	1	3rd PM	8-N	8-E
NICELY	**17**	3	3rd PM	5-N	9-E
NICHOLAS	**15**	7	2nd PM	6-N	14-W
" "	**17**	1	3rd PM	5-N	9-E
NICHOLS	**1**	15	3rd PM	8-N	8-E
" "	**15**	2	2nd PM	6-N	14-W
" "	**18**	1	3rd PM	5-N	10-E
" "	**6**	1	3rd PM	7-N	8-E
" "	**2**	1	3rd PM	8-N	9-E
NIGHT	**12**	1	3rd PM	6-N	9-E
NOEL	**10**	2	2nd PM	7-N	14-W
NORRIS	**3**	3	3rd PM	8-N	10-E
NORTON	**3**	1	3rd PM	8-N	10-E
NOTINGHAM	**17**	2	3rd PM	5-N	9-E
NUTT	**11**	1	3rd PM	6-N	8-E
OBRIEN	**6**	2	3rd PM	7-N	8-E
OCHELTREE	**16**	2	3rd PM	5-N	8-E
OCONNOR	**6**	1	3rd PM	7-N	8-E
ODELL	**1**	1	3rd PM	8-N	8-E
" "	**2**	1	3rd PM	8-N	9-E
ODLE	**5**	2	2nd PM	8-N	14-W
ODONNELL	**20**	1	2nd PM	5-N	14-W
ODOR	**20**	1	2nd PM	5-N	14-W
OGDEN	**8**	3	3rd PM	7-N	10-E
" "	**7**	1	3rd PM	7-N	9-E
OKEAN	**12**	3	3rd PM	6-N	9-E
" "	**19**	2	3rd PM	5-N	11-E
" "	**11**	2	3rd PM	6-N	8-E
" "	**7**	2	3rd PM	7-N	9-E
OKEEN	**11**	2	3rd PM	6-N	8-E
" "	**6**	2	3rd PM	7-N	8-E
OLDAKER	**12**	1	3rd PM	6-N	9-E
ORR	**5**	1	2nd PM	8-N	14-W
OSBORN	**3**	2	3rd PM	8-N	10-E
OSBURN	**3**	1	3rd PM	8-N	10-E
OST	**15**	1	2nd PM	6-N	14-W
" "	**18**	1	3rd PM	5-N	10-E
OURY	**5**	3	2nd PM	8-N	14-W
OWEN	**15**	1	2nd PM	6-N	14-W

Surname	Map Group	Parcels of Land	Meridian/Township/Range		
OWEN (Cont'd)	**16**	1	3rd PM	5-N	8-E
OWRY	**5**	1	2nd PM	8-N	14-W
PAGE	**18**	3	3rd PM	5-N	10-E
PAIN	**13**	3	3rd PM	6-N	10-E
PAINE	**8**	1	3rd PM	7-N	10-E
PARENT	**8**	1	3rd PM	7-N	10-E
PARKER	**5**	2	2nd PM	8-N	14-W
" "	**16**	2	3rd PM	5-N	8-E
" "	**15**	1	2nd PM	6-N	14-W
" "	**11**	1	3rd PM	6-N	8-E
" "	**3**	1	3rd PM	8-N	10-E
PARR	**8**	3	3rd PM	7-N	10-E
" "	**7**	3	3rd PM	7-N	9-E
PARRENT	**8**	4	3rd PM	7-N	10-E
PARSHALL	**16**	2	3rd PM	5-N	8-E
PARSONS	**2**	3	3rd PM	8-N	9-E
" "	**5**	1	2nd PM	8-N	14-W
" "	**7**	1	3rd PM	7-N	9-E
PATEE	**8**	2	3rd PM	7-N	10-E
PATRICK	**3**	7	3rd PM	8-N	10-E
" "	**7**	5	3rd PM	7-N	9-E
" "	**13**	1	3rd PM	6-N	10-E
" "	**1**	1	3rd PM	8-N	8-E
PATTERSON	**8**	1	3rd PM	7-N	10-E
" "	**3**	1	3rd PM	8-N	10-E
PAUGH	**3**	3	3rd PM	8-N	10-E
PAULUS	**7**	4	3rd PM	7-N	9-E
" "	**8**	1	3rd PM	7-N	10-E
PAYNE	**3**	4	3rd PM	8-N	10-E
" "	**13**	3	3rd PM	6-N	10-E
" "	**2**	1	3rd PM	8-N	9-E
PEARPOINT	**12**	2	3rd PM	6-N	9-E
PECKLE	**6**	1	3rd PM	7-N	8-E
PENHORWOOD	**5**	1	2nd PM	8-N	14-W
PENNINGTON	**2**	1	3rd PM	8-N	9-E
PERISHO	**4**	4	3rd PM	8-N	11-E
" "	**5**	2	2nd PM	8-N	14-W
" "	**3**	2	3rd PM	8-N	10-E
PETERSON	**12**	10	3rd PM	6-N	9-E
" "	**7**	5	3rd PM	7-N	9-E
" "	**1**	3	3rd PM	8-N	8-E
" "	**13**	2	3rd PM	6-N	10-E
" "	**16**	1	3rd PM	5-N	8-E
" "	**6**	1	3rd PM	7-N	8-E
PEYTON	**15**	1	2nd PM	6-N	14-W
PHELPS	**15**	1	2nd PM	6-N	14-W
PHILIPS	**10**	1	2nd PM	7-N	14-W
PHILLIPS	**7**	1	3rd PM	7-N	9-E
PICQUET	**13**	37	3rd PM	6-N	10-E
" "	**18**	19	3rd PM	5-N	10-E
" "	**14**	12	3rd PM	6-N	11-E
" "	**15**	10	2nd PM	6-N	14-W
" "	**8**	4	3rd PM	7-N	10-E
" "	**7**	4	3rd PM	7-N	9-E
" "	**20**	2	2nd PM	5-N	14-W
" "	**19**	2	3rd PM	5-N	11-E
PIECUIT	**15**	2	2nd PM	6-N	14-W
PIEQUET	**15**	4	2nd PM	6-N	14-W
PIKE	**7**	2	3rd PM	7-N	9-E
PINDELL	**13**	2	3rd PM	6-N	10-E

Surname	Map Group	Parcels of Land	Meridian/Township/Range		
PING	**15**	16	2nd PM	6-N	14-W
" "	**10**	7	2nd PM	7-N	14-W
PIQUET	**15**	1	2nd PM	6-N	14-W
" "	**14**	1	3rd PM	6-N	11-E
PLANK	**17**	3	3rd PM	5-N	9-E
POLLIS	**20**	1	2nd PM	5-N	14-W
POMEROT	**16**	1	3rd PM	5-N	8-E
POMEROY	**16**	5	3rd PM	5-N	8-E
POOR	**3**	2	3rd PM	8-N	10-E
POWELL	**2**	5	3rd PM	8-N	9-E
" "	**11**	3	3rd PM	6-N	8-E
" "	**12**	3	3rd PM	6-N	9-E
" "	**17**	2	3rd PM	5-N	9-E
" "	**3**	2	3rd PM	8-N	10-E
" "	**18**	1	3rd PM	5-N	10-E
" "	**7**	1	3rd PM	7-N	9-E
PRENTISS	**11**	2	3rd PM	6-N	8-E
PRESTON	**16**	8	3rd PM	5-N	8-E
" "	**5**	5	2nd PM	8-N	14-W
" "	**10**	4	2nd PM	7-N	14-W
" "	**15**	3	2nd PM	6-N	14-W
" "	**17**	1	3rd PM	5-N	9-E
" "	**13**	1	3rd PM	6-N	10-E
PRICE	**3**	4	3rd PM	8-N	10-E
" "	**2**	3	3rd PM	8-N	9-E
" "	**15**	1	2nd PM	6-N	14-W
" "	**14**	1	3rd PM	6-N	11-E
" "	**11**	1	3rd PM	6-N	8-E
" "	**8**	1	3rd PM	7-N	10-E
PRINCE	**12**	1	3rd PM	6-N	9-E
PRINTZ	**1**	2	3rd PM	8-N	8-E
PROSE	**3**	1	3rd PM	8-N	10-E
PRUET	**16**	1	3rd PM	5-N	8-E
" "	**11**	1	3rd PM	6-N	8-E
PULLIAM	**16**	1	3rd PM	5-N	8-E
PULLIS	**13**	1	3rd PM	6-N	10-E
PURSELL	**6**	1	3rd PM	7-N	8-E
PUTTROFF	**17**	1	3rd PM	5-N	9-E
RAEF	**20**	7	2nd PM	5-N	14-W
" "	**18**	2	3rd PM	5-N	10-E
" "	**19**	2	3rd PM	5-N	11-E
" "	**15**	1	2nd PM	6-N	14-W
RAFE	**19**	5	3rd PM	5-N	11-E
" "	**20**	3	2nd PM	5-N	14-W
" "	**13**	3	3rd PM	6-N	10-E
RAINES	**8**	2	3rd PM	7-N	10-E
RAMSEY	**11**	1	3rd PM	6-N	8-E
RANDOLPH	**6**	1	3rd PM	7-N	8-E
RANOLPH	**6**	1	3rd PM	7-N	8-E
RAPER	**1**	2	3rd PM	8-N	8-E
RAWLINGS	**12**	3	3rd PM	6-N	9-E
RAY	**3**	2	3rd PM	8-N	10-E
" "	**2**	1	3rd PM	8-N	9-E
RAYLE	**17**	3	3rd PM	5-N	9-E
REA	**7**	2	3rd PM	7-N	9-E
REDFORD	**2**	5	3rd PM	8-N	9-E
" "	**1**	2	3rd PM	8-N	8-E
" "	**7**	1	3rd PM	7-N	9-E
REDMAN	**16**	1	3rd PM	5-N	8-E
REED	**6**	5	3rd PM	7-N	8-E

Surname	Map Group	Parcels of Land	Meridian/Township/Range
REED (Cont'd)	**11**	4	3rd PM 6-N 8-E
REEDS	**6**	1	3rd PM 7-N 8-E
REEGLE	**20**	3	2nd PM 5-N 14-W
REEGLESBARGER	**7**	1	3rd PM 7-N 9-E
REELHORN	**17**	4	3rd PM 5-N 9-E
REEVES	**12**	1	3rd PM 6-N 9-E
REFFIT	**1**	2	3rd PM 8-N 8-E
" "	**6**	1	3rd PM 7-N 8-E
REIGELSBERGER	**13**	4	3rd PM 6-N 10-E
REIGLE	**20**	3	2nd PM 5-N 14-W
REILEY	**20**	1	2nd PM 5-N 14-W
REILLEY	**20**	1	2nd PM 5-N 14-W
REILLY	**20**	1	2nd PM 5-N 14-W
REINS	**9**	2	3rd PM 7-N 11-E
" "	**10**	1	2nd PM 7-N 14-W
" "	**3**	1	3rd PM 8-N 10-E
REISNER	**8**	3	3rd PM 7-N 10-E
RENICK	**6**	2	3rd PM 7-N 8-E
REPETTO	**20**	1	2nd PM 5-N 14-W
" "	**15**	1	2nd PM 6-N 14-W
REYNOLDS	**6**	4	3rd PM 7-N 8-E
" "	**13**	1	3rd PM 6-N 10-E
" "	**1**	1	3rd PM 8-N 8-E
RHEA	**5**	1	2nd PM 8-N 14-W
RHOADES	**6**	5	3rd PM 7-N 8-E
RHOADS	**6**	1	3rd PM 7-N 8-E
RIBLER	**7**	1	3rd PM 7-N 9-E
RICE	**2**	2	3rd PM 8-N 9-E
RICENER	**8**	1	3rd PM 7-N 10-E
RICHARD	**7**	1	3rd PM 7-N 9-E
RICHARDS	**12**	6	3rd PM 6-N 9-E
" "	**11**	3	3rd PM 6-N 8-E
" "	**7**	1	3rd PM 7-N 9-E
RICHEY	**7**	1	3rd PM 7-N 9-E
RICK	**1**	1	3rd PM 8-N 8-E
RICKMAN	**8**	3	3rd PM 7-N 10-E
" "	**7**	1	3rd PM 7-N 9-E
RIDENHOUR	**11**	4	3rd PM 6-N 8-E
RIDENOUR	**11**	7	3rd PM 6-N 8-E
RIDLEN	**15**	3	2nd PM 6-N 14-W
" "	**8**	3	3rd PM 7-N 10-E
" "	**17**	2	3rd PM 5-N 9-E
" "	**14**	2	3rd PM 6-N 11-E
RIDLON	**15**	3	2nd PM 6-N 14-W
RIFE	**16**	5	3rd PM 5-N 8-E
" "	**13**	2	3rd PM 6-N 10-E
" "	**11**	2	3rd PM 6-N 8-E
RIFFETT	**6**	1	3rd PM 7-N 8-E
RIGDON	**8**	2	3rd PM 7-N 10-E
RIGGLE	**20**	1	2nd PM 5-N 14-W
RIGHT	**7**	2	3rd PM 7-N 9-E
RILEY	**11**	4	3rd PM 6-N 8-E
" "	**10**	3	2nd PM 7-N 14-W
" "	**6**	2	3rd PM 7-N 8-E
RINJWALD	**11**	1	3rd PM 6-N 8-E
RIPPETO	**20**	1	2nd PM 5-N 14-W
" "	**18**	1	3rd PM 5-N 10-E
ROACH	**13**	1	3rd PM 6-N 10-E
" "	**9**	1	3rd PM 7-N 11-E
ROBBINS	**8**	2	3rd PM 7-N 10-E

Surname	Map Group	Parcels of Land	Meridian/Township/Range		
ROBBINS (Cont'd)	12	1	3rd PM	6-N	9-E
" "	7	1	3rd PM	7-N	9-E
ROBE	1	1	3rd PM	8-N	8-E
ROBERSON	1	2	3rd PM	8-N	8-E
ROBERTS	10	11	2nd PM	7-N	14-W
" "	5	6	2nd PM	8-N	14-W
" "	3	6	3rd PM	8-N	10-E
" "	11	3	3rd PM	6-N	8-E
" "	16	1	3rd PM	5-N	8-E
" "	17	1	3rd PM	5-N	9-E
" "	12	1	3rd PM	6-N	9-E
" "	4	1	3rd PM	8-N	11-E
" "	1	1	3rd PM	8-N	8-E
ROBERTSON	8	3	3rd PM	7-N	10-E
ROBINSON	5	3	2nd PM	8-N	14-W
" "	8	3	3rd PM	7-N	10-E
ROCH	13	1	3rd PM	6-N	10-E
RODGERS	8	4	3rd PM	7-N	10-E
ROGERS	15	2	2nd PM	6-N	14-W
ROONEY	18	1	3rd PM	5-N	10-E
ROPER	1	2	3rd PM	8-N	8-E
ROSS	13	6	3rd PM	6-N	10-E
" "	1	4	3rd PM	8-N	8-E
" "	3	2	3rd PM	8-N	10-E
" "	12	1	3rd PM	6-N	9-E
ROW	3	3	3rd PM	8-N	10-E
ROWLAND	16	1	3rd PM	5-N	8-E
ROYAL	10	2	2nd PM	7-N	14-W
RUDDELL	15	1	2nd PM	6-N	14-W
RUSING	17	2	3rd PM	5-N	9-E
RUSSEL	17	1	3rd PM	5-N	9-E
RUTHERFORD	15	2	2nd PM	6-N	14-W
RYA	10	1	2nd PM	7-N	14-W
RYAN	10	3	2nd PM	7-N	14-W
" "	15	1	2nd PM	6-N	14-W
" "	5	1	2nd PM	8-N	14-W
" "	4	1	3rd PM	8-N	11-E
RYON	10	1	2nd PM	7-N	14-W
SAIGER	7	1	3rd PM	7-N	9-E
SAMPSON	17	4	3rd PM	5-N	9-E
" "	11	2	3rd PM	6-N	8-E
" "	6	1	3rd PM	7-N	8-E
SANDERS	20	1	2nd PM	5-N	14-W
SANDS	17	1	3rd PM	5-N	9-E
SCHACKMAN	8	8	3rd PM	7-N	10-E
" "	13	2	3rd PM	6-N	10-E
SCHACKMANN	8	2	3rd PM	7-N	10-E
SCHAMHART	11	1	3rd PM	6-N	8-E
SCHATTMAN	1	1	3rd PM	8-N	8-E
SCHEALDBANER	8	1	3rd PM	7-N	10-E
SCHEDLBANER	8	3	3rd PM	7-N	10-E
SCHELDBANER	19	2	3rd PM	5-N	11-E
" "	8	2	3rd PM	7-N	10-E
" "	18	1	3rd PM	5-N	10-E
SCHIFFERSTEIN	13	3	3rd PM	6-N	10-E
" "	15	1	2nd PM	6-N	14-W
" "	19	1	3rd PM	5-N	11-E
" "	14	1	3rd PM	6-N	11-E
SCHOTTMANN	1	5	3rd PM	8-N	8-E
SCHROADER	3	2	3rd PM	8-N	10-E

Surname	Map Group	Parcels of Land	Meridian/Township/Range
SCHUFFENSTUN	**15**	3	2nd PM 6-N 14-W
"	**8**	3	3rd PM 7-N 10-E
SCHUHK	**19**	1	3rd PM 5-N 11-E
SCHUMACHER	**6**	1	3rd PM 7-N 8-E
SCHWAGER	**15**	1	2nd PM 6-N 14-W
SCIFRES	**13**	1	3rd PM 6-N 10-E
SCOTT	**16**	5	3rd PM 5-N 8-E
" "	**12**	3	3rd PM 6-N 9-E
" "	**7**	3	3rd PM 7-N 9-E
SCRADER	**8**	1	3rd PM 7-N 10-E
SCREWS	**1**	1	3rd PM 8-N 8-E
SCRIVEN	**6**	1	3rd PM 7-N 8-E
SEAMON	**5**	3	2nd PM 8-N 14-W
SEARSE	**1**	1	3rd PM 8-N 8-E
SEGELER	**8**	1	3rd PM 7-N 10-E
SEITH	**6**	1	3rd PM 7-N 8-E
SELBY	**11**	11	3rd PM 6-N 8-E
" "	**10**	4	2nd PM 7-N 14-W
" "	**8**	4	3rd PM 7-N 10-E
" "	**6**	2	3rd PM 7-N 8-E
SELF	**6**	1	3rd PM 7-N 8-E
SELLERS	**7**	2	3rd PM 7-N 9-E
SERIGHT	**7**	2	3rd PM 7-N 9-E
SEXTON	**6**	1	3rd PM 7-N 8-E
SHACKLEE	**10**	1	2nd PM 7-N 14-W
SHAFER	**15**	1	2nd PM 6-N 14-W
SHAMHART	**11**	5	3rd PM 6-N 8-E
SHAMHEART	**11**	2	3rd PM 6-N 8-E
SHARICK	**7**	9	3rd PM 7-N 9-E
" "	**8**	3	3rd PM 7-N 10-E
SHARP	**7**	2	3rd PM 7-N 9-E
SHAW	**12**	1	3rd PM 6-N 9-E
SHEALY	**9**	1	3rd PM 7-N 11-E
SHEARS	**7**	1	3rd PM 7-N 9-E
SHELL	**3**	1	3rd PM 8-N 10-E
SHEPHERD	**11**	1	3rd PM 6-N 8-E
SHERER	**5**	1	2nd PM 8-N 14-W
SHERMAN	**1**	1	3rd PM 8-N 8-E
SHERWOOD	**2**	4	3rd PM 8-N 9-E
SHIPLEY	**20**	1	2nd PM 5-N 14-W
" "	**18**	1	3rd PM 5-N 10-E
SHIRDEN	**8**	1	3rd PM 7-N 10-E
SHIRLEY	**14**	1	3rd PM 6-N 11-E
SHOOK	**5**	1	2nd PM 8-N 14-W
SHORT	**5**	3	2nd PM 8-N 14-W
" "	**17**	1	3rd PM 5-N 9-E
SHOWALTER	**5**	2	2nd PM 8-N 14-W
SHUE	**19**	1	3rd PM 5-N 11-E
SHUH	**19**	1	3rd PM 5-N 11-E
SHY	**12**	1	3rd PM 6-N 9-E
" "	**1**	1	3rd PM 8-N 8-E
SICKMEN	**17**	1	3rd PM 5-N 9-E
SIDDINS	**1**	1	3rd PM 8-N 8-E
SIEFKEN	**1**	1	3rd PM 8-N 8-E
SIGLER	**8**	1	3rd PM 7-N 10-E
SILLS	**6**	3	3rd PM 7-N 8-E
SIMMS	**5**	1	2nd PM 8-N 14-W
SIMONS	**8**	1	3rd PM 7-N 10-E
SIMPSON	**11**	8	3rd PM 6-N 8-E
" "	**3**	1	3rd PM 8-N 10-E

Surname	Map Group	Parcels of Land	Meridian/Township/Range
SIMS	**8**	3	3rd PM 7-N 10-E
SINCLAIR	**10**	3	2nd PM 7-N 14-W
SINK	**2**	5	3rd PM 8-N 9-E
" "	**1**	1	3rd PM 8-N 8-E
SKELTON	**12**	4	3rd PM 6-N 9-E
SKIDMORE	**10**	2	2nd PM 7-N 14-W
SKINNER	**8**	2	3rd PM 7-N 10-E
SLAVEN	**5**	1	2nd PM 8-N 14-W
SMALL	**8**	5	3rd PM 7-N 10-E
SMALLWOOD	**16**	5	3rd PM 5-N 8-E
SMART	**6**	4	3rd PM 7-N 8-E
SMITH	**2**	9	3rd PM 8-N 9-E
" "	**3**	7	3rd PM 8-N 10-E
" "	**6**	4	3rd PM 7-N 8-E
" "	**12**	3	3rd PM 6-N 9-E
" "	**8**	2	3rd PM 7-N 10-E
" "	**20**	1	2nd PM 5-N 14-W
" "	**15**	1	2nd PM 6-N 14-W
" "	**10**	1	2nd PM 7-N 14-W
" "	**17**	1	3rd PM 5-N 9-E
" "	**13**	1	3rd PM 6-N 10-E
" "	**1**	1	3rd PM 8-N 8-E
SNEARLEY	**5**	2	2nd PM 8-N 14-W
SNEARLY	**5**	1	2nd PM 8-N 14-W
SNIDER	**10**	5	2nd PM 7-N 14-W
" "	**5**	1	2nd PM 8-N 14-W
SNODGRASS	**8**	1	3rd PM 7-N 10-E
SNYDER	**10**	1	2nd PM 7-N 14-W
" "	**11**	1	3rd PM 6-N 8-E
SOHEDLBANER	**8**	1	3rd PM 7-N 10-E
SONG	**11**	2	3rd PM 6-N 8-E
SONGER	**3**	1	3rd PM 8-N 10-E
SOURS	**2**	6	3rd PM 8-N 9-E
SOWERS	**1**	1	3rd PM 8-N 8-E
SPEARS	**1**	3	3rd PM 8-N 8-E
" "	**12**	2	3rd PM 6-N 9-E
SPIESL	**8**	1	3rd PM 7-N 10-E
SPITZER	**20**	1	2nd PM 5-N 14-W
SPIVEY	**3**	1	3rd PM 8-N 10-E
SPOON	**6**	2	3rd PM 7-N 8-E
" "	**2**	1	3rd PM 8-N 9-E
STAELCUP	**6**	1	3rd PM 7-N 8-E
STAFFORD	**10**	2	2nd PM 7-N 14-W
STALLCUP	**6**	2	3rd PM 7-N 8-E
STANDISH	**20**	1	2nd PM 5-N 14-W
STAPP	**16**	2	3rd PM 5-N 8-E
" "	**11**	1	3rd PM 6-N 8-E
STARLING	**13**	2	3rd PM 6-N 10-E
" "	**12**	1	3rd PM 6-N 9-E
STARNIS	**2**	1	3rd PM 8-N 9-E
STATER	**6**	1	3rd PM 7-N 8-E
STEEL	**13**	14	3rd PM 6-N 10-E
" "	**15**	4	2nd PM 6-N 14-W
" "	**5**	2	2nd PM 8-N 14-W
" "	**18**	1	3rd PM 5-N 10-E
" "	**12**	1	3rd PM 6-N 9-E
" "	**8**	1	3rd PM 7-N 10-E
STEPHENS	**8**	1	3rd PM 7-N 10-E
STEPHENSON	**6**	1	3rd PM 7-N 8-E
STERCHY	**19**	1	3rd PM 5-N 11-E

Surname	Map Group	Parcels of Land	Meridian/Township/Range		
STEVENS	**8**	11	3rd PM	7-N	10-E
" "	**12**	6	3rd PM	6-N	9-E
" "	**5**	1	2nd PM	8-N	14-W
" "	**6**	1	3rd PM	7-N	8-E
" "	**7**	1	3rd PM	7-N	9-E
" "	**1**	1	3rd PM	8-N	8-E
STEWARD	**15**	1	2nd PM	6-N	14-W
STEWART	**17**	7	3rd PM	5-N	9-E
" "	**10**	6	2nd PM	7-N	14-W
" "	**16**	3	3rd PM	5-N	8-E
STIENER	**1**	1	3rd PM	8-N	8-E
STILWELL	**11**	2	3rd PM	6-N	8-E
STINE	**6**	1	3rd PM	7-N	8-E
STIPP	**8**	2	3rd PM	7-N	10-E
" "	**7**	1	3rd PM	7-N	9-E
STIVERS	**16**	1	3rd PM	5-N	8-E
" "	**12**	1	3rd PM	6-N	9-E
STOCKWELL	**6**	5	3rd PM	7-N	8-E
STONEBARGER	**18**	3	3rd PM	5-N	10-E
STOUGHTON	**16**	1	3rd PM	5-N	8-E
STOVER	**5**	1	2nd PM	8-N	14-W
STRATTON	**3**	6	3rd PM	8-N	10-E
" "	**11**	5	3rd PM	6-N	8-E
" "	**4**	2	3rd PM	8-N	11-E
" "	**8**	1	3rd PM	7-N	10-E
STROLE	**2**	3	3rd PM	8-N	9-E
" "	**7**	1	3rd PM	7-N	9-E
STRONG	**3**	1	3rd PM	8-N	10-E
STRUBING	**6**	1	3rd PM	7-N	8-E
STUBNER	**15**	1	2nd PM	6-N	14-W
STUMP	**8**	6	3rd PM	7-N	10-E
" "	**9**	3	3rd PM	7-N	11-E
STURNS	**8**	1	3rd PM	7-N	10-E
SUDDUTH	**12**	2	3rd PM	6-N	9-E
SUTER	**13**	7	3rd PM	6-N	10-E
SUTTON	**12**	9	3rd PM	6-N	9-E
" "	**11**	5	3rd PM	6-N	8-E
" "	**8**	4	3rd PM	7-N	10-E
" "	**2**	4	3rd PM	8-N	9-E
" "	**15**	2	2nd PM	6-N	14-W
" "	**3**	1	3rd PM	8-N	10-E
SWAIN	**11**	2	3rd PM	6-N	8-E
SWAK	**3**	1	3rd PM	8-N	10-E
SWANEY	**8**	1	3rd PM	7-N	10-E
SWANK	**11**	1	3rd PM	6-N	8-E
SWARTZ	**16**	1	3rd PM	5-N	8-E
SWEET	**8**	1	3rd PM	7-N	10-E
SWICK	**3**	6	3rd PM	8-N	10-E
" "	**2**	1	3rd PM	8-N	9-E
SWIM	**3**	1	3rd PM	8-N	10-E
SWINEHEART	**12**	1	3rd PM	6-N	9-E
SWOPE	**15**	6	2nd PM	6-N	14-W
" "	**8**	4	3rd PM	7-N	10-E
" "	**14**	1	3rd PM	6-N	11-E
TARR	**16**	3	3rd PM	5-N	8-E
TATE	**11**	3	3rd PM	6-N	8-E
" "	**12**	3	3rd PM	6-N	9-E
TAYLOR	**10**	2	2nd PM	7-N	14-W
" "	**17**	1	3rd PM	5-N	9-E
TEDFORD	**15**	1	2nd PM	6-N	14-W

Surname	Map Group	Parcels of Land	Meridian/Township/Range		
TEMPLE	**5**	1	2nd PM	8-N	14-W
TENNERY	**5**	5	2nd PM	8-N	14-W
TERREL	**15**	6	2nd PM	6-N	14-W
TERWILLIGER	**1**	1	3rd PM	8-N	8-E
THADDAUS	**8**	2	3rd PM	7-N	10-E
THARP	**5**	1	2nd PM	8-N	14-W
THINOS	**11**	1	3rd PM	6-N	8-E
THOM	**12**	1	3rd PM	6-N	9-E
THOMAS	**15**	4	2nd PM	6-N	14-W
" "	**7**	3	3rd PM	7-N	9-E
" "	**13**	1	3rd PM	6-N	10-E
" "	**8**	1	3rd PM	7-N	10-E
" "	**9**	1	3rd PM	7-N	11-E
" "	**1**	1	3rd PM	8-N	8-E
" "	**2**	1	3rd PM	8-N	9-E
THOMPSON	**3**	6	3rd PM	8-N	10-E
" "	**2**	5	3rd PM	8-N	9-E
" "	**1**	1	3rd PM	8-N	8-E
THORNBURY	**7**	1	3rd PM	7-N	9-E
THORNTON	**17**	3	3rd PM	5-N	9-E
THROCKMORTON	**11**	2	3rd PM	6-N	8-E
TICHENOR	**11**	1	3rd PM	6-N	8-E
TICHNER	**12**	1	3rd PM	6-N	9-E
TIMMONS	**2**	1	3rd PM	8-N	9-E
TINDAL	**10**	1	2nd PM	7-N	14-W
TINDALL	**12**	4	3rd PM	6-N	9-E
TINGLEY	**15**	1	2nd PM	6-N	14-W
TIPPIT	**18**	3	3rd PM	5-N	10-E
" "	**12**	2	3rd PM	6-N	9-E
TOBIN	**6**	1	3rd PM	7-N	8-E
TODD	**17**	3	3rd PM	5-N	9-E
" "	**15**	2	2nd PM	6-N	14-W
" "	**10**	2	2nd PM	7-N	14-W
" "	**8**	2	3rd PM	7-N	10-E
" "	**13**	1	3rd PM	6-N	10-E
" "	**9**	1	3rd PM	7-N	11-E
TOELLNER	**6**	1	3rd PM	7-N	8-E
TOLES	**10**	2	2nd PM	7-N	14-W
" "	**5**	1	2nd PM	8-N	14-W
TOLIVER	**17**	1	3rd PM	5-N	9-E
TOMPKINS	**1**	2	3rd PM	8-N	8-E
TOTTEN	**20**	1	2nd PM	5-N	14-W
TOWNSAND	**12**	3	3rd PM	6-N	9-E
TOWNSEND	**7**	1	3rd PM	7-N	9-E
TRACY	**2**	1	3rd PM	8-N	9-E
TRAINER	**20**	5	2nd PM	5-N	14-W
TRAVIS	**3**	1	3rd PM	8-N	10-E
TREXLER	**11**	13	3rd PM	6-N	8-E
" "	**6**	2	3rd PM	7-N	8-E
" "	**16**	1	3rd PM	5-N	8-E
TRIMBLE	**2**	2	3rd PM	8-N	9-E
TROBAUGH	**14**	1	3rd PM	6-N	11-E
TROUTMAN	**2**	2	3rd PM	8-N	9-E
TROWBRIDGE	**8**	4	3rd PM	7-N	10-E
TRUITT	**3**	1	3rd PM	8-N	10-E
TUCKER	**16**	5	3rd PM	5-N	8-E
" "	**1**	3	3rd PM	8-N	8-E
TURNER	**13**	4	3rd PM	6-N	10-E
" "	**3**	1	3rd PM	8-N	10-E
TUSING	**11**	1	3rd PM	6-N	8-E

Surname	Map Group	Parcels of Land	Meridian/Township/Range		
UHL	**13**	5	3rd PM	6-N	10-E
UNDERHILL	**18**	2	3rd PM	5-N	10-E
" "	**17**	1	3rd PM	5-N	9-E
VAN LUE	**15**	2	2nd PM	6-N	14-W
VANATTA	**3**	2	3rd PM	8-N	10-E
VANCE	**12**	4	3rd PM	6-N	9-E
VANDERHOFF	**13**	2	3rd PM	6-N	10-E
VANDERHOOF	**13**	2	3rd PM	6-N	10-E
" "	**8**	2	3rd PM	7-N	10-E
VANLIEU	**15**	1	2nd PM	6-N	14-W
VANLUE	**15**	6	2nd PM	6-N	14-W
VANMETER	**7**	5	3rd PM	7-N	9-E
" "	**8**	2	3rd PM	7-N	10-E
" "	**15**	1	2nd PM	6-N	14-W
VANNATA	**2**	4	3rd PM	8-N	9-E
" "	**3**	2	3rd PM	8-N	10-E
VANNATTAR	**13**	1	3rd PM	6-N	10-E
VANNETTA	**2**	2	3rd PM	8-N	9-E
VANOLMAN	**20**	1	2nd PM	5-N	14-W
VANRANT	**5**	1	2nd PM	8-N	14-W
" "	**4**	1	3rd PM	8-N	11-E
VANSANDT	**6**	2	3rd PM	7-N	8-E
VANSANT	**5**	1	2nd PM	8-N	14-W
" "	**4**	1	3rd PM	8-N	11-E
VANWINKLE	**17**	1	3rd PM	5-N	9-E
VAROLE	**1**	1	3rd PM	8-N	8-E
VARVIL	**1**	3	3rd PM	8-N	8-E
VARVILLE	**1**	1	3rd PM	8-N	8-E
VAUGHAN	**16**	3	3rd PM	5-N	8-E
" "	**2**	2	3rd PM	8-N	9-E
VAUGHEN	**11**	1	3rd PM	6-N	8-E
VAUGHN	**2**	1	3rd PM	8-N	9-E
VAUN	**11**	2	3rd PM	6-N	8-E
VICKREY	**11**	1	3rd PM	6-N	8-E
VIXLER	**16**	2	3rd PM	5-N	8-E
VOGEL	**13**	3	3rd PM	6-N	10-E
VON OLMAN	**20**	1	2nd PM	5-N	14-W
WADDLE	**15**	4	2nd PM	6-N	14-W
" "	**7**	1	3rd PM	7-N	9-E
WADE	**13**	1	3rd PM	6-N	10-E
" "	**12**	1	3rd PM	6-N	9-E
" "	**7**	1	3rd PM	7-N	9-E
WAGLE	**1**	6	3rd PM	8-N	8-E
WAGNER	**8**	1	3rd PM	7-N	10-E
WAGONER	**8**	2	3rd PM	7-N	10-E
WAITE	**13**	2	3rd PM	6-N	10-E
WAKEFIELD	**17**	1	3rd PM	5-N	9-E
WALKER	**12**	7	3rd PM	6-N	9-E
" "	**10**	5	2nd PM	7-N	14-W
" "	**13**	4	3rd PM	6-N	10-E
" "	**7**	2	3rd PM	7-N	9-E
WALL	**7**	2	3rd PM	7-N	9-E
" "	**1**	2	3rd PM	8-N	8-E
WALLACE	**1**	2	3rd PM	8-N	8-E
WAPLES	**5**	2	2nd PM	8-N	14-W
WARD	**2**	6	3rd PM	8-N	9-E
" "	**3**	5	3rd PM	8-N	10-E
" "	**16**	1	3rd PM	5-N	8-E
WARNER	**8**	1	3rd PM	7-N	10-E
WARREN	**3**	4	3rd PM	8-N	10-E

Surname	Map Group	Parcels of Land	Meridian/Township/Range
WARREN (Cont'd)	**11**	2	3rd PM 6-N 8-E
WATSON	**17**	1	3rd PM 5-N 9-E
WAYLE	**1**	2	3rd PM 8-N 8-E
WAYMAN	**16**	2	3rd PM 5-N 8-E
WEATHERINGTON	**8**	1	3rd PM 7-N 10-E
WEAVER	**10**	2	2nd PM 7-N 14-W
" "	**17**	1	3rd PM 5-N 9-E
" "	**3**	1	3rd PM 8-N 10-E
WEBB	**10**	2	2nd PM 7-N 14-W
WEBSTER	**10**	3	2nd PM 7-N 14-W
" "	**16**	1	3rd PM 5-N 8-E
WEIMERT	**8**	2	3rd PM 7-N 10-E
WEISCOPF	**20**	1	2nd PM 5-N 14-W
WELDAM	**8**	3	3rd PM 7-N 10-E
" "	**13**	1	3rd PM 6-N 10-E
" "	**3**	1	3rd PM 8-N 10-E
WELLS	**1**	2	3rd PM 8-N 8-E
" "	**8**	1	3rd PM 7-N 10-E
WELTY	**6**	1	3rd PM 7-N 8-E
WEST	**11**	1	3rd PM 6-N 8-E
WHEELELER	**6**	1	3rd PM 7-N 8-E
WHEELER	**7**	5	3rd PM 7-N 9-E
" "	**2**	3	3rd PM 8-N 9-E
" "	**6**	2	3rd PM 7-N 8-E
" "	**12**	1	3rd PM 6-N 9-E
" "	**4**	1	3rd PM 8-N 11-E
WHIGHT	**5**	2	2nd PM 8-N 14-W
WHITE	**5**	4	2nd PM 8-N 14-W
" "	**10**	2	2nd PM 7-N 14-W
" "	**13**	2	3rd PM 6-N 10-E
" "	**8**	2	3rd PM 7-N 10-E
" "	**16**	1	3rd PM 5-N 8-E
" "	**11**	1	3rd PM 6-N 8-E
" "	**12**	1	3rd PM 6-N 9-E
" "	**6**	1	3rd PM 7-N 8-E
WHITECHURCH	**11**	1	3rd PM 6-N 8-E
WHITEHURST	**5**	5	2nd PM 8-N 14-W
WHITENACK	**20**	1	2nd PM 5-N 14-W
WHITLOCK	**11**	1	3rd PM 6-N 8-E
WHORTON	**17**	2	3rd PM 5-N 9-E
WICHARD	**1**	1	3rd PM 8-N 8-E
WICOFF	**8**	1	3rd PM 7-N 10-E
" "	**7**	1	3rd PM 7-N 9-E
WILDAM	**8**	1	3rd PM 7-N 10-E
WILES	**6**	1	3rd PM 7-N 8-E
WILFONG	**5**	1	2nd PM 8-N 14-W
WILKERSON	**20**	2	2nd PM 5-N 14-W
WILKINSON	**20**	1	2nd PM 5-N 14-W
WILLIAM	**11**	1	3rd PM 6-N 8-E
WILLIAMS	**1**	4	3rd PM 8-N 8-E
" "	**12**	2	3rd PM 6-N 9-E
" "	**11**	1	3rd PM 6-N 8-E
WILLIAMSON	**5**	2	2nd PM 8-N 14-W
WILLOUGHBY	**17**	3	3rd PM 5-N 9-E
WILSON	**10**	3	2nd PM 7-N 14-W
" "	**8**	2	3rd PM 7-N 10-E
" "	**2**	2	3rd PM 8-N 9-E
" "	**20**	1	2nd PM 5-N 14-W
" "	**15**	1	2nd PM 6-N 14-W
" "	**13**	1	3rd PM 6-N 10-E

Surname	Map Group	Parcels of Land	Meridian/Township/Range
WILSON (Cont'd)	11	1	3rd PM 6-N 8-E
" "	12	1	3rd PM 6-N 9-E
" "	6	1	3rd PM 7-N 8-E
" "	1	1	3rd PM 8-N 8-E
WINDSOR	12	2	3rd PM 6-N 9-E
WINES	10	1	2nd PM 7-N 14-W
" "	13	1	3rd PM 6-N 10-E
WINTERS	2	3	3rd PM 8-N 9-E
WISELEY	2	2	3rd PM 8-N 9-E
WISEMORE	5	3	2nd PM 8-N 14-W
WISHARD	2	11	3rd PM 8-N 9-E
" "	1	4	3rd PM 8-N 8-E
" "	6	1	3rd PM 7-N 8-E
WISNER	1	2	3rd PM 8-N 8-E
WITSMAN	16	2	3rd PM 5-N 8-E
" "	11	2	3rd PM 6-N 8-E
WOHLTMANN	6	1	3rd PM 7-N 8-E
WOLF	1	2	3rd PM 8-N 8-E
" "	18	1	3rd PM 5-N 10-E
" "	17	1	3rd PM 5-N 9-E
WOLFE	20	7	2nd PM 5-N 14-W
WOLLACE	1	1	3rd PM 8-N 8-E
WOOD	17	3	3rd PM 5-N 9-E
" "	5	2	2nd PM 8-N 14-W
" "	6	2	3rd PM 7-N 8-E
" "	16	1	3rd PM 5-N 8-E
" "	12	1	3rd PM 6-N 9-E
" "	4	1	3rd PM 8-N 11-E
WOODARD	10	2	2nd PM 7-N 14-W
WOODFORD	17	2	3rd PM 5-N 9-E
WOODS	12	7	3rd PM 6-N 9-E
" "	8	3	3rd PM 7-N 10-E
" "	17	2	3rd PM 5-N 9-E
WOODWORTH	7	2	3rd PM 7-N 9-E
WOOLLEY	17	2	3rd PM 5-N 9-E
WORKS	17	2	3rd PM 5-N 9-E
WORMAN	6	1	3rd PM 7-N 8-E
" "	2	1	3rd PM 8-N 9-E
WORTHEY	11	5	3rd PM 6-N 8-E
WRIGHT	15	5	2nd PM 6-N 14-W
" "	5	4	2nd PM 8-N 14-W
" "	8	2	3rd PM 7-N 10-E
" "	2	2	3rd PM 8-N 9-E
" "	6	1	3rd PM 7-N 8-E
" "	1	1	3rd PM 8-N 8-E
WYANT	13	3	3rd PM 6-N 10-E
YAEGER	8	1	3rd PM 7-N 10-E
YAKELEY	1	1	3rd PM 8-N 8-E
YAW	2	8	3rd PM 8-N 9-E
YOUNG	2	4	3rd PM 8-N 9-E
" "	5	1	2nd PM 8-N 14-W
" "	8	1	3rd PM 7-N 10-E
" "	1	1	3rd PM 8-N 8-E
ZELL	18	3	3rd PM 5-N 10-E
" "	20	2	2nd PM 5-N 14-W
ZIEGLER	12	2	3rd PM 6-N 9-E
ZIMMERLEE	8	1	3rd PM 7-N 10-E
" "	9	1	3rd PM 7-N 11-E

– Part II –

Township Map Groups

Map Group 1: Index to Land Patents

Township 8-North Range 8-East (3rd PM)

After you locate an individual in this Index, take note of the Section and Section Part then proceed to the Land Patent map on the pages immediately following. You should have no difficulty locating the corresponding parcel of land.

The "For More Info" Column will lead you to more information about the underlying Patents. See the *Legend* at right, and the "How to Use this Book" chapter, for more information.

```
                    LEGEND
          "For More Info . . . " column
G = Group  (Multi-Patentee Patent, see Appendix "C")
R = Residence
S = Social Status


See Appendix A for list of abbreviations used by the
Illinois State Archives in describing the place and
nature of these land patents.

Note: if the Abbreviations contain "L", "BL", "LOT",
or "BLOCK", the exact whereabouts of the parcel within
the section is not known.
```

ID	Individual in Patent	Sec.	Sec. Part	Purchase Date	Sale Type	IL Aliquot Part	For More Info . . .
165	ALEXANDER, Jesse J	28	W½NW	1851-08-21	FD	W2NW	
166	" "	29	NESE	1851-08-21	FD	NESE	
167	" "	29	SENE	1851-08-21	FD	SENE	
287	ALEXANDER, William	16	L1	1852-08-09	SC	LOT1E2NE	
288	" "	29	NENE	1853-01-04	FD	NENE	
169	ANDERSON, John	10	NWSW	1851-05-05	FD	NWSW	R:JASPER
265	ANDERSON, Samuel	32	NWNW	1850-01-29	FD	NWNW	R:JASPER
262	" "	21	E½NW	1850-01-30	FD	E2NW	
264	" "	21	NWNW	1850-01-30	FD	NWNW	
263	" "	21	NESW	1850-01-30	FD	NESW	
64	ARNOLD, Fletcher	21	SWNW	1853-01-25	FD	SWNW	
89	ARNOLD, Henry	23	NENE	1854-01-20	FD	NENE	
117	ARNOLD, James	29	NWNW	1853-02-26	FD	NWNW	
170	ARNOLD, John	10	E½NE	1839-12-07	FD	E2NE	R:JASPER
195	ARNOLD, Joseph	29	NENW	1851-10-26	FD	NENW	R:JASPER
260	ARNOLD, Robert	5	NWSE	1839-06-24	FD	NWSE	R:COLES
289	ARNOLD, William	10	NWSE	1840-01-28	FD	NWSE	R:COLES
203	ASHER, Kellar	33	NENE	1853-02-23	FD	NENE	
204	" "	33	SENE	1853-04-04	FD	SENE	
196	ATKINS, Joseph Hazard	10	W½NE	1839-12-07	FD	W2NE	R:COLES
103	" "	10	W½NE	1839-12-07	FD	W2NE	R:COLES
118	AUSTIN, James	27	NESE	1854-03-10	FD	NESE	R:CUMBERLAND
274	BADGER, Stephen	26	N½SE	1873-02-28	RR	N2SE	
59	BARBER, Elam	33	SW	1853-02-01	FD	SW	
225	BARTLETT, Martin S	1	NE	1851-09-23	FD	NEFR	
226	BERRY, Mathias	21	NENE	1850-10-01	FD	NENE	
227	" "	21	NWSE	1850-10-01	FD	NWSE	
228	" "	21	W½NE	1850-10-01	FD	W2NE	
229	" "	31	N½NE	1850-12-12	FD	N2NEFR	R:JASPER
315	BERRY, Wyatt S	17	E½NW	1852-10-20	FD	E2NW	
302	BLAKE, William J	16	L3	1852-08-09	SC	LOT3NW	
301	" "	16	L2	1852-08-09	SC	LOT2W2NE	
171	BLIDE, John	34	NWSW	1864-09-22	RR	NWSW	
24	BOWEN, Anthony	22	NENE	1877-04-20	RR	NENE	
121	BRADSHAW, James	13	SWSE	1852-09-09	FD	SWSE	
120	" "	13	NWSE	1852-09-09	FD	NWSE	
125	" "	25	NENE	1853-01-14	FD	NENE	
126	" "	25	NWNE	1853-01-14	FD	NWNE	
119	" "	13	E½NE	1853-01-14	FD	E2NE	
127	" "	25	SENE	1853-01-14	FD	SENE	
128	" "	25	SWNE	1853-01-14	FD	SWNE	
122	" "	13	W½NE	1853-01-14	FD	W2NE	
124	" "	24	S½SE	1853-03-14	FD	S2SE	
123	" "	23	E½SW	1854-01-31	FD	E2SW	R:JASPER
92	BREWER, Henry	36	SESE	1850-06-06	FD	SESE	R:JASPER
90	" "	36	NESE	1852-11-18	FD	NESE	

ID	Individual in Patent	Sec.	Sec. Part	Purchase Date	Sale Type	IL Aliquot Part	For More Info . . .
91	BREWER, Henry (Cont'd)	36	NESW	1853-01-21	FD	NESW	
61	BRIGHT, Elkanah	4	NESE	1848-02-27	FD	NESE	R:CUMBERLAND
8	CALDWELL, Albert G	16	L5	1852-08-09	SC	LOT5W2SW	
10	" "	16	L7	1852-08-09	SC	LOT7W2SE	
11	" "	16	L8	1852-08-09	SC	LOT8E2SE	
9	" "	16	L6	1852-08-09	SC	LOT6E2SW	
18	" "	6	NE	1869-02-27	RR	NEFR	
17	" "	6	N½SE	1869-02-27	RR	N2SEFR	
15	" "	28	NESW	1870-02-28	RR	NESW	
14	" "	28	NENW	1870-07-30	RR	NENW	
19	" "	28	NE	1870-10-31	RR	NE	G:16
12	" "	22	SWSW	1871-02-28	RR	SWSW	
13	" "	28	N½SE	1871-02-28	RR	N2SE	
16	" "	28	SENW	1873-05-31	RR	SENW	
7	" "	14	SWNE	1875-03-23	RR	SWNE	S:F
19	CALDWELL, Robert J	28	NE	1870-10-31	RR	NE	G:16
303	CARSON, William J	15	NW	1849-08-16	FD	NW	
99	COAN, Hiram S	34	NWNW	1874-11-13	RR	NWNW	
68	COLLINS, George	34	SWSW	1866-11-08	RR	SWSW	
104	COOLEY, Isaiah	14	E½NW	1858-07-03	RR	E2NW	
115	COZARD, Jacob	32	NWNE	1863-07-22	RR	NWNE	
147	CREWS, James L	9	NESW	1851-09-06	FD	NESW	R:JASPER
148	" "	9	SWNE	1851-09-06	FD	SWNE	R:JASPER
141	" "	29	SWSE	1853-01-14	FD	SWSE	
135	" "	21	W½SW	1853-01-14	FD	W2SW	
138	" "	29	E½SW	1853-01-14	FD	E2SW	
140	" "	29	SWNW	1853-01-14	FD	SWNW	
142	" "	29	SWSW	1853-01-14	FD	SWSW	
143	" "	29	W½NE	1853-01-14	FD	W2NE	
139	" "	29	NWSW	1853-01-14	FD	NWSW	
134	" "	20	W½SE	1864-04-22	RR	W2SE	
144	" "	30	N½NE	1872-10-31	RR	NFRNE	
136	" "	24	NWNW	1874-03-31	RR	NWNW	
132	" "	14	SWSW	1874-06-15	RR	SWSW	
133	" "	20	NENW	1874-06-20	RR	NENW	
137	" "	26	NWSW	1874-08-03	RR	NWSW	
131	" "	14	SESW	1876-03-03	RR	SESW	
145	" "	30	N½SE	1880-12-24	RR	NFR2SEFR	
146	" "	30	S½NE	1880-12-24	RR	S2NEFR	
130	" "	10	SWSE	1881-02-03	RR	SWSE	
256	CRITTENDEN, Richard H	17	S½	1852-10-18	FD	S2	R:INDIANA
258	" "	27	NWSW	1852-10-21	FD	NWSW	R:INDIANA
257	" "	27	N½	1852-10-21	FD	N2	R:INDIANA
151	CRUSE, James L	9	NWNE	1850-01-03	FD	NWNE	
150	" "	4	W½SE	1850-01-03	FD	W2SE	
149	" "	4	NESW	1850-01-03	FD	NESW	
6	DITTEMOORE, Adam	11	W½SW	1849-08-16	FD	W2SW	
5	" "	10	E½SE	1849-08-16	FD	E2SE	
291	DITTEMOORE, William	15	NE	1849-08-16	FD	NE	
88	DITTEMORE, Greenbury	11	NE	1849-08-16	FD	NE	
153	DITTEMORE, James M	12	NWNW	1871-09-30	RR	NWNW	
292	DITTEMORE, William	10	SWSW	1849-12-01	FD	SWSW	R:JASPER
293	" "	15	NESE	1853-01-12	FD	NESE	
294	" "	15	NWSE	1853-01-25	FD	NWSE	
113	DUNEGAN, Jackson	16	L4	1852-08-09	SC	LOT4NW	
29	DUTELL, August	14	NWNW	1872-11-30	RR	NWNW	
30	" "	14	SWNW	1875-03-29	RR	SWNW	
28	" "	14		1875-03-29	RR	NENE2	
190	ECKARDT, John W	26	SWSE	00/00/1871	RR	SWSE	
241	ELLIOTT, Michael D	20	SWSW	1871-02-28	RR	SWSW	
211	EPPERSON, Lewis	7	SEN½	1852-10-30	FD	S2NE	
210	" "	7	SE	1852-10-30	FD	SE	
209	" "	7	N½NE	1852-10-30	FD	N2NE	
208	EPPERSON, Lewis E	5	SWSE	1853-02-22	FD	SWSE	
222	EPPERSON, Louis	2	NENW	1894-09-06	RR	NENW	
152	EVANS, James L	31	S½NE	1852-09-09	FD	S2NEFR	
270	FATOOT, Silas	12	N½SE	1869-03-31	RR	N2SE	
35	FELDKAMP, Bernhard	8	SESE	1870-06-30	RR	SESE	
34	" "	8	NESE	1871-04-29	RR	NESE	
93	FENTONSPREAD, Henry	6	S½SE	1874-03-23	RR	S2SE	
87	FITHIAN, Glover	36	SWSE	1849-11-26	FD	SWSE	
192	FOSTER, John W	34	S½SE	1872-10-09	RR	S2SE	
191	" "	34	E½SW	1872-10-09	RR	E2SW	

ID	Individual in Patent	Sec.	Sec. Part	Purchase Date	Sale Type	IL Aliquot Part	For More Info . . .
275	FOSTER, Thomas	25	E½NE	1853-03-05	FD	E2NEVOID	
276	" "	35	E½NE	1854-03-10	FD	E2NE	
32	FOUST, Benjamin	35	E½SW	1853-05-30	FD	E2SW	G:29
31	" "	35	E½NW	1853-05-30	FD	E2NW	G:29
32	FOUST, Charles	35	E½SW	1853-05-30	FD	E2SW	G:29
31	" "	35	E½NW	1853-05-30	FD	E2NW	G:29
23	GARDNER, William	2	SE	1849-11-21	FD	SE	G:30
299	GARDNER, William H	2	SENW	1851-07-08	FD	SENWFR	R:JASPER
297	" "	11	NESW	1852-09-09	FD	NESW	
298	" "	11	NWSE	1852-09-09	FD	NWSE	
178	GILLHAM, John	1	NWSE	1852-11-19	FD	NWSE	
176	" "	1	NESE	1853-01-24	FD	NESE	
177	" "	1	NESW	1853-01-24	FD	NESW	
277	GLOUR, Thomas	15	SWSE	1853-01-24	FD	SWSE	
23	GLOVER, Andrew J	2	SE	1849-11-21	FD	SE	G:30
66	GOSS, Fredrick	3	W½NW	1849-08-20	FD	W2NWFR	R:INDIANA
65	" "	3	NE	1849-08-20	FD	NEFR	R:INDIANA
223	HALFHILL, Mandervile	15	W½SW	1853-01-24	FD	W2SW	
20	HANNA, Albert G	34	E½NW	1874-12-04	RR	E2NW	
51	HARRAH, Daniel T	26	W½NW	1864-06-22	RR	W2NW	
50	" "	26	E½NW	1864-09-22	RR	E2NW	
305	HARRAH, William N	9	E½NW	1853-01-14	FD	E2NW	
308	" "	9	NWSW	1853-01-14	FD	NWSW	
307	" "	9	NWSE	1853-01-14	FD	NWSE	
306	" "	9	NWNW	1853-01-14	FD	NWNW	
309	" "	9	SWNW	1853-01-14	FD	SWNW	
212	HAYES, Lewis M	13	E½SW	1853-01-17	FD	E2SW	
215	HAYS, Lewis M	11	SWSE	1852-09-09	FD	SWSE	
214	" "	11	SESW	1852-09-09	FD	SESW	
213	" "	11	E½SE	1852-09-09	FD	E2SE	
220	" "	21	SENE	1852-09-10	FD	SENE	
219	" "	21	S½SE	1852-09-10	FD	S2SE	
218	" "	21	NESE	1852-09-10	FD	NESE	
217	" "	15	SESE	1853-01-08	FD	SESE	
221	" "	21	SESW	1853-01-25	FD	SESW	
216	" "	13	W½SW	1853-01-25	FD	W2SW	
182	HEFFERNAN, John	32	SWNE	1886-07-01	RR	SWNE	
52	HENSLEY, David M	24	NWSW	1875-02-16	RR	NWSW	
53	" "	24	SWNW	1875-02-16	RR	SWNW	
69	HENSLEY, George	13	SESE	1850-06-08	FD	SESE	
70	" "	24	E½NE	1850-06-08	FD	E2NE	
71	" "	24	NESE	1850-06-08	FD	NESE	
72	" "	24	SESW	1873-06-30	RR	SESW	
269	HESS, Sarah J	34	N½SE	1872-10-31	RR	N2SE	S:F
62	KIBLER, Emanuel C	36	W½SW	1853-01-22	FD	W2SW	
73	KIBLER, George	25	S½SE	1853-01-07	FD	S2SE	
74	" "	25	SESW	1853-01-07	FD	SESW	
75	" "	36	NENW	1853-01-07	FD	NENW	
76	" "	36	SENW	1853-01-13	FD	SENW	
205	KOEBELE, Landolin	20	E½NE	1870-09-30	RR	E2NE	
154	KUYKENDALL, James M	14	NWSW	1876-03-11	RR	NWSW	
33	LAKE, Benjamin	33	NESE	1853-02-25	FD	NESE	
259	LAUGHLIN, Richard	9	S½NW	1853-01-24	FD	S2NW	
206	LEE, Levi	32	SENE	1849-12-14	FD	SENE	R:JASPER
207	" "	33	SWNW	1853-06-25	FD	SWNW	
60	LINK, Eli	23	SE	1853-02-11	FD	SE	
197	MAMMOPER, Joseph	28	SESW	1864-05-23	RR	SESW	
199	MAMMOSER, Joseph	28	SWSE	1872-03-30	RR	SWSE	
198	" "	28	SESE	1874-06-15	RR	SESE	
155	MARK, James	25	NW	1852-09-10	FD	NW	
44	MARRS, Christopher	31	NESE	1849-11-20	FD	NESEFR	R:EFFINGHAM
45	" "	31	SWSE	1852-11-17	FD	SWSE	R:EFFINGHAM
48	MAURER, Daniel S	12	NWSW	1871-03-31	RR	NWSW	
49	" "	2	SENE	1874-11-20	RR	SENE	
193	MAURER, John W	12	NESW	1874-05-15	RR	NESW	
174	MCCOY, John G	20	SENW	1872-02-29	RR	SENW	
175	" "	20	W½NW	1872-02-29	RR	W2NW	
173	" "	20	NWSW	1872-02-29	RR	NWSW	
243	MCQUAID, Milton	23	W½SW	1853-05-16	FD	W2SW	
244	" "	35	W½NW	1853-05-16	FD	W2NW	
245	MCQUAID, Mitlon	35	W½SW	1853-05-16	FD	W2SW	
230	MEINHART, Mathias	22	N½SW	1874-02-28	RR	N2SW	
231	" "	22	NW	1874-12-15	RR	NW	

ID	Individual in Patent	Sec.	Sec. Part	Purchase Date	Sale Type	IL Aliquot Part	For More Info . . .
235	MEINHART, Matthias	22	SE	1864-08-22	RR	SE	
236	" "	22	SESW	1865-06-22	RR	SESW	
234	" "	2	SWNE	1867-12-31	RR	SWNE	
42	MEISLAHN, Christian	18	S½SE	1871-09-30	RR	S2SE	S:F
43	" "	18	SEN½	1871-09-30	RR	S2NE	S:F
22	MILLER, Allen O	12	SWSW	1875-09-20	RR	SWSW	
224	MILLER, Marshall	14	NESW	1876-05-26	RR	NESW	
252	MITCHELL, O H	26	SESW	1873-09-30	RR	SESW	S:I
251	" "	26	NESW	1875-02-10	RR	NESW	S:I
314	MITCHELL, Willis T	23	SENE	1853-01-08	FD	SENE	
129	MYERS, James G	33	S½SE	1853-02-26	FD	S2SE	
250	MYERS, Noah	24	W½NE	1850-01-23	FD	W2NE	
249	" "	24	E½NW	1850-01-23	FD	E2NW	
247	" "	14	E½SE	1873-10-31	RR	E2SE	
248	" "	14	SWSE	1874-03-31	RR	SWSE	
279	MYERS, Thomas	14	NWSE	1875-02-27	RR	NWSE	
295	MYERS, William F T	9	NESE	1849-08-11	FD	NESE	R:JASPER
296	" "	9	SENE	1849-08-11	FD	SENE	R:JASPER
4	NEWLIN, Absalom	24	S½SW	1873-06-30	RR	S2SW	
300	NEWLIN, William H	26	NWNE	1873-02-28	RR	NWNE	
290	NEWTON, William D	15	E½SW	1853-01-08	FD	E2SW	
67	NICHOLS, Garret	3	E½NW	1846-07-09	FD	E2NW	R:JASPER
79	NICHOLS, George	5	NE	1839-04-25	FD	NEFR	R:COLES
78	" "	4	NW	1839-04-25	FD	NWFR	R:COLES
77	" "	3	SWSE	1839-10-25	FD	SWSE	R:JASPER
111	NICHOLS, Israel	4	NE	1839-04-25	FD	NEFR	R:COLES
110	" "	33	NENW	1853-01-07	FD	NENW	
109	NICHOLS, Israel M	32	W½SE	1849-08-24	FD	W2SE	
105	" "	28	W½SW	1849-08-24	FD	W2SW	
106	" "	29	SESE	1849-08-24	FD	SESE	
108	" "	32	NENE	1849-08-24	FD	NENE	
107	" "	32	E½SW	1849-08-24	FD	E2SW	
112	NICHOLS, Israil	33	NWNE	1853-02-25	FD	NWNE	
156	NICHOLS, James	10	NENW	1839-10-21	FD	NENW	R:JASPER
183	NICHOLS, John	33	NWNW	1853-01-04	FD	NWNW	
184	" "	33	SENW	1853-01-04	FD	SENW	
282	ODELL, Washington	35	E½SE	1854-03-10	FD	E2SE	
38	PATRICK, Charles	36	NE	1849-12-22	FD	NE	
2	PETERSON, Abner M	23	W½NW	1853-12-27	FD	W2NW	R:JASPER
1	" "	19		1853-12-27	FD	SC	R:JASPER
3	" "	27	SWSW	1853-12-27	FD	SWSW	R:JASPER
37	PRINTZ, Calvin F	34	N½NE	1869-01-30	RR	N2NE	
98	PRINTZ, Hiram M	34	SEN½	1869-02-27	RR	S2NE	
100	RAPER, Holley	35	W½NE	1854-03-10	FD	W2NE	
101	" "	35	W½SE	1854-03-10	FD	W2SE	R:OHIO
158	REDFORD, James	25	NESW	1853-02-25	FD	NESW	
157	" "	23	N½SE	1853-02-25	FD	N2SE	
201	REFFIT, Joseph	33	SWNE	1852-12-07	FD	SWNE	
200	" "	33	NWSE	1852-12-07	FD	NWSE	
168	REYNOLDS, Jesse S P	12	SWNW	1872-01-31	RR	SWNW	
63	RICK, Enoch	32	SESE	1886-07-16	RR	SESE	
310	ROBE, William	5	NW	1852-09-10	FD	NWFR	R:INDIANA
185	ROBERSON, John	12	E½NW	1868-10-31	RR	E2NW	
186	" "	26	SWSW	1874-10-02	RR	SWSW	
254	ROBERTS, Peter H	13	NW	1853-02-10	FD	NW	
102	ROPER, Holley	25	W½NE	1853-03-05	FD	W2NEVOID	S:F
266	ROPER, Samuel	25	W½SE	1853-03-05	FD	W2SEVOID	
237	ROSS, Meredith B	1	NWSW	1851-06-23	FD	NWSW	R:CUMBERLAND
239	" "	1	SWSW	1852-09-09	FD	SWSW	
238	" "	1	SESW	1853-01-25	FD	SESW	
240	ROSS, Meridith	1	S½SE	1853-01-04	FD	S2SE	
187	SCHATTMAN, John	8	SWSW	1864-04-22	RR	SWSW	
84	SCHOTTMANN, Gerhard	8	NWSW	1870-04-30	RR	NWSW	
85	" "	8	W½SE	1870-04-30	RR	W2SE	
83	" "	22	W½NE	1875-06-04	RR	W2NE	
189	SCHOTTMANN, John	8	SESW	1870-04-30	RR	SESW	
188	" "	8	NESW	1871-03-31	RR	NESW	
159	SCREWS, James	29	SENW	1853-02-26	FD	SENW	
103	SEARSE, Isaac	10	W½NE	1840-06-19	FD	W2NE	R:JASPER
196	" "	10	W½NE	1840-06-19	FD	W2NE	R:JASPER
246	SHERMAN, Nelson	20	NESE	1871-04-29	RR	NESE	
114	SHY, Jacob Cantrel	29	NWSE	1838-06-16	FD	NWSE	R:JASPER
278	SIDDINS, Thomas J	5	E½SE	1853-02-09	FD	E2SE	

ID	Individual in Patent	Sec.	Sec. Part	Purchase Date	Sale Type	IL Aliquot Part	For More Info . . .
86	SIEFKEN, Gerhard	30	S½SE	1880-12-20	RR	SFR2SE	
253	SINK, Paul	13	NESE	1851-09-12	FD	NESE	R:JASPER
267	SMITH, Samuel	36	SESW	1852-09-10	FD	SESW	
242	SOWERS, Michael M	24	NWSE	1872-11-30	RR	NWSE	
41	SPEARS, Charles	36	SWNW	1853-01-04	FD	SWNW	G:56
311	"	36	SWNW	1853-01-04	FD	SWNW	G:56
40	"	36	NWNW	1853-01-24	FD	NWNW	G:56
39	"	25	W½SW	1853-03-04	FD	W2SW	
41	SPEARS, William	36	SWNW	1852-01-04	FD	SWNW	
311	"	36	SWNW	1852-01-04	FD	SWNW	
41	SPEARS, William M	36	SWNW	1853-01-04	FD	SWNW	G:56
311	"	36	SWNW	1853-01-04	FD	SWNW	G:56
40	"	36	NWNW	1853-01-24	FD	NWNW	G:56
255	STEVENS, Plowdon	8	N½	1874-03-31	RR	N2	
202	STIENER, Joseph	32	NESE	1873-06-30	RR	NESE	
58	TERWILLIGER, David	20	W½NE	1873-04-30	RR	W2NE	
172	THOMAS, John D	36	NWSE	1849-08-24	FD	NWSE	R:JASPER
261	THOMPSON, Robert	22	SENE	1875-11-11	RR	SENE	
46	TOMPKINS, Christopher	11	NW	1849-08-16	FD	NW	
47	"	3	NESE	1849-11-08	FD	NESE	R:JASPER
54	TUCKER, David M	17	NE	1852-10-18	FD	NE	
55	"	17	NE	1852-10-18	FD	NE	
57	"	27	NESW	1852-12-07	FD	NESW	
56	"	17	W½NW	1853-02-09	FD	W2NW	
54	"	17	NE	1853-08-10	FD	NE	
55	"	17	NE	1853-08-10	FD	NE	
36	VAROLE, Brice M	20	SESE	1871-03-31	RR	SESE	
179	VARVIL, John H	27	NWSE	1853-03-17	FD	NWSE	
180	"	27	S½SE	1853-03-17	FD	S2SE	
181	"	27	SESW	1853-03-17	FD	SESW	
81	VARVILLE, George W	23	E½NW	1853-02-12	FD	E2NW	
25	WAGLE, Asa	10	SENW	1839-10-25	FD	SENW	R:IOWA
26	"	3	NWSE	1839-10-25	FD	NWSE	R:IOWA
27	"	9	NENE	1849-08-16	FD	NENE	R:JASPER
161	WAGLE, James	3	E½SW	1839-10-25	FD	E2SW	R:IOWA
160	"	14	SENE	1875-11-15	RR	SENE	
116	WAGLE, James A	14	N½NE	1875-11-15	RR	N2NE	
95	WALL, Henry	3	SESE	1840-01-28	FD	SESE	R:COLES
94	"	10	E½SW	1840-01-28	FD	E2SW	R:COLES
162	WALLACE, James	9	S½SE	1853-01-07	FD	S2SE	
304	WALLACE, William L	20	NESW	1867-08-26	RR	NESW	
164	WAYLE, James	3	W½SW	1849-02-16	FD	W2SW	R:JASPER
163	"	10	W½NW	1849-02-16	FD	W2NW	R:JASPER
80	WELLS, George T	34	SWNW	1870-01-31	RR	SWNW	
194	WELLS, John	4	SESE	1000-02-26	FD	SESE	R:COLES
271	WICHARD, Silas W	12	W½NE	1863-11-23	RR	W2NE	
283	WILLIAMS, Wiley	2	SW	1849-10-09	FD	SW	
284	"	2	W½NW	1849-10-09	FD	W2NW	R:INDIANA
285	"	32	S½NW	1849-10-09	FD	S2NW	
286	"	32	W½SW	1849-10-09	FD	W2SW	
280	WILSON, Thomas	23	W½NE	1853-02-11	FD	W2NE	
272	WISHARD, Silas W	12	NENE	1868-10-31	RR	NENE	
273	"	12	SENE	1870-01-31	RR	SENE	
312	WISHARD, William	12	S½SE	1867-10-25	RR	S2SE	
313	"	12	SESW	1880-12-11	RR	SESW	
233	WISNER, Mathias	4	W½SW	1864-05-23	RR	W2SW	
232	"	4	SESW	1864-05-23	RR	SESW	
96	WOLF, Henry	18	N½NE	1871-02-28	RR	N2NEFR	
97	"	18	N½SE	1871-02-28	RR	N2SEFR	
21	WOLLACE, Alexander As	20	SESW	1866-03-27	RR	SESW	
82	WRIGHT, George	32	NENW	1868-06-30	RR	NENW	
268	YAKELEY, Samuel	1	NW	1849-12-05	FD	NWFR	
281	YOUNG, Timothy E	26	NENE	00/00/1871	RR	NENE	

Patent Map

T8-N R8-E
3rd PM Meridian

Map Group 1

Township Statistics

Parcels Mapped	:	315
Number of Patents	:	1
Number of Individuals	:	172
Patentees Identified	:	170
Number of Surnames	:	125
Multi-Patentee Parcels	:	6
Oldest Patent Date	:	2/26/1000
Most Recent Patent	:	9/6/1894
Block/Lot Parcels	:	9
Cities and Towns	:	1
Cemeteries	:	2

6
CALDWELL Albert G 1869
CALDWELL Albert G 1869
ROBE William 1852
FENTONSPREAD Henry 1874
5
NICHOLS George 1839
ARNOLD Robert 1839
EPPERSON Lewis E 1853
SIDDINS Thomas J 1853
NICHOLS George 1839
WISNER Mathias 1864
CRUSE James L 1850
WISNER Mathias 1864
4
NICHOLS Israel 1839
CRUSE James L 1850
BRIGHT Elkanah 1848
WELLS John 1000

7
EPPERSON Lewis 1852
EPPERSON Lewis 1852
EPPERSON Lewis 1852
STEVENS Plowdon 1874
SCHOTTMANN Gerhard 1870
SCHOTTMANN John 1871
SCHATTMAN John 1864
SCHOTTMANN John 1870
8
SCHOTTMANN Gerhard 1870
FELDKAMP Bernhard 1871
FELDKAMP Bernhard 1870
HARRAH William N 1853
HARRAH William N 1853
HARRAH William N 1853
HARRAH William N 1853
HARRAH William N 1853
LAUGHLIN Richard 1853
CRUSE James L 1850
CRUSE James L 1850
CREWS James L 1851
CREWS James L 1851
9
WAGLE Asa 1849
MYERS William F T 1849
HARRAH William N 1853
MYERS William F T 1849
WALLACE James 1853

18
WOLF Henry 1871
MEISLAHN Christian 1871
WOLF Henry 1871
MEISLAHN Christian 1871
TUCKER David M 1853
BERRY Wyatt S 1852
CRITTENDEN Richard H 1852
17
TUCKER David M 1853
TUCKER David M 1852

Lots-Sec. 16
L1 ALEXANDER, William 1852
L2 BLAKE, William J 1852
L3 BLAKE, William J 1852
L4 DUNEGAN, Jackson 1852
L5 CALDWELL, Albert G 1852
L6 CALDWELL, Albert G 1852
L7 CALDWELL, Albert G 1852
L8 CALDWELL, Albert G 1852
16

19
PETERSON Abner M 1853
MCCOY John G 1872
MCCOY John G 1872
MCCOY John G 1872
CREWS James L 1874
MCCOY John G 1872
20
WALLACE William L 1867
ELLIOTT Michael D 1871
WOLLACE Alexander As 1866
TERWILLIGER David 1873
CREWS James L 1864
KOEBELE Landolin 1870
SHERMAN Nelson 1871
VAROLE Brice M 1871
ANDERSON Samuel 1850
ARNOLD Fletcher 1853
CREWS James L 1853
ANDERSON Samuel 1850
ANDERSON Samuel 1850
BERRY Mathias 1850
BERRY Mathias 1850
HAYS Lewis M 1853
21
BERRY Mathias 1850
HAYS Lewis M 1852
BERRY Mathias 1850
HAYS Lewis M 1852
HAYS Lewis M 1852

30
CREWS James L 1872
CREWS James L 1880
CREWS James L 1880
SIEFKEN Gerhard 1880
ARNOLD James 1853
CREWS James L 1853
CREWS James L 1853
CREWS James L 1853
ARNOLD Joseph 1851
SCREWS James 1853
CREWS James L 1853
29
CREWS James L 1853
SHY Jacob Cantrel 1838
CREWS James L 1853
ALEXANDER William 1853
ALEXANDER Jesse J 1851
ALEXANDER Jesse J 1851
NICHOLS Israel M 1849
ALEXANDER Jesse J 1851
CALDWELL Albert G 1870
CALDWELL Albert G 1873
CALDWELL Albert G 1870
MAMMOPER Joseph 1864
CALDWELL [16] Albert G 1870
28
CALDWELL Albert G 1871
MAMMOSER Joseph 1872
MAMMOSER Joseph 1874

31
BERRY Mathias 1850
EVANS James L 1852
MARRS Christopher 1849
MARRS Christopher 1849
ANDERSON Samuel 1850
WILLIAMS Wiley 1849
WILLIAMS Wiley 1849
WRIGHT George 1868
HEFFERNAN John 1886
NICHOLS Israel M 1849
COZARD Jacob 1863
32
LEE Levi 1849
NICHOLS Israel M 1849
STIENER Joseph 1873
RICK Enoch 1886
NICHOLS Israel M 1849
NICHOLS John 1853
LEE Levi 1853
BARBER Elam 1853
NICHOLS Israel 1853
NICHOLS John 1853
NICHOLS Israel 1853
REFFIT Joseph 1852
REFFIT Joseph 1852
33
ASHER Kellar 1853
ASHER Kellar 1853
LAKE Benjamin 1853
MYERS James G 1853

Section 3
GOSS Fredrick 1849
NICHOLS Garret 1846
GOSS Fredrick 1849
3
WAYLE James 1849
WAGLE James 1839
WAGLE Asa 1839
TOMPKINS Christopher 1849
NICHOLS George 1839
WALL Henry 1840

Section 2
WILLIAMS Wiley 1849
EPPERSON Louis 1894
GARDNER William H 1851
MEINHART Matthias 1867
MAURER Daniel S 1874
2
WILLIAMS Wiley 1849
GLOVER [30] Andrew J 1849

Section 1
YAKELEY Samuel 1849
1
BARTLETT Martin S 1851
ROSS Meredith B 1851
GILLHAM John 1853
GILLHAM John 1852
GILLHAM John 1853
ROSS Meredith B 1852
ROSS Meredith B 1853
ROSS Meridith 1853

Section 10
NICHOLS James 1839
ATKINS Joseph Hazard 1839
WAYLE James 1849
WAGLE Asa 1839
SEARSE Isaac 1840
ARNOLD John 1839
10
ANDERSON John 1851
WALL Henry 1840
ARNOLD William 1840
DITTEMORE William 1849
CREWS James L 1881
DITTEMOORE Adam 1849

Section 11
TOMPKINS Christopher 1849
DITTEMORE Greenbury 1849
11
DITTEMOORE Adam 1849
GARDNER William H 1852
GARDNER William H 1852
HAYS Lewis M 1852
HAYS Lewis M 1852
HAYS Lewis M 1852

Section 12
DITTEMORE James M 1871
ROBERSON John 1868
WICHARD Silas W 1863
WISHARD Silas W 1868
REYNOLDS Jesse S P 1872
WISHARD Silas W 1870
12
MAURER Daniel S 1871
MAURER John W 1874
FATOOT Silas 1869
MILLER Allen O 1875
WISHARD William 1880
WISHARD William 1867

Section 15
CARSON William J 1849
DITTEMOORE William 1849
15
HALFHILL Mandervile 1853
DITTEMORE William 1853
DITTEMORE William 1853
NEWTON William D 1853
GLOUR Thomas 1853
HAYS Lewis M 1853

Section 14
DUTELL August 1872
COOLEY Isaiah 1858
WAGLE James A 1875
DUTELL August 1875
DUTELL August 1875
CALDWELL Albert G 1875
WAGLE James 1875
14
KUYKENDALL James M 1876
MILLER Marshall 1876
MYERS Thomas 1875
MYERS Noah 1873
CREWS James L 1874
CREWS James L 1876
MYERS Noah 1874

Section 13
ROBERTS Peter H 1853
BRADSHAW James 1853
BRADSHAW James 1853
13
HAYS Lewis M 1853
BRADSHAW James 1852
SINK Paul 1851
HAYES Lewis M 1852
BRADSHAW James 1852
HENSLEY George 1850

Section 22
MEINHART Mathias 1874
SCHOTTMANN Gerhard 1875
BOWEN Anthony 1877
THOMPSON Robert 1875
22
MEINHART Mathias 1874
MEINHART Matthias 1864
CALDWELL Albert G 1871
MEINHART Matthias 1865

Section 23
PETERSON Abner M 1853
VARVILLE George W 1853
WILSON Thomas 1853
ARNOLD Henry 1854
23
MITCHELL Willis T 1853
BRADSHAW James 1854
REDFORD James 1853
MCQUAID Milton 1853
LINK Eli 1853

Section 24
CREWS James L 1874
HENSLEY David M 1875
MYERS Noah 1850
MYERS Noah 1850
HENSLEY George 1850
HENSLEY David M 1875
SOWERS Michael M 1872
HENSLEY George 1850
24
NEWLIN Absalom 1873
HENSLEY George 1873
BRADSHAW James 1853

Section 27
CRITTENDEN Richard H 1852
27
CRITTENDEN Richard H 1852
TUCKER David M 1852
VARVIL John H 1853
AUSTIN James 1854
PETERSON Abner M 1853
VARVIL John H 1853
VARVIL John H 1853

Section 26
HARRAH Daniel T 1864
HARRAH Daniel T 1864
NEWLIN William H 1873
YOUNG Timothy E 00/0
26
CREWS James L 1874
MITCHELL O H 1875
BADGER Stephen 1873
ROBERSON John 1874
MITCHELL O H 1873
ECKARDT John W 00/0

Section 25
MARK James 1852
BRADSHAW James 1853
BRADSHAW James 1853
FOSTER Thomas 1853
BRADSHAW James 1853
ROPER Holley 1853
BRADSHAW James 1853
25
SPEARS Charles 1853
REDFORD James 1853
ROPER Samuel 1853
KIBLER George 1853

Section 34
COAN Hiram S 1874
HANNA Albert G 1874
PRINTZ Calvin F 1869
WELLS George T 1870
PRINTZ Hiram M 1869
34
BLIDE John 1864
HESS Sarah J 1872
FOSTER John W 1872
COLLINS George 1866
FOSTER John W 1872

Section 35
MCQUAID Milton 1853
FOUST [29] Benjamin 1853
RAPER Holley 1854
FOSTER Thomas 1854
35
FOUST [29] Benjamin 1853
RAPER Holley 1854
ODELL Washington 1854
MCQUAID Mitlon 1853

Section 36
SPEARS [56] Charles 1853
KIBLER George 1853
SPEARS William 1852
SPEARS [56] Charles 1853
KIBLER George 1853
PATRICK Charles 1849
KIBLER George 1853
36
KIBLER Emanuel C 1853
BREWER Henry 1853
THOMAS John D 1849
BREWER Henry 1852
SMITH Samuel 1852
FITHIAN Glover 1849
BREWER Henry 1850

Helpful Hints

1. This Map's INDEX can be found on the preceding pages.

2. Refer to Map "C" to see where this Township lies within Jasper County, Illinois.

3. Numbers within square brackets [ ] denote a multi-patentee land parcel (multi-owner). Refer to Appendix "C" for a full list of members in this group.

4. Areas that look to be crowded with Patentees usually indicate multiple sales of the same parcel (re-issues), cancellations or voided transactions (that we map, anyway) or overlapping parcels. We opt to show even these ambiguous parcels, which oftentimes lead to research avenues not yet taken.

Legend

———— Patent Boundary

━━━━ Section Boundary

No Patents Found (or Outside County)

1., 2., 3., ... Lot Numbers (when beside a name)

[ ] Group Number (see Appendix "C")

Scale: Section = 1 mile X 1 mile (generally, with some exceptions)

Road Map

T8-N R8-E
3rd PM Meridian

Map Group 1

Cities & Towns
Island Grove

Cemeteries
Brewer Cemetery
Island Creek Cemetery

E 2200th Ave

6

5

E 2160th Ave

4

E 2100th Ave

7

8

9

E 2000th Ave

18

17

16

N 200th St

E 1900th Ave

19

20

21

N 100th St

30

29

28

E 1700th Ave

Island Grove

Brewer
Cem.

31

32

33

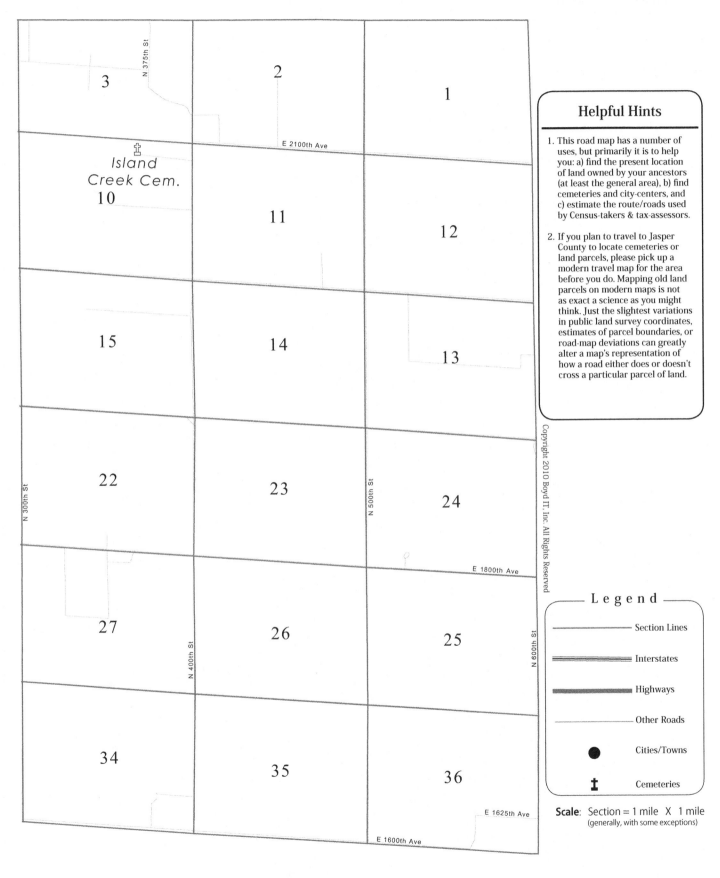

Helpful Hints

1. This road map has a number of uses, but primarily it is to help you: a) find the present location of land owned by your ancestors (at least the general area), b) find cemeteries and city-centers, and c) estimate the route/roads used by Census-takers & tax-assessors.

2. If you plan to travel to Jasper County to locate cemeteries or land parcels, please pick up a modern travel map for the area before you do. Mapping old land parcels on modern maps is not as exact a science as you might think. Just the slightest variations in public land survey coordinates, estimates of parcel boundaries, or road-map deviations can greatly alter a map's representation of how a road either does or doesn't cross a particular parcel of land.

Legend

————————	Section Lines
═══════	Interstates
━━━━━━	Highways
————————	Other Roads
●	Cities/Towns
♰	Cemeteries

Scale: Section = 1 mile X 1 mile
(generally, with some exceptions)

Island Creek Cem.

N 375th St

E 2100th Ave

N 300th St

N 400th St

N 500th St

N 600th St

E 1800th Ave

E 1625th Ave

E 1600th Ave

3 2 1
10 11 12
15 14 13
22 23 24
27 26 25
34 35 36

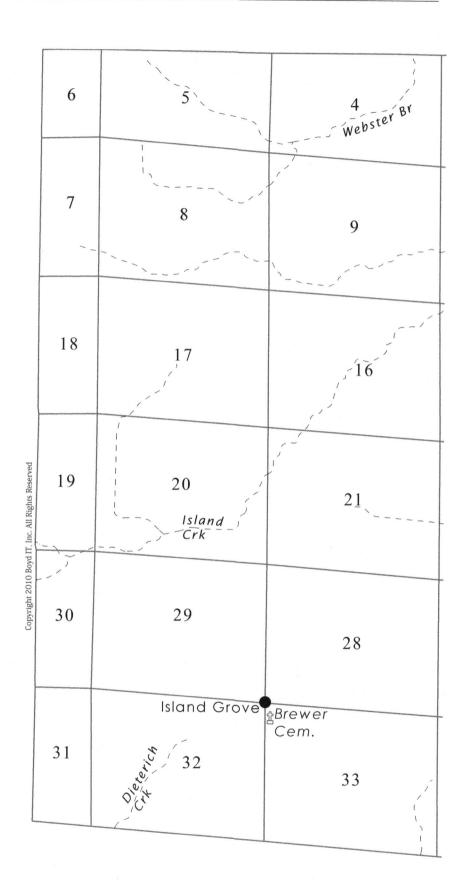

Historical Map

T8-N R8-E
3rd PM Meridian

Map Group 1

Cities & Towns
Island Grove

Cemeteries
Brewer Cemetery
Island Creek Cemetery

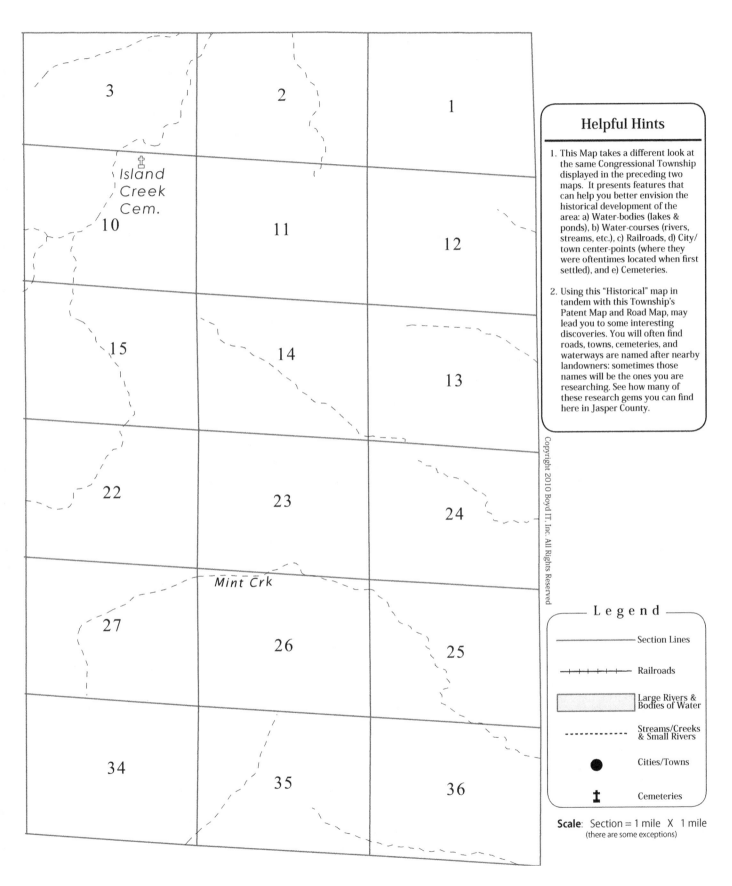

1. This Map takes a different look at the same Congressional Township displayed in the preceding two maps. It presents features that can help you better envision the historical development of the area: a) Water-bodies (lakes & ponds), b) Water-courses (rivers, streams, etc.), c) Railroads, d) City/town center-points (where they were oftentimes located when first settled), and e) Cemeteries.

2. Using this "Historical" map in tandem with this Township's Patent Map and Road Map, may lead you to some interesting discoveries. You will often find roads, towns, cemeteries, and waterways are named after nearby landowners: sometimes those names will be the ones you are researching. See how many of these research gems you can find here in Jasper County.

Legend
Section Lines
Railroads
Large Rivers & Bodies of Water
Streams/Creeks & Small Rivers
Cities/Towns
Cemeteries

Scale: Section = 1 mile X 1 mile
(there are some exceptions)

Map Group 2: Index to Land Patents

Township 8-North Range 9-East (3rd PM)

After you locate an individual in this Index, take note of the Section and Section Part then proceed to the Land Patent map on the pages immediately following. You should have no difficulty locating the corresponding parcel of land.

The "For More Info" Column will lead you to more information about the underlying Patents. See the *Legend* at right, and the "How to Use this Book" chapter, for more information.

```
┌─────────────────────────────────────────────────────┐
│                      LEGEND                           │
│          "For More Info . . . " column                │
│ G = Group  (Multi-Patentee Patent, see Appendix "C")  │
│ R = Residence                                         │
│ S = Social Status                                     │
│                                                       │
│                                                       │
│ See Appendix A for list of abbreviations used by the  │
│ Illinois State Archives in describing the place and   │
│ nature of these land patents.                         │
│                                                       │
│ Note: if the Abbreviations contain "L", "BL", "LOT",  │
│ or "BLOCK", the exact whereabouts of the parcel within│
│ the section is not known.                             │
└─────────────────────────────────────────────────────┘
```

ID	Individual in Patent	Sec.	Sec. Part	Purchase Date	Sale Type	IL Aliquot Part	For More Info . . .
466	ADKINS, Jackson	3	S½SE	1852-10-19	FD	S2SE	
465	" "	10	NWNE	1852-10-19	FD	NWNE	
492	ANDREWS, Jasin	13	NWSW	1848-04-03	FD	NWSW	R:JASPER
470	BAILEY, James	22	NWNW	1852-12-01	FD	NWNW	
469	" "	15	SWSW	1852-12-01	FD	SWSW	
441	BAIN, George	11	NENE	1850-04-17	FD	NENE	R:JASPER
502	BAIN, John	19	E½SE	1837-09-25	FD	E2SE	R:INDIANA
498	" "	10	E½SW	1837-09-25	FD	E2SW	R:INDIANA
499	" "	15	E½NW	1837-09-25	FD	E2NW	R:INDIANA
500	" "	15	NWNW	1837-09-25	FD	NWNW	R:INDIANA
501	" "	19	E½NE	1837-09-25	FD	E2NE	R:INDIANA
503	" "	20	NW	1837-09-25	FD	NW	R:INDIANA
504	" "	20	SW	1837-09-25	FD	SW	R:INDIANA
505	" "	29	NW	1837-09-25	FD	NW	R:INDIANA
448	BARRETT, Harvey B	34	E½NE	1853-09-13	FD	E2NE	R:INDIANA
604	BARRETT, Samuel	21	W½NE	1852-09-28	FD	W2NE	
601	" "	21	E½NW	1852-09-28	FD	E2NW	
602	" "	21	NENE	1852-09-28	FD	NENE	
603	" "	21	SENE	1853-09-13	FD	SENE	R:INDIANA
587	BARTLETT, Robert L	21	S½SW	1850-05-24	FD	S2SW	
588	" "	28	W½NW	1850-05-24	FD	W2NW	
651	BAXTER, William	35	SWSW	1853-09-21	FD	SWSW	R:INDIANA
558	BORING, Michael	16	L11	1853-10-15	SC	LOT11NESW	
405	BOYD, David	9	SENE	1832-10-25	FD	SENE	R:COLES
554	BRACKNEY, Levi	30	N½NE	1850-12-11	FD	N2NE	
552	" "	17	SWSE	1850-12-11	FD	SWSE	R:INDIANA
553	" "	19	W½SE	1850-12-11	FD	W2SE	
476	BRADSHAW, James	7	SWSE	1852-08-20	FD	SWSE	
475	" "	7	SW	1852-08-20	FD	SW	R:TENNESSEE
474	" "	18	NW	1852-08-20	FD	NW	R:TENNESSEE
472	" "	17	NWNW	1852-08-20	FD	NWNW	
471	" "	17	N½SW	1852-08-20	FD	N2SW	R:TENNESSEE
417	" "	17	N½SW	1852-08-20	FD	N2SW	R:TENNESSEE
473	" "	17	S½NW	1852-08-23	FD	S2NW	
366	BUTLER, Amos C	21	E½SE	1853-09-28	FD	E2SE	
605	BUTLER, Samuel C	27	W½SE	1853-09-28	FD	W2SE	
637	BUTLER, Warren	21	W½SE	1853-09-28	FD	W2SE	
506	BYRD, John	29	NE	1851-09-03	FD	NE	
398	CAREY, Coonrod W	4	SWSE	1852-09-15	FD	SWSE	
568	CARR, Milam C	13	SESE	1849-07-26	FD	SESE	R:OHIO
612	CATLIN, Seth	28	NE	1851-10-01	FD	NE	
595	CHANEY, Robert Y	6	SESE	1851-06-20	FD	SESE	
596	" "	7	NENE	1851-06-20	FD	NENE	
597	" "	7	W½NE	1851-06-20	FD	W2NE	
435	CLAWSON, Ephraim	31	W½NE	1837-11-15	FD	W2NE	R:INDIANA G:18
434	" "	31	W½	1837-11-15	FD	W2	R:INDIANA G:18

ID	Individual in Patent	Sec.	Sec. Part	Purchase Date	Sale Type	IL Aliquot Part	For More Info . . .
433	CLAWSON, Ephraim (Cont'd)	31	SE	1837-11-15	FD	SE	R:INDIANA G:18
435	CLAWSON, Josiah	31	W½NE	1837-11-15	FD	W2NE	R:INDIANA G:18
434	" "	31	W½	1837-11-15	FD	W2	R:INDIANA G:18
433	" "	31	SE	1837-11-15	FD	SE	R:INDIANA G:18
541	CODD, Joseph	24	NWNW	1850-12-12	FD	NWNW	R:JASPER
497	COGGESHALL, Job	4	W½NE	1839-04-13	FD	W2NE	R:INDIANA
507	COGGESHALL, John	10	E½NW	1839-05-21	FD	E2NW	R:INDIANA
508	" "	10	NWNW	1839-05-21	FD	NWNW	R:INDIANA
509	" "	4	NENW	1839-05-21	FD	NENW	R:INDIANA
413	CURTISS, E H	34	NENW	1865-05-12	SW	NENW	
384	DAVIS, Benjamin	6	SWNE	1849-11-06	FD	SWNE	R:INDIANA
381	" "	5	SWNW	1849-11-06	FD	SWNW	R:INDIANA
383	" "	6	E½NE	1849-11-06	FD	E2NE	R:INDIANA
382	" "	6		1849-12-29	FD	E2NEWA	R:INDIANA
551	DODD, Kendle B	36	SESE	1851-02-25	FD	SESE	R:JASPER
640	DOWNS, William A	16	L6	1853-12-08	SC	LOT6SENW	
641	" "	16	L7	1853-12-08	SC	LOT7SWNE	
351	EAGLETON, Alexander	32	NWNW	1851-08-21	FD	NWNW	
352	EAGLETON, Alexander M	28	E½NW	1849-06-16	FD	E2NW	
353	" "	28	N½SW	1849-06-16	FD	N2SW	
652	EAGLETON, William	29	SWSW	1851-09-19	FD	SWSW	R:INDIANA
403	EDWARDS, Daniel P	11	W½NW	1850-01-17	FD	W2NW	
401	" "	11	NWSW	1850-01-17	FD	NWSW	
402	" "	11	SENW	1850-01-17	FD	SENW	
400	" "	1	NESW	1850-04-17	FD	NESW	R:JASPER
519	ELDER, John L	35	SWNW	1852-10-20	FD	SWNW	
494	ELY, Jerard	23	NENE	1846-02-18	FD	NENE	R:EDGAR
411	FARIS, David Jr	15	W½SE	1839-08-26	FD	W2SE	R:COLES
412	FARRIS, David Jr	15	E½SW	1839-11-16	FD	E2SW	R:COLES
606	FOREMAN, Samuel	28	E½SE	1850-11-21	FD	E2SE	
607	" "	28	SWSE	1850-11-22	FD	SWSE	
608	" "	33	NENE	1850-11-22	FD	NENE	
542	FOUST, Joseph	23	SENE	1847-04-20	FD	SENE	R:JASPER
372	FRAZIER, Arlindo	8	SWSE	1852-08-24	FD	SWSE	
371	" "	17	N½NE	1852-09-14	FD	N2NE	R:JASPER
656	GALBREATH, William	34	SENW	1852-08-27	FD	SENW	R:INDIANA
655	" "	30	NW	1852-08-27	FD	NW	R:INDIANA
667	GILLMORE, William J	5	NWNW	1852-09-15	FD	NWNW	R:OHIO
668	GILMORE, William J	4	E½E½	1852-09-15	FD	E2E2	R:OHIO
407	GOLDSBY, David	9	NENW	1853-01-20	FD	NENW	
510	GORRELL, John	23	NW	1849-05-19	FD	NW	
444	GOSNELL, George	35	NENE	1850-02-28	FD	NENE	R:JASPER
445	" "	35	NENE	1850-02-28	FD	NENE	R:JASPER
442	" "	25	NWSW	1850-10-22	FD	NWSW	R:JASPER
444	" "	35	NENE	1850-10-22	FD	NENE	R:JASPER
443	" "	26	SESE	1850-10-22	FD	SESE	R:JASPER
445	" "	35	NENE	1850-10-22	FD	NENE	R:JASPER
638	GOSNELL, Washington	25	SESW	1851-06-17	FD	SESW	R:JASPER
354	GRAY, Alexander M	35	SESE	1852-08-20	FD	SESE	
322	GREEN, Abner C	36	N½SW	1849-10-25	FD	N2SW	G:33
323	" "	36	S½NW	1849-10-25	FD	S2NW	G:33
323	GREEN, Jeremiah	36	S½NW	1849-10-25	FD	S2NW	G:33
322	" "	36	N½SW	1849-10-25	FD	N2SW	G:33
396	GRIFFITH, Charles	35	NESW	1850-10-22	FD	NESW	
395	" "	35	E½NW	1850-10-22	FD	E2NW	
397	" "	35	SWNE	1850-10-22	FD	SWNE	
449	HAGY, Henry	9	S½NW	1852-11-20	FD	S2NW	
609	HANKINS, Samuel	22	NWSE	1853-09-28	FD	NWSE	
328	HARDING, Abraham	3	SENE	1850-04-17	FD	SENE	R:JASPER
326	" "	2	S½NW	1850-04-17	FD	S2NW	R:JASPER
327	" "	3	NESE	1850-04-17	FD	NESE	R:JASPER
324	" "	2		1850-05-31	FD	S2NWWA	R:JASPER
325	" "	2	NESW	1852-12-28	FD	NESW	
375	HARDING, Aron	15	NWNE	1853-08-05	FD	NWNE	
635	HARDING, Thomas H	2	SESE	1849-11-16	FD	SESE	R:INDIANA
634	" "	2	NWSE	1850-04-29	FD	NWSE	R:JASPER
633	" "	2	NESE	1851-02-03	FD	NESE	R:JASPER
660	HARPER, William	16	L8	1858-05-03	SC	LOT08SENE	
329	HARRIS, Addison	24	E½SE	1840-06-09	FD	E2SE	R:JASPER
330	" "	25	W½SE	1840-06-09	FD	W2SE	R:JASPER
343	HARRIS, Addison S	27	E½NW	1837-08-05	FD	E2NW	R:CRAWFORD
344	" "	27	E½SW	1837-08-05	FD	E2SW	R:CRAWFORD
334	" "	22	SWSW	1837-08-05	FD	SWSW	R:CRAWFORD

ID	Individual in Patent	Sec.	Sec. Part	Purchase Date	Sale Type	IL Aliquot Part	For More Info . . .
333	HARRIS, Addison S (Cont'd)	22	NE	1837-08-05	FD	NE	R:CRAWFORD
332	" "	22	E½SW	1837-08-05	FD	E2SW	R:CRAWFORD
342	" "	26	W½SW	1838-02-12	FD	W2SW	R:CRAWFORD
346	" "	27	SENE	1838-04-04	FD	SENE	R:CRAWFORD
331	" "	22	E½SE	1840-03-24	FD	E2SE	R:JASPER
337	" "	25	NWNW	1848-06-28	FD	NWNW	R:JASPER
340	" "	26	SENW	1848-06-28	FD	SENW	R:JASPER
335	" "	24	E½SW	1848-10-03	FD	E2SW	R:JASPER
336	" "	24	SENE	1849-11-02	FD	SENE	R:JASPER
338	" "	25	SWNW	1851-04-15	FD	SWNW	
339	" "	26	E½NE	1851-04-15	FD	E2NE	
341	" "	26	SWNE	1851-04-15	FD	SWNE	
345	" "	27	NENE	1853-01-20	FD	NENE	
347	" "	27	W½NE	1865-05-09	SW	W2NE	
646	HARRIS, William A	27	E½SE	1838-04-04	FD	E2SE	R:CRAWFORD
650	" "	34	W½NE	1838-04-04	FD	W2NE	R:CRAWFORD
645	" "	26	SWNW	1838-04-06	FD	SWNW	R:CRAWFORD
649	" "	34	SE	1839-12-06	FD	SE	R:JASPER
647	" "	27	W½NW	1839-12-06	FD	W2NW	R:JASPER
648	" "	27	W½SW	1839-12-06	FD	W2SW	R:JASPER
644	" "	26	E½SW	1840-03-24	FD	E2SW	R:JASPER
643	" "	25	NE	1840-06-09	FD	NE	R:JASPER
642	" "	25	E½NW	1848-06-28	FD	E2NW	R:JASPER
477	HAYS, James	11	NENW	1841-11-10	FD	NENW	R:JASPER
479	" "	2	NENW	1841-11-10	FD	NENW	R:JASPER
478	" "	11	NWNE	1849-10-24	FD	NWNE	R:JASPER
567	HAYS, Michael S	2	SWSE	1851-10-02	FD	SWSE	R:JASPER
679	HAYS, William W	2	SESW	1851-09-24	FD	SESW	R:JASPER
423	HICKS, Ellis	29	NESW	1850-06-24	FD	NESW	R:COLES
422	" "	29	N½SE	1850-06-24	FD	N2SE	R:COLES
569	HILLS, Moses	10	SWNW	1832-10-04	FD	SWNW	R:CRAWFORD
364	HILLYER, Alvin	32	NENW	1850-10-31	FD	NENW	R:SHELBY
363	" "	28	NWSE	1850-10-31	FD	NWSE	R:SHELBY
426	HINTON, Ellis	20	SE	1850-10-03	FD	SE	
424	" "	17	N½SE	1852-08-23	FD	N2SE	
425	" "	17	SEN½	1852-08-23	FD	S2NE	
512	HOGUE, John	11	SESW	1848-09-11	FD	SESW	
511	" "	11	SESE	1848-09-11	FD	SESE	
533	" "	11	SESE	1848-09-11	FD	SESE	
513	" "	11	W½SE	1848-09-11	FD	W2SE	
350	HOLSCHER, Franie	33	W½NE	1846-02-28	FD	W2NE	R:EFFINGHAM
483	" "	33	NWSE	1846-02-28	FD	NWSE	R:EFFINGHAM
436	" "	33	NWSE	1846-02-28	FD	NWSE	R:EFFINGHAM
437	" "	33	W½NE	1846-02-28	FD	W2NE	R:EFFINGHAM
543	HUNT, Joseph	1	E½NE	1843-11-25	FD	E2NE	R:JASPER
532	HURING, John R	11	NWSE	1861-09-26	FD	NWSE	
511	" "	11	SESE	1861-09-26	FD	SESE	
533	" "	11	SESE	1861-09-26	FD	SESE	
514	HURST, John	17	SESW	1851-09-08	FD	SESW	R:INDIANA
515	" "	30	NESE	1851-09-13	FD	NESE	R:INDIANA
456	HUTSON, Isaac	11	SWNE	1852-12-11	FD	SWNE	
545	HUTSON, Joseph	12	E½NW	1850-10-19	FD	E2NW	R:JASPER
546	" "	12	NWNW	1850-10-19	FD	NWNW	R:JASPER
547	" "	12	W½NE	1850-10-19	FD	W2NE	R:JASPER
544	" "	12		1850-11-30	FD	PTW2NEWA	R:JASPER
663	HUTSON, William	12	SWNW	1840-12-21	FD	SWNW	R:JASPER
662	" "	11	SWSW	1852-08-20	FD	SWSW	
664	" "	14	NENW	1852-08-20	FD	NENW	
661	" "	11	SENE	1852-08-20	FD	SENE	
665	" "	2	NWNW	1852-08-20	FD	NWNW	
666	" "	23	SESE	1852-08-20	FD	SESE	
585	ISLEY, Philip	33	SWSW	1850-10-02	FD	SWSW	R:INDIANA
584	" "	32	SE	1850-10-02	FD	SE	R:INDIANA
583	" "	32	E½SW	1850-10-02	FD	E2SW	R:INDIANA
496	JACK, Jeremiah	16	L16	1853-10-15	SC	LOT16SESE	
495	" "	16	L15	1853-10-15	SC	LOT15SWSE	
408	JONES, David	3	NESW	1853-02-04	FD	NESW	R:OHIO
409	" "	3	SENW	1853-02-04	FD	SENW	R:OHIO
410	" "	3	W½NW	1853-02-04	FD	W2NW	R:OHIO
555	KELLY, Matilda	15	NESE	1839-09-23	FD	NESE	R:COLES S:F
517	KERN, John	30	W½SE	1852-08-20	FD	W2SE	
516	" "	30	SEN½	1852-08-20	FD	S2NE	
468	KIBLER, Jacob	23	SWSE	1847-09-02	FD	SWSE	R:JASPER

ID	Individual in Patent	Sec.	Sec. Part	Purchase Date	Sale Type	IL Aliquot Part	For More Info . . .
467	KIBLER, Jacob E	24	SWSW	1851-02-01	FD	SWSW	R:JASPER
627	KIBLER, Theobald	22	SWSE	1854-02-09	FD	SWSE	R:JASPER
628	KIBLER, Theobold	24	SWNW	1849-05-17	FD	SWNW	R:JASPER
670	KIBLER, William M	25	SWSW	1848-09-27	FD	SWSW	R:VIRGINIA
671	"	36	NWNW	1848-09-27	FD	NWNW	R:VIRGINIA
518	KILLGORE, John	3	NENW	1852-08-20	FD	NENW	R:CUMBERLAND
620	LARIMER, Smith	25	E½SE	1839-05-16	FD	E2SE	R:OHIO
686	LAUGHTER, Yewen H	8	NW	1850-03-14	FD	NW	
421	LEACH, Elizabeth	19	N½NW	1853-07-29	FD	N2NW	R:JASPER S:F G:43
421	LEACH, Joseph N	19	N½NW	1853-07-29	FD	N2NW	R:JASPER S:F G:43
421	LEACH, Mary Ann	19	N½NW	1853-07-29	FD	N2NW	R:JASPER S:F G:43
421	LEACH, Nancy N	19	N½NW	1853-07-29	FD	N2NW	R:JASPER S:F G:43
421	LEACH, Nathaniel	19	N½NW	1853-07-29	FD	N2NW	R:JASPER S:F G:43
421	LEACH, Richard	19	N½NW	1853-07-29	FD	N2NW	R:JASPER S:F G:43
421	LEACH, Thomas	19	N½NW	1853-07-29	FD	N2NW	R:JASPER S:F G:43
421	LEACH, Walter	19	N½NW	1853-07-29	FD	N2NW	R:JASPER S:F G:43
561	LIDEY, Michael	12	NESW	1850-04-18	FD	NESW	
562	"	12	NWSE	1850-04-18	FD	NWSE	
563	"	12	S½SE	1850-04-18	FD	S2SE	
565	"	13	NENW	1850-04-18	FD	NENW	
566	"	13	NWNE	1850-04-18	FD	NWNE	
564	"	12	W½SW	1850-04-18	FD	W2SW	
560	"	12	NESE	1850-10-09	FD	NESE	
559	"	12	E½NE	1850-10-09	FD	E2NE	
619	LINTHIEUM, Slingsby	29	SWSE	1850-12-03	FD	SWSE	R:COLES
618	"	29	SESW	1850-12-03	FD	SESW	R:COLES
446	LITTLE, George	35	NWSW	1853-06-15	FD	NWSW	R:JASPER
520	LITTLE, John	35	SESW	1851-09-24	FD	SESW	R:JASPER
440	LITTON, Fulton	16	L5	1817-11-17	SC	LOT5SWNW	
386	LONG, Benjamin	24	NWSE	1847-03-03	FD	NWSE	R:JASPER
385	"	23	N½SE	1847-03-03	FD	N2SE	R:JASPER
388	"	26	SWSE	1851-04-05	FD	SWSE	
387	"	26	NWNE	1851-04-05	FD	NWNE	
669	LONG, William	36	E½NE	1840-07-01	FD	E2NE	R:JASPER
548	LYONS, Joseph	15	NWSW	1852-10-06	FD	NWSW	
549	"	15	SWNW	1852-10-06	FD	SWNW	
438	MARKWELL, French	2	NE	1849-01-20	FD	NE	
439	"	2	NE	1849-01-20	FD	NE	
438	"	2	NE	1849-02-28	FD	NE	R:INDIANA
439	"	2	NE	1849-02-28	FD	NE	R:INDIANA
539	MATHEW, Jonah	19	N½SW	1850-12-10	FD	N2SW	R:JASPER
540	"	19	S½SW	1853-09-23	FD	S2SW	R:JASPER
357	MCBATH, Alexander	6	W½	1852-08-20	FD	W2	R:TENNESSEE
359	"	7	NW	1852-08-20	FD	NW	R:TENNESSEE
356	"	6	NWNE	1852-08-20	FD	NWNE	R:TENNESSEE
355	"	6	NESE	1852-08-20	FD	NESE	
358	"	6	W½SE	1852-08-20	FD	W2SE	R:TENNESSEE
394	MCCOMAS, Charles C	2	SWSW	1849-10-17	FD	SWSW	R:JASPER
481	MCCOMAS, James M	2	NWSW	1851-01-14	FD	NWSW	R:JASPER
521	MCDANIEL, John	35	NESE	1851-05-16	FD	NESE	R:INDIANA
522	"	35	SENE	1851-05-16	FD	SENE	R:INDIANA
523	"	36	SWSE	1851-05-16	FD	SWSE	R:INDIANA
361	MERITT, Allen	1	SESW	1850-11-08	FD	SESW	R:JASPER
360	"	1	NENW	1852-08-20	FD	NENW	R:JASPER
362	MERRITT, Allen	1	W½NE	1852-08-20	FD	W2NE	R:JASPER
685	MITCHELL, Willis T	8	SWSW	1852-09-07	FD	SWSW	R:INDIANA
524	MONDON, John	14	W½SW	1852-08-20	FD	W2SW	R:INDIANA
393	MOORE, Benjamin D	21	W½NW	1851-09-08	FD	W2NW	
380	"	21	W½NW	1851-09-08	FD	W2NW	
379	"	20	W½NE	1851-09-08	FD	W2NE	R:INDIANA
418	MOORE, Elias	25	NESW	1850-10-22	FD	NESW	R:JASPER
419	"	35	NWNE	1850-10-22	FD	NWNE	R:JASPER
447	MOORE, Harrison	35	NWNW	1852-10-18	FD	NWNW	R:INDIANA
672	MOORE, William	30	SESE	1852-10-09	FD	SESE	
621	MUSGRAVE, Stephen	1		1849-07-31	FD	N2SEWA	R:JASPER
622	"	13		1849-07-31	FD	SENWWA	R:JASPER
622	"	13		1849-07-31	FD	NESWWA	R:JASPER
625	MUSGROVE, Stephen	13	SENW	1849-06-30	FD	SENW	R:JASPER
623	"	13	N½SE	1849-06-30	FD	N2SE	R:JASPER
626	"	13	SWNE	1849-06-30	FD	SWNE	R:JASPER
624	"	13	NESW	1849-06-30	FD	NESW	R:JASPER
406	MYERS, David C	8	W½NE	1850-04-09	FD	W2NE	R:INDIANA
414	MYERS, Eli	5	SW	1850-04-09	FD	SW	

ID	Individual in Patent	Sec.	Sec. Part	Purchase Date	Sale Type	IL Aliquot Part	For More Info . . .
415	MYERS, Eli (Cont'd)	8	SENE	1850-04-09	FD	SENE	R:INDIANA
431	MYERS, Enoch	18	SW	1850-02-01	FD	SW	R:INDIANA
432	" "	8	SESE	1852-08-30	FD	SESE	
525	MYERS, John	16	SENE	1872-09-21	SC	SENE	G:49
570	MYERS, Noah	18	SWSE	1850-02-01	FD	SWSE	R:INDIANA
573	" "	19	W½NE	1850-02-01	FD	W2NE	R:INDIANA
572	" "	19	E½NW	1850-02-01	FD	E2NW	R:INDIANA
574	" "	19	W½NW	1850-02-01	FD	W2NW	R:INDIANA
571	" "	19		1850-03-31	FD	PTE2NWWA	R:INDIANA
636	MYERS, Thomas	21	NWSW	1850-04-26	FD	NWSW	R:JASPER
454	NICHOLS, Hiram	10	E½SE	1839-09-02	FD	E2SE	R:INDIANA
639	ODELL, Washington	22	NENW	1852-11-24	FD	NENW	
393	PARSONS, Catharine Jr	21	W½NW	1849-08-04	FD	W2NWVOID	S:F
392	" "	21	NWNE	1849-08-04	FD	NWNEVOID	S:F
391	" "	21	NENW	1849-08-04	FD	NENWVOID	S:F
380	" "	21	W½NW	1849-08-04	FD	W2NWVOID	S:F
581	PAYNE, Othniel H	11	NESW	1851-04-14	FD	NESW	R:JASPER
416	PENNINGTON, Eli	4	NWSE	1840-10-26	FD	NWSE	R:OHIO
376	POWELL, Asahel W	11	NESE	1841-11-26	FD	NESE	R:JASPER
528	POWELL, John	1	SENW	1843-11-25	FD	SENW	R:JASPER
527	" "	1	NWSE	1843-11-25	FD	NWSE	R:JASPER
526	" "	1	E½SE	1849-11-12	FD	E2SE	
529	" "	1	SWSE	1849-11-12	FD	SWSE	
531	PRICE, John	9	W½NE	1852-11-12	FD	W2NE	
530	" "	9	NESE	1853-05-23	FD	NESE	R:JASPER
673	PRICE, William	9	NENE	1838-02-02	FD	NENE	R:COLES
589	RAY, Robert	12	SESW	1841-10-25	FD	SESW	R:JASPER
489	REDFORD, James	32	SWSW	1852-08-20	FD	SWSW	
488	" "	32	SWNW	1852-08-20	FD	SWNW	R:JASPER
487	" "	32	NWSW	1852-08-20	FD	NWSW	R:JASPER
486	" "	31	E½NE	1852-08-20	FD	E2NE	R:JASPER
485	" "	30	SW	1852-08-26	FD	SW	R:JASPER
534	RICE, John	3	NWSE	1852-11-06	FD	NWSE	
680	RICE, William W	3	W½NE	1852-11-06	FD	W2NE	R:INDIANA
629	SHERWOOD, Thomas C	9	N½SW	1865-05-11	SW	N2SW	
630	" "	9	S½SW	1865-05-11	SW	S2SW	
631	" "	9	SESE	1865-05-11	SW	SESE	
632	" "	9	W½SE	1865-05-11	SW	W2SE	
471	SINK, Eli	17	N½SW	1852-09-14	FD	N2SW	R:JASPER
417	" "	17	N½SW	1852-09-14	FD	N2SW	R:JASPER
430	SINK, Emsley	9	NWNW	1852-08-24	FD	NWNW	
429	" "	8	NENE	1852-08-24	FD	NENE	
535	SINK, John	20	NENE	1850-06-04	FD	NENE	R:INDIANA
582	SINK, Paul	17	SWSW	1851-09-04	FD	SWSW	R:INDIANA
370	SMITH, Archibald	3	W½SW	1839-08-22	FD	W2SW	R:INDIANA
369	" "	10	E½NE	1839-08-22	FD	E2NE	R:INDIANA
389	SMITH, Benjamin	32	SENW	1850-11-22	FD	SENW	
390	" "	33	SENE	1850-11-22	FD	SENE	R:INDIANA
404	SMITH, Daniel P	32	NE	1850-01-16	FD	NE	
451	SMITH, Henry	34	W½NW	1839-10-23	FD	W2NW	R:INDIANA
592	SMITH, Robert	34	W½SW	1839-10-17	FD	W2SW	R:OHIO
591	" "	34	SESW	1839-10-17	FD	SESW	R:OHIO
590	" "	33	NESE	1839-10-17	FD	NESE	R:OHIO
575	SOURS, Noah	13	S½SW	1848-11-04	FD	S2SW	R:OHIO
576	" "	13	SWSE	1848-11-04	FD	SWSE	R:OHIO
577	" "	14	SESW	1848-11-04	FD	SESW	R:OHIO
578	" "	23	NWNE	1848-11-04	FD	NWNE	R:OHIO
579	" "	24	NENE	1849-10-15	FD	NENE	R:JASPER
580	" "	24	NWSW	1850-12-05	FD	NWSW	R:JASPER
399	SPOON, Daniel A	3	SESW	1839-04-08	FD	SESW	R:COLES
586	STARNIS, Phillip	16	N½SE	1868-07-11	SC	N2SE	
350	STROLE, Albert H	33	W½NE	1850-04-08	FD	W2NE	R:INDIANA
349	" "	33	N½SW	1850-04-08	FD	N2SW	R:INDIANA
437	" "	33	W½NE	1850-04-08	FD	W2NE	R:INDIANA
348	" "	33	E½NW	1850-04-08	FD	E2NW	R:INDIANA
365	SUTTON, Amariah	36	NESE	1851-02-24	FD	NESE	R:INDIANA
452	SUTTON, Henry	15	SESE	1850-11-04	FD	SESE	R:JASPER
610	SUTTON, Samuel	14	NESW	1850-10-30	FD	NESW	R:INDIANA
611	" "	14	SENW	1850-10-30	FD	SENW	R:INDIANA
316	SWICK, Aaron	14	NENE	1849-06-06	FD	NENE	R:JASPER
525	THOMAS, John	16	SENE	1872-09-21	SC	SENE	G:49
598	THOMPSON, Roseline	20	SENE	1851-06-02	FD	SENE	R:COLES S:F
599	THOMPSON, Rufus H	35	W½SE	1851-05-16	FD	W2SE	R:INDIANA

ID	Individual in Patent	Sec.	Sec. Part	Purchase Date	Sale Type	IL Aliquot Part	For More Info . . .
600	THOMPSON, Rufus H (Cont'd)	36	S½SW	1851-05-16	FD	S2SW	R:INDIANA
674	THOMPSON, William	21	NESW	1852-08-20	FD	NESW	R:JASPER
675	"	29	NWSW	1852-09-25	FD	NWSW	
482	TIMMONS, James M	10	W½SE	1839-09-02	FD	W2SE	R:INDIANA
455	TRACY, Hiram	22	NWSW	1853-09-28	FD	NWSW	
594	TRIMBLE, Robert	33	W½NW	1849-06-13	FD	W2NW	
593	"	28	S½SW	1849-06-13	FD	S2SW	
676	TROUTMAN, William	26	NESE	1851-10-06	FD	NESE	
677	"	26	W½SE	1851-10-06	FD	W2SE	
319	VANNATA, Aaron	14	W½NE	1849-06-30	FD	W2NE	
318	"	14	SENE	1849-06-30	FD	SENE	
317	"	13	SWNW	1849-06-30	FD	SWNW	
457	VANNATA, Isaac	13	NENE	1848-08-17	FD	NENE	R:JASPER
320	VANNETTA, Aaron	13	NWNW	1841-07-08	FD	NWNW	R:JASPER
321	"	13	SENE	1841-07-08	FD	SENE	R:JASPER
653	VAUGHAN, William G	1	W½NW	1848-07-29	FD	W2NW	
654	"	1	W½SW	1848-07-29	FD	W2SW	
678	VAUGHN, William	15	NENE	1851-04-05	FD	NENE	R:JASPER
373	WARD, Armstead	14	W½NW	1851-02-06	FD	W2NW	
374	"	15	SEN½	1851-02-06	FD	S2NE	
453	WARD, Henry	14	SE	1848-05-03	FD	SE	
493	WARD, Jeniah	23	NESW	1851-04-05	FD	NESW	R:INDIANA
537	WARD, John	24	W½NE	1848-05-03	FD	W2NE	
536	"	24	E½NW	1848-05-03	FD	E2NW	
480	WHEELER, James Jerry	33	SWSE	1845-07-19	FD	SWSE	R:JASPER
484	WHEELER, James P	33	SESW	1850-05-22	FD	SESW	R:JASPER
436	"	33	NWSE	1850-09-25	FD	NWSE	R:JASPER
483	"	33	NWSE	1850-09-25	FD	NWSE	R:JASPER
490	WILSON, James	16	L14	1853-10-15	SC	LOT14SESW	
550	WILSON, Josiah C	34	NESW	1852-09-22	FD	NESW	
368	WINTERS, Andrew J	8	N½SW	1850-07-19	FD	N2SW	
367	"	8	N½SE	1850-07-19	FD	N2SE	
450	WINTERS, Henry L	17	SESE	1852-09-27	FD	SESE	R:JASPER
557	WISELEY, Matilda	4	SENW	1852-09-21	FD	SENW	R:CUMBERLAND S:F
556	"	18	NWSE	1852-09-21	FD	NWSE	R:CUMBERLAND S:F
378	WISHARD, Beacham R	22	SWNW	1852-11-20	FD	SWNW	
377	"	22	SENW	1852-11-20	FD	SENW	
538	WISHARD, John	16	L3	1864-05-17	SC	LOT03NENW	
614	WISHARD, Silas W	18	E½NE	1850-02-15	FD	E2NE	
615	"	18	E½SE	1850-02-15	FD	E2SE	
613	"	17	NENW	1852-08-23	FD	NENW	
617	"	18	SWNE	1852-08-23	FD	SWNE	
616	"	18	NWNE	1852-08-23	FD	NWNE	
659	WISHARD, William H	7	SENE	1851-03-29	FD	SENE	
658	"	7	NWSE	1851-03-29	FD	NWSE	
657	"	7	E½SE	1851-03-29	FD	E2SE	
491	WORMAN, James	8	SESW	1852-09-09	FD	SESW	
427	WRIGHT, Elston	29	SESE	1850-09-26	FD	SESE	R:COLES
428	WRIGHT, Elstron	16	L4	1859-02-26	SC	LOT4NWNW	
420	YAW, Elias	3	NENE	1853-05-06	FD	NENE	
463	YAW, Isaac	5	SE	1850-05-25	FD	SE	R:INDIANA
462	"	5	E½NW	1850-05-25	FD	E2NW	R:INDIANA
461	"	5	E½NE	1850-05-25	FD	E2NE	R:INDIANA
459	"	4	W½NW	1850-05-25	FD	W2NW	R:INDIANA
458	"	4	SW	1850-05-25	FD	SW	R:INDIANA
464	"	5	W½NE	1850-05-25	FD	W2NE	R:INDIANA
460	"	5		1850-06-30	FD	E2NWWA	R:INDIANA
460	"	5		1850-06-30	FD	PTE2NEWA	R:INDIANA
682	YOUNG, William	23	S½SW	1849-04-18	FD	S2SW	
684	"	26	N½NW	1849-04-18	FD	N2NW	
683	"	24	SWSE	1851-04-10	FD	SWSE	R:JASPER
681	"	23	NWSW	1852-12-13	FD	NWSW	

Patent Map

T8-N R9-E
3rd PM Meridian

Map Group 2

Township Statistics

Parcels Mapped	:	371
Number of Patents	:	1
Number of Individuals	:	192
Patentees Identified	:	182
Number of Surnames	:	126
Multi-Patentee Parcels	:	7
Oldest Patent Date	:	11/17/1817
Most Recent Patent	:	9/21/1872
Block/Lot Parcels	:	10
Cities and Towns	:	1
Cemeteries	:	8

Copyright 2010 Boyd IT, Inc. All Rights Reserved

Section 6
MCBATH Alexander 1852
MCBATH Alexander 1852
CHANEY Robert Y 1851
MCBATH Robert 1852
MCBATH Alexander 1852
DAVIS Benjamin 1849
DAVIS Benjamin 1849
GILLMORE William J 1852
DAVIS Benjamin 1849
YAW Isaac 1850
YAW Isaac 1850

Section 5
YAW Isaac 1850
YAW Isaac 1850
YAW Isaac 1850
MYERS Eli 1850

Section 4
YAW Isaac 1850
YAW Isaac 1850
YAW Isaac 1850
COGGESHALL John 1839
COGGESHALL Job 1839
WISELEY Matilda 1852
PENNINGTON Eli 1840
GILMORE William J 1852
CAREY Coonrod W 1852

Section 7
MCBATH Alexander 1852
CHANEY Robert Y 1851
CHANEY Robert Y 1851
WISHARD William H 1851
BRADSHAW James 1852
WISHARD William H 1851
BRADSHAW James 1852
WISHARD William H 1851

Section 8
LAUGHTER Yewen H 1850
MYERS David C 1850
SINK Emsley 1852
MYERS Eli 1850
WINTERS Andrew J 1850
WINTERS Andrew J 1850
MITCHELL Willis T 1852
WORMAN James 1852
FRAZIER Arlindo 1852
MYERS Enoch 1852

Section 9
SINK Emsley 1852
GOLDSBY David 1853
HAGY Henry 1852
SHERWOOD Thomas C 1865
SHERWOOD Thomas C 1865
PRICE John 1852
PRICE William 1838
BOYD David 1832
PRICE John 1853
SHERWOOD Thomas C 1865
SHERWOOD Thomas C 1865

Section 18
BRADSHAW James 1852
WISHARD Silas W 1852
WISHARD Silas W 1850
WISHARD Silas W 1852
WISELEY Matilda 1852
WISHARD Silas W 1850
MYERS Enoch 1850
MYERS Noah 1850

Section 17
BRADSHAW James 1852
WISHARD Silas W 1852
FRAZIER Arlindo 1852
BRADSHAW James 1852
HINTON Ellis 1852
SINK Eli 1852
BRADSHAW James 1852
HINTON Ellis 1852
SINK Paul 1851
HURST John 1851
BRACKNEY Levi 1850
WINTERS Henry L 1852

Section 16
Lots-Sec. 16
L3 WISHARD, John 1864
L4 WRIGHT, Elstron 1859
L5 LITTON, Fulton 1817
L6 DOWNS, William A 1853
L7 DOWNS, William A 1853
L8 HARPER, William 1858
L11 BORING, Michael 1853
L14 WILSON, James 1853
L15 JACK, Jeremiah 1853
L16 JACK, Jeremiah 1853
MYERS [49] John 1872
STARNIS Phillip 1868

Section 19
LEACH [43] Elizabeth 1853
MYERS Noah 1850
MYERS Noah 1850
MYERS Noah 1850
MYERS Noah 1850
BAIN John 1837
MATHEW Jonah 1850
MATHEW Jonah 1853
BRACKNEY Levi 1850
BAIN John 1837

Section 20
BAIN John 1837
MOORE Benjamin D 1851
SINK John 1850
THOMPSON Roseline 1851
MOORE Benjamin D 1851
BAIN John 1837
HINTON Ellis 1850

Section 21
PARSONS Catharine Jr 1849
PARSONS Catharine Jr 1849
PARSONS Catharine Jr 1849
BARRETT Samuel 1852
BARRETT Samuel 1852
BARRETT Samuel 1852
BARRETT Samuel 1853
MYERS Thomas 1850
THOMPSON William 1852
BARTLETT Robert L 1850
BUTLER Warren 1853
BUTLER Amos C 1853

Section 30
GALBREATH William 1852
BRACKNEY Levi 1850
KERN John 1852
REDFORD James 1852
KERN John 1852
HURST John 1851
MOORE William 1852

Section 29
BAIN John 1837
BYRD John 1851
THOMPSON William 1852
HICKS Ellis 1850
HICKS Ellis 1850
EAGLETON William 1851
LINTHIEUM Slingsby 1850
LINTHIEUM Slingsby 1850
WRIGHT Elston 1850

Section 28
BARTLETT Robert L 1850
EAGLETON Alexander M 1849
CATLIN Seth 1851
EAGLETON Alexander M 1849
HILLYER Alvin 1850
FOREMAN Samuel 1850
TRIMBLE Robert 1849
FOREMAN Samuel 1850

Section 31
CLAWSON [18] Ephraim 1837
REDFORD James 1852
CLAWSON [18] Ephraim 1837
CLAWSON [18] Ephraim 1837

Section 32
EAGLETON Alexander 1851
HILLYER Alvin 1850
SMITH Daniel P 1850
REDFORD James 1852
SMITH Benjamin 1850
REDFORD James 1852
ISLEY Philip 1850
ISLEY Philip 1850

Section 33
TRIMBLE Robert 1849
STROLE Albert H 1850
HOLSCHER Franie 1846
FOREMAN Samuel 1850
STROLE Albert H 1850
SMITH Benjamin 1850
STROLE Albert H 1850
WHEELER James P 1850
HOLSCHER Franie 1846
SMITH Robert 1839
ISLEY Philip 1850
WHEELER James P 1850
WHEELER James Jerry 1845

Helpful Hints

1. This Map's INDEX can be found on the preceding pages.

2. Refer to Map "C" to see where this Township lies within Jasper County, Illinois.

3. Numbers within square brackets [ ] denote a multi-patentee land parcel (multi-owner). Refer to Appendix "C" for a full list of members in this group.

4. Areas that look to be crowded with Patentees usually indicate multiple sales of the same parcel (re-issues), cancellations or voided transactions (that we map, anyway) or overlapping parcels. We opt to show even these ambiguous parcels, which oftentimes lead to research avenues not yet taken.

Legend

- Patent Boundary
- Section Boundary
- No Patents Found (or Outside County)
- 1., 2., 3., ... Lot Numbers (when beside a name)
- [ ] Group Number (see Appendix "C")

Scale: Section = 1 mile X 1 mile (generally, with some exceptions)

Section 3
- KILLGORE John 1852
- JONES David 1853
- RICE William W 1852
- YAW Elias 1853
- JONES David 1853
- HARDING Abraham 1850
- JONES David 1853
- RICE John 1852
- HARDING Abraham 1850
- SMITH Archibald 1839
- SPOON Daniel A 1839
- ADKINS Jackson 1852

Section 2
- HUTSON William 1852
- HAYS James 1841
- MARKWELL French 1849
- HARDING Abraham 1850
- HARDING Abraham 1850
- MARKWELL French 1849
- MCCOMAS James M 1851
- HARDING Abraham 1852
- HARDING Thomas H 1850
- HARDING Thomas H 1851
- MCCOMAS Charles C 1849
- HAYS William W 1851
- HAYS Michael S 1851
- HARDING Thomas H 1849

Section 1
- MERITT Allen 1852
- MERRITT Allen 1852
- HUNT Joseph 1843
- VAUGHAN William G 1848
- POWELL John 1843
- EDWARDS Daniel P 1850
- POWELL John 1843
- MUSGRAVE Stephen 1849
- VAUGHAN William G 1848
- MERITT Allen 1850
- POWELL John 1849
- POWELL John 1849

Section 10
- COGGESHALL John 1839
- COGGESHALL John 1839
- ADKINS Jackson 1852
- SMITH Archibald 1839
- HILLS Moses 1832
- BAIN John 1837
- TIMMONS James M 1839
- NICHOLS Hiram 1839

Section 11
- EDWARDS Daniel P 1850
- HAYS James 1841
- HAYS James 1849
- BAIN George 1850
- EDWARDS Daniel P 1850
- HUTSON Isaac 1852
- HUTSON William 1852
- EDWARDS Daniel P 1850
- PAYNE Othniel H 1851
- HURING John R 1861
- POWELL Asahel W 1841
- HUTSON William 1852
- HOGUE John 1848
- HOGUE John 1848
- HURING John R 1861
- HOGUE John 1848

Section 12
- HUTSON Joseph 1850
- HUTSON Joseph 1850
- LIDEY Michael 1850
- HUTSON Joseph 1850
- HUTSON Joseph 1850
- HUTSON William 1840
- HUTSON Joseph 1850
- LIDEY Michael 1850
- LIDEY Michael 1850
- LIDEY Michael 1850
- LIDEY Michael 1850
- RAY Robert 1841
- LIDEY Michael 1850

Section 15
- BAIN John 1837
- BAIN John 1837
- HARDING Aron 1853
- VAUGHN William 1851
- LYONS Joseph 1852
- WARD Armstead 1851
- LYONS Joseph 1852
- FARRIS David Jr 1839
- FARIS David Jr 1839
- KELLY Matilda 1839
- BAILEY James 1852
- SUTTON Henry 1850

Section 14
- WARD Armstead 1851
- HUTSON William 1852
- VANNATA Aaron 1849
- SWICK Aaron 1849
- SUTTON Samuel 1850
- VANNATA Aaron 1849
- SUTTON Samuel 1850
- MONDON John 1852
- SOURS Noah 1848
- WARD Henry 1848

Section 13
- VANNETTA Aaron 1841
- LIDEY Michael 1850
- LIDEY Michael 1850
- VANNATA Isaac 1848
- VANNATA Aaron 1849
- VANNATA Aaron 1849
- MUSGRAVE Stephen 1849
- MUSGROVE Stephen 1849
- VANNETTA Aaron 1841
- LIDEY Michael 1850
- MUSGROVE Stephen 1849
- ANDREWS Jasin 1848
- MUSGROVE Stephen 1849
- MUSGROVE Stephen 1849
- MUSGROVE Stephen 1849
- SOURS Noah 1848
- SOURS Noah 1848
- CARR Milam C 1849

Section 22
- BAILEY James 1852
- ODELL Washington 1852
- HARRIS Addison S 1837
- WISHARD Beacham R 1852
- WISHARD Beacham R 1852
- TRACY Hiram 1853
- HANKINS Samuel 1853
- HARRIS Addison S 1840
- HARRIS Addison S 1837
- HARRIS Addison S 1837
- KIBLER Theobald 1854

Section 23
- GORRELL John 1849
- SOURS Noah 1848
- ELY Jerard 1846
- FOUST Joseph 1847
- YOUNG William 1852
- WARD Jeniah 1851
- LONG Benjamin 1847
- YOUNG William 1849
- KIBLER Jacob 1847
- HUTSON William 1852

Section 24
- CODD Joseph 1850
- WARD John 1848
- SOURS Noah 1849
- KIBLER Theobold 1849
- WARD John 1848
- HARRIS Addison S 1849
- SOURS Noah 1850
- LONG Benjamin 1847
- KIBLER Jacob E 1851
- HARRIS Addison S 1848
- YOUNG William 1851
- HARRIS Addison 1840

Section 27
- HARRIS William A 1839
- HARRIS Addison S 1837
- HARRIS Addison S 1865
- HARRIS Addison S 1853
- HARRIS Addison S 1838
- HARRIS William A 1839
- HARRIS Addison S 1837
- BUTLER Samuel C 1853
- HARRIS William A 1838

Section 26
- YOUNG William 1849
- LONG Benjamin 1851
- HARRIS Addison S 1851
- HARRIS William A 1838
- HARRIS Addison S 1848
- HARRIS Addison S 1851
- HARRIS William A 1840
- TROUTMAN William 1851
- TROUTMAN William 1851
- HARRIS Addison S 1838
- LONG Benjamin 1851
- GOSNELL George 1850

Section 25
- HARRIS Addison S 1848
- HARRIS William A 1848
- HARRIS William A 1840
- HARRIS Addison S 1851
- GOSNELL George 1850
- MOORE Elias 1850
- KIBLER William M 1848
- GOSNELL Washington 1851
- HARRIS Addison 1840
- LARIMER Smith 1839

Section 34
- CURTISS E H 1865
- HARRIS William A 1838
- BARRETT Harvey B 1853
- SMITH Henry 1839
- GALBREATH William 1852
- SMITH Robert 1839
- WILSON Josiah C 1852
- HARRIS William A 1839
- SMITH Robert 1839

Section 35
- MOORE Harrison 1852
- MOORE Elias 1850
- GOSNELL George 1850
- GOSNELL George 1850
- GRIFFITH Charles 1850
- GRIFFITH Charles 1850
- KIBLER William M 1848
- ELDER John L 1852
- MCDANIEL John 1851
- LITTLE George 1853
- GRIFFITH Charles 1850
- THOMPSON Rufus H 1851
- MCDANIEL John 1851
- BAXTER William 1853
- LITTLE John 1851

Section 36
- KIBLER William M 1848
- GREEN [33] Abner C 1849
- LONG William 1840
- GREEN [33] Abner C 1849
- SUTTON Amariah 1851
- GRAY Alexander M 1852
- THOMPSON Rufus H 1851
- MCDANIEL John 1851
- DODD Kendle B 1851

Road Map

T8-N R9-E
3rd PM Meridian

Map Group 2

Cities & Towns
Gila

Cemeteries
Diel Cemetery
Fairfield Cemetery
Gila Lutheran Cemetery
Hayes Cemetery
Hicks Cemetery
Myer Cemetery
Songer Cemetery
Ward Cemetery

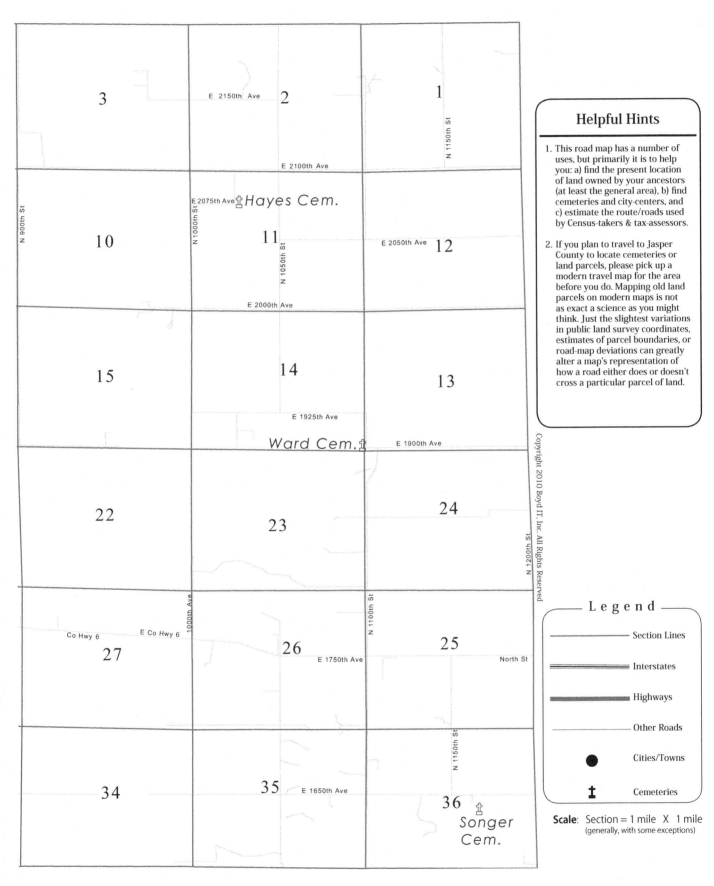

Helpful Hints

1. This road map has a number of uses, but primarily it is to help you: a) find the present location of land owned by your ancestors (at least the general area), b) find cemeteries and city-centers, and c) estimate the route/roads used by Census-takers & tax-assessors.

2. If you plan to travel to Jasper County to locate cemeteries or land parcels, please pick up a modern travel map for the area before you do. Mapping old land parcels on modern maps is not as exact a science as you might think. Just the slightest variations in public land survey coordinates, estimates of parcel boundaries, or road-map deviations can greatly alter a map's representation of how a road either does or doesn't cross a particular parcel of land.

L e g e n d

————	Section Lines
═══════	Interstates
━━━━━━	Highways
————	Other Roads
●	Cities/Towns
✝	Cemeteries

Scale: Section = 1 mile X 1 mile
(generally, with some exceptions)

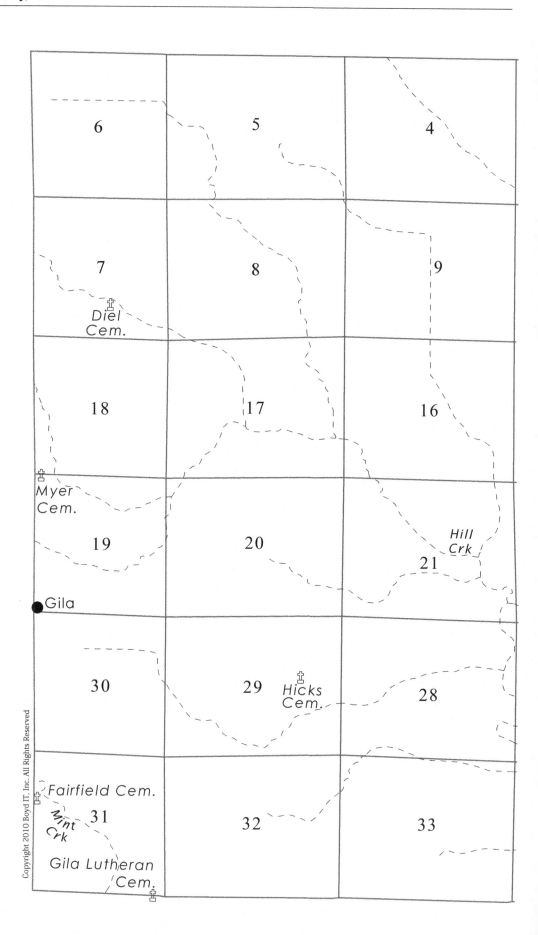

Historical Map

T8-N R9-E
3rd PM Meridian

Map Group 2

Cities & Towns
Gila

Cemeteries
Diel Cemetery
Fairfield Cemetery
Gila Lutheran Cemetery
Hayes Cemetery
Hicks Cemetery
Myer Cemetery
Songer Cemetery
Ward Cemetery

6

5

4

7

8

9

Diel
Cem.

18

17

16

Myer
Cem.

19

20

Hill
Crk

21

Gila

30

29

Hicks
Cem.

28

Fairfield Cem.

31

Mint
Crk

32

33

Gila Lutheran
Cem.

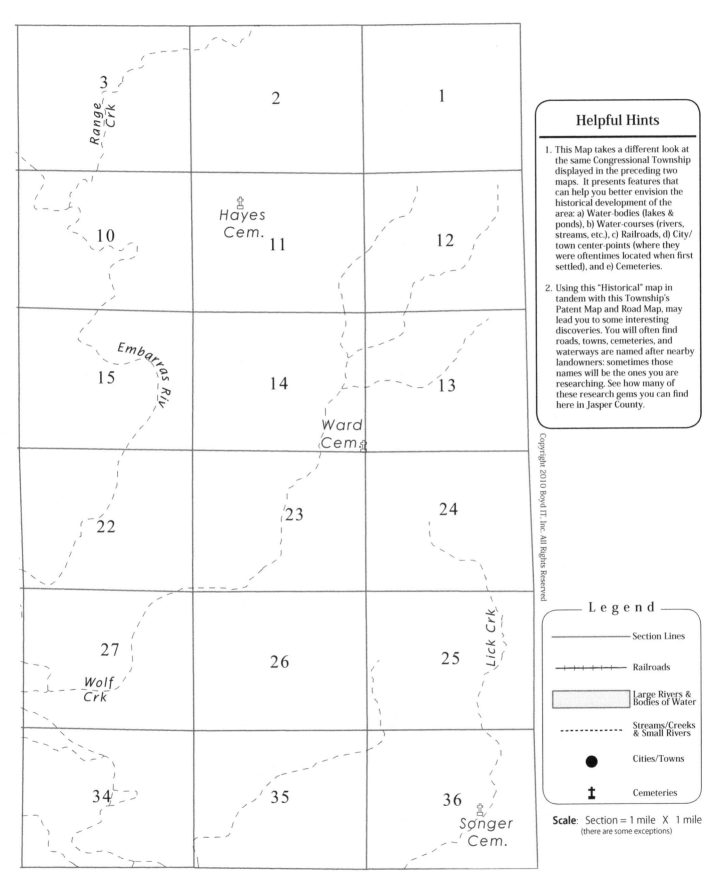

3

2

1

Range
Crk

10

✝
Hayes
Cem. 11

12

Embarras Riv

15

14

13

Ward
Cem.✝

22

23

24

Lick Crk

27

26

25

Wolf
Crk

34

35

36

✝
Songer
Cem.

Helpful Hints

1. This Map takes a different look at the same Congressional Township displayed in the preceding two maps. It presents features that can help you better envision the historical development of the area: a) Water-bodies (lakes & ponds), b) Water-courses (rivers, streams, etc.), c) Railroads, d) City/ town center-points (where they were oftentimes located when first settled), and e) Cemeteries.

2. Using this "Historical" map in tandem with this Township's Patent Map and Road Map, may lead you to some interesting discoveries. You will often find roads, towns, cemeteries, and waterways are named after nearby landowners: sometimes those names will be the ones you are researching. See how many of these research gems you can find here in Jasper County.

Legend

————————	Section Lines
+++++++	Railroads
▭	Large Rivers & Bodies of Water
- - - - - -	Streams/Creeks & Small Rivers
●	Cities/Towns
✝	Cemeteries

Scale: Section = 1 mile X 1 mile
(there are some exceptions)

Map Group 3: Index to Land Patents

Township 8-North Range 10-East (3rd PM)

After you locate an individual in this Index, take note of the Section and Section Part then proceed to the Land Patent map on the pages immediately following. You should have no difficulty locating the corresponding parcel of land.

The "For More Info" Column will lead you to more information about the underlying Patents. See the *Legend* at right, and the "How to Use this Book" chapter, for more information.

```
                        LEGEND
              "For More Info . . . " column
    G = Group  (Multi-Patentee Patent, see Appendix "C")
    R = Residence
    S = Social Status

    See Appendix A for list of abbreviations used by the
    Illinois State Archives in describing the place and
    nature of these land patents.

    Note: if the Abbreviations contain "L", "BL", "LOT",
    or "BLOCK", the exact whereabouts of the parcel within
    the section is not known.
```

ID	Individual in Patent	Sec.	Sec. Part	Purchase Date	Sale Type	IL Aliquot Part	For More Info . . .
843	ADAMS, James	18		1850-03-31	FD	PTNENWWA	R:INDIANA
710	"	18		1850-03-31	FD	PTNENWWA	R:INDIANA
847	ADAMS, James C	7	SWSE	1850-09-04	FD	SWSE	R:INDIANA
846	" "	7	SESW	1850-09-04	FD	SESW	R:INDIANA
845	" "	18	NWNE	1850-09-04	FD	NWNE	R:INDIANA
844	" "	18	NENW	1850-09-04	FD	NENW	R:INDIANA
874	ADAMS, John B	26	SWNW	1851-07-18	FD	SWNW	R:CRAWFORD
875	"	29	SENE	1851-07-18	FD	SENE	R:CRAWFORD
714	ADKISSON, Alexander	25	S½NW	1851-09-01	FD	S2NW	R:KENTUCKY
768	ANDREWS, Elias	28	NE	1848-09-24	FD	NE	
769	" "	28	SENW	1849-08-16	FD	SENW	R:JASPER
770	" "	29	NESE	1852-10-30	FD	NESE	
1093	ANDREWS, William P	19	SWNE	1847-07-06	FD	SWNE	R:INDIANA
1090	" "	16	L13	1849-01-25	SC	LOT13SWSW	
1091	" "	16	L14	1849-01-25	SC	LOT14SWSW	
1092	" "	18	SWSE	1852-03-08	FD	SWSE	R:JASPER
829	AVERY, Homer T	31	SWSW	1851-01-18	FD	SWSW	R:JASPER
1064	BEELES, William	33	SWSW	1853-08-12	FD	SWSW	R:JASPER
1063	" "	32	SESE	1853-08-12	FD	SESE	R:JASPER
750	BIRT, David H	32	NWNW	1851-12-19	FD	NWNW	R:JASPER
906	BLACK, John Jr	4	NWNW	1852-10-09	FD	NWNW	R:OHIO
907	" "	4	SWNW	1852-10-09	FD	SWNW	R:OHIO
835	BLAKE, Isaac	31	SWSE	1847-10-26	FD	SWSE	R:INDIANA
834	"	31	SESE	1850-12-07	FD	SESE	R:JASPER
948	BONHAM, Levi	26	E½NW	1839-07-17	FD	E2NW	R:CLARK
949	" "	26	W½NW	1849-03-13	FD	W2NWVOID	
950	" "	27	E½NE	1849-03-13	FD	E2NEVOID	
952	BONHAM, Levi M	26	NWNW	1851-05-27	FD	NWNW	R:JASPER
951	"	23	NWSW	1851-12-02	FD	NWSW	R:JASPER
989	BONHAM, Richard	26	W½SE	1839-09-03	FD	W2SE	R:CLARK
987	" "	26	E½SW	1839-09-03	FD	E2SW	R:CLARK
988	" "	26	NESE	1852-06-19	FD	NESE	
758	BREES, Doctor F	14	NWSW	1852-08-14	FD	NWSW	
759	"	15	NESE	1852-08-14	FD	NESE	
967	BROOKS, Nelson	6	W½NW	1844-01-22	FD	W2NW	R:JASPER
1039	BROOKS, Thomas	17	SW	1841-02-15	FD	SW	R:CRAWFORD
1040	" "	20	NENW	1841-02-25	FD	NENW	R:CRAWFORD
747	CARMEAN, Edward	10	W½SW	1851-09-03	FD	W2SW	R:JASPER
764	" "	10	W½SW	1851-09-03	FD	W2SW	R:JASPER
961	CARR, Milam C	8	SWNW	1849-07-26	FD	SWNW	R:OHIO
933	CHAPMAN, Joseph	25	NENW	1841-10-28	FD	NENW	R:EDGAR
928	" "	23	SESW	1841-12-09	FD	SESW	R:EDGAR
929	" "	23	SWSE	1847-10-18	FD	SWSE	R:JASPER
932	" "	24	SESW	1849-01-06	FD	SESW	R:JASPER
926	" "	23	NESW	1849-01-06	FD	NESW	R:JASPER
930	" "	23	SWSW	1850-03-14	FD	SWSW	R:JASPER

ID	Individual in Patent	Sec.	Sec. Part	Purchase Date	Sale Type	IL Aliquot Part	For More Info . . .
931	CHAPMAN, Joseph (Cont'd)	24	NESW	1850-11-04	FD	NESW	R:JASPER
935	" "	26	NWNE	1851-11-12	FD	NWNE	R:JASPER
927	" "	23	NWSE	1852-08-26	FD	NWSE	
934	" "	26	NENE	1853-06-07	FD	NENE	R:JASPER
975	CHAPMAN, Perry	24	E½SE	1849-10-31	FD	E2SE	
976	" "	25	E½NE	1849-10-31	FD	E2NE	
991	CHAPMAN, Robert	25	SWNE	1851-09-11	FD	SWNE	R:JASPER
1005	CHAPMAN, Samuel	13	W½SW	1840-03-16	FD	W2SW	R:EDGAR
1006	" "	14	E½SE	1840-03-16	FD	E2SE	R:EDGAR
1009	" "	24	NWNW	1840-04-18	FD	NWNW	R:JASPER
1007	" "	23	E½NE	1840-04-18	FD	E2NE	R:JASPER
1008	" "	23	E½SE	1840-06-02	FD	E2SE	R:JASPER
1010	" "	24	W½SW	1840-06-02	FD	W2SW	R:JASPER
1045	CHAPMAN, Thomas	35	SESW	1851-11-28	FD	SESW	R:JASPER
1068	CHAPMAN, William	36	W½NW	1849-06-20	FD	W2NW	
1067	" "	35	SENE	1849-06-20	FD	SENE	
1066	" "	35	NESE	1849-06-20	FD	NESE	
767	CHRISMAN, Edwin L	30	SWSE	1844-02-08	FD	SWSE	R:EDGAR
765	" "	30	N½SE	1845-11-07	FD	N2SE	R:EDGAR
766	" "	30	NESW	1848-09-23	FD	NESW	R:JASPER
726	CLARK, Austin	24	E½NW	1851-08-26	FD	E2NW	
723	" "	13	E½SW	1851-08-26	FD	E2SW	
724	" "	13	N½SE	1851-08-26	FD	N2SE	
725	" "	13	SEN½	1851-08-26	FD	S2NE	
818	CLARK, Henry	25	SW	1851-08-26	FD	SW	
890	CLARK, John	14	NESW	1852-08-04	FD	NESW	
957	CLARK, Margaret E	35	NENE	1854-04-03	FD	NENE	R:JASPER S:F
891	COALE, John	1	W½NW	1839-11-22	FD	W2NW	R:CLARK
892	" "	2	E½NE	1839-11-22	FD	E2NE	R:CLARK
1035	COHOON, Stephen	24	SENE	1840-10-24	FD	SENE	R:OHIO
895	CUMMANS, John	20	NWSW	1838-08-24	FD	NWSW	R:JASPER
894	" "	20	NWNW	1842-01-28	FD	NWNW	R:JASPER
893	" "	18	NWSE	1850-09-03	FD	NWSE	R:JASPER
936	CUMMINS, Joseph	34	NWSE	1844-01-05	FD	NWSE	R:JASPER
997	CUMMINS, Robert	34	NW	1839-06-28	FD	NW	R:EDGAR
996	" "	34	E½SW	1839-06-28	FD	E2SW	R:EDGAR
994	" "	34	E½NE	1839-06-28	FD	E2NE	R:EDGAR
995	" "	34	E½SE	1839-08-14	FD	E2SE	R:EDGAR
993	" "	33	NE	1839-08-14	FD	NE	R:EDGAR
999	" "	34	SWSE	1839-08-14	FD	SWSE	R:EDGAR
992	" "	28	E½SE	1839-08-14	FD	E2SE	R:EDGAR
998	" "	34	NWNE	1844-01-05	FD	NWNE	R:JASPER
937	CUMMONS, Joseph	27	SWSW	1849-07-27	FD	SWSW	R:JASPER
925	CURTIS, Joseph C	25	NWNW	1854-10-18	FD	NWNW	R:JASPER
1069	DAILEY, William	25	W½SE	1840-11-06	FD	W2SE	R:OHIO
748	DAVIS, David	24	SWNE	1853-09-21	FD	SWNE	R:CLARK
849	DAVIS, James	23	NW	1849-06-11	FD	NW	
848	" "	13	NW	1849-06-11	FD	NW	
825	DAVISSON, Hezekiah	10	NENE	1839-09-07	FD	NENE	R:COLES
826	" "	2	SWSE	1839-09-07	FD	SWSE	R:COLES
982	DEBORD, Reuben	5	NE	1851-11-14	FD	NE	R:INDIANA
924	DENMAN, Jonathan B	3	NWSE	1852-11-07	FD	NWSE	R:JASPER
1070	DUGAN, William	1	N½NE	1849-05-23	FD	N2NE	R:OHIO
819	DULGOR, Henry	16	L2	1850-11-04	SC	LOT2NWNE	
863	EDWARDS, James N	28	SWNW	1852-12-15	FD	SWNW	
837	ERVIN, Isaac	9	SENE	1852-01-17	FD	SENE	R:JASPER
836	" "	9	NENE	1852-09-04	FD	NENE	
749	FAWCETT, David F	21	SWSE	1850-02-18	FD	SWSE	R:INDIANA
903	FAWSETT, John H	16	L17	1850-01-23	SC	LOT17S2SE	
902	" "	16	L16	1850-01-23	SC	L16S2SE	
904	" "	16	L15	1850-11-21	SC	LOT15SESW	
745	FINEY, Damon	3	SWSW	1852-09-02	FD	SWSW	
1072	FISHER, William	32	W½SE	1837-12-25	FD	W2SE	R:INDIANA
1071	" "	32	E½SW	1837-12-25	FD	E2SW	R:INDIANA
696	FLINT, Abigail	9	E½SW	1851-11-03	FD	E2SW	S:F G:28
696	FLINT, John	9	E½SW	1851-11-03	FD	E2SW	S:F G:28
696	FLINT, Sarah	9	E½SW	1851-11-03	FD	E2SW	S:F G:28
713	FORESMAN, George	9	NWSW	1851-06-02	FD	NWSW	
794	" "	9	SWNE	1851-06-02	FD	SWNE	
788	" "	8	SE	1851-06-02	FD	SE	
793	" "	9	S½NW	1851-06-02	FD	S2NW	
792	" "	9	NWSW	1851-06-02	FD	NWSW	
790	" "	9	N½NW	1851-11-04	FD	N2NW	

ID	Individual in Patent	Sec.	Sec. Part	Purchase Date	Sale Type	IL Aliquot Part	For More Info . . .
786	FORESMAN, George (Cont'd)	5	S½SE	1851-11-04	FD	S2SE	
791	" "	9	NWNE	1851-11-04	FD	NWNE	R:OHIO
789	" "	8	W½NE	1851-11-04	FD	W2NE	
787	" "	8	E½NE	1851-11-04	FD	E2NE	
795	" "	9	SWSW	1852-10-15	FD	SWSW	
1060	FRENCH, Will V	6		1848-01-28	FD	PTS2NE	R:SHELBY
687	" "	6		1848-01-28	FD	PTS2NE	R:SHELBY
1059	" "	6		1848-01-28	FD	PTS2NE	R:SHELBY
1062	" "	6	SEN½	1848-04-08	FD	S2NE	
1061	" "	6	N½SE	1848-04-08	FD	N2SE	
687	" "	6		1848-04-28	FD	PTN2SW	R:SHELBY
1060	" "	6		1848-04-28	FD	PTN2SW	R:SHELBY
1059	" "	6		1848-04-28	FD	PTN2SW	R:SHELBY
820	GARDWAIN, Henry	36	W½SW	1840-08-21	FD	W2SW	R:JASPER
737	GIBSON, Calvin	5	N½NW	1852-08-31	FD	N2NW	R:CRAWFORD
779	GORSLINE, Fletcher	29	NWNE	1853-06-16	FD	NWNE	R:INDIANA
900	GREEN, John	17	E½SE	1837-09-29	FD	E2SE	R:INDIANA
901	" "	17	SWSE	1837-09-29	FD	SWSE	R:INDIANA
1017	GROVES, Septor	12	SENE	1851-11-22	FD	SENE	R:JASPER
1075	HACKNEY, William	5	NWSW	1851-09-09	FD	NWSW	R:JASPER
717	HAMMER, Andrew	19	SENE	1838-06-02	FD	SENE	R:JASPER
751	HAMMER, David	27	NWSW	1848-08-25	FD	NWSW	R:JASPER
753	" "	28	NWSE	1849-06-18	FD	NWSE	R:JASPER
752	" "	28	NESW	1850-09-02	FD	NESW	R:JASPER
755	" "	28	SESW	1851-01-22	FD	SESW	R:JASPER
754	" "	28	NWSW	1852-10-30	FD	NWSW	
756	" "	29	SESE	1853-05-11	FD	SESE	
757	" "	32	NENE	1853-05-11	FD	NENE	
782	HAMMER, Frederick	20	NWSE	1837-12-25	FD	NWSE	R:INDIANA
783	" "	29	NESW	1837-12-25	FD	NESW	R:INDIANA
784	" "	32	E½NW	1837-12-25	FD	E2NW	R:INDIANA
785	" "	32	W½NE	1837-12-25	FD	W2NE	R:INDIANA
781	" "	20	NESW	1837-12-25	FD	NESW	R:INDIANA
1060	HARDING, Aaron	6		1850-10-31	FD	PTSESWWA	R:JASPER
687	" "	6		1850-10-31	FD	PTSESWWA	R:JASPER
1059	" "	6		1850-10-31	FD	PTSESWWA	R:JASPER
690	HARDING, Aaron M	7	NWNE	1850-09-19	FD	NWNE	R:JASPER
689	" "	6	SESW	1850-09-19	FD	SESW	R:JASPER
688	" "	6	S½SE	1850-09-19	FD	S2SE	R:JASPER
697	HARDING, Abraham	7	NENW	1850-04-29	FD	NENW	R:JASPER
707	HARRIS, Addison	11	E½SE	1839-06-28	FD	E2SE	R:JASPER
708	HARRIS, Addison S	10	W½NE	1839-04-22	FD	W2NE	R:JASPER
709	" "	11	NWNE	1839-04-22	FD	NWNE	R:JASPER
792	" "	9	NWSW	1849-01-06	FD	NWSW	R:JASPER
713	" "	9	NWSW	1849-01-06	FD	NWSW	R:JASPER
711	" "	18	W½SW	1849-11-03	FD	W2SW	R:JASPER
712	" "	19	W½NW	1849-11-03	FD	W2NW	R:JASPER
843	" "	18		1849-12-29	FD	W2SWWA	R:JASPER
710	" "	18		1849-12-29	FD	W2SWWA	R:JASPER
838	HARRISON, Jacob	35	SESE	1849-05-18	FD	SESE	R:JASPER
760	HASKET, Edmund C	12	NESE	1853-07-30	FD	NESE	
761	" "	12	NWSE	1853-08-01	FD	NWSE	
763	HASKET, Edward C	13	NENE	1853-07-30	FD	NENE	
762	" "	12	SESE	1853-07-30	FD	SESE	
872	HEARD, Jesse M	11	SWNE	1838-08-06	FD	SWNE	R:JASPER
963	HENDERSON, Milton	33	W½NW	1852-11-17	FD	W2NW	
962	" "	28	SWSW	1853-05-03	FD	SWSW	
811	HEPNER, Green Berry	35	W½SW	1852-09-03	FD	W2SW	
905	HOUGE, John	7	SWNW	1848-08-04	FD	SWNW	R:EDGAR
852	HOWARD, James	5	NESW	1851-10-22	FD	NESW	R:CRAWFORD
853	" "	5	NWSE	1851-10-22	FD	NWSE	R:CRAWFORD
854	" "	5	S½NW	1851-10-22	FD	S2NW	R:CRAWFORD
1103	HUDSON, William W	2	E½SE	1840-03-21	FD	E2SE	R:EDGAR
771	HUNT, Elihu	36	SWSE	1849-09-01	FD	SWSE	R:JASPER
1029	HUNT, Stephanas	27	SE	1838-10-29	FD	SE	R:JASPER
1027	" "	26	NWSW	1838-11-26	FD	NWSW	R:JASPER
1028	" "	27	NWNW	1840-10-09	FD	NWNW	R:JASPER
1030	HUNT, Stephanus	22	E½SW	1838-09-29	FD	E2SW	R:JASPER
1031	" "	26	SWSW	1841-10-12	FD	SWSW	R:JASPER
1032	" "	27	E½SW	1841-10-12	FD	E2SW	R:JASPER
1033	" "	27	SWNW	1841-10-12	FD	SWNW	R:JASPER
1034	" "	35	W½NW	1841-10-12	FD	W2NW	R:JASPER
1036	HUNT, Stephen	24	NWSE	1850-12-25	FD	NWSE	R:JASPER

ID	Individual in Patent	Sec.	Sec. Part	Purchase Date	Sale Type	IL Aliquot Part	For More Info . . .
1078	HUNT, William	22	W½SE	1838-09-29	FD	W2SE	R:JASPER
1076	" "	13	SWSE	1849-07-13	FD	SWSE	R:JASPER
1077	" "	22	SESE	1849-07-13	FD	SESE	R:JASPER
1079	" "	27	NENE	1851-05-27	FD	NENE	R:JASPER
1107	HUNT, Zimri	36	NWSE	1849-06-12	FD	NWSE	R:JASPER
1106	" "	36	NESE	1853-01-21	FD	NESE	R:JASPER
1026	HUNTER, Spencer K	10	NW	1852-02-20	FD	NW	
738	HUSSONG, Calvin	16	L9	1850-01-23	SC	LOT9NESE	
1080	HUTSON, William	27	E½NW	1838-09-29	FD	E2NW	R:JASPER
851	JAMES, James E	31	SWNW	1839-09-24	FD	SWNW	R:JASPER
850	" "	31	SENW	1842-08-31	FD	SENW	R:JASPER
773	" "	31	SENW	1842-08-31	FD	SENW	R:JASPER
1094	JAMES, William P	31	N½NW	1839-09-24	FD	N2NW	R:JASPER
877	KELLEY, John B	1	W½SE	1853-03-03	FD	W2SE	R:CUMBERLAND
878	" "	12	NWNE	1853-03-03	FD	NWNE	R:CUMBERLAND
876	" "	1	SWNE	1853-03-03	FD	SWNE	R:CUMBERLAND
728	KELLY, Benjamin F	15	SWSW	1852-09-09	FD	SWSW	
856	KELLY, James M	11	NW	1849-07-13	FD	NW	
858	" "	22	E½NE	1852-08-10	FD	E2NE	
860	" "	22	W½NE	1852-08-10	FD	W2NE	
859	" "	22	SENW	1852-08-10	FD	SENW	
857	" "	15	SESW	1852-08-25	FD	SESW	
884	KELLY, John B	2	NWSE	1852-03-09	FD	NWSE	R:CUMBERLAND
885	" "	2	SWNW	1852-03-09	FD	SWNW	R:CUMBERLAND
883	" "	2	N½SW	1852-03-09	FD	N2SW	R:CUMBERLAND
887	" "	4	E½NE	1852-05-29	FD	E2NE	R:CUMBERLAND
886	" "	3	W½NW	1852-05-29	FD	W2NW	R:CUMBERLAND
889	" "	4	SWNE	1852-09-09	FD	SWNE	R:CUMBERLAND
888	" "	4	NWNE	1852-09-09	FD	NWNE	R:CUMBERLAND
882	" "	12	SWNE	1853-03-09	FD	SWNE	
880	" "	1	E½SW	1853-03-09	FD	E2SW	
812	" "	1		1854-09-14	FD	SWNERP	R:CUMBERLAND
812	" "	1		1854-09-14	FD	W2SERP	R:CUMBERLAND
879	" "	1		1854-09-14	FD	W2SERP	R:CUMBERLAND
879	" "	1		1854-09-14	FD	SWNERP	R:CUMBERLAND
881	" "	12		1854-09-14	FD	NWNERP	R:CUMBERLAND
1082	KELLY, William	3	NE	1851-06-07	FD	NE	R:CUMBERLAND
1081	" "	3		1851-08-31	FD	NEWA	R:CUMBERLAND
1065	KELLY, William C	15	S½SE	1852-08-10	FD	S2SE	
704	KIBLER, Adam	20	SWNW	1838-05-28	FD	SWNW	R:JASPER
705	" "	29	NWNW	1838-05-28	FD	NWNW	R:JASPER
703	" "	20	SESW	1839-04-10	FD	SESW	R:JASPER
706	" "	30	SENE	1846-03-05	FD	SENE	R:JASPER
702	" "	19	NENW	1849-06-12	FD	NENW	R:JASPER
839	KIBLER, Jacob	19	E½SE	1837-09-29	FD	E2SE	R:INDIANA
840	" "	21	NW	1837-09-29	FD	NW	R:INDIANA
842	" "	30	NENE	1837-09-29	FD	NENE	R:INDIANA
841	" "	29	SESW	1837-09-29	FD	SESW	R:INDIANA
873	KIBLER, Joel	9	NESE	1849-08-30	FD	NESE	R:JASPER
897	KIBLER, John F	29	SWSW	1844-11-26	FD	SWSW	R:JASPER
896	" "	19	SWSW	1848-12-19	FD	SWSW	R:JASPER
959	KIBLER, Martin	32	W½SW	1838-05-24	FD	W2SW	R:INDIANA
981	KIBLER, Reben	33	E½NW	1844-12-11	FD	E2NW	R:JASPER
983	KIBLER, Reuben	29	NENW	1838-09-06	FD	NENW	R:JASPER
984	" "	29	NWSW	1839-04-10	FD	NWSW	R:JASPER
986	" "	8	SWSE	1849-07-27	FD	SWSE	R:JASPER
985	" "	33	NESW	1852-04-30	FD	NESW	R:JASPER
1020	KIBLER, Solomon	19	SWSE	1837-12-28	FD	SWSE	R:INDIANA
1023	" "	30	NWNE	1838-09-06	FD	NWNE	R:JASPER
1021	" "	20	SWSE	1842-01-28	FD	SWSE	R:JASPER
1025	" "	30	SWNE	1844-12-11	FD	SWNE	R:JASPER
1019	" "	19	NWNE	1846-03-05	FD	NWNE	R:JASPER
1024	" "	30	SENW	1847-09-02	FD	SENW	R:JASPER
1022	" "	30	NENW	1848-12-19	FD	NENW	R:JASPER
1087	KIBLER, William M	30	SWNW	1848-09-27	FD	SWNW	R:VIRGINIA
1086	" "	30	NWNW	1848-10-04	FD	NWNW	R:VIRGINIA
909	KILBOURN, John	6	SENW	1849-11-12	FD	SENW	
908	" "	6	N½SW	1849-11-12	FD	N2SW	
739	KILGORE, Charles	27	W½NE	1838-09-29	FD	W2NE	R:JASPER
1083	KILLGORE, William	34	SWNE	1853-01-08	FD	SWNE	R:JASPER
1047	KIRKWOOD, Thomas	31	N½SE	1843-05-03	FD	N2SE	R:JASPER
1073	LAND, William H	11	N½SW	1850-09-21	FD	N2SW	R:INDIANA
1074	" "	14	E½NE	1850-09-21	FD	E2NE	R:INDIANA

ID	Individual in Patent	Sec.	Sec. Part	Purchase Date	Sale Type	IL Aliquot Part	For More Info . . .
1018	LARIMER, Smith	30	W½SW	1839-05-16	FD	W2SW	R:OHIO
775	LEACH, Elizabeth	24	NENE	1853-07-29	FD	NENE	R:JASPER S:F G:43
774	"	13	SESE	1853-07-29	FD	SESE	R:JASPER S:F G:43
855	LEACH, James	24	SWSE	1852-09-03	FD	SWSE	
774	LEACH, Joseph N	13	SESE	1853-07-29	FD	SESE	R:JASPER S:F G:43
775	"	24	NENE	1853-07-29	FD	NENE	R:JASPER S:F G:43
775	LEACH, Mary Ann	24	NENE	1853-07-29	FD	NENE	R:JASPER S:F G:43
774	"	13	SESE	1853-07-29	FD	SESE	R:JASPER S:F G:43
774	LEACH, Nancy N	13	SESE	1853-07-29	FD	SESE	R:JASPER S:F G:43
775	"	24	NENE	1853-07-29	FD	NENE	R:JASPER S:F G:43
775	LEACH, Nathaniel	24	NENE	1853-07-29	FD	NENE	R:JASPER S:F G:43
774	"	13	SESE	1853-07-29	FD	SESE	R:JASPER S:F G:43
774	LEACH, Richard	13	SESE	1853-07-29	FD	SESE	R:JASPER S:F G:43
775	"	24	NENE	1853-07-29	FD	NENE	R:JASPER S:F G:43
775	LEACH, Thomas	24	NENE	1853-07-29	FD	NENE	R:JASPER S:F G:43
774	"	13	SESE	1853-07-29	FD	SESE	R:JASPER S:F G:43
775	LEACH, Walter	24	NENE	1853-07-29	FD	NENE	R:JASPER S:F G:43
774	"	13	SESE	1853-07-29	FD	SESE	R:JASPER S:F G:43
871	LEWIS, James W	26	SESE	1852-05-13	FD	SESE	
870	"	23	NWNE	1852-05-13	FD	NWNE	
869	"	14	SESW	1852-05-13	FD	SESW	
960	LIDEY, Michael	7	NWSW	1850-10-09	FD	NWSW	
773	LONG, Elisha	31	SENW	1842-01-25	FD	SENW	R:JASPER
850	"	31	SENW	1842-01-25	FD	SENW	R:JASPER
1084	LONG, William	20	SENW	1839-08-22	FD	SENW	R:JASPER
1085	"	30	SESW	1840-07-01	FD	SESW	R:JASPER
1108	LORANCE, Zimri	31	N½SW	1845-11-15	FD	N2SW	R:JASPER
938	LYONS, Joseph	4	NENW	1852-10-09	FD	NENW	R:OHIO
939	"	4	SENW	1852-10-09	FD	SENW	R:OHIO
730	MALLORY, Benjamin	29	SWNE	1853-06-21	FD	SWNE	
718	MANNING, Hiram	16	L3	1851-06-17	SC	LOT3NENW	
827	"	16	L3	1851-06-17	SC	LOT3NENW	
828	"	16	L4	1851-06-17	SC	LOT4NWNW	
1105	MARKLAND, Zadock	3	NESE	1850-11-26	FD	NESE	R:JASPER
1104	"	14	SWNE	1853-09-07	FD	SWNE	R:JASPER
740	MARTIN, Charles	10	E½SW	1839-09-07	FD	E2SW	R:INDIANA
741	"	10	SENE	1839-09-07	FD	SENE	R:INDIANA
742	"	11	SWSE	1839-10-16	FD	SWSE	R:INDIANA
1056	MARTIN, Wesley	10	NWSE	1839-09-07	FD	NWSE	R:INDIANA
1057	"	11	NWSE	1839-09-07	FD	NWSE	R:INDIANA
1058	"	2	NWNE	1841-04-22	FD	NWNE	R:JASPER
1055	"	10	NESE	1850-06-24	FD	NESE	R:JASPER
1011	MAZE, Samuel	2	SWNE	1840-10-27	FD	SWNE	R:INDIANA
1012	"	3	SESE	1840-10-27	FD	SESE	R:INDIANA
911	MCCAIN, John	36	E½NE	1849-06-13	FD	E2NE	R:OHIO
910	"	25	E½SE	1849-06-13	FD	E2SE	R:OHIO
743	MCCOMAS, Christian S	20	SWSW	1837-12-28	FD	SWSW	R:INDIANA S:A
816	MCCOMAS, Henly C	19	NWSE	1838-02-24	FD	NWSE	R:JASPER
965	MCCOMAS, Napoleon B	20	NWNE	1839-08-22	FD	NWNE	R:JASPER
744	MCCOMMIS, Clinton	7	SENW	1851-09-29	FD	SENW	R:JASPER
817	MCCORNAS, Henly C	19	SENW	1848-12-19	FD	SENW	R:JASPER
954	MCCRACKEN, Lorenzo	14	NWNE	1840-06-11	FD	NWNE	R:CLARK
953	"	14	E½NW	1840-06-11	FD	E2NW	R:CLARK
1088	MCCULLOUGH, William M	2	SESW	1853-01-03	FD	SESW	
861	MCGARNEY, James	16	L11	1849-03-03	SC	LOT11NESW	
862	"	16	L12	1849-03-03	SC	LOT12NWSW	
833	MCILWAIN, Hugh	15	SWNE	1851-11-04	FD	SWNE	
832	"	15	NWSE	1851-11-04	FD	NWSE	
830	"	15	E½NE	1851-11-04	FD	E2NE	
831	"	15	NWNE	1852-08-24	FD	NWNE	
969	MILLIS, Nichoson	3	E½NE	1838-05-28	FD	E2NE	R:INDIANA
968	"	2	W½NW	1838-06-16	FD	W2NW	R:INDIANA
1089	MINTON, William	8	SENW	1851-10-31	FD	SENW	
797	MITCHELL, George	34	W½SW	1839-04-08	FD	W2SW	R:INDIANA
796	"	33	NESE	1849-12-26	FD	NESE	R:JASPER
800	MOCK, Gotlieb	9	W½SE	1844-09-19	FD	W2SE	R:JASPER
799	"	9	SESE	1844-09-19	FD	SESE	R:JASPER
805	MOCK, Gotliep	20	E½NE	1837-10-30	FD	E2NE	R:OHIO
810	"	29	E½NE	1837-10-30	FD	E2NE	R:OHIO
806	"	20	E½SE	1837-10-30	FD	E2SE	R:OHIO
807	"	20	SWNE	1838-09-06	FD	SWNE	R:JASPER
804	"	19	NENE	1842-10-24	FD	NENE	R:CRAWFORD
801	"	17	SWNW	1848-10-03	FD	SWNW	

ID	Individual in Patent	Sec.	Sec. Part	Purchase Date	Sale Type	IL Aliquot Part	For More Info . . .
802	MOCK, Gotliep (Cont'd)	18	E½SE	1848-10-03	FD	E2SE	
803	" "	18	SENE	1848-10-03	FD	SENE	
809	" "	22	N½NW	1849-08-20	FD	N2NW	
808	" "	21	N½NE	1849-08-20	FD	N2NE	
1048	MOORE, Thomas L	4	SE	1851-10-31	FD	SE	
1049	" "	4	SW	1851-10-31	FD	SW	
990	MORELAND, Richard	3	SWSE	1851-08-25	FD	SWSE	
974	MORGAN, Parker	3	N½SW	1852-04-13	FD	N2SW	R:NEW HAMPSHIRE
973	" "	3	E½NW	1852-04-13	FD	E2NW	R:NEW HAMPSHIRE
1038	MUSGRAVE, Stephen	21	NWSE	1851-10-30	FD	NWSE	R:JASPER
1037	" "	21	E½SW	1852-08-23	FD	E2SW	
735	NORRIS, Caleb	35	NWSE	1853-12-17	FD	NWSE	
736	" "	35	SWNE	1853-12-17	FD	SWNE	
947	NORRIS, Letta	35	NESW	1853-12-17	FD	NESW	
716	NORTON, Amos	10	S½SE	1851-11-04	FD	S2SE	R:INDIANA
945	OSBORN, Joshua J	11	S½SW	1852-08-30	FD	S2SW	R:JASPER
955	OSBORN, Lucy	14	W½NW	1852-08-30	FD	W2NW	R:JASPER S:F
956	OSBURN, Lucy	25	NWNE	1852-10-11	FD	NWNE	S:F
764	PARKER, Daniel	10	W½SW	1832-07-30	FD	W2SW	R:CRAWFORD
747	" "	10	W½SW	1832-07-30	FD	W2SW	R:CRAWFORD
1043	PATRICK, Thomas C	31	W½NE	1843-09-22	FD	W2NE	R:JASPER
1042	" "	31	E½NE	1843-10-18	FD	E2NE	R:JASPER
1041	" "	19	E½SW	1846-11-30	FD	E2SW	R:JASPER
1044	" "	32	SWNW	1851-04-10	FD	SWNW	R:JASPER
1095	PATRICK, William	12	E½SW	1852-06-01	FD	E2SW	
1097	" "	12	SWSE	1852-06-01	FD	SWSE	
1096	" "	12	SENW	1852-06-01	FD	SENW	
780	PATTERSON, Francis	18	SWNE	1851-04-05	FD	SWNE	
866	PAUGH, James	15	W½NW	1851-05-28	FD	W2NW	R:INDIANA
865	" "	15	NENW	1851-05-28	FD	NENW	R:INDIANA
864	" "	12	SWSW	1851-05-28	FD	SWSW	R:INDIANA
699	PAYNE, Absalom	8	NWNW	1851-04-04	FD	NWNW	R:JASPER
700	PAYNE, Absolom	5	NENW	1852-08-02	FD	NENW	
701	" "	5	SESW	1852-08-02	FD	SESW	
972	PAYNE, Othmiel H	5	SWSW	1852-08-02	FD	SWSW	
941	PERISHO, Joseph	13	NWNE	1843-11-07	FD	NWNE	R:JASPER
940	" "	12	NWSW	1849-10-15	FD	NWSW	R:JASPER
966	POOR, Nathaniel	16	L10	1852-08-26	SC	LOT10NWSE	
1050	POOR, Thomas	17	NENE	1851-11-22	FD	NENE	R:EDGAR
1098	POOR, William	16	L5	1851-12-29	SC	LOT5SWNW	
912	POWELL, John	6	SWSW	1849-11-12	FD	SWSW	
913	" "	7	NWNW	1851-11-14	FD	NWNW	R:JASPER
731	PRICE, Benjamin	15	SENW	1852-09-27	FD	SENW	
732	" "	24	SWNW	1854-02-09	FD	SWNW	R:JASPER
733	" "	26	SENE	1854-04-17	FD	SENE	R:JASPER
1013	PRICE, Samuel	26	SWNE	1853-07-22	FD	SWNE	
746	PROSE, Daniel Ii	29	W½SE	1840-12-15	FD	W2SE	R:OHIO
698	RAY, Abraham	21	W½SW	1840-11-12	FD	W2SW	R:OHIO
914	RAY, John	28	NENW	1849-10-16	FD	NENW	R:JASPER
727	REINS, Bartley	35	SWSE	1851-11-28	FD	SWSE	R:JASPER
729	ROBERTS, Benjamin F	1	SENE	1850-12-21	FD	SENE	R:JASPER
814	ROBERTS, Harrison	1	NWSW	1841-11-24	FD	NWSW	R:CLARK
815	" "	1	SESE	1841-11-24	FD	SESE	R:CLARK
812	" "	1		1844-07-12	FD	SWSWTYNT	R:JASPER
879	" "	1		1844-07-12	FD	SWSWTYNT	R:JASPER
813	" "	1	NESE	1849-10-01	FD	NESE	R:JASPER
1046	ROBERTS, Thomas D	5	NESE	1852-07-12	FD	NESE	
1000	ROSS, Robert	30	SESE	1845-01-18	FD	SESE	R:EDGAR
1001	" "	31	SESW	1847-08-18	FD	SESW	R:JASPER
1003	ROW, Robert	33	SESW	1852-02-03	FD	SESW	
1004	" "	33	W½SE	1852-02-03	FD	W2SE	
1002	" "	33	SESE	1852-02-03	FD	SESE	
734	SCHROADER, Bernard	36	E½NW	1840-08-21	FD	E2NW	R:JASPER
942	SCHROADER, Joseph	36	E½SW	1840-08-21	FD	E2SW	R:OHIO
1099	SHELL, William	6	NENE	1851-10-18	FD	NENE	R:INDIANA
715	SIMPSON, Allan	29	S½NW	1838-11-05	FD	S2NW	R:INDIANA
867	SMITH, James	7	NENE	1851-10-27	FD	NENE	
970	SMITH, Noah J	32	NESE	1853-08-02	FD	NESE	R:OHIO
971	" "	32	SENE	1853-08-02	FD	SENE	R:OHIO
1051	SMITH, Thomas	7	NESW	1851-10-31	FD	NESW	
1052	" "	7	SWNE	1851-10-31	FD	SWNE	
1100	SMITH, William	11	SENE	1849-11-16	FD	SENE	R:JASPER
1101	" "	3	SESW	1849-11-16	FD	SESW	R:JASPER

ID	Individual in Patent	Sec.	Sec. Part	Purchase Date	Sale Type	IL Aliquot Part	For More Info . . .
958	SONGER, Marion	33	NWSW	1852-05-17	FD	NWSW	R:JASPER S:F
915	SPIVEY, John	22	NENW	1851-10-29	FD	NENW	R:CRAWFORD
823	STRATTON, Henry J	22	SWNW	1850-08-26	FD	SWNW	
822	" "	21	SENE	1850-08-26	FD	SENE	
824	" "	22	W½SW	1850-08-26	FD	W2SW	
821	" "	21	E½SE	1850-08-26	FD	E2SE	R:EDGAR
899	STRATTON, John F	36	SESE	1852-08-23	FD	SESE	
898	" "	21	SWNE	1852-08-23	FD	SWNE	
964	STRONG, Moses	15	N½SW	1851-10-20	FD	N2SW	R:INDIANA
1014	SUTTON, Samuel	18	E½SW	1850-10-30	FD	E2SW	R:INDIANA
693	SWAK, Aaron	17	NWNE	1848-11-04	FD	NWNE	R:JASPER
695	SWICK, Aaron	8	S½SW	1849-08-21	FD	S2SW	
694	" "	17	E½NW	1849-08-21	FD	E2NW	
718	SWICK, Andrew	16	L3	1850-10-15	SC	L3NENWVOID	
827	" "	16	L3	1850-10-15	SC	L3NENWVOID	
917	SWICK, John	17	NWSW	1839-06-11	FD	NWSW	R:JASPER
918	" "	17	SWNE	1839-06-11	FD	SWNE	R:JASPER
916	" "	16	L6	1851-11-28	SC	LOT6SENW	
978	SWICK, Peter	16	L7	1850-10-15	SC	LOT7SWNE	
979	" "	16	L8	1850-10-15	SC	LOT8SENE	
977	" "	16	L1	1850-10-15	SC	LOT1NENE	
1102	SWICK, William	17	SENE	1852-10-08	FD	SENE	
943	SWIM, Joseph	35	NWNE	1853-01-21	FD	NWNE	R:CLARK
772	THOMPSON, Elijah	2	SENW	1852-04-13	FD	SENW	R:NEW HAMPSHIRE
777	THOMPSON, Enoch	1	W½NE	1838-05-28	FD	W2NE	R:INDIANA
778	" "	2	E½NW	1838-05-28	FD	E2NW	R:INDIANA
776	" "	1	E½NW	1838-05-28	FD	E2NW	R:INDIANA
1053	THOMPSON, Wallace	24	NWNE	1850-12-11	FD	NWNE	R:JASPER
1054	THOMPSON, Wallis	14	SWSW	1852-04-15	FD	SWSW	
946	TRAVIS, Josiah	2	SWSW	1851-06-02	FD	SWSW	R:JASPER
868	TRUITT, James	2	N½NW	1851-10-22	FD	N2NW	R:INDIANA
798	TURNER, George	35	E½NW	1855-02-01	FD	E2NW	R:JASPER
691	VANATTA, Aaron Sen	18	SENW	1850-06-03	FD	SENW	
692	" "	18	W½NW	1850-06-03	FD	W2NW	
1016	VANNATA, Samuel	6	NWNE	1848-09-17	FD	NWNE	
1015	" "	6	NENW	1848-09-17	FD	NENW	
719	WARD, Armstead	17	NWNW	1851-02-06	FD	NWNW	R:INDIANA
720	" "	18	NENE	1851-02-06	FD	NENE	
721	" "	7	E½SE	1851-02-06	FD	E2SE	
722	" "	7	SENE	1851-02-06	FD	SENE	
920	WARD, John	8	N½SW	1851-04-05	FD	N2SW	
921	WARREN, John	11	NENE	1850-06-11	FD	NENE	
922	" "	12	NENW	1850-06-11	FD	NENW	
923	" "	12	W½NW	1850-06-11	FD	W2NW	
919	WARREN, John T	12	NENE	1851-10-16	FD	NENE	R:JASPER
980	WEAVER, Peter	28	NWNW	1851-12-24	FD	NWNW	R:JASPER
944	WELDAM, Joseph	36	W½NE	1840-08-21	FD	W2NE	R:JASPER

Patent Map

T8-N R10-E
3rd PM Meridian

Map Group 3

Township Statistics

Parcels Mapped	:	422
Number of Patents	:	1
Number of Individuals	:	217
Patentees Identified	:	208
Number of Surnames	:	137
Multi-Patentee Parcels	:	3
Oldest Patent Date	:	7/30/1832
Most Recent Patent	:	2/1/1855
Block/Lot Parcels	:	18
Cities and Towns	:	4
Cemeteries	:	9

Lots-Sec. 16

L1	SWICK, Peter	1850
L2	DULGOR, Henry	1850
L3	SWICK, Andrew	1850
L3	MANNING, Hiram	1851
L4	MANNING, Hiram	1851
L5	POOR, William	1851
L6	SWICK, John	1851
L7	SWICK, Peter	1850
L8	SWICK, Peter	1850
L9	HUSSONG, Calvin	1850
L10	POOR, Nathaniel	1852
L11	MCGARNEY, James	1849
L12	MCGARNEY, James	1849
L13	ANDREWS, William P	1849

Map — Township 8-N Range 10-E (3rd PM)

Section 3
KELLY John B 1852
MORGAN Parker 1852
KELLY William 1851
KELLY William 1851 | MILLIS Nichoson 1838
MORGAN Parker 1852
DENMAN Jonathan B 1852 | MARKLAND Zadock 1850
FINEY Damon 1852
SMITH William 1849
MORELAND Richard 1851
MAZE Samuel 1840

Section 2
MILLIS Nichoson 1838 | TRUITT James 1851 | THOMPSON Enoch 1838
KELLY John B 1852 | THOMPSON Elijah 1852 | MAZE Samuel 1840
KELLY John B 1852
KELLY John B 1852
TRAVIS Josiah 1851
MCCULLOUGH William M 1853
DAVISSON Hezekiah 1839
HUDSON William W 1840

Section 1
MARTIN Wesley 1841
COALE John 1839
COALE John 1839
THOMPSON Enoch 1838
THOMPSON Enoch 1838
KELLEY John B 1853
KELLY John B 1854
ROBERTS Benjamin F 1850
ROBERTS Harrison 1841
KELLY John B 1853
ROBERTS Harrison 1849
ROBERTS Harrison 1844
KELLEY John B 1853
KELLY John B 1854
ROBERTS Harrison 1841

Section 10
HUNTER Spencer K 1852
HARRIS Addison S 1839
DAVISSON Hezekiah 1839
MARTIN Charles 1839
PARKER Daniel 1832
MARTIN Charles 1839
MARTIN Wesley 1839
MARTIN Wesley 1850
NORTON Amos 1851
CARMEAN Edward 1851

Section 11
KELLY James M 1849
HARRIS Addison S 1839
HEARD Jesse M 1838
WARREN John 1850
SMITH William 1849
LAND William H 1850
MARTIN Wesley 1839
OSBORN Joshua J 1852
MARTIN Charles 1839
HARRIS Addison 1839

Section 12
WARREN John 1850
WARREN John 1850
WARREN John 1850
PATRICK William 1852
KELLEY John B 1853
KELLY John B 1853
KELLY John B 1854
WARREN John T 1851
GROVES Septor 1851
PERISHO Joseph 1849
PATRICK William 1852
PAUGH James 1851
HASKET Edmund C 1853
HASKET Edmund C 1853
PATRICK William 1852
HASKET Edward C 1853

Section 15
PAUGH James 1851
PAUGH James 1851
MCILWAIN Hugh 1852
PRICE Benjamin 1852
MCILWAIN Hugh 1851
MCILWAIN Hugh 1851
STRONG Moses 1851
MCILWAIN Hugh 1851
BREES Doctor F 1852
KELLY Benjamin F 1852
KELLY James M 1852
KELLY William C 1852

Section 14
OSBORN Lucy 1852
MCCRACKEN Lorenzo 1840
MCCRACKEN Lorenzo 1840
MARKLAND Zadock 1853
LAND William H 1850
BREES Doctor F 1852
CLARK John 1852
THOMPSON Wallis 1852
LEWIS James W 1852

Section 13
DAVIS James 1849
PERISHO Joseph 1843
CLARK Austin 1851
HASKET Edward C 1853
CLARK Austin 1851
CHAPMAN Samuel 1840
CLARK Austin 1851
HUNT William 1849
LEACH [43] Elizabeth 1853

Section 22
MOCK Gotliep 1849
SPIVEY John 1851
KELLY James M 1852
STRATTON Henry J 1850
KELLY James M 1852
KELLY James M 1852
DAVIS James 1849

Section 23
LEWIS James W 1852
CHAPMAN Samuel 1840
CHAPMAN Samuel 1840

Section 24
CHAPMAN Samuel 1840
CLARK Austin 1851
THOMPSON Wallace 1850
LEACH [43] Elizabeth 1853
PRICE Benjamin 1854
DAVIS David 1853
COHOON Stephen 1840

Section 27
STRATTON Henry J 1850
HUNT Stephanus 1838
HUNT William 1838
HUNT William 1849
HUNT Stephanus 1840
HUTSON William 1838
KILGORE Charles 1838
HUNT William 1851
BONHAM Levi 1849
HUNT Stephanus 1841
HAMMER David 1848
CUMMONS Joseph 1849
HUNT Stephanus 1841
HUNT Stephanas 1838

Section 26
BONHAM Levi M 1851
CHAPMAN Joseph 1849
CHAPMAN Joseph 1852
CHAPMAN Joseph 1850
CHAPMAN Joseph 1841
CHAPMAN Joseph 1847
BONHAM Levi M 1851
BONHAM Levi 1849
BONHAM Levi 1839
ADAMS John B 1851
CHAPMAN Joseph 1851
CHAPMAN Joseph 1853
PRICE Samuel 1853
PRICE Benjamin 1854
HUNT Stephanus 1838
BONHAM Richard 1839
HUNT Stephanus 1841
BONHAM Richard 1852
LEWIS James W 1852

Section 25
CHAPMAN Samuel 1840
CHAPMAN Samuel 1840
CHAPMAN Samuel 1840
CHAPMAN Joseph 1850
CHAPMAN Joseph 1849
HUNT Stephen 1850
LEACH James 1852
CHAPMAN Perry 1849
CURTIS Joseph C 1854
CHAPMAN Joseph 1841
OSBURN Lucy 1852
CHAPMAN Perry 1849
ADKISSON Alexander 1851
CHAPMAN Robert 1851
BONHAM Richard 1852
CLARK Henry 1851
DAILEY William 1840
MCCAIN John 1849

Section 34
CUMMINS Robert 1839
CUMMINS Robert 1844
KILLGORE William 1853
CUMMINS Robert 1839
CUMMINS Joseph 1844
CUMMINS Robert 1839
MITCHELL George 1839
CUMMINS Robert 1839
CUMMINS Robert 1839

Section 35
HUNT Stephanus 1841
TURNER George 1855
SWIM Joseph 1853
CLARK Margaret E 1854
NORRIS Caleb 1853
CHAPMAN William 1849
HEPNER Green Berry 1852
NORRIS Letta 1853
NORRIS Caleb 1853
CHAPMAN William 1849
CHAPMAN Thomas 1851
REINS Bartley 1851
HARRISON Jacob 1849

Section 36
CHAPMAN William 1849
SCHROADER Bernard 1840
WELDAM Joseph 1840
MCCAIN John 1849
MCCAIN John 1849
GARDWAIN Henry 1840
SCHROADER Joseph 1840
HUNT Zimri 1849
HUNT Zimri 1853
HUNT Elihu 1849
STRATTON John F 1852

Helpful Hints

1. This Map's INDEX can be found on the preceding pages.

2. Refer to Map "C" to see where this Township lies within Jasper County, Illinois.

3. Numbers within square brackets [ ] denote a multi-patentee land parcel (multi-owner). Refer to Appendix "C" for a full list of members in this group.

4. Areas that look to be crowded with Patentees usually indicate multiple sales of the same parcel (re-issues), cancellations or voided transactions (that we map, anyway) or overlapping parcels. We opt to show even these ambiguous parcels, which oftentimes lead to research avenues not yet taken.

Legend

— Patent Boundary

— Section Boundary

No Patents Found (or Outside County)

1., 2., 3., ...   Lot Numbers (when beside a name)

[ ]   Group Number (see Appendix "C")

Scale: Section = 1 mile X 1 mile (generally, with some exceptions)

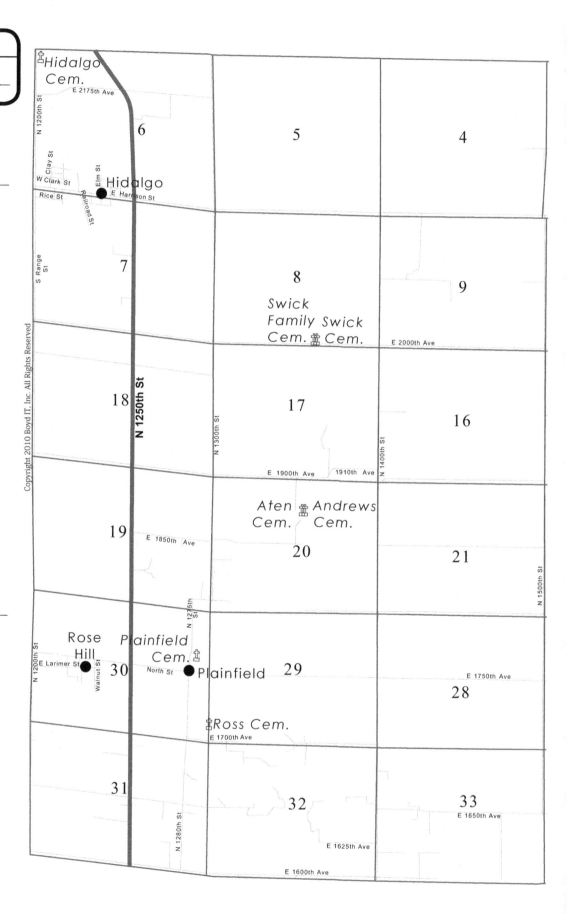

Road Map

T8-N R10-E
3rd PM Meridian

Map Group 3

Cities & Towns
Hidalgo
Plainfield
Point Pleasant
Rose Hill

Cemeteries
Andrews Cemetery
Aten Cemetery
Brown Cemetery
Hidalgo Cemetery
Kilgore Cemetery
Plainfield Cemetery
Ross Cemetery
Swick Cemetery
Swick Family Cemetery

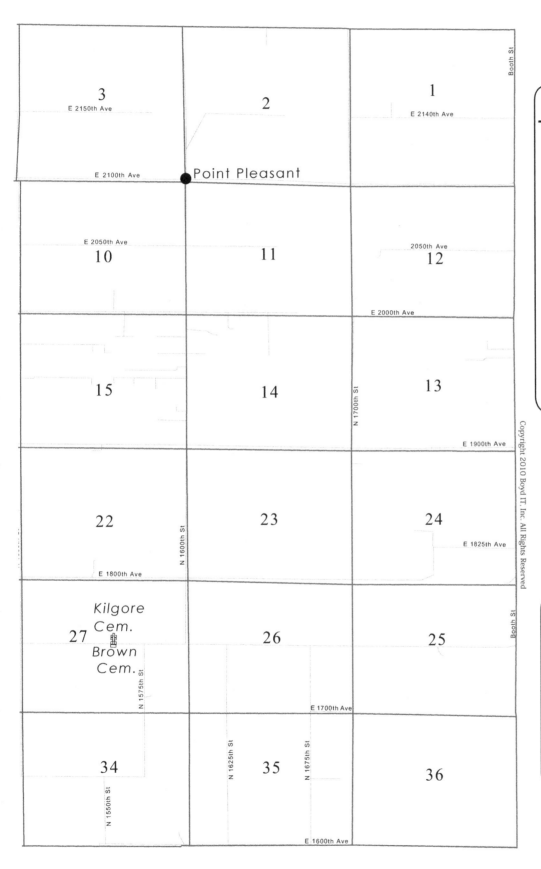

3
E 2150th Ave

2

1
E 2140th Ave

Booth St

E 2100th Ave
● Point Pleasant

E 2050th Ave
10

11

2050th Ave
12

E 2000th Ave

15

14

N 1700th St

13

E 1900th Ave

22

N 1600th St

23

24

E 1825th Ave

E 1800th Ave

Kilgore
Cem.
27 ✝
Brown
Cem.

N 1575th St

26

25

Booth St

E 1700th Ave

34

N 1550th St

N 1625th St

35

N 1675th St

36

E 1600th Ave

Helpful Hints

1. This road map has a number of uses, but primarily it is to help you: a) find the present location of land owned by your ancestors (at least the general area), b) find cemeteries and city-centers, and c) estimate the route/roads used by Census-takers & tax-assessors.

2. If you plan to travel to Jasper County to locate cemeteries or land parcels, please pick up a modern travel map for the area before you do. Mapping old land parcels on modern maps is not as exact a science as you might think. Just the slightest variations in public land survey coordinates, estimates of parcel boundaries, or road-map deviations can greatly alter a map's representation of how a road either does or doesn't cross a particular parcel of land.

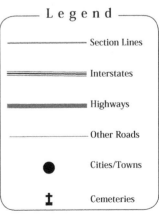

L e g e n d

_____ Section Lines

═══════ Interstates

▓▓▓▓▓▓ Highways

_____ Other Roads

● Cities/Towns

✝ Cemeteries

Scale: Section = 1 mile X 1 mile
(generally, with some exceptions)

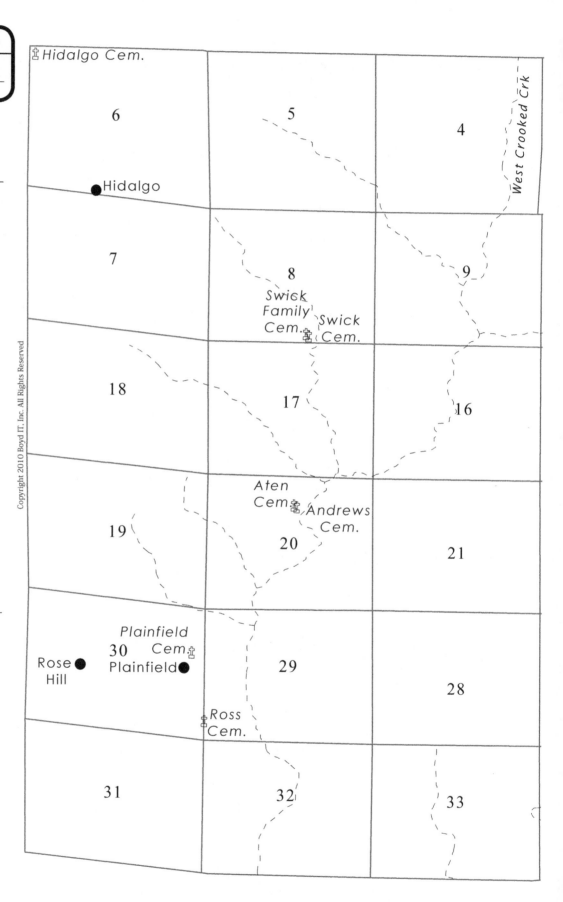

Historical Map

T8-N R10-E
3rd PM Meridian

Map Group 3

Cities & Towns
Hidalgo
Plainfield
Point Pleasant
Rose Hill

Cemeteries
Andrews Cemetery
Aten Cemetery
Brown Cemetery
Hidalgo Cemetery
Kilgore Cemetery
Plainfield Cemetery
Ross Cemetery
Swick Cemetery
Swick Family Cemetery

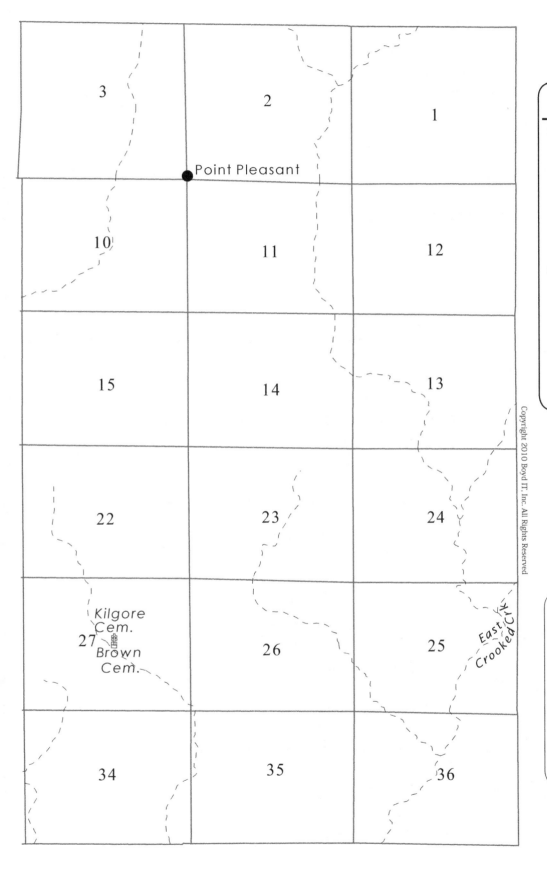

3

2

1

● Point Pleasant

10

11

12

15

14

13

22

23

24

Kilgore
Cem.

27   Brown
Cem.

26

25

East
Crooked Crk

34

35

36

Helpful Hints

1. This Map takes a different look at the same Congressional Township displayed in the preceding two maps. It presents features that can help you better envision the historical development of the area: a) Water-bodies (lakes & ponds), b) Water-courses (rivers, streams, etc.), c) Railroads, d) City/town center-points (where they were oftentimes located when first settled), and e) Cemeteries.

2. Using this "Historical" map in tandem with this Township's Patent Map and Road Map, may lead you to some interesting discoveries. You will often find roads, towns, cemeteries, and waterways are named after nearby landowners: sometimes those names will be the ones you are researching. See how many of these research gems you can find here in Jasper County.

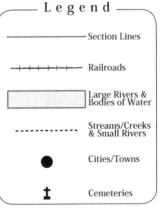

L e g e n d

——————— Section Lines

+++++++ Railroads

Large Rivers & Bodies of Water

- - - - - - - Streams/Creeks & Small Rivers

● Cities/Towns

✝ Cemeteries

Scale: Section = 1 mile X 1 mile
(there are some exceptions)

Map Group 4: Index to Land Patents

Township 8-North Range 11-East (3rd PM)

After you locate an individual in this Index, take note of the Section and Section Part then proceed to the Land Patent map on the pages immediately following. You should have no difficulty locating the corresponding parcel of land.

The "For More Info" Column will lead you to more information about the underlying Patents. See the *Legend* at right, and the "How to Use this Book" chapter, for more information.

```
                        LEGEND
            "For More Info . . . " column
G = Group   (Multi-Patentee Patent, see Appendix "C")
R = Residence
S = Social Status


See Appendix A for list of abbreviations used by the
Illinois State Archives in describing the place and
nature of these land patents.

Note: if the Abbreviations contain "L", "BL", "LOT",
or "BLOCK", the exact whereabouts of the parcel within
the section is not known.
```

ID	Individual in Patent	Sec.	Sec. Part	Purchase Date	Sale Type	IL Aliquot Part	For More Info . . .
1161	ADAMS, Timothy R B	7	NE	1848-09-26	FD	NE	
1169	ADAMSON, Zedakiah	6	SWNE	1850-06-20	FD	SWNE	R:INDIANA
1168	" "	6	S½NW	1850-06-20	FD	S2NW	R:INDIANA
1167	" "	6	NWSE	1850-06-20	FD	NWSE	R:INDIANA
1112	ADKINSON, Alexander	30	E½SE	1851-08-23	FD	E2SE	R:KENTUCKY
1119	ALLEN, David	19	SESE	1850-10-30	FD	SESE	R:JASPER
1132	BENSON, John	30	SENE	1851-09-04	FD	SENE	R:JASPER
1154	BUCKINGHAM, Samuel	18	S½SW	1852-05-25	FD	S2SW	R:JASPER
1133	BUSSELL, John	7	NESE	1841-02-27	FD	NESE	R:JASPER
1129	CARTER, James B	18	L4	1853-01-28	SC	LOT4SESE	
1128	" "	18	L3	1853-01-28	SC	LOT3SWSE	
1127	" "	18	L2	1853-01-28	SC	LOT2NWSE	
1142	CHAPAN, Margaret	31		1849-06-30	FD	W2NEWA	R:JASPER S:F
1145	" "	31		1849-06-30	FD	W2NEWA	R:JASPER S:F
1147	CHAPMAN, Margaret	31	W½NE	1849-05-31	FD	W2NE	R:JASPER S:F
1144	" "	30	S½SW	1849-05-31	FD	S2SW	R:JASPER S:F
1146	" "	31	N½NW	1849-05-31	FD	N2NW	R:JASPER S:F
1143	" "	30		1849-06-30	FD	S2SWWA	R:JASPER S:F
1145	" "	31		1849-06-30	FD	N2NWWA	R:JASPER S:F
1139	" "	30		1849-06-30	FD	S2SWWA	R:JASPER S:F
1142	" "	31		1849-06-30	FD	N2NWWA	R:JASPER S:F
1149	CHAPMAN, Perry	31	S½NW	1852-10-18	FD	S2NW	R:JASPER
1153	CHAPMAN, Robert	30	NWSE	1851-07-16	FD	NWSE	R:JASPER
1160	CHAPMAN, Thomas	31	S½SW	1852-10-28	FD	S2SW	R:JASPER
1124	CLARK, Henry	31	E½NE	1851-08-26	FD	E2NE	R:INDIANA
1123	" "	30	SWSE	1852-09-13	FD	SWSE	
1157	COHOON, Stephen	19	SWNE	1840-10-24	FD	SWNE	R:OHIO
1156	" "	18	E½NE	1840-10-24	FD	E2NE	R:OHIO
1120	DAVIS, David	19	SWNW	1853-09-23	FD	SWNW	R:CLARK
1164	DUGAN, William	6	NWNE	1849-10-24	FD	NWNE	R:CUMBERLAND
1163	" "	6	N½NW	1849-10-24	FD	N2NW	R:CUMBERLAND
1121	GEDDES, George P	6	NW	1839-09-03	FD	NW	R:CLARK
1130	GEDDES, James R	6	N½NE	1839-09-04	FD	N2NE	R:CLARK
1118	GOSNELL, Daniel	19	NENE	1851-11-13	FD	NENE	R:JASPER
1165	GOSNELL, William	30	N½SW	1854-01-11	FD	N2SW	R:JASPER
1141	GRAVES, Lewis	19	SW	1840-03-24	FD	SW	R:KENTUCKY
1115	GROVE, Christopher	18	NW	1839-12-05	FD	NW	R:COLES
1117	" "	7	SW	1839-12-05	FD	SW	R:COLES
1116	" "	7	SESE	1840-09-22	FD	SESE	R:JASPER
1155	GROVE, Septor	7	W½NW	1849-05-25	FD	W2NW	R:JASPER
1150	GROVES, Perry	18	L1	1853-01-28	SC	LOT1NESE	
1162	HARRISON, Washington	30	NW	1853-01-17	FD	NW	R:JASPER
1113	HUDDLESTON, Barnet G	7	SENW	1850-07-01	FD	SENW	R:JASPER
1110	HUDDLESTUN, Abram S	6	SWSE	1850-01-07	FD	SWSE	
1109	" "	6	SW	1850-01-07	FD	SW	
1111	" "	7	NENW	1850-01-07	FD	NENW	

ID	Individual in Patent	Sec.	Sec. Part	Purchase Date	Sale Type	IL Aliquot Part	For More Info . . .
1170	HUNT, Zimpi	31	N½SW	1851-09-30	FD	N2SW	R:JASPER
1131	HURD, Jesse M	7	W½SE	1840-03-04	FD	W2SE	R:JASPER
1166	LEWIS, William T	18	N½SW	1854-11-02	FD	N2SW	R:JASPER
1151	MCCUBBINS, Phebe	19	NWSE	1847-07-01	FD	NWSE	R:EDGAR S:F
1152	" "	19	SENE	1851-09-02	FD	SENE	R:JASPER S:F
1159	MONRONEY, Sylvester	19	SENW	1853-11-12	FD	SENW	R:JASPER
1158	" "	19	NWNE	1853-11-12	FD	NWNE	R:JASPER
1125	PERISHO, Isaac	6	E½NE	1840-09-09	FD	E2NE	R:EDGAR
1126	" "	6	NESE	1841-01-04	FD	NESE	R:JASPER
1137	PERISHO, Joseph	18	NWNE	1842-08-22	FD	NWNE	R:JASPER
1138	" "	18	SWNE	1850-03-11	FD	SWNE	R:JASPER
1114	ROBERTS, Benjamin F	6	SESE	1844-07-12	FD	SESE	R:JASPER
1136	RYAN, John	19	NESE	1851-05-28	FD	NESE	R:CRAWFORD
1135	STRATTON, John F	31	W½SE	1852-11-06	FD	W2SE	
1134	" "	31	E½SE	1852-11-06	FD	E2SE	
1139	VANRANT, Joseph	30		1849-06-30	FD	N2NEWA	R:JASPER
1143	" "	30		1849-06-30	FD	N2NEWA	R:JASPER
1140	VANSANT, Joseph	30	N½NE	1849-05-22	FD	N2NE	R:JASPER
1122	WHEELER, George W	19	SWSE	1853-10-06	FD	SWSE	R:COLES
1148	WOOD, Noble W	30	SWNE	1852-09-17	FD	SWNE	

Patent Map

T8-N R11-E
3rd PM Meridian

Map Group 4

Township Statistics

Parcels Mapped	:	62
Number of Patents	:	1
Number of Individuals	:	42
Patentees Identified	:	42
Number of Surnames	:	35
Multi-Patentee Parcels	:	0
Oldest Patent Date	:	9/3/1839
Most Recent Patent	:	11/2/1854
Block/Lot Parcels	:	4
Cities and Towns	:	1
Cemeteries	:	1

Note: the area contained in this map amounts to far less than a full Township. Therefore, its contents are completely on this single page (instead of a "normal" 2-page spread).

Legend

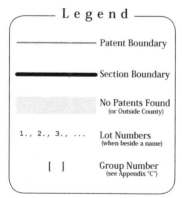

	Patent Boundary
	Section Boundary
	No Patents Found (or Outside County)
1., 2., 3., ...	Lot Numbers (when beside a name)
[ ]	Group Number (see Appendix "C")

Scale: Section = 1 mile X 1 mile
(generally, with some exceptions)

Section 6
DUGAN William 1849
GEDDES George P 1839
DUGAN William 1849
GEDDES James R 1839
ADAMSON Zedakiah 1850
ADAMSON Zedakiah 1850
PERISHO Isaac 1840
HUDDLESTUN Abram S 1850
ADAMSON Zedakiah 1850
PERISHO Isaac 1841
HUDDLESTUN Abram S 1850
ROBERTS Benjamin F 1844

Section 7
HUDDLESTUN Abram S 1850
GROVE Septor 1849
HUDDLESTON Barnet G 1850
ADAMS Timothy R B 1848
GROVE Christopher 1839
HURD Jesse M 1840
BUSSELL John 1841
GROVE Christopher 1840

Section 18
GROVE Christopher 1839
PERISHO Joseph 1842
PERISHO Joseph 1850
COHOON Stephen 1840
LEWIS William T 1854
BUCKINGHAM Samuel 1852
Lots-Sec. 18
L1 GROVES, Perry 1853
L2 CARTER, James B 1853
L3 CARTER, James B 1853
L4 CARTER, James B 1853

Section 19
MONRONEY Sylvester 1853
GOSNELL Daniel 1851
DAVIS David 1853
MONRONEY Sylvester 1853
COHOON Stephen 1840
MCCUBBINS Phebe 1851
GRAVES Lewis 1840
MCCUBBINS Phebe 1847
RYAN John 1851
WHEELER George W 1853
ALLEN David 1850

Section 30
HARRISON Washington 1853
VANRANT Joseph 1849
VANSANT Joseph 1849
WOOD Noble W 1852
BENSON John 1851
GOSNELL William 1854
CHAPMAN Robert 1851
CHAPMAN Margaret 1849
CHAPMAN Margaret 1849
CLARK Henry 1852
ADKINSON Alexander 1851

Section 31
CHAPMAN Margaret 1849
CHAPMAN Margaret 1849
CHAPMAN Margaret 1849
CHAPMAN Perry 1852
CHAPMAN Margaret 1849
CLARK Henry 1851
HUNT Zimpi 1851
STRATTON John F 1852
CHAPMAN Thomas 1852
STRATTON John F 1852

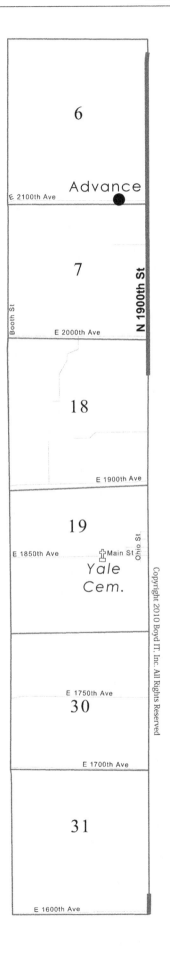

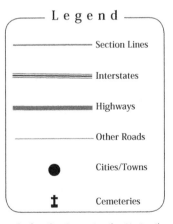

Road Map

T8-N R11-E
3rd PM Meridian

M a p   G r o u p   4

Note: the area contained in this map amounts to far less than a full Township. Therefore, its contents are completely on this single page (instead of a "normal" 2-page spread).

Cities & Towns
Advance

Cemeteries
Yale Cemetery

L e g e n d

———————— Section Lines

═══════════ Interstates

━━━━━━━━━━ Highways

———————— Other Roads

● Cities/Towns

✝ Cemeteries

Scale: Section = 1 mile X 1 mile
(generally, with some exceptions)

Historical Map

T8-N R11-E
3rd PM Meridian

Map Group 4

Note: the area contained in this map amounts to far less than a full Township. Therefore, its contents are completely on this single page (instead of a "normal" 2-page spread).

Cities & Towns
Advance

Cemeteries
Yale Cemetery

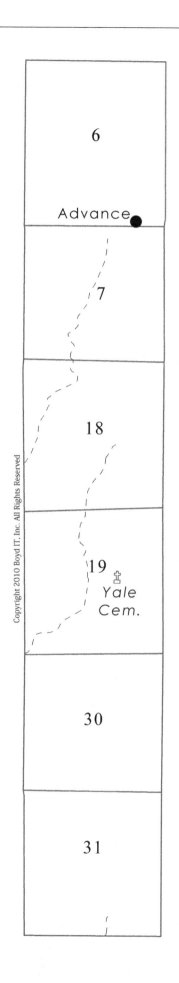

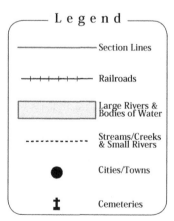

Legend

——————— Section Lines

+++++++ Railroads

Large Rivers & Bodies of Water

----------- Streams/Creeks & Small Rivers

● Cities/Towns

☩ Cemeteries

Scale: Section = 1 mile X 1 mile
(there are some exceptions)

Map Group 5: Index to Land Patents

Township 8-North Range 14-West (2nd PM)

After you locate an individual in this Index, take note of the Section and Section Part then proceed to the Land Patent map on the pages immediately following. You should have no difficulty locating the corresponding parcel of land.

The "For More Info" Column will lead you to more information about the underlying Patents. See the *Legend* at right, and the "How to Use this Book" chapter, for more information.

```
┌─────────────────────────────────────────────────────┐
│                      LEGEND                            │
│           "For More Info . . . " column                │
│ G = Group  (Multi-Patentee Patent, see Appendix "C")   │
│ R = Residence                                          │
│ S = Social Status                                      │
│                                                        │
│ See Appendix A for list of abbreviations used by the   │
│ Illinois State Archives in describing the place and    │
│ nature of these land patents.                          │
│                                                        │
│ Note: if the Abbreviations contain "L", "BL", "LOT",   │
│ or "BLOCK", the exact whereabouts of the parcel within │
│ the section is not known.                              │
└─────────────────────────────────────────────────────┘
```

ID	Individual in Patent	Sec.	Sec. Part	Purchase Date	Sale Type	IL Aliquot Part	For More Info . . .
1300	ADAMS, Jeremiah	3	SWNW	1851-11-18	FD	SWNW	R:JASPER
1299	" "	3	NESW	1851-11-18	FD	NESW	R:JASPER
1301	" "	4	NENE	1851-11-18	FD	NENE	R:JASPER
1401	ADAMS, Timothy R B	5	W½SE	1849-06-16	FD	W2SE	
1400	" "	5	SESW	1849-06-16	FD	SESW	
1402	" "	8	NENW	1849-06-16	FD	NENW	
1466	ADAMSON, Zedakiah	7	NENE	1850-06-20	FD	NENE	R:INDIANA
1468	ADAMSON, Zedekiah	7	SENE	1852-09-10	FD	SENE	
1467	" "	6	SESE	1853-02-14	FD	SESE	
1180	ADKINSON, Alexander	30	NESW	1851-08-23	FD	NESW	R:KENTUCKY
1181	" "	30	W½SW	1851-08-23	FD	W2SW	R:KENTUCKY
1334	ALLENTHARP, Joseph P	33	NWNE	1854-09-18	FD	NWNE	R:INDIANA
1187	ALLISON, Andrew	27	SENE	1851-11-04	FD	SENE	
1188	" "	27	W½NE	1851-11-04	FD	W2NE	
1219	ALLISON, David	33	NENW	1840-10-27	FD	NENW	R:JASPER
1217	" "	21	NESW	1845-11-12	FD	NESW	R:JASPER
1218	" "	29	SWSW	1845-11-12	FD	SWSW	R:JASPER
1387	ALLISON, Sarah	34	SWNW	1851-10-10	FD	SWNW	R:OHIO
1344	AMES, Leonard	16	L8	1850-10-24	SC	LOT8SENE	
1341	" "	16	L1	1850-10-24	SC	LOT1NENE	
1342	" "	16	L2	1850-10-24	SC	LOT2NWNE	
1343	" "	16	L7	1850-10-24	SC	LOT7SWNE	
1212	ARCHER, Daniel E	20	SESW	1852-02-13	FD	SESW	R:JASPER
1309	ARCHER, John C	20	W½SW	1843-04-24	FD	W2SW	R:JASPER
1308	" "	20	SWNW	1843-04-24	FD	SWNW	R:JASPER
1307	" "	20	SENE	1843-04-24	FD	SENE	R:JASPER
1327	ARCHER, John W	17	NWSE	1847-11-11	FD	NWSE	R:JASPER
1347	BAILEY, Loyd Jr	33	NWSE	1852-05-12	FD	NWSE	R:JASPER
1382	BAILEY, Samuel Jr	28	E½SE	1851-11-17	FD	E2SE	R:OHIO
1393	BAILEY, Sudwell	33	SESE	1853-09-06	FD	SESE	R:JASPER
1420	BARLOW, William	34	SENW	1851-01-25	FD	SENW	R:CRAWFORD
1348	BATES, Lubin	10	SENE	1852-05-28	FD	SENE	
1349	BOWMAN, Michael	15	NENW	1854-10-11	FD	NENW	R:CRAWFORD
1415	BOWMAN, William B	15	SENE	1854-08-25	FD	SENE	R:CRAWFORD
1419	" "	15	W½SW	1854-09-27	FD	W2SW	R:CRAWFORD
1416	" "	15	SESW	1854-09-27	FD	SESW	R:CRAWFORD
1418	" "	15	W½SE	1854-09-28	FD	W2SE	R:CRAWFORD
1417	" "	15	SWNE	1854-09-28	FD	SWNE	R:CRAWFORD
1305	BUSSELL, John	7	NWSE	1841-02-27	FD	NWSE	R:JASPER
1306	" "	8	SENW	1841-02-27	FD	SENW	R:JASPER
1255	CALDWELL, Hugh	34	N½SW	1851-06-04	FD	N2SW	R:CRAWFORD
1250	CLARK, Henry	31	W½NW	1851-08-26	FD	W2NW	R:INDIANA
1249	CLEMANS, Hamilton J	21	SESW	1845-10-27	FD	SESW	R:OHIO
1404	CLEMENS, Walden	28	W½NW	1845-04-26	FD	W2NW	R:JASPER
1357	CLEMENTS, Owzzy	29	W½SE	1839-11-15	FD	W2SE	R:EDGAR
1358	" "	32	E½NW	1839-11-15	FD	E2NW	R:EDGAR

ID	Individual in Patent	Sec.	Sec. Part	Purchase Date	Sale Type	IL Aliquot Part	For More Info . . .
1359	CLEMENTS, Oyzy	33	NWSW	1843-10-19	FD	NWSW	R:JASPER
1405	CLEMMONS, Warden	29	NWSW	1843-10-31	FD	NWSW	R:EDGAR
1406	"	"	30	NWSE	1848-06-07	FD	NWSE	R:JASPER
1407	"	"	30	SESE	1849-10-05	FD	SESE	R:JASPER
1408	CLEMONS, Warden	30	NESE	1843-12-27	FD	NESE	R:EDGAR
1410	"	"	30	SWSE	1850-12-19	FD	SWSE	R:JASPER
1409	"	"	30	SESW	1851-06-12	FD	SESW	R:JASPER
1411	"	"	31	NENW	1851-09-08	FD	NENW	R:JASPER
1412	"	"	31	NWNE	1851-10-24	FD	NWNE	R:JASPER
1413	"	"	31	SWNW	1852-05-31	FD	SWNW	R:JASPER
1391	COHOON, Stephen	18	W½SW	1840-10-24	FD	W2SW	R:OHIO
1272	COMSTOCK, Norman	21	SEN½	1854-01-04	FD	S2NE	R:JASPER G:19
1204	COOPER, Chrisley	27	SENW	1851-06-16	FD	SENW	R:CRAWFORD
1205	"	"	27	SWNW	1853-01-06	FD	SWNW	R:JASPER
1203	"	"	27	NENE	1951-10-10	FD	NENE	R:CRAWFORD
1302	COX, Jesse	15	SESE	1853-09-15	FD	SESE	
1389	COX, Solomon	22	SWNW	1838-11-03	FD	SWNW	R:INDIANA
1388	"	"	22	NWSW	1838-11-03	FD	NWSW	R:INDIANA
1184	CRAMER, Alvin	21	W½NW	1852-11-13	FD	W2NW	
1264	CRAMER, Isaiah	19	SWNE	1847-05-13	FD	SWNE	R:JASPER
1263	"	"	19	SE	1847-05-13	FD	SE	R:JASPER
1265	"	"	20	NENE	1847-05-31	FD	NENE	R:JASPER
1266	"	"	20	SENW	1847-05-31	FD	SENW	R:JASPER
1268	"	"	21	E½NW	1847-05-31	FD	E2NW	R:JASPER
1267	"	"	20	SWNE	1847-05-31	FD	SWNE	R:JASPER
1324	CRAMER, John R	20	SESE	1853-02-08	FD	SESE	
1360	CRAMER, Peter Jr	8	E½SE	1840-12-08	FD	E2SE	R:OHIO
1370	CRAMER, Reuben N	30	SWNE	1851-10-11	FD	SWNE	R:JASPER
1369	"	"	21	SWSW	1853-01-12	FD	SWSW	
1394	CRAMER, Thomas	20	NESW	1853-12-05	FD	NESW	R:JASPER
1197	DAVIS, Benjamin	33	NWNW	1839-09-30	FD	NWNW	R:EDGAR
1339	DAVIS, Joshua	32	NESE	1839-09-30	FD	NESE	R:EDGAR
1390	DAVIS, Solomon	32	NE	1839-09-30	FD	NE	R:EDGAR
1376	DEBOW, Robert W	17	W½NW	1839-11-15	FD	W2NW	R:EDGAR
1377	"	"	18	E½SE	1839-12-27	FD	E2SE	R:JASPER
1189	DILLMON, Andrew	32	S½SE	1850-10-30	FD	S2SE	R:JASPER
1353	DORN, Nichodemus	22	E½SW	1848-11-27	FD	E2SW	
1354	"	"	22	W½SW	1848-11-27	FD	W2SW	
1234	DOWELL, George	16	L13	1850-11-16	SC	LOT13SWSW	
1235	"	"	29	SESW	1853-01-12	FD	SESW	
1371	DOWELL, Riley	16	L14	1850-11-16	SC	LOT14SESW	
1372	"	"	31	NENE	1850-11-18	FD	NENE	R:JASPER
1175	EATON, Absalom	28	W½SE	1840-04-06	FD	W2SE	R:JASPER
1331	EATON, Joseph	34	W½SE	1852-09-11	FD	W2SE	
1278	EMBODY, James	5	E½SE	1853-05-18	FD	E2SE	
1210	"	"	5	E½SE	1853-05-18	FD	E2SE	
1231	FARLEY, Forest	30	NWNE	1848-09-27	FD	NWNE	R:JASPER
1230	"	"	29	SWNW	1848-09-27	FD	SWNW	R:JASPER
1286	FARLEY, James M	17	SWSE	1847-11-11	FD	SWSE	R:JASPER
1287	"	"	18	SWSE	1848-09-27	FD	SWSE	R:JASPER
1279	FEARS, James	16	L10	1851-05-16	SC	LOT10NWSE	
1280	"	"	31	N½SE	1851-05-17	FD	N2SELS	R:INDIANA
1332	FEARS, Joseph	31	S½SE	1851-06-18	FD	S2SE	R:EDGAR
1421	FEARS, William	16	L9	1851-06-17	SC	LOT9NESE	
1312	FRANCIS, John	16	L5	1853-02-14	SC	LOT5SWNW	
1311	"	"	16	L15	1853-02-14	SC	LOT15SWSE	
1310	"	"	16	L12	1853-02-14	SC	L12NWSW	
1232	FRY, Frederick	18	NWNE	1839-10-15	FD	NWNE	R:INDIANA
1422	FULLER, William	8	NESW	1853-05-07	FD	NESW	
1423	GARRET, William	5	NW	1851-10-22	FD	NW	R:INDIANA
1237	GEDDES, George P	6	W½NW	1840-09-04	FD	W2NW	R:CLARK
1294	GEDDES, James R	6	W½NE	1840-09-04	FD	W2NE	R:CLARK
1213	GOSNELL, Daniel	19	NWNW	1848-08-24	FD	NWNW	R:JASPER
1246	GOSNELL, Greenberry	18	E½NE	1839-10-31	FD	E2NE	R:EDGAR
1247	"	"	18	SWNE	1839-10-31	FD	SWNE	R:EDGAR
1248	"	"	7	E½SE	1839-10-31	FD	E2SE	R:EDGAR
1245	"	"	17	NWNE	1840-12-28	FD	NWNE	R:JASPER
1340	GOSNELL, Joshua G	18	NWSE	1850-03-15	FD	NWSE	R:JASPER
1345	GRAVES, Lewis	19	E½NW	1840-06-18	FD	E2NW	R:KENTUCKY
1201	GULLION, Charles D	33	E½SW	1839-04-24	FD	E2SW	R:JASPER
1251	HAMPSTEN, Henry	15	NWNW	1845-11-15	FD	NWNW	R:JASPER
1252	"	"	9	SESE	1845-11-15	FD	SESE	R:JASPER
1206	HAMPSTON, Christian F	4	SESW	1850-06-12	FD	SESW	R:JASPER S:F

ID	Individual in Patent	Sec.	Sec. Part	Purchase Date	Sale Type	IL Aliquot Part	For More Info . . .
1179	HARRIS, Alderson	3	SENE	1852-08-06	FD	SENE	R:JASPER
1185	HARRIS, Amos	3	NESE	1845-03-25	FD	NESE	R:JASPER
1186	" "	3	SESW	1850-04-18	FD	SESW	R:JASPER
1403	HARRIS, Valentine	3	NENE	1851-05-08	FD	NENE	R:JASPER
1297	HELMICK, James W	22	NWNW	1853-10-06	FD	NWNW	R:INDIANA
1296	" "	21	N½NE	1853-10-06	FD	N2NE	R:INDIANA
1333	HETON, Joseph	27	N½NW	1851-05-31	FD	N2NW	
1304	HOLMES, John B	15	NESE	1853-08-20	FD	NESE	R:CLARK
1427	HOLT, William	8	NENE	1853-09-03	FD	NENE	R:OHIO
1202	HOUSE, Charles	22	SWSW	1851-07-14	FD	SWSW	R:JASPER
1381	HOWARD, Samuel	17	SENE	1852-03-29	FD	SENE	
1380	" "	17	NESE	1852-03-29	FD	NESE	
1174	HUDDLESTON, Abram S	5	SWSW	1850-07-01	FD	SWSW	R:JASPER
1298	HUSSONG, James W	31	SEN½	1851-05-17	FD	S2NE	R:INDIANA
1244	JARED, Granville	32	NWNW	1850-12-16	FD	NWNW	R:JASPER
1243	" "	28	NWSW	1853-02-15	FD	NWSW	R:JASPER
1269	JARED, Israel	32	SWNW	1851-11-15	FD	SWNW	R:JASPER
1303	JARED, Joel	28	SWSW	1853-01-19	FD	SWSW	
1428	JARED, William	32	NWSE	1849-11-10	FD	NWSE	R:JASPER
1270	JARRED, Israel	20	NESE	1853-11-21	FD	NESE	R:JASPER
1271	" "	21	NWSW	1853-11-21	FD	NWSW	R:JASPER
1220	JONES, David	15	NWSE	1851-10-04	FD	NWSE	R:CRAWFORD
1221	" "	21	NENE	1851-10-04	FD	NENE	R:CRAWFORD
1236	JORDON, George	34	SWNE	1851-04-12	FD	SWNE	R:CRAWFORD
1429	JORDON, William	34	NWNE	1851-04-28	FD	NWNE	R:JASPER
1457	KESTERSON, Willis	17	NENE	1852-03-29	FD	NENE	
1316	LAKE, John	33	SWNE	1854-10-17	FD	SWNE	R:JASPER
1283	LAMASTERS, James	22	NESE	1853-01-29	FD	NESE	
1284	" "	22	SENE	1853-01-29	FD	SENE	
1273	LAMB, Jacob	22	SESE	1853-01-26	FD	SESE	R:CRAWFORD
1199	LEAMON, Benjamin	3	NWSE	1850-04-18	FD	NWSE	R:JASPER
1200	" "	3	SWSE	1852-07-05	FD	SWSE	
1285	LEAMON, James	4	SWSE	1853-03-09	FD	SWSE	
1432	LEAMON, William	4		1849-04-30	FD	E2NWEC	R:CHAMPAIGN
1432	" "	4		1849-04-30	FD	NWNWEC	R:JASPER
1436	" "	5		1849-04-30	FD	NENEEC	R:JASPER
1439	" "	9	W½NE	1850-12-28	FD	W2NE	
1437	" "	9	NWSE	1850-12-28	FD	NWSE	
1438	" "	9	SENE	1850-12-28	FD	SENE	
1431	" "	3	NWNW	1851-04-03	FD	NWNW	
1430	" "	3		1851-06-30	FD	NWNWWA	R:CRAWFORD
1433	" "	4	NESW	1852-06-28	FD	NESW	
1434	" "	4	NWSE	1852-06-28	FD	NWSE	
1435	" "	4	W½SW	1852-06-28	FD	W2SW	
1441	LEMON, William	5	E½NE	1839-04-22	FD	E2NE	R:CLARK
1440	" "	4	W½NE	1840-08-29	FD	W2NE	R:CLARK
1195	LEVINGSTON, Andrew	22	NWNE	1849-10-08	FD	NWNE	R:OHIO
1194	" "	22	NENW	1851-10-16	FD	NENW	R:OHIO
1193	" "	22	NENE	1852-02-27	FD	NENE	R:OHIO
1192	LEVINGSTON, Andrew Jr	34	SWSW	1851-10-22	FD	SWSW	R:OHIO
1317	MACY, John	29	NENW	1841-08-20	FD	NENW	R:JASPER
1183	MALONE, Alfred	17	SENW	1854-09-27	FD	SENW	R:CRAWFORD
1182	" "	17	NENW	1854-10-03	FD	NENW	R:CRAWFORD
1442	MANLEY, William	20	NWNE	1851-07-25	FD	NWNE	
1443	MARTIN, William	17	SESE	1853-03-01	FD	SESE	R:JASPER
1258	MATHENY, Isaac	16	L4	1850-10-12	SC	LOT4NWNW	
1288	MATHENY, James P	10	SESW	1854-03-13	FD	SESW	R:JASPER
1318	MATHENY, John	16	L3	1850-10-12	SC	LOT3NENW	
1383	MAYSEY, Samuel	29	NWNW	1851-11-24	FD	NWNW	
1379	MAYSEY, Samuel B	30	E½NE	1843-07-06	FD	E2NE	R:JASPER
1378	" "	29	NWNE	1843-07-06	FD	NWNE	R:JASPER
1384	MAYSEY, Samuel R	29	NENE	1853-01-12	FD	NENE	
1385	" "	29	SWNE	1854-01-25	FD	SWNE	R:JASPER
1444	MCCABE, William	33	SWSW	1852-02-05	FD	SWSW	
1319	MCCAIN, John	31	SW	1849-06-13	FD	SW	R:OHIO
1375	MCCARTY, Robert	34	E½SE	1849-08-18	FD	E2SE	
1374	" "	34	E½NE	1849-08-18	FD	E2NE	
1320	MCCLAIN, John	31		1849-07-31	FD	SWWA	R:OHIO
1445	MCCOY, William	16	L6	1850-10-12	SC	LOT6SENW	
1464	MCCUBBIN, Zack H	19	NWSW	1849-08-23	FD	NWSW	R:JASPER
1272	MCCUBBINS, Jack H	21	SEN½	1854-01-04	FD	S2NE	R:JASPER G:19
1366	MCCUBBINS, Phebe	19	S½SW	1847-07-01	FD	S2SW	R:EDGAR S:F
1365	" "	17	SWNE	1851-12-23	FD	SWNE	R:JASPER S:F

ID	Individual in Patent	Sec.	Sec. Part	Purchase Date	Sale Type	IL Aliquot Part	For More Info . . .
1462	MCCUBBINS, Zach H	19	SWNW	1850-02-13	FD	SWNW	R:JASPER
1463	" "	30	S½NW	1850-06-25	FD	S2NW	R:JASPER
1465	MCCUBBINS, Zack H	16	L11	1850-10-12	SC	LOT11NESW	
1313	MCKEE, John H	10	NENE	1854-09-27	FD	NENE	R:CLARK
1225	MEAKER, Edward S	10	NESW	1853-12-26	FD	NESW	R:CUMBERLAND
1224	MEEKER, Edward	10	SWNW	1853-08-18	FD	SWNW	
1198	METHENY, Benjamin F	29	SESE	1854-10-17	FD	SESE	R:JASPER
1291	METHENY, James P	9	W½NW	1851-01-11	FD	W2NW	
1289	" "	9	NESW	1851-01-11	FD	NESW	
1290	" "	9	SENW	1851-01-11	FD	SENW	
1321	MIKWORTH, John	5	W½NE	1853-05-23	FD	W2NE	R:CRAWFORD
1173	MILLER, Aaron	29	SENE	1839-04-24	FD	SENE	R:JASPER
1172	" "	29	NESE	1839-04-24	FD	NESE	R:JASPER
1171	" "	28	E½SW	1840-04-06	FD	E2SW	R:JASPER
1254	MILLER, Henry	28	E½NW	1839-04-24	FD	E2NW	R:JASPER
1322	MILLER, John	17	SWNW	1851-11-17	FD	SWNW	R:CRAWFORD
1323	" "	34	SESW	1851-11-26	FD	SESW	R:JASPER
1315	MILLER, John Jr	29	SENW	1839-04-24	FD	SENW	R:JASPER
1314	" "	29	NESW	1839-04-24	FD	NESW	R:JASPER
1367	MOORMAN, Pleasant	28	E½NE	1851-12-13	FD	E2NE	S:A
1425	NEIBARGER, William H	17	E½SW	1852-11-30	FD	E2SW	
1426	" "	17	W½SW	1852-11-30	FD	W2SW	
1424	" "	16	L16	1852-12-28	SC	LOT16SESE	
1256	ODLE, Isaac L	18	NW	1839-11-15	FD	NW	R:EDGAR
1257	" "	8	W½SW	1839-11-15	FD	W2SW	R:EDGAR
1196	ORR, Anthony	8	W½NE	1845-12-01	FD	W2NE	R:JASPER
1176	OURY, Adam	15	SENW	1842-12-14	FD	SENW	R:JASPER
1177	" "	15	SWNW	1842-12-14	FD	SWNW	R:JASPER
1207	OURY, Christopher	15	NESW	1842-12-14	FD	NESW	R:JASPER
1178	OWRY, Adam	9	NENW	1850-08-26	FD	NENW	R:JASPER
1293	PARKER, James	28	W½NE	1854-09-13	FD	W2NE	
1292	" "	21	W½SE	1854-09-13	FD	W2SE	
1414	PARSONS, Willard L	4	SENE	1848-07-06	FD	SENE	R:CLARK
1446	PENHORWOOD, William	3	SESE	1853-09-01	FD	SESE	R:OHIO
1259	PERISHO, Isaac	6	E½NE	1840-09-09	FD	E2NE	R:EDGAR
1260	" "	6	E½NW	1840-09-09	FD	E2NW	R:EDGAR
1191	PRESTON, Andrew J	27	SE	1851-01-14	FD	SE	
1190	" "	21	E½SE	1852-09-15	FD	E2SE	
1211	PRESTON, Cyprian	5	SWSE	1851-10-29	FD	SWSE	
1210	" "	5	E½SE	1851-10-29	FD	E2SE	
1278	" "	5	E½SE	1851-10-29	FD	E2SE	
1238	PRESTON, George R	10	W½NE	1853-06-27	FD	W2NE	
1373	RHEA, Robert M	18	NESW	1852-02-27	FD	NESW	R:EDGAR
1215	ROBERTS, Daniel	6	NWSW	1839-12-07	FD	NWSW	R:CLARK
1216	" "	6	SWSW	1841-11-24	FD	SWSW	R:CLARK
1214	" "	6	NESE	1841-11-24	FD	NESE	R:CLARK
1325	ROBERTS, John	6	SESW	1842-08-24	FD	SESW	R:JASPER
1451	ROBERTS, William S	6	W½SE	1839-11-15	FD	W2SE	R:OHIO
1450	" "	6	NESW	1839-11-15	FD	NESW	R:OHIO
1336	ROBINSON, Joseph	4	E½NW	1839-10-03	FD	E2NW	R:CLARK
1452	" "	4	E½NW	1839-10-03	FD	E2NW	R:CLARK
1335	" "	3	E½NW	1840-09-29	FD	E2NW	R:CLARK
1449	ROBINSON, William	3	NWNE	1841-11-05	FD	NWNE	R:CLARK
1326	RYAN, John	8	W½NW	1852-09-06	FD	W2NW	
1336	SEAMON, William	4	E½NW	1849-03-19	FD	E2NW	
1453	" "	4	NWNW	1849-03-19	FD	NWNW	
1454	" "	5	NENE	1849-03-19	FD	NENE	
1452	" "	4	E½NW	1849-03-19	FD	E2NW	
1295	SHERER, James	20	W½SE	1841-04-21	FD	W2SE	R:VIRGINIA
1274	SHOOK, Jacob	15	NWNE	1842-12-14	FD	NWNE	R:JASPER
1352	SHORT, Nancy	9	W½SW	1851-10-28	FD	W2SW	S:F
1350	" "	9	SESW	1851-10-28	FD	SESW	S:F
1351	" "	9	SWSE	1851-10-28	FD	SWSE	S:F
1362	SHOWALTER, Peter	4	NESE	1840-11-02	FD	NESE	R:OHIO
1361	" "	3	W½SW	1840-11-02	FD	W2SW	R:OHIO
1355	SIMMS, Noah	33	S½NW	1854-10-06	FD	S2NW	R:CLARK
1455	SLAVEN, William	4	SWNW	1849-10-01	FD	SWNW	R:JASPER
1240	SNEARLEY, George	10	NWNW	1850-04-26	FD	NWNW	R:JASPER
1239	" "	10	NENW	1851-04-16	FD	NENW	R:JASPER
1241	SNEARLY, George	10	SENW	1853-03-04	FD	SENW	
1253	SNIDER, Henry Jr	33	SWSE	1853-02-14	FD	SWSE	
1281	STEEL, James H	27	SWSW	1853-12-16	FD	SWSW	R:CRAWFORD
1282	" "	34	NWNW	1853-12-16	FD	NWNW	R:CRAWFORD

ID	Individual in Patent	Sec.	Sec. Part	Purchase Date	Sale Type	IL Aliquot Part	For More Info . . .
1392	STEVENS, Stephen	18	SESW	1852-02-27	FD	SESW	R:JASPER
1222	STOVER, David	5	SENE	1851-12-25	FD	SENE	R:CLARK
1223	TEMPLE, David	22	SWNE	1853-02-25	FD	SWNE	
1395	TENNERY, Thomas	19	NESW	1846-08-24	FD	NESW	R:EDGAR
1458	TENNERY, Wilson S	19	E½NE	1840-09-02	FD	E2NE	R:EDGAR
1461	" "	20	NWNW	1840-09-02	FD	NWNW	R:EDGAR
1460	" "	20	NENW	1840-12-29	FD	NENW	R:EDGAR
1459	" "	19	NWNE	1847-07-27	FD	NWNE	R:JASPER
1386	THARP, Samuel	22	SENW	1851-03-25	FD	SENW	R:CRAWFORD
1346	TOLES, Lot B	27	NWSW	1854-10-14	FD	NWSW	R:CRAWFORD
1337	VANRANT, Joseph	30		1849-06-30	FD	N2NWWA	R:JASPER
1338	VANSANT, Joseph	30	N½NW	1849-05-22	FD	N2NW	R:JASPER
1364	WAPLES, Peter	8	SESW	1840-11-06	FD	SESW	R:OHIO
1363	" "	7	W½SW	1840-11-06	FD	W2SW	R:OHIO
1227	WHIGHT, Eva	33	NESE	1852-12-31	FD	NESE	R:RICHLAND S:F G:59
1448	" "	33	E½NE	1852-12-31	FD	E2NE	R:RICHLAND S:F G:59
1226	" "	33	E½NE	1852-12-31	FD	E2NE	R:RICHLAND S:F G:59
1229	" "	33	NESE	1852-12-31	FD	NESE	R:RICHLAND S:F G:59
1228	" "	33	E½NE	1852-12-31	FD	E2NE	R:RICHLAND S:F G:59
1227	WHIGHT, William R	33	NESE	1852-12-31	FD	NESE	R:RICHLAND S:F G:59
1226	" "	33	E½NE	1852-12-31	FD	E2NE	R:RICHLAND S:F G:59
1229	" "	33	NESE	1852-12-31	FD	NESE	R:RICHLAND S:F G:59
1448	" "	33	E½NE	1852-12-31	FD	E2NE	R:RICHLAND S:F G:59
1228	" "	33	E½NE	1852-12-31	FD	E2NE	R:RICHLAND S:F G:59
1229	WHITE, Eve	33	NESE	1852-12-11	FD	NESE	S:F
1448	" "	33	E½NE	1852-12-11	FD	E2NE	S:F
1226	" "	33	E½NE	1852-12-11	FD	E2NE	S:F
1228	" "	33	E½NE	1852-12-11	FD	E2NE	S:F
1227	" "	33	NESE	1852-12-11	FD	NESE	S:F
1368	WHITE, Providence	19		1850-03-31	FD	PTNWWA	R:INDIANA S:F
1448	WHITE, William R	33	E½NE	1852-12-11	FD	E2NEAC	
1226	" "	33	E½NE	1852-12-11	FD	E2NEAC	
1228	" "	33	E½NE	1852-12-11	FD	E2NEAC	
1447	" "	33		1852-12-11	FD	NESEAC	
1276	WHITEHURST, Jacob	8	W½SE	1840-08-24	FD	W2SE	R:JASPER
1277	" "	9	NENE	1841-04-23	FD	NENE	R:JASPER
1275	" "	4	SESE	1841-04-23	FD	SESE	R:JASPER
1329	WHITEHURST, John	7	SWSE	1839-10-29	FD	SWSE	R:CLARK
1328	" "	7	E½SW	1839-10-29	FD	E2SW	R:CLARK
1242	WILFONG, George	27	NESW	1849-11-30	FD	NESW	R:CLARK
1208	WILLIAMSON, Cornelius	7	NW	1839-11-15	FD	NW	R:CLARK
1209	" "	7	W½NE	1839-11-15	FD	W2NE	R:CLARK
1397	WISEMORE, Thomas	32	SW	1845-02-28	FD	SW	R:EDGAR
1398	" "	34	NENW	1845-07-17	FD	NENW	R:EDGAR
1396	" "	27	SESW	1845-07-17	FD	SESW	R:EDGAR
1233	WOOD, George B	15	NENE	1847-05-13	FD	NENE	R:CLARK
1356	WOOD, Noble W	10	SE	1850-11-29	FD	SE	
1262	WRIGHT, Isaac	9	NESE	1845-03-25	FD	NESE	R:JASPER
1261	" "	10	SWSW	1851-07-15	FD	SWSW	R:JASPER
1330	WRIGHT, Jonathan	8	SENE	1849-11-03	FD	SENE	R:JASPER
1456	WRIGHT, William	10	NWSW	1850-04-24	FD	NWSW	R:JASPER
1399	YOUNG, Thompson G	3	SWNE	1848-12-04	FD	SWNE	R:INDIANA

Patent Map

T8-N R14-W
2nd PM Meridian

Map Group 5

Township Statistics

Parcels Mapped	:	298
Number of Patents	:	1
Number of Individuals	:	186
Patentees Identified	:	184
Number of Surnames	:	126
Multi-Patentee Parcels	:	3
Oldest Patent Date	:	11/3/1838
Most Recent Patent	:	10/10/1951
Block/Lot Parcels	:	16
Cities and Towns	:	1
Cemeteries	:	5

Section 6
GEDDES George P 1840
PERISHO Isaac 1840
GEDDES James R 1840
PERISHO Isaac 1840
ROBERTS Daniel 1839
ROBERTS William S 1839
ROBERTS William S 1839
ROBERTS Daniel 1841
ROBERTS Daniel 1841
ROBERTS John 1842
ADAMSON Zedekiah 1853

Section 5
GARRET William 1851
MIKWORTH John 1853
SEAMON William 1849
LEMON William 1849
LEMON William 1839
STOVER David 1851
ADAMS Timothy R B 1849
PRESTON Cyprian 1851
HUDDLESTON Abram S 1850
ADAMS Timothy R B 1849
PRESTON Cyprian 1851
EMBODY James 1853

Section 4
SEAMON William 1849
ROBINSON Joseph 1839
LEAMON William 1849
SLAVEN William 1849
ADAMS Jeremiah 1851
PARSONS Willard L 1848
LEMON William 1840
LEAMON William 1852
LEAMON William 1852
SHOWALTER Peter 1840
LEAMON William 1852
HAMPSTON Christian F 1850
LEAMON James 1853
WHITEHURST Jacob 1841

Section 7
WILLIAMSON Cornelius 1839
WILLIAMSON Cornelius 1839
ADAMSON Zedakiah 1850
ADAMSON Zedekiah 1852
WAPLES Peter 1840
WHITEHURST John 1839
BUSSELL John 1841
WHITEHURST John 1839

Section 8
RYAN John 1852
ADAMS Timothy R B 1849
BUSSELL John 1841
ORR Anthony 1845
GOSNELL Greenberry 1839
FULLER William 1853
ODLE Isaac L 1839
WAPLES Peter 1840
WHITEHURST Jacob 1840
HOLT William 1853
WRIGHT Jonathan 1849
CRAMER Peter Jr 1840

Section 9
METHENY James P 1851
OWRY Adam 1850
LEAMON William 1850
METHENY James P 1851
SHORT Nancy 1851
METHENY James P 1851
LEAMON William 1850
SHORT Nancy 1851
SHORT Nancy 1851
WHITEHURST Jacob 1841
LEAMON William 1850
WRIGHT Isaac 1845
HAMPSTEN Henry 1845

Section 18
ODLE Isaac L 1839
FRY Frederick 1839
GOSNELL Greenberry 1839
GOSNELL Greenberry 1839
COHOON Stephen 1840
RHEA Robert M 1852
GOSNELL Joshua G 1850
STEVENS Stephen 1852
FARLEY James M 1848

Section 17
DEBOW Robert W 1839
MALONE Alfred 1854
MILLER John 1851
MALONE Alfred 1854
DEBOW Robert W 1839
NEIBARGER William H 1852
NEIBARGER William H 1852
GOSNELL Greenberry 1840
MCCUBBINS Phebe 1851
ARCHER John W 1847
FARLEY James M 1847
KESTERSON Willis 1852
HOWARD Samuel 1852
HOWARD Samuel 1852
MARTIN William 1853

Section 16 — Lots-Sec. 16
L1 AMES, Leonard 1850
L2 AMES, Leonard 1850
L3 MATHENY, John 1850
L4 MATHENY, Isaac 1850
L5 FRANCIS, John 1853
L6 MCCOY, William 1850
L7 AMES, Leonard 1850
L8 AMES, Leonard 1850
L9 FEARS, William 1851
L10 FEARS, James 1851
L11 MCCUBBINS, Zack H 1850
L12 FRANCIS, John 1853
L13 DOWELL, George 1850
DOWELL, Riley 1853
FRANCIS, John 1853
NEIBARGER, William H 1852
L14 L15 L16

Section 19
GOSNELL Daniel 1848
TENNERY Wilson S 1847
TENNERY Wilson S 1840
GRAVES Lewis 1840
CRAMER Isaiah 1847
MCCUBBIN Zack H 1850
WHITE Providence 1850
MCCUBBIN Zack H 1849
TENNERY Thomas 1846
MCCUBBINS Phebe 1847
CRAMER Isaiah 1847

Section 20
TENNERY Wilson S 1840
TENNERY Wilson S 1840
MANLEY William 1851
ARCHER John C 1843
CRAMER Isaiah 1847
CRAMER Isaiah 1847
ARCHER John C 1843
CRAMER Thomas 1853
ARCHER John C 1843
SHERER James 1841
ARCHER Daniel E 1852

Section 21
CRAMER Isaiah 1847
CRAMER Alvin 1852
CRAMER Isaiah 1847
HELMICK James W 1853
JONES David 1851
MCCUBBINS [19] Jack H 1854
JARRED Israel 1853
JARRED Israel 1853
CRAMER Reuben N 1853
ALLISON David 1845
CLEMANS Hamilton J 1845
JARRED Israel 1853
CRAMER John R 1853
PARKER James 1854
PRESTON Andrew J 1852

Section 30
VANSANT Joseph 1849
VANRANT Joseph 1849
FARLEY Forest 1848
MCCUBBINS Zach H 1850
CRAMER Reuben N 1851
ADKINSON Alexander 1851
ADKINSON Alexander 1851
CLEMONS Warden 1848
CLEMONS Warden 1851
CLEMONS Warden 1849
CLEMONS Warden 1850

Section 29
MAYSEY Samuel B 1843
MAYSEY Samuel 1851
FARLEY Forest 1848
MILLER John Jr 1839
MACY John 1841
MILLER John Jr 1839
MAYSEY Samuel B 1843
MAYSEY Samuel R 1854
MAYSEY Samuel R 1853
MILLER Aaron 1839
CLEMMONS Warden 1843
CLEMMONS Warden 1843
ALLISON David 1845
MILLER John Jr 1839
DOWELL George 1853
MILLER Aaron 1839
CLEMENTS Owzzy 1839
METHENY Benjamin F 1854

Section 28
CLEMENS Walden 1845
MILLER Henry 1839
MILLER Aaron 1840
JARED Granville 1853
JARED Joel 1853
PARKER James 1854
EATON Absalom 1840
MOORMAN Pleasant 1851
BAILEY Samuel Jr 1851

Section 31
CLARK Henry 1851
CLEMONS Warden 1851
CLEMONS Warden 1851
DOWELL Riley 1850
CLEMONS Warden 1852
HUSSONG James W 1851
MCCAIN John 1849
FEARS James 1851
MCCLAIN John 1849
FEARS Joseph 1851

Section 32
JARED Granville 1850
JARED Israel 1851
CLEMENTS Owzzy 1839
CLEMENTS Owzzy 1839
JARED William 1849
WISEMORE Thomas 1845
DAVIS Solomon 1839
DAVIS Joshua 1839
DILLMON Andrew 1850

Section 33
DAVIS Benjamin 1839
SIMMS Noah 1854
CLEMENTS Oyzy 1843
ALLISON David 1840
LAKE John 1854
BAILEY Loyd Jr 1852
MCCABE William 1852
GULLION Charles D 1839
ALLENTHARP Joseph P 1854
SNIDER Henry Jr 1853
WHITE Eve 1852
WHITE William R 1852
WHIGHT [59] Eva 1852
WHITE William R 1852
WHITE Eve 1852
WHIGHT [59] Eva 1852
BAILEY Sudwell 1853

LEAMON William / LEAMON 1851 William 1851	ROBINSON Joseph 1840	ROBINSON William 1841	HARRIS Valentine 1851	
ADAMS Jeremiah 1851		YOUNG Thompson G 1848	HARRIS Alderson 1852	2
SHOWALTER Peter 1840	ADAMS Jeremiah 1851 3	LEAMON Benjamin 1850	HARRIS Amos 1845	
	HARRIS Amos 1850	LEAMON Benjamin 1852	PENHORWOO William 1853	

2   **1**

Jasper   *Crawford*

SNEARLEY George 1850	SNEARLEY George 1851	PRESTON George R 1853	MCKEE John H 1854
MEEKER Edward 1853	SNEARLY George 1853 10		BATES Lubin 1852
WRIGHT William 1850	MEAKER Edward S 1853	WOOD Noble W 1850	
WRIGHT Isaac 1851	MATHENY James P 1854		

11   **12**

HAMPSTEN Henry 1845	BOWMAN Michael 1854	SHOOK Jacob 1842	WOOD George B 1847
OURY Adam 1842	OURY Adam 1842 15	BOWMAN William B 1854	BOWMAN William B 1854
BOWMAN William B 1854	OURY Christopher 1842	JONES David 1851	HOLMES John B 1853
	BOWMAN William B 1854	BOWMAN William B 1854	COX Jesse 1853

14   **13**

HELMICK James W 1853	LEVINGSTON Andrew 1851	LEVINGSTON Andrew 1849	LEVINGSTON Andrew 1852
COX Solomon 1838	THARP Samuel 1851 22	TEMPLE David 1853	LAMASTERS James 1853
COX Solomon 1838	DORN Nichodemus 1848		LAMASTERS James 1853
DORN Nichodemus HOUSE 1848 Charles 1851			LAMB Jacob 1853

23   **24**

	HETON Joseph 1851	ALLISON Andrew 1851	COOPER Chrisley 1951
COOPER Chrisley 1853	COOPER Chrisley 1851 27		ALLISON Andrew 1851
TOLES Lot B 1854	WILFONG George 1849	PRESTON Andrew J 1851	
STEEL James H 1853	WISEMORE Thomas 1845		

26   **25**

STEEL James H 1853	WISEMORE Thomas 1845	JORDON William 1851	MCCARTY Robert 1849
ALLISON Sarah 1851	BARLOW William 1851	JORDON George 1851 34	
CALDWELL Hugh 1851		EATON Joseph 1852	MCCARTY Robert 1849
LEVINGSTON Andrew Jr 1851	MILLER John 1851		

35   **36**

Legend

————————	Patent Boundary
▬▬▬▬▬▬	Section Boundary
	No Patents Found (or Outside County)
1., 2., 3., ...	Lot Numbers (when beside a name)
[ ]	Group Number (see Appendix "C")

Scale: Section = 1 mile X 1 mile (generally, with some exceptions)

Road Map

T8-N R14-W
2nd PM Meridian

Map Group 5

Cities & Towns
Yale

Cemeteries
Backbone Cemetery
Bethel Cemetery
Debord Cemetery
Leamon Cemetery
McFadden Cemetery

Leamon
Cem.

N 2175th St

6

Debord
Cem.

5

E 2150th Ave

4

N 2000th St

E 2100th Ave

E 2050th Av.

7

8

9

E 2000th Ave

McFadden
Cem.

18

17

N 2100th St

16

E 1900th Ave

1890th Ave

W Main St

19

E 1850th Ave

20

21

Yale

Range St

E 1800th Ave

E Co Hwy 6

N 1900th St

30

29

28

Bethel Cem.

E 1700 Ave

N 2000th St

31

32

33

E 1600th Ave

3

2

1

N 2200th St

10

Backbone
Cem.

11

12

Crawford County

15

14

13

22

23

24

Jasper County

27

26

25

N 2200th St

34

35

36

Helpful Hints

1. This road map has a number of uses, but primarily it is to help you: a) find the present location of land owned by your ancestors (at least the general area), b) find cemeteries and city-centers, and c) estimate the route/roads used by Census-takers & tax-assessors.

2. If you plan to travel to Jasper County to locate cemeteries or land parcels, please pick up a modern travel map for the area before you do. Mapping old land parcels on modern maps is not as exact a science as you might think. Just the slightest variations in public land survey coordinates, estimates of parcel boundaries, or road-map deviations can greatly alter a map's representation of how a road either does or doesn't cross a particular parcel of land.

Legend

————————	Section Lines
════════════	Interstates
————————	Highways
————————	Other Roads
●	Cities/Towns
✝	Cemeteries

Scale: Section = 1 mile X 1 mile
(generally, with some exceptions)

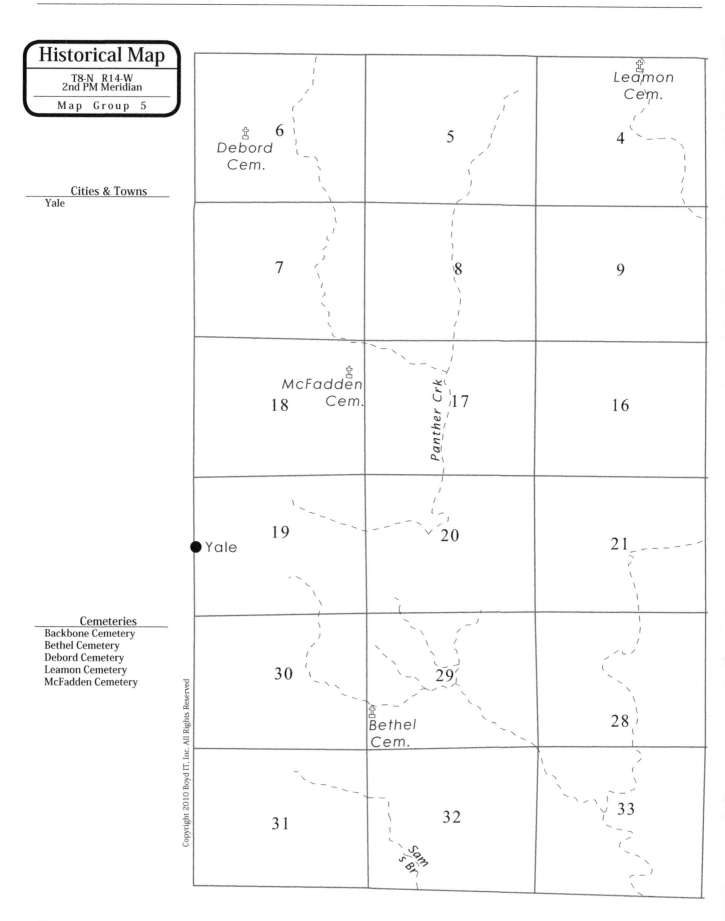

Historical Map

T8-N R14-W
2nd PM Meridian

Map Group 5

Cities & Towns
Yale

Cemeteries
Backbone Cemetery
Bethel Cemetery
Debord Cemetery
Leamon Cemetery
McFadden Cemetery

Copyright 2010 Boyd IT, Inc. All Rights Reserved

| 3 | 2 | 1 |

Helpful Hints

1. This Map takes a different look at the same Congressional Township displayed in the preceding two maps. It presents features that can help you better envision the historical development of the area: a) Water-bodies (lakes & ponds), b) Water-courses (rivers, streams, etc.), c) Railroads, d) City/ town center-points (where they were oftentimes located when first settled), and e) Cemeteries.

2. Using this "Historical" map in tandem with this Township's Patent Map and Road Map, may lead you to some interesting discoveries. You will often find roads, towns, cemeteries, and waterways are named after nearby landowners: sometimes those names will be the ones you are researching. See how many of these research gems you can find here in Jasper County.

✝
Backbone
Cem.

| 10 | 11 | 12 |

| 15 | 14 | 13 |

North Fork
Embarras Riv

| 22 | 23 | 24 |

Jasper Crawford

| 27 | 26 | 25 |

No Business Crk

| 34 | 35 | 36 |

Legend

———————	Section Lines
+++++++	Railroads
☐	Large Rivers & Bodies of Water
- - - - - - -	Streams/Creeks & Small Rivers
●	Cities/Towns
✝	Cemeteries

Scale: Section = 1 mile X 1 mile
(there are some exceptions)

115

Map Group 6: Index to Land Patents

Township 7-North Range 8-East (3rd PM)

After you locate an individual in this Index, take note of the Section and Section Part then proceed to the Land Patent map on the pages immediately following. You should have no difficulty locating the corresponding parcel of land.

The "For More Info" Column will lead you to more information about the underlying Patents. See the *Legend* at right, and the "How to Use this Book" chapter, for more information.

```
                    LEGEND
         "For More Info . . ." column
G = Group   (Multi-Patentee Patent, see Appendix "C")
R = Residence
S = Social Status

See Appendix A for list of abbreviations used by the
Illinois State Archives in describing the place and
nature of these land patents.

Note: if the Abbreviations contain "L", "BL", "LOT",
or "BLOCK", the exact whereabouts of the parcel within
the section is not known.
```

ID	Individual in Patent	Sec.	Sec. Part	Purchase Date	Sale Type	IL Aliquot Part	For More Info . . .
1691	ABELS, Martin D	28	E½SW	1864-12-26	RR	E2SW	
1636	ALEXANDER, Joshua H	15	SE	1853-02-28	FD	SE	G:1
1648	"	"	9	SE	1853-02-28	FD	SE	G:1
1638	"	"	17	S½SE	1853-02-28	FD	S2SE	G:1
1637	"	"	15	SW	1853-02-28	FD	SW	G:1
1647	"	"	9	NE	1853-02-28	FD	NE	G:1
1639	"	"	17	S½SW	1853-02-28	FD	S2SW	G:1
1640	"	"	23	NE	1853-02-28	FD	NE	G:1
1626	"	"	11	NE	1853-02-28	FD	NE	G:1
1641	"	"	23	NW	1853-02-28	FD	NW	G:1
1629	"	"	13	SWNW	1853-03-03	FD	SWNW	G:1
1644	"	"	24	NW	1853-03-03	FD	NW	G:1
1635	"	"	14	W½NE	1853-03-03	FD	W2NE	G:1
1643	"	"	23	SW	1853-03-03	FD	SW	G:1
1642	"	"	23	SE	1853-03-03	FD	SE	G:1
1633	"	"	14	SENE	1853-03-03	FD	SENE	G:1
1507	"	"	3	L2	1853-03-03	FD	LOT2NW	G:2
1627	"	"	11	NW	1853-03-03	FD	NW	G:1
1628	"	"	11	SW	1853-03-03	FD	SW	G:1
1630	"	"	13	W½SW	1853-03-03	FD	W2SW	G:1
1687	"	"	13	SESW	1853-03-03	FD	SESW	G:4
1499	"	"	3	L2 (W½)	1853-03-03	FD	W2LOT2NE	G:3
1508	"	"	3	L2 (W½)	1853-03-03	FD	W2LOT2NE	G:3
1634	"	"	14	SW	1853-03-03	FD	SW	G:1
1506	"	"	3	L1 (E½)	1853-03-03	FD	E2LOT1NE	G:2
1631	"	"	14	NW	1853-03-03	FD	NW	G:1
1646	"	"	26	NW	1853-03-03	FD	NW	G:1
1632	"	"	14	SE	1853-03-03	FD	SE	G:1
1688	"	"	13	SWSE	1853-03-03	FD	SWSE	G:4
1500	"	"	11	W½SE	1853-03-03	FD	W2SE	G:2
1501	"	"	15	NE	1853-03-03	FD	NE	G:2
1502	"	"	15	NW	1853-03-03	FD	NW	G:2
1503	"	"	3	NESE	1853-03-03	FD	NESE	G:2
1504	"	"	3	S½SE	1853-03-03	FD	S2SE	G:2
1505	"	"	3	S½SW	1853-03-03	FD	S2SW	G:2
1645	"	"	24	SW	1853-03-03	FD	SW	G:1
1591	ANDERSON, Jacob	21	W½SE	1839-07-23	FD	W2SE	R:FAYETTE G:6
1618	ANDERSON, John	33	NWSE	1839-08-08	FD	NWSE	R:JASPER
1697	ARMSTRONG, Melvin	8	W½NW	1871-03-31	RR	W2NW	
1551	ARNOLD, Fletcher	5	NWSE	1853-01-15	FD	NWSE	
1637	AVERY, John H	15	SW	1853-02-28	FD	SW	G:1
1636	"	"	15	SE	1853-02-28	FD	SE	G:1
1626	"	"	11	NE	1853-02-28	FD	NE	G:1
1625	"	"	15	N½NW	1853-02-28	FD	N2NW	
1624	"	"	15	N½NE	1853-02-28	FD	N2NE	
1638	"	"	17	S½SE	1853-02-28	FD	S2SE	G:1

ID	Individual in Patent	Sec.	Sec. Part	Purchase Date	Sale Type	IL Aliquot Part	For More Info . . .
1639	AVERY, John H (Cont'd)	17	S½SW	1853-02-28	FD	S2SW	G:1
1640	" "	23	NE	1853-02-28	FD	NE	G:1
1641	" "	23	NW	1853-02-28	FD	NW	G:1
1647	" "	9	NE	1853-02-28	FD	NE	G:1
1648	" "	9	SE	1853-02-28	FD	SE	G:1
1643	" "	23	SW	1853-03-03	FD	SW	G:1
1644	" "	24	NW	1853-03-03	FD	NW	G:1
1645	" "	24	SW	1853-03-03	FD	SW	G:1
1635	" "	14	W½NE	1853-03-03	FD	W2NE	G:1
1646	" "	26	NW	1853-03-03	FD	NW	G:1
1634	" "	14	SW	1853-03-03	FD	SW	G:1
1642	" "	23	SE	1853-03-03	FD	SE	G:1
1632	" "	14	SE	1853-03-03	FD	SE	G:1
1631	" "	14	NW	1853-03-03	FD	NW	G:1
1630	" "	13	W½SW	1853-03-03	FD	W2SW	G:1
1628	" "	11	SW	1853-03-03	FD	SW	G:1
1627	" "	11	NW	1853-03-03	FD	NW	G:1
1629	" "	13	SWNW	1853-03-03	FD	SWNW	G:1
1633	" "	14	SENE	1853-03-03	FD	SENE	G:1
1536	BARBER, Elam	5	W½NE	1852-09-20	FD	W2NE	
1748	BARLOW, William H	6	N½NE	1883-05-12	RR	N2NE	
1731	BARTELLS, Sophia	8	SENW	1877-08-29	RR	SENW	S:F
1483	BATMAN, Alexander B	12	SESW	1850-03-12	FD	SESW	R:JASPER
1657	BENFORD, John M	21	E½SW	1853-01-05	FD	E2SW	
1756	BERRY, Wyatt L	27	W½SW	1853-10-20	FD	W2SW	R:FAYETTE
1760	BERRY, Wyatt S	31	L2	1853-02-01	FD	LOT2SE	
1759	" "	31	L1	1853-02-01	FD	S2LOT1SE	
1761	" "	33	W½NE	1853-03-17	FD	W2NE	
1762	" "	36	E½SW	1853-03-17	FD	E2SW	
1763	" "	7	N½	1853-06-01	FD	N2	
1757	" "	21	NENE	1853-12-05	FD	NENE	R:FAYETTE
1758	" "	21	SESE	1853-12-05	FD	SESE	R:FAYETTE
1607	BLAKE, Jefferson	27	SESW	1853-04-11	FD	SESW	R:JASPER
1517	BOSTER, Claindo	32	NWNE	1876-03-07	RR	NWNE	
1530	BRIDGES, Edmund R	13	E½SE	1853-01-05	FD	E2SE	
1531	" "	13	SENE	1853-01-15	FD	SENE	
1658	BRIDGES, John M	24	NENE	1853-07-21	FD	NENE	R:JASPER
1527	BROWN, David L	1	L2(W½)	1852-09-09	FD	W2LOT2NW	
1526	" "	1	L1(W½)	1852-09-09	FD	W2LOT1NW	
1723	" "	1	L1(W½)	1852-09-09	FD	W2LOT1NW	
1525	" "	1	N½SW	1852-09-09	FD	N2SW	
1524	BUHLER, David	28	NWSW	1886-02-18	RR	NWSW	
1659	BUHLER, John M	30	NWSE	1874-07-16	RR	NWSEFR	
1619	BURFORD, John	16	L25	1854-09-15	SC	LOT25LI5SWSE	
1620	" "	16	L26	1854-09-15	SC	LOT26LI5SWSE	
1606	BURNHAM, Jasper N	2	SENE	1876-12-28	RR	SENE	
1596	CALDWELL, Abbert G	5	L1(E½)	1852-09-09	FD	E2LOT1NE	
1470	" "	5	L1(E½)	1852-09-09	FD	E2LOT1NE	
1482	CALDWELL, Albert S	4	NWNE	1865-02-22	RR	NWNE	
1621	CAROTHERS, John	34	W½SW	1852-12-08	FD	W2SW	
1571	CASJENS, Harm E	32	SWNW	1864-07-22	RR	SWNW	
1570	CLARK, Grandison	11	E½SE	1853-03-14	FD	E2SE	
1741	CLARK, William	13	NWNW	1853-01-22	FD	NWNW	
1742	" "	14	NENE	1853-01-22	FD	NENE	
1743	CORRIGAM, William	22	N½NW	1860-09-10	RR	N2NW	
1744	CORRIGAN, William	22	NWSW	1864-06-22	RR	NWSW	
1745	" "	22	SWSW	1864-06-22	RR	SWSW	
1599	CREWS, James L	28	SWNE	1869-05-31	RR	SWNE	
1719	" "	28	SWNE	1869-05-31	RR	SWNE	
1598	" "	28	E½SE	1869-12-31	RR	E2SE	
1601	" "	6	N½SE	1873-02-28	RR	N2SEFR	
1600	" "	4	E½SE	1874-06-05	RR	E2SE	
1622	CULNANE, John	4	E½SW	1870-09-30	RR	E2SW	
1562	CUMMING, George	16	L9	1854-09-15	SC	LOT9NESE	
1561	" "	16	L10	1854-09-15	SC	LOT10NWSE	
1686	DABBINS, Joshua	16	L1	1854-10-19	SC	LOT01NENE	
1746	DECKER, William	13	NENW	1850-03-30	FD	NENW	
1747	" "	13	NWNE	1850-03-30	FD	NWNE	
1677	DELOTT, Jonah F	16	L16	1854-09-15	SC	LOT16SESE	G:26
1676	" "	16	L15	1854-09-15	SC	LOT15SWSE	G:26
1677	DELOTT, Nancy Jane	16	L16	1854-09-15	SC	LOT16SESE	G:26
1676	" "	16	L15	1854-09-15	SC	LOT15SWSE	G:26
1594	DOBBINS, Jacob H	34	E½SW	1853-01-05	FD	E2SW	

117

ID	Individual in Patent	Sec.	Sec. Part	Purchase Date	Sale Type	IL Aliquot Part	For More Info . . .
1592	DOERR, Jacob	22	N½SE	1874-01-31	RR	N2SE	
1512	EBALING, Christian	20	SWSW	1876-12-26	RR	SWSW	S:A
1519	EBALING, Coonrad	20	SESE	1873-01-31	RR	SESE	
1518	EBELING, Conrad	20	SENE	1883-06-05	RR	SENE	
1573	EILERS, Helene	32	NWSW	1886-10-25	RR	NWSW	S:F
1574	" "	32	NWSW	1886-10-25	RR	NWSW	S:F
1574	" "	32	NWSW	1887-08-03	RR	NWSW	S:F
1573	" "	32	NWSW	1887-08-03	RR	NWSW	S:F
1520	ELSON, Corneluis J	13	NENE	1849-10-29	FD	NENE	R:JASPER
1705	ELSON, Moses	12	SENW	1849-10-02	FD	SENW	
1706	" "	12	W½SW	1849-10-02	FD	W2SW	
1704	" "	12	NESW	1849-10-02	FD	NESW	
1709	FICKLIN, Orlando B	19	SESE	1853-02-08	FD	SESE	
1711	" "	29	W½NW	1853-03-07	FD	W2NW	
1710	" "	29	SENW	1853-03-11	FD	SENW	
1565	FITHIAN, George W	2	NESE	1881-05-07	RR	NESE	
1568	FITHIAN, Glover	1	E½NE	1849-11-26	FD	E2NE	
1569	" "	1	NWNE	1849-11-26	FD	NWNE	
1514	FOGLER, Christian	33	SENW	1853-02-09	FD	SENW	R:INDIANA S:A
1513	" "	33	N½SW	1853-02-09	FD	N2SW	R:INDIANA
1498	FOUST, Benjamin	25	NE	1853-06-24	FD	NE	G:29
1498	FOUST, Charles	25	NE	1853-06-24	FD	NE	G:29
1593	FOUST, Jacob	25	E½NW	1853-06-23	FD	E2NW	
1563	GOULD, George E	8	NWSW	1873-09-10	RR	NWSW	
1499	GREELY, Carlos	3	L2 (W½)	1852-03-03	FD	W2LOT2NE	
1508	" "	3	L2 (W½)	1852-03-03	FD	W2LOT2NE	
1504	GREELY, Carlos S	3	S½SE	1853-03-03	FD	S2SE	G:2
1506	" "	3	L1 (E½)	1853-03-03	FD	E2LOT1NE	G:2
1503	" "	3	NESE	1853-03-03	FD	NESE	G:2
1502	" "	15	NW	1853-03-03	FD	NW	G:2
1507	" "	3	L2	1853-03-03	FD	LOT2NW	G:2
1500	" "	11	W½SE	1853-03-03	FD	W2SE	G:2
1505	" "	3	S½SW	1853-03-03	FD	S2SW	G:2
1501	" "	15	NE	1853-03-03	FD	NE	G:2
1535	GROOTHINS, Eildert	30	SWNE	1881-12-23	RR	SWNE	
1609	GROVE, Jesse	16	L7	1856-03-03	SC	LOT07SWNE	
1660	" "	16	L7	1856-03-03	SC	LOT07SWNE	
1508	GRRELY, Carlos S	3	L2 (W½)	1853-03-03	FD	W2LOT2NE	G:3
1499	" "	3	L2 (W½)	1853-03-03	FD	W2LOT2NE	G:3
1692	HANNEMANN, Martin	22	NE	1870-11-30	RR	NE	
1693	" "	32	NENW	1870-11-30	RR	NENW	
1602	HARLAND, James M	29	SESE	1853-02-17	FD	SESE	
1485	HARTING, Alexander	20	NWSW	1863-11-23	RR	NWSW	
1484	" "	20	NESE	1865-02-22	RR	NESE	
1740	HAYES, William C	21	SENE	1853-01-15	FD	SENE	
1739	" "	21	NESE	1853-01-15	FD	NESE	
1604	HENDERSON, James S	10	SESE	1874-12-17	RR	SESE	
1603	" "	10	NESE	1876-06-07	RR	NESE	
1511	HILDERBRAND, Christ	30	NESE	1884-06-04	RR	NESE	
1564	HOARE, George E	21	NWNE	1853-06-22	FD	NWNE	
1474	HOLLOM, Adam	33	W½NW	1853-08-01	FD	W2NW	R:JASPER
1481	HOLM, Adam	33	NENW	1852-12-10	FD	NENW	
1477	" "	29	NESE	1853-01-05	FD	NESE	
1478	" "	29	W½SE	1853-01-26	FD	W2SE	
1476	" "	16	L28	1854-09-15	SC	LOT28LISWSE	
1475	" "	16	L21	1854-09-15	SC	LOT21LISWSE	
1479	" "	32	NENE	1865-02-22	RR	NENE	
1480	" "	32	SENE	1865-04-22	RR	SENE	
1549	HUNT, Eri	27	N½NE	1853-04-01	FD	N2NE	
1550	" "	27	SEN½	1853-04-01	FD	S2NE	
1718	INGLE, Renney	16	L14	1854-09-15	SC	LOT14SESW	
1587	" "	16	L14	1854-09-15	SC	LOT14SESW	
1752	INGLE, Renney C	16	L13	1854-09-15	SC	LOT13SWSW	
1716	" "	16	L11	1854-09-15	SC	LOT11NESW	
1717	" "	16	L13	1854-09-15	SC	LOT13SWSW	
1651	JACKSON, John	26	SE	1853-07-27	FD	SE	
1649	" "	25	SE	1853-07-27	FD	SE	
1650	" "	25	SW	1853-07-27	FD	SW	
1653	" "	35	NW	1853-07-27	FD	NW	R:OHIO
1654	" "	36	NE	1853-07-27	FD	NE	
1655	" "	36	NW	1853-07-27	FD	NW	
1652	" "	27	SWSE	1853-08-08	FD	SWSE	
1656	" "	36	SE	1853-08-08	FD	SE	

ID	Individual in Patent	Sec.	Sec. Part	Purchase Date	Sale Type	IL Aliquot Part	For More Info . . .
1718	JARED, Israel	16	L14	1854-03-01	SC	LOT14LISWSE	
1588	" "	16	L22	1854-03-01	SC	LOT22LISWSE	
1587	" "	16	L14	1854-03-01	SC	LOT14LISWSE	
1486	JOHNSTON, Alexander	25	W½NW	1853-07-12	FD	W2NW	
1487	"	26	NE	1853-08-08	FD	NE	
1544	JOURDAN, Elizabeth	21	SWNE	1851-09-26	FD	SWNE	R:JASPER S:F
1543	"	21	SENW	1851-09-26	FD	SENW	R:JASPER S:F
1548	KECK, Enoch	10	N½NE	1871-08-31	RR	N2NE	G:40
1548	KECK, Frederick	10	N½NE	1871-08-31	RR	N2NE	G:40
1579	KEENE, Henry L	8	NENW	1873-08-30	RR	NENW	
1733	KEENE, Sumner	8	NWNE	1873-07-31	RR	NWNE	
1751	KENEIPP, William M	32	NWNW	1887-02-25	RR	NWNW	
1493	KOONTZ, Andrew J	2	NENW	1868-04-30	RR	NENW	
1494	" "	2	NWNW	1868-04-30	RR	NWNW	
1515	KRAASS, Christopher	31	NE	1853-02-09	FD	NE	
1473	LAMBERT, Abraham	4	SWSW	1872-11-30	RR	SWSW	
1715	LEATH, Reason	20	W½NE	1851-09-16	FD	W2NE	R:JASPER
1720	LEATH, Samuel	20	NENW	1851-09-16	FD	NENW	R:JASPER
1576	LETURRO, Henry F	10	SEN½	1874-08-27	RR	S2NE	
1584	LEWIS, Howel	9	SW	1853-10-27	FD	SW	R:JASPER
1582	" "	17	N½SE	1853-10-28	FD	N2SE	R:JASPER
1583	" "	17	NE	1853-10-28	FD	NE	R:JASPER
1572	LOVE, Harvey N	28	NENE	1864-09-22	RR	NENE	
1680	LUSTIG, Joseph	8	SWSW	1886-01-25	RR	SWSW	
1725	LUX, Sebastian	2	NWSE	1874-06-03	RR	NWSE	
1728	" "	2	SWNE	1874-06-03	RR	SWNE	
1727	" "	2	SW	1874-06-03	RR	SW	
1726	" "	2	S½NW	1874-06-03	RR	S2NW	
1552	MACHER, Frederick	19	N½SE	1853-02-09	FD	N2SE	R:INDIANA
1553	" "	19	SWSE	1853-02-09	FD	SWSE	R:INDIANA
1616	MAIER, Johan	18	S½NE	1876-07-13	RR	SFR2NE	S:F
1682	MAIER, Joseph	18	S½SE	1870-08-31	RR	S2SEFR	
1681	" "	18	N½SE	1870-08-31	RR	N2SEFR	
1610	MARKS, Jesse	33	E½SE	1852-09-09	FD	E2SE	
1612	" "	33	SWSE	1852-09-09	FD	SWSE	
1611	" "	33	SENE	1852-09-09	FD	SENE	
1516	MARTIN, Christopher	32	SWSE	1880-10-25	RR	SWSE	
1556	MASCHER, Frederick	30	E½NE	1863-03-23	RR	E2NE	
1555	" "	20	SENW	1863-04-22	RR	SENW	
1554	" "	20	NENE	1864-06-22	RR	NENE	
1557	" "	30	NWNE	1869-08-31	RR	NWNE	
1558	MASCHER, Fredrick	16	L292	1854-09-15	SC	LOT29LI5SWSE	
1559	" "	16	L30,15	1854-09-15	SC	SCLOT30LI5SW	
1560	" "	16	L12, 15	1854-09-21	SC	LOT12LI5SWSE	
1660	MCCABE, John	16	L7	1854-10-23	SC	LOT7SWNE	
1609	" "	16	L7	1854-10-23	SC	LOT7SWNE	
1661	MCCARTHY, John	4	W½SE	1870-09-30	RR	W2SE	
1689	MCCOY, L H	32	SESW	1893-04-29	RR	SESW	S:I
1765	MCCUBBINS, Z	16	L3	1854-11-07	SC	SCLOT03NENW	S:I
1764	" "	16	L2	1854-11-07	SC	LOT02NWNE	S:I
1766	" "	16	L8	1854-11-07	SC	LOT08SENE	S:I
1608	" "	16	L4	1857-11-07	SC	LOT04NWNW	S:I
1767	" "	16	L4	1857-11-07	SC	LOT04NWNW	S:I
1662	MCMANAMY, John	10	W½	1869-12-31	RR	W2	
1701	MCQUAID, Milton	3	L2 (E½)	1853-05-16	FD	E2LOT2NE	
1537	MICHELL, Elihu	16	L19	1854-09-15	SC	LOT19LISWSE	
1538	" "	16	L20	1854-09-15	SC	LOT20LISWSE	
1510	MILLER, Charles	32	SWSW	00/00/1871	RR	SWSW	
1521	MILLER, Daniel Sen	35	SE	1853-01-04	FD	SE	
1522	" "	36	W½SW	1853-02-09	FD	W2SW	
1534	MINOR, Edward D	33	SWSW	1853-01-05	FD	SWSW	
1533	" "	33	SESW	1853-01-07	FD	SESW	
1532	" "	33	NENE	1853-02-17	FD	NENE	
1539	MITCHELL, Elihu	34	SE	1853-02-11	FD	SE	
1707	MONELL, Ogden	4	NW	1864-04-22	RR	NW	
1737	MOORE, Turner	28	NW	1851-06-11	FD	NW	
1734	MULGUEEN, Thomas	4	SWNE	1870-04-30	RR	SWNE	
1497	MUSGRAVE, Arma	22	SESW	1877-02-12	RR	SESW	
1596	MYRES, James G	5	L1 (E½)	1852-10-02	FD	E2LOT1NW	
1597	" "	5	L2 (E½)	1852-10-02	FD	E2LOT2NW	
1470	" "	5	L1 (E½)	1852-10-02	FD	E2LOT1NW	
1589	NICHOLS, Israel	5	NESE	1852-12-10	FD	NESE	
1749	OBRIEN, William H	8	NWSE	1871-02-28	RR	NWSE	

ID	Individual in Patent	Sec.	Sec. Part	Purchase Date	Sale Type	IL Aliquot Part	For More Info . . .
1750	OBRIEN, William H (Cont'd)	8	SWSE	1873-07-31	RR	SWSE	
1623	OCONNOR, John F	4	E½NE	1871-12-30	RR	E2NE	
1702	OKEEN, Mortimore	24	SENE	1853-11-13	FD	SENE	R:JASPER
1703	" "	24	W½NE	1853-11-13	FD	W2NE	R:JASPER
1696	PECKLE, Matthias	34	NW	1853-02-11	FD	NW	
1472	PETERSON, Abner M	5	L2 (W½)	1853-12-27	FD	W2LOT2NW	R:JASPER
1471	" "	5	L1 (W½)	1853-12-27	FD	W2LOT1NW	R:JASPER
1752	PURSELL, William	16	L13	1854-10-12	SC	LOT13L1SWSE	
1717	" "	16	L13	1854-10-12	SC	LOT13L1SWSE	
1663	RANDOLPH, John	22	S½SE	1872-03-30	RR	S2SE	
1714	RANOLPH, Payton	22	SWSW	1873-10-31	RR	SWSW	
1490	REED, Allen	17	SENW	1853-11-26	FD	SENW	R:INDIANA
1492	" "	7	SE	1853-11-26	FD	SEFR	R:INDIANA
1489	" "	17	NENW	1853-11-26	FD	NENW	
1488	" "	17	N½SW	1853-11-26	FD	N2SW	R:INDIANA
1491	" "	19	NE	1853-11-26	FD	NEFR	R:INDIANA
1753	REEDS, William T	6	S½SE	1871-02-28	RR	S2SEFR	
1683	REFFIT, Joseph	5	S½SW	1852-12-07	FD	S2SW	
1688	RENICK, Robert M	13	SWSE	1853-03-03	FD	SWSE	G:4
1687	" "	13	SESW	1853-03-03	FD	SESW	G:4
1577	REYNOLDS, Henry I M	20	E½SW	1839-06-10	FD	E2SW	R:WABASH
1578	" "	20	W½SE	1839-06-10	FD	W2SE	R:WABASH
1665	REYNOLDS, John	29	NWNE	1838-10-18	FD	NWNE	R:JASPER
1664	" "	29	NENW	1838-10-18	FD	NENW	R:JASPER
1542	RHOADES, Elisha E	12	N½NW	1850-06-06	FD	N2NW	
1541	" "	12	E½SE	1850-06-06	FD	E2SE	R:JASPER
1540	" "	1	S½SW	1850-06-06	FD	S2SW	
1585	RHOADES, Isaac H	2	SESE	1870-04-30	RR	SESE	
1586	" "	2	SWSE	1875-06-04	RR	SWSE	
1754	RHOADS, William W	1	SE	1849-11-09	FD	SE	
1684	RIFFETT, Joseph	5	SESW	1852-12-10	FD	SESW	
1666	RILEY, John	22	NESW	1863-06-02	RR	NESW	G:51
1667	" "	22	SENW	1863-06-02	RR	SENW	G:51
1667	RILEY, Owen	22	SENW	1863-06-02	RR	SENW	G:51
1666	" "	22	NESW	1863-06-02	RR	NESW	G:51
1605	SAMPSON, James	12	SWNW	1853-01-22	FD	SWNW	
1685	SCHUMACHER, Joseph	18	N½NE	1874-01-31	RR	N2NE	
1755	SCRIVEN, Willis M	8	E½SE	1873-07-31	RR	E2SE	
1721	SEITH, Samuel	31	NESE	1853-02-08	FD	NESE	
1614	SELBY, Jesse	35	W½SW	1853-02-04	FD	W2SW	
1613	" "	35	E½SW	1853-02-04	FD	E2SW	
1608	SELF, Jeremiah	16	L4	1856-02-17	SC	LOT4NWNW	
1767	" "	16	L4	1856-02-17	SC	LOT4NWNW	
1736	SEXTON, Thomas	10	W½SE	1870-10-17	RR	W2SE	
1545	SILLS, Elizabeth	3	NWSE	1853-02-26	FD	NWSE	S:F
1546	" "	3	L1 (W½)	1853-02-26	FD	W2LOT1NE	S:F
1669	SILLS, John	3	L1	1853-03-02	FD	LOT1NW	
1668	" "	3	N½SW	1853-03-02	FD	N2SW	
1670	SMART, John	13	NESW	1849-10-02	FD	NESW	
1671	" "	13	NWSE	1849-10-02	FD	NWSE	
1672	" "	13	SENW	1849-10-02	FD	SENW	
1673	" "	13	SWNE	1849-10-02	FD	SWNE	
1523	SMITH, Daniel	28	W½SE	1864-12-26	RR	W2SE	
1674	SMITH, John W	2	NWNE	00/00/1871	RR	NWNE	
1722	SMITH, Samuel	1	E½NW	1852-09-10	FD	E2NW	
1526	" "	1	L1 (W½)	1852-09-10	FD	W2LOT1NE	
1723	" "	1	L1 (W½)	1852-09-10	FD	W2LOT1NE	
1595	SPOON, Jacob L	21	NWNW	1853-12-10	FD	NWNW	R:JASPER
1738	SPOON, William A	28	SWSW	1870-12-31	RR	SWSW	
1719	STAELCUP, S	28	SWNE	1869-05-01	RR	SWNE	S:I
1599	" "	28	SWNE	1869-05-01	RR	SWNE	S:I
1730	STALLCUP, Solomon	28	SENE	1866-02-23	RR	SENE	
1729	" "	28	NWNE	1868-12-31	RR	NWNE	
1566	STATER, Andrew	16	L5	1856-03-03	SC	LOT5SWNW	
1496	" "	16	L6	1856-03-03	SC	LOT6SENW	
1567	" "	16	L6	1856-03-03	SC	LOT6SENW	
1495	" "	16	L5	1856-03-03	SC	LOT5SWNW	
1591	STEPHENSON, William H	21	W½SE	1839-07-23	FD	W2SE	R:FAYETTE G:6
1732	STEVENS, Stephen	16	L12	1854-11-07	SC	LOT12NWSW	
1690	STINE, Louis	6	S½NE	1874-08-03	RR	S2NEFR	
1694	STOCKWELL, Martin	21	SWSW	1853-01-05	FD	SWSW	
1695	" "	29	SENE	1853-01-05	FD	SENE	
1700	STOCKWELL, Michael	29	NENE	1853-02-01	FD	NENE	R:JASPER

ID	Individual in Patent	Sec.	Sec. Part	Purchase Date	Sale Type	IL Aliquot Part	For More Info . . .
1699	STOCKWELL, Michael (Cont'd)	21	SWNW	1853-03-03	FD	SWNW	
1698	" "	21	NWSW	1853-03-03	FD	NWSW	
1617	STRUBING, Johann	20	W½NW	1874-02-11	RR	W2NW	
1713	TOBIN, Patrick	8	E½SW	1874-02-28	RR	E2SW	
1615	TOELLNER, Joachim	8	SEN½	1877-01-08	RR	S2NE	
1590	TREXLER, Jackson	34	SEN½	1853-03-17	FD	S2NE	
1675	TREXLER, Johnson	34	N½NE	1853-03-21	FD	N2NE	
1581	VANSANDT, Hiram G	32	SENW	1886-06-05	RR	SENW	
1580	" "	32	NESW	1886-06-05	RR	NESW	
1469	WELTY, Aaron	4	NWSW	1873-07-31	RR	NWSW	
1495	WHEELELER, George	16	L5	1854-10-30	SC	LOT5SWNW	
1566	" "	16	L5	1854-10-30	SC	LOT5SWNW	
1567	" "	16	L6	1854-10-30	SC	LOT6SENW	
1496	" "	16	L6	1854-10-30	SC	LOT6SENW	
1708	WHEELER, Orde H	29	SW	1853-02-05	FD	SW	
1712	WHEELER, Orrel H	30	S½SE	1865-04-22	RR	S2SE	
1735	WHITE, Thomas Q	8	NENE	1872-11-30	RR	NENE	
1575	WILES, Henry C	29	SWNE	1852-12-04	FD	SWNE	
1724	WILSON, Sarah R	32	N½SE	1883-03-20	RR	N2SE	S:F
1679	WISHARD, Joseph E	12	NE	1849-12-22	FD	NE	
1509	WOHLTMANN, Carston	32	SESE	1864-07-22	RR	SESE	G:60
1509	WOHLTMANN, Johann	32	SESE	1864-07-22	RR	SESE	G:60
1529	WOOD, David	5	SWSW	1853-05-27	FD	SWSW	
1528	" "	5	NWSW	1853-05-27	FD	NWSW	
1678	WORMAN, Joseph B	32	SWNE	1883-05-26	RR	SWNE	
1547	WRIGHT, Elston	5	NESW	1853-02-01	FD	NESW	

Patent Map

T7-N R8-E
3rd PM Meridian

Map Group 6

Township Statistics

Parcels Mapped	:	299
Number of Patents	:	1
Number of Individuals	:	176
Patentees Identified	:	170
Number of Surnames	:	145
Multi-Patentee Parcels	:	42
Oldest Patent Date	:	10/18/1838
Most Recent Patent	:	4/29/1893
Block/Lot Parcels	:	49
Cities and Towns	:	1
Cemeteries	:	1

Map detail (sections 4–33), names and dates as labeled:

Section 6: BARLOW William H 1883; STINE Louis 1874; CREWS James L 1873; REEDS William T 1871; BERRY Wyatt S 1853

Lots-Sec. 5: L1(E½) CALDWELL, Abbert G 1852; L1(E½) MYRES, James G 1852; L1(W½) PETERSON, Abner M 1853; L2(E½) MYRES, James G 1852; L2(W½) PETERSON, Abner M 1853

Section 5: BARBER Elam 1852; WOOD David 1853; WRIGHT Elston 1853; ARNOLD Fletcher 1853; NICHOLS Israel 1852; WOOD David 1853; REFFIT Joseph 1852; RIFFETT Joseph 1852

Section 4: MONELL Ogden 1864; CALDWELL Albert S 1865; OCONNOR John F 1871; MULGUEEN Thomas 1870; WELTY Aaron 1873; CULNANE John 1870; MCCARTHY John 1870; LAMBERT Abraham 1872; CREWS James L 1874

Section 7: BERRY Wyatt S 1853; ARMSTRONG Melvin 1871; KEENE Henry L 1873; KEENE Sumner 1873; WHITE Thomas Q 1872; BARTELLS Sophia 1877; REED Allen 1853; GOULD George E 1873; LUSTIG Joseph 1886; TOBIN Patrick 1874

Section 8: TOELLNER Joachim 1877; OBRIEN William H 1871; SCRIVEN Willis M 1873; OBRIEN William H 1873

Section 9: AVERY [1] John H 1853; LEWIS Howel 1853; AVERY [1] John H 1853

Section 18: SCHUMACHER Joseph 1874; MAIER Johan 1876; MAIER Joseph 1870; MAIER Joseph 1870

Section 17: REED Allen 1853; REED Allen 1853; REED Allen 1853; AVERY [1] John H 1853; LEWIS Howel 1853; LEWIS Howel 1853; AVERY [1] John H 1853

Lots-Sec. 16: L1 DABBINS, Joshua 1854; L2 MCCUBBINS, Z 1854; L3 MCCUBBINS, Z 1854; L4 SELF, Jeremiah 1856; L4 MCCUBBINS, Z 1857; L5 WHEELELER, George 1854; L5 STATER, Andrew 1856; L6 WHEELELER, George 1854; L6 STATER, Andrew 1856; L7 GROVE, Jesse 1856; L7 MCCABE, John 1854; L8 MCCUBBINS, Z 1854; L9 CUMMING, George 1854; L10 CUMMING, George 1854; L11 INGLE, Renney C 1854; L12 STEVENS, Stephen 1854; L12, 15 MASCHER, Fredrick 1854; L13 INGLE, Renney C 1854; L13 PURSELL, William 1854; L14 JARED, Israel 1854; L14 INGLE, Renney 1854; L15 DELOTT, Jonah F [26]1854; L16 DELOTT, Jonah F [26]1854; L19 MICHELL, Elihu 1854; L20 MICHELL, Elihu 1854; L21 HOLM, Adam 1854; L22 JARED, Israel 1854; L25 BURFORD, John 1854; L26 BURFORD, John 1854; L28 HOLM, Adam 1854; L292 MASCHER, Fredrick 1854; L30,15 MASCHER, Fredrick 1854

Section 19: REED Allen 1853; STRUBING Johann 1874; MACHER Frederick 1853; HARTING Alexander 1863; EBALING Christian 1876; LEATH Samuel 1851; MASCHER Frederick 1863; LEATH Reason 1851; REYNOLDS Henry I M 1839

Section 20: MASCHER Frederick 1864; SPOON Jacob L 1853; EBELING Conrad 1883; STOCKWELL Michael 1853; HARTING Alexander 1865; STOCKWELL Michael 1853; EBALING Coonrad 1873; STOCKWELL Martin 1853

Section 21: HOARE George E 1853; BERRY Wyatt S 1853; JOURDAN Elizabeth 1851; JOURDAN Elizabeth 1851; HAYES William C 1853; ANDERSON [6] Jacob 1839; BENFORD John M 1853; HAYES William C 1853; BERRY Wyatt S 1853

Section 30: MASCHER Frederick 1869; MACHER Frederick 1881; GROOTHINS Eildert 1874; MASCHER Frederick 1863; BUHLER John M 1874; HILDEBRAND Christ 1884; FICKLIN Orlando B 1853; WHEELER Orrel H 1865

Section 29: FICKLIN Orlando B 1853; FICKLIN Orlando B 1853; WHEELER Orde H 1853; REYNOLDS John 1838; REYNOLDS John 1838; WILES Henry C 1852; HOLM Adam 1853; STOCKWELL Michael 1853; STOCKWELL Martin 1853; HOLM Adam 1853; HARLAND James M 1853

Section 28: MOORE Turner 1851; SPOON William A 1870; BUHLER David 1886; STALLCUP Solomon 1868; STAELCUPS 1869; CREWS James L 1869; LOVE Harvey N 1864; STALLCUP Solomon 1866; ABELS Martin D 1864; SMITH Daniel 1864; CREWS James L 1869

Section 31: Lots-Sec. 31; L1 BERRY, Wyatt S 1853; L2 BERRY, Wyatt S 1853; KRAASS Christopher 1853; KENEIPP William M 1887; CASJENS Harm E 1864; SEITH Samuel 1853; EILERS Helene 1887; EILERS Helene 1886; VANSANDT Hiram G 1886; MILLER Charles 00/0

Section 32: HANNEMANN Martin 1870; BOSTER Claindo 1876; HOLM Adam 1865; VANSANDT Hiram G 1886; WORMAN Joseph B 1883; HOLM Adam 1865; MCCOY L H 1893; MARTIN Christopher 1880; WILSON Sarah R 1883; WOHLTMANN [60] Carston 1864

Section 33: HOLM Adam 1852; HOLLOM Adam 1853; FOGLER Christian 1853; BERRY Wyatt S 1853; FOGLER Christian 1853; ANDERSON John 1839; MINOR Edward D 1853; MINOR Edward D 1853; MINOR Edward D 1853; MARKS Jesse 1852; MARKS Jesse 1852; MARKS Jesse 1852

Lots-Sec. 3
L1   SILLS, John   1853
L1(E½) ALEXANDER, Joshua[2]1853
L1(W½) SILLS, Elizabeth   1853
L2   ALEXANDER, Joshua[2]1853
L2(E½) MCQUAID, Milton   1853
L2(W½) ALEXANDER, Joshua[3]1853
L2(W½) GREELY, Carlos   1852

		KOONTZ Andrew J 1868	KOONTZ Andrew J 1868	SMITH John W 00/0		SMITH Samuel 1852	FITHIAN Glover 1849	FITHIAN Glover 1849

SILLS John 1853 **3**
SILLS Elizabeth 1853
GREELY [2] Carlos S 1853

LUX Sebastian 1874
LUX Sebastian 1874 **2**
BURNHAM Jasper N 1876

SMITH Samuel 1852 **1**

GREELY [2] Carlos S 1853
GREELY [2] Carlos S 1853

LUX Sebastian 1874
LUX Sebastian 1874
FITHIAN George W 1881

BROWN David L 1852
RHOADS William W 1849

LUX Sebastian 1874
RHOADES Isaac H 1875
RHOADES Isaac H 1870
RHOADES Elisha E 1850

Lots-Sec 1
L1(W½) SMITH, Samuel   1852
L1(W½) BROWN, David L   1852
L2(W½) BROWN, David L   1852

KECK [40] Enoch 1871
LETURRO Henry F 1874 **10**
MCMANAMY John 1869
SEXTON Thomas 1870
HENDERSON James S 1876
HENDERSON James S 1874

AVERY [1] John H 1853 **11**
AVERY [1] John H 1853
AVERY [1] John H 1853
GREELY [2] Carlos S 1853
CLARK Grandison 1853

RHOADES Elisha E 1850
SAMPSON James 1853
ELSON Moses 1849 **12**
ELSON Moses 1849
ELSON Moses 1849
BATMAN Alexander B 1850

WISHARD Joseph E 1849
RHOADES Elisha E 1850

AVERY John H 1853
AVERY John H 1853 **15**
GREELY [2] Carlos S 1853
GREELY [2] Carlos S 1853

AVERY [1] John H 1853 **14**
AVERY [1] John H 1853
AVERY [1] John H 1853
AVERY [1] John H 1853

CLARK William 1853
CLARK William 1853
AVERY [1] John H 1853
AVERY [1] John H 1853

DECKER William 1850
SMART John 1849
SMART John 1849

DECKER William 1850
ELSON Corneluis J 1849 **13**
SMART John 1849
BRIDGES Edmund R 1853
SMART John 1849
BRIDGES Edmund R 1853
ALEXANDER [4] Joshua H 1853
ALEXANDER [4] Joshua H 1853

AVERY [1] John H 1853
AVERY [1] John H 1853
AVERY [1] John H 1853

CORRIGAM William 1860
HANNEMANN Martin 1870
RILEY [51] John 1863
CORRIGAN William 1864 **22**
CORRIGAN William 1864
RILEY John 1863
DOERR Jacob 1874
RANOLPH Payton 1873
MUSGRAVE Arma 1877
RANDOLPH John 1872

AVERY [1] John H 1853 **23**
AVERY [1] John H 1853
AVERY [1] John H 1853
AVERY [1] John H 1853

AVERY [1] John H 1853
AVERY [1] John H 1853 **24**
OKEEN Mortimore 1853
OKEEN Mortimore 1853
BRIDGES John M 1853

HUNT Eri 1853
HUNT Eri 1853 **27**
BERRY Wyatt L 1853
BLAKE Jefferson 1853
JACKSON John 1853

AVERY [1] John H 1853 **26**
JOHNSTON Alexander 1853
JACKSON John 1853

JOHNSTON Alexander 1853
FOUST Jacob 1853 **25**
JACKSON John 1853
JACKSON John 1853

FOUST [29] Benjamin 1853
JACKSON John 1853

TREXLER Johnson 1853 **34**
PECKLE Matthias 1853
TREXLER Jackson 1853
CAROTHERS John 1852
DOBBINS Jacob H 1853
MITCHELL Elihu 1853

JACKSON John 1853 **35**
SELBY Jesse 1853
SELBY Jesse 1853
MILLER Daniel Sen 1853

JACKSON John 1853
JACKSON John 1853 **36**
MILLER Daniel Sen 1853
BERRY Wyatt S 1853
JACKSON John 1853

JACKSON John 1853

Helpful Hints

1. This Map's INDEX can be found on the preceding pages.

2. Refer to Map "C" to see where this Township lies within Jasper County, Illinois.

3. Numbers within square brackets [ ] denote a multi-patentee land parcel (multi-owner). Refer to Appendix "C" for a full list of members in this group.

4. Areas that look to be crowded with Patentees usually indicate multiple sales of the same parcel (re-issues), cancellations or voided transactions (that we map, anyway) or overlapping parcels. We opt to show even these ambiguous parcels, which oftentimes lead to research avenues not yet taken.

Legend

— Patent Boundary

━ Section Boundary

No Patents Found (or Outside County)

1., 2., 3., ...   Lot Numbers (when beside a name)

[ ]   Group Number (see Appendix "C")

Scale: Section = 1 mile X 1 mile (generally, with some exceptions)

Road Map

T7-N R8-E
3rd PM Meridian

Map Group 6

Cities & Towns

Wheeler

Cemeteries

Wheeler Cemetery

N 2400th St

6

5

4

N 300th St

E 1500th Ave

7

8

9

E 1400th Ave

State Rte 33

18

17

16

N Main St

Love St

Elm St

N Mill St

Center St

Mason St

E 1300th Ave

19

N 100th St

20

N 200th St

21

E 1200th Ave

30

29

28

E 1100th Ave

31

32

33

Copyright 2010 Boyd IT, Inc. All Rights Reserved

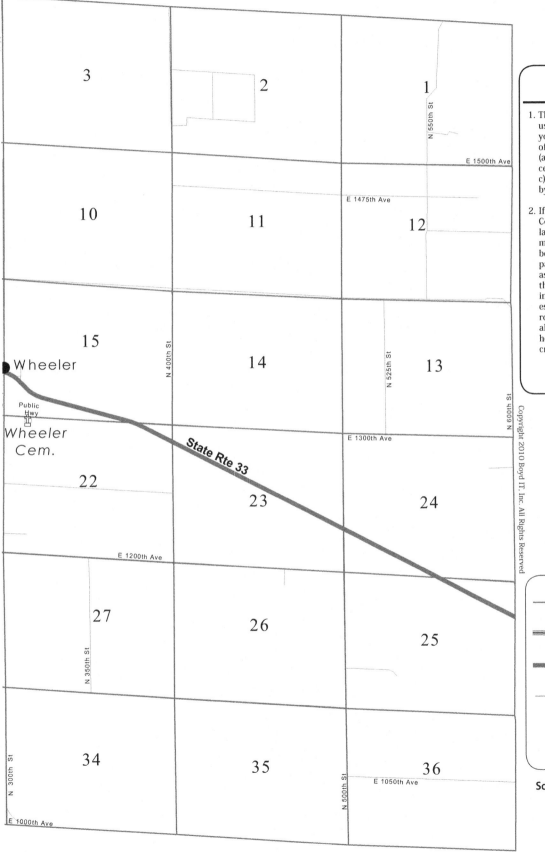

3

2

1

N 550th St

E 1500th Ave

10

11

E 1475th Ave

12

15

N 400th St

14

N 525th St

13

● Wheeler

Public
Hwy

*Wheeler
Cem.*

22

State Rte 33

23

E 1300th Ave

N 500th St

24

E 1200th Ave

27

N 350th St

26

25

N 300th St

34

35

N 500th St

E 1050th Ave

36

E 1000th Ave

Helpful Hints

1. This road map has a number of uses, but primarily it is to help you: a) find the present location of land owned by your ancestors (at least the general area), b) find cemeteries and city-centers, and c) estimate the route/roads used by Census-takers & tax-assessors.

2. If you plan to travel to Jasper County to locate cemeteries or land parcels, please pick up a modern travel map for the area before you do. Mapping old land parcels on modern maps is not as exact a science as you might think. Just the slightest variations in public land survey coordinates, estimates of parcel boundaries, or road-map deviations can greatly alter a map's representation of how a road either does or doesn't cross a particular parcel of land.

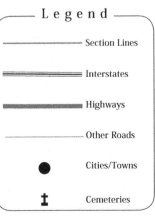

L e g e n d

——————— Section Lines

═══════ Interstates

━━━━━━━ Highways

——————— Other Roads

● Cities/Towns

♰ Cemeteries

Scale: Section = 1 mile X 1 mile
(generally, with some exceptions)

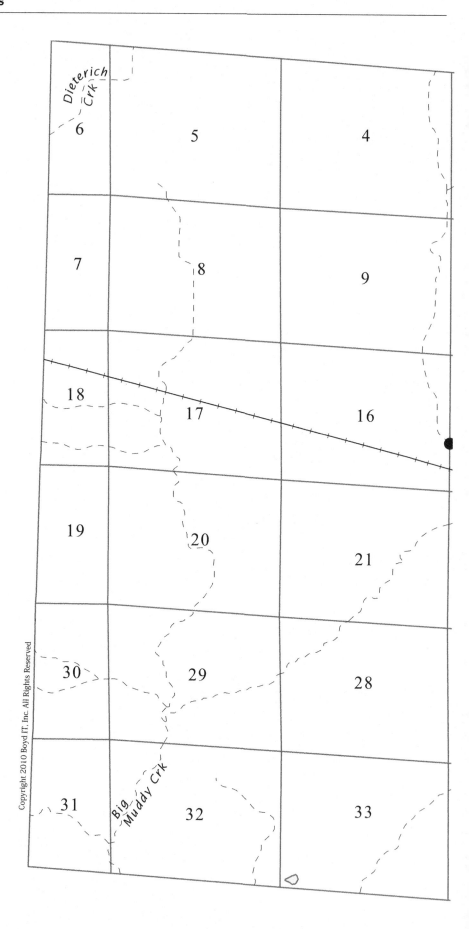

Historical Map

T7-N R8-E
3rd PM Meridian

Map Group 6

Cities & Towns
Wheeler

Cemeteries
Wheeler Cemetery

Copyright 2010 Boyd IT, Inc. All Rights Reserved

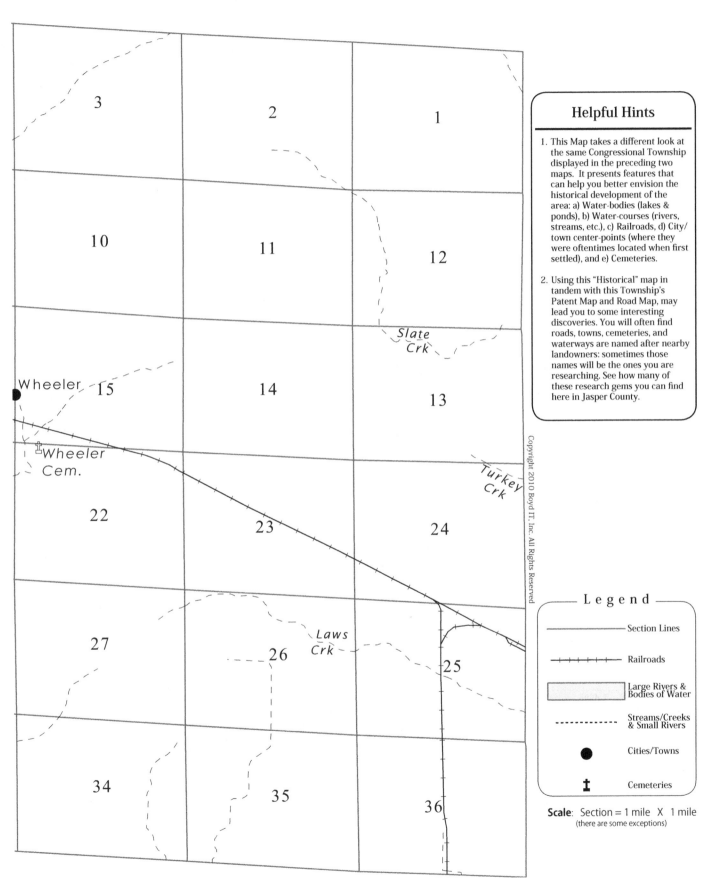

Helpful Hints

1. This Map takes a different look at the same Congressional Township displayed in the preceding two maps. It presents features that can help you better envision the historical development of the area: a) Water-bodies (lakes & ponds), b) Water-courses (rivers, streams, etc.), c) Railroads, d) City/town center-points (where they were oftentimes located when first settled), and e) Cemeteries.

2. Using this "Historical" map in tandem with this Township's Patent Map and Road Map, may lead you to some interesting discoveries. You will often find roads, towns, cemeteries, and waterways are named after nearby landowners: sometimes those names will be the ones you are researching. See how many of these research gems you can find here in Jasper County.

Legend

————————	Section Lines
+—+—+—+—+	Railroads
▭	Large Rivers & Bodies of Water
- - - - - - -	Streams/Creeks & Small Rivers
●	Cities/Towns
‡	Cemeteries

Scale: Section = 1 mile X 1 mile
(there are some exceptions)

Map Group 7: Index to Land Patents

Township 7-North Range 9-East (3rd PM)

After you locate an individual in this Index, take note of the Section and Section Part then proceed to the Land Patent map on the pages immediately following. You should have no difficulty locating the corresponding parcel of land.

The "For More Info" Column will lead you to more information about the underlying Patents. See the *Legend* at right, and the "How to Use this Book" chapter, for more information.

```
            LEGEND
      "For More Info . . . " column
G = Group  (Multi-Patentee Patent, see Appendix "C")
R = Residence
S = Social Status

See Appendix A for list of abbreviations used by the
Illinois State Archives in describing the place and
nature of these land patents.

Note: if the Abbreviations contain "L", "BL", "LOT",
or "BLOCK", the exact whereabouts of the parcel within
the section is not known.
```

ID	Individual in Patent	Sec.	Sec. Part	Purchase Date	Sale Type	IL Aliquot Part	For More Info . . .
1902	ADAMS, Gilbert D	23	E½SW	1848-06-23	FD	E2SW	
1903	" "	23	W½SE	1848-06-23	FD	W2SE	
1929	ALLEN, James C	32	S½NW	1853-06-23	FD	S2NW	G:5
1928	" "	32	NESW	1853-06-23	FD	NESW	R:CRAWFORD G:5
1930	" "	32	SWNW	1853-06-23	FD	SWNW	R:CRAWFORD G:5
1931	ARBUCKELL, James	13	NWNW	1852-11-08	FD	NWNW	R:JASPER
1773	ARBUCKLE, Abraham	2	E½SW	1851-09-24	FD	E2SW	
1774	" "	2	W½SE	1851-09-24	FD	W2SE	
1932	ARBUCKLE, James	24	SWSE	1852-10-08	FD	SWSE	
1933	" "	25	NWNE	1852-10-08	FD	NWNE	
2082	BADGER, Stephen	16	L1	1851-09-15	SC	LOT1NENE	
2083	" "	16	L2	1851-09-15	SC	LOT2NWNE	
1777	BAKER, Absalom	15	NENE	1852-11-01	FD	NENE	R:OHIO
1776	" "	10	SESE	1852-11-01	FD	SESE	R:OHIO
1951	BAKER, Jeptha	16	L11	1850-04-15	SC	LOT11NESW	
1788	BALL, Amos W	24	NW	1850-05-03	FD	NW	
1787	" "	13	NENE	1851-02-08	FD	NENE	R:JASPER
2045	BARKLEY, Peyton H	18	NE	1849-08-29	FD	NE	
2046	" "	7	SE	1849-08-29	FD	SE	
2067	BARRET, Samuel	19	W½NE	1851-10-10	FD	W2NE	R:INDIANA
1914	BARRETT, Harvey	15	SESW	1853-09-13	FD	SESW	R:INDIANA
1912	BARRETT, Harvey B	16	L7	1851-10-09	SC	LOT7SWNE	
1911	" "	16	L3	1851-10-09	SC	LOT3NENW	
1910	" "	11	SENW	1853-09-13	FD	SENW	R:INDIANA
1913	" "	23	SENE	1853-09-13	FD	SENE	R:INDIANA
2068	BARRETT, Samuel	15	W½NW	1851-10-10	FD	W2NW	
2069	" "	18	S½SW	1851-10-10	FD	S2SW	R:INDIANA
2071	" "	28	NW	1851-10-10	FD	NW	R:INDIANA
2070	" "	19	S½NW	1851-11-20	FD	S2NW	R:INDIANA
2118	BARRETT, William E	15	NESW	1865-05-08	SW	NESW	
1909	BATMAN, Greenberry	7		1849-11-30	FD	W2WA	R:INDIANA
2031	BLACK, Milton	14	W½NW	1837-11-15	FD	W2NW	R:INDIANA
2030	" "	11	SESW	1837-11-15	FD	SESW	R:INDIANA
2029	" "	11	NESW	1837-11-16	FD	NESW	R:INDIANA
1998	BOWERS, Joseph	12	W½NW	1852-02-10	FD	W2NW	R:JASPER
1997	" "	11	NENE	1852-02-10	FD	NENE	R:JASPER
1851	BREWER, David L	6	W½SE	1849-11-13	FD	W2SE	R:INDIANA
1850	" "	6	SW	1849-11-13	FD	SW	R:INDIANA
1853	BREWER, David S	6		1849-12-31	FD	SWWA	R:INDIANA
1916	BREWER, Henry	6	S½NW	1850-01-28	FD	S2NW	R:INDIANA
1915	" "	6	NE	1850-01-28	FD	NE	R:INDIANA
1954	BRIDGES, John	16	L10	1851-01-15	SC	LOT10NWSE	
1955	" "	16	L14	1851-01-15	SC	LOT14SESW	
1956	" "	16	L9	1851-01-15	SC	LOT9NESE	
2110	BRIDGES, William	16	L12	1850-04-15	SC	LOT12W2SW	
2111	" "	16	L13	1850-04-15	SC	LOT13W2SW	

ID	Individual in Patent	Sec.	Sec. Part	Purchase Date	Sale Type	IL Aliquot Part	For More Info . . .
1789	BRISTOL, Andrew E	19	SW	1853-11-29	FD	SW	R:CRAWFORD
1790	" "	30	NW	1853-11-29	FD	NW	R:CRAWFORD
1812	BROWN, Bullard W	10	NESE	1851-10-23	FD	NESE	R:INDIANA
1872	BROWN, Felix	36	NWNE	1835-06-13	FD	NWNE	R:WABASH
1871	" "	25	SWSE	1835-06-13	FD	SWSE	R:WABASH
1919	BUEL, Henry L	27	NENW	1849-09-04	FD	NENW	
1921	" "	27	W2NW	1849-09-04	FD	W2NW	
1920	" "	27	NWSW	1849-09-04	FD	NWSW	
2026	BUTLER, Melvin	3	NESE	1852-08-30	FD	NESE	
2023	" "	12	NESW	1852-08-30	FD	NESW	
2024	" "	12	SENW	1852-08-30	FD	SENW	
2025	" "	2	NWSW	1852-08-30	FD	NWSW	
1995	CARR, Jonathan	32	W2SW	1851-09-15	FD	W2SW	
1994	" "	32	SESW	1851-09-15	FD	SESW	
2112	CARTER, William	10	E2NE	1839-10-28	FD	E2NE	R:JASPER
2113	" "	17	NWNW	1847-03-20	FD	NWNW	R:JASPER
2115	" "	17	SWNW	1848-02-25	FD	SWNW	R:JASPER
2114	" "	17	SWNE	1849-09-07	FD	SWNE	R:JASPER
1908	CLARK, Grandison	7	NE	1849-10-02	FD	NE	
2072	COMER, Samuel	28	E2SW	1852-01-30	FD	E2SW	
1934	COTTINGHAM, James	22	S2SW	1851-01-21	FD	S2SW	R:INDIANA
1898	COURE, George W	27	NE	1851-03-19	FD	NE	G:20
1898	COURE, William	27	NE	1851-03-19	FD	NE	G:20
1907	COX, Godfrey	14	SWNE	1851-05-03	FD	SWNE	
1906	" "	14	SENW	1851-05-03	FD	SENW	
1905	" "	14	NWSE	1851-05-03	FD	NWSE	
1904	" "	14	NESW	1851-05-03	FD	NESW	
2080	COX, Solomon Jr	26	NENE	1838-10-30	FD	NENE	R:CLARK
2079	" "	23	NESE	1838-10-30	FD	NESE	R:CLARK
2081	COX, Solomon Sen	23	SESE	1838-10-30	FD	SESE	R:CLARK
2116	COX, William	14	SESE	1851-10-16	FD	SESE	R:JASPER
2109	CREASON, William B	24	NENE	1848-09-14	FD	NENE	R:JASPER
1887	CURRIE, George	32	E2SE	1853-06-23	FD	E2SE	
1886	" "	31	NW	1853-06-23	FD	NW	R:INDIANA
1885	" "	30	SW	1853-06-23	FD	SW	R:INDIANA
1888	" "	32	SENE	1853-06-23	FD	SENE	
1889	" "	33	NWSW	1853-06-23	FD	NWSW	
1865	CURTIS, Eli	24	E2SW	1853-03-12	FD	E2SW	R:JASPER G:22
1867	DUGAN, Elisha	9	NENW	1851-02-03	FD	NENW	R:INDIANA
1869	DUNGAN, Elisha	4	W2SE	1849-10-13	FD	W2SE	
1868	" "	4	E2SW	1849-10-13	FD	E2SW	
2117	DURKEY, William	11	SE	1849-11-10	FD	SE	
1978	ELDER, John L	1	NWSW	1852-09-07	FD	NWSW	R:INDIANA
1999	ELDER, Joseph	11	NENW	1852-09-07	FD	NENW	R:INDIANA
2000	" "	11	NWNE	1852-09-07	FD	NWNE	R:INDIANA
1805	FERGUSON, Benjamin	2	E2SE	1851-10-22	FD	E2SE	R:INDIANA
1803	" "	1	W2NW	1852-07-10	FD	W2NW	R:IOWA
1804	" "	2	E2NE	1852-07-10	FD	E2NE	R:IOWA
1917	FISHER, Henry	33	E2SW	1852-09-17	FD	E2SW	
1918	" "	33	W2SE	1852-09-17	FD	W2SE	
2077	FITHIAN, Smith	35	W2SE	1836-09-30	FD	W2SE	R:WARREN
1925	FLETCHER, Jacob	14	SWSW	1836-02-29	FD	SWSW	R:LAWRENCE
2010	FLETCHER, Lazarus	23	NWNW	1838-07-20	FD	NWNW	R:JASPER
2011	" "	23	SWNW	1838-07-24	FD	SWNW	R:JASPER
1893	FOLTZ, George	8	E2NE	1850-03-21	FD	E2NE	R:JASPER
1892	" "	5	SENE	1850-03-21	FD	SENE	R:JASPER
1891	" "	5	SE	1850-03-21	FD	SE	R:JASPER
1894	" "	8	NESE	1850-03-21	FD	NESE	R:JASPER
2054	FOLTZ, Reuben	28	SE	1851-08-13	FD	SE	R:JASPER
2051	" "	22	N2SW	1851-08-13	FD	N2SW	R:JASPER
2053	" "	27	SWSW	1851-08-13	FD	SWSW	R:JASPER
2052	" "	22	SWNW	1851-08-13	FD	SWNW	R:JASPER
2078	FOLTZ, Solomon	15	NWNE	1851-10-22	FD	NWNE	
2120	FOLTZ, William	9	SWNW	1850-03-21	FD	SWNW	R:JASPER
2119	" "	4	NWSW	1850-03-21	FD	NWSW	R:JASPER
1801	FOOT, Barnard	8	SW	1850-02-28	FD	SW	
1800	" "	18	N2SW	1850-10-14	FD	N2SW	R:JASPER
1820	FOOT, Charles W	17	SWSE	1850-03-01	FD	SWSE	R:INDIANA
1835	FOOT, Dan	17	N2NE	1850-09-28	FD	N2NE	R:JASPER
1836	" "	17	SENW	1850-09-28	FD	SENW	R:JASPER
1834	" "	16	L4	1850-10-14	SC	LOT4NWNW	
2035	FRAKES, Nathan	28	E2NE	1851-08-02	FD	E2NE	R:INDIANA
1878	FULLER, Francis	34	NESW	1851-09-15	FD	NESW	

ID	Individual in Patent	Sec.	Sec. Part	Purchase Date	Sale Type	IL Aliquot Part	For More Info . . .
1881	FULLER, Francis (Cont'd)	34	W½SE	1851-09-15	FD	W2SE	
1879	" "	34	SESE	1851-09-15	FD	SESE	
1873	" "	29	NWNE	1852-05-04	FD	NWNE	R:JASPER
1880	" "	34	SESW	1852-07-19	FD	SESW	
1877	" "	32	NWNE	1852-09-02	FD	NWNE	
1875	" "	29	W½SE	1852-09-02	FD	W2SE	
1874	" "	29	SWNE	1852-09-02	FD	SWNE	
1876	" "	32	NENE	1853-06-23	FD	NENE	R:JASPER
1992	GARRISON, John V	23	W½NE	1839-06-10	FD	W2NE	R:OHIO
1991	" "	23	E½NW	1839-06-10	FD	E2NW	R:OHIO
2091	GARWOOD, Thomas	36	E½SW	1830-12-11	FD	E2SW	R:CLARK
2092	" "	36	SWSW	1836-04-08	FD	SWSW	R:JASPER
2090	" "	21	E½SW	1837-11-13	FD	E2SW	R:JASPER
2089	" "	20	SWNW	1839-06-11	FD	SWNW	R:JASPER
1947	GOOD, James W	8	NWNW	1850-12-18	FD	NWNW	R:VIRGINIA
1945	" "	5	E½SW	1850-12-18	FD	E2SW	R:VIRGINIA
1946	" "	5	SWSW	1850-12-18	FD	SWSW	R:VIRGINIA
1896	GORNELL, George	21	N½N½	1849-08-18	FD	N2N2	R:INDIANA
1895	" "	17	SW	1849-09-25	FD	SW	R:INDIANA
2104	GOSNELL, Washington	17	SENE	1851-06-17	FD	SENE	R:JASPER
2102	" "	17	E½SE	1851-06-17	FD	E2SE	R:JASPER
2103	" "	17	NWSE	1851-06-17	FD	NWSE	R:JASPER
2108	" "	8	SWNW	1851-08-02	FD	SWNW	R:JASPER
2107	" "	5	SWNW	1851-08-02	FD	SWNW	R:JASPER
2106	" "	5	NWSW	1851-08-02	FD	NWSW	R:JASPER
2105	" "	5	E½NW	1851-08-02	FD	E2NW	R:JASPER
2123	GOSNELL, William	26	W½NW	1851-01-21	FD	W2NW	R:INDIANA
2121	" "	22	S½SE	1851-01-21	FD	S2SE	R:INDIANA
2122	" "	23	SWSW	1851-01-21	FD	SWSW	R:INDIANA
1882	GREEN, Francis M	12	SWSW	1852-09-24	FD	SWSW	R:JASPER
2027	GROVE, Michael	11	SWNE	1852-04-02	FD	SWNE	R:JASPER
2008	HALLENBECK, Lawrence	36	E½NE	1838-08-04	FD	E2NE	R:JASPER
2009	" "	36	SWNE	1838-08-04	FD	SWNE	R:JASPER
2001	HARMON, Joseph	13	NESW	1856-05-01	FD	NESW	R:RICHLAND
1786	HARRIS, Addison S	36	NWSW	1838-02-12	FD	NWSW	R:CRAWFORD
1785	" "	34	W½SW	1852-09-04	FD	W2SW	
1780	" "	30	N½NE	1852-09-04	FD	N2NE	
1779	" "	19	W½SE	1852-09-04	FD	W2SE	
1784	" "	33	E½SE	1852-09-04	FD	E2SE	
1781	" "	31	E½NE	1853-06-22	FD	E2NE	R:JASPER
1783	" "	31	SW	1853-06-22	FD	SW	R:JASPER
1782	" "	31	N½SE	1853-06-22	FD	N2SE	R:JASPER
1811	HARRIS, Benjamin	35	SWNW	1836-11-25	FD	SWNW	R:OHIO G:37
1808	" "	35	E½SE	1836-11-25	FD	E2SE	R:OHIO G:37
1807	" "	35	E½NW	1836-11-25	FD	E2NW	R:OHIO G:37
1810	" "	35	SW	1836-11-25	FD	SW	R:OHIO G:37
1809	" "	35	NE	1836-11-25	FD	NE	R:OHIO G:37
1806	" "	26	NWSW	1839-11-21	FD	NWSW	R:JASPER
1802	HARRIS, Benjamin F	31	W½NE	1853-06-22	FD	W2NE	G:36
1818	HARRIS, Bushrod W	34	E½NW	1837-06-12	FD	E2NW	R:VIRGINIA
1817	" "	27	SESW	1837-06-12	FD	SESW	R:VIRGINIA
1816	" "	27	SE	1837-06-12	FD	SE	R:VIRGINIA
1815	" "	26	SWSW	1837-06-12	FD	SWSW	R:VIRGINIA
1813	" "	20	E½SE	1840-03-04	FD	E2SE	R:JASPER
1814	" "	21	W½SW	1840-03-04	FD	W2SW	R:JASPER
1802	" "	31	W½NE	1853-06-22	FD	W2NE	G:36
1961	HARRIS, John	28	W½NW	1840-06-19	FD	W2NW	R:VIRGINIA
1960	" "	28	SENW	1840-06-19	FD	SENW	R:VIRGINIA
1802	HARRIS, William C	31	W½NE	1853-06-22	FD	W2NE	G:36
2073	HENSLEY, Samuel	12	SESW	1851-10-06	FD	SESW	R:JASPER
2074	" "	13	NENW	1853-03-02	FD	NENW	R:JASPER
1810	HERRON, John	35	SW	1836-11-25	FD	SW	R:OHIO G:37
1808	" "	35	E½SE	1836-11-25	FD	E2SE	R:OHIO G:37
1811	" "	35	SWNW	1836-11-25	FD	SWNW	R:OHIO G:37
1809	" "	35	NE	1836-11-25	FD	NE	R:OHIO G:37
1807	" "	35	E½NW	1836-11-25	FD	E2NW	R:OHIO G:37
2129	HILLS, William	16	L5	1850-04-15	SC	LOT5SWNW	
1890	HOARE, George E	21	NENW	1853-06-22	FD	NENW	
1837	HOLLOPETERS, Daniel	12	SE	1849-06-05	FD	SE	
1926	HOWARD, Jacob	33	W½NW	1853-05-16	FD	W2NW	
1858	HOWE, Edward	13	E½SW	1849-06-05	FD	E2SW	
1860	" "	13	SWSE	1849-06-05	FD	SWSE	
1859	" "	13	SENW	1849-06-05	FD	SENW	

ID	Individual in Patent	Sec.	Sec. Part	Purchase Date	Sale Type	IL Aliquot Part	For More Info . . .
1937	HUNT, James	13	SWSW	1849-07-11	FD	SWSW	R:JASPER
2093	HUNT, Thomas	13	NWSE	1848-07-04	FD	NWSE	R:INDIANA
2094	" "	13	SENE	1850-11-18	FD	SENE	R:JASPER
2039	HUSHAW, Peter	8	E½NW	1851-09-03	FD	E2NW	
2040	" "	8	NWNE	1851-09-03	FD	NWNE	R:INDIANA
2038	" "	5	SWNE	1851-09-03	FD	SWNE	R:INDIANA
2049	ISLEY, Philip	9	SENE	1850-10-02	FD	SENE	R:INDIANA
2050	" "	9	W½NE	1850-10-02	FD	W2NE	R:INDIANA
2047	" "	10	NWSW	1850-10-02	FD	NWSW	R:INDIANA
2048	" "	10	SWNW	1850-10-02	FD	SWNW	R:INDIANA
1962	JACKSON, John	10	NENW	1853-12-08	FD	NENW	R:OHIO
1935	JAMES, James E	1	E½NW	1851-02-25	FD	E2NW	R:JASPER
1799	JASPER, Augustine	9	SENW	1850-03-21	FD	SENW	R:JASPER
1798	" "	4	SWSW	1850-03-21	FD	SWSW	R:JASPER
1899	JEFFERS, George W	3	SESE	1852-09-10	FD	SESE	R:JASPER
1833	JONES, Constant B	31	S½SE	1852-05-29	FD	S2SE	S:F
1883	JONES, Francis S	29	NENE	1851-11-11	FD	NENE	
2007	JONES, Laban	13	SESE	1848-05-03	FD	SESE	R:INDIANA
2057	JONES, Robert C	29	SENE	1851-11-11	FD	SENE	
2058	" "	29	SESE	1852-05-05	FD	SESE	R:JASPER
2059	JONES, Robert E	29	NESE	1851-02-05	FD	NESE	R:JASPER
2061	JONES, Robert H	16	L16	1850-04-15	SC	LOT16S2SE	
2060	" "	16	L15	1850-04-15	SC	LOT15S2SE	
2128	JORDON, William H	9	SE	1849-10-13	FD	SE	
2020	JOURDEN, Lewis W	36	NENW	1837-07-03	FD	NENW	R:JASPER
2019	" "	25	SESW	1837-07-03	FD	SESW	R:JASPER
2032	KEAN, Mortimer O	14	SESW	1843-11-27	FD	SESW	R:JASPER
1963	KEBLER, John	16	L6	1850-04-15	SC	LOT6SENW	
1778	KIBLER, Adam	26	NENW	1839-07-06	FD	NENW	R:JASPER
1843	KIBLER, Daniel	21	SWNE	1849-12-29	FD	SWNE	
1842	" "	21	S½NW	1849-12-29	FD	S2NW	
1838	" "	20	NENE	1849-12-29	FD	NENE	
1839	" "	20	NWSE	1849-12-29	FD	NWSE	
1840	" "	20	SENE	1849-12-29	FD	SENE	
1841	" "	20	W½NE	1849-12-29	FD	W2NE	
1972	KIBLER, John	21	NWSE	1849-12-29	FD	NWSE	
1977	" "	29	S½NW	1849-12-29	FD	S2NW	
1976	" "	29	N½SW	1849-12-29	FD	N2SW	
1975	" "	29	N½NW	1849-12-29	FD	N2NW	
1973	" "	21	SENE	1849-12-29	FD	SENE	
1971	" "	21	E½SE	1849-12-29	FD	E2SE	
1969	" "	20	SWSE	1849-12-29	FD	SWSE	
1968	" "	20	SESW	1849-12-29	FD	SESW	
1966	" "	19	E½SE	1849-12-29	FD	E2SE	
1965	" "	19	E½NE	1849-12-29	FD	E2NE	
1964	" "	18	SE	1849-12-29	FD	SE	
1967	" "	20	NWNW	1850-03-21	FD	NWNW	R:JASPER
1970	" "	20	SWSW	1850-06-22	FD	SWSW	R:JASPER
1974	" "	21	SWSE	1850-06-22	FD	SWSE	R:JASPER
1844	KIBLINGER, Daniel	15	E½NW	1851-10-22	FD	E2NW	
1928	KITCHELL, James A	32	NESW	1853-06-23	FD	NESW	R:CRAWFORD G:5
1930	" "	32	SWNW	1853-06-23	FD	SWNW	R:CRAWFORD G:5
1929	" "	32	S½NW	1853-06-23	FD	S2NW	G:5
1794	KOONTZ, Andrew	9	NWNW	1853-12-20	FD	NWNW	R:JASPER
2064	LEACH, Robert	10	SWNE	1865-05-09	SW	SWNE	
2063	" "	10	SESW	1865-05-09	SW	SESW	
2065	" "	15	NESE	1865-05-09	SW	NESE	
2062	" "	10	NESW	1865-05-09	SW	NESW	
1768	LEE, Abbit	3	E½NE	1836-06-14	FD	E2NE	R:JASPER
1769	LEE, Abbot	10	NWNE	1839-05-07	FD	NWNE	R:JASPER
1770	" "	2	W½NW	1853-08-18	FD	W2NW	R:JASPER
1771	LEE, Abbott	2	SENW	1852-09-07	FD	SENW	R:JASPER
2016	LEE, Levi	26	SENE	1836-04-18	FD	SENE	R:JASPER
2017	" "	35	NWNW	1836-11-16	FD	NWNW	R:JASPER
2018	LEE, Levie	25	SWNW	1839-04-11	FD	SWNW	R:JASPER
1900	LEISURE, George W	24	NESE	1850-05-03	FD	NESE	R:INDIANA
1901	" "	24	SENE	1850-05-03	FD	SENE	R:INDIANA
2085	LEMASTERS, Surbrina	26	SWNE	1837-09-07	FD	SWNE	R:JASPER S:F
2084	" "	25	NESW	1837-12-30	FD	NESW	R:JASPER S:F
2095	LEMAY, Thomas M	22	NWSE	1852-12-01	FD	NWSE	
1857	LEONARD, Edward F	32	SWNE	1861-04-01	FD	SWNELS	
2100	LOY, Thomas Moore	36	SWSE	1835-03-17	FD	SWSE	R:JASPER
2086	MARSH, Sylvester	30	SEN½	1852-09-06	FD	S2NE	

ID	Individual in Patent	Sec.	Sec. Part	Purchase Date	Sale Type	IL Aliquot Part	For More Info . . .
2132	MARSH, William	29	S½SW	1852-09-06	FD	S2SW	
2133	" "	32	N½NW	1852-09-06	FD	N2NW	
1821	MCCALL, Chrisley	24	SESE	1851-09-15	FD	SESE	R:JASPER
1830	MCCALL, Christley	14	NWNE	1853-06-23	FD	NWNE	S:F
1831	" "	11	NWNW	1853-09-06	FD	NWNW	S:F G:45
1832	" "	2	SWSW	1853-09-06	FD	SWSW	S:F G:45
1832	MCCALL, William P	2	SWSW	1853-09-06	FD	SWSW	S:F G:45
1831	" "	11	NWNW	1853-09-06	FD	NWNW	S:F G:45
1988	MCCARTY, John S	16	L8	1852-03-02	SC	LOT8SENE	
1792	MCDANIEL, Andrew	5	N½NE	1850-06-30	FD	N2NELS	R:INDIANA
1795	" "	5	N½NE	1850-06-30	FD	N2NELS	R:INDIANA
1791	MCDANIEL, Andrew J	4	W½NW	1850-05-21	FD	W2NW	R:INDIANA
1792	" "	5	N½NE	1850-05-21	FD	N2NE	R:INDIANA
1795	" "	5	N½NE	1850-05-21	FD	N2NE	R:INDIANA
1979	MCDANIEL, John	10	NWNW	1850-05-21	FD	NWNW	R:INDIANA
1984	" "	9	NENE	1850-05-21	FD	NENE	R:INDIANA
1983	" "	4	E½SE	1850-05-21	FD	E2SE	
1982	" "	3	W½SW	1850-05-21	FD	W2SW	
1981	" "	3	SESW	1851-10-23	FD	SESW	
1980	" "	19	N½NW	1851-10-23	FD	N2NW	R:INDIANA
2134	MCDANIEL, William	4		1850-06-30	FD	PTE2NEWA	R:JASPER
2134	" "	4		1850-06-30	FD	PTW2NEWA	R:JASPER
2127	MCDANIEL, William H H	4	W½NE	1850-05-27	FD	W2NE	R:JASPER
2124	" "	3	W½NW	1850-05-27	FD	W2NW	R:JASPER
2126	" "	4	E½NW	1850-05-27	FD	E2NW	R:JASPER
2125	" "	4	E½NE	1850-05-27	FD	E2NE	R:JASPER
1845	MCKINNEY, Daniel	25	NWSW	1835-12-14	FD	NWSW	R:FAYETTE
1989	" "	25	NWSW	1835-12-14	FD	NWSW	R:FAYETTE
2136	MCKINSTER, William	3	SWSE	1837-10-03	FD	SWSE	R:JASPER
2135	" "	11	W½SW	1837-10-09	FD	W2SW	R:JASPER
2138	MCQUISTON, William	33	E½NE	1852-01-30	FD	E2NE	R:INDIANA
2137	" "	15	NWSW	1852-01-30	FD	NWSW	R:INDIANA
2139	" "	34	W½NW	1852-01-30	FD	W2NW	R:INDIANA
2066	MOORE, Robert	16	SENW	1853-11-22	FD	SENW	R:INDIANA
2099	MOORE, Thomas	34	NESE	1838-10-19	FD	NESE	R:INDIANA
2097	" "	26	SENW	1838-10-19	FD	SENW	R:INDIANA
2098	" "	26	W½SE	1838-10-19	FD	W2SE	R:INDIANA
2096	" "	26	E½SW	1838-10-19	FD	E2SW	R:INDIANA
1870	MORRIS, Ervin	25	SENE	1852-03-01	FD	SENE	R:JASPER
2006	NAGELY, Josiah	36	E½SE	1838-03-12	FD	E2SE	R:OHIO
1996	OGDEN, Jonathan	24	NWSE	1851-09-26	FD	NWSE	R:INDIANA
2033	OKEAN, Mortimer	25	NWSE	1852-02-12	FD	NWSE	R:JASPER
2034	OKEAN, Mortimore	10	W½SE	1853-12-08	FD	W2SE	
2044	PARR, Peterson K	8	W½SE	1850-10-31	FD	W2SE	
2042	" "	8	SESE	1850-10-31	FD	SESE	
2043	" "	8	SWNE	1850-10-31	FD	SWNE	
2075	PARSONS, Samuel	2	W½NE	1851-09-24	FD	W2NE	R:INDIANA
1819	PATRICK, Charles	6	SESE	1851-01-28	FD	SESE	R:JASPER
1862	PATRICK, Eleanor	28	W½SW	1852-03-30	FD	W2SW	R:JASPER S:F
1864	" "	33	NWNE	1852-03-30	FD	NWNE	R:JASPER S:F
1863	" "	33	NENW	1852-03-30	FD	NENW	R:JASPER S:F
1861	" "	22	SENW	1852-12-01	FD	SENW	R:JASPER S:F
1847	PAULUS, Daniel	22	E½NE	1852-09-06	FD	E2NE	
1848	" "	22	NESE	1852-09-06	FD	NESE	
1849	" "	30	SE	1852-09-06	FD	SE	
1846	" "	15	SESE	1852-09-06	FD	SESE	
1772	PETERSON, Abner M	6	NESE	1854-01-07	FD	NESE	R:JASPER
1942	PETERSON, James	22	SWNE	1852-12-02	FD	SWNE	
1941	" "	22	NWNE	1852-12-02	FD	NWNE	
1940	" "	15	W½SE	1852-12-15	FD	W2SE	
1943	" "	33	SWSW	1853-05-20	FD	SWSW	R:JASPER
1852	PHILLIPS, David	34	E½NE	1831-09-28	FD	E2NE	R:WHITE
2005	PICQUET, Joseph	36	W½NW	1839-04-10	FD	W2NW	R:JASPER
2004	" "	26	SESE	1839-04-10	FD	SESE	R:JASPER
2003	" "	26	NWNE	1839-04-10	FD	NWNE	R:JASPER
2002	" "	25	SWSW	1839-04-10	FD	SWSW	R:JASPER
1796	PIKE, Asher	36	NWSE	1837-11-23	FD	NWSE	R:JASPER
1797	" "	36	SENW	1837-11-23	FD	SENW	R:JASPER
1865	POWELL, John	24	E½SW	1853-03-12	FD	E2SW	R:JASPER G:22
2087	REA, Thomas G	20	NESW	1839-10-23	FD	NESW	R:JASPER
2088	" "	20	SENW	1839-10-23	FD	SENW	R:JASPER
1944	REDFORD, James	5	NWNW	1852-05-22	FD	NWNW	R:JASPER
2076	REEGLESBARGER, Samuel	14	NWSW	1865-05-09	SW	NWSW	

ID	Individual in Patent	Sec.	Sec. Part	Purchase Date	Sale Type	IL Aliquot Part	For More Info . . .
1985	RIBLER, John	20	NENW	1850-04-08	FD	NENW	R:JASPER
2130	RICHARD, William M	34	W½NE	1831-08-30	FD	W2NE	R:CRAWFORD
2131	RICHARDS, William M	27	NESW	1839-08-02	FD	NESW	R:JASPER
1793	RICHEY, Andrew J	2	NENW	1852-10-08	FD	NENW	R:IOWA
2140	RICKMAN, William	13	NESE	1839-05-06	FD	NESE	R:JASPER
1987	RIGHT, John	14	NESE	1850-10-21	FD	NESE	R:JASPER
1986	" "	13	NWSW	1850-10-21	FD	NWSW	R:JASPER
2022	ROBBINS, Maria Ann	14	SWSE	1851-03-11	FD	SWSE	R:JASPER S:F
2041	SAIGER, Peter	15	SEN½	1851-10-22	FD	S2NE	
1854	SCOTT, David	32	W½SE	1853-06-22	FD	W2SE	R:JASPER
1856	" "	33	SWNE	1853-07-19	FD	SWNE	R:JASPER
1855	" "	33	SENW	1853-07-19	FD	SENW	R:JASPER
1831	SELLERS, Mary	11	NWNW	1853-09-06	FD	NWNW	S:F G:45
1832	" "	2	SWSW	1853-09-06	FD	SWSW	S:F G:45
1897	SERIGHT, George	27	SENW	1851-11-01	FD	SENW	
1924	SERIGHT, Isaac	10	SWSW	1852-02-09	FD	SWSW	
1824	SHARICK, Christian	1	NWSE	1845-01-13	FD	NWSE	R:EDGAR S:F
1823	" "	1	NESW	1847-04-12	FD	NESW	R:JASPER S:F
1822	" "	1	NESE	1847-12-29	FD	NESE	R:JASPER S:F
1826	SHARICK, Christian W	1	SESE	1847-07-28	FD	SESE	R:JASPER S:F
1827	" "	1	SWSE	1848-11-15	FD	SWSE	S:F
1828	" "	12	NENW	1848-11-15	FD	NENW	S:F
1825	" "	1	S½SW	1848-11-15	FD	S2SW	S:F
1829	" "	12	NWSW	1852-07-20	FD	NWSW	R:JASPER S:F
2028	SHARICK, Michael	11	SENE	1852-02-10	FD	SENE	R:JASPER
1953	SHARP, Job H	28	W½NE	1837-11-09	FD	W2NE	R:OHIO
1952	" "	28	NENW	1837-11-09	FD	NENW	R:OHIO
2036	SHEARS, Nathan H	24	NWSW	1852-10-15	FD	NWSW	
2101	STEVENS, Uriah G	14	NENW	1848-12-12	FD	NENW	R:JASPER
1775	STIPP, Abraham	1	NE	1843-11-27	FD	NE	R:EDGAR
1927	STROLE, Jacob	15	SWSW	1852-01-30	FD	SWSW	
1957	THOMAS, John D	25	NESE	1837-06-16	FD	NESE	R:JASPER
1958	" "	25	NWNW	1837-07-04	FD	NWNW	R:JASPER
1959	" "	6	N½NW	1849-06-14	FD	N2NW	R:JASPER
1866	THORNBURY, Elijah	23	NENE	1851-10-11	FD	NENE	R:OHIO
1936	TOWNSEND, James F	9	SW	1849-09-25	FD	SW	
2012	VANMETER, Lemuel W	24	SWSW	1839-06-10	FD	SWSW	R:OHIO
2014	" "	25	SESE	1839-06-10	FD	SESE	R:OHIO
2013	" "	25	E½NW	1839-06-10	FD	E2NW	R:OHIO
2015	" "	25	SWNE	1839-06-10	FD	SWNE	R:OHIO
2055	VANMETER, Richard B	25	NENE	1838-02-12	FD	NENE	R:JASPER
1993	WADDLE, John	22	N½NW	1853-05-16	FD	N2NW	
2021	WADE, Lorenzo Dow	20	NWSW	1838-06-16	FD	NWSW	R:JASPER
1923	WALKER, Isaac H	23	NWSW	1853-12-08	FD	NWSW	R:JASPER
1922	" "	11	SWNW	1865-05-09	SW	SWNW	
1884	WALL, Francis	13	SWNW	1853-03-02	FD	SWNW	R:JASPER
2056	WALL, Richard B	14	E½NE	1852-07-15	FD	E2NE	
1949	WHEELER, James	3	SENW	1837-04-29	FD	SENW	R:JASPER
1948	" "	3	NENW	1838-12-26	FD	NENW	R:JASPER
1950	" "	3	W½NE	1839-04-10	FD	W2NE	R:JASPER
1939	WHEELER, James P	3	NWSE	1851-12-09	FD	NWSE	R:JASPER
2037	WHEELER, Perry	3	NESW	1838-10-01	FD	NESW	R:JASPER
1938	WICOFF, James L	24	W½NE	1849-03-06	FD	W2NE	R:INDIANA
1990	WOODWORTH, John S	26	NESE	1836-10-24	FD	NESE	R:CRAWFORD
1989	" "	25	NWSW	1836-10-24	FD	NWSW	R:CRAWFORD
1845	" "	25	NWSW	1836-10-24	FD	NWSW	R:CRAWFORD

Patent Map

T7-N R9-E
3rd PM Meridian

Map Group 7

Township Statistics

Parcels Mapped	:	373
Number of Patents	:	1
Number of Individuals	:	189
Patentees Identified	:	184
Number of Surnames	:	133
Multi-Patentee Parcels	:	13
Oldest Patent Date	:	12/11/1830
Most Recent Patent	:	5/9/1865
Block/Lot Parcels	:	16
Cities and Towns	:	1
Cemeteries	:	7

Section 6: THOMAS John D 1849; BREWER Henry 1850; BREWER Henry 1850; BREWER David S 1849; BREWER David L 1849; PETERSON Abner M 1854; BREWER David L 1849; PATRICK Charles 1851

Section 5: REDFORD James 1852; GOSNELL Washington 1851; GOSNELL Washington 1851; HUSHAW Peter 1851; FOLTZ George 1850; GOSNELL Washington 1851; GOOD James W 1850; GOOD James W 1850; FOLTZ George 1850

Section 4: MCDANIEL Andrew J 1850; MCDANIEL Andrew 1850; MCDANIEL Andrew J 1850; MCDANIEL William H H 1850; MCDANIEL William 1850; MCDANIEL William 1850; MCDANIEL William H H 1850; MCDANIEL William H H 1850; FOLTZ William 1850; DUNGAN Elisha 1849; JASPER Augustine 1850; DUNGAN Elisha 1849; MCDANIEL John 1850

Section 7: BATMAN Greenberry 1849; CLARK Grandison 1849; BARKLEY Peyton H 1849

Section 8: GOOD James W 1850; GOSNELL Washington 1851; HUSHAW Peter 1851; HUSHAW Peter 1851; PARR Peterson K 1850; PARR Peterson K 1850; FOOT Barnard 1850; FOLTZ George 1850; FOLTZ George 1850; PARR Peterson K 1850

Section 9: KOONTZ Andrew 1853; DUGAN Elisha 1851; FOLTZ William 1850; JASPER Augustine 1850; ISLEY Philip 1850; MCDANIEL John 1850; ISLEY Philip 1850; TOWNSEND James F 1849; JORDON William H 1849

Section 18: BARKLEY Peyton H 1849; FOOT Barnard 1850; KIBLER John 1849; BARRETT Samuel 1851

Section 17: CARTER William 1847; CARTER William 1848; FOOT Dan 1850; FOOT Dan 1850; GORNELL George 1849; CARTER William 1849; GOSNELL Washington 1851; GOSNELL Washington 1851; FOOT Charles W 1850

Section 16:
Lots-Sec. 16
L1	BADGER, Stephen		1851
L2	BADGER, Stephen		1851
L3	BARRETT, Harvey B		1851
L4	FOOT, Dan		1850
L5	HILLS, William		1850
L6	KEBLER, John		1850
L7	BARRETT, Harvey B		1851
L8	MCCARTY, John S		1852
L9	BRIDGES, John		1851
L10	BRIDGES, John		1851
L11	BAKER, Jeptha		1850
L12	BRIDGES, William		1850
L13	BRIDGES, William		1850
L14	BRIDGES, John		1851
L15	JONES, Robert H		1850
L16	JONES, Robert H		1850

MOORE Robert 1853

Section 19: MCDANIEL John 1851; BARRETT Samuel 1851; BARRET Samuel 1851; KIBLER John 1849; BRISTOL Andrew E 1853; HARRIS Addison S 1852; KIBLER John 1849

Section 20: KIBLER John 1850; RIBLER John 1850; GARWOOD Thomas 1839; REA Thomas G 1839; WADE Lorenzo Dow 1838; REA Thomas G 1839; KIBLER John 1850; KIBLER John 1849; KIBLER Daniel 1849; KIBLER Daniel 1849; KIBLER John 1849

Section 21: KIBLER Daniel 1849; KIBLER Daniel 1849; HOARE George E 1853; GORNELL George 1849; KIBLER Daniel 1849; KIBLER Daniel 1849; KIBLER John 1849; HARRIS Bushrod W 1840; GARWOOD Thomas 1837; KIBLER John 1849; KIBLER John 1850; KIBLER John 1849

Section 30: BRISTOL Andrew E 1853; HARRIS Addison S 1852; MARSH Sylvester 1852; CURRIE George 1853; PAULUS Daniel 1852

Section 29: KIBLER John 1849; KIBLER John 1849; KIBLER John 1849; MARSH William 1852

Section 28: FULLER Francis 1852; JONES Francis S 1851; HARRIS John 1840; SHARP Job H 1837; FULLER Francis 1852; JONES Robert C 1851; BARRETT Samuel 1851; HARRIS John 1840; SHARP Job H 1837; FRAKES Nathan 1851; JONES Robert E 1851; PATRICK Eleanor 1852; COMER Samuel 1852; FOLTZ Reuben 1851; FULLER Francis 1852; JONES Robert C 1852

Section 31: CURRIE George 1853; HARRIS [36] Benjamin F 1853; HARRIS Addison S 1853; HARRIS Addison S 1853; HARRIS Addison S 1853; JONES Constant B 1852

Section 32: MARSH William 1852; KITCHELL [5] James A 1853; KITCHELL [5] James A 1853; LEONARD Edward F 1861; FULLER Francis 1853; CURRIE George 1853; KITCHELL [5] James A 1853; CARR Jonathan 1851; CARR Jonathan 1851; SCOTT David 1853; CURRIE George 1853

Section 33: FULLER Francis 1853; HOWARD Jacob 1853; PATRICK Eleanor 1852; PATRICK Eleanor 1852; MCQUISTON William 1852; SCOTT David 1853; SCOTT David 1853; CURRIE George 1853; PETERSON James 1853; FISHER Henry 1852; FISHER Henry 1852; HARRIS Addison S 1852

Section 3
- MCDANIEL William H H 1850
- WHEELER James 1838
- WHEELER James 1839
- WHEELER James 1837
- LEE Abbit 1836
- MCDANIEL John 1850
- WHEELER Perry 1838
- WHEELER James P 1851
- BUTLER Melvin 1852
- MCDANIEL John 1851
- MCKINSTER William 1837
- JEFFERS George W 1852

Section 2
- LEE Abbot 1853
- RICHEY Andrew J 1852
- PARSONS Samuel 1851
- LEE Abbott 1852
- FERGUSON Benjamin 1852
- FERGUSON Benjamin 1851
- MCCALL [45] Christley 1853
- ARBUCKLE Abraham 1851
- ARBUCKLE Abraham 1851

Section 1
- FERGUSON Benjamin 1852
- JAMES James E 1851
- STIPP Abraham 1843
- ELDER John L 1852
- SHARICK Christian 1847
- SHARICK Christian 1845
- SHARICK Christian 1847
- SHARICK Christian W 1848
- SHARICK Christian W 1848
- SHARICK Christian W 1847

Section 10
- MCDANIEL John 1850
- JACKSON John 1853
- LEE Abbot 1839
- ISLEY Philip 1850
- LEACH Robert 1865
- CARTER William 1839
- ISLEY Philip 1850
- LEACH Robert 1865
- BROWN Bullard W 1851
- OKEAN Mortimore 1853
- SERIGHT Isaac 1852
- LEACH Robert 1865
- BAKER Absalom 1852

Section 11
- MCCALL [45] Christley 1853
- ELDER Joseph 1852
- ELDER Joseph 1852
- BOWERS Joseph 1852
- WALKER Isaac H 1865
- BARRETT Harvey B 1853
- GROVE Michael 1852
- SHARICK Michael 1852
- BLACK Milton 1837
- DURKEY William 1849
- MCKINSTER William 1837
- BLACK Milton 1837

Section 12
- BOWERS Joseph 1852
- SHARICK Christian W 1848
- BUTLER Melvin 1852
- SHARICK Christian W 1852
- BUTLER Melvin 1852
- GREEN Francis M 1852
- HENSLEY Samuel 1851
- HOLLOPETERS Daniel 1849

Section 15
- BARRETT Samuel 1851
- KIBLINGER Daniel 1851
- FOLTZ Solomon 1851
- BAKER Absalom 1852
- SAIGER Peter 1851
- MCQUISTON William 1852
- BARRETT William E 1865
- PETERSON James 1852
- LEACH Robert 1865
- STROLE Jacob 1852
- BARRETT Harvey 1853
- PAULUS Daniel 1852

Section 14
- BLACK Milton 1837
- STEVENS Uriah G 1848
- MCCALL Christley 1853
- WALL Richard B 1852
- COX Godfrey 1851
- COX Godfrey 1851
- REEGLESBARGER Samuel 1865
- COX Godfrey 1851
- COX Godfrey 1851
- RIGHT John 1850
- FLETCHER Jacob 1836
- KEAN Mortimer O 1843
- ROBBINS Maria Ann 1851
- COX William 1851

Section 13
- ARBUCKELL James 1852
- HENSLEY Samuel 1853
- BALL Amos W 1851
- WALL Francis 1853
- HOWE Edward 1849
- HUNT Thomas 1850
- RIGHT John 1850
- HARMON Joseph 1856
- HUNT Thomas 1848
- RICKMAN William 1839
- HUNT James 1849
- HOWE Edward 1849
- HOWE Edward 1849
- JONES Laban 1848

Section 22
- WADDLE John 1853
- PETERSON James 1852
- PAULUS Daniel 1852
- FOLTZ Reuben 1851
- PATRICK Eleanor 1852
- PETERSON James 1852
- FOLTZ Reuben 1851
- LEMAY Thomas M 1852
- PAULUS Daniel 1852
- COTTINGHAM James 1851
- GOSNELL William 1851

Section 23
- FLETCHER Lazarus 1838
- GARRISON John V 1839
- GARRISON John V 1839
- THORNBURY Elijah 1851
- BARRETT Harvey B 1853
- FLETCHER Lazarus 1838
- WALKER Isaac H 1853
- ADAMS Gilbert D 1848
- ADAMS Gilbert D 1848
- COX Solomon Jr 1838
- GOSNELL William 1851
- COX Solomon Sen 1838

Section 24
- BALL Amos W 1850
- WICOFF James L 1849
- CREASON William B 1848
- LEISURE George W 1850
- SHEARS Nathan H 1852
- CURTIS [22] Eli 1853
- OGDEN Jonathan 1851
- LEISURE George W 1850
- VANMETER Lemuel W 1839
- ARBUCKLE James 1852
- MCCALL Chrisley 1851

Section 27
- BUEL Henry L 1849
- BUEL Henry L 1849
- SERIGHT George 1851
- COURE [20] George W 1851
- BUEL Henry L 1849
- RICHARDS William M 1839
- HARRIS Bushrod W 1837
- FOLTZ Reuben 1851
- HARRIS Bushrod W 1837

Section 26
- GOSNELL William 1851
- KIBLER Adam 1839
- PICQUET Joseph 1839
- COX Solomon Jr 1838
- MOORE Thomas 1838
- LEMASTERS Surbrina 1837
- LEE Levi 1836
- HARRIS Benjamin 1839
- MOORE Thomas 1838
- WOODWORTH John S 1836
- MOORE Thomas 1838
- HARRIS Bushrod W 1837
- PICQUET Joseph 1839

Section 25
- THOMAS John D 1837
- VANMETER Lemuel W 1839
- ARBUCKLE James 1852
- VANMETER Richard B 1838
- LEE Levie 1837
- VANMETER Lemuel W 1839
- MORRIS Ervin 1852
- MCKINNEY Daniel 1835
- WOODWORTH John S 1836
- LEMASTERS Surbrina 1837
- OKEAN Mortimore 1852
- THOMAS John D 1837
- PICQUET Joseph 1839
- JOURDEN Lewis W 1837
- BROWN Felix 1835
- VANMETER Lemuel W 1839

Section 34
- MCQUISTON William 1852
- HARRIS Bushrod W 1837
- RICHARD William M 1831
- PHILLIPS David 1831
- HARRIS [37] Benjamin 1836
- HARRIS [37] Benjamin 1836
- HARRIS Addison S 1852
- FULLER Francis 1851
- FULLER Francis 1851
- MOORE Thomas 1838
- FULLER Francis 1851

Section 35
- HARRIS [37] Benjamin 1836
- HARRIS [37] Benjamin 1836
- HARRIS [37] Benjamin 1836
- HARRIS [37] Benjamin 1836
- FITHIAN Smith 1836

Section 36
- JOURDEN Lewis W 1837
- BROWN Felix 1835
- HALLENBECK Lawrence 1838
- PICQUET Joseph 1839
- PIKE Asher 1837
- HALLENBECK Lawrence 1838
- PIKE Asher 1837
- HARRIS Addison S 1838
- GARWOOD Thomas 1836
- GARWOOD Thomas 1830
- LOY Thomas Moore 1835
- NAGELY Josiah 1838

Helpful Hints

1. This Map's INDEX can be found on the preceding pages.

2. Refer to Map "C" to see where this Township lies within Jasper County, Illinois.

3. Numbers within square brackets [ ] denote a multi-patentee land parcel (multi-owner). Refer to Appendix "C" for a full list of members in this group.

4. Areas that look to be crowded with Patentees usually indicate multiple sales of the same parcel (re-issues), cancellations or voided transactions (that we map, anyway) or overlapping parcels. We opt to show even these ambiguous parcels, which oftentimes lead to research avenues not yet taken.

Legend

- ——— Patent Boundary
- ▬▬▬ Section Boundary
- No Patents Found (or Outside County)
- 1., 2., 3., ... Lot Numbers (when beside a name)
- [ ] Group Number (see Appendix "C")

Scale: Section = 1 mile X 1 mile (generally, with some exceptions)

Road Map

T7-N R9-E
3rd PM Meridian

Map Group 7

Cities & Towns
Lis

Cemeteries
Bowers Cemetery
Brick Cemetery
Chaple Cemetery
Coburn Cemetery
Jones Cemetery
Kibler Cemetery
Redford Cemetery

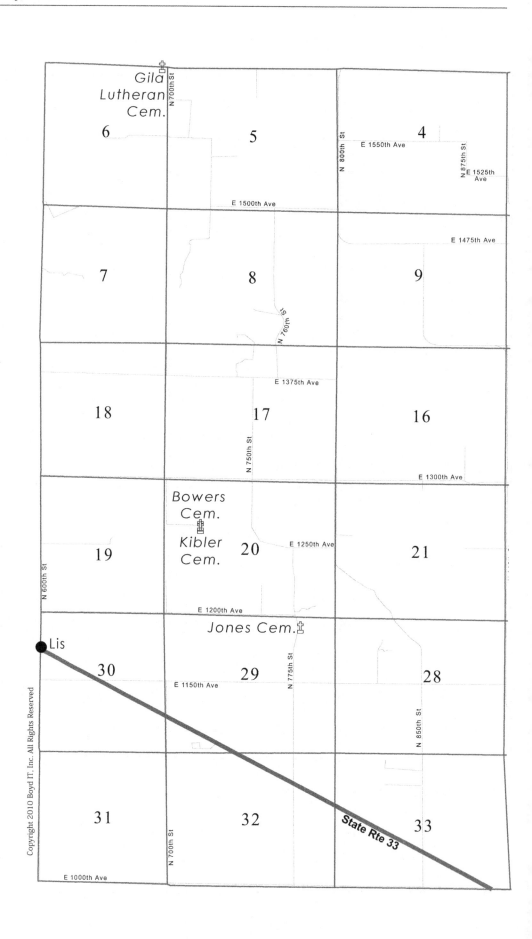

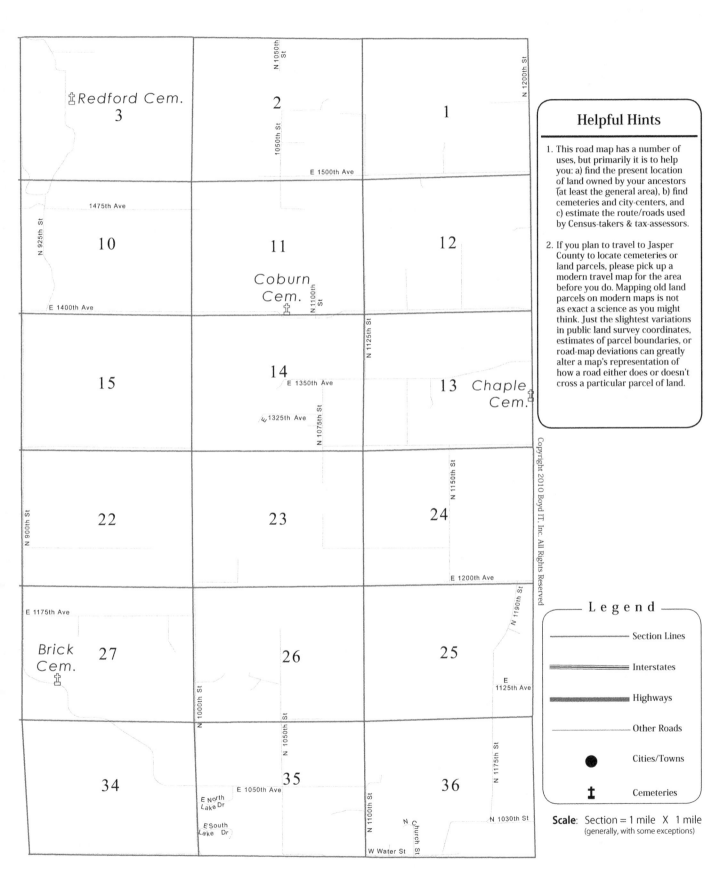

‡Redford Cem.
3

N 1050th St

2

N 1200th St

1

1050th St

E 1500th Ave

1475th Ave

N 925th St

10

11

12

Coburn
Cem.
‡

N 1100th St

N 1125th St

E 1400th Ave

15

14

E 1350th Ave

13 Chaple
Cem.‡

E 1325th Ave

N 1075th St

N 1150th St

N 900th St

22

23

24

E 1200th Ave

E 1175th Ave

N 1190th St

Brick
Cem.
‡

27

26

25

E
1125th Ave

N 1000th St

N 1050th St

N 1175th St

34

35

E 1050th Ave

36

E North
Lake Dr

E South
Lake Dr

N 1100th St

N Church St

N 1030th St

W Water St

Helpful Hints

1. This road map has a number of uses, but primarily it is to help you: a) find the present location of land owned by your ancestors (at least the general area), b) find cemeteries and city-centers, and c) estimate the route/roads used by Census-takers & tax-assessors.

2. If you plan to travel to Jasper County to locate cemeteries or land parcels, please pick up a modern travel map for the area before you do. Mapping old land parcels on modern maps is not as exact a science as you might think. Just the slightest variations in public land survey coordinates, estimates of parcel boundaries, or road-map deviations can greatly alter a map's representation of how a road either does or doesn't cross a particular parcel of land.

L e g e n d

————————	Section Lines
═══════════	Interstates
▬▬▬▬▬▬▬	Highways
————————	Other Roads
●	Cities/Towns
‡	Cemeteries

Scale: Section = 1 mile X 1 mile
(generally, with some exceptions)

Historical Map

T7-N R9-E
3rd PM Meridian

Map Group 7

Cities & Towns
Lis

Cemeteries
Bowers Cemetery
Brick Cemetery
Chaple Cemetery
Coburn Cemetery
Jones Cemetery
Kibler Cemetery
Redford Cemetery

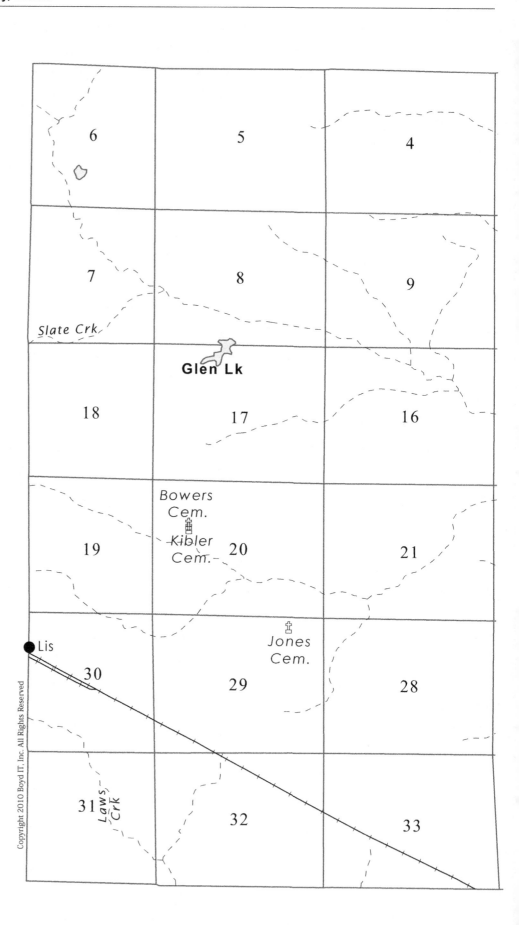

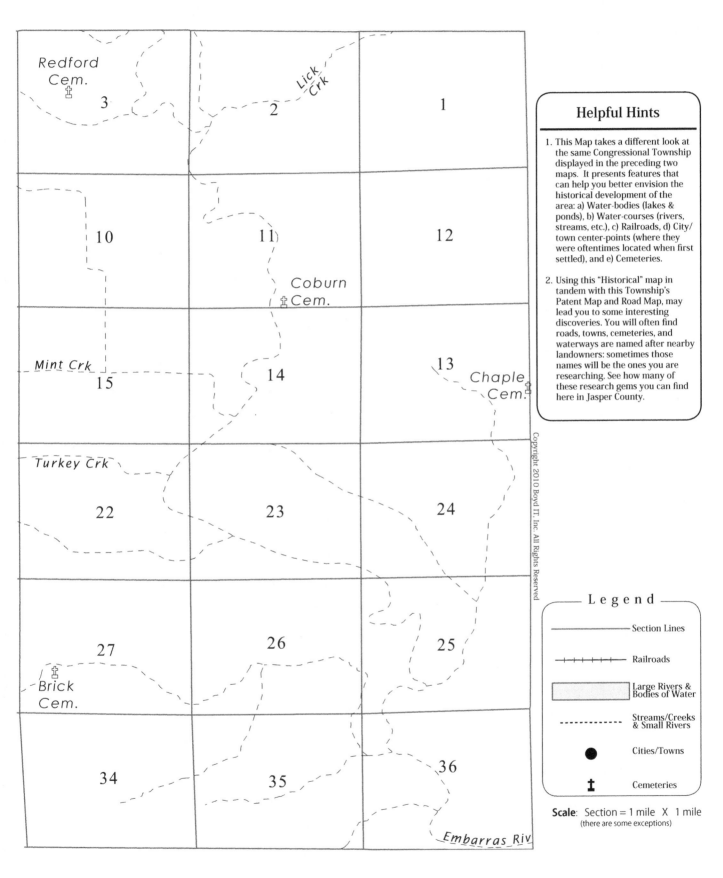

1. This Map takes a different look at the same Congressional Township displayed in the preceding two maps. It presents features that can help you better envision the historical development of the area: a) Water-bodies (lakes & ponds), b) Water-courses (rivers, streams, etc.), c) Railroads, d) City/town center-points (where they were oftentimes located when first settled), and e) Cemeteries.

2. Using this "Historical" map in tandem with this Township's Patent Map and Road Map, may lead you to some interesting discoveries. You will often find roads, towns, cemeteries, and waterways are named after nearby landowners: sometimes those names will be the ones you are researching. See how many of these research gems you can find here in Jasper County.

L e g e n d

————————	Section Lines
—+—+—+—+—	Railroads
▭	Large Rivers & Bodies of Water
- - - - - - - -	Streams/Creeks & Small Rivers
●	Cities/Towns
✝	Cemeteries

Scale: Section = 1 mile X 1 mile
(there are some exceptions)

Map Group 8: Index to Land Patents

Township 7-North Range 10-East (3rd PM)

After you locate an individual in this Index, take note of the Section and Section Part then proceed to the Land Patent map on the pages immediately following. You should have no difficulty locating the corresponding parcel of land.

The "For More Info" Column will lead you to more information about the underlying Patents. See the *Legend* at right, and the "How to Use this Book" chapter, for more information.

```
┌─────────────────────────────────────────────────────────┐
│                        LEGEND                             │
│            "For More Info . . . " column                  │
│  G = Group   (Multi-Patentee Patent, see Appendix "C")    │
│  R = Residence                                            │
│  S = Social Status                                        │
│                                                           │
│  See Appendix A for list of abbreviations used by the     │
│  Illinois State Archives in describing the place and      │
│  nature of these land patents.                            │
│                                                           │
│  Note: if the Abbreviations contain "L", "BL", "LOT",     │
│  or "BLOCK", the exact whereabouts of the parcel within   │
│  the section is not known.                                │
└─────────────────────────────────────────────────────────┘
```

ID	Individual in Patent	Sec.	Sec. Part	Purchase Date	Sale Type	IL Aliquot Part	For More Info . . .
2460	ADAMS, Matthew	33	W½NW	1845-11-21	FD	W2NW	R:JASPER
2290	AVERY, Homer T	22	NWNE	1848-05-11	FD	NWNE	R:JASPER
2291	" "	22	SENW	1848-05-11	FD	SENW	R:JASPER
2293	" "	23	NWSE	1848-06-24	FD	NWSE	R:JASPER
2292	" "	23	NESE	1848-10-07	FD	NESE	R:JASPER
2313	BAILEY, Jacob	36	NE	1849-08-29	FD	NE	
2170	BAKER, Peter	28	E½SE	1849-05-17	FD	E2SE	G:7
2169	"	27	W½SW	1849-05-17	FD	W2SW	G:7
2321	BARNES, James	29	N½SE	1849-04-26	FD	N2SE	R:JASPER
2158	BARTLEY, Amos	23	SWSE	1849-04-21	FD	SWSE	R:INDIANA
2197	BARTLEY, David	10	SWNE	1850-01-12	FD	SWNE	R:JASPER G:8
2363	BARTLEY, John	23	SWNE	1846-01-03	FD	SWNE	R:INDIANA
2362	" "	23	E½NE	1849-06-16	FD	E2NE	
2361	" "	14	E½SE	1849-06-16	FD	E2SE	
2397	BARTLEY, John P	23	E½NW	1839-11-06	FD	E2NW	R:INDIANA
2398	" "	23	SW	1839-11-06	FD	SW	R:INDIANA
2396	" "	22	W½SE	1840-03-23	FD	W2SE	R:INDIANA
2394	" "	15	E½SE	1840-03-23	FD	E2SE	R:INDIANA
2395	" "	22	E½SW	1840-11-05	FD	E2SW	R:INDIANA
2197	" "	10	SWNE	1850-01-12	FD	SWNE	R:JASPER G:8
2251	BATMAN, Greenberry	7	W½	1849-10-02	FD	W2	R:INDIANA
2164	BECKWITH, Benjamin	11	NWSW	1845-12-17	FD	NWSW	R:CRAWFORD
2163	" "	10	SESE	1845-12-17	FD	SESE	R:CRAWFORD
2165	" "	11	SWNW	1846-03-11	FD	SWNW	R:JASPER
2171	BECKWITH, Benjamin Jr	13	SWNW	1851-03-13	FD	SWNW	R:JASPER
2438	BEMUSDOFFER, Joseph V	2	E½NE	1849-04-21	FD	E2NE	R:INDIANA
2440	" "	2	SWNE	1849-04-21	FD	SWNE	R:INDIANA
2439	" "	2	SENW	1849-04-21	FD	SENW	R:INDIANA
2312	BENEFIELD, Israel	12	W½SE	1852-09-21	FD	W2SE	
2310	" "	12	NESE	1852-09-21	FD	NESE	
2311	" "	12	SESW	1852-09-21	FD	SESW	
2508	BERCASTLE, Susannah	33	SESW	1845-02-25	FD	SESW	R:JASPER S:F
2441	BEUSDOFFER, Joseph V	2		1849-05-31	FD	SENWWA	R:INDIANA
2441	" "	2		1849-05-31	FD	SWNEWA	R:INDIANA
2441	" "	2		1849-05-31	FD	E2NEWA	R:INDIANA
2411	" "	2		1849-05-31	FD	E2NEWA	R:INDIANA
2411	" "	2		1849-05-31	FD	SENWWA	R:INDIANA
2411	" "	2		1849-05-31	FD	SWNEWA	R:INDIANA
2198	BIRT, David H	7	NESW	1851-12-19	FD	NESW	R:JASPER
2265	BIRT, Henry	9	SWSW	1852-09-01	FD	SWSW	
2264	" "	19	W½SW	1852-09-01	FD	W2SW	R:INDIANA
2297	BLAKE, Isaac	8	SWNE	1843-10-03	FD	SWNE	R:JASPER
2155	BLISS, Alvin C	4	SW	1850-03-30	FD	SW	
2521	BONER, Uriah	11	NESW	1851-12-11	FD	NESW	R:INDIANA
2217	BOWERS, Frederick	20	E½SW	1844-11-30	FD	E2SW	R:OHIO
2286	BROCK, Holland L	16	L8	1853-03-09	SC	LOT8SENE	

ID	Individual in Patent	Sec.	Sec. Part	Purchase Date	Sale Type	IL Aliquot Part	For More Info . . .
2287	BROCK, Hollen L	14	SWSW	1848-02-07	FD	SWSW	R:JASPER
2288	BROCK, Hollon L	14	SESW	1847-10-18	FD	SESW	R:JASPER
2289	" "	23	NWNE	1847-10-18	FD	NWNE	R:JASPER
2494	BROCK, Richard H	14	SWSE	1847-09-06	FD	SWSE	R:EDGAR
2493	" "	14	NWSW	1847-09-06	FD	NWSW	R:EDGAR
2492	" "	14	NWSE	1847-10-18	FD	NWSE	R:JASPER
2491	" "	14	NESW	1847-10-18	FD	NESW	R:JASPER
2495	" "	16	L14	1853-02-14	SC	LOT14S2SE	
2144	BRODERICK, Aaron M	13	NWNW	1849-05-05	FD	NWNW	
2142	" "	12	E½SE	1849-05-05	FD	E2SE	
2143	" "	12	SWSW	1849-05-05	FD	SWSW	
2148	BRODERICK, Abraham P	34	SEN½	1849-02-05	FD	S2NE	
2147	" "	34	S½NW	1849-02-05	FD	S2NW	
2154	BRODERICK, Alvah P	23	SESE	1849-02-05	FD	SESE	R:INDIANA
2322	BROOK, James	16	L3	1852-03-08	SC	LOT3NENW	
2152	BROOKS, Alfred J F	27	SWSE	1836-01-04	FD	SWSE	R:FAYETTE
2542	" "	27	SWSE	1836-01-04	FD	SWSE	R:FAYETTE
2205	BROOKS, Elliphaz	6	E½NE	1842-01-31	FD	E2NE	R:JASPER
2207	" "	6	SWNE	1842-01-31	FD	SWNE	R:JASPER
2206	" "	6	NWSE	1842-01-31	FD	NWSE	R:JASPER
2299	BROOKS, Isaac	7	SEN½	1849-06-19	FD	S2NE	
2301	" "	8	W½NW	1849-06-19	FD	W2NW	
2298	" "	5	SW	1850-05-20	FD	SW	
2300	" "	7	SENW	1851-02-25	FD	SENW	R:JASPER
2325	BROOKS, James	9	W½NW	1840-08-19	FD	W2NW	R:CRAWFORD
2324	" "	8	E½NE	1840-08-19	FD	E2NE	R:CRAWFORD
2323	" "	5	W½SE	1840-08-19	FD	W2SE	R:CRAWFORD
2372	BROOKS, John	8	SE	1840-10-12	FD	SE	R:JASPER
2369	" "	20	SE	1840-12-12	FD	SE	R:JASPER
2368	" "	20	NENE	1841-02-25	FD	NENE	R:JASPER
2371	" "	6	SWSE	1846-03-30	FD	SWSE	R:JASPER
2370	" "	6	NESE	1846-03-30	FD	NESE	R:JASPER
2367	" "	17	NWNE	1846-07-01	FD	NWNE	R:JASPER
2365	" "	17	E½SE	1847-07-06	FD	E2SE	R:JASPER
2366	" "	17	NENE	1847-07-06	FD	NENE	R:JASPER
2364	" "	16	L2	1851-03-18	SC	LOT2NWNE	
2515	BROOKS, Thomas	6	NWNE	00/20/1850	FD	NWNE	R:JASPER
2548	BROWN, William M	30	SENW	1846-04-23	FD	SENW	R:JASPER
2556	BROWNING, William P	30	NENW	1850-07-04	FD	NENW	R:JASPER
2173	BRYER, Bernard	19	SWNE	1849-07-13	FD	SWNE	R:JASPER
2501	BUCHANAN, Samuel	8	E½NW	1852-01-12	FD	E2NW	R:JASPER
2424	BURCHAM, Joseph	15	SWNE	1851-10-25	FD	SWNE	R:INDIANA
2162	BURFORD, Basel B	19	SENW	1852-04-06	FD	SENW	R:JASPER
2534	BURT, William	4	S½NW	1851-09-30	FD	S2NW	R:JASPER
2374	BYRD, John	9	E½SE	1842-02-02	FD	E2SE	R:JASPER
2373	" "	10	W½SW	1842-02-02	FD	W2SW	R:JASPER
2210	CHAPMAN, Enoch	3	SE	1848-07-06	FD	SE	
2209	" "	10	NWNW	1850-02-01	FD	NWNW	R:JASPER
2208	" "	10	NENE	1852-01-02	FD	NENE	R:JASPER
2302	CHAPMAN, Isaac	3	NWNE	1853-12-06	FD	NWNE	R:JASPER
2328	CHAPMAN, James	3	SWNE	1848-06-06	FD	SWNE	R:JASPER
2326	" "	3	NESW	1849-05-14	FD	NESW	R:JASPER
2327	" "	3	SENW	1850-03-26	FD	SENW	R:JASPER
2329	" "	3	SWSW	1851-03-08	FD	SWSW	R:JASPER
2375	CHAPMAN, John	2	SWSW	1850-02-01	FD	SWSW	R:JASPER
2146	CHRISS, Abraham	34	NENE	1850-09-11	FD	NENE	R:INDIANA
2220	CHRISS, George	26	SWSE	1849-05-05	FD	SWSE	R:INDIANA
2225	" "	35	S½NW	1849-05-05	FD	S2NW	
2224	" "	35	N½SW	1849-05-05	FD	N2SW	
2223	" "	35	N½NW	1849-05-05	FD	N2NW	
2222	" "	35	N½NE	1849-05-05	FD	N2NE	
2226	" "	35	S½SW	1849-06-21	FD	S2SW	
2221	" "	35	E½SE	1849-06-21	FD	E2SE	
2245	" "	35	E½SE	1849-06-21	FD	E2SE	
2219	" "	26	NWNE	1850-10-01	FD	NWNE	R:JASPER
2320	CONDE, James B	36	W½SE	1849-08-27	FD	W2SE	
2319	" "	36	W½NE	1849-08-27	FD	W2NE	
2514	" "	36	W½SE	1849-08-27	FD	W2SE	
2536	COX, William	21	SWSE	1851-03-11	FD	SWSE	R:JASPER
2376	CUMMINS, John	11	NWNW	1851-11-04	FD	NWNW	
2426	CUMMINS, Joseph	9	NENE	1850-07-20	FD	NENE	R:JASPER
2425	" "	3	NENE	1852-08-07	FD	NENE	R:EDGAR
2387	DE GAEGER, THEODORE	32	SWNE	1844-09-11	FD	SWNE	R:JASPER G:25

ID	Individual in Patent	Sec.	Sec. Part	Purchase Date	Sale Type	IL Aliquot Part	For More Info . . .
2386	DE GAEGER, THEODORE (Cont'd)	32	E½NE	1844-09-11	FD	E2NE	R:JASPER G:25
2252	DE YAEGER, GREGOR	29	SESE	1850-07-02	FD	SESE	R:JASPER
2463	DHOM, Michael V	34	W½SE	1839-05-09	FD	W2SE	R:JASPER
2462	" "	34	SW	1839-05-09	FD	SW	R:JASPER
2336	DIXON, James H	34	NWNE	1848-11-13	FD	NWNE	G:27
2335	" "	34	NENW	1848-11-13	FD	NENW	G:27
2334	" "	27	E½SW	1848-11-13	FD	E2SW	G:27
2333	" "	26	SWSW	1852-06-07	FD	SWSW	R:JASPER
2341	DIXON, James L	26	SESW	1852-05-24	FD	SESW	R:JASPER
2216	DORN, Franz	32	NWNE	1851-08-11	FD	NWNE	R:JASPER
2540	DRYSDALE, William	17	SENE	1849-12-22	FD	SENE	R:INDIANA
2537	" "	16	L4	1850-10-21	SC	LOT4NWNW	
2538	" "	16	L5	1850-10-21	SC	LOT5SWNW	
2539	" "	17	NENW	1851-10-29	FD	NENW	R:INDIANA
2266	EARNEST, Henry F	16	L11	1851-01-27	SC	LOT11NWSN	
2267	" "	16	L7	1853-01-08	SC	LOT7SWNE	
2461	EDERER, Michael	21	SWSW	1852-11-03	FD	SWSW	
2379	FAWCETT, John H	4	SWSE	1850-02-18	FD	SWSE	R:INDIANA
2332	FEAR, James	24	SW	1849-11-14	FD	SW	
2331	" "	22	NWSW	1850-03-29	FD	NWSW	R:JASPER
2356	FERGUSON, Jeremiah	36	SENW	1848-05-27	FD	SENW	R:INDIANA
2355	" "	36	NENW	1850-02-07	FD	NENW	R:JASPER
2503	FERGUSON, Samuel	35	W½SE	1851-10-28	FD	W2SE	
2504	FERGUSON, Sandford	15	SWSE	1851-08-01	FD	SWSE	R:JASPER
2531	FERGUSON, Will	24	E½SW	1848-12-19	FD	E2SWVOID	
2532	" "	24	SWSW	1848-12-19	FD	SWSWVOID	
2533	" "	27	SESE	1848-12-19	FD	SESEVOID	
2541	" "	27	SESE	1848-12-19	FD	SESEVOID	
2152	FERGUSON, William	27	SWSE	1848-12-19	FD	SWSE	R:JASPER
2542	" "	27	SWSE	1848-12-19	FD	SWSE	R:JASPER
2533	" "	27	SESE	1852-07-15	FD	SESE	
2541	" "	27	SESE	1852-07-15	FD	SESE	
2166	FITHIAN, Benjamin	19	NWNE	1839-07-15	FD	NWNE	R:JASPER
2228	FOGLE, George	11	N½NE	1849-05-02	FD	N2NE	
2227	" "	11	E½NW	1849-05-02	FD	E2NW	
2377	FRANKE, John	31	W½NE	1852-02-17	FD	W2NE	R:JASPER
2378	" "	32	SWSW	1852-08-12	FD	SWSW	
2253	FREEMAN, Gustavus F	18	NESW	1852-09-02	FD	NESW	R:INDIANA
2427	FRUCHTEL, Joseph	19	SESW	1852-09-06	FD	SESW	R:JASPER
2428	FRUICHTEL, Joseph	30	NENE	1850-10-03	FD	NENE	R:JASPER
2271	GARDENWINE, Henry	29	SWNW	1850-10-28	FD	SWNW	R:JASPER
2274	GARDEWAIN, Henry	29	SESW	1842-02-03	FD	SESW	R:JASPER
2272	" "	29	E½NW	1846-01-06	FD	E2NW	R:JASPER
2273	" "	29	NESW	1849-06-18	FD	NESW	R:JASPER
2358	GARRETSON, Jeremiah	19	NENW	1852-09-14	FD	NENW	R:JASPER
2357	" "	18	SESW	1852-09-14	FD	SESW	R:JASPER
2417	GARRISON, John V	30	SWNW	1839-06-10	FD	SWNW	R:OHIO
2305	GIFFORD, Isaac M	1	SESE	1840-10-08	FD	SESE	R:COLES
2306	" "	1	SWSE	1840-11-14	FD	SWSE	R:COLES
2307	" "	2	NWNE	1849-04-21	FD	NWNE	R:JASPER
2303	" "	1	NESW	1850-03-26	FD	NESW	R:JASPER
2304	" "	1	NWSE	1851-12-23	FD	NWSE	R:JASPER
2452	GIFFORD, Levi	12	W½NE	1840-10-08	FD	W2NE	R:COLES
2451	" "	1	W½SW	1840-10-08	FD	W2SW	R:COLES
2516	GRIFFING, Thomas C	13	SESE	1851-10-13	FD	SESE	R:JASPER
2518	GRIFFING, Thomas G	15	NWSE	1848-05-03	FD	NWSE	R:INDIANA
2517	" "	13	SWSE	1848-10-19	FD	SWSE	R:JASPER
2449	HALLENBECK, Lawrence	30	NWSW	1838-08-04	FD	NWSW	R:JASPER
2141	HARLEN, Aaron	24	SE	1849-08-27	FD	SE	
2314	HARRISON, Jacob	1	SESE	1849-06-27	FD	SESE	R:JASPER
2315	" "	12	NENW	1852-01-03	FD	NENW	R:JASPER
2316	" "	12	NWNW	1853-12-03	FD	NWNW	R:JASPER
2190	HARRISON, Richard	9	NENW	1851-11-04	FD	NENW	
2497	" "	9	NWNE	1851-11-04	FD	NWNE	
2496	" "	9	NENW	1851-11-04	FD	NENW	
2229	HAWLEY, George	31	NESE	1837-06-28	FD	NESE	R:JASPER
2338	HAWS, James	14	SWNW	1848-02-07	FD	SWNW	R:JASPER
2342	HAWS, James L	14	SENW	1847-10-18	FD	SENW	R:JASPER
2343	" "	14	SWNE	1847-10-18	FD	SWNE	R:JASPER
2475	HAYS, Oliver	9	NWSE	1851-08-06	FD	NWSE	R:JASPER
2476	" "	9	SWNE	1851-08-06	FD	SWNE	R:JASPER
2191	" "	9	NWSE	1851-08-06	FD	NWSE	R:JASPER
2555	HAYS, William O	5	E½SE	1851-10-02	FD	E2SE	R:JASPER

ID	Individual in Patent	Sec.	Sec. Part	Purchase Date	Sale Type	IL Aliquot Part	For More Info . . .
2554	HAYS, William O (Cont'd)	30	NWSE	1851-10-13	FD	NWSE	R:JASPER
2553	" "	18	SWSE	1852-08-03	FD	SWSE	
2472	HAZELTON, Newton	7	SWNW	1849-11-10	FD	SWNW	
2473	" "	7	W½SW	1849-11-10	FD	W2SW	
2250	HEFNER, Green Berry	1	NENE	1852-09-21	FD	NENE	
2480	HELVET, Peter	29	SWSE	1849-07-13	FD	SWSE	R:JASPER
2543	HENRICK, William	7	N½NE	1840-03-16	FD	N2NE	R:JASPER
2192	HOLLOPETERS, Daniel	9	W½NE	1849-06-05	FD	W2NEVOID	
2191	" "	9	NWSE	1849-06-05	FD	NWSEVOID	
2496	" "	9	NENW	1849-06-05	FD	NENWVOID	
2190	" "	9	NENW	1849-06-05	FD	NENWVOID	
2475	" "	9	NWSE	1849-06-05	FD	NWSEVOID	
2159	HOUSE, Andrew	14	SENE	1849-08-21	FD	SENE	R:JASPER
2177	HOUSE, Charles	14	NENE	1848-10-03	FD	NENE	R:JASPER
2201	HOUSE, Eleanor	15	NWNE	1846-12-21	FD	NWNE	R:JASPER S:F
2167	HUME, Benjamin	26	NENW	1849-01-19	FD	NENW	R:INDIANA
2169	" "	27	W½SW	1849-05-17	FD	W2SW	G:7
2170	" "	28	E½SE	1849-05-17	FD	E2SE	G:7
2168	" "	34	NWNW	1851-04-09	FD	NWNW	R:JASPER
2381	HUME, John	27	NWNE	1848-10-07	FD	NWNE	R:INDIANA
2380	" "	26	SWNE	1848-10-07	FD	SWNE	R:INDIANA
2545	HUME, William	27	SWNE	1848-10-07	FD	SWNE	R:INDIANA
2544	" "	26	SENW	1848-10-07	FD	SENW	R:INDIANA
2453	HUMES, Lewis	15	NENE	1852-05-24	FD	NENE	R:JASPER
2157	HUNT, Amaziah	18	NWNW	1851-01-06	FD	NWNW	R:INDIANA
2339	HUNT, James	18	NENW	1848-07-04	FD	NENW	R:INDIANA
2340	" "	18	SWNW	1848-07-04	FD	SWNW	R:INDIANA
2519	HUNT, Thomas	7	SESW	1848-07-04	FD	SESW	R:INDIANA
2276	INGLE, Henry	3	SESW	1851-12-29	FD	SESW	R:JASPER
2275	" "	16	L6	1852-12-28	SC	LOT6SENW	
2382	INGLE, John	10	NENW	1851-07-28	FD	NENW	
2383	" "	10	NWNE	1851-07-28	FD	NWNE	
2330	JAMES, James E	6	NWSW	1850-12-21	FD	NWSW	R:JASPER
2242	JEFFERS, George W	26	SWNW	1849-01-11	FD	SWNW	
2244	" "	27	SENE	1849-01-11	FD	SENE	
2241	" "	26	NWSW	1849-01-11	FD	NWSW	
2243	" "	27	NESE	1849-01-11	FD	NESE	
2240	" "	22	SWSW	1849-09-01	FD	SWSW	R:JASPER
2221	JOHNSON, George W	35	E½SE	1849-05-14	FD	E2SE	
2246	" "	35	SEN½	1849-05-14	FD	S2NE	
2245	" "	35	E½SE	1849-05-14	FD	E2SE	
2215	JONES, Ezekiel	24	NW	1849-10-19	FD	NW	
2214	" "	13	SEN½	1849-11-16	FD	S2NE	
2213	" "	13	N½SE	1849-11-16	FD	N2SE	
2447	JONES, Laban	18	NWNE	1848-05-03	FD	NWNE	R:INDIANA
2547	JONES, William	7	SESE	1848-05-03	FD	SESE	R:INDIANA
2550	JONES, William M	8	NWNE	1847-09-03	FD	NWNE	R:INDIANA
2549	" "	7	NESE	1847-09-03	FD	NESE	R:INDIANA
2551	" "	8	NWSW	1847-09-03	FD	NWSW	R:INDIANA
2469	KEAN, Mortimer O	19	W½NW	1852-07-10	FD	W2NW	R:JASPER
2470	" "	21	SESW	1852-07-12	FD	SESW	
2498	KELLY, Robert S	5	E½NE	1852-05-24	FD	E2NE	R:IOWA
2392	KIBLER, John M	10	SWSE	1849-02-22	FD	SWSE	R:JASPER
2391	" "	10	NWSE	1852-01-16	FD	NWSE	R:JASPER
2456	KIBLER, Martin	5	N½NW	1838-05-24	FD	N2NW	R:INDIANA
2455	" "	15	SENE	1852-05-31	FD	SENE	
2488	KIBLER, Reuben	4	NWSE	1849-01-20	FD	NWSE	R:JASPER
2487	" "	4	NESE	1850-02-09	FD	NESE	R:JASPER
2489	" "	4	SESE	1850-12-25	FD	SESE	R:JASPER
2179	KINTZEL, Charles	32	SWNW	1841-02-27	FD	SWNW	R:JASPER
2178	" "	32	NWSW	1841-04-23	FD	NWSW	R:JASPER
2248	LEISURE, George W	19	W½SE	1850-05-03	FD	W2SE	R:INDIANA
2247	" "	19	SESE	1851-02-06	FD	SESE	R:INDIANA
2145	LEMASTERS, Abbot A	30	W½NE	1839-04-08	FD	W2NE	R:JASPER
2151	LEWIS, Adam C	22	SWNE	1851-03-10	FD	SWNE	R:JASPER
2230	LIPTRAP, George	29	SWNE	1839-04-08	FD	SWNE	R:INDIANA
2399	MADDEN, John P	15	E½SW	1849-10-04	FD	E2SW	
2400	" "	22	N½NW	1849-10-04	FD	N2NW	
2546	MADDEN, William J	13	SW	1849-10-04	FD	SW	
2346	MARSHALL, James	9	SWSE	1852-01-09	FD	SWSE	
2345	" "	9	SESW	1852-01-09	FD	SESW	
2348	MARTIN, James	12	NWSW	1843-04-12	FD	NWSW	R:JASPER
2347	" "	11	SWSE	1843-04-12	FD	SWSE	R:JASPER

ID	Individual in Patent	Sec.	Sec. Part	Purchase Date	Sale Type	IL Aliquot Part	For More Info . . .
2182	MATTHEWS, Christian	2	W½SE	1848-10-28	FD	W2SE	R:OHIO S:A
2231	MCKINLEY, George	31	W½NW	1841-02-26	FD	W2NW	R:JASPER
2514	MCNAIR, Thomas A	36	W½SE	1849-05-15	FD	W2SE	
2513	" "	36	E½SW	1849-05-15	FD	E2SW	
2512	" "	36	E½SE	1849-05-15	FD	E2SE	
2320	" "	36	W½SE	1849-05-15	FD	W2SE	
2181	MICHAEL, Chatarina	28	W½NW	1850-05-23	FD	W2NW	R:JASPER S:F
2180	" "	28	NENW	1850-05-23	FD	NENW	R:JASPER S:F
2474	MICHAEL, Nicholas	28	SENE	1851-08-12	FD	SENE	R:JASPER
2390	MIRES, John L	27	NWSE	1850-01-23	FD	NWSE	R:INDIANA
2389	" "	26	N½SE	1850-01-23	FD	N2SE	
2388	" "	26	E½NE	1850-01-23	FD	E2NE	
2203	MITCHELL, Elihu	18	NWSE	1849-10-29	FD	NWSE	R:JASPER
2202	" "	16	L9	1851-04-10	SC	LOT9N2SE	
2233	MITCHELL, George	3	W½NW	1839-04-08	FD	W2NW	R:INDIANA
2232	" "	3	NENW	1849-12-26	FD	NENW	R:JASPER
2294	MOSCHENROSS, Ignace	28	SENW	1845-04-26	FD	SENW	R:JASPER
2295	" "	28	SWNE	1845-04-26	FD	SWNE	R:JASPER
2296	" "	28	W½SE	1845-04-26	FD	W2SE	R:JASPER
2552	MULVANY, William	17	NWSW	1850-02-11	FD	NWSW	R:JASPER
2446	NAGELY, Josiah	31	W½SW	1838-03-12	FD	W2SW	R:CLARK
2421	OGDEN, Jonathan	18	NWSW	1851-09-26	FD	NWSW	R:INDIANA
2422	" "	18	SENW	1851-09-26	FD	SENW	R:INDIANA
2423	" "	18	SWSW	1852-10-25	FD	SWSW	R:JASPER
2176	PAINE, Casius M	3	SENE	1854-01-13	FD	SENE	R:LAWRENCE
2199	PARENT, David	29	N½NE	1839-04-08	FD	N2NE	R:INDIANA
2481	PARR, Peterson K	11	SESW	1849-10-19	FD	SESW	
2482	" "	14	N½NW	1849-10-19	FD	N2NW	
2483	" "	14	NWNE	1849-10-19	FD	NWNE	
2200	PARRENT, David	29	SENE	1848-10-30	FD	SENE	R:JASPER
2454	PARRENT, Maria Ann	28	NWSW	1848-10-30	FD	NWSW	R:JASPER S:F
2557	PARRENT, William	20	SWSW	1837-11-10	FD	SWSW	R:CRAWFORD
2558	" "	29	NWNW	1837-11-10	FD	NWNW	R:CRAWFORD
2402	PATEE, John	10	SENW	1852-03-27	FD	SENW	
2401	" "	10	NESW	1852-03-27	FD	NESW	
2309	PATTERSON, Isaac	16	L13	1851-09-17	SC	LOT13SESW	
2308	" "	16	L12	1851-09-17	SC	LOT12SWSW	
2161	PAULUS, Anthony	32	NWNW	1842-08-15	FD	NWNW	R:JASPER
2429	PICQUET, Joseph	2	NW	1838-05-07	FD	NW	R:JASPER
2432	" "	31	W½SE	1839-04-10	FD	W2SE	R:JASPER
2431	" "	31	SESE	1839-04-10	FD	SESE	R:JASPER
2430	" "	31	E½SW	1839-04-10	FD	E2SW	R:JASPER
2393	PRICE, John M	3	NWSW	1852-08-26	FD	NWSW	
2153	RAINES, Allen	12	E½NE	1851-10-18	FD	E2NE	
2285	RAINES, Henry W	2	NWNW	1851-10-18	FD	NWNW	R:EDGAR
2183	REISNER, Christian	21	NWNE	1844-03-02	FD	NWNE	R:JASPER S:F
2184	" "	21	NWNW	1844-03-02	FD	NWNW	R:JASPER S:F
2185	" "	21	SWNW	1850-11-01	FD	SWNW	R:JASPER S:F
2186	RICENER, Christian	21	E½NW	1842-02-02	FD	E2NW	R:JASPER
2194	RICKMAN, Daniel	20	SWNW	1839-05-01	FD	SWNW	R:JASPER
2193	" "	20	NWSW	1839-05-01	FD	NWSW	R:JASPER
2559	RICKMAN, William	18	SWNE	1839-05-06	FD	SWNE	R:JASPER
2505	RIDLEN, Stephen T	26	E½SE	1849-05-05	FD	E2SE	
2507	" "	27	NENE	1849-05-05	FD	NENE	
2506	" "	26	NWNW	1849-05-05	FD	NWNW	
2349	RIGDON, James	11	NWSE	1852-03-01	FD	NWSE	
2350	" "	11	SWNE	1852-03-01	FD	SWNE	
2404	ROBBINS, John	20	SENE	1837-10-16	FD	SENE	R:JASPER
2403	" "	20	NWNE	1837-10-16	FD	NWNE	R:JASPER
2479	ROBERTSON, Oliver P	30	SESE	1849-05-17	FD	SESE	
2477	" "	29	SWSW	1849-05-17	FD	SWSW	
2478	" "	30	E½NE	1849-05-17	FD	E2NE	
2270	ROBINSON, Henry G	12	S½NW	1849-04-18	FD	S2NW	
2269	" "	12	NESW	1849-04-18	FD	NESW	
2268	" "	11	SENE	1849-04-18	FD	SENE	
2353	RODGERS, James W	15	SWSW	1846-07-23	FD	SWSW	R:JASPER
2352	" "	15	NWSW	1849-06-18	FD	NWSW	R:JASPER
2354	" "	21	NENE	1851-03-28	FD	NENE	R:JASPER
2351	" "	12	SESE	1852-09-01	FD	SESE	R:JASPER
2236	SCHACKMAN, George	33	SWSE	1840-07-17	FD	SWSE	R:JASPER
2235	" "	21	SWNE	1851-09-15	FD	SWNE	R:JASPER
2234	" "	21	NESW	1851-10-03	FD	NESW	R:JASPER
2409	SCHACKMAN, John	33	E½SE	1848-02-03	FD	E2SE	R:JASPER

ID	Individual in Patent	Sec.	Sec. Part	Purchase Date	Sale Type	IL Aliquot Part	For More Info . . .
2405	SCHACKMAN, John (Cont'd)	21	E½SE	1849-04-24	FD	E2SE	
2406	" "	21	NWSE	1849-04-24	FD	NWSE	
2407	" "	28	NENE	1849-04-24	FD	NENE	
2408	" "	28	NWNE	1851-09-09	FD	NWNE	R:JASPER
2237	SCHACKMANN, George	33	NWSE	1844-08-19	FD	NWSE	R:JASPER
2384	SCHACKMANN, John Jr	21	NWSW	1852-10-18	FD	NWSW	R:JASPER
2457	SCHEALDBANER, Martin	33	E½NE	1852-06-28	FD	E2NE	R:JASPER
2434	SCHEDLBANER, Joseph	22	SWNW	1848-02-05	FD	SWNW	R:JASPER
2433	" "	21	SENE	1848-02-05	FD	SENE	R:JASPER
2435	" "	32	NWSE	1848-02-05	FD	NWSE	R:JASPER
2436	SCHELDBANER, Joseph	32	NESE	1848-03-23	FD	NESE	R:JASPER
2445	SCHELDBANER, Joshep	32	SESE	1849-04-17	FD	SESE	R:JASPER
2509	SCHUFFENSTUN, Theodor	28	E½SW	1849-10-11	FD	E2SW	
2510	" "	28	SWSW	1849-10-11	FD	SWSW	
2511	" "	33	NENW	1849-10-11	FD	NENW	
2174	SCRADER, Bernhard	32	NENW	1842-03-16	FD	NENW	R:JASPER
2360	SEGELER, John B	33	SENW	1849-12-18	FD	SENW	R:JASPER G:53
2334	SELBY, Laban	27	E½SW	1848-11-13	FD	E2SW	G:27
2336	" "	34	NWNE	1848-11-13	FD	NWNE	G:27
2335	" "	34	NENW	1848-11-13	FD	NENW	G:27
2448	" "	26	NESW	1852-05-24	FD	NESW	R:JASPER
2187	SHARICK, Christian	6	SWSW	1848-03-11	FD	SWSW	R:JASPER S:F
2189	SHARICK, Christian W	7	N½NW	1849-06-14	FD	N2NW	S:F
2188	" "	6	SESW	1849-06-14	FD	SESW	S:F
2204	SHIRDEN, Eliza Jane	17	SWNW	1848-12-20	FD	SWNW	R:JASPER S:F
2359	SIGLER, Johann B	33	W½NE	1847-06-24	FD	W2NE	R:JASPER S:F G:54
2359	SIGLER, Johann H	33	W½NE	1847-06-24	FD	W2NE	R:JASPER S:F G:54
2282	SIMONS, Henry	31	SENW	1851-10-13	FD	SENW	R:JASPER
2464	SIMS, Milton	22	E½NE	1849-10-24	FD	E2NE	
2465	" "	23	W½NW	1849-10-24	FD	W2NW	
2466	" "	25	SE	1850-11-23	FD	SE	
2195	SKINNER, Daniel	13	E½NW	1851-10-11	FD	E2NW	
2196	" "	13	N½NE	1851-10-11	FD	N2NE	
2256	SMALL, Henry A	17	SWSW	1845-12-25	FD	SWSW	R:JASPER
2258	" "	18	SESE	1847-10-14	FD	SESE	R:JASPER
2259	" "	20	NWNW	1850-04-15	FD	NWNW	R:JASPER
2257	" "	18	SENE	1850-04-24	FD	SENE	R:JASPER
2254	" "	16	L1	1851-01-16	SC	LOT1NENE	
2255	" "	16	L10	1851-01-16	SC	LOT10NESW	
2502	SMITH, Samuel D	8	E½SW	1846-04-06	FD	E2SW	R:JASPER
2535	SMITH, William C	8	SWSW	1849-06-02	FD	SWSW	R:JASPER
2218	SNODGRASS, Garret	4	E½NE	1839-04-08	FD	E2NE	R:INDIANA
2437	SOHEDLBANER, Joseph	32	SWSE	1851-02-07	FD	SWSE	R:JASPER
2410	SPIESL, John	29	NWSW	1850-10-24	FD	NWSW	R:JASPER
2337	STEEL, James H	15	SENW	1852-07-28	FD	SENW	
2524	STEPHENS, Uriah	17	SWSE	1847-06-19	FD	SWSE	R:JASPER
2212	STEVENS, Eunice	17	SWNE	1845-09-08	FD	SWNE	R:JASPER S:F
2211	" "	17	SENW	1845-10-15	FD	SENW	R:JASPER S:F
2468	STEVENS, Mirhynna	17	NWSE	1845-09-08	FD	NWSE	R:JASPER
2467	" "	17	NESW	1845-09-08	FD	NESW	R:JASPER
2529	STEVENS, Uriah	9	NESW	1845-09-08	FD	NESW	R:JASPER
2525	" "	17	SESW	1848-08-24	FD	SESW	R:JASPER
2526	" "	20	NENW	1849-06-20	FD	NENW	R:JASPER
2528	" "	20	SWNE	1850-01-01	FD	SWNE	R:JASPER
2527	" "	20	SENW	1850-01-07	FD	SENW	R:JASPER
2523	STEVENS, Uriah G	9	SENW	1845-09-08	FD	SENW	R:JASPER
2522	" "	30	NESW	1846-04-02	FD	NESW	R:JASPER
2149	STIPP, Abraham	6	NESW	1843-11-27	FD	NESW	R:EDGAR
2150	" "	6	NW	1843-11-27	FD	NW	R:EDGAR
2277	STRATTON, Henry J	5	S½NW	1850-08-26	FD	S2NW	R:EDGAR
2172	STUMP, Benjamin	2	NENW	1851-04-02	FD	NENW	R:JASPER
2283	STUMP, Henry	1	SENW	1853-12-28	FD	SENW	R:JASPER
2278	STUMP, Henry S	1	NENW	1848-10-28	FD	NENW	R:CRAWFORD
2280	" "	1	NWNE	1851-12-23	FD	NWNE	R:JASPER
2279	" "	1	NESE	1852-08-23	FD	NESE	
2281	" "	1	SEN½	1852-09-13	FD	S2NE	
2530	STURNS, Uriah	9	NWSW	1843-06-26	FD	NWSW	R:JASPER
2156	SUTTON, Amariah	5	NWNE	1851-02-24	FD	NWNE	R:INDIANA
2560	SUTTON, William	17	NWNW	1851-02-24	FD	NWNW	R:INDIANA
2561	" "	18	NENE	1851-02-24	FD	NENE	R:INDIANA
2562	" "	5	SWNE	1851-02-24	FD	SWNE	R:INDIANA
2471	SWANEY, Nathan	19	SENE	1851-07-25	FD	SENE	
2284	SWEET, Henry	10	NESE	1842-08-27	FD	NESE	R:OHIO

ID	Individual in Patent	Sec.	Sec. Part	Purchase Date	Sale Type	IL Aliquot Part	For More Info . . .
2412	SWOPE, John	2	E½SW	1849-05-28	FD	E2SW	R:INDIANA
2414	" "	2	NWSW	1849-05-28	FD	NWSW	R:INDIANA
2415	" "	2	SWNW	1849-05-28	FD	SWNW	R:INDIANA
2413	" "	2	E½SW	1849-05-28	FD	E2SW	R:INDIANA
2412	" "	2	E½SW	1849-06-30	FD	E2SWWA	R:INDIANA
2411	" "	2		1849-06-30	FD	NWSWWA	R:INDIANA
2413	" "	2	E½SW	1849-06-30	FD	E2SWWA	R:INDIANA
2441	" "	2		1849-06-30	FD	NWSWWA	R:INDIANA
2441	" "	2		1849-06-30	FD	SWNWWA	R:INDIANA
2411	" "	2		1849-06-30	FD	SWNWWA	R:INDIANA
2387	THADDAUS, John Juda	32	SWNE	1844-09-11	FD	SWNE	R:JASPER G:25
2386	" "	32	E½NE	1844-09-11	FD	E2NE	R:JASPER G:25
2416	THOMAS, John	25	NE	1849-10-24	FD	NE	
2499	TODD, Samuel B	25	NW	1848-09-21	FD	NW	
2500	" "	25	SW	1848-09-21	FD	SW	
2263	TROWBRIDGE, Henry B	24	NE	1849-11-02	FD	NE	
2260	" "	10	SESW	1849-11-02	FD	SESW	
2261	" "	15	NENW	1849-11-02	FD	NENW	
2262	" "	15	W½NW	1849-11-02	FD	W2NW	
2238	VANDERHOOF, George	30	NESE	1850-10-28	FD	NESE	R:JASPER
2239	" "	30	SENE	1850-10-28	FD	SENE	R:JASPER
2450	VANMETER, Lemuel W	30	SWSW	1839-06-10	FD	SWSW	R:OHIO
2490	VANMETER, Richard B	30	NWNW	1838-11-26	FD	NWNW	R:INDIANA
2160	WAGNER, Andrew	30	SWSE	1851-11-06	FD	SWSE	R:JASPER
2318	WAGONER, Jacob L	31	NENW	1851-11-06	FD	NENW	R:JASPER
2317	" "	30	SESW	1851-11-06	FD	SESW	R:JASPER
2484	WARNER, Philip	10	SENE	1849-05-03	FD	SENE	R:JASPER
2520	WEATHERINGTON, Thomas	19	NESW	1852-09-11	FD	NESW	R:INDIANA
2458	WEIMERT, Mathaus	32	SENW	1849-07-02	FD	SENW	R:JASPER
2459	WEIMERT, Mathias	32	SESW	1851-03-15	FD	SESW	R:JASPER
2443	WELDAM, Joseph	33	SWSW	1842-02-03	FD	SWSW	R:JASPER
2442	" "	33	NESW	1848-02-29	FD	NESW	R:JASPER
2360	" "	33	SENW	1849-12-18	FD	SENW	R:JASPER G:53
2249	WELLS, George	6	SESE	1852-09-09	FD	SESE	
2486	WHITE, Providence	2	E½SE	1850-02-01	FD	E2SE	R:INDIANA S:F
2485	" "	1	W½NW	1850-07-01	FD	W2NW	R:INDIANA S:F
2344	WICOFF, James L	7	W½SE	1849-03-06	FD	W2SE	R:INDIANA
2444	WILDAM, Joseph	33	NWSW	1847-12-04	FD	NWSW	R:JASPER
2563	WILSON, William	10	SWNW	1850-02-14	FD	SWNW	R:JASPER
2564	" "	9	SENE	1850-04-18	FD	SENE	R:JASPER
2418	WOODS, John	4	NENW	1852-09-01	FD	NENW	R:INDIANA
2419	" "	4	NWNW	1852-09-01	FD	NWNW	R:INDIANA
2420	" "	4	W½NE	1852-09-01	FD	W2NE	R:INDIANA
2565	WRIGHT, William	19	NENE	1849-08-16	FD	NENE	R:JASPER
2566	" "	19	NESE	1851-08-11	FD	NESE	R:JASPER
2385	YAEGER, John Juda T D	32	NESW	1852-07-19	FD	NESW	
2175	YOUNG, Canner R	26	SESE	1851-05-26	FD	SESE	R:JASPER
2567	ZIMMERLEE, William	11	SWSW	1852-08-09	FD	SWSW	

Patent Map

T7-N R10-E
3rd PM Meridian

Map Group 8

Township Statistics

Parcels Mapped	:	427
Number of Patents	:	1
Number of Individuals	:	233
Patentees Identified	:	232
Number of Surnames	:	170
Multi-Patentee Parcels	:	10
Oldest Patent Date	:	1/4/1836
Most Recent Patent	:	1/13/1854
Block/Lot Parcels	:	14
Cities and Towns	:	2
Cemeteries	:	5

Section 6
STIPP Abraham 1843
BROOKS Thomas 00/2
BROOKS Elliphaz 1842
BROOKS Elliphaz 1842
JAMES James E 1850
STIPP Abraham 1843
BROOKS Elliphaz 1842
BROOKS John 1846
SHARICK Christian 1848
SHARICK Christian W 1849
BROOKS John 1846
WELLS George 1852

Section 5
KIBLER Martin 1838
STRATTON Henry J 1850
SUTTON Amariah 1851
SUTTON William 1851
KELLY Robert S 1852
BROOKS Isaac 1850
BROOKS James 1840
HAYS William O 1851

Section 4
WOODS John 1852
WOODS John 1852
BURT William 1851
WOODS John 1852
SNODGRASS Garret 1839
BLISS Alvin C 1850
KIBLER Reuben 1849
KIBLER Reuben 1850
FAWCETT John H 1850
KIBLER Reuben 1850

Section 7
SHARICK Christian W 1849
HENRICK William 1840
HAZELTON Newton 1849
BROOKS Isaac 1851
BROOKS Isaac 1849
BATMAN Greenberry 1849
BIRT David H 1851
JONES William M 1847
HAZELTON Newton 1849
WICOFF James L 1849
HUNT Thomas 1848
JONES William 1848

Section 8
BROOKS Isaac 1849
BUCHANAN Samuel 1852
JONES William M 1847
BLAKE Isaac 1843
JONES William M 1847
SMITH William C 1849
JONES William M 1847
SMITH Samuel D 1846
BROOKS John 1840

Section 9
HOLLOPETERS Daniel 1849
HARRISON Richard 1851
CUMMINS Joseph 1850
HOLLOPETERS Richard 1851
STEVENS Uriah G 1845
HOLLOPETERS Daniel 1849
HAYS Oliver 1851
WILSON William 1850
BROOKS James 1840
BROOKS James 1840
STURNS Uriah 1843
STEVENS Uriah 1845
HOLLOPETERS Daniel 1849
HAYS Oliver 1851
BYRD John 1842
BIRT Henry 1852
MARSHALL James 1852
MARSHALL James 1852

Section 18
HUNT Amaziah 1851
HUNT James 1848
JONES Laban 1848
SUTTON William 1851
HUNT James 1848
OGDEN Jonathan 1851
RICKMAN William 1839
SMALL Henry A 1850
OGDEN Jonathan 1851
FREEMAN Gustavus F 1852
MITCHELL Elihu 1849
OGDEN Jonathan 1852
GARRETSON Jeremiah 1852
HAYS William O 1852
SMALL Henry A 1847

Section 17
SUTTON William 1851
DRYSDALE William 1851
BROOKS John 1846
BROOKS John 1847
SHIRDEN Eliza Jane 1848
STEVENS Eunice 1845
STEVENS Eunice 1845
DRYSDALE William 1849
MULVANY William 1850
STEVENS Mirhynna 1845
STEVENS Mirhynna 1845
SMALL Henry A 1845
STEVENS Uriah 1848
STEPHENS Uriah 1847
BROOKS John 1847

Section 16 — Lots-Sec. 16
L1	SMALL, Henry A	1851
L2	BROOKS, John	1851
L3	BROOK, James	1852
L4	DRYSDALE, William	1850
L5	DRYSDALE, William	1850
L6	INGLE, Henry	1852
L7	EARNEST, Henry F	1853
L8	BROCK, Holland L	1853
L9	MITCHELL, Elihu	1851
L10	SMALL, Henry A	1851
L11	EARNEST, Henry F	1851
L12	PATTERSON, Isaac	1851
L13	PATTERSON, Isaac	1851
L14	BROCK, Richard H	1853

Section 19
KEAN Mortimer O 1852
GARRETSON Jeremiah 1852
FITHIAN Benjamin 1839
WRIGHT William 1849
BURFORD Basel B 1852
BRYER Bernard 1849
SWANEY Nathan 1851
WEATHERINGTON Thomas 1852
WRIGHT William 1851
BIRT Henry 1852
FRUCHTEL Joseph 1852
LEISURE George W 1850
LEISURE George W 1851

Section 20
SMALL Henry A 1850
STEVENS Uriah 1849
ROBBINS John 1837
BROOKS John 1841
RICKMAN Daniel 1839
STEVENS Uriah 1850
STEVENS Uriah 1850
ROBBINS John 1837
RICKMAN Daniel 1839
BOWERS Frederick 1844
BROOKS John 1840
PARRENT William 1837

Section 21
REISNER Christian 1844
RICENER Christian 1842
REISNER Christian 1844
RODGERS James W 1851
REISNER Christian 1850
SCHACKMAN George 1851
SCHEDLBANER Joseph 1848
SCHACKMANN John Jr 1852
SCHACKMAN George 1851
SCHACKMAN John 1849
EDERER Michael 1852
KEAN Mortimer O 1852
COX William 1851
SCHACKMAN John 1849

Section 30
VANMETER Richard B 1838
BROWNING William P 1850
LEMASTERS Abbot A 1839
FRUCHTEL Joseph 1850
ROBERTSON Oliver P 1849
GARRISON John V 1839
BROWN William M 1846
VANDERHOOF George 1850
HALLENBECK Lawrence 1838
STEVENS Uriah G 1846
HAYS William O 1851
VANDERHOOF George 1850
VANMETER Lemuel W 1839
WAGONER Jacob L 1851
WAGNER Andrew 1851
ROBERTSON Oliver P 1849

Section 29
PARRENT William 1837
GARDEWAIN Henry 1846
PARENT David 1839
GARDENWINE Henry 1850
LIPTRAP George 1839
PARRENT David 1848
SPIESL John 1850
GARDEWAIN Henry 1849
BARNES James 1849
ROBERTSON Oliver P 1849
GARDEWAIN Henry 1849
HELVET Peter 1849
YAEGER Gregor De 1850

Section 28
MICHAEL Chatarina 1850
MICHAEL Chatarina 1850
SCHACKMAN John 1851
SCHACKMAN John 1849
MOSCHENROSS Ignace 1845
MOSCHENROSS Ignace 1845
MICHAEL Nicholas 1851
PARRENT Maria Ann 1848
SCHUFFENSTUN Theodor 1849
MOSCHENROSS Ignace 1845
SCHUFFENSTUN Theodor 1849
HUME [7] Benjamin 1849

Section 31
MCKINLEY George 1841
WAGONER Jacob L 1851
FRANKE John 1852
SIMONS Henry 1851
NAGELY Josiah 1838
PICQUET Joseph 1839
PICQUET Joseph 1839
HAWLEY George 1837
PICQUET Joseph 1839

Section 32
PAULUS Anthony 1842
SCRADER Bernhard 1842
DORN Franz 1851
KINTZEL Charles 1841
WEIMERT Mathaus 1849
THADDAUS [25] John Juda 1844
THADDAUS [25] John Juda 1844
YAEGER John Juda T D 1852
SCHEDLBANER Joseph 1848
SCHELDBANER Joseph 1848
KINTZEL Charles 1841
FRANKE John 1852
WEIMERT Mathias 1851
SOHEDLBANER Joseph 1851
SCHELDBANER Joshep 1849

Section 33
ADAMS Matthew 1845
SCHUFFENSTUN Theodor 1849
SIGLER [54] Johann B 1847
SCHEALDBANER Martin 1852
SEGELER [53] John B 1849
WILDAM Joseph 1847
WELDAM Joseph 1848
SCHACKMANN George 1844
WELDAM Joseph 1842
BERCASTLE Susannah 1845
SCHACKMAN George 1840
SCHACKMAN John 1848

Section 3
- MITCHELL George 1839
- MITCHELL George 1849
- CHAPMAN Isaac 1853
- CUMMINS Joseph 1852
- CHAPMAN James 1850
- CHAPMAN James 1848
- PAINE Casius M 1854
- PRICE John M 1852
- CHAPMAN James 1849
- CHAPMAN Enoch 1848
- CHAPMAN James 1851
- INGLE Henry 1851

Section 2
- RAINES Henry W 1851
- PICQUET Joseph 1838
- STUMP Benjamin 1851
- GIFFORD Isaac M 1849
- BEUSDOFFER Joseph V
- SWOPE John 1849
- SWOPE John 1849
- BEMUSDOFFER Joseph V 1849
- BEUSDOFFER Joseph V 1849
- BEUSDOFFER Joseph V
- SWOPE John 1849 / SWOPE John 1849
- SWOPE John 1849
- MATTHEWS Christian 1848
- WHITE Providence 1850
- CHAPMAN John 1850
- SWOPE John 1849

Section 1
- WHITE Providence 1850
- STUMP Henry S 1848
- STUMP Henry S 1851
- HEFNER Green Berry 1852
- STUMP Henry 1853
- STUMP Henry S 1852
- GIFFORD Levi 1840
- GIFFORD Isaac M 1850
- GIFFORD Isaac M 1851
- STUMP Henry S 1852
- GIFFORD Isaac M 1840
- GIFFORD Isaac M 1851
- HARRISON Jacob 1849

Section 10
- CHAPMAN Enoch 1850
- INGLE John 1851
- INGLE John 1851
- CHAPMAN Enoch 1852
- WILSON William 1850
- PATEE John 1852
- BARTLEY [8] David 1850
- WARNER Philip 1849
- BYRD John 1842
- PATEE John 1852
- KIBLER John M 1852
- SWEET Henry 1842
- TROWBRIDGE Henry B 1849
- KIBLER John M 1849
- BECKWITH Benjamin 1845

Section 11
- CUMMINS John 1851
- FOGLE George 1849
- FOGLE George 1849
- RIGDON James 1852
- ROBINSON Henry G 1849
- BECKWITH Benjamin 1846
- BECKWITH Benjamin 1845
- BONER Uriah 1851
- RIGDON James 1852
- ZIMMERLEE William 1852
- PARR Peterson K 1849
- MARTIN James 1843

Section 12
- HARRISON Jacob 1853
- HARRISON Jacob 1852
- GIFFORD Levi 1840
- RAINES Allen 1851
- ROBINSON Henry G 1849
- MARTIN James 1843
- ROBINSON Henry G 1849
- BENEFIELD Israel 1852
- BRODERICK Aaron M 1849
- BENEFIELD Israel 1852
- BENEFIELD Israel 1852
- RODGERS James W 1852
- BRODERICK Aaron M 1849

Section 15
- TROWBRIDGE Henry B 1849
- HOUSE Eleanor 1852
- HUMES Lewis 1852
- TROWBRIDGE Henry B 1849
- STEEL James H 1852
- BURCHAM Joseph 1851
- KIBLER Martin 1852
- RODGERS James W 1849
- MADDEN John P 1849
- GRIFFING Thomas G 1848
- BARTLEY John P 1840
- RODGERS James W 1846
- FERGUSON Sandford 1851

Section 14
- PARR Peterson K 1849
- PARR Peterson K 1849
- HOUSE Charles 1848
- HAWS James 1848
- HAWS James L 1847
- HAWS James L 1847
- HOUSE Andrew 1849
- BROCK Richard H 1847
- BROCK Richard H 1847
- BROCK Richard H 1847
- BARTLEY John 1849
- BROCK Hollen L 1848
- BROCK Hollen L 1847
- BROCK Richard H 1847

Section 13
- BRODERICK Aaron M 1849
- SKINNER Daniel 1851
- SKINNER Daniel 1851
- BECKWITH Benjamin 1851
- JONES Ezekiel 1849
- MADDEN William J 1849
- JONES Ezekiel 1849
- GRIFFING Thomas G 1848
- GRIFFING Thomas C 1851

Section 22
- MADDEN John P 1849
- AVERY Homer T 1848
- SIMS Milton 1849
- SCHEDLBANER Joseph 1848
- AVERY Homer T 1848
- LEWIS Adam C 1851
- FEAR James 1850
- JEFFERS George W 1849
- BARTLEY John P 1840
- BARTLEY John P 1840

Section 23
- SIMS Milton 1849
- BARTLEY John P 1839
- BARTLEY John 1846
- BARTLEY John P 1839
- AVERY Homer T 1848
- AVERY Homer T 1848
- BARTLEY Amos 1849
- BRODERICK Alvah P 1849

Section 24
- BROCK Hollen L 1847
- JONES Ezekiel 1849
- BARTLEY John 1849
- TROWBRIDGE Henry B 1849
- FEAR James 1849
- FERGUSON Will 1848
- FERGUSON Will 1848
- HARLEN Aaron 1849

Section 27
- HUME John 1848
- RIDLEN Stephen T 1849
- HUME William 1848
- JEFFERS George W 1849
- HUME [7] Benjamin 1849
- DIXON [27] James H 1848
- MIRES John L 1850
- JEFFERS George W 1849
- BROOKS Alfred J F 1836
- FERGUSON Will 1848
- FERGUSON William 1852

Section 26
- RIDLEN Stephen T 1849
- HUME Benjamin 1849
- CHRISS George 1850
- JEFFERS George W 1849
- HUME William 1848
- HUME John 1848
- MIRES John L 1850
- JEFFERS George W 1849
- SELBY Laban 1852
- MIRES John L 1850
- RIDLEN Stephen T 1849
- DIXON James H 1852
- DIXON James L 1852
- CHRISS George 1849
- YOUNG Canner R 1851

Section 25
- TODD Samuel B 1848
- THOMAS John 1849
- TODD Samuel B 1848
- SIMS Milton 1850

Section 34
- HUME Benjamin 1851
- DIXON [27] James H 1848
- DIXON [27] James H 1850
- CHRISS Abraham 1850
- BRODERICK Abraham P 1849
- BRODERICK Abraham P 1849
- DHOM Michael V 1839
- DHOM Michael V 1839

Section 35
- CHRISS George 1849
- CHRISS George 1849
- CHRISS George 1849
- JOHNSON George W 1849
- CHRISS George 1849
- FERGUSON Samuel 1851
- CHRISS George 1849
- CHRISS George 1849
- JOHNSON George W 1849

Section 36
- FERGUSON Jeremiah 1850
- BAILEY Jacob 1849
- FERGUSON Jeremiah 1848
- CONDE James B 1849
- MCNAIR Thomas A 1849
- MCNAIR Thomas A 1849
- MCNAIR Thomas A 1849
- CONDE James B 1849

Helpful Hints

1. This Map's INDEX can be found on the preceding pages.

2. Refer to Map "C" to see where this Township lies within Jasper County, Illinois.

3. Numbers within square brackets [ ] denote a multi-patentee land parcel (multi-owner). Refer to Appendix "C" for a full list of members in this group.

4. Areas that look to be crowded with Patentees usually indicate multiple sales of the same parcel (re-issues), cancellations or voided transactions (that we map, anyway) or overlapping parcels. We opt to show even these ambiguous parcels, which oftentimes lead to research avenues not yet taken.

Legend
- Patent Boundary
- Section Boundary
- No Patents Found (or Outside County)
- 1., 2., 3., ... Lot Numbers (when beside a name)
- [ ] Group Number (see Appendix "C")

Scale: Section = 1 mile X 1 mile (generally, with some exceptions)

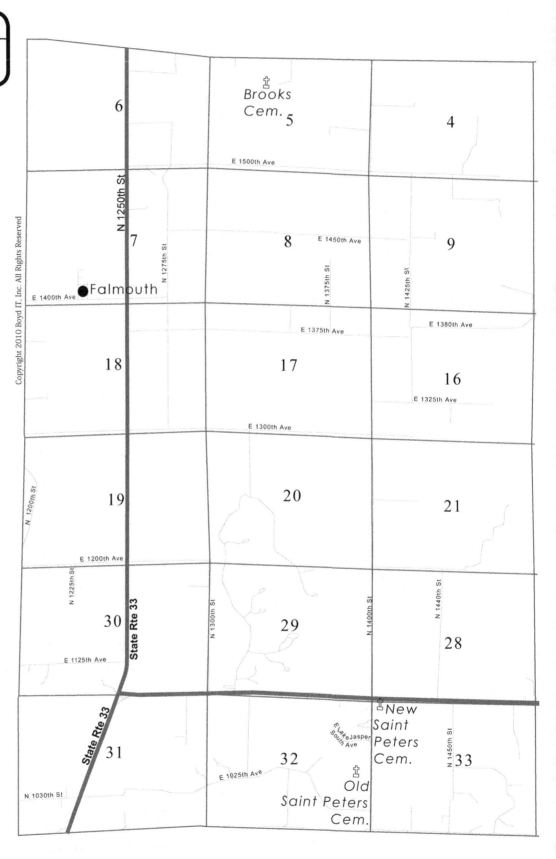

Road Map

T7-N R10-E
3rd PM Meridian

Map Group 8

Cities & Towns
Brookville
Falmouth

Cemeteries
Brockville Cemetery
Brooks Cemetery
Madison Cemetery
New Saint Peters Cemetery
Old Saint Peters Cemetery

Helpful Hints

1. This road map has a number of uses, but primarily it is to help you: a) find the present location of land owned by your ancestors (at least the general area), b) find cemeteries and city-centers, and c) estimate the route/roads used by Census-takers & tax-assessors.

2. If you plan to travel to Jasper County to locate cemeteries or land parcels, please pick up a modern travel map for the area before you do. Mapping old land parcels on modern maps is not as exact a science as you might think. Just the slightest variations in public land survey coordinates, estimates of parcel boundaries, or road-map deviations can greatly alter a map's representation of how a road either does or doesn't cross a particular parcel of land.

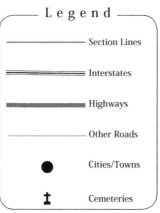

L e g e n d

Section Lines

Interstates

Highways

Other Roads

Cities/Towns

Cemeteries

Scale: Section = 1 mile X 1 mile
(generally, with some exceptions)

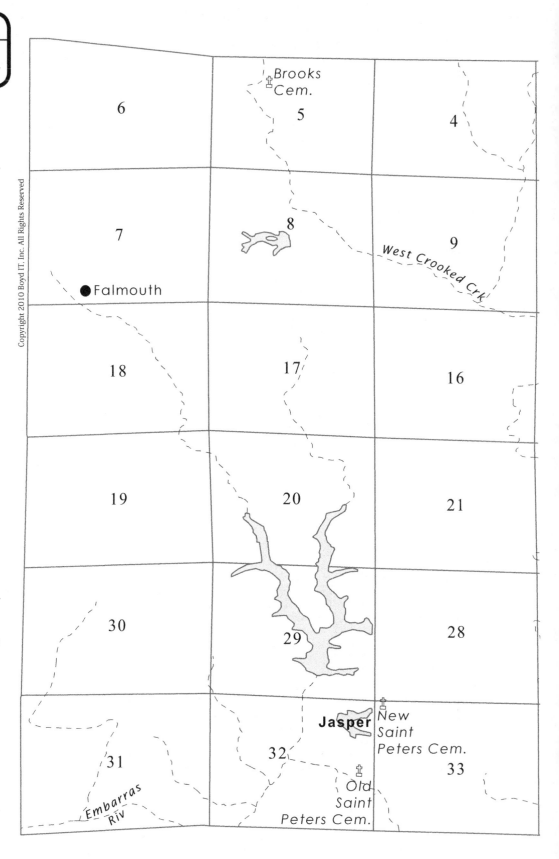

Historical Map

T7-N R10-E
3rd PM Meridian

Map Group 8

Copyright 2010 Boyd IT. Inc. All Rights Reserved

Cities & Towns
Brookville
Falmouth

Cemeteries
Brockville Cemetery
Brooks Cemetery
Madison Cemetery
New Saint Peters Cemetery
Old Saint Peters Cemetery

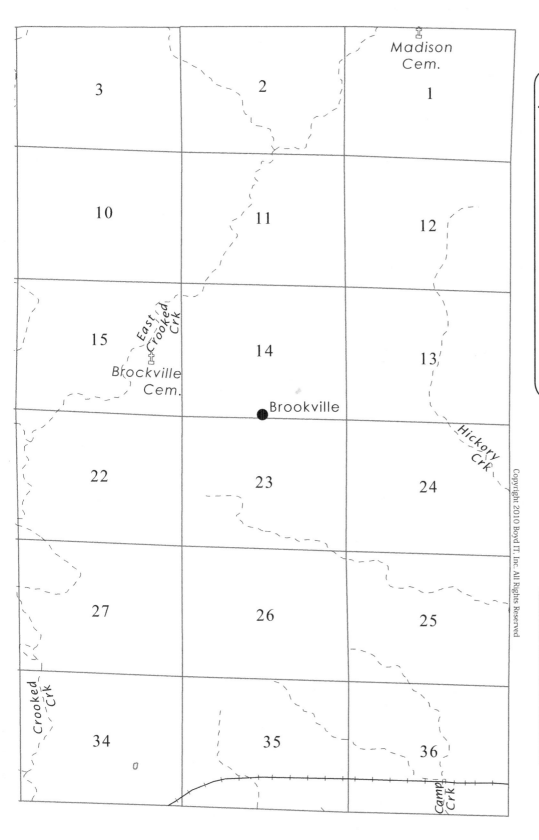

3

2

1

Madison
Cem.

10

11

12

15

East Crooked Crk

Brockville
Cem.

14

13

Brookville

22

23

24

Hickory Crk

27

26

25

Crooked Crk

34

35

36

Camp Crk

Helpful Hints

1. This Map takes a different look at the same Congressional Township displayed in the preceding two maps. It presents features that can help you better envision the historical development of the area: a) Water-bodies (lakes & ponds), b) Water-courses (rivers, streams, etc.), c) Railroads, d) City/town center-points (where they were oftentimes located when first settled), and e) Cemeteries.

2. Using this "Historical" map in tandem with this Township's Patent Map and Road Map, may lead you to some interesting discoveries. You will often find roads, towns, cemeteries, and waterways are named after nearby landowners: sometimes those names will be the ones you are researching. See how many of these research gems you can find here in Jasper County.

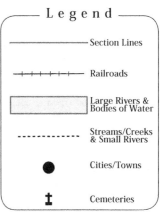

Legend

——————— Section Lines

+++++++++ Railroads

Large Rivers &
Bodies of Water

------------ Streams/Creeks
& Small Rivers

● Cities/Towns

☦ Cemeteries

Scale: Section = 1 mile X 1 mile
(there are some exceptions)

Map Group 9: Index to Land Patents

Township 7-North Range 11-East (3rd PM)

After you locate an individual in this Index, take note of the Section and Section Part then proceed to the Land Patent map on the pages immediately following. You should have no difficulty locating the corresponding parcel of land.

The "For More Info" Column will lead you to more information about the underlying Patents. See the *Legend* at right, and the "How to Use this Book" chapter, for more information.

```
                        LEGEND
              "For More Info . . . " column
G = Group  (Multi-Patentee Patent, see Appendix "C")
R = Residence
S = Social Status

See Appendix A for list of abbreviations used by the
Illinois State Archives in describing the place and
nature of these land patents.

Note: if the Abbreviations contain "L", "BL", "LOT",
or "BLOCK", the exact whereabouts of the parcel within
the section is not known.
```

ID	Individual in Patent	Sec.	Sec. Part	Purchase Date	Sale Type	IL Aliquot Part	For More Info . . .
2608	BIRD, William	19	W½SE	1851-11-19	FD	W2SE	
2591	BROOKS, Joseph H	31	L1	1854-06-24	SC	L1NESE	
2600	BURCHARD, Solomon	30	SE	1848-02-21	FD	SE	
2587	CALDWELL, John	19	W½NE	1851-10-01	FD	W2NE	
2590	CARPENTER, John M	31	L3	1854-06-24	SC	L3SWSE	
2609	CHAPAN, William	7	S½NW	1850-07-01	FD	S2NW	R:JASPER
2607	CHAPMAN, Thomas	6	N½NW	1852-10-28	FD	N2NW	R:JASPER
2610	CHAPMAN, William	7	N½NW	1851-09-11	FD	N2NW	R:JASPER
2588	CHURCH, John	7	NE	1849-04-21	FD	NE	
2577	DAVIS, Precilla	6	SE	1851-12-24	FD	SE	G:24
2584	FEESER, James	31	NE	1849-03-02	FD	NE	
2599	FERGUSON, Sandford	19	SWNW	1851-08-01	FD	SWNW	R:JASPER
2598	" "	19	NWSW	1851-08-01	FD	NWSW	R:JASPER
2568	HARLEN, Aaron	19	E½NE	1852-02-20	FD	E2NE	R:JASPER
2570	" "	19	SWSW	1852-02-20	FD	SWSW	R:JASPER
2569	" "	19	E½SW	1852-02-20	FD	E2SW	R:JASPER
2592	HESLER, Joseph	19	E½SE	1851-11-21	FD	E2SE	R:INDIANA
2578	HUME, John	18	SWNE	1853-05-15	FD	SWNE	G:39
2594	HUME, Lewis	19	NWNW	1852-05-29	FD	NWNW	
2593	" "	19	E½NW	1852-05-29	FD	E2NW	
2580	JOHNSON, George W	31	SESW	1852-02-09	FD	SESW	R:JASPER
2573	MARTIN, Alfred	7	W½SE	1849-05-02	FD	W2SE	R:JASPER
2572	" "	7	SW	1849-05-02	FD	SW	R:JASPER
2571	" "	7		1849-06-30	FD	SWWA	R:JASPER
2571	" "	7		1849-06-30	FD	W2SEWA	R:JASPER
2585	MARTIN, James	18	NWNE	1853-01-29	FD	NWNE	
2577	MATHEWS, David W	6	SE	1851-12-24	FD	SE	G:24
2577	MATHEWS, James	6	SE	1851-12-24	FD	SE	G:24
2577	MATHEWS, Joseph	6	SE	1851-12-24	FD	SE	G:24
2577	MATHEWS, Rebecca	6	SE	1851-12-24	FD	SE	G:24
2577	MATHEWS, Sarah	6	SE	1851-12-24	FD	SE	G:24
2577	MATHEWS, Thomas	6	SE	1851-12-24	FD	SE	G:24
2586	MCKEE, Jefferson	7	E½SE	1850-02-01	FD	E2SE	R:INDIANA
2589	MCNAIR, John H	31	L2	1854-06-24	SC	L2NWSE	
2605	MCNAIR, Thomas A	31	NW	1849-02-05	FD	NW	
2602	" "	30	SW	1849-02-05	FD	SW	
2603	" "	31		1849-03-19	FD	NEEC	R:JASPER
2601	" "	30		1849-03-19	FD	SWEC	R:JASPER
2606	" "	31	W½SW	1849-05-15	FD	W2SW	
2604	" "	31	NESW	1849-05-15	FD	NESW	
2578	MONRONEY, George	18	SWNE	1853-05-15	FD	SWNE	G:39
2579	MORONEY, George	18	W½	1852-09-23	FD	W2	R:FULTON
2574	REINS, Bartley Y	6	E½NE	1852-11-06	FD	E2NE	
2575	" "	6	W½NE	1852-11-06	FD	W2NE	
2581	ROACH, Henry Jr	30	NE	1849-04-21	FD	NE	
2595	SHEALY, Phebe	18	E½NE	1851-12-13	FD	E2NE	S:F

ID	Individual in Patent	Sec.	Sec. Part	Purchase Date	Sale Type	IL Aliquot Part	For More Info . . .
2576	STUMP, Benjamin	6	S½NW	1851-04-09	FD	S2NW	R:JASPER
2582	STUMP, Henry S	6	N½SW	1848-10-28	FD	N2SW	R:CRAWFORD
2583	" "	6	S½SW	1849-06-18	FD	S2SW	R:JASPER
2596	THOMAS, Reuben	30	NW	1849-10-24	FD	NW	R:INDIANA
2597	TODD, Samuel B	31	L4	1854-06-24	SC	L4SESE	
2611	ZIMMERLEE, William	18	SE	1852-08-09	FD	SE	

Patent Map

T7-N R11-E
3rd PM Meridian

Map Group 9

Township Statistics

Parcels Mapped	:	44
Number of Patents	:	1
Number of Individuals	:	38
Patentees Identified	:	31
Number of Surnames	:	28
Multi-Patentee Parcels	:	2
Oldest Patent Date	:	2/21/1848
Most Recent Patent	:	6/24/1854
Block/Lot Parcels	:	4
Cities and Towns	:	2
Cemeteries	:	1

Note: the area contained in this map amounts to far less than a full Township. Therefore, its contents are completely on this single page (instead of a "normal" 2-page spread).

Legend

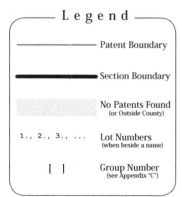

——————— Patent Boundary

━━━━━━━ Section Boundary

No Patents Found
(or Outside County)

1., 2., 3., ...   Lot Numbers
(when beside a name)

[ ]   Group Number
(see Appendix "C")

Scale: Section = 1 mile X 1 mile
(generally, with some exceptions)

Section 6
CHAPMAN Thomas 1852	REINS Bartley Y 1852
STUMP Benjamin 1851	REINS Bartley Y 1852
STUMP Henry S 1848	MATHEWS [24] David W 1851
STUMP Henry S 1849	

Section 7
CHAPMAN William 1851	CHURCH John 1849	
CHAPAN William 1850		
MARTIN Alfred 1849	MARTIN Alfred 1849	MCKEE Jefferson 1850
MARTIN Alfred 1849	MARTIN Alfred 1849	

Section 18
MORONEY George 1852	MARTIN James 1853	SHEALY Phebe 1851
	MONRONEY [39] George 1853	
	ZIMMERLEE William 1852	

Section 19
HUME Lewis 1852	HUME Lewis 1852	CALDWELL John 1851	HARLEN Aaron 1852
FERGUSON Sandford 1851			
FERGUSON Sandford 1851	HARLEN Aaron 1852	BIRD William 1851	HESLER Joseph 1851
HARLEN Aaron 1852			

Section 30
THOMAS Reuben 1849	ROACH Henry Jr. 1849
MCNAIR Thomas A 1849	BURCHARD Solomon 1848
MCNAIR Thomas A 1849	

Section 31
MCNAIR Thomas A 1849	MCNAIR Thomas A 1849	
		FEESER James 1849
MCNAIR Thomas A 1849	MCNAIR Thomas A 1849	
	JOHNSON George W 1852	

Lots-Sec. 31
L1 BROOKS, Joseph H 1854
L2 MCNAIR, John H 1854
L3 CARPENTER, John M 1854
L4 TODD, Samuel B 1854

Road Map

T7-N R11-E
3rd PM Meridian

M a p   G r o u p   9

Note: the area contained in this map amounts to far less than a full Township. Therefore, its contents are completely on this single page (instead of a "normal" 2-page spread).

Cities & Towns
Hunt City
Willow Hill

Cemeteries
Edison Cemetery

L e g e n d

Section Lines

Interstates

Highways

Other Roads

● Cities/Towns

✝ Cemeteries

Scale: Section = 1 mile X 1 mile
(generally, with some exceptions)

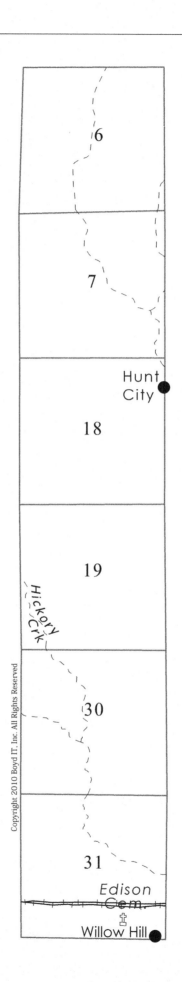

Historical Map

T7-N R11-E
3rd PM Meridian

Map Group 9

Note: the area contained in this map amounts to far less than a full Township. Therefore, its contents are completely on this single page (instead of a "normal" 2-page spread).

Cities & Towns
Hunt City
Willow Hill

Cemeteries
Edison Cemetery

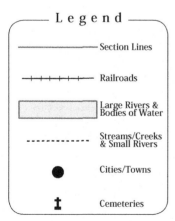

L e g e n d

—————— Section Lines

+++++++ Railroads

Large Rivers & Bodies of Water

- - - - - - Streams/Creeks & Small Rivers

● Cities/Towns

‡ Cemeteries

Scale: Section = 1 mile X 1 mile
(there are some exceptions)

Map Group 10: Index to Land Patents

Township 7-North Range 14-West (2nd PM)

After you locate an individual in this Index, take note of the Section and Section Part then proceed to the Land Patent map on the pages immediately following. You should have no difficulty locating the corresponding parcel of land.

The "For More Info" Column will lead you to more information about the underlying Patents. See the *Legend* at right, and the "How to Use this Book" chapter, for more information.

```
                        LEGEND
            "For More Info . . . " column
 G = Group   (Multi-Patentee Patent, see Appendix "C")
 R = Residence
 S = Social Status

 See Appendix A for list of abbreviations used by the
 Illinois State Archives in describing the place and
 nature of these land patents.

 Note: if the Abbreviations contain "L", "BL", "LOT",
 or "BLOCK", the exact whereabouts of the parcel within
 the section is not known.
```

ID	Individual in Patent	Sec.	Sec. Part	Purchase Date	Sale Type	IL Aliquot Part	For More Info . . .
2695	ARDERY, James	20	E½SW	1852-01-14	FD	E2SW	
2744	BAILEY, John L	18	E½NW	1851-12-12	FD	E2NW	R:OHIO
2745	" "	18	NESW	1851-12-12	FD	NESW	R:OHIO
2746	" "	18	SWNW	1851-12-12	FD	SWNW	R:OHIO
2749	" "	4	SENE	1852-05-12	FD	SENE	R:JASPER
2748	" "	3	W½NW	1852-05-12	FD	W2NW	R:JASPER
2747	" "	3	SENW	1852-05-12	FD	SENW	R:JASPER
2806	BAILEY, Ludwill	4	NENE	1852-03-16	FD	NENE	R:JASPER
2807	" "	8	SENW	1852-03-16	FD	SENW	R:JASPER
2809	" "	9	NWNE	1852-03-16	FD	NWNE	R:JASPER
2810	" "	9	SENE	1852-05-12	FD	SENE	R:JASPER
2808	" "	8	SESE	1852-11-05	FD	SESE	R:JASPER
2860	BAILEY, William	17	NWNE	1852-06-23	FD	NWNE	
2861	" "	8	NESW	1852-06-23	FD	NESW	
2862	" "	8	W½SE	1852-06-23	FD	W2SE	
2811	BALEY, Ludwill	9	NENE	1853-02-15	FD	NENE	
2619	BEESON, Allen	34	NESE	1853-02-01	FD	NESE	R:JASPER
2688	BEESON, Igal	22	NESE	1851-01-22	FD	NESE	R:CRAWFORD
2689	" "	34	SESW	1851-01-28	FD	SESW	R:CRAWFORD
2690	" "	34	SWSW	1851-02-26	FD	SWSW	R:CRAWFORD
2743	BOYD, Robert	3	W½SW	1839-08-17	FD	W2SW	R:JASPER G:12
2680	BROOKS, Henry	31	SE	1848-10-20	FD	SE	
2723	BUFFINGTON, John	3	NWNE	1851-12-11	FD	NWNE	R:OHIO
2722	" "	3	NENW	1851-12-11	FD	NENW	R:OHIO
2786	BURCHAM, Joseph	30	SESE	1852-12-02	FD	SESE	
2725	BUTLER, John	15	SWNW	1850-01-23	FD	SWNW	R:INDIANA
2728	" "	21	E½NW	1850-01-23	FD	E2NW	
2730	" "	21	W½NE	1850-01-23	FD	W2NE	
2729	" "	21	NWNW	1851-10-27	FD	NWNW	R:INDIANA
2727	" "	16	L7	1851-10-28	SC	LOT7SWNE	
2726	" "	16	L10	1851-10-28	SC	LOT10NWSE	
2724	" "	15	NWSE	1851-11-03	FD	NWSE	
2847	BYRNE, Thomas	4	SWNE	1854-11-01	FD	SWNE	R:CRAWFORD
2858	CHAPMAN, Washington	5	NENW	1850-04-13	FD	NENW	R:JASPER
2859	" "	5	SWNW	1851-09-11	FD	SWNW	R:JASPER
2636	CLARK, Austin	6	S½NW	1852-09-13	FD	S2NW	R:INDIANA
2635	" "	6	E½SW	1852-09-13	FD	E2SW	R:INDIANA
2681	CLARK, Henry	6	NENW	1853-08-17	FD	NENW	R:JASPER
2673	CLEMANS, Hamilton J	5	W½NE	1845-10-27	FD	W2NE	R:OHIO
2672	" "	4	NWNE	1845-10-27	FD	NWNE	R:OHIO
2857	CLEMENS, Walden	5	E½SE	1845-04-26	FD	E2SE	R:JASPER
2662	COLEMAN, Elias	5	SESE	1851-10-29	FD	SESE	R:CUMBERLAND
2877	COX, William K	9	S½NW	1850-06-06	FD	S2NW	
2875	" "	9	N½SW	1850-06-06	FD	N2SW	
2878	" "	9	SESW	1850-06-06	FD	SESW	R:JASPER
2879	" "	9	SWNE	1850-09-13	FD	SWNE	

ID	Individual in Patent	Sec.	Sec. Part	Purchase Date	Sale Type	IL Aliquot Part	For More Info . . .
2876	COX, William K (Cont'd)	9	NWSE	1850-09-13	FD	NWSE	
2874	" "	9	E½SE	1850-09-13	FD	E2SE	
2836	CRAIG, Samuel	32	NESW	1850-08-16	FD	NESW	
2838	" "	32	SENW	1850-08-16	FD	SENW	
2839	" "	32	SWNE	1850-08-16	FD	SWNE	
2837	" "	32	NWSE	1850-08-16	FD	NWSE	
2632	CURTIS, Asa	10	NENE	1851-02-13	FD	NENE	
2633	" "	3	SESE	1851-02-13	FD	SESE	
2661	CURTIS, Eli	3	SWSE	1849-11-29	FD	SWSE	R:CRAWFORD
2732	DAVIS, John D	6	SESE	1852-09-18	FD	SESE	R:INDIANA
2866	DAY, William	27	S½SW	1851-10-22	FD	S2SW	
2614	DECKER, Abijah	30	SWSW	1851-09-08	FD	SWSW	R:INDIANA
2623	DILLMAN, Andrew	4	E½NW	1839-04-16	FD	E2NW	R:JASPER
2624	DILLMON, Andrew	5	SWSE	1850-10-30	FD	SWSE	R:JASPER
2731	DURHAM, John C	17	SESE	1841-05-05	FD	SESE	R:CLARK
2631	EAMES, Armstead	31	W½NE	1851-10-25	FD	W2NE	
2825	EATON, Richard	34	W½SE	1828-09-22	FD	W2SE	R:CRAWFORD
2733	EDGERTON, John D	28	NESW	1852-11-19	FD	NESW	R:INDIANA
2734	" "	28	NWSE	1852-11-19	FD	NWSE	R:INDIANA
2645	EDWARDS, Charles	29	NENE	1849-10-30	FD	NENE	R:JASPER
2644	" "	21	SWSW	1849-11-19	FD	SWSW	R:JASPER
2796	ELLIOTT, Joseph W	17	S½SE	1852-08-27	FD	S2SE	
2799	" "	22	SESW	1852-08-27	FD	SESW	
2798	" "	22	NENW	1852-09-23	FD	NENW	
2797	" "	17	SESW	1852-09-25	FD	SESW	
2616	EVERMAN, Alfred	22	NESW	1849-10-23	FD	NESW	R:JASPER
2617	" "	22	NWSW	1850-02-14	FD	NWSW	R:JASPER
2615	" "	21	NESE	1851-10-09	FD	NESE	R:JASPER
2618	" "	22	SENW	1852-03-20	FD	SENW	R:JASPER
2867	EVERMAN, William	21	W½SE	1823-11-07	FD	W2SE	R:CRAWFORD
2787	FEARS, Joseph	5	NWNW	1851-06-18	FD	NWNW	R:EDGAR
2869	FEARS, William	6	NENE	1851-06-18	FD	NENE	R:EDGAR
2868	" "	6		1851-08-31	FD	NENEWA	R:EDGAR
2701	FEESER, James	31	NW	1848-12-18	FD	NW	
2834	" "	31		1849-01-31	FD	PTNW	R:INDIANA
2700	" "	31		1849-01-31	FD	PTNW	R:INDIANA
2699	" "	30	SWSE	1851-09-18	FD	SWSE	R:JASPER
2648	FOX, Daniel	6	W½SE	1852-07-27	FD	W2SE	
2650	GRIFFY, David B	20	S½NW	1851-10-03	FD	S2NW	R:INDIANA
2718	GRIFFY, Jobe H	22	NWNE	1853-05-07	FD	NWNE	
2826	GUYNN, Richard	30	N½NE	1852-12-20	FD	N2NE	
2849	HAMILTON, Thomas	32	SESW	1849-09-27	FD	SESW	R:INDIANA
2850	" "	32	W½SW	1849-09-27	FD	W2SW	R:INDIANA
2870	HARBERT, William	18	NWNW	1840-04-13	FD	NWNW	R:JASPER
2737	HARMON, John	15	NENE	1839-04-08	FD	NENE	R:JASPER
2738	" "	15	NWNE	1839-05-03	FD	NWNE	R:JASPER
2743	" "	3	W½SW	1839-08-17	FD	W2SW	R:JASPER G:12
2739	" "	15	SENE	1847-03-30	FD	SENE	R:JASPER
2736	" "	10	SWSW	1850-08-31	FD	SWSW	R:JASPER
2742	" "	9	SWSE	1850-09-11	FD	SWSE	R:JASPER
2740	" "	16	L1	1851-01-25	SC	LOT1NENE	
2741	" "	16	L2	1851-01-25	SC	LOT2NWNE	
2735	" "	10	NWSE	1852-02-17	FD	NWSE	R:JASPER
2759	HARMON, John P	16	L11	1851-01-25	SC	LOT11NESW	
2760	" "	16	L12	1851-01-25	SC	LOT12NWSW	
2788	HARMON, Joseph	10	SWSE	1839-05-03	FD	SWSE	R:JASPER
2871	HARMON, William	16	L5	1851-01-25	SC	LOT5SWNW	
2884	HAWKINS, William S	20	SE	1849-11-03	FD	SE	
2649	HENDRICKSON, Daniel	30	W½NW	1852-10-07	FD	W2NW	R:IOWA
2671	HEPNER, Green Berry	6	W½SW	1852-09-03	FD	W2SW	R:INDIANA
2789	HESLER, Joseph	19	SW	1851-11-21	FD	SW	R:INDIANA
2790	" "	30	E½NW	1852-10-25	FD	E2NW	R:JASPER
2750	HILL, John M L	7	E½SW	1853-06-07	FD	E2SW	R:CRAWFORD
2856	HINMAN, Titus	16	L3	1854-09-21	SC	LOT3NENW	
2800	" "	16	L3	1854-09-21	SC	LOT3NENW	
2827	IRELAND, Richard	31	W½SW	1849-10-19	FD	W2SW	R:JASPER
2668	JEFFERS, George W	10	S½NW	1852-10-12	FD	S2NW	
2667	" "	10	N½SW	1852-10-12	FD	N2SW	
2780	JENKINS, Jonathan	19	NE	1852-05-12	FD	NE	
2775	JENKINS, Jonathan H	18	SESW	1852-05-11	FD	SESW	R:OHIO
2776	" "	18	SWNE	1852-05-11	FD	SWNE	R:OHIO
2777	" "	18	W½SE	1852-05-11	FD	W2SE	R:OHIO
2774	" "	18	SENE	1852-08-13	FD	SENE	

ID	Individual in Patent	Sec.	Sec. Part	Purchase Date	Sale Type	IL Aliquot Part	For More Info . . .
2773	JENKINS, Jonathan H (Cont'd)	17	SWNW	1852-10-08	FD	SWNW	
2778	" "	19	NENW	1852-10-22	FD	NENW	R:OHIO
2779	" "	19	SENW	1853-07-05	FD	SENW	R:OHIO
2845	JONES, Sarah E	17	SENW	1853-02-01	FD	SENW	S:F
2846	"	17	SWNE	1853-02-01	FD	SWNE	S:F
2873	JONES, William	21	SWNW	1851-05-12	FD	SWNW	R:JASPER
2872	" "	21	NESW	1852-07-12	FD	NESW	
2628	KEIF, Andrew	34	SWNE	1851-10-20	FD	SWNE	R:INDIANA
2820	KEIFF, Patrick	34	N½NE	1850-11-26	FD	N2NE	
2819	" "	34	E½NW	1850-11-26	FD	E2NW	
2818	" "	27	SESE	1850-11-26	FD	SESE	R:INDIANA
2821	KEIFFE, Patrick	34	SENE	1852-07-14	FD	SENE	
2641	KELLY, Benjamin F	8	SWSW	1852-10-09	FD	SWSW	
2638	" "	17	NENW	1852-10-09	FD	NENW	
2639	" "	17	NWNW	1852-10-09	FD	NWNW	
2640	" "	8	SESW	1852-10-09	FD	SESW	
2676	KELLY, Hannah	8	W½NW	1852-09-18	FD	W2NW	S:F
2675	" "	8	NWSW	1852-09-18	FD	NWSW	S:F
2674	" "	8	NENW	1852-09-18	FD	NENW	S:F
2714	KINSLOW, James T	15	SESE	1840-03-10	FD	SESE	R:CRAWFORD
2715	" "	22	NENE	1840-10-16	FD	NENE	R:JASPER
2851	KIRKWOOD, Thomas	27	E½NW	1851-02-25	FD	E2NW	
2852	" "	27	N½NE	1851-02-25	FD	N2NE	
2646	LAGOW, Clark B	10	SENE	1852-06-26	FD	SENE	R:CRAWFORD
2703	LEACH, James	18	NWNE	1852-09-03	FD	NWNE	
2702	" "	18	NENE	1852-09-03	FD	NENE	
2704	" "	7	SE	1852-09-03	FD	SE	
2781	LENEX, Jonathan	16	L6	1851-01-25	SC	LOT6SENW	
2802	MCALLISTER, Lewis	29	N½SE	1849-10-19	FD	N2SE	R:INDIANA
2801	" "	28	NWSW	1849-10-19	FD	NWSW	R:INDIANA
2751	MCCABE, John	9	SWSW	1851-04-28	FD	SWSW	
2880	MCCABE, William	3	NENE	1853-05-05	FD	NENE	R:CLARK
2706	MCCARTY, James	33	NWNE	1852-09-06	FD	NWNE	
2707	" "	33	W½NW	1852-09-06	FD	W2NW	
2705	" "	33	NENW	1852-09-06	FD	NENW	
2840	MCCLELLAND, Samuel	10	NWNW	1842-12-22	FD	NWNW	R:KENTUCKY
2629	MCCORMICK, Andrew M	34	NESW	1837-11-17	FD	NESW	R:OHIO
2630	" "	34	NWSW	1838-05-07	FD	NWSW	R:OHIO
2752	MCCRILLIS, John	33	SWSW	1850-10-26	FD	SWSW	R:CRAWFORD
2816	MCGINNESS, Orvill S	7	E½NE	1852-07-23	FD	E2NE	
2817	MCGINNESS, Orville	7	W½NE	1852-07-13	FD	W2NE	
2830	MCKEE, Robert	28	NENW	1851-09-18	FD	NENW	
2829	" "	28	N½NE	1851-09-18	FD	N2NE	
2828	" "	21	SESW	1851-09-18	FD	SESW	
2696	MEANS, James B	21	SESE	1852-08-27	FD	SESE	
2652	MEERE, David	33	SEN½	1850-04-04	FD	S2NE	
2653	" "	34	W½NW	1850-04-04	FD	W2NW	
2654	MEESE, David	22	SENE	1851-09-27	FD	SENE	R:INDIANA
2708	MEESE, James	33	NENE	1852-12-08	FD	NENE	
2613	MILLER, Aaron	28	SENE	1852-08-23	FD	SENE	
2612	" "	27	NWSE	1852-08-23	FD	NWSE	
2677	MILLER, Harrison	27	SEN½	1852-08-23	FD	S2NE	R:INDIANA
2679	" "	28	SWNE	1852-09-04	FD	SWNE	
2678	" "	28	SENW	1852-09-04	FD	SENW	
2682	MILLER, Henry	4	S½SE	1839-08-31	FD	S2SE	R:JASPER
2683	" "	8	NENE	1851-10-29	FD	NENE	R:JASPER
2756	MILLER, John	9	N½NW	1837-10-07	FD	N2NW	R:INDIANA
2755	" "	4	SW	1837-10-07	FD	SW	R:INDIANA
2754	" "	4	NWSE	1845-10-27	FD	NWSE	R:JASPER
2753	" "	4	NESE	1851-11-26	FD	NESE	R:JASPER
2824	MILLER, Rebecca	3	NESW	1852-08-24	FD	NESW	R:CRAWFORD S:F
2881	MILLER, William	31	SESW	1839-08-20	FD	SESW	R:CRAWFORD
2643	MONROE, Caleb	29	NWNE	1852-08-23	FD	NWNE	
2642	" "	29	N½NW	1852-08-23	FD	N2NW	
2854	NEAL, Thomas	31	E½NE	1851-08-09	FD	E2NE	R:INDIANA
2853	" "	10	NESE	1851-10-03	FD	NESE	R:JASPER
2855	" "	32	SWNW	1852-10-21	FD	SWNW	
2656	NOEL, David	29	SEN½	1849-11-03	FD	S2NE	
2655	" "	28	W½NW	1849-11-03	FD	W2NW	
2651	PHILIPS, David C	5	SENW	1851-08-29	FD	SENW	R:JASPER
2622	PING, Anderson S	33	W½SE	1849-08-16	FD	W2SE	R:INDIANA
2634	PING, Asa	33	E½SW	1850-06-01	FD	E2SW	R:JASPER
2764	PING, John	33	W½SW	1849-08-16	FD	W2SW	R:INDIANA

ID	Individual in Patent	Sec.	Sec. Part	Purchase Date	Sale Type	IL Aliquot Part	For More Info . . .
2761	PING, John (Cont'd)	32	SESE	1849-11-03	FD	SESE	R:INDIANA
2762	" "	32	SWSE	1849-12-08	FD	SWSE	R:JASPER
2763	" "	33	SENW	1852-07-12	FD	SENW	
2831	PING, Robert	33	E½SE	1849-09-24	FD	E2SE	R:INDIANA
2626	PRESTON, Andrew J	10	SESE	1851-02-03	FD	SESE	R:CRAWFORD
2627	" "	3	SESW	1852-11-23	FD	SESW	
2625	" "	10	NENW	1852-11-23	FD	NENW	
2647	PRESTON, Cyprian	8	NE	1851-10-30	FD	NE	
2637	REINS, Bartlett Y	6	NWNW	1852-08-31	FD	NWNW	R:JASPER
2771	RILEY, John W	19	SESE	1852-06-23	FD	SESE	
2772	" "	19	W½SE	1852-06-23	FD	W2SE	
2770	" "	19	NESE	1853-03-10	FD	NESE	
2657	ROBERTS, David	16	L9	1851-02-10	SC	LOT9NESE	
2658	" "	30	SENE	1852-10-09	FD	SENE	
2659	" "	30	SWNE	1852-10-09	FD	SWNE	
2686	ROBERTS, Henry	22	SWNW	1853-12-21	FD	SWNW	R:JASPER
2767	ROBERTS, John	21	NENE	1837-10-07	FD	NENE	R:INDIANA
2768	" "	22	NWNW	1837-10-07	FD	NWNW	R:INDIANA
2765	" "	16	L15	1851-01-25	SC	LOT15SWSE	
2766	" "	16	L16	1851-01-25	SC	LOT16SESE	
2769	ROBERTS, John Sen	21	NWSW	1850-11-15	FD	NWSW	R:JASPER
2782	ROBERTS, Jonathan	16	L14	1851-01-25	SC	LOT14SESW	
2785	" "	30	SESW	1851-09-05	FD	SESW	R:JASPER
2784	" "	30	NWSE	1852-10-09	FD	NWSE	
2783	" "	30	NESE	1852-10-09	FD	NESE	
2795	ROBERTS, Joseph	15	SWNE	1853-12-21	FD	SWNE	R:JASPER
2882	ROYAL, William	15	SW	1849-11-28	FD	SW	
2883	" "	20	NE	1849-11-28	FD	NE	
2815	RYA, N John N	20	N½NW	1851-09-18	FD	N2NW	R:ADAMS
2757	RYAN, John N	17	W½SW	1851-09-18	FD	W2SW	R:CLARK
2758	" "	18	E½SE	1851-09-18	FD	E2SE	R:CLARK
2832	RYAN, William G	34	SESE	1839-04-30	FD	SESE	R:JASPER G:52
2848	RYON, Thomas F	16	L13	1851-01-25	SC	LOT13SWSW	
2794	SELBY, Joseph J	32	N½NW	1849-06-20	FD	N2NW	
2792	" "	29	S½SW	1849-06-20	FD	S2SW	
2793	" "	32	N½NE	1849-06-20	FD	N2NE	
2791	" "	29	S½SE	1849-06-20	FD	S2SE	
2709	SHACKLEE, James	5	NWSE	1852-03-16	FD	NWSE	R:JASPER
2720	SINCLAIR, Joel	6	SENE	1851-11-17	FD	SENE	R:JASPER
2721	" "	6	W½NE	1851-11-17	FD	W2NE	R:JASPER
2719	" "	6	NESE	1851-12-09	FD	NESE	R:JASPER
2698	SKIDMORE, James B	16	L8	1851-01-25	SC	LOT8SENE	
2697	" "	10	SESW	1854-02-06	FD	SESW	R:JASPER
2660	SMITH, David	28	SWSW	1852-08-24	FD	SWSW	
2663	SNIDER, Fendol P	4	W½NW	1850-10-17	FD	W2NW	R:JASPER
2664	" "	5	SENE	1850-10-17	FD	SENE	R:JASPER
2687	SNIDER, Henry	15	NENW	1853-02-01	FD	NENW	
2685	SNIDER, Henry P	5	SW	1851-09-16	FD	SW	R:KENTUCKY G:55
2684	" "	17	E½NE	1852-11-27	FD	E2NE	
2685	SNYDER, Henry P	5	SW	1851-09-16	FD	SW	R:KENTUCKY G:55
2670	STAFFORD, Gideon	19	W½NW	1853-01-27	FD	W2NW	R:INDIANA
2669	" "	18	W½SW	1853-01-27	FD	W2SW	R:INDIANA
2710	STEWART, James	22	SWNE	1851-10-21	FD	SWNE	R:INDIANA
2712	" "	27	NESE	1851-10-22	FD	NESE	R:INDIANA
2713	" "	27	W½NW	1851-10-22	FD	W2NW	
2711	" "	27	N½SW	1851-10-22	FD	N2SW	
2843	STEWART, Sanford C	17	SWSE	1851-10-21	FD	SWSE	R:INDIANA
2844	" "	22	NWSE	1851-10-21	FD	NWSE	R:INDIANA
2716	TAYLOR, James	29	N½SW	1849-12-03	FD	N2SW	
2717	" "	29	S½NW	1849-12-03	FD	S2NW	
2832	TINDAL, Robert	34	SESE	1839-04-30	FD	SESE	R:JASPER G:52
2835	TODD, Samuel B	31	NESW	1848-12-18	FD	NESW	
2834	" "	31		1849-01-31	FD	PTNESW	R:INDIANA
2700	" "	31		1849-01-31	FD	PTNESW	R:INDIANA
2804	TOLES, Lott	3	SEN½	1851-07-08	FD	S2NE	R:JASPER
2803	" "	3	N½SE	1851-07-08	FD	N2SE	R:JASPER
2694	WALKER, Isaac H	28	SWSE	1852-08-23	FD	SWSE	
2692	" "	28	E½SE	1852-08-23	FD	E2SE	
2693	" "	28	SESW	1852-08-23	FD	SESW	
2691	" "	22	SWSW	1853-02-02	FD	SWSW	
2833	WALKER, Sam	15	NWNW	1839-11-04	FD	NWNW	R:JASPER
2856	WEAVER, Joshua	16	L3	1851-01-25	SC	LOT3NENW	
2800	" "	16	L3	1851-01-25	SC	LOT3NENW	

ID	Individual in Patent	Sec.	Sec. Part	Purchase Date	Sale Type	IL Aliquot Part	For More Info . . .
2841	WEAVER, Samuel	10	W½NE	1841-11-17	FD	W2NE	R:JASPER
2842	" "	16	L4	1851-01-25	SC	LOT4NWNW	
2620	WEBB, Amasiah M	15	SWSE	1853-08-09	FD	SWSE	R:INDIANA
2621	WEBB, Amaziah	17	N½SE	1852-09-14	FD	N2SE	
2813	WEBSTER, Lyman	32	NESE	1849-10-22	FD	NESE	R:JASPER
2814	" "	32	SENE	1850-05-28	FD	SENE	R:JASPER
2812	" "	22	SESE	1852-10-13	FD	SESE	R:JASPER
2823	WHITE, Providence	7	W½SW	1850-02-01	FD	W2SW	R:INDIANA S:F
2822	"	7	NW	1850-02-02	FD	NW	R:INDIANA S:F
2863	WILSON, William C	15	NESE	1851-11-15	FD	NESE	R:JASPER
2865	" "	22	SWSE	1853-01-21	FD	SWSE	
2864	" "	17	NESW	1853-11-05	FD	NESW	R:JASPER
2805	WINES, Louisiana	30	N½SW	1851-11-21	FD	N2SW	R:INDIANA S:F
2666	WOODARD, Franklin	21	SENE	1850-01-23	FD	SENE	R:INDIANA
2665	" "	15	SENW	1850-01-23	FD	SENW	R:INDIANA

Patent Map

T7-N R14-W
2nd PM Meridian

Map Group 10

Township Statistics

Parcels Mapped	:	273
Number of Patents	:	1
Number of Individuals	:	141
Patentees Identified	:	140
Number of Surnames	:	103
Multi-Patentee Parcels	:	3
Oldest Patent Date	:	11/7/1823
Most Recent Patent	:	11/1/1854
Block/Lot Parcels	:	17
Cities and Towns	:	0
Cemeteries	:	4

Section 6
- REINS Bartlett Y 1852
- CLARK Henry 1853
- CLARK Austin 1852
- SINCLAIR Joel 1851
- FEARS William 1851
- FEARS William 1851
- SINCLAIR Joel 1851
- HEPNER Green Berry 1852
- CLARK Austin 1852
- FOX Daniel 1852
- SINCLAIR Joel 1851

Section 5
- FEARS Joseph 1851
- CHAPMAN Washington 1850
- CHAPMAN Washington 1851
- PHILIPS David C 1851
- SNIDER Henry P 1851
- DAVIS John D 1852
- SHACKLEE James 1852
- COLEMAN Elias 1851
- DILLMON Andrew 1850

Section 4
- CLEMANS Hamilton J 1845
- SNIDER Fendol P 1850
- SNIDER Fendol P 1850
- DILLMAN Andrew 1839
- CLEMANS Hamilton J 1845
- BYRNE Thomas 1854
- BAILEY Ludwill 1852
- BAILEY John L 1852
- MILLER John 1837
- MILLER John 1845
- MILLER John 1851
- MILLER Henry 1839

Section 7
- WHITE Providence 1850
- MCGINNESS Orville 1852
- MCGINNESS Orvill S 1852
- WHITE Providence 1850
- HILL John M L 1853
- LEACH James 1852

Section 8
- KELLY Hannah 1852
- KELLY Hannah 1852
- PRESTON Cyprian 1851
- MILLER Henry 1851
- BAILEY Ludwill 1852
- CLEMENS Walden 1845
- KELLY Hannah 1852
- BAILEY William 1852
- BAILEY William 1852
- KELLY Benjamin F 1852
- KELLY Benjamin F 1852
- BAILEY Ludwill 1852

Section 9
- MILLER John 1837
- BAILEY Ludwill 1852
- BALEY Ludwill 1853
- COX William K 1850
- COX William K 1850
- BAILEY Ludwill 1852
- COX William K 1850
- COX William K 1850
- COX William K 1850
- MCCABE John 1851
- COX William K 1850
- HARMON John 1850

Section 18
- HARBERT William 1840
- BAILEY John L 1851
- LEACH James 1852
- LEACH James 1852
- BAILEY John L 1851
- JENKINS Jonathan H 1852
- JENKINS Jonathan H 1852
- BAILEY John L 1851
- STAFFORD Gideon 1853
- JENKINS Jonathan H 1852
- JENKINS Jonathan H 1852

Section 17
- KELLY Benjamin F 1852
- KELLY Benjamin F 1852
- BAILEY William 1852
- JENKINS Jonathan H 1852
- JONES Sarah E 1853
- JONES Sarah E 1853
- SNIDER Henry P 1852
- WILSON William C 1853
- WEBB Amaziah 1852
- RYAN John N 1851
- ELLIOTT Joseph W 1852
- STEWART Sanford C 1851
- ELLIOTT Joseph W 1852
- DURHAM John C 1841

Lots-Sec. 16
- L1 HARMON, John 1851
- L2 HARMON, John 1851
- L3 WEAVER, Joshua 1851
- L3 HINMAN, Titus 1854
- L4 WEAVER, Samuel 1851
- L5 HARMON, William 1851
- L6 LENEX, Jonathan 1851
- L7 BUTLER, John 1851
- L8 SKIDMORE, James B 1851
- L9 ROBERTS, David 1851
- L10 BUTLER, John 1851
- L11 HARMON, John P 1851
- L12 HARMON, John P 1851
- L13 RYON, Thomas F 1851
- L14 ROBERTS, Jonathan 1851
- L15 ROBERTS, John 1851
- L16 ROBERTS, John 1851

16

Jasper

Section 19
- JENKINS Jonathan H 1852
- JENKINS Jonathan 1852
- STAFFORD Gideon 1853
- JENKINS Jonathan H 1853
- HESLER Joseph 1851
- RILEY John W 1852
- RILEY John W 1853
- RILEY John W 1852

Section 20
- RYAN John N 1851
- ROYAL William 1849
- GRIFFY David B 1851
- ARDERY James 1852
- HAWKINS William S 1849

Section 21
- BUTLER John 1851
- BUTLER John 1850
- BUTLER John 1850
- ROBERTS John 1837
- JONES William 1851
- WOODARD Franklin 1850
- ROBERTS John Sen 1850
- JONES William 1852
- EVERMAN William 1823
- EVERMAN Alfred 1851
- EDWARDS Charles 1849
- MCKEE Robert 1851
- MEANS James B 1852

Section 30
- HENDRICKSON Daniel 1852
- HESLER Joseph 1852
- GUYNN Richard 1852
- ROBERTS David 1852
- ROBERTS David 1852
- WINES Louisiana 1851
- ROBERTS Jonathan 1852
- ROBERTS Jonathan 1852
- DECKER Abijah 1851
- ROBERTS Jonathan 1851
- FEESER James 1851

Section 29
- MONROE Caleb 1852
- MONROE Caleb 1852
- EDWARDS Charles 1849
- TAYLOR James 1849
- NOEL David 1849
- TAYLOR James 1849
- MCALLISTER Lewis 1849
- BURCHAM Joseph 1852
- SELBY Joseph J 1849
- SELBY Joseph J 1849

Section 28
- MCKEE Robert 1851
- MCKEE Robert 1851
- NOEL David 1849
- MILLER Harrison 1852
- MILLER Harrison 1852
- MILLER Aaron 1852
- MCALLISTER Lewis 1849
- EDGERTON John D 1852
- EDGERTON John D 1852
- SMITH David 1852
- WALKER Isaac H 1852
- WALKER Isaac H 1852
- WALKER Isaac H 1852

Section 31
- FEESER James 1848
- FEESER James 1849
- EAMES Armstead 1851
- NEAL Thomas 1851
- TODD Samuel B 1848
- TODD Samuel B 1849
- IRELAND Richard 1849
- MILLER William 1839
- BROOKS Henry 1848

Section 32
- SELBY Joseph J 1849
- SELBY Joseph J 1849
- NEAL Thomas 1852
- CRAIG Samuel 1850
- CRAIG Samuel 1850
- WEBSTER Lyman 1850
- HAMILTON Thomas 1849
- CRAIG Samuel 1850
- CRAIG Samuel 1850
- WEBSTER Lyman 1849
- HAMILTON Thomas 1849
- PING John 1849
- PING John 1849

Section 33
- MCCARTY James 1852
- MCCARTY James 1852
- MCCARTY James 1852
- MEESE James 1852
- PING John 1852
- MEERE David 1850
- PING John 1849
- MCCRILLIS John 1850
- PING Asa 1849
- PING Anderson S 1849
- PING Robert 1849

BAILEY John L 1852	BUFFINGTON John 1851	BUFFINGTON John 1851	MCCABE William 1853
	BAILEY John L 1852 **3**	TOLES Lott 1851	
HARMON [12] John 1839	MILLER Rebecca 1852		TOLES Lott 1851
	PRESTON Andrew J 1852	CURTIS Eli 1849	CURTIS Asa 1851

Sections: **2**, **1**

MCCLELLAND Samuel 1842	PRESTON Andrew J 1852	WEAVER Samuel 1841	CURTIS Asa 1851
JEFFERS George W 1852 **10**			LAGOW Clark B 1852
JEFFERS George W 1852	HARMON John 1852	NEAL Thomas 1851	

Sections: **11**, **12**

HARMON John 1850	SKIDMORE James B 1854	HARMON Joseph 1839	PRESTON Andrew J 1851
WALKER Sam 1839	SNIDER Henry 1853	HARMON John 1839	HARMON John 1839
BUTLER John 1850 **15**	WOODARD Franklin 1850	ROBERTS Joseph 1853	HARMON John 1847
	ROYAL William 1849	BUTLER John 1851	WILSON William C 1851
		WEBB Amasiah M 1853	KINSLOW James T 1840

Sections: **14**, **13**

Crawford

ROBERTS John 1837	ELLIOTT Joseph W 1852	GRIFFY Jobe H 1853	KINSLOW James T 1840
ROBERTS Henry 1853	EVERMAN Alfred 1852 **22**	STEWART James 1851	MEESE David 1851
EVERMAN Alfred 1850	EVERMAN Alfred 1849	STEWART Sanford C 1851	BEESON Igal 1851
WALKER Isaac H 1853	ELLIOTT Joseph W 1852	WILSON William C 1853	WEBSTER Lyman 1852

Sections: **23**, **24**

	KIRKWOOD Thomas 1851		KIRKWOOD Thomas 1851
STEWART James 1851 **27**		MILLER Harrison 1852	
STEWART James 1851		MILLER Aaron 1852	STEWART James 1851
DAY William 1851			KEIFF Patrick 1850

Sections: **26**, **25**

MEERE David 1850	KEIFF Patrick 1850	KEIFF Patrick 1850	
	34	KEIF Andrew 1851	KEIFFE Patrick 1852
MCCORMICK Andrew M 1838	MCCORMICK Andrew M 1837	EATON Richard 1828	BEESON Allen 1853
BEESON Igal 1851	BEESON Igal 1851		TINDAL [52] Robert 1839

Sections: **35**, **36**

Helpful Hints

1. This Map's INDEX can be found on the preceding pages.

2. Refer to Map "C" to see where this Township lies within Jasper County, Illinois.

3. Numbers within square brackets [ ] denote a multi-patentee land parcel (multi-owner). Refer to Appendix "C" for a full list of members in this group.

4. Areas that look to be crowded with Patentees usually indicate multiple sales of the same parcel (re-issues), cancellations or voided transactions (that we map, anyway) or overlapping parcels. We opt to show even these ambiguous parcels, which oftentimes lead to research avenues not yet taken.

Legend

— Patent Boundary

— Section Boundary

No Patents Found (or Outside County)

1., 2., 3., ... Lot Numbers (when beside a name)

[   ] Group Number (see Appendix "C")

Scale: Section = 1 mile X 1 mile (generally, with some exceptions)

Road Map

T7-N R14-W
2nd PM Meridian

Map Group 10

Cities & Towns
None

Cemeteries
Baily Cemetery
Mound Cemetery
Sand Rock Cemetery
Todd Cemetery

6

5   E 1575th Ave

4

N 2100th St

E 1550th Ave

N 2000th St

E 1500th Ave

7

8

Baily Cem.

9

N 2175th St

18

17

E 1350th Ave

16

E 1325th St

19

20

E 1250th Ave

21

Mound Cem.

E 1200th Ave

30

29

28

N 1900th St

N 1100th St

31
Cemetery

E 1050 Ave   E 1050th Ave

Todd Cem.

North St
Green St

1000 N

32

33

E 1000th Ave

3

2

1

Sand Rock Cem. ✝

N 2275th St

10

11

12

E 1375th Ave

2300 E

15

14

13

Crawford

N 2200th St

22

Jasper

23

24

N 2250th St

E 1150th Ave

27

26

25

N 1100th St

34

N 2275th St

35

36

E 102 0th Ave

Helpful Hints

1. This road map has a number of uses, but primarily it is to help you: a) find the present location of land owned by your ancestors (at least the general area), b) find cemeteries and city-centers, and c) estimate the route/roads used by Census-takers & tax-assessors.

2. If you plan to travel to Jasper County to locate cemeteries or land parcels, please pick up a modern travel map for the area before you do. Mapping old land parcels on modern maps is not as exact a science as you might think. Just the slightest variations in public land survey coordinates, estimates of parcel boundaries, or road-map deviations can greatly alter a map's representation of how a road either does or doesn't cross a particular parcel of land.

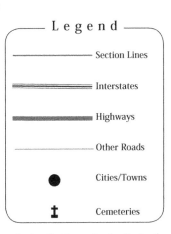

L e g e n d

———— Section Lines

══════ Interstates

━━━━━ Highways

———— Other Roads

● Cities/Towns

✝ Cemeteries

Scale: Section = 1 mile X 1 mile
(generally, with some exceptions)

169

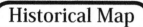

Historical Map

T7-N R14-W
2nd PM Meridian

Map Group 10

<u>Cities & Towns</u>
None

<u>Cemeteries</u>
Baily Cemetery
Mound Cemetery
Sand Rock Cemetery
Todd Cemetery

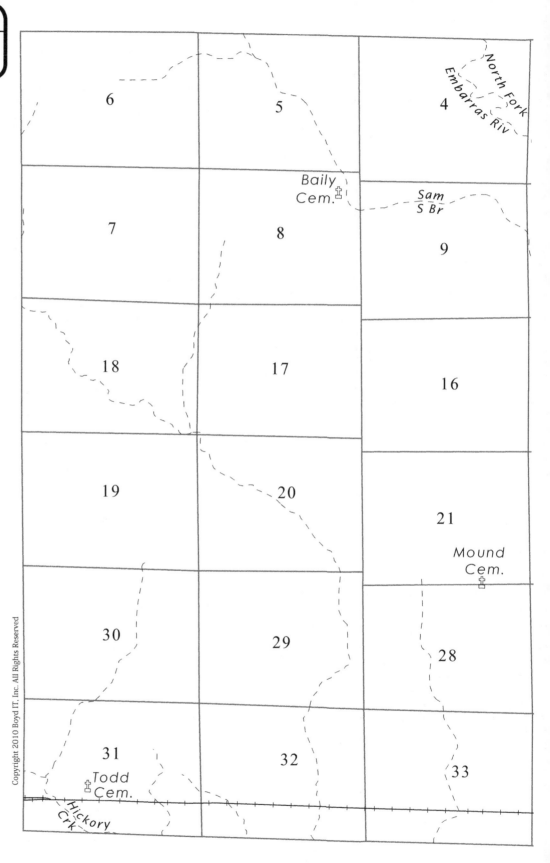

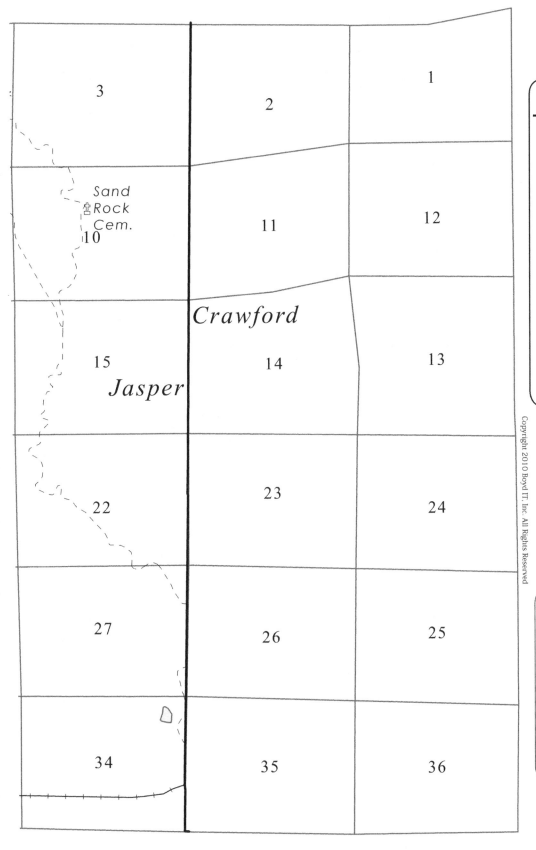

3

2

1

Sand
🏛*Rock*
Cem.
10

11

12

Crawford

15

14

13

Jasper

22

23

24

27

26

25

34

35

36

Helpful Hints

1. This Map takes a different look at the same Congressional Township displayed in the preceding two maps. It presents features that can help you better envision the historical development of the area: a) Water-bodies (lakes & ponds), b) Water-courses (rivers, streams, etc.), c) Railroads, d) City/ town center-points (where they were oftentimes located when first settled), and e) Cemeteries.

2. Using this "Historical" map in tandem with this Township's Patent Map and Road Map, may lead you to some interesting discoveries. You will often find roads, towns, cemeteries, and waterways are named after nearby landowners: sometimes those names will be the ones you are researching. See how many of these research gems you can find here in Jasper County.

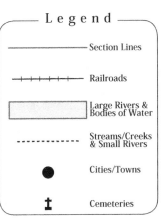

Legend

——————— Section Lines

+++++++ Railroads

Large Rivers & Bodies of Water

----------- Streams/Creeks & Small Rivers

● Cities/Towns

🏛 Cemeteries

Scale: Section = 1 mile X 1 mile
(there are some exceptions)

Map Group 11: Index to Land Patents

Township 6-North Range 8-East (3rd PM)

After you locate an individual in this Index, take note of the Section and Section Part then proceed to the Land Patent map on the pages immediately following. You should have no difficulty locating the corresponding parcel of land.

The "For More Info" Column will lead you to more information about the underlying Patents. See the *Legend* at right, and the "How to Use this Book" chapter, for more information.

```
                    LEGEND
         "For More Info . . . " column
G = Group   (Multi-Patentee Patent, see Appendix "C")
R = Residence
S = Social Status

See Appendix A for list of abbreviations used by the
Illinois State Archives in describing the place and
nature of these land patents.

Note: if the Abbreviations contain "L", "BL", "LOT",
or "BLOCK", the exact whereabouts of the parcel within
the section is not known.
```

ID	Individual in Patent	Sec.	Sec. Part	Purchase Date	Sale Type	IL Aliquot Part	For More Info . . .
2903	ADAMSON, Asa	32	SWSE	1840-01-27	FD	SWSE	R:CLAY
3044	ADAMSON, James	9	NESE	1852-12-10	FD	NESE	
3258	" "	2	L1 (E½)	1853-02-11	FD	E2LOT1NW	
3043	" "	2	L1 (W½)	1853-02-11	FD	W2LOT1NE	
3042	" "	2	L1 (E½)	1853-02-11	FD	E2LOT1NW	
3250	" "	2	L1 (W½)	1853-02-11	FD	W2LOT1NE	
3041	" "	2	NWSE	1853-02-25	FD	NWSE	
3197	ADAMSON, William	8	W½SW	1840-06-03	FD	W2SW	R:IOWA
3260	ADAMSON, Zedekiah	2	L3	1852-11-01	FD	LOT3NW	
3260	" "	2	L3	1852-11-01	FD	LOT3NE	
3259	" "	2	L2	1852-11-01	FD	LOT2NE	
3259	" "	2	L2	1852-11-01	FD	LOT2NW	
3258	" "	2	L1 (E½)	1852-11-01	FD	E2LOT1NE	
3257	" "	2	NESE	1852-11-01	FD	NESE	
3042	" "	2	L1 (E½)	1852-11-01	FD	E2LOT1NE	
3261	" "	4	NESE	1852-12-03	FD	NESE	
2932	AKIN, Daniel	29	NESW	1840-01-20	FD	NESW	R:EFFINGHAM
2953	AKIN, Edmund	9	SWNW	1853-03-17	FD	SWNW	
2952	" "	9	NWSW	1853-03-17	FD	NWSW	
2979	ARCHER, Evander	29	SESE	1853-02-21	FD	SESE	
3069	BAKER, Jeptha	26	E½NW	1853-01-17	FD	E2NW	
3068	" "	23	E½SW	1853-01-17	FD	E2SW	
3030	BALEY, Jacob	5	L3	1852-09-09	FD	LOT3NE	R:JASPER
3031	" "	5	L1	1853-01-03	FD	LOT1NE	
3035	" "	5	L3 (E½)	1853-01-03	FD	E2LOT3NW	
3034	" "	5	L2 (E½)	1853-01-03	FD	E2LOT2NW	
3032	" "	5	L1 (E½)	1853-01-03	FD	E2LOT1NW	
3029	" "	5	W½SE	1853-01-03	FD	W2SE	
3028	" "	5	SW	1853-01-03	FD	SW	
3033	" "	5	L2	1853-01-03	FD	LOT2NE	
3199	BARTEE, William	35	S½SW	1853-03-19	FD	S2SWVOID	
3209	BARTEE, William J	35	S½SE	1854-10-26	FD	S2SE	
3137	BERRY, Myatt	22	SENE	1853-04-18	FD	SENE	G:10
3235	BERRY, Wyatt	22	E½NW	1853-04-25	FD	E2NW	
3234	" "	22		1853-04-25	FD	FDW2NE	
3236	" "	7	NWSE	1853-04-30	FD	NWSE	R:FAYETTE
3233	" "	20	NESE	1853-10-21	FD	NESE	R:FAYETTE
3249	BERRY, Wyatt S	2	W½SW	1852-09-13	FD	W2SW	
3254	" "	3	SESW	1852-10-04	FD	SESW	
3250	" "	2	L1 (W½)	1852-10-18	FD	W2LOT1NW	
3043	" "	2	L1 (W½)	1852-10-18	FD	W2LOT1NW	
3244	" "	14	NWNE	1852-10-20	FD	NWNE	
3238	" "	11	NENE	1852-10-20	FD	NENE	
3241	" "	12	W½SW	1852-10-20	FD	W2SW	
3239	" "	11	NESE	1852-10-20	FD	NESE	
3242	" "	13	W½SW	1852-12-08	FD	W2SW	

ID	Individual in Patent	Sec.	Sec. Part	Purchase Date	Sale Type	IL Aliquot Part	For More Info . . .
3243	BERRY, Wyatt S (Cont'd)	14	E½SE	1852-12-08	FD	E2SE	
3251	" "	23	E½NW	1852-12-09	FD	E2NW	
3237	" "	10	E½NW	1852-12-10	FD	E2NW	
3247	" "	17	SW	1853-01-07	FD	SW	
3246	" "	14	SWNE	1853-01-07	FD	SWNE	
3245	" "	14	NWSE	1853-01-07	FD	NWSE	
3240	" "	11	SENW	1853-01-07	FD	SENW	
3248	" "	2	SWSE	1853-02-03	FD	SWSE	
3252	" "	24	W½SW	1853-03-21	FD	W2SW	
3137	" "	22	SENE	1853-04-18	FD	SENE	G:10
3256	" "	5	NESE	1853-08-01	FD	NESE	R:FAYETTE
3255	" "	32	NENE	1853-10-10	FD	NENE	R:FAYETTE
3253	" "	26	S½SW	1854-01-05	FD	S2SW	R:FAYETTE
3119	BIDEL, Joseph E	29	NESE	1853-02-21	FD	NESE	
3067	BLAKE, Jefferson	3	L3 (W½)	1853-04-11	FD	W2LOT3NW	R:JASPER
3204	BONE, William E	29	NWSW	1853-05-19	FD	NWSW	R:SHELBY
3203	" "	29	NWSE	1853-05-19	FD	NWSE	R:SHELBY
2970	BRADBERRY, Elijah	5	L1 (W½)	1852-12-18	FD	W2LOT1NW	
2974	BRADBERRY, Elisha	6	NESE	1851-08-29	FD	NESE	R:JASPER
2973	" "	5	L2 (W½)	1852-12-18	FD	W2LOT2NW	
2890	BREWER, Abraham	34	E½SE	1853-01-17	FD	E2SE	
2891	BRIGES, Absalom	16	L4	1856-04-28	SC	LOT04NWNW	
2892	" "	16	L5	1857-03-01	SC	LOT05SWNW	
3158	BRUMFIED, Richard T	31	NESE	1852-09-09	FD	NESE	R:JASPER
3154	BRUMFIELD, Richard	31	SENE	1852-09-09	FD	SENE	R:JASPER
3200	BRYAN, William	4	W½SW	1853-08-01	FD	W2SW	R:JASPER
3198	BRYAN, William B	4	L1 (W½)	1853-01-28	FD	W2LOT1NW	
3188	" "	4	L1 (W½)	1853-01-28	FD	W2LOT1NW	
3176	BUNTAIN, Smith B	18	NENE	1873-05-31	RR	NENE	
3072	BURCHAM, John	11	SENE	1851-06-09	FD	SENE	R:JASPER
3074	" "	2	SESE	1851-08-11	FD	SESE	R:JASPER
3073	" "	16	L8	1855-12-06	SC	LOT08SENE	
2902	CARRELL, Archibald	31	NENE	1840-02-25	FD	NENEFR	R:JASPER
2904	CASSITY, Ashley C	9	NESW	1853-10-10	FD	NESW	
3004	CATERS, Green	16	L13	1855-12-06	SC	LOT13SWSW	
2998	CATHEN, Green B	20	SESE	1853-03-04	FD	SESE	
3001	CATHER, Green B	20	SWNE	1853-01-03	FD	SWNE	
2999	" "	20	E½NW	1853-01-22	FD	E2NW	
3000	" "	20	NWSE	1853-01-22	FD	NWSE	
3003	" "	21	SWSW	1853-01-22	FD	SWSW	
3002	" "	20	W½NW	1853-08-01	FD	W2NW	R:JASPER
3138	CATHER, Nathan	33	NESW	1853-10-10	FD	NESW	R:JASPER
3220	CATHER, William R	7	E½SE	1853-01-07	FD	E2SE	
3221	" "	9	SENE	1853-01-07	FD	SENE	
3078	CHEEK, John	26	SWNW	1853-02-14	FD	SWNW	
3077	" "	26	NWNW	1853-02-14	FD	NWNW	
3022	CHESMETT, Ibby	29	NWNW	1853-02-19	FD	NWNW	
3016	CHESNUT, Hey Jane	19	SESE	1852-09-09	FD	SESE	R:JASPER S:F
3144	CHESNUT, Polly	32	SWSW	1845-04-28	FD	SWSW	R:JASPER S:F
2914	CHOATE, Benjamin H	4	SESW	1852-12-18	FD	SESW	
2915	" "	9	NWNW	1852-12-18	FD	NWNW	
2980	CLARK, Frederick A	32	SWNW	1853-02-24	FD	SWNW	R:INDIANA
3177	CLARK, Thomas	32	NESE	1853-03-02	FD	NESE	
3178	" "	33	NWSW	1853-03-02	FD	NWSW	
3179	" "	33	SENE	1853-08-24	FD	SENE	R:INDIANA
3124	COCHRAN, Josiah	14	E½NW	1853-03-05	FD	E2NW	
2977	CORBIN, Ephraim	10	SESE	1852-12-18	FD	SESE	
2976	" "	10	NESE	1852-12-18	FD	NESE	
2978	" "	12	NW	1853-02-12	FD	NW	
3110	COWGER, Jonathan	19	SWSW	1852-10-16	FD	SWSW	R:INDIANA
3111	" "	20	SWSE	1853-02-09	FD	SWSE	
2963	CURTISS, Eli	26	W½SE	1853-03-21	FD	W2SE	R:JASPER G:23
3047	DALE, James	13	NESW	1853-02-26	FD	NESW	
3048	" "	14	SWSE	1853-02-26	FD	SWSE	
3005	DENMAN, Hampton	27	NENE	1853-02-16	FD	NENE	
2986	DICKMAN, George H	32	NESW	1854-04-29	FD	NESW	R:FAYETTE
3036	DOBBINS, Jacob H	4	L2 (E½)	1853-01-07	FD	E2LOT2NE	
3201	DOGGETT, William	15	E½NW	1853-02-09	FD	E2NW	
3202	" "	15	E½SW	1853-02-09	FD	E2SW	
2984	DOUTHIT, George	20	NWNE	1839-02-22	FD	NWNE	R:CLINTON
2985	" "	20	SESW	1839-06-21	FD	SESW	R:CLAY
2898	DOVEL, Andrew	23	N½NE	1853-03-11	FD	N2NE	
2897	" "	22	NENE	1853-03-11	FD	NENE	

ID	Individual in Patent	Sec.	Sec. Part	Purchase Date	Sale Type	IL Aliquot Part	For More Info . . .
2899	DOVEL, Andrew (Cont'd)	23	NWSW	1853-03-11	FD	NWSW	
2901	DOVEL, Andrew J	1	NW	1852-11-08	FD	NW	
3156	DRAKE, Richard J	33	SWSE	1853-09-07	FD	SWSE	R:INDIANA
3155	" "	33	SESW	1853-09-07	FD	SESW	R:INDIANA
2964	DUNCAN, Eli	9	S½SE	1853-02-05	FD	S2SE	
3214	ELDER, William M	25	NENE	1853-01-15	FD	NENE	
3213	" "	24	SESE	1853-01-15	FD	SESE	
2923	EVANS, Brison J	9	SESW	1853-02-23	FD	SESW	R:JASPER
2924	EVANS, Caleb	32	SESW	1853-02-23	FD	SESW	R:JASPER
3132	EVANS, Mary E	30	SWSE	1882-02-11	RR	SWSE	S:F
2921	FIELD, Benton	29	NENE	1852-09-09	FD	NENE	R:JASPER
2922	" "	29	SWSW	1852-09-09	FD	SWSW	R:JASPER
3081	FIELD, John	29	SENW	1842-04-19	FD	SENW	R:JASPER
3082	" "	30	E½SE	1842-04-19	FD	E2SE	R:JASPER
3083	FIELDS, John	29	SWNW	1839-05-27	FD	SWNW	R:CLAY
3160	FOSTER, Samuel	23	SENE	1851-06-02	FD	SENE	
3164	" "	24	W½NE	1851-06-02	FD	W2NE	
3162	" "	24	SENW	1851-06-02	FD	SENW	
3161	" "	24	N½NW	1851-06-02	FD	N2NW	
3159	" "	13	SWNE	1851-06-02	FD	SWNE	
3163	" "	24	SWNW	1851-06-02	FD	SWNW	
3165	" "	3	NWSE	1851-08-11	FD	NWSE	R:JASPER
3166	FOSTER, Samuel Jr	25	NWNW	1853-10-27	FD	NWNW	R:JASPER
3183	FOSTER, Thomas	11	SWNE	1851-06-02	FD	SWNE	R:OHIO
3182	" "	11	SESE	1851-06-02	FD	SESE	R:OHIO
3180	" "	11	NESW	1851-06-02	FD	NESW	
3184	" "	11	W½SW	1851-06-02	FD	W2SW	
3009	" "	11	NWSE	1851-06-02	FD	NWSE	
3181	" "	11	NWSE	1851-06-02	FD	NWSE	
3188	" "	4	L1 (W½)	1853-01-24	FD	W2LOT1NE	
3187	" "	4	NWSE	1853-01-24	FD	NWSE	
3198	" "	4	L1 (W½)	1853-01-24	FD	W2LOT1NE	
3186	" "	15	NENE	1853-01-28	FD	NENE	
3185	" "	14	NWNW	1853-01-28	FD	NWNW	
3102	FREEMAN, John W	19	SWNE	1853-01-03	FD	SWNE	
3101	" "	19	N½NE	1853-01-03	FD	N2NE	
3103	" "	21	NWNE	1853-01-03	FD	NWNE	
3104	" "	29	NENW	1853-02-18	FD	NENW	
3105	" "	8	E½NE	1866-11-08	RR	E2NE	
3232	GAMBRIEL, Woodford	24	SENE	1853-01-07	FD	SENE	
3215	GAREE, William M	30	E½NE	1870-04-30	RR	E2NE	
3216	" "	30	NWSE	1870-04-30	RR	NWSE	
3217	" "	30	SWNE	1870-04-30	RR	SWNE	
3141	GARS, Peter	9	NWSE	1852-10-20	FD	NWSE	R:INDIANA
3142	GHURST, Peter	25	NWNE	1853-03-17	FD	NWNE	
2933	GREGORY, Daniel	33	E½SE	1853-10-20	FD	E2SE	R:FAYETTE
3088	HAGEMAN, John	33	W½NW	1852-09-09	FD	W2NW	
3087	" "	32	SENE	1852-09-09	FD	SENE	
3086	" "	28	SWSW	1852-09-09	FD	SWSW	
2995	HAGIMAN, George W	27	SESW	1853-02-26	FD	SESW	
2996	" "	27	SWSE	1853-02-26	FD	SWSE	
3174	HAGIMAN, Simon	27	SWSW	1853-02-26	FD	SWSW	
3175	" "	34	NWNW	1853-02-26	FD	NWNW	
3066	HALL, Jasper	8	N½SE	1885-12-01	RR	N2SE	
3014	HAWKS, Henry	36	SWNE	1853-03-17	FD	SWNE	
3013	" "	36	NWSE	1853-03-17	FD	NWSE	
3205	HAYES, William	24	NENE	1852-01-07	FD	NENE	
3218	HAYES, William O	13	N½SE	1853-01-07	FD	N2SE	
3219	" "	13	SESE	1853-01-07	FD	SESE	
3207	HIGGINS, William	27	SENE	1853-03-19	FD	SENE	
3206	" "	23	NWSE	1853-03-19	FD	NWSE	
3208	" "	27	SWNE	1853-03-21	FD	SWNE	
2983	HILL, George B	13	E½NE	1853-01-24	FD	E2NE	
3189	HILL, Thomas J	32	SESE	1853-03-05	FD	SESE	
3190	" "	33	SWSW	1853-03-05	FD	SWSW	
2938	HINDS, Daniel T	24	NESE	1852-11-05	FD	NESE	
3089	HOLLINGSWORTH, John	5	SESE	1851-08-18	FD	SESE	
2981	HUFF, Gabril	10	SWSE	1853-03-09	FD	SWSE	
2982	" "	15	NWNE	1853-03-09	FD	NWNE	
3023	HUGGINS, Isaac	20	N½SW	1853-02-15	FD	N2SW	
2900	IRVIN, Andrew	16	L16	1855-12-06	SC	LOT16SESE	
3212	JAYCON, William	33	NENE	1853-10-10	FD	NENE	R:JASPER
3026	JAYCOX, Isaiah	21	N½SW	1852-09-24	FD	N2SW	

ID	Individual in Patent	Sec.	Sec. Part	Purchase Date	Sale Type	IL Aliquot Part	For More Info . . .
3025	JAYCOX, Isaiah (Cont'd)	21	E½NW	1852-09-24	FD	E2NW	
3024	" "	20	E½NE	1853-02-14	FD	E2NE	
3027	" "	21	W½NW	1853-02-14	FD	W2NW	
2941	JOHNSON, David L	18	W½NE	1877-05-28	RR	W2NE	
2940	" "	18	NWSE	1877-10-27	RR	NWSEFR	
3046	JOHNSON, James B	24	E½SW	1853-03-21	FD	E2SW	
3045	" "	13	SESW	1853-03-21	FD	SESW	
2925	JONES, Charles Floyd	1	L1 (E½)	1852-10-05	FD	E2LOT1NW	
2929	" "	9	NWNE	1853-02-19	FD	NWNE	
2930	" "	9	SENW	1853-02-19	FD	SENW	
2928	" "	9	NENW	1853-02-19	FD	NENW	
2931	" "	9	SWNE	1853-02-19	FD	SWNE	
2927	" "	36	NWNE	1853-03-21	FD	NWNE	
2926	" "	36	NENW	1853-03-21	FD	NENW	
3007	JONES, Harter S	35	N½SE	1853-03-21	FD	N2SE	
3012	KEPLEY, Henry B	20	SWSW	1884-07-14	RR	SWSW	
2975	KESTER, Ellen N	8	SESE	1888-06-28	RR	SESE	
2916	KRUZAN, Benjamin	3	L2 (E½)	1853-03-03	FD	E2LOT2NW	R:JASPER
2918	" "	4	L3 (E½)	1853-03-03	FD	E2LOT3NW	R:JASPER
2917	" "	3	L3 (E½)	1853-03-03	FD	E2LOT3NW	R:JASPER
2949	LAMBERT, Eaden	16	L9	1856-08-25	SC	LOT09NESE	
2950	LAMBERT, Eden	15	NWNW	1853-01-08	FD	NWNW	
2951	" "	16	L1	1855-12-06	SC	LOT01NENE	
3194	LAMBERT, Watson	1	S½SW	1852-09-29	FD	S2SW	
3195	" "	1	W½SE	1852-09-29	FD	W2SE	
3196	" "	10	W½SW	1853-01-22	FD	W2SW	
2954	LEONARD, Edward F	30		1867-10-29	FD	NWSVB2IVFR	
2886	LUERSEN, A H August	6	L2	1864-06-22	RR	LOT2NEMA	
2885	" "	6	L1	1864-06-22	RR	LOT1NEMA	
2887	" "	6	L3	1864-06-22	RR	LOT3NEMA	
3018	MANNING, Hiram	24	NWSE	1853-03-11	FD	NWSEVOID	
3017	" "	24	NWSE	1853-03-11	FD	NWSEVOID	
3018	" "	24	NWSE	1853-12-12	FD	NWSE	R:JASPER
3017	" "	24	NWSE	1853-12-12	FD	NWSE	R:JASPER
3128	MATHEWS, Levi	7	SWSE	1853-01-29	FD	SWSE	R:JASPER
3058	MATLOCK, James M	8	NENW	1868-12-31	RR	NENW	
3059	" "	8	NWNE	1873-02-28	RR	NWNE	
3084	MATTINGLEY, John G	27	NWNE	1853-11-13	FD	NWNE	R:JASPER
3062	MCNUTT, James	29	SWSE	1853-03-02	FD	SWSE	
3075	MCQUEEN, John C	31	SESE	1852-09-09	FD	SESE	R:JASPER
3076	" "	32	NWSE	1853-02-01	FD	NWSE	R:JASPER
3019	MICHELL, Hiram	16	L10	1856-01-29	SC	LOT10NWSE	
3020	" "	16	L15	1985-01-12	SC	LOT15SWSE	R:BUREAU
2934	MILLER, Daniel Sen	10	NWSE	1853-02-09	FD	NWSE	
3063	MILLER, James	15	SWSW	1853-02-09	FD	SWSW	
2935	MILLIN, Daniel Sen	15	NWSW	1853-02-05	FD	NWSW	
2936	" "	15	SWNW	1853-02-05	FD	SWNW	
2968	MITCHELL, Elihu	4	L2 (W½)	1852-12-10	FD	W2LOT2NW	
2969	" "	4	L2 (W½)	1852-12-10	FD	W2LOT2NW	
2968	" "	4	L2 (W½)	1853-01-29	FD	W2LOT2NE	
2969	" "	4	L2 (W½)	1853-01-29	FD	W2LOT2NE	
3055	MITCHELL, James J	4	L1	1852-12-08	FD	LOT1NW	
3056	" "	4	L2	1852-12-08	FD	LOT2NW	
3057	" "	4	L3	1853-02-02	FD	LOT3NE	
3054	" "	3	L2 (W½)	1853-02-18	FD	W2LOT2NW	
3210	MONAHAN, William J	18	SWSE	1881-12-29	RR	SWSE	
3006	MORRIS, Harmony	25	SW	1853-02-25	FD	SW	
3139	MORRIS, Oliver P	25	NWSE	1853-02-25	FD	NWSE	
3122	NEAL, Joseph R	4	L1 (E½)	1853-03-21	FD	E2LOT1NE	
3123	NEALE, Joseph R	3	L1 (W½)	1853-01-07	FD	W2LOT1NW	
2943	NESSLEY, David	21	SESW	1853-02-22	FD	SESW	
2942	" "	12	SESE	1853-02-24	FD	SESE	
3060	NUTT, James M	32	W½NE	1853-03-02	FD	W2NE	
3133	OKEAN, Mortimer	27	N½SW	1853-04-23	FD	N2SW	
3134	" "	27	W½NW	1853-04-23	FD	W2NW	
3136	OKEEN, Mortimore	33	NWSE	1853-11-13	FD	NWSE	R:JASPER
3135	" "	25	NESE	1853-11-13	FD	NESE	R:JASPER
3090	PARKER, John	31	W½NW	1839-05-23	FD	W2NW	R:CLAY
2963	POWELL, John	26	W½SE	1853-03-21	FD	W2SE	R:JASPER G:23
3121	POWELL, Joseph	4	L3 (W½)	1853-03-01	FD	W2LOT3NW	R:JASPER
3120	" "	3	N½SW	1853-03-01	FD	N2SW	
2956	PRENTISS, Edward	19	SENE	1855-01-27	FD	SENE	
2955	" "	19	N½SE	1855-01-27	FD	N2SE	

ID	Individual in Patent	Sec.	Sec. Part	Purchase Date	Sale Type	IL Aliquot Part	For More Info . . .
3021	PRICE, Hiram	34	SWNW	1853-10-10	FD	SWNW	R:JASPER
2893	PRUET, Adinston	34	SW	1853-10-26	FD	SW	
3191	RAMSEY, Thomas	17	NE	1853-02-26	FD	NE	
3223	REED, William	35	N½NE	1853-04-04	FD	N2NE	
3222	" "	35	E½SW	1853-04-04	FD	E2SW	
3224	" "	35	N½NW	1853-04-04	FD	N2NW	
3225	" "	35	S½NW	1853-04-04	FD	S2NW	
2945	RICHARDS, David	11	NWNE	1853-01-06	FD	NWNE	
2944	" "	11	NENW	1853-01-06	FD	NENW	
2946	" "	36	NESE	1853-08-25	FD	NESE	R:JASPER
2987	RIDENHOUR, George	21	SENE	1853-02-09	FD	SENE	
3172	RIDENHOUR, Sarah	21	SWNE	1853-02-09	FD	SWNE	S:F
3170	" "	12	NWNE	1853-02-09	FD	NWNE	S:F
3171	" "	21	NWSE	1853-02-09	FD	NWSE	S:F
3091	RIDENOUR, John	12	SENE	1853-02-10	FD	SENE	
3093	" "	21	NENE	1853-02-10	FD	NENE	
3092	" "	12	SWNE	1853-02-10	FD	SWNE	
3168	RIDENOUR, Samuel	21	SESE	1853-02-10	FD	SESE	
3167	" "	12	N½SE	1853-02-10	FD	N2SE	
3169	" "	21	SWSE	1853-02-10	FD	SWSE	
3173	RIDENOUR, Sarah	12	NENE	1852-12-13	FD	NENE	
2888	RIFE, Aaron	17	E½SE	1853-01-07	FD	E2SE	
2889	" "	17	W½SE	1853-01-17	FD	W2SE	
3008	RILEY, Hedgeman	1		1853-06-30	FD	SEST	
3009	RILEY, Hedgemon	11	NWSE	1853-02-08	FD	NWSE	
3181	" "	11	NWSE	1853-02-08	FD	NWSE	
3010	RILEY, Hedgman	11	SESW	1853-02-12	FD	SESW	
3011	" "	11	SWSE	1853-02-12	FD	SWSE	
3085	RINJWALD, John G	6	W½SE	1874-05-15	RR	W2SE	
3061	ROBERTS, James M	35	SEN½	1853-03-17	FD	S2NE	
3126	ROBERTS, Lavina M	25	SWSE	1853-03-17	FD	SWSE	
3193	ROBERTS, Warrington L	36	E½SW	1853-03-17	FD	E2SW	
2971	SAMPSON, Elijah	14	NENE	1853-02-16	FD	NENE	
2972	" "	23	NWNW	1853-02-16	FD	NWNW	
2988	SCHAMHART, George	8	SWNE	1872-02-29	RR	SWNE	
2909	SELBY, Benjamin F	13	W½NW	1853-02-21	FD	W2NW	
2908	" "	13	W½NE	1853-02-21	FD	W2NE	
2913	" "	15	SWSE	1853-02-21	FD	SWSE	
2910	" "	14	E½SW	1853-02-21	FD	E2SW	
2912	" "	15	E½SE	1853-02-21	FD	E2SE	
2911	" "	14	W½SW	1853-02-21	FD	W2SW	
2907	" "	13	E½NW	1853-02-21	FD	E2NW	
2906	" "	12	SWSE	1853-02-21	FD	SWSE	
2905	" "	12	SESW	1853-02-21	FD	SESW	
3071	SELBY, Jesse	22	SWNW	1853-02-04	FD	SWNW	
3070	" "	11	SWNW	1853-02-14	FD	SWNW	
2992	SHAMHART, George	8	SENW	1870-07-30	RR	SENW	
2991	" "	6	SESE	1871-09-30	RR	SESE	
2989	" "	18	SENE	1875-07-09	RR	SENE	
2990	" "	18	SESE	1877-09-21	RR	SESE	
3145	SHAMHART, Reason H	18	NESE	1872-06-29	RR	NESE	
2994	SHAMHEART, George	8	SWNW	1865-04-22	RR	SWNW	
2993	" "	8	NWNW	1865-04-22	RR	NWNW	
3064	SHEPHERD, James S	34	SWNE	1853-09-02	FD	SWNE	R:JASPER
3157	SIMPSON, Richard	22	W½SW	1853-04-23	FD	W2SW	
3151	SIMPSON, Richard B	3	L1	1852-09-13	FD	LOT1NE	
3152	" "	3	L2	1852-09-13	FD	LOT2NE	
3146	" "	10	NE	1852-09-13	FD	NE	
3150	" "	3	SWSE	1853-01-27	FD	SWSE	
3147	" "	11	NWNW	1853-01-27	FD	NWNW	
3149	" "	3	E½SE	1853-01-27	FD	E2SE	
3148	" "	23	SWNE	1853-01-27	FD	SWNE	
3153	" "	4	NESW	1853-03-01	FD	NESW	
3143	SNYDER, Philip	28	N½SE	1853-02-21	FD	N2SE	
3037	SONG, Jacob	21	NESE	1853-02-08	FD	NESE	
3140	SONG, Paul	2	E½SW	1853-02-08	FD	E2SW	
3065	STAPP, James T B	34	W½SE	1853-10-27	FD	W2SE	R:FAYETTE
3094	STILWELL, John	17	NW	1851-09-29	FD	NW	
3095	" "	22	NWNW	1852-09-09	FD	NWNW	
3097	STRATTON, John	5	L3 (W½)	1853-02-02	FD	W2LOT3NW	R:JASPER
3098	" "	7	NE	1853-02-18	FD	NE	
3096	" "	16	L12	1855-12-06	SC	LOT12NWSW	
3079	STRATTON, John F	19	E½NE	1853-08-01	FD	E2NE	R:JASPER

ID	Individual in Patent	Sec.	Sec. Part	Purchase Date	Sale Type	IL Aliquot Part	For More Info . . .
3080	STRATTON, John F (Cont'd)	19	NWNE	1853-10-21	FD	NWNE	R:CLAY
2895	SUTTON, Amariah	10	SESW	1852-10-16	FD	SESW	R:INDIANA
2896	" "	25	SWNW	1853-01-19	FD	SWNW	
2894	" "	10	NESW	1853-02-09	FD	NESW	
3015	SUTTON, Henry	29	NWNE	1853-02-09	FD	NWNE	
3226	SUTTON, William	35	NENW	1853-03-04	FD	NENW	
2919	SWAIN, Bennet	28	N½SW	1853-02-20	FD	N2SW	
2920	SWAIN, Bennett	33	E½NW	1853-10-11	FD	E2NW	R:JASPER
2937	SWANK, Daniel	23	NESE	1853-02-28	FD	NESE	
3227	TATE, William	25	SENW	1852-09-09	FD	SENW	R:JASPER
3229	" "	36	E½NE	1852-09-09	FD	E2NE	R:JASPER
3228	" "	25	SWNE	1852-09-09	FD	SWNE	R:JASPER
2939	THINOS, Daniel	24	SWSE	1853-03-11	FD	SWSE	
3130	THROCKMORTON, Lewis	23	S½SE	1853-01-08	FD	S2SE	
3131	" "	26	N½NE	1853-01-08	FD	N2NE	
2962	TICHENOR, Edward	16	L7	1856-01-29	SC	LOT7SWNE	
2961	" "	16	L6	1856-01-29	SC	LOT6SENW	
2960	" "	16	L3	1856-01-29	SC	LOT3NENW	
2958	" "	16	L11	1856-01-29	SC	LOT11NESW	
2957	" "	16	L-	1856-01-29	SC	LOT	
2959	" "	16	L14	1856-01-29	SC	LOT14SESW	
3100	TREXLER, John	28	NW	1853-05-10	FD	NW	
3099	" "	1	NE	1853-05-10	FD	NE	
3107	TREXLER, Johnson	10	W½NW	1853-01-07	FD	W2NW	
3108	" "	3	SWSW	1853-01-07	FD	SWSW	
3109	" "	9	NENE	1853-01-07	FD	NENE	
3113	TREXLER, Jonathan	14	SENE	1852-11-10	FD	SENE	R:OHIO
3112	" "	12	NESW	1852-11-10	FD	NESW	R:OHIO
3114	" "	14	SWNW	1853-01-18	FD	SWNW	
3117	" "	15	SWNE	1853-01-18	FD	SWNE	
3115	" "	15	NWSE	1853-01-18	FD	NWSE	
3116	" "	15	SENE	1853-01-18	FD	SENE	
3118	" "	4	SESE	1853-01-28	FD	SESE	
3192	TREXLER, Vinton	27	E½NW	1853-03-21	FD	E2NW	
2967	TUSING, Elias	22	NESW	1853-03-23	FD	NESW	
3125	VAUGHEN, Josiah	29	SEN½	1853-07-25	FD	S2NE	R:MARION
2948	VAUN, David	27	N½SE	1853-03-05	FD	N2SE	
2947	" "	26	N½SW	1853-03-05	FD	N2SW	
3106	VICKREY, John Washing	8	E½SW	1840-03-12	FD	E2SW	R:JASPER
2966	WARREN, Eli	9	SWSW	1853-03-02	FD	SWSW	
2965	" "	4	SWSE	1853-03-18	FD	SWSE	
3211	WEST, William J	19	L1(S½)	1847-06-04	FD	S2LOT1SW	R:COLES
2997	WHITE, George	25	SENE	1853-03-07	FD	SENE	
3230	WHITECHURCH, William	8	SWSE	1888-07-09	RR	SWSE	
3040	WHITLOCK, James A	22	SESW	1853-03-23	FD	SESW	
3127	WILLIAM, Levi Linn	29	SESW	1839-03-29	FD	SESW	R:CLAY
3129	WILLIAMS, Levi S	31	W½SE	1853-01-24	FD	W2SE	
3231	WILSON, William	35	W½SW	1853-01-24	FD	W2SW	
3038	WITSMAN, Jacob	32	E½NW	1839-05-27	FD	E2NW	R:CLAY
3039	" "	32	NWSW	1839-05-27	FD	NWSW	R:CLAY
3049	WORTHEY, James F	22	SE	1853-04-04	FD	SE	
3051	" "	23	SWSW	1853-04-04	FD	SWSW	
3052	" "	26	E½SE	1853-04-04	FD	E2SE	
3053	" "	26	SEN½	1853-04-04	FD	S2NE	
3050	" "	23	SWNW	1853-04-04	FD	SWNW	

Patent Map

T6-N R8-E
3rd PM Meridian

Map Group 11

Township Statistics

Parcels Mapped	:	377
Number of Patents	:	1
Number of Individuals	:	188
Patentees Identified	:	187
Number of Surnames	:	140
Multi-Patentee Parcels	:	2
Oldest Patent Date	:	2/22/1839
Most Recent Patent	:	1/12/1985
Block/Lot Parcels	:	54
Cities and Towns	:	1
Cemeteries	:	8

Lots-Sec. 6
L1 LUERSEN, A H August 1864
L2 LUERSEN, A H August 1864
L3 LUERSEN, A H August 1864

Lots-Sec. 5
L1   BALEY, Jacob   1853
L1(E½) BALEY, Jacob   1853
L1(W½) BRADBERRY, Elijah 1852
L2   BALEY, Jacob   1853
L2(E½) BALEY, Jacob   1853
L2(W½) BRADBERRY, Elisha 1852
L3   BALEY, Jacob   1852
L3(E½) BALEY, Jacob   1853
L3(W½) STRATTON, John 1853

Lots-Sec. 4
L1   MITCHELL, James J 1852
L1(E½) NEAL, Joseph R 1853
L1(W½) BRYAN, William B 1853
L1(W½) FOSTER, Thomas 1853
L2   MITCHELL, James J 1852
L2(E½) DOBBINS, Jacob H 1853
L2(W½) MITCHELL, Elihu 1853
L2(W½) MITCHELL, Elihu 1852
L3   MITCHELL, James J 1853
L3(E½) KRUZAN, Benjamin 1853
L3(W½) POWELL, Joseph 1853

6

RINJWALD
John G
1874

SHAMHART
George
1871

BRADBERRY
Elisha
1851

BALEY
Jacob
1853

5

BALEY
Jacob
1853

BERRY
Wyatt S
1853

HOLLINGSWORTH
John 1851

BRYAN
William
1853

SIMPSON
Richard B
1853

4

FOSTER
Thomas
1853

ADAMSON
Zedekiah
1852

CHOATE
Benjamin H
1852

WARREN
Eli
1853

TREXLER
Jonathan
1853

7

STRATTON
John
1853

BERRY
Wyatt
1853

MATHEWS
Levi
1853

CATHER
William R
1853

SHAMHEART
George
1865

SHAMHEART
George
1865

MATLOCK
James M
1868

SHAMHART
George
1870

VICKREY
John Washing
1840

ADAMSON
William
1840

8

MATLOCK
James M
1873

SCHAMHART
George
1872

HALL
Jasper
1885

WHITECHURCH
William
1888

FREEMAN
John W
1866

KESTER
Ellen N
1888

CHOATE
Benjamin H
1852

AKIN
Edmund
1853

AKIN
Edmund
1853

WARREN
Eli
1853

JONES
Charles Floyd
1853

JONES
Charles Floyd
1853

CASSITY
Ashley C
1853

EVANS
Brison J
1853

9

JONES
Charles Floyd
1853

JONES
Charles Floyd
1853

GARS
Peter
1852

TREXLER
Johnson
1853

CATHER
William R
1853

ADAMSON
James
1852

DUNCAN
Eli
1853

18

JOHNSON
David L
1877

JOHNSON
David L
1877

MONAHAN
William J
1881

SHAMHART
George
1875

SHAMHART
Reason H
1872

BUNTAIN
Smith B
1873

SHAMHART
George
1877

17

STILWELL
John
1851

BERRY
Wyatt S
1853

RAMSEY
Thomas
1853

RIFE
Aaron
1853

RIFE
Aaron
1853

Lots-Sec. 16
L- TICHENOR, Edward 1856
L1 LAMBERT, Eden 1855
L3 TICHENOR, Edward 1856
L4 BRIGES, Absalom 1856
L5 BRIGES, Absalom 1857
L6 TICHENOR, Edward 1856
L7 TICHENOR, Edward 1856
L8 BURCHAM, John 1855
L9 LAMBERT, Eaden 1856
L10 MICHELL, Hiram 1856
L11 TICHENOR, Edward 1856
L12 STRATTON, John 1855
L13 CATERS, Green 1855
L14 TICHENOR, Edward 1856
L15 MICHELL, Hiram 1985
L16 IRVIN, Andrew 1855

16

19

COWGER
Jonathan
1852

WEST, William J 1847

STRATTON
John F
1853

FREEMAN
John W
1853

PRENTISS
Edward
1855

Lots-Sec. 19
L1(S½)

CHESNUT
Hey Jane
1852

PRENTISS
Edward
1855

CATHER
Green B
1853

STRATTON
John F
1853

HUGGINS
Isaac
1853

KEPLEY
Henry B
1884

20

CATHER
Green B
1853

CATHER
Green B
1853

DOUTHIT
George
1839

CATHER
Green B
1853

CATHER
Green B
1853

COWGER
Jonathan
1853

DOUTHIT
George
1839

DOUTHIT
George
1839

BERRY
Wyatt
1853

CATHEN
Green B
1853

JAYCOX
Isaiah
1853

JAYCOX
Isaiah
1853

JAYCOX
Isaiah
1852

JAYCOX
Isaiah
1852

CATHER
Green B
1853

JAYCOX
Isaiah
1852

RIDENHOUR
Sarah
1853

NESSLEY
David
1853

FREEMAN
John W
1853

RIDENHOUR
Sarah
1853

21

RIDENOUR
John
1853

RIDENHOUR
George
1853

SONG
Jacob
1853

RIDENOUR
Samuel
1853

RIDENOUR
Samuel
1853

30

LEONARD
Edward F
1867

GAREE
William M
1870

GAREE
William M
1870

GAREE
William M
1870

FIELD
John
1842

EVANS
Mary E
1882

CHESMETT
Ibby
1853

FIELDS
John
1839

BONE
William E
1853

FIELD
Benton
1852

FREEMAN
John W
1853

FIELD
John
1842

AKIN
Daniel
1840

WILLIAM
Levi Linn
1839

29

SUTTON
Henry
1853

VAUGHEN
Josiah
1853

BONE
William E
1853

MCNUTT
James
1853

FIELD
Benton
1852

BIDEL
Joseph E
1853

ARCHER
Evander
1853

TREXLER
John
1853

SWAIN
Bennet
1853

HAGEMAN
John
1852

28

SNYDER
Philip
1853

31

PARKER
John
1839

WILLIAMS
Levi S
1853

MCQUEEN
John C
1852

BRUMFIELD
Richard T
1852

BRUMFIELD
Richard T
1852

CARRELL
Archibald
1840

CLARK
Frederick A
1853

WITSMAN
Jacob
1839

CHESNUT
Polly
1845

WITSMAN
Jacob
1839

DICKMAN
George H
1854

EVANS
Caleb
1853

32

NUTT
James M
1853

MCQUEEN
John C
1853

ADAMSON
Asa
1840

BERRY
Wyatt S
1853

HAGEMAN
John
1852

CLARK
Thomas
1853

HILL
Thomas J
1853

HAGEMAN
John
1852

SWAIN
Bennett
1853

CLARK
Thomas
1853

HILL
Thomas J
1853

CATHER
Nathan
1853

33

OKEEN
Mortimore
1853

DRAKE
Richard J
1853

JAYCON
William
1853

CLARK
Thomas
1853

GREGORY
Daniel
1853

DRAKE
Richard J
1853

Lots-Sec. 3
L1   SIMPSON, Richard B 1852
L1(W½) NEALE, Joseph R 1853
L2   SIMPSON, Richard B 1852
L2(E½) KRUZAN, Benjamin 1853
L2(W½) MITCHELL, James J 1853
L3(E½) KRUZAN, Benjamin 1853
L3(W½) BLAKE, Jefferson 1853

Lots-Sec. 2
L1(E½) ADAMSON, James   1853
L1(E½) ADAMSON, Zedekiah 1852
L1(W½) ADAMSON, James   1853
L1(W½) BERRY, Wyatt S   1852
L2   ADAMSON, Zedekiah 1852
L3   ADAMSON, Zedekiah 1852

Lots-Sec. 1
L1(E½) JONES, Charles Floyd 1852

Section 3

POWELL Joseph 1853

FOSTER Samuel 1851

SIMPSON Richard B 1853

TREXLER Johnson 1853

BERRY Wyatt S 1852

SIMPSON Richard B 1853

Section 2

BERRY Wyatt S 1852

SONG Paul 1853

ADAMSON James 1853

ADAMSON Zedekiah 1852

BERRY Wyatt S 1853

BURCHAM John 1851

DOVEL Andrew J 1852

TREXLER John 1853

Section 1

LAMBERT Watson 1852

LAMBERT Watson 1852

RILEY Hedgeman 1853

Section 10

TREXLER Johnson 1853

BERRY Wyatt S 1852

SIMPSON Richard B 1852

SUTTON Amariah 1853

MILLER Daniel Sen 1852

CORBIN Ephraim 1852

LAMBERT Watson 1853

SUTTON Amariah 1852

HUFF Gabril 1852

CORBIN Ephraim 1852

Section 11

SIMPSON Richard B 1853

RICHARDS David 1853

RICHARDS David 1853

BERRY Wyatt S 1852

SELBY Jesse 1853

BERRY Wyatt S 1853

FOSTER Thomas 1851

BURCHAM John 1851

FOSTER Thomas 1851

FOSTER Thomas 1851

RILEY Hedgemon 1853

BERRY Wyatt S 1852

FOSTER Thomas 1851

RILEY Hedgman 1853

Section 12

CORBIN Ephraim 1853

RIDENHOUR Sarah 1853

RIDENOUR Sarah 1852

RIDENOUR John 1853

RIDENOUR John 1853

TREXLER Jonathan 1852

RIDENOUR Samuel 1853

BERRY Wyatt S 1852

SELBY Benjamin F 1853

SELBY Benjamin F 1853

NESSLEY David 1853

Section 15

LAMBERT Eden 1853

DOGGETT William 1853

HUFF Gabril 1853

FOSTER Thomas 1853

FOSTER Thomas 1853

MILLIN Daniel Sen 1853

TREXLER Jonathan 1853

TREXLER Jonathan 1853

MILLIN Daniel Sen 1853

DOGGETT William 1853

TREXLER Jonathan 1853

SELBY Benjamin F

MILLER James 1853

SELBY Benjamin F 1853

Section 14

COCHRAN Josiah 1853

SELBY Benjamin F 1853

SELBY Benjamin F 1853

BERRY Wyatt S 1852

SAMPSON Elijah 1853

BERRY Wyatt S 1853

TREXLER Jonathan 1852

BERRY Wyatt S 1853

DALE James 1853

BERRY Wyatt S 1852

Section 13

SELBY Benjamin F 1853

SELBY Benjamin F 1853

SELBY Benjamin F 1853

SELBY Benjamin F 1853

HILL George B 1853

FOSTER Samuel 1851

BERRY Wyatt S 1852

DALE James 1853

JOHNSON James B 1853

HAYES William O 1853

HAYES William O 1853

Section 22

STILWELL John 1852

BERRY Wyatt 1853

BERRY Wyatt 1853

DOVEL Andrew 1853

SELBY Jesse 1853

BERRY [10] Myatt 1853

TUSING Elias 1853

WORTHEY James F 1853

SIMPSON Richard 1853

WHITLOCK James A 1853

Section 23

SAMPSON Elijah 1853

BERRY Wyatt S 1852

DOVEL Andrew 1853

WORTHEY James F 1853

DOVEL Andrew 1853

SIMPSON Richard B 1853

FOSTER Samuel 1851

HIGGINS William 1853

SWANK Daniel 1853

WORTHEY James F 1853

BAKER Jeptha 1853

THROCKMORTON Lewis 1853

Section 24

FOSTER Samuel 1851

FOSTER Samuel 1851

FOSTER Samuel 1851

FOSTER Samuel 1851

FOSTER Samuel 1851

HAYES William 1852

GAMBRIEL Woodford 1853

MANNING Hiram 1853

MANNING Hiram 1853

HINDS Daniel T 1852

BERRY Wyatt S 1853

JOHNSON James B 1853

THINOS Daniel 1853

ELDER William M 1853

Section 27

OKEAN Mortimer 1853

TREXLER Vinton 1853

MATTINGLEY John G 1853

HIGGINS William 1853

HIGGINS William 1853

OKEAN Mortimer 1853

VAUN David 1853

HAGIMAN Simon 1853

HAGIMAN George W 1853

HAGIMAN George W 1853

HAGIMAN Simon 1853

PRICE Hiram 1853

Section 34

SHEPHERD James S 1853

STAPP James T B 1853

PRUET Adinston 1853

BREWER Abraham 1853

Section 26

DENMAN Hampton 1853

CHEEK John 1853

CHEEK John 1853

CHEEK John 1853

BAKER Jeptha 1853

THROCKMORTON Lewis 1853

WORTHEY James F 1853

VAUN David 1853

CURTISS [23] Eli 1853

WORTHEY James F 1853

BERRY Wyatt S 1854

Section 35

REED William 1853

SUTTON William 1853

REED William 1853

REED William 1853

ROBERTS James M 1853

WILSON William 1853

REED William 1853

JONES Harter S 1853

BARTEE William 1853

BARTEE William J 1854

Section 25

FOSTER Samuel Jr 1853

GHURST Peter 1853

ELDER William M 1853

SUTTON Amariah 1853

TATE William 1852

TATE William 1852

WHITE George 1853

MORRIS Harmony 1853

MORRIS Oliver P 1853

OKEEN Mortimore 1853

ROBERTS Lavina M 1853

Section 36

JONES Charles Floyd 1853

JONES Charles Floyd 1853

TATE William 1852

HAWKS Henry 1853

ROBERTS Warrington L 1853

HAWKS Henry 1853

RICHARDS David 1853

Helpful Hints

1. This Map's INDEX can be found on the preceding pages.

2. Refer to Map "C" to see where this Township lies within Jasper County, Illinois.

3. Numbers within square brackets [ ] denote a multi-patentee land parcel (multi-owner). Refer to Appendix "C" for a full list of members in this group.

4. Areas that look to be crowded with Patentees usually indicate multiple sales of the same parcel (re-issues), cancellations or voided transactions (that we map, anyway) or overlapping parcels. We opt to show even these ambiguous parcels, which oftentimes lead to research avenues not yet taken.

Legend

———— Patent Boundary

━━━━ Section Boundary

No Patents Found (or Outside County)

1., 2., 3., ...   Lot Numbers (when beside a name)

[ ]   Group Number (see Appendix "C")

Scale: Section = 1 mile X 1 mile (generally, with some exceptions)

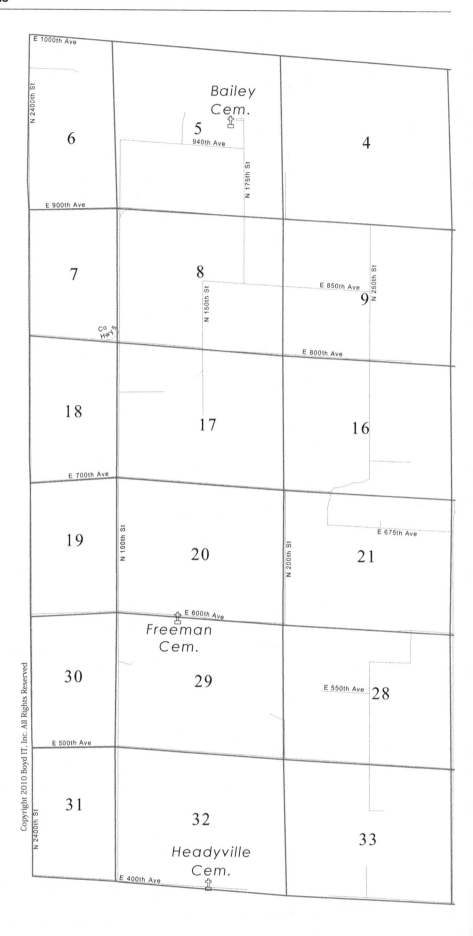

Road Map

T6-N R8-E
3rd PM Meridian

Map Group 11

Cities & Towns
Latona

Cemeteries
Bailey Cemetery
Foster Cemetery
Freeman Cemetery
Headyville Cemetery
Kedron Cemetery
Texler Cemetery
Worthey Cemetery
Worthy Cemetery

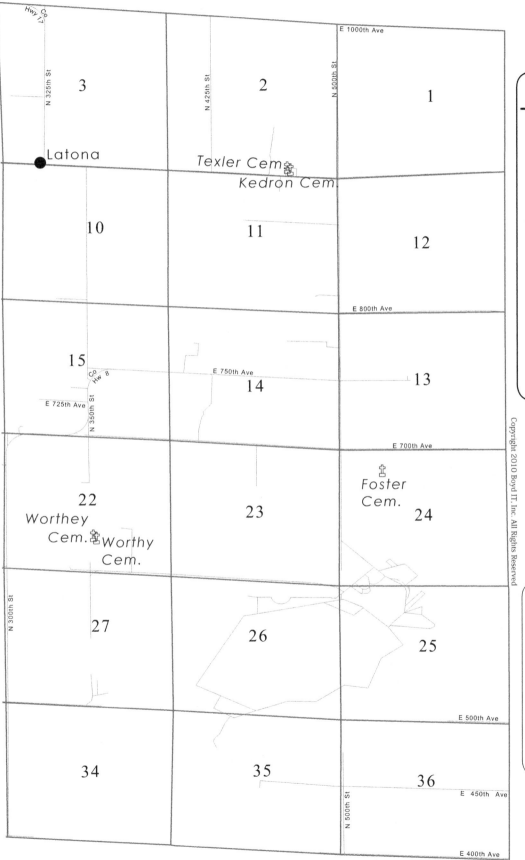

| 3 | 2 | 1 |

● Latona

Texler Cem. ✝
Kedron Cem.

| 10 | 11 | 12 |

E 1000th Ave

N 325th St
N 425th St
N 500th St

E 800th Ave

| 15 | 14 | 13 |

Co Hw 8
E 750th Ave
E 725th Ave
N 350th St

E 700th Ave

✝ Foster Cem.

| 22 | 23 | 24 |

Worthey Cem. ✝ Worthy Cem.

N 300th St

| 27 | 26 | 25 |

E 500th Ave

| 34 | 35 | 36 |

N 500th St
E 450th Ave
E 400th Ave

Helpful Hints

1. This road map has a number of uses, but primarily it is to help you: a) find the present location of land owned by your ancestors (at least the general area), b) find cemeteries and city-centers, and c) estimate the route/roads used by Census-takers & tax-assessors.

2. If you plan to travel to Jasper County to locate cemeteries or land parcels, please pick up a modern travel map for the area before you do. Mapping old land parcels on modern maps is not as exact a science as you might think. Just the slightest variations in public land survey coordinates, estimates of parcel boundaries, or road-map deviations can greatly alter a map's representation of how a road either does or doesn't cross a particular parcel of land.

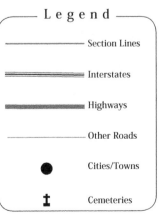

Legend

———————	Section Lines
══════════	Interstates
━━━━━━━━━	Highways
———————	Other Roads
●	Cities/Towns
✝	Cemeteries

Scale: Section = 1 mile X 1 mile
(generally, with some exceptions)

Historical Map

T6-N R8-E
3rd PM Meridian

Map Group 11

Cities & Towns
Latona

Cemeteries
Bailey Cemetery
Foster Cemetery
Freeman Cemetery
Headyville Cemetery
Kedron Cemetery
Texler Cemetery
Worthey Cemetery
Worthy Cemetery

Big Muddy Crk

6	5 Bailey Cem.	4
7	8	9
18	17	16
19	20	21
30	29	28
31	32	33

Crabapple Crk

Freeman Cem.

Headyville Cem.

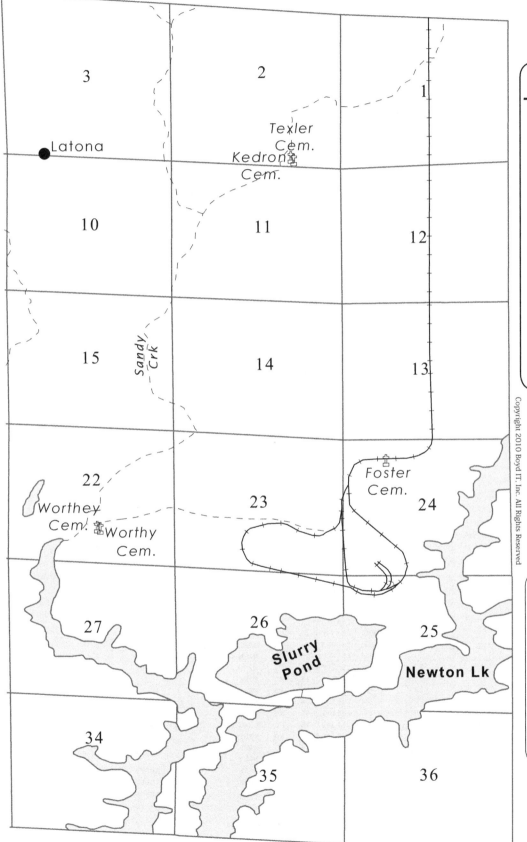

Helpful Hints

1. This Map takes a different look at the same Congressional Township displayed in the preceding two maps. It presents features that can help you better envision the historical development of the area: a) Water-bodies (lakes & ponds), b) Water-courses (rivers, streams, etc.), c) Railroads, d) City/ town center-points (where they were oftentimes located when first settled), and e) Cemeteries.

2. Using this "Historical" map in tandem with this Township's Patent Map and Road Map, may lead you to some interesting discoveries. You will often find roads, towns, cemeteries, and waterways are named after nearby landowners: sometimes those names will be the ones you are researching. See how many of these research gems you can find here in Jasper County.

Legend

——————	Section Lines
+–+–+–+–+	Railroads
▭	Large Rivers & Bodies of Water
- - - - - -	Streams/Creeks & Small Rivers
●	Cities/Towns
‡	Cemeteries

Scale: Section = 1 mile X 1 mile
(there are some exceptions)

Map Group 12: Index to Land Patents

Township 6-North Range 9-East (3rd PM)

After you locate an individual in this Index, take note of the Section and Section Part then proceed to the Land Patent map on the pages immediately following. You should have no difficulty locating the corresponding parcel of land.

The "For More Info" Column will lead you to more information about the underlying Patents. See the *Legend* at right, and the "How to Use this Book" chapter, for more information.

```
                        LEGEND
            "For More Info . . . " column
  G = Group  (Multi-Patentee Patent, see Appendix "C")
  R = Residence
  S = Social Status

  See Appendix A for list of abbreviations used by the
  Illinois State Archives in describing the place and
  nature of these land patents.

  Note: if the Abbreviations contain "L", "BL", "LOT",
  or "BLOCK", the exact whereabouts of the parcel within
  the section is not known.
```

ID	Individual in Patent	Sec.	Sec. Part	Purchase Date	Sale Type	IL Aliquot Part	For More Info . . .
3313	ADAMS, Clark	7	E½NE	1849-12-22	FD	E2NE	
3314	" "	7	NESE	1849-12-22	FD	NESE	
3315	" "	8	NWSW	1849-12-22	FD	NWSW	
3318	ADAMS, Daniel	19	NW	1850-07-08	FD	NW	R:OHIO
3370	ADAMS, Gilbert D	3	NENE	1848-05-23	FD	NENE	R:OHIO
3454	ADAMS, John Q	7	W½SE	1849-12-22	FD	W2SE	
3453	" "	7	SWNE	1849-12-22	FD	SWNE	
3452	" "	7	SESE	1849-12-22	FD	SESE	
3516	ADAMS, Philip	10	NW	1850-07-08	FD	NW	
3517	" "	8	SWNW	1850-07-08	FD	SWNW	R:OHIO
3560	ADAMS, Timothy R B	3	E½SE	1850-07-03	FD	E2SE	
3558	" "	19	NWNE	1850-07-03	FD	NWNE	R:JASPER
3559	" "	2	N½SW	1850-07-03	FD	N2SW	
3547	ALLEN, Thomas	35	NENW	1838-10-10	FD	NENW	R:COLES
3263	AMES, Aaron H	33	NE	1852-06-02	FD	NE	
3264	" "	33	NESE	1852-06-02	FD	NESE	
3265	" "	33	NWSE	1852-06-02	FD	NWSE	
3262	" "	28	SESE	1852-10-27	FD	SESE	
3322	ANSPACK, David	15	NE	1851-12-01	FD	NE	
3546	ANTON, Susannah	31	SWSE	1851-10-31	FD	SWSE	R:INDIANA S:F
3545	" "	31	S½SW	1851-10-31	FD	S2SW	R:INDIANA S:F
3392	ASHCRAFT, James	17	NENW	1849-06-11	FD	NENW	
3401	ASHCROFT, James	18	SEN½	1849-06-11	FD	S2NE	
3400	" "	18	S½SE	1849-06-11	FD	S2SE	
3393	" "	17	E½SW	1849-06-11	FD	E2SW	
3402	" "	20	NWNW	1849-06-11	FD	NWNW	
3394	" "	17	NWSE	1849-06-11	FD	NWSE	
3395	" "	17	NWSW	1849-06-11	FD	NWSW	
3398	" "	18	N½SE	1849-06-11	FD	N2SE	
3397	" "	17	W½NW	1849-06-11	FD	W2NW	
3396	" "	17	SWSW	1849-06-11	FD	SWSW	
3399	" "	18	NENE	1849-06-11	FD	NENE	
3273	BAKER, Absalom	9	SESE	1852-11-01	FD	SESE	R:OHIO
3430	BARNES, John	1	NESW	1836-11-25	FD	NESW	R:JASPER
3341	BARRETT, Elias A	27	W½NW	1852-08-11	FD	W2NW	
3342	" "	28	E½NE	1852-08-11	FD	E2NE	
3343	" "	28	W½NE	1852-08-11	FD	W2NE	
3528	BARRETT, Samuel	22	NW	1852-06-04	FD	NW	
3323	BASORE, David	14	NW	1851-12-01	FD	NW	
3267	BLACK, Abner	34	S½SW	1853-01-18	FD	S2SW	
3274	BOGARD, Alfred	19	SENE	1852-04-12	FD	SENE	R:JASPER
3404	BOGARD, James	30	SWSE	1852-06-16	FD	SWSE	
3405	" "	31	NWNE	1852-06-16	FD	NWNE	
3403	" "	30	SESW	1853-06-14	FD	SESW	R:JASPER
3572	BOOTH, Beeber	12	SWSE	1851-09-05	FD	SWSE	R:JASPER G:11
3286	" "	12	SESW	1851-09-05	FD	SESW	R:JASPER G:11

ID	Individual in Patent	Sec.	Sec. Part	Purchase Date	Sale Type	IL Aliquot Part	For More Info . . .
3287	BOOTH, Beeber (Cont'd)	12	SWSE	1851-09-05	FD	SWSE	R:JASPER G:11
3351	" "	12	SESW	1851-09-05	FD	SESW	R:JASPER G:11
3328	BOWMAN, David W	14	E½E½	1852-06-23	FD	E2E2	
3510	BOWMAN, Peter	25	S½NW	1852-06-14	FD	S2NW	
3509	" "	25	E½SW	1852-06-14	FD	E2SW	
3511	" "	25	W½NE	1852-06-14	FD	W2NE	
3512	" "	25	W½SE	1852-06-14	FD	W2SE	
3508	" "	13	W½NW	1852-06-14	FD	W2NW	
3330	BRIDGES, Edmund R	2	NWSE	1850-03-28	FD	NWSE	R:JASPER
3447	BRIDGES, John M	11	NWNE	1851-08-16	FD	NWNE	R:JASPER
3448	" "	2	SWSE	1851-08-16	FD	SWSE	R:JASPER
3280	BRISTOL, Andrew E	36	S½SW	1853-05-20	FD	S2SW	G:13
3279	" "	34	NESW	1853-09-21	FD	NESW	R:CRAWFORD
3280	BRISTOL, Orla H	36	S½SW	1853-05-20	FD	S2SW	G:13
3431	BROOKS, John	22	E½SW	1852-06-04	FD	E2SW	R:INDIANA
3432	" "	22	W½SE	1852-06-04	FD	W2SE	
3433	" "	3	W½NW	1852-08-12	FD	W2NW	
3456	BRYAN, John S	24	NENE	1852-07-17	FD	NENE	
3457	" "	24	SEN½	1852-07-17	FD	S2NE	
3455	" "	13	SESE	1852-07-17	FD	SESE	
3444	BRYANT, John J	32	N½SW	1851-10-31	FD	N2SW	
3446	" "	32	SWNW	1851-10-31	FD	SWNW	
3445	" "	32	NWSE	1851-10-31	FD	NWSE	
3382	BULEY, Isaac	9	W½SW	1838-02-01	FD	W2SW	R:JASPER
3312	BUSH, Christopher	9	NWNW	1851-09-03	FD	NWNW	R:JASPER
3365	BUSH, George F	8	SWSE	1851-09-03	FD	SWSE	R:JASPER
3366	" "	9	NENW	1852-09-01	FD	NENW	G:14
3434	BUSH, John	5	SESW	1851-09-03	FD	SESW	R:JASPER
3366	BUSH, Margaret	9	NENW	1852-09-01	FD	NENW	G:14
3529	BUSH, Samuel	5	SESE	1851-09-03	FD	SESE	R:JASPER
3605	BUSH, William S Y	4	SWSW	1852-06-24	FD	SWSW	
3606	" "	5	NWNE	1852-07-24	FD	NWNE	
3466	CARR, Jonathan	5	NENW	1851-09-15	FD	NENW	R:INDIANA
3353	CARTER, Francis	13	NE	1837-06-19	FD	NE	R:JASPER
3355	" "	13	W½SE	1837-06-19	FD	W2SE	R:JASPER
3351	" "	12	SESW	1837-06-19	FD	SESW	R:JASPER
3354	" "	13	NENW	1837-06-19	FD	NENW	R:JASPER
3286	" "	12	SESW	1837-06-19	FD	SESW	R:JASPER
3291	" "	12	E½SE	1839-07-10	FD	E2SE	R:JASPER G:17
3350	" "	12	NWSE	1839-07-10	FD	NWSE	R:JASPER
3352	" "	12	W½SW	1839-11-05	FD	W2SW	R:JASPER
3287	CARTER, William	12	SWSE	1837-11-13	FD	SWSE	R:JASPER
3572	" "	12	SWSE	1837-11-13	FD	SWSE	R:JASPER
3571	" "	12	NESW	1838-04-12	FD	NESW	R:JASPER
3573	" "	13	NESE	1838-04-26	FD	NESE	R:JASPER
3574	" "	13	SENW	1839-12-05	FD	SENW	R:JASPER
3575	" "	24	NENW	1848-02-25	FD	NENW	R:JASPER
3576	" "	5	NESW	1852-06-22	FD	NESW	
3601	CARTER, William S	11	SW	1852-05-18	FD	SW	
3438	CHEEK, John	26	SWNW	1852-10-23	FD	SWNW	
3436	" "	26	SW	1852-10-23	FD	SW	
3437	" "	26	SWNE	1852-10-23	FD	SWNE	
3435	" "	26	SENW	1852-10-23	FD	SENW	
3549	CHITTENDAN, Thomas	34	W½NE	1853-01-20	FD	W2NE	
3548	" "	34	E½NW	1853-01-20	FD	E2NW	
3335	CURTIS, Eli	35	N½NE	1853-03-12	FD	N2NE	R:JASPER G:22
3336	" "	36	NWNW	1853-03-12	FD	NWNW	R:JASPER G:22
3338	CURTIS, Eli W	16	L11	1853-11-26	SC	LOT11NESW	G:21
3337	" "	16	L10	1853-11-26	SC	LOT10NWSE	G:21
3340	" "	16	L16	1853-11-26	SC	LOT16SESE	G:21
3339	" "	16	L12	1853-11-26	SC	LOT12NWSW	G:21
3565	CURTIS, Van Raanselel	12	NENW	1851-09-18	FD	NENW	R:JASPER
3287	CURTIS, Van Ranseler	12	SWSE	1851-09-05	FD	SWSE	R:JASPER G:11
3351	" "	12	SESW	1851-09-05	FD	SESW	R:JASPER G:11
3572	" "	12	SWSE	1851-09-05	FD	SWSE	R:JASPER G:11
3286	" "	12	SESW	1851-09-05	FD	SESW	R:JASPER G:11
3586	DENMAN, William J	27	N½SE	1852-10-23	FD	N2SE	
3358	DENNIS, Francis	26	N½NE	1852-04-24	FD	N2NE	R:OHIO
3357	" "	25	NWNW	1852-04-24	FD	NWNW	R:OHIO
3356	" "	23	SESE	1852-04-24	FD	SESE	R:OHIO
3471	DENNIS, Joseph	25	NENW	1852-04-24	FD	NENW	R:OHIO
3467	" "	23	N½SE	1852-04-24	FD	N2SE	R:OHIO
3468	" "	23	SEN½	1852-04-24	FD	S2NE	R:OHIO

ID	Individual in Patent	Sec.	Sec. Part	Purchase Date	Sale Type	IL Aliquot Part	For More Info . . .
3469	DENNIS, Joseph (Cont'd)	24	E½SW	1852-04-24	FD	E2SW	R:OHIO
3470	" "	24	S½NW	1852-04-24	FD	S2NW	R:OHIO
3363	DUVAL, Gabriel	18	SWSW	1852-08-23	FD	SWSW	R:JASPER
3364	DUVALL, Gabriel	7	NW	1852-08-23	FD	NW	R:JASPER
3518	EATON, Richard	3	E½NW	1851-09-05	FD	E2NW	
3519	" "	3	W½NE	1851-09-05	FD	W2NE	
3592	ELDER, William M	33	S½SE	1852-05-27	FD	S2SE	
3593	" "	33	SWSW	1852-05-27	FD	SWSW	R:INDIANA
3591	" "	33	E½SW	1852-05-27	FD	E2SW	
3472	EVANS, Joseph	25	E½E½	1852-07-31	FD	E2E2	
3537	FASSETT, Sarah	35	W½NW	1853-01-20	FD	W2NW	S:F
3536	" "	34	E½NE	1853-01-20	FD	E2NE	S:F
3406	FINCH, James	5	SENW	1851-03-25	FD	SENW	R:JASPER
3381	FITCH, Horatio	3	W½SE	1851-09-05	FD	W2SE	
3380	" "	3	E½SW	1851-09-05	FD	E2SW	
3390	FITHIAN, Israel	1	SESE	1836-09-27	FD	SESE	R:OHIO
3281	FOLTZ, Andrew	15	NWSW	1852-06-03	FD	NWSW	
3282	" "	15	SWSW	1852-06-03	FD	SWSW	
3407	FOLTZ, James	11	SESE	1852-11-01	FD	SESE	
3500	FORCE, Moses C	19	SWNE	1852-09-25	FD	SWNE	
3440	FRAZIER, John	31	NENE	1847-11-22	FD	NENE	R:COLES
3538	" "	31	NENE	1847-11-22	FD	NENE	R:COLES
3348	FULLER, Frances	16	L14	1853-11-26	SC	LOT14SESW	S:F
3349	" "	16	L15	1853-11-26	SC	LOT15SWSE	S:F
3360	FULLER, Francis	28	NESE	1853-01-22	FD	NESE	
3361	" "	28	W½SE	1853-01-22	FD	W2SE	
3359	" "	27	NWSW	1853-01-22	FD	NWSW	
3362	" "	32	SWSE	1853-05-06	FD	SWSE	
3443	GARWOOD, John	12	E½NE	1833-06-06	FD	E2NE	R:OHIO
3577	GASS, William	21	NWNW	1844-11-16	FD	NWNW	R:EDGAR
3513	GHAIST, Peter	20	NESE	1852-09-16	FD	NESE	
3514	GHARST, Peter	20	SESE	1852-09-10	FD	SESE	
3515	" "	20	SWNE	1853-08-03	FD	SWNE	R:JASPER
3506	GOODWIN, Nelson	33	NW	1852-06-02	FD	NW	
3346	GORE, Esteline	6	SEN½	1853-05-23	FD	S2NE	S:F G:31
3346	GORE, James W	6	SEN½	1853-05-23	FD	S2NE	S:F G:31
3429	GORE, John A	6	W½SE	1853-05-14	FD	W2SE	G:32
3346	" "	6	SEN½	1853-05-23	FD	S2NE	S:F G:31
3429	GORE, Silas M	6	W½SE	1853-05-14	FD	W2SE	G:32
3485	GREGORY, Liles	18	NW	1851-10-07	FD	NW	S:F
3487	" "	7	SESW	1851-10-07	FD	SESW	S:F
3486	" "	18	NWNE	1851-10-07	FD	NWNE	S:F
3367	GROVE, George	32	S½SW	1849-06-08	FD	S2SW	
3440	GROVE, Silas	31	NENE	1851-12-27	FD	NENE	R:JASPER
3538	" "	31	NENE	1851-12-27	FD	NENE	R:JASPER
3582	HANDER, William	21	N½NE	1852-06-04	FD	N2NE	
3583	" "	21	SENE	1852-06-04	FD	SENE	
3584	" "	21	SWNE	1852-06-04	FD	SWNE	
3585	" "	8	SESE	1852-06-07	FD	SESE	
3368	HARRINGTON, George W	14	SW	1852-04-24	FD	SW	
3292	HARRIS, Benjamin	1	NWSW	1836-11-25	FD	NWSW	R:OHIO G:37
3294	" "	2	NESE	1836-11-25	FD	NESE	R:OHIO G:37
3293	" "	12	NWNW	1836-11-26	FD	NWNW	R:OHIO G:37
3289	" "	1	SWSE	1838-07-14	FD	SWSE	R:JASPER
3288	" "	1	SESW	1838-07-14	FD	SESW	R:JASPER
3291	" "	12	E½SE	1839-07-10	FD	E2SE	R:JASPER G:17
3290	" "	2	SESE	1840-03-04	FD	SESE	R:JASPER
3296	HARRIS, Benjamin J	1	NWSE	1837-04-29	FD	NWSE	R:JASPER
3297	" "	12	SWNW	1837-11-30	FD	SWNW	R:JASPER
3301	HARRIS, Bushrod W	2	E½NW	1837-06-12	FD	E2NW	R:VIRGINIA
3302	" "	2	W½NW	1839-11-21	FD	W2NW	R:JASPER
3344	HARRIS, Elizabeth	24	NWNE	1841-02-06	FD	NWNE	R:JASPER S:F
3488	HARRIS, Louiza	9	SESW	1853-02-22	FD	SESW	R:JASPER S:F
3524	HARRIS, Richard P	3	SENE	1852-01-17	FD	SENE	R:JASPER
3541	HARRIS, Stephen	8	NESE	1847-10-08	FD	NESE	R:JASPER
3542	" "	9	SWNW	1850-12-05	FD	SWNW	R:JASPER
3600	HAYS, William O	5	SWNE	1852-06-16	FD	SWNE	
3599	" "	20	E½NE	1852-08-03	FD	E2NE	
3295	HEADY, Benjamin	34	SE	1852-05-06	FD	SE	
3294	HERRON, John	2	NESE	1836-11-25	FD	NESE	R:OHIO G:37
3292	" "	1	NWSW	1836-11-25	FD	NWSW	R:OHIO G:37
3293	" "	12	NWNW	1836-11-26	FD	NWNW	R:OHIO G:37
3319	HINDS, Daniel T	29	E½SE	1852-11-08	FD	E2SE	

ID	Individual in Patent	Sec.	Sec. Part	Purchase Date	Sale Type	IL Aliquot Part	For More Info . . .
3320	HINDS, Daniel T (Cont'd)	29	SWNE	1852-11-08	FD	SWNE	
3321	" "	29	W½SE	1852-11-08	FD	W2SE	
3459	HONEY, John W	30	SWSW	1851-10-09	FD	SWSW	R:JASPER
3458	" "	29	SESW	1851-10-09	FD	SESW	R:JASPER
3283	HYATT, Andrew	31	S½NW	1851-11-11	FD	S2NW	R:JASPER
3522	JOHNSON, Richard	36	N½SW	1852-08-11	FD	N2SW	
3520	" "	35	N½SE	1852-08-11	FD	N2SE	
3521	" "	35	SEN½	1852-08-11	FD	S2NE	
3523	" "	36	S½NW	1852-08-11	FD	S2NW	
3587	JOHNSON, William K	25	W½SW	1853-05-04	FD	W2SW	
3588	" "	26	SE	1853-05-04	FD	SE	
3317	JONES, Constant	6	N½NE	1852-05-29	FD	N2NE	S:F
3483	JOURDEN, Lewis W	1	NW	1831-05-03	FD	NW	R:CRAWFORD
3484	" "	1	W½NE	1831-05-30	FD	W2NE	R:CRAWFORD
3298	LAMM, Benjamin	1	NESE	1832-10-06	FD	NESE	R:CRAWFORD
3492	LAWALL, Michael	4	E½NE	1852-09-04	FD	E2NE	R:INDIANA
3473	LAWRENCE, Joseph	36	NE	1852-10-23	FD	NE	
3589	LAWRENCE, William	36	SE	1852-10-15	FD	SE	
3412	LAWS, James	8	W½NE	1831-03-17	FD	W2NE	R:LAWRENCE
3411	" "	5	W½SE	1831-03-17	FD	W2SE	R:LAWRENCE
3415	LEMAY, James	21	W½SE	1852-06-04	FD	W2SE	
3416	" "	22	W½SW	1852-06-04	FD	W2SW	
3413	" "	21	E½SE	1852-06-04	FD	E2SE	
3414	" "	21	E½SW	1852-06-04	FD	E2SW	
3417	" "	4	W½SE	1852-08-12	FD	W2SE	
3551	LEMAY, Thomas	3	W½SW	1852-08-11	FD	W2SW	
3552	" "	4	E½SE	1852-08-11	FD	E2SE	
3553	LEMAY, Thomas M	16	L13	1853-11-26	SC	LOT13SWSW	
3278	LEVI, Amasa	11	S½NW	1852-05-13	FD	S2NW	R:OHIO
3543	LEWIS, Stephen	21	NWSW	1851-12-31	FD	NWSW	
3544	" "	21	SWNW	1851-12-31	FD	SWNW	
3557	LILLY, Thomas W	20	SWNW	1851-04-11	FD	SWNW	R:RICHLAND
3556	" "	20	NWNE	1851-04-11	FD	NWNE	R:RICHLAND
3555	" "	19	NENE	1851-04-11	FD	NENE	R:RICHLAND
3554	" "	17	SWSE	1851-04-11	FD	SWSE	R:RICHLAND
3590	LLOYD, William	32	SESE	1852-07-28	FD	SESE	
3375	MANNING, Hiram	20	S½SW	1852-10-29	FD	S2SW	
3550	MARTIN, Thomas J	16	L5	1853-11-26	SC	LOT5SWNW	
3441	MATTINGLY, John G	8	NENW	1851-10-25	FD	NENW	R:JASPER
3597	MATTINGLY, William	8	SENW	1851-11-26	FD	SENW	
3329	MAXWELL, Easther	11	SWSE	1852-02-18	FD	SWSE	S:F
3598	MCCLURE, William	8	E½NE	1836-10-31	FD	E2NE	R:INDIANA
3316	MCCOOMAS, Clinton B	26	SENE	1853-06-02	FD	SENE	
3568	MCCULLOUGH, Walter R	31	NWSE	1852-10-27	FD	NWSE	
3569	" "	34	W½NW	1852-10-27	FD	W2NW	
3594	MCCULLOUGH, William M	32	NE	1852-06-02	FD	NE	
3595	" "	32	NESE	1853-01-03	FD	NESE	
3596	" "	33	NWSW	1853-01-03	FD	NWSW	
3502	MCDONALD, Nancy	29	SENW	1852-02-16	FD	SENW	S:F
3501	" "	29	NESW	1852-02-16	FD	NESW	S:F
3373	MEEK, Hamilton	35	S½S½	1853-05-04	FD	S2S2	
3371	" "	35	E½NW	1853-05-04	FD	E2NW	
3372	" "	35	N½SW	1853-05-04	FD	N2SW	
3345	MILLER, Elizabeth	23	N½NW	1852-04-24	FD	N2NW	S:F
3581	MORRIS, William H	20	NWSW	1851-03-03	FD	NWSW	R:INDIANA
3580	" "	19	W½SE	1851-03-03	FD	W2SE	R:INDIANA
3578	" "	19	NESE	1851-03-03	FD	NESE	R:INDIANA
3579	" "	19	SW	1851-03-03	FD	SW	R:INDIANA
3299	MURPHEY, Benjamin	2	E½NE	1831-05-06	FD	E2NE	R:LAWRENCE
3300	" "	2	NWNE	1832-08-10	FD	NWNE	R:LAWRENCE
3507	NATION, Obediah	10	SE	1852-05-26	FD	SE	
3451	NIGHT, John	15	W½NW	1852-06-03	FD	W2NW	
3497	OKEAN, Mortimar	11	N½SE	1852-02-12	FD	N2SE	
3498	" "	11	SEN½	1852-02-12	FD	S2NE	
3499	OKEAN, Mortimor	2	SWNE	1841-01-23	FD	SWNE	R:JASPER
3489	OLDAKER, Martin G	8	SWSW	1840-05-15	FD	SWSW	R:JASPER
3308	PEARPOINT, Charles	17	NESE	1851-04-04	FD	NESE	R:JASPER
3309	" "	9	SENW	1851-10-31	FD	SENW	R:JASPER
3270	PETERSON, Abner M	9	NESW	1852-06-14	FD	NESW	
3271	" "	9	W½SE	1852-06-14	FD	W2SE	
3269	" "	9	NESE	1852-06-14	FD	NESE	
3268	" "	17	SENW	1852-06-14	FD	SENW	
3419	PETERSON, James	10	NE	1852-04-29	FD	NE	

ID	Individual in Patent	Sec.	Sec. Part	Purchase Date	Sale Type	IL Aliquot Part	For More Info . . .
3422	PETERSON, James (Cont'd)	17	NE	1852-04-29	FD	NE	
3424	" "	9	NE	1852-06-08	FD	NE	
3421	" "	14	W½SE	1852-06-17	FD	W2SE	
3420	" "	14	W½NE	1852-06-17	FD	W2NE	
3423	" "	23	N½NE	1852-12-15	FD	N2NE	
3335	POWELL, John	35	N½NE	1853-03-12	FD	N2NE	R:JASPER G:22
3336	" "	36	NWNW	1853-03-12	FD	NWNW	R:JASPER G:22
3339	" "	16	L12	1853-11-26	SC	LOT12NWSW	G:21
3337	" "	16	L10	1853-11-26	SC	LOT10NWSE	G:21
3338	" "	16	L11	1853-11-26	SC	LOT11NESW	G:21
3340	" "	16	L16	1853-11-26	SC	LOT16SESE	G:21
3272	PRINCE, Abraham	8	NWSE	1852-06-03	FD	NWSE	
3442	RAWLINGS, John G	21	E½NW	1852-09-01	FD	E2NW	
3460	RAWLINGS, John W	18	NESW	1852-09-01	FD	NESW	R:JASPER
3504	RAWLINGS, Nathan	17	SESE	1851-11-06	FD	SESE	R:JASPER
3425	REEVES, James	28	E½SW	1852-11-22	FD	E2SW	
3284	RICHARDS, Anna	32	NWNW	1851-10-07	FD	NWNW	R:JASPER S:F
3285	" "	32	SENW	1851-10-07	FD	SENW	R:JASPER S:F
3326	RICHARDS, David	31	SENE	1851-12-27	FD	SENE	R:JASPER
3327	" "	31	SWNE	1852-07-05	FD	SWNE	
3324	" "	19	SESE	1853-06-20	FD	SESE	R:JASPER
3325	" "	20	NENW	1853-06-20	FD	NENW	R:JASPER
3347	ROBBINS, Ezra	11	NENE	1850-10-12	FD	NENE	R:JASPER
3310	ROBERTS, Charles	32	NENW	1853-06-09	FD	NENW	
3426	ROSS, James	1	E½NE	1836-08-29	FD	E2NE	R:OHIO
3439	SCOTT, John E	15	W½SE	1852-05-31	FD	W2SE	
3530	SCOTT, Samuel	15	E½SE	1852-05-31	FD	E2SE	
3531	" "	15	E½SW	1852-06-14	FD	E2SW	
3266	SHAW, Aaron	36	NENW	1853-05-03	FD	NENW	
3391	SHY, Jacob C	1	SWSW	1841-01-29	FD	SWSW	R:JASPER
3494	SKELTON, Morgan	28	NWNW	1852-11-11	FD	NWNW	
3495	" "	28	SENW	1852-11-11	FD	SENW	
3496	" "	28	SWNW	1852-11-11	FD	SWNW	
3493	" "	28	NENW	1852-11-22	FD	NENW	
3526	SMITH, Robert B	8	E½SW	1840-05-15	FD	E2SW	R:JASPER
3527	" "	8	NWNW	1850-06-10	FD	NWNW	R:JASPER
3525	" "	5	SWSW	1851-10-31	FD	SWSW	R:JASPER
3505	SPEARS, Nathan	5	NWNW	1851-07-01	FD	NWNW	R:INDIANA
3503	SPEARS, Nathan H	18	NWSW	1852-02-19	FD	NWSW	R:JASPER
3607	STARLING, William	24	W½SW	1837-11-13	FD	W2SW	R:JASPER
3408	STEEL, James H	10	SW	1852-04-30	FD	SW	
3564	STEVENS, Uriah	12	NWNE	1849-06-08	FD	NWNE	R:JASPER
3562	STEVENS, Uriah G	2	SWSW	1850-07-03	FD	SWSW	R:JASPER
3561	" "	11	NWNW	1851-09-05	FD	NWNW	R:JASPER
3563	" "	22	E½SE	1851-12-30	FD	E2SE	R:JASPER
3567	STEVENS, W Gilbert	2	SESW	1849-11-02	FD	SESW	R:JASPER
3566	" "	11	NENW	1849-11-02	FD	NENW	R:JASPER
3374	STIVERS, Harrison	31	E½SE	1852-07-07	FD	E2SE	
3409	SUDDUTH, James H	23	N½SW	1852-05-31	FD	N2SW	
3410	" "	23	S½NW	1852-05-31	FD	S2NW	
3277	SUTTON, Amariah	29	NENW	1852-11-05	FD	NENW	R:JASPER
3275	SUTTON, Amariah Jr	30	N½SW	1851-03-03	FD	N2SW	R:INDIANA
3276	" "	30	NWSE	1851-03-03	FD	NWSE	R:INDIANA
3306	SUTTON, Chapman	30	N½	1851-03-03	FD	N2	R:INDIANA G:57
3304	" "	29	NWSW	1851-03-03	FD	NWSW	R:INDIANA G:57
3307	" "	30	NESE	1851-03-03	FD	NESE	R:INDIANA G:57
3305	" "	29	W½NW	1851-03-03	FD	W2NW	R:INDIANA G:57
3303	" "	29	N½NE	1852-11-05	FD	N2NE	R:INDIANA
3304	SUTTON, Hester E	29	NWSW	1851-03-03	FD	NWSW	R:INDIANA G:57
3307	" "	30	NESE	1851-03-03	FD	NESE	R:INDIANA G:57
3306	" "	30	N½	1851-03-03	FD	N2	R:INDIANA G:57
3305	" "	29	W½NW	1851-03-03	FD	W2NW	R:INDIANA G:57
3304	SUTTON, Isaiah	29	NWSW	1851-03-03	FD	NWSW	R:INDIANA G:57
3305	" "	29	W½NW	1851-03-03	FD	W2NW	R:INDIANA G:57
3306	" "	30	N½	1851-03-03	FD	N2	R:INDIANA G:57
3307	" "	30	NESE	1851-03-03	FD	NESE	R:INDIANA G:57
3306	SUTTON, Nancy	30	N½	1851-03-03	FD	N2	R:INDIANA G:57
3304	" "	29	NWSW	1851-03-03	FD	NWSW	R:INDIANA G:57
3307	" "	30	NESE	1851-03-03	FD	NESE	R:INDIANA G:57
3305	" "	29	W½NW	1851-03-03	FD	W2NW	R:INDIANA G:57
3306	SUTTON, Susan E	30	N½	1851-03-03	FD	N2	R:INDIANA G:57
3305	" "	29	W½NW	1851-03-03	FD	W2NW	R:INDIANA G:57
3304	" "	29	NWSW	1851-03-03	FD	NWSW	R:INDIANA G:57

ID	Individual in Patent	Sec.	Sec. Part	Purchase Date	Sale Type	IL Aliquot Part	For More Info . . .
3307	SUTTON, Susan E (Cont'd)	30	NESE	1851-03-03	FD	NESE	R:INDIANA G:57
3608	SUTTON, William	18	SESW	1851-12-31	FD	SESW	R:JASPER
3311	SWINEHEART, Christina	15	E½NW	1852-01-17	FD	E2NW	S:A
3540	TATE, Stephen B	29	SENE	1853-07-21	FD	SENE	R:JASPER
3539	"	21	SWSW	1853-07-21	FD	SWSW	R:JASPER
3609	TATE, William	31	N½NW	1852-09-13	FD	N2NW	R:INDIANA
3610	THOM, William W	34	NWSW	1852-10-27	FD	NWSW	
3333	TICHNER, Edward J	16	L8	1853-11-26	SC	LOT8SENE	
3334	" "	16	L9	1853-11-26	SC	LOT9NESE	
3332	" "	16	L7	1853-11-26	SC	LOT7SWNE	
3331	" "	16	L6	1853-11-26	SC	LOT6SENW	
3449	TINDALL, John M	7	NWNE	1853-05-14	FD	NWNE	R:INDIANA
3450	" "	7	W½NE	1853-05-14	FD	W2NE	R:INDIANA
3462	TINDALL, John W	6	SW	1853-05-14	FD	SW	R:INDIANA
3461	" "	6	NW	1853-05-14	FD	NW	R:INDIANA
3491	TIPPIT, Mathew L	30	SESE	1851-12-19	FD	SESE	R:RICHLAND
3490	" "	29	SWSW	1851-12-19	FD	SWSW	R:RICHLAND
3604	TOWNSAND, William S	5	NESE	1852-06-15	FD	NESE	
3603	" "	5	E½NE	1852-06-15	FD	E2NE	
3602	" "	4	NW	1852-06-15	FD	NW	
3534	VANCE, Sarah A	13	SWSW	1852-06-15	FD	SWSW	S:F
3535	" "	24	NWNW	1852-06-15	FD	NWNW	S:F
3532	" "	13	E½SW	1852-06-15	FD	E2SW	S:F
3533	" "	13	NWSW	1852-08-23	FD	NWSW	R:CRAWFORD S:F
3376	WADE, Hiram	16	L1	1853-11-26	SC	LOT1NENE	
3377	" "	16	L2	1853-11-26	SC	LOT2NWNE	
3378	" "	16	L3	1853-11-26	SC	LOT3NENW	
3379	" "	16	L4	1853-11-26	SC	LOT4NWNW	
3387	WALKER, Isaac H	5	SWNW	1853-03-01	FD	SWNW	R:JASPER
3383	" "	4	N½SW	1853-03-01	FD	N2SW	
3385	" "	4	W½NE	1853-03-01	FD	W2NE	
3386	" "	5	NWSW	1853-03-01	FD	NWSW	R:JASPER
3384	" "	4	SESW	1853-05-10	FD	SESW	R:JASPER
3388	" "	6	NESE	1853-05-10	FD	NESE	R:JASPER
3389	" "	6	SESE	1853-08-17	FD	SESE	R:JASPER
3418	WHEELER, James P	33	SESE	1853-02-26	FD	SESE	R:JASPER
3369	WHITE, George	28	W½SW	1852-11-15	FD	W2SW	
3464	WILLIAMS, John W	20	SENW	1852-10-29	FD	SENW	
3463	" "	20	NESW	1852-10-29	FD	NESW	
3570	WILSON, William C	31	N½SW	1853-09-16	FD	N2SW	R:CRAWFORD
3475	WINDSOR, Joseph M	27	SWSE	1853-09-10	FD	SWSE	
3474	" "	27	SESE	1853-09-10	FD	SESE	
3465	WOOD, John	20	W½SE	1852-09-10	FD	W2SE	
3479	WOODS, Joseph	27	E½NW	1852-06-04	FD	E2NW	R:INDIANA
3476	" "	23	S½SW	1852-06-04	FD	S2SW	
3481	" "	27	NE	1852-06-04	FD	NE	
3478	" "	26	N½NW	1852-06-04	FD	N2NW	
3477	" "	23	SWSE	1852-10-14	FD	SWSE	
3480	" "	27	E½SW	1852-12-20	FD	E2SW	
3482	" "	27	SWSW	1853-05-07	FD	SWSW	
3428	ZIEGLER, Joel	24	W½SE	1852-06-14	FD	W2SE	
3427	" "	24	E½SE	1852-06-14	FD	E2SE	

Patent Map

T6-N R9-E
3rd PM Meridian

Map Group 12

Township Statistics

Parcels Mapped	:	349
Number of Patents	:	1
Number of Individuals	:	184
Patentees Identified	:	178
Number of Surnames	:	127
Multi-Patentee Parcels	:	20
Oldest Patent Date	:	3/17/1831
Most Recent Patent	:	11/26/1853
Block/Lot Parcels	:	16
Cities and Towns	:	2
Cemeteries	:	6

Section 6

- TINDALL John W 1853
- JONES Constant 1852
- GORE [31] Esteline 1853
- SPEARS Nathan 1851
- CARR Jonathan 1851
- BUSH William S Y 1852
- WALKER Isaac H 1853
- TINDALL John W 1853
- GORE [32] John A 1853
- WALKER Isaac H 1853
- WALKER Isaac H 1853
- SMITH Robert B 1851

Section 5

- TOWNSAND William S 1852
- WALKER Isaac H 1853
- FINCH James 1851
- HAYS William O 1852
- CARTER William 1852
- LAWS James 1831
- BUSH John 1851
- TOWNSAND William S 1852
- BUSH Samuel 1851

Section 4

- WALKER Isaac H 1853
- LAWALL Michael 1852
- TOWNSAND William S 1852
- WALKER Isaac H 1853
- LEMAY James 1852
- BUSH William S Y 1852
- WALKER Isaac H 1853
- LEMAY Thomas 1852

Section 7

- DUVALL Gabriel 1852
- TINDALL John M 1853
- TINDALL John M 1853
- ADAMS John Q 1849
- ADAMS Clark 1849
- ADAMS John Q 1849
- ADAMS Clark 1849
- GREGORY Liles 1851
- ADAMS John Q 1849
- ADAMS Clark 1849

Section 8

- SMITH Robert B 1850
- MATTINGLY John G 1851
- ADAMS Philip 1850
- MATTINGLY William 1851
- ADAMS Clark 1849
- SMITH Robert B 1840
- OLDAKER Martin G 1840
- LAWS James 1831
- MCCLURE William 1836
- PRINCE Abraham 1852
- HARRIS Stephen 1847
- BUSH George F 1851

Section 9

- BUSH Christopher 1851
- BUSH [14] George F 1852
- HARRIS Stephen 1850
- PEARPOINT Charles 1851
- PETERSON James 1852
- BULEY Isaac 1838
- PETERSON Abner M 1852
- PETERSON Abner M 1852
- PETERSON Abner M 1852
- HARRIS Louiza 1853
- HANDER William 1852
- BAKER Absalom 1852

Section 18

- GREGORY Liles 1851
- GREGORY Liles 1851
- ASHCROFT James 1849
- ASHCROFT James 1849
- ASHCROFT James 1849
- SPEARS Nathan H 1852
- RAWLINGS John W 1852
- ASHCROFT James 1849
- DUVAL Gabriel 1852
- SUTTON William 1851
- ASHCROFT James 1849

Section 17

- ASHCRAFT James 1849
- PETERSON Abner M 1852
- PETERSON James 1852
- ASHCROFT James 1849
- ASHCROFT James 1849
- ASHCROFT James 1849
- LILLY Thomas W 1851
- ASHCROFT James 1849
- PEARPOINT Charles 1851
- RAWLINGS Nathan 1851

Section 16

Lots-Sec. 16
- L1 WADE, Hiram 1853
- L2 WADE, Hiram 1853
- L3 WADE, Hiram 1853
- L4 WADE, Hiram 1853
- L5 MARTIN, Thomas J 1853
- L6 TICHNER, Edward J 1853
- L7 TICHNER, Edward J 1853
- L8 TICHNER, Edward J 1853
- L9 TICHNER, Edward J 1853
- L10 CURTIS, Eli W [21]1853
- L11 CURTIS, Eli W [21]1853
- L12 CURTIS, Eli W [21]1853
- L13 LEMAY, Thomas M 1853
- L14 FULLER, Frances 1853
- L15 FULLER, Frances 1853
- L16 CURTIS, Eli W [21]1853

Section 19

- ADAMS Daniel 1850
- ADAMS Timothy R B 1850
- LILLY Thomas W 1851
- FORCE Moses C 1852
- BOGARD Alfred 1852
- MORRIS William H 1851
- MORRIS William H 1851
- MORRIS William H 1851
- RICHARDS David 1853

Section 20

- ASHCROFT James 1849
- RICHARDS David 1853
- LILLY Thomas W 1851
- LILLY Thomas W 1851
- WILLIAMS John W 1852
- GHARST Peter 1853
- WILLIAMS John W 1852
- MANNING Hiram 1852
- WOOD John 1852

Section 21

- LILLY Thomas W 1851
- HAYS William O 1852
- GASS William 1844
- RAWLINGS John G 1852
- HANDER William 1852
- LEWIS Stephen 1851
- HANDER William 1852
- HANDER William 1852
- GHAIST Peter 1852
- LEWIS Stephen 1851
- TATE Stephen B 1853
- GHARST Peter 1852
- LEMAY James 1852
- LEMAY James 1852
- LEMAY James 1852

Section 30

- SUTTON [57] Chapman 1851
- SUTTON Amariah Jr 1851
- SUTTON Amariah Jr 1851
- SUTTON [57] Chapman 1851
- HONEY John W 1851
- BOGARD James 1853
- BOGARD James 1852
- TIPPIT Mathew L 1851

Section 29

- SUTTON Amariah 1852
- SUTTON Chapman 1852
- SUTTON [57] Chapman 1851
- MCDONALD Nancy 1852
- HINDS Daniel T 1852
- SUTTON [57] Chapman 1851
- MCDONALD Nancy 1852
- TIPPIT Mathew L 1851
- HONEY John W 1851
- HINDS Daniel T 1852
- HINDS Daniel T 1852

Section 28

- SKELTON Morgan 1852
- SKELTON Morgan 1852
- BARRETT Elias A 1852
- TATE Stephen B 1853
- SKELTON Morgan 1852
- SKELTON Morgan 1852
- BARRETT Elias A 1852
- WHITE George 1852
- REEVES James 1852
- FULLER Francis 1853
- FULLER Francis 1853
- AMES Aaron H 1852

Section 31

- TATE William 1852
- BOGARD James 1852
- FRAZIER John 1847
- GROVE Silas 1851
- RICHARDS Anna 1851
- HYATT Andrew 1851
- RICHARDS David 1852
- RICHARDS David 1851
- BRYANT John J 1851
- WILSON William C 1853
- MCCULLOUGH Walter R 1852
- STIVERS Harrison 1852
- ANTON Susannah 1851
- ANTON Susannah 1851
- GROVE George 1849

Section 32

- RICHARDS Anna 1851
- ROBERTS Charles 1853
- RICHARDS Anna 1851
- MCCULLOUGH William M 1852
- BRYANT John J 1851
- BRYANT John J 1851
- MCCULLOUGH William M 1853
- FULLER Francis 1853
- LLOYD William 1852

Section 33

- GOODWIN Nelson 1852
- AMES Aaron H 1852
- MCCULLOUGH William M 1853
- ELDER William M 1852
- ELDER William M 1853
- AMES Aaron H 1852
- AMES Aaron H 1852
- AMES Aaron H 1852
- ELDER William M 1852
- WHEELER James P 1853

Section 3
- BROOKS John 1852
- EATON Richard 1851
- EATON Richard 1851
- ADAMS Gilbert D 1848
- HARRIS Richard P 1852
- LEMAY Thomas 1852
- FITCH Horatio 1851
- FITCH Horatio 1851
- ADAMS Timothy R B 1850

Section 2
- HARRIS Bushrod W 1839
- HARRIS Bushrod W 1837
- MURPHEY Benjamin 1832
- OKEAN Mortimor 1841
- ADAMS Timothy R B 1850
- BRIDGES Edmund R 1850
- STEVENS Uriah G 1850
- STEVENS W Gilbert 1849
- BRIDGES John M 1851
- HARRIS Benjamin 1840

Section 1
- MURPHEY Benjamin 1831
- JOURDEN Lewis W 1831
- JOURDEN Lewis W 1831
- ROSS James 1836
- HARRIS [37] Benjamin 1836
- HARRIS [37] Benjamin 1836
- BARNES John 1836
- HARRIS Benjamin J 1837
- LAMM Benjamin 1832
- SHY Jacob C 1841
- HARRIS Benjamin 1838
- HARRIS Benjamin 1838
- FITHIAN Israel 1836

Section 10
- ADAMS Philip 1850
- PETERSON James 1852
- STEEL James H 1852
- NATION Obediah 1852

Section 11
- STEVENS Uriah G 1851
- STEVENS W Gilbert 1849
- BRIDGES John M 1851
- ROBBINS Ezra 1850
- LEVI Amasa 1852
- OKEAN Mortimar 1852
- CARTER William S 1852
- OKEAN Mortimar 1852
- MAXWELL Easther 1852
- FOLTZ James 1852

Section 12
- HARRIS [37] Benjamin 1836
- STEVENS Uriah 1849
- GARWOOD John 1833
- HARRIS Benjamin J 1837
- CURTIS Van Raanselel 1851
- CARTER Francis 1839
- CARTER William 1838
- CARTER Francis 1839
- HARRIS [17] Benjamin 1839
- CARTER Francis 1837
- BOOTH [11] Beeber 1851
- BOOTH [11] Beeber 1851
- CARTER William 1837

Section 15
- SWINEHEART Christina 1852
- ANSPACK David 1851
- NIGHT John 1852
- FOLTZ Andrew 1852
- SCOTT Samuel 1852
- SCOTT Samuel 1852
- SCOTT John E 1852
- FOLTZ Andrew 1852

Section 14
- BASORE David 1851
- PETERSON James 1852
- CARTER William S 1852
- PETERSON James 1852
- HARRINGTON George W 1852
- BOWMAN David W 1852

Section 13
- BOWMAN Peter 1852
- CARTER Francis 1837
- CARTER William 1839
- CARTER Francis 1837
- VANCE Sarah A 1852
- VANCE Sarah A 1852
- VANCE Sarah A 1852
- CARTER Francis 1837
- CARTER William 1838
- BRYAN John S 1852

Section 22
- BARRETT Samuel 1852
- LEMAY James 1852
- BROOKS John 1852
- BROOKS John 1852
- STEVENS Uriah G 1851

Section 23
- MILLER Elizabeth 1852
- PETERSON James 1852
- SUDDUTH James H 1852
- DENNIS Joseph 1852
- SUDDUTH James H 1852
- DENNIS Joseph 1852
- WOODS Joseph 1852
- WOODS Joseph 1852
- DENNIS Francis 1852

Section 24
- VANCE Sarah A 1852
- CARTER William 1848
- HARRIS Elizabeth 1841
- BRYAN John S 1852
- DENNIS Joseph 1852
- BRYAN John S 1852
- STARLING William 1837
- DENNIS Joseph 1852
- ZIEGLER Joel 1852
- ZIEGLER Joel 1852

Section 27
- WOODS Joseph 1852
- WOODS Joseph 1852
- BARRETT Elias A 1852
- FULLER Francis 1853
- WOODS Joseph 1852
- DENMAN William J 1853
- WOODS Joseph 1853
- WINDSOR Joseph M 1853
- WINDSOR Joseph M 1853

Section 26
- WOODS Joseph 1852
- DENNIS Francis 1852
- CHEEK John 1852
- CHEEK John 1852
- CHEEK John 1852
- MCCOOMAS Clinton B 1853
- CHEEK John 1852
- JOHNSON William K 1853

Section 25
- DENNIS Francis 1852
- DENNIS Joseph 1852
- BOWMAN Peter 1852
- BOWMAN Peter 1852
- JOHNSON William K 1853
- BOWMAN Peter 1852
- BOWMAN Peter 1852
- EVANS Joseph 1852

Section 34
- MCCULLOUGH Walter R 1852
- CHITTENDAN Thomas 1853
- CHITTENDAN Thomas 1853
- FASSETT Sarah 1853
- FASSETT Sarah 1853
- THOM William W 1852
- BRISTOL Andrew E 1853
- HEADY Benjamin 1852
- BLACK Abner 1853

Section 35
- ALLEN Thomas 1838
- CURTIS [22] Eli 1853
- MEEK Hamilton 1853
- JOHNSON Richard 1852
- CHEEK John 1852
- JOHNSON William K 1853
- MEEK Hamilton 1853
- JOHNSON Richard 1852
- MEEK Hamilton 1853

Section 36
- CURTIS [22] Eli 1853
- SHAW Aaron 1853
- LAWRENCE Joseph 1852
- JOHNSON Richard 1852
- JOHNSON Richard 1852
- LAWRENCE William 1852
- BRISTOL [13] Andrew E 1853

Helpful Hints

1. This Map's INDEX can be found on the preceding pages.

2. Refer to Map "C" to see where this Township lies within Jasper County, Illinois.

3. Numbers within square brackets [ ] denote a multi-patentee land parcel (multi-owner). Refer to Appendix "C" for a full list of members in this group.

4. Areas that look to be crowded with Patentees usually indicate multiple sales of the same parcel (re-issues), cancellations or voided transactions (that we map, anyway) or overlapping parcels. We opt to show even these ambiguous parcels, which oftentimes lead to research avenues not yet taken.

Legend

- ——— Patent Boundary
- ▬▬▬ Section Boundary
- No Patents Found (or Outside County)
- 1., 2., 3., ... Lot Numbers (when beside a name)
- [ ] Group Number (see Appendix "C")

Scale: Section = 1 mile X 1 mile (generally, with some exceptions)

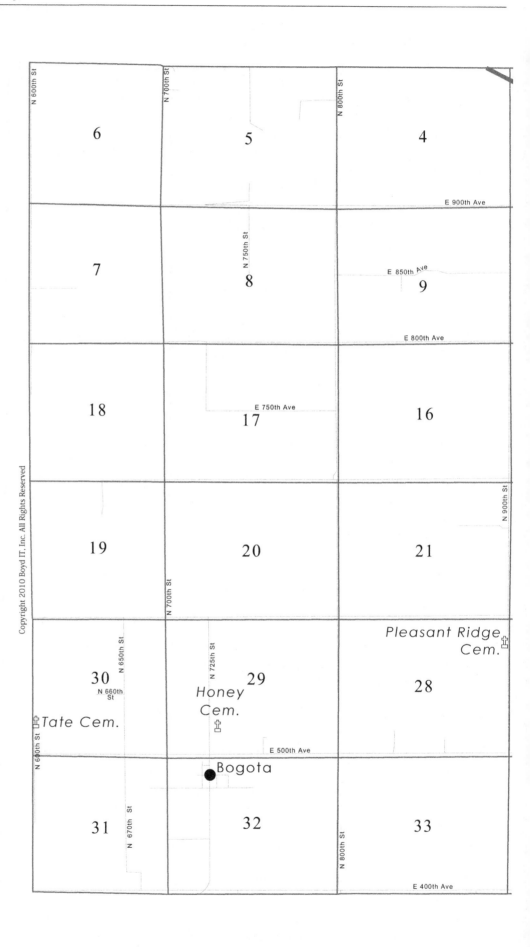

Road Map

T6-N R9-E
3rd PM Meridian

Map Group 12

Cities & Towns
Bogota
Newton

Cemeteries
Cummins Cemetery
Honey Cemetery
Pleasant Ridge Cemetery
Riverside Cemetery
Tate Cemetery
West Lawn Cemetery

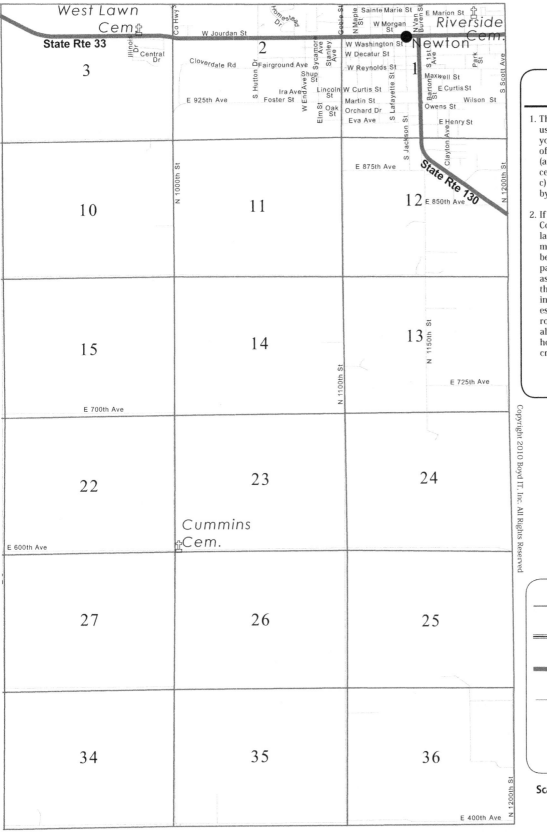

West Lawn Cem
State Rte 33
3
Illinois Dr
Central Dr
Cloverdale Rd
2
Homestead Dr
W Jourdan St
Goble St
N Maple St
Sainte Marie St
W Morgan St
E Marion St
Riverside Cem.
Newton
W Washington St
W Decatur St
W Reynolds St
Fairground Ave
S Hutton Dr
Sycamore Ave
Shup St
Stanley Ave
E 925th Ave
Ira Ave
W End Ave
Foster St
Lincoln St
W Curtis St
Martin St
Orchard Dr
Eva Ave
Elm St
Oak St
S Lafayette St
Barton St
N Van Buren St
N 1st Ave
Maxwell St
E Curtis St
Wilson St
Owens St
E Henry St
Park St
S Scott Ave
1
E 875th Ave
S Jackson St
State Rte 130
Clayton Ave
12 E 850th Ave
N 1200th St
N 1000th St
10
11
15
14
13
N 1150th St
E 725th Ave
N 1100th St
E 700th Ave
22
23
24
Cummins Cem.
E 600th Ave
27
26
25
34
35
36
N 1200th St
E 400th Ave

Helpful Hints

1. This road map has a number of uses, but primarily it is to help you: a) find the present location of land owned by your ancestors (at least the general area), b) find cemeteries and city-centers, and c) estimate the route/roads used by Census-takers & tax-assessors.

2. If you plan to travel to Jasper County to locate cemeteries or land parcels, please pick up a modern travel map for the area before you do. Mapping old land parcels on modern maps is not as exact a science as you might think. Just the slightest variations in public land survey coordinates, estimates of parcel boundaries, or road-map deviations can greatly alter a map's representation of how a road either does or doesn't cross a particular parcel of land.

L e g e n d

————————	Section Lines
═══════════	Interstates
▬▬▬▬▬▬▬▬	Highways
————————	Other Roads
●	Cities/Towns
✝	Cemeteries

Scale: Section = 1 mile X 1 mile
(generally, with some exceptions)

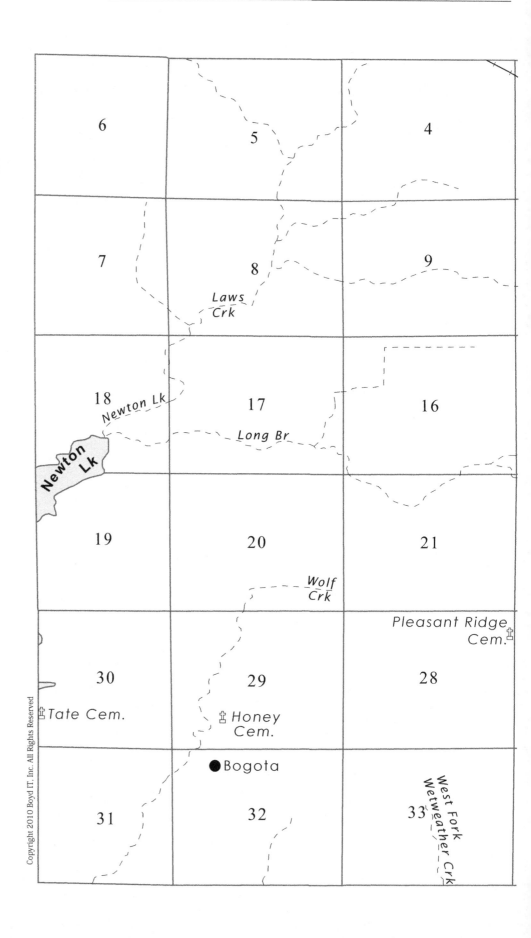

Historical Map

T6-N R9-E
3rd PM Meridian

Map Group 12

Cities & Towns
Bogota
Newton

Cemeteries
Cummins Cemetery
Honey Cemetery
Pleasant Ridge Cemetery
Riverside Cemetery
Tate Cemetery
West Lawn Cemetery

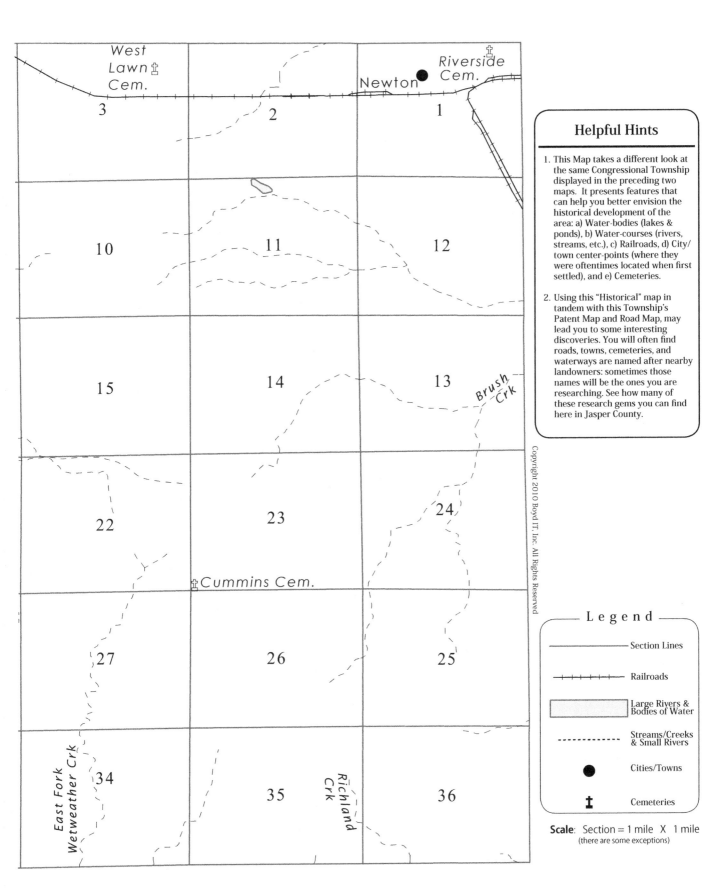

Helpful Hints

1. This Map takes a different look at the same Congressional Township displayed in the preceding two maps. It presents features that can help you better envision the historical development of the area: a) Water-bodies (lakes & ponds), b) Water-courses (rivers, streams, etc.), c) Railroads, d) City/town center-points (where they were oftentimes located when first settled), and e) Cemeteries.

2. Using this "Historical" map in tandem with this Township's Patent Map and Road Map, may lead you to some interesting discoveries. You will often find roads, towns, cemeteries, and waterways are named after nearby landowners: sometimes those names will be the ones you are researching. See how many of these research gems you can find here in Jasper County.

Legend

————————	Section Lines
+++++++	Railroads
▭	Large Rivers & Bodies of Water
- - - - - - -	Streams/Creeks & Small Rivers
●	Cities/Towns
☨	Cemeteries

Scale: Section = 1 mile X 1 mile
(there are some exceptions)

Map Group 13: Index to Land Patents

Township 6-North Range 10-East (3rd PM)

After you locate an individual in this Index, take note of the Section and Section Part then proceed to the Land Patent map on the pages immediately following. You should have no difficulty locating the corresponding parcel of land.

The "For More Info" Column will lead you to more information about the underlying Patents. See the *Legend* at right, and the "How to Use this Book" chapter, for more information.

```
                              LEGEND
                    "For More Info . . . " column
  G = Group   (Multi-Patentee Patent, see Appendix "C")
  R = Residence
  S = Social Status

  See Appendix A for list of abbreviations used by the
  Illinois State Archives in describing the place and
  nature of these land patents.

  Note: if the Abbreviations contain "L", "BL", "LOT",
  or "BLOCK", the exact whereabouts of the parcel within
  the section is not known.
```

ID	Individual in Patent	Sec.	Sec. Part	Purchase Date	Sale Type	IL Aliquot Part	For More Info . . .
3844	ADAMI, Nicholas	3	E½NE	1848-02-03	FD	E2NE	R:JASPER
3845	" "	3	NWNE	1849-08-20	FD	NWNE	R:JASPER
3917	ADAMS, Waldo T	35	W½NE	1852-07-15	FD	W2NE	
3916	" "	35	NESE	1852-07-15	FD	NESE	
3915	" "	35	E½NE	1852-07-15	FD	E2NE	
3913	" "	26	S½NW	1852-08-03	FD	S2NW	
3914	" "	26	W½SW	1852-08-03	FD	W2SW	
3789	ALLENTHARP, Joseph P	3	SWNE	1854-09-18	FD	SWNE	R:INDIANA
3856	BAILEY, Philip	1	NESE	1842-02-14	FD	NESE	R:JASPER
3822	BANTA, Lawrence	15	W½SW	1852-09-15	FD	W2SW	
3686	BARNS, James	5	NENW	1842-02-03	FD	NENW	R:JASPER
3733	BARNS, John	7	NWSW	1836-11-10	FD	NWSW	R:JASPER
3918	BLACK, William	19	SENE	1853-05-06	FD	SENE	
3919	"	20	SWNW	1853-05-06	FD	SWNW	
3705	BLACKBURN, James M	20	SENE	1852-07-01	FD	SENE	
3707	" "	20	SWNE	1852-07-01	FD	SWNE	
3706	" "	20	SENW	1852-07-01	FD	SENW	
3703	" "	20	E½SW	1852-07-01	FD	E2SW	
3704	" "	20	SE	1852-07-06	FD	SE	
3830	BOLENDER, Louis	36	SENE	1852-03-12	FD	SENE	R:JASPER
3776	BOOS, Joseph	28	SWSW	1839-11-19	FD	SWSW	R:JASPER
3774	" "	28	SWNW	1844-08-19	FD	SWNW	R:JASPER
3771	" "	28	SENW	1852-02-04	FD	SENW	R:JASPER
3775	" "	28	SWSE	1852-05-10	FD	SWSE	R:JASPER
3773	" "	28	SWNE	1852-06-19	FD	SWNE	
3770	" "	28	NWSE	1852-06-19	FD	NWSE	
3777	" "	29	SENE	1852-07-31	FD	SENE	
3772	" "	28	SESE	1852-09-02	FD	SESE	
3778	BOSS, Joseph	3	SWNW	1865-05-09	SW	SWNW	
3648	BRIDGES, Edmund R	1	NENE	1843-11-24	FD	NENE	R:JASPER
3647	" "	1	N½SW	1848-12-19	FD	N2SW	
3646	" "	1	N½SW	1848-12-19	FD	N2SW	
3649	" "	1	W½NW	1848-12-19	FD	W2NW	
3650	" "	1	W½NW	1848-12-19	FD	W2NW	
3650	" "	1	W½NW	1849-01-31	FD	W2NW	R:JASPER
3649	" "	1	W½NW	1849-01-31	FD	W2NW	R:JASPER
3646	" "	1	N½SW	1849-01-31	FD	N2SW	R:JASPER
3647	" "	1	N½SW	1849-01-31	FD	N2SW	R:JASPER
3831	BRIDGES, Mathew	5	NWSW	1851-11-14	FD	NWSW	R:JASPER
3734	BROOKS, John	1	NENW	1848-09-23	FD	NENW	R:INDIANA
3739	" "	1	W½NE	1848-10-23	FD	W2NE	
3737	" "	1	SENW	1848-10-23	FD	SENW	
3740	" "	1	W½NE	1848-10-23	FD	W2NE	
3738	" "	1	SENW	1848-10-23	FD	SENW	
3736	" "	1	SENE	1848-10-23	FD	SENE	
3737	" "	1	SENW	1848-10-31	FD	SENW	R:INDIANA

ID	Individual in Patent	Sec.	Sec. Part	Purchase Date	Sale Type	IL Aliquot Part	For More Info . . .
3738	BROOKS, John (Cont'd)	1	SENW	1848-10-31	FD	SENW	R:INDIANA
3740	" "	1	W½NE	1848-10-31	FD	W2NE	R:INDIANA
3739	" "	1	W½NE	1848-10-31	FD	W2NE	R:INDIANA
3735	" "	1	SE	1848-10-31	FD	SE	R:INDIANA
3765	BRYAN, John S	19	N½SW	1852-10-20	FD	N2SW	
3766	" "	19	S½NW	1852-10-20	FD	S2NW	R:PENNSYLVANIA
3644	BURCHAM, David	1	SWSW	1851-10-25	FD	SWSW	R:INDIANA
3757	BURFORD, John M	5	S½NW	1839-07-18	FD	S2NW	R:JASPER
3869	CALDWELL, Samuel	19	SESE	1852-06-22	FD	SESE	
3743	CARSON, John	24	NWSW	1852-06-24	FD	NWSW	
3744	" "	24	SWSW	1852-06-24	FD	SWSW	
3653	CARTER, Francis	6	E½SW	1839-11-08	FD	E2SW	R:JASPER
3730	CATT, Job	5	S½SE	1852-02-12	FD	S2SE	R:JASPER
3731	" "	9	NWSW	1852-02-12	FD	NWSW	R:JASPER
3745	CATT, John	8	SESE	1852-03-02	FD	SESE	R:JASPER
3665	CHABLE, Henry	6	S½SE	1854-01-13	FD	S2SE	R:JASPER
3862	CHAPMAN, Robert	23	SWNE	1851-09-27	FD	SWNE	R:JASPER
3929	CHASTAIN, William L	6	NESE	1840-03-16	FD	NESE	R:JASPER
3870	CRAIG, Samuel	3	NENW	1850-08-24	FD	NENW	R:INDIANA
3723	CRUME, James W	30	W½NE	1852-10-30	FD	W2NE	
3842	CRUME, Nancy	30	NENE	1852-10-30	FD	NENE	S:F
3746	DAVIS, John	4	W½NW	1839-11-05	FD	W2NW	R:JASPER
3655	EICHER, Francis	10	SWNE	1840-06-13	FD	SWNE	R:OHIO
3654	" "	10	S½SE	1840-06-13	FD	S2SE	R:OHIO
3726	EMERSON, Jesse O	21	E½SW	1852-07-27	FD	E2SW	
3727	" "	21	SE	1852-07-27	FD	SE	
3728	" "	21	SEN½	1852-07-27	FD	S2NE	
3729	" "	21	SENW	1852-07-27	FD	SENW	
3781	EVANS, Joseph	27	NWSW	1852-07-31	FD	NWSW	
3780	" "	27	NW	1852-07-31	FD	NW	
3784	" "	30	W½W½	1852-07-31	FD	W2W2	R:OHIO
3783	" "	28	NESE	1852-07-31	FD	NESE	
3782	" "	28	E½NE	1852-07-31	FD	E2NE	
3779	" "	27	NESW	1853-01-01	FD	NESW	
3909	EVANS, Thomas	20	W½SW	1852-06-12	FD	W2SW	
3908	" "	19	NESE	1852-06-12	FD	NESE	
3662	FITHIAN, Glover	9	E½NE	1839-05-27	FD	E2NE	R:JASPER
3663	" "	9	E½SE	1839-05-27	FD	E2SE	R:JASPER
3661	" "	3	SESW	1852-03-02	FD	SESW	R:JASPER
3660	" "	3	NWNW	1852-03-02	FD	NWNW	R:JASPER
3685	FITHIAN, Israel	7	W½SE	1836-09-30	FD	W2SE	R:OHIO
3684	" "	7	E½SW	1836-09-30	FD	E2SW	R:OHIO
3683	" "	7	E½SE	1837-05-31	FD	E2SE	R:JASPER
3682	" "	6	NWSW	1837-05-31	FD	NWSW	R:JASPER
3748	FOX, John	33	S½SE	1852-11-27	FD	S2SE	R:PENNSYLVANIA
3747	" "	33	NESE	1852-12-03	FD	NESE	
3755	FREEMAN, John L	10	E½SW	1838-09-07	FD	E2SW	R:JASPER
3940	FREEMAN, William W	10	NWSE	1837-06-26	FD	NWSE	R:JASPER
3749	GARWOOD, John	6	SWSW	1833-06-06	FD	SWSW	R:OHIO
3871	GARWOOD, Samuel	10	NENW	1836-04-08	FD	NENW	R:JASPER
3911	GARWOOD, Timothy	7	NWNW	1837-11-04	FD	NWNW	R:JASPER
3843	GILBRETH, Nancy	17	NESW	1852-06-12	FD	NESW	S:F
3750	GRUB, John	34	NW	1852-11-08	FD	NW	
3751	" "	34	SW	1852-11-08	FD	SW	
3651	GUERIN, Edward	7	SWNE	1838-04-26	FD	SWNE	R:JASPER
3823	HALLENBECK, Lawrence	6	NWNW	1836-11-25	FD	NWNW	R:JASPER
3721	HALSEY, James S	34	SE	1852-09-15	FD	SE	
3722	" "	35	W½SE	1852-09-15	FD	W2SE	
3642	HAMPELMAN, Daniel H	4	W½SE	1838-03-12	FD	W2SE	R:CLARK
3641	" "	4	E½SW	1838-03-12	FD	E2SW	R:CLARK
3925	HANNAH, William	8	SENW	1837-10-14	FD	SENW	R:INDIANA
3671	HARMON, John	6	SWNE	1840-03-16	FD	SWNE	R:JASPER G:35
3624	HARRIS, Benjamin	5	E½NE	1836-11-25	FD	E2NE	R:OHIO G:37
3626	" "	6	NWSE	1836-11-25	FD	NWSE	R:OHIO G:37
3622	" "	6	SWNW	1836-11-25	FD	SWNW	R:OHIO
3625	" "	6	E½NW	1836-11-25	FD	E2NW	R:OHIO G:37
3623	" "	4	W½SW	1836-11-25	FD	W2SW	R:OHIO G:37
3753	" "	6	SWNW	1836-11-25	FD	SWNW	R:OHIO
3621	" "	6	E½NE	1838-11-30	FD	E2NE	R:JASPER
3883	HARTRICH, Theodore	26	E½NE	1852-06-22	FD	E2NE	
3884	" "	26	SWNE	1852-06-22	FD	SWNE	
3885	HARTRICK, Theodore	13	E½	1845-02-21	FD	E2	R:JASPER
3890	" "	25	W½SE	1851-07-18	FD	W2SE	R:JASPER

ID	Individual in Patent	Sec.	Sec. Part	Purchase Date	Sale Type	IL Aliquot Part	For More Info . . .
3889	HARTRICK, Theodore (Cont'd)	23	SWSE	1852-03-12	FD	SWSE	R:JASPER
3888	" "	23	SESW	1852-03-12	FD	SESW	R:JASPER
3886	" "	15	W½SE	1852-08-12	FD	W2SE	
3891	" "	26	NWNW	1852-08-12	FD	NWNW	
3887	" "	23	NENW	1852-08-12	FD	NENW	
3725	HAYDEN, Jerom	25	E½SE	1845-09-18	FD	E2SE	R:JASPER
3937	HAYS, William O	8	NESE	1852-03-24	FD	NESE	R:JASPER
3624	HERRON, John	5	E½NE	1836-11-25	FD	E2NE	R:OHIO G:37
3625	" "	6	E½NW	1836-11-25	FD	E2NW	R:OHIO G:37
3623	" "	4	W½SW	1836-11-25	FD	W2SW	R:OHIO G:37
3626	" "	6	NWSE	1836-11-25	FD	NWSE	R:OHIO G:37
3622	" "	6	SWNW	1836-11-26	FD	SWNW	R:OHIO
3753	" "	6	SWNW	1836-11-26	FD	SWNW	R:OHIO
3752	" "	5	W½NE	1839-11-21	FD	W2NE	R:OHIO
3629	HOLINGER, Charles	15	SENE	1851-03-22	FD	SENE	R:JASPER
3612	HOLM, Adam	4	W½NE	1841-01-06	FD	W2NE	R:JASPER
3724	HOWELL, Jane	19	W½SE	1852-06-22	FD	W2SE	S:F
3702	JORDAN, James	8	SWSE	1837-07-15	FD	SWSE	R:JASPER
3701	" "	17	NWNE	1839-05-21	FD	NWNE	R:JASPER
3639	KAUFFMAN, Cyriac	33	N½NE	1852-07-12	FD	N2NE	
3640	" "	33	SENE	1852-07-12	FD	SENE	
3620	KAUFMANN, Anthony	33	NWSE	1852-08-31	FD	NWSE	
3846	KELLER, Nicholas	36	NWSW	1852-08-02	FD	NWSW	
3847	KEPLER, Nicholas	4	SENE	1851-01-06	FD	SENE	R:JASPER
3850	KESSLER, Nicholas	9	NWSE	1845-02-25	FD	NWSE	R:JASPER
3851	" "	9	SENW	1848-02-03	FD	SENW	R:JASPER
3848	" "	4	NESE	1852-01-27	FD	NESE	R:JASPER
3849	" "	9	NESW	1852-02-17	FD	NESW	R:JASPER
3852	" "	9	SESW	1852-06-17	FD	SESW	R:JASPER
3676	KING, Ira	27	S½SW	1853-09-27	FD	S2SW	R:CRAWFORD
3677	" "	33	SWNE	1853-11-02	FD	SWNE	R:CRAWFORD
3668	KRITOSER, Henry R	2	N½SE	1849-01-23	FD	N2SE	
3669	" "	2	N½SW	1849-01-23	FD	N2SW	
3785	LAWRENCE, Joseph	31	NW	1852-11-30	FD	NW	
3930	LAWRENCE, William	31	SW	1853-02-17	FD	SW	
3931	" "	31	W½SE	1853-02-18	FD	W2SE	
3928	LEE, William J	1	W½SE	1849-11-20	FD	W2SE	
3926	" "	1	SESE	1849-11-20	FD	SESE	
3927	" "	1	SESW	1849-11-20	FD	SESW	
3912	LEINHART, Valentine	36	SWNE	1851-12-19	FD	SWNE	R:JASPER
3756	LOBMAIER, John	5	NESE	1853-10-26	FD	NESE	R:JASPER
3932	MAGILL, William	14	NESE	1832-11-27	FD	NESE	R:CRAWFORD
3865	MASON, Sampson	34	NE	1852-07-20	FD	NE	
3867	" "	35	SW	1852-07-20	FD	SW	
3866	" "	35	NW	1852-07-20	FD	NW	
3652	MATTINGLY, Edward	31	NE	1852-11-18	FD	NE	G:44
3652	MATTINGLY, James	31	NE	1852-11-18	FD	NE	G:44
3652	MATTINGLY, Jane	31	NE	1852-11-18	FD	NE	G:44
3652	MATTINGLY, John	31	NE	1852-11-18	FD	NE	G:44
3742	MAXWELL, John C	19	N½NW	1852-05-21	FD	N2NW	R:JASPER
3741	" "	18	S½SW	1852-05-21	FD	S2SW	R:JASPER
3933	MAXWELL, William	17	S½SW	1852-03-13	FD	S2SW	
3936	" "	20	N½NW	1852-03-13	FD	N2NW	
3934	" "	18	S½SE	1852-04-12	FD	S2SE	
3935	" "	19	N½NE	1852-04-12	FD	N2NE	
3732	MAY, John A	5	NWNW	1852-02-20	FD	NWNW	R:JASPER
3910	MCDONNEL, Thomas F	2	SESE	1843-10-04	FD	SESE	R:JASPER
3635	MCILVOY, Charles	23	W½SW	1852-06-21	FD	W2SW	
3632	" "	22	E½SE	1852-06-21	FD	E2SE	
3630	" "	11	E½SE	1852-06-21	FD	E2SE	
3633	" "	23	NESW	1852-06-29	FD	NESW	R:KENTUCKY
3634	" "	23	SENW	1852-06-29	FD	SENW	R:KENTUCKY
3636	" "	3	NESW	1852-06-29	FD	NESW	R:KENTUCKY
3637	" "	3	SENW	1852-06-29	FD	SENW	R:KENTUCKY
3631	" "	22	E½NE	1852-06-29	FD	E2NE	R:KENTUCKY
3759	MCKINLEY, John	7	E½NW	1839-11-05	FD	E2NW	R:JASPER
3758	" "	18	N½NE	1849-09-06	FD	N2NE	R:JASPER
3829	MCKINLEY, Lewis	5	NWSE	1845-07-17	FD	NWSE	R:JASPER
3826	" "	17	SWNW	1845-07-17	FD	SWNW	R:JASPER
3825	" "	17	NWSW	1852-03-13	FD	NWSW	R:JASPER
3827	" "	18	NESE	1852-03-24	FD	NESE	R:JASPER
3824	" "	17	NWSE	1852-08-02	FD	NWSE	R:JASPER
3828	" "	18	NWSW	1852-08-02	FD	NWSW	R:JASPER

ID	Individual in Patent	Sec.	Sec. Part	Purchase Date	Sale Type	IL Aliquot Part	For More Info . . .
3656	MCKINLY, George	17	E½SE	1852-06-18	FD	E2SE	
3657	" "	8	NWNE	1852-06-18	FD	NWNE	
3761	MILLER, John	9	NWNW	1840-06-23	FD	NWNW	R:JASPER
3760	" "	17	NENE	1840-06-23	FD	NENE	R:JASPER
3762	" "	9	SWNW	1851-04-18	FD	SWNW	R:JASPER
3787	MILLER, Joseph	29	W½NW	1852-10-21	FD	W2NW	
3786	" "	29	E½NW	1852-10-21	FD	E2NW	
3788	" "	8	NENW	1852-10-21	FD	NENW	
3833	MILLER, Mathias	36	SESW	1849-06-06	FD	SESW	R:JASPER
3832	" "	36	NESW	1850-06-20	FD	NESW	R:JASPER
3643	MURVIN, Daniel	28	E½SW	1831-09-26	FD	E2SW	R:WABASH
3820	NAGELY, Josiah	3	W½SW	1838-03-12	FD	W2SW	R:CLARK
3821	" "	4	SESE	1838-03-12	FD	SESE	R:CLARK
3763	PAIN, John	8	NESW	1837-09-16	FD	NESW	R:INDIANA
3764	" "	8	SWNE	1837-10-14	FD	SWNE	R:INDIANA
3921	PAIN, William F	17	SENW	1843-09-13	FD	SENW	R:JASPER
3905	PATRICK, Thomas C	16	L7	1853-10-08	SC	LOT7SWNE	
3898	" "	16	L15	1853-10-08	SC	LOT15SWSE	
3907	" "	16	L9	1853-10-08	SC	LOT9NESE	
3906	" "	16	L8	1853-10-08	SC	LOT8SENE	
3904	" "	16	L6	1853-10-08	SC	LOT6SENW	
3903	" "	16	L5	1853-10-08	SC	LOT5SWNW	
3902	" "	16	L4	1853-10-08	SC	LOT4NWNW	
3901	" "	16	L3	1853-10-08	SC	LOT3NENW	
3899	" "	16	L16	1853-10-08	SC	LOT16SESE	
3897	" "	16	L14	1853-10-08	SC	LOT14SESW	
3896	" "	16	L13	1853-10-08	SC	LOT13SWSW	
3895	" "	16	L12	1853-10-08	SC	LOT12NWSW	
3894	" "	16	L11	1853-10-08	SC	LOT11NESW	
3893	" "	16	L10	1853-10-08	SC	LOT10NWSE	
3892	" "	16	L1	1853-10-08	SC	LOT1NENE	
3900	" "	16	L2	1853-10-08	SC	LOT2NWNE	
3922	PAYNE, William F	17	NWNW	1849-07-23	FD	NWNW	R:JASPER
3923	" "	5	E½SW	1851-11-14	FD	E2SW	R:JASPER
3924	" "	9	SWSW	1852-07-02	FD	SWSW	
3611	PETERSON, Abner M	30	SENE	1854-01-07	FD	SENE	R:JASPER
3708	PETERSON, James	19	S½SW	1853-05-20	FD	S2SW	R:JASPER
3664	PICQUET, Havier	36	NWNW	1852-06-29	FD	NWNW	
3716	PICQUET, James	36	NWSE	1840-03-17	FD	NWSE	R:JASPER
3715	" "	36	E½NW	1852-05-11	FD	E2NW	
3713	" "	25	W½SW	1852-05-27	FD	W2SW	
3712	" "	15	W½NW	1852-06-29	FD	W2NW	
3711	" "	15	SENW	1852-06-29	FD	SENW	
3710	" "	15	NESW	1852-06-29	FD	NESW	
3709	" "	12	NENE	1852-06-29	FD	NENE	
3717	" "	36	SWSW	1852-06-29	FD	SWSW	
3718	" "	9	SWSE	1852-06-29	FD	SWSE	
3714	" "	35	SESE	1852-06-29	FD	SESE	
3807	PICQUET, Joseph	31	E½SE	1837-10-07	FD	E2SE	R:JASPER
3797	" "	23	NE	1837-10-07	FD	NE	R:JASPER
3791	" "	11	N½	1837-10-07	FD	N2	R:JASPER
3792	" "	11	SW	1837-10-07	FD	SW	R:JASPER
3793	" "	12		1837-10-07	FD	SEC	R:JASPER
3794	" "	13	W½	1837-10-07	FD	W2	R:JASPER
3809	" "	32	E½NW	1837-10-07	FD	E2NW	R:JASPER
3795	" "	14		1837-10-07	FD	SEC	R:JASPER
3811	" "	33	W½	1837-10-07	FD	W2	R:JASPER
3798	" "	24	E½SW	1837-10-07	FD	E2SW	R:JASPER
3799	" "	24	N½	1837-10-07	FD	N2	R:JASPER
3800	" "	24	SE	1837-10-07	FD	SE	R:JASPER
3806	" "	29	SE	1837-10-07	FD	SE	R:JASPER
3808	" "	32	E½	1837-10-07	FD	E2	R:JASPER
3810	" "	32	SW	1837-10-07	FD	SW	R:JASPER
3790	" "	10	SENW	1839-04-10	FD	SENW	R:JASPER
3814	" "	36	SWSE	1840-01-08	FD	SWSE	R:JASPER
3812	" "	36	E½SE	1840-01-08	FD	E2SE	R:JASPER
3801	" "	25	E½NE	1840-04-04	FD	E2NE	R:JASPER
3803	" "	25	W½NE	1843-10-16	FD	W2NE	R:JASPER
3802	" "	25	E½NW	1843-10-16	FD	E2NW	R:JASPER
3813	" "	36	N½NE	1852-05-11	FD	N2NE	
3805	" "	26	SE	1852-06-29	FD	SE	
3804	" "	26	E½SW	1852-06-29	FD	E2SW	
3796	" "	2	SWSE	1865-05-10	SW	SWSE	

ID	Individual in Patent	Sec.	Sec. Part	Purchase Date	Sale Type	IL Aliquot Part	For More Info . . .
3944	PICQUET, Xavier	25	E½SW	1852-03-23	FD	E2SW	R:JASPER
3858	PINDELL, Richard	29	N½NE	1852-11-18	FD	N2NE	
3857	" "	28	N½NW	1852-11-18	FD	N2NW	
3658	PRESTON, George R	30	E½SW	1853-08-29	FD	E2SW	R:CRAWFORD
3754	PULLIS, John J	6	NWNE	1839-07-15	FD	NWNE	R:JASPER
3834	RAFE, Mathias	29	NESW	1852-08-31	FD	NESW	
3836	" "	32	W½NW	1853-05-21	FD	W2NW	
3835	" "	29	W½SW	1853-05-21	FD	W2SW	
3619	REIGELSBERGER, Anthon	15	NWNE	1842-11-28	FD	NWNE	R:JASPER
3618	" "	15	NENW	1851-01-28	FD	NENW	R:JASPER
3617	" "	10	NWNW	1852-01-23	FD	NWNW	R:JASPER
3839	REIGELSBERGER, Meinra	10	SENE	1844-12-30	FD	SENE	R:JASPER
3666	REYNOLDS, Henry J M	7	SWSW	1838-03-20	FD	SWSW	R:WABASH
3837	RIFE, Mathias	29	SESW	1847-11-29	FD	SESW	R:PENNSYLVANIA
3838	" "	29	SWNE	1853-09-29	FD	SWNE	R:JASPER
3667	ROACH, Henry Jr	2	NE	1848-02-21	FD	NE	
3670	ROCH, Henry	2		1848-02-29	FD	PTNE	R:INDIANA
3720	ROSS, James	8	SENE	1839-05-21	FD	SENE	R:JASPER
3719	" "	17	SWNE	1839-05-21	FD	SWNE	R:JASPER
3768	ROSS, John T	17	SWSE	1852-03-24	FD	SWSE	R:JASPER
3769	" "	20	NWNE	1852-03-24	FD	NWNE	R:JASPER
3863	ROSS, Robert	18	NW	1836-08-29	FD	NW	R:OHIO
3864	" "	18	NWSE	1851-12-26	FD	NWSE	R:JASPER
3659	SCHACKMAN, George	4	SENW	1848-03-10	FD	SENW	R:JASPER
3767	SCHACKMAN, John	4	NENE	1844-09-11	FD	NENE	R:JASPER
3882	SCHIFFERSTEIN, Theodo	25	W½NW	1852-06-29	FD	W2NW	
3881	" "	23	NWSE	1852-07-20	FD	NWSE	
3880	" "	23	E½SE	1852-07-20	FD	E2SE	
3638	SCIFRES, Colmon L	30	E½NW	1852-10-30	FD	E2NW	R:KENTUCKY
3853	SMITH, Nicholas	36	SWNW	1852-06-03	FD	SWNW	R:JASPER
3939	STARLING, William	8	SWNW	1839-05-07	FD	SWNW	R:KENTUCKY
3938	" "	7	SENE	1839-05-07	FD	SENE	R:KENTUCKY
3694	STEEL, James H	22	SW	1852-10-07	FD	SW	
3687	" "	10	NESE	1852-10-20	FD	NESE	
3699	" "	27	W½SE	1852-10-20	FD	W2SE	
3698	" "	27	W½NE	1852-10-20	FD	W2NE	
3697	" "	27	E½SE	1852-10-20	FD	E2SE	
3695	" "	22	W½SE	1852-10-20	FD	W2SE	
3696	" "	27	E½NE	1852-10-20	FD	E2NE	
3691	" "	21	NWSW	1853-05-06	FD	NWSW	
3692	" "	21	SWNW	1853-05-06	FD	SWNW	
3690	" "	20	NENE	1853-05-06	FD	NENE	
3693	" "	21	SWSW	1853-05-09	FD	SWSW	
3700	" "	28	NWNE	1853-05-20	FD	NWNE	R:CRAWFORD
3689	" "	19	SWNE	1853-05-20	FD	SWNE	R:CRAWFORD
3688	" "	15	SESW	1853-09-02	FD	SESW	R:CRAWFORD
3873	SUTER, Solomon	11	W½SE	1852-06-17	FD	W2SE	
3879	" "	23	W½NW	1852-06-17	FD	W2NW	
3876	" "	22	E½NW	1852-07-17	FD	E2NW	
3878	" "	22	W½NW	1852-07-17	FD	W2NW	
3877	" "	22	W½NE	1852-07-17	FD	W2NE	
3875	" "	21	N½N½	1852-10-20	FD	N2N2	
3874	" "	2	SWSW	1852-11-30	FD	SWSW	
3627	THOMAS, Benjamin	8	NENE	1840-01-14	FD	NENE	R:OHIO
3872	TODD, Samuel B	2	NW	1848-06-27	FD	NW	
3868	" "	2	NW	1848-06-27	FD	NW	
3872	TODD, Samuel R	2	NW	1848-06-30	FD	NWFR	R:INDIANA
3868	" "	2	NW	1848-06-30	FD	NWFR	R:INDIANA
3616	TURNER, Alexander	8	W½SW	1837-11-29	FD	W2SW	R:EDGAR
3615	" "	8	SESW	1837-11-29	FD	SESW	R:EDGAR
3613	" "	17	NENW	1838-03-20	FD	NENW	R:JASPER
3614	" "	8	NWSE	1838-03-26	FD	NWSE	R:JASPER
3673	UHL, Hugh	3	S½SE	1850-08-23	FD	S2SE	
3672	" "	10	N½NE	1850-08-23	FD	N2NE	
3674	UHL, Hugo	15	NESE	1845-07-28	FD	NESE	R:JASPER
3675	" "	15	SESE	1852-06-28	FD	SESE	
3815	UHL, Joseph	15	SWNE	1850-07-30	FD	SWNE	R:JASPER
3860	VANDERHOFF, Richard	18	NE	1839-05-22	FD	NEVOID	R:OHIO G:58
3859	" "	18	SEN½	1839-11-04	FD	S2NE	R:JASPER
3860	VANDERHOOF, Richard	18	NE	1839-05-22	FD	NEVOID	R:OHIO G:58
3861	" "	17	SENE	1852-07-31	FD	SENE	
3628	VANNATTAR, Benjamin	7	SWNW	1837-11-03	FD	SWNW	R:JASPER
3816	VOGEL, Joseph	10	SWNW	1840-09-03	FD	SWNW	R:OHIO

ID	Individual in Patent	Sec.	Sec. Part	Purchase Date	Sale Type	IL Aliquot Part	For More Info . . .
3817	VOGEL, Joseph (Cont'd)	10	W½SW	1840-09-03	FD	W2SW	R:OHIO
3818	" "	15	NENE	1842-11-28	FD	NENE	R:JASPER
3671	WADE, Hiram	6	SWNE	1840-03-16	FD	SWNE	R:JASPER G:35
3671	WADE, Lorenzo D	6	SWNE	1840-03-16	FD	SWNE	R:JASPER G:35
3854	WAITE, Paul	26	NENW	1843-07-07	FD	NENW	R:JASPER
3855	" "	26	NWNE	1843-07-07	FD	NWNE	R:JASPER
3678	WALKER, Isaac H	5	SWSW	1865-05-09	SW	SWSW	
3679	" "	7	NENE	1865-05-09	SW	NENE	
3680	" "	7	NWNE	1865-05-09	SW	NWNE	
3681	" "	8	NWNW	1865-05-09	SW	NWNW	
3819	WELDAM, Joseph	4	NENW	1848-02-29	FD	NENW	R:JASPER
3841	WHITE, Miles	30	S½SE	1852-08-05	FD	S2SE	R:BALTIMORE
3840	" "	30	N½SE	1852-08-05	FD	N2SE	R:BALTIMORE
3920	WILSON, William C	3	N½SE	1850-09-11	FD	N2SE	R:INDIANA
3645	WINES, David	2	SESW	1852-06-08	FD	SESW	R:INDIANA
3941	WYANT, William	28	NWSW	1836-04-02	FD	NWSW	R:JASPER
3942	" "	9	NENW	1839-09-02	FD	NENW	R:JASPER
3943	" "	9	W½NE	1839-09-02	FD	W2NE	R:JASPER

Patent Map

T6-N R10-E
3rd PM Meridian

Map Group 13

Township Statistics

Parcels Mapped	:	334
Number of Patents	:	1
Number of Individuals	:	142
Patentees Identified	:	139
Number of Surnames	:	112
Multi-Patentee Parcels	:	7
Oldest Patent Date	:	9/26/1831
Most Recent Patent	:	5/10/1865
Block/Lot Parcels	:	18
Cities and Towns	:	1
Cemeteries	:	2

Section 6

HALLENBECK Lawrence 1836
HERRON John
HARRIS Benjamin 1836
HARRIS [37] Benjamin 1836
PULLIS John J 1839
WADE [35] Hiram 1840
HARRIS Benjamin 1838

FITHIAN Israel 1837
CARTER Francis 1839
HARRIS [37] Benjamin 1836
CHASTAIN William L 1840
CHABLE Henry 1854
GARWOOD John 1833

Section 5

MAY John A 1852
BARNS James 1842
HERRON John 1839
BURFORD John M 1839
BRIDGES Mathew 1851
PAYNE William F 1851
MCKINLEY Lewis 1845
LOBMAIER John 1853
CATT Job 1852
WALKER Isaac H 1865

Section 4

WELDAM Joseph 1848
HOLM Adam 1841
SCHACKMAN John 1844
HARRIS [37] Benjamin 1836
DAVIS John 1839
SCHACKMAN George 1848
KEPLER Nicholas 1851
KESSLER Nicholas 1852
HARRIS [37] Benjamin 1836
HAMPELMAN Daniel H 1838
NAGELY Josiah 1838

Section 7

GARWOOD Timothy 1837
MCKINLEY John 1839
VANNATTAR Benjamin 1837
WALKER Isaac H 1865
WALKER Isaac H 1865
GUERIN Edward 1838
STARLING William 1839
BARNS John 1836
FITHIAN Israel 1836
REYNOLDS Henry J M 1838
FITHIAN Israel 1836
FITHIAN Israel 1837

Section 8

WALKER Isaac H 1865
MILLER Joseph 1852
STARLING William 1839
HANNAH William 1837
PAIN John 1837
PAIN John 1837
TURNER Alexander 1838
TURNER Alexander 1837
TURNER Alexander 1837
JORDAN James 1837

Section 9

MCKINLY George 1852
THOMAS Benjamin 1840
MILLER John 1840
WYANT William 1839
WYANT William 1839
FITHIAN Glover 1839
ROSS James 1839
MILLER John 1851
KESSLER Nicholas 1848
HAYS William O 1852
CATT Job 1852
KESSLER Nicholas 1845
KESSLER Nicholas
CATT John 1852
PAYNE William F 1852
KESSLER Nicholas 1852
PICQUET James 1852
FITHIAN Glover 1839

Section 18

ROSS Robert 1836
MCKINLEY Lewis 1852
MAXWELL John C 1852
ROSS Robert 1851
MCKINLEY Lewis 1852

Section 17

MCKINLEY John 1849
VANDERHOFF [58] Richard 1839
VANDERHOFF Richard 1839
PAYNE William F
TURNER Alexander 1838
JORDAN James 1839
MCKINLEY Lewis 1845
PAIN William F 1843
ROSS James 1839
MCKINLEY Lewis 1852
GILBRETH Nancy 1852
MCKINLEY Lewis 1852
MILLER John 1840
VANDERHOOF Richard 1852
MCKINLY George 1852
ROSS John T 1852
MAXWELL William 1852
MAXWELL William 1852

Section 16

Lots-Sec. 16
L1 PATRICK, Thomas C 1853
L2 PATRICK, Thomas C 1853
L3 PATRICK, Thomas C 1853
L4 PATRICK, Thomas C 1853
L5 PATRICK, Thomas C 1853
L6 PATRICK, Thomas C 1853
L7 PATRICK, Thomas C 1853
L8 PATRICK, Thomas C 1853
L9 PATRICK, Thomas C 1853
L10 PATRICK, Thomas C 1853
L11 PATRICK, Thomas C 1853
L12 PATRICK, Thomas C 1853
L13 PATRICK, Thomas C 1853
L14 PATRICK, Thomas C 1853
L15 PATRICK, Thomas C 1853
L16 PATRICK, Thomas C 1853

Section 19

MAXWELL John C 1852
BRYAN John S 1852
STEEL James H 1853
BLACK William 1853
BRYAN John S 1852
HOWELL Jane 1852
EVANS Thomas 1852
CALDWELL Samuel 1852
PETERSON James 1853

Section 20

MAXWELL William 1852
BLACK William 1853
BLACKBURN James M 1852
BLACKBURN James M 1852
BLACKBURN James M 1852
EVANS Thomas 1852
BLACKBURN James M 1852
BLACKBURN James M 1852

Section 21

ROSS John T 1852
STEEL James H 1853
SUTER Solomon 1852
STEEL James H 1853
EMERSON Jesse O 1852
EMERSON Jesse O 1852
STEEL James H 1853
EMERSON Jesse O 1852
EMERSON Jesse O 1852
STEEL James H 1853

Section 30

SCIFRES Colmon L 1852
CRUME James W 1852
CRUME Nancy 1852
PETERSON Abner M 1854
EVANS Joseph 1852
PRESTON George R 1853
WHITE Miles 1852
WHITE Miles 1852

Section 29

MILLER Joseph 1852
MILLER Joseph 1852
RAFE Mathias 1852
RAFE Mathias 1853
RIFE Mathias 1853
BOOS Joseph 1852
PICQUET Joseph 1837
RIFE Mathias 1847

Section 28

PINDELL Richard 1852
PINDELL Richard 1852
STEEL James H 1853
EVANS Joseph 1852
BOOS Joseph 1844
BOOS Joseph 1852
BOOS Joseph 1852
WYANT William 1836
MURVIN Daniel 1831
BOOS Joseph 1852
EVANS Joseph 1852
BOOS Joseph 1839
BOOS Joseph 1852
BOOS Joseph 1852

Section 31

MATTINGLY [44] Edward 1852
LAWRENCE Joseph 1852
LAWRENCE William 1853
LAWRENCE William 1853
PICQUET Joseph 1837

Section 32

RAFE Mathias 1853
PICQUET Joseph 1837
PICQUET Joseph 1837
PICQUET Joseph 1837

Section 33

PICQUET Joseph 1837
KAUFFMAN Cyriac 1852
KING Ira 1853
KAUFFMAN Cyriac 1852
KAUFMANN Anthony 1852
FOX John 1852
FOX John 1852

FITHIAN Glover 1852	CRAIG Samuel 1850	ADAMI Nicholas 1849	ADAMI Nicholas 1848	TODD Samuel B 1848		ROACH Henry Jr 1848	BRIDGES Edmund R 1848	BROOKS John 1848	BROOKS John 1848	BRIDGES Edmund R 1843

Section 3:
- BOSS Joseph 1865
- MCILVOY Charles 1852
- ALLENTHARP Joseph P 1854
- ADAMI Nicholas 1848
- NAGELY Josiah 1838
- MCILVOY Charles 1852
- WILSON William C 1850
- FITHIAN Glover 1852
- UHL Hugh 1850

Section 2:
- TODD Samuel R 1848
- 2
- ROCH Henry 1848
- KRITOSER Henry R 1849
- KRITOSER Henry R 1849
- SUTER Solomon 1852
- WINES David 1852
- PICQUET Joseph 1865
- MCDONNEL Thomas F 1843

Section 1:
- BRIDGES Edmund R 1848
- BRIDGES Edmund R 1849
- BROOKS John BROOKS John 1848
- BROOKS John 1848
- BROOKS John 1848
- BRIDGES Edmund R 1848
- LEE William J 1849
- BAILEY Philip 1842
- BURCHAM David 1851
- LEE William J 1849
- BROOKS John 1848
- LEE William J 1849
- PICQUET James 1852

Section 10:
- REIGELSBERGER Anthon 1852
- GARWOOD Samuel 1836
- UHL Hugh 1850
- VOGEL Joseph 1840
- PICQUET Joseph 1839
- EICHER Francis 1840
- 10
- REIGELSBERGER Melnra 1844
- VOGEL Joseph 1840
- FREEMAN John L 1838
- FREEMAN William W 1837
- STEEL James H 1852
- EICHER Francis 1840

Section 11:
- 11
- PICQUET Joseph 1837
- PICQUET Joseph 1837
- SUTER Solomon 1852
- MCILVOY Charles 1852

Section 12:
- PICQUET Joseph 1837
- 12

Section 15:
- PICQUET James 1852
- REIGELSBERGER Anthon 1851
- REIGELSBERGER Anthon 1842
- VOGEL Joseph 1842
- PICQUET James 1852
- UHL Joseph 1850
- HOLINGER Charles 1851
- 15
- BANTA Lawrence 1852
- PICQUET James 1852
- HARTRICK Theodore 1852
- UHL Hugo 1845
- STEEL James H 1853
- UHL Hugo 1852

Section 14:
- 14
- PICQUET Joseph 1837
- MAGILL William 1832

Section 13:
- PICQUET Joseph 1837
- 13
- HARTRICK Theodore 1845

Section 22:
- SUTER Solomon 1852
- SUTER Solomon 1852
- SUTER Solomon 1852
- MCILVOY Charles 1852
- 22
- STEEL James H 1852
- STEEL James H 1852
- MCILVOY Charles 1852

Section 23:
- SUTER Solomon 1852
- HARTRICK Theodore 1852
- MCILVOY Charles 1852
- CHAPMAN Robert 1851
- PICQUET Joseph 1837
- MCILVOY Charles 1852
- SCHIFFERSTEIN Theodo 1852
- 23
- SCHIFFERSTEIN Theodo 1852
- MCILVOY Charles 1852
- HARTRICK Theodore 1852
- HARTRICK Theodore 1852

Section 24:
- PICQUET Joseph 1837
- 24
- CARSON John 1852
- PICQUET Joseph 1837
- PICQUET Joseph 1837
- CARSON John 1852

Section 27:
- EVANS Joseph 1852
- STEEL James H 1852
- STEEL James H 1852
- 27
- EVANS Joseph 1852
- EVANS Joseph 1853
- STEEL James H 1852
- STEEL James H 1852
- KING Ira 1853

Section 26:
- HARTRICK Theodore 1852
- WAITE Paul 1843
- WAITE Paul 1843
- HARTRICK Theodore 1852
- ADAMS Waldo T 1852
- 26
- HARTRICH Theodore 1852
- ADAMS Waldo T 1852
- PICQUET Joseph 1852
- PICQUET Joseph 1852

Section 25:
- SCHIFFERSTEIN Theodo 1852
- PICQUET Joseph 1843
- PICQUET Joseph 1843
- PICQUET Joseph 1840
- 25
- HAYDEN Jerom 1845
- PICQUET James 1852
- PICQUET Xavier 1852
- HARTRICK Theodore 1851

Section 34:
- GRUB John 1852
- 34
- MASON Sampson 1852
- HALSEY James S 1852
- GRUB John 1852

Section 35:
- MASON Sampson 1852
- ADAMS Waldo T 1852
- 35
- ADAMS Waldo T 1852
- PICQUET Joseph 1852
- PICQUET Joseph 1852
- MASON Sampson 1852
- HALSEY James S 1852
- PICQUET James 1852

Section 36:
- ADAMS Waldo T 1852
- PICQUET Joseph 1852
- PICQUET James 1852
- SMITH Nicholas 1852
- 36
- LEINHART Valentine 1851
- BOLENDER Louis 1852
- KELLER Nicholas 1852
- MILLER Mathias 1850
- PICQUET James 1840
- PICQUET James 1852
- MILLER Mathias 1849
- PICQUET Joseph 1840

Helpful Hints

1. This Map's INDEX can be found on the preceding pages.

2. Refer to Map "C" to see where this Township lies within Jasper County, Illinois.

3. Numbers within square brackets [ ] denote a multi-patentee land parcel (multi-owner). Refer to Appendix "C" for a full list of members in this group.

4. Areas that look to be crowded with Patentees usually indicate multiple sales of the same parcel (re-issues), cancellations or voided transactions (that we map, anyway) or overlapping parcels. We opt to show even these ambiguous parcels, which oftentimes lead to research avenues not yet taken.

Legend

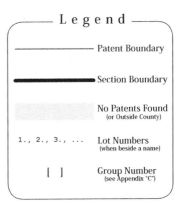

— Patent Boundary

— Section Boundary

No Patents Found (or Outside County)

1., 2., 3., ... Lot Numbers (when beside a name)

[ ] Group Number (see Appendix "C")

Scale: Section = 1 mile X 1 mile (generally, with some exceptions)

Road Map

T6-N R10-E
3rd PM Meridian

Map Group 13

Cities & Towns

Boos

Cemeteries

Shiloh Cemetery
Vanderhoof Cemetery

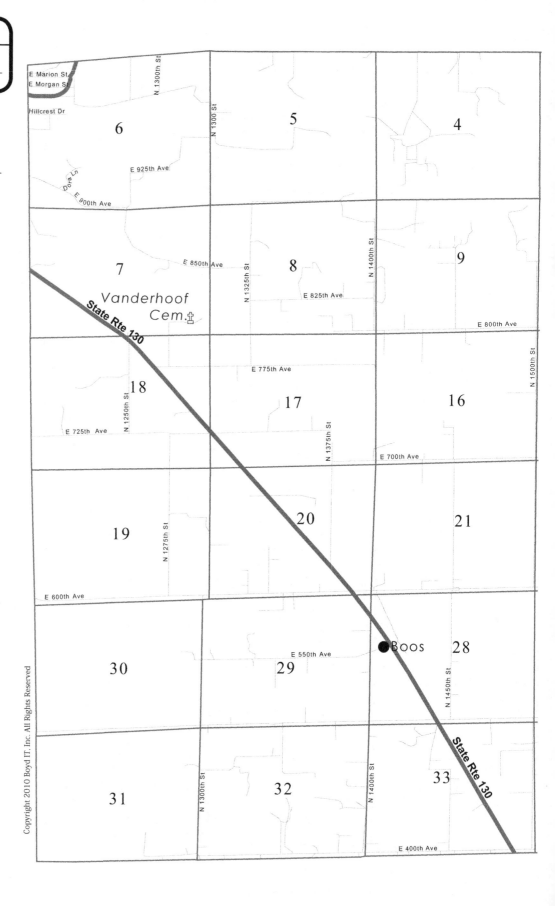

Shiloh Cem.

950 N

3

2

1

E 950th Ave

E 900th Ave

10

11

12

E 850th Ave

15

14

13

E 675th Ave

22

23

24

E 600th Ave

27

26

25

E 500th Ave

34

35

36

E 430th Ave

E 425th Ave

N 1700th St
N 1750th St
N 1800th St
N 1725th St
N 1775th St
N 1600th St
N 1700th St

Helpful Hints

1. This road map has a number of uses, but primarily it is to help you: a) find the present location of land owned by your ancestors (at least the general area), b) find cemeteries and city-centers, and c) estimate the route/roads used by Census-takers & tax-assessors.

2. If you plan to travel to Jasper County to locate cemeteries or land parcels, please pick up a modern travel map for the area before you do. Mapping old land parcels on modern maps is not as exact a science as you might think. Just the slightest variations in public land survey coordinates, estimates of parcel boundaries, or road-map deviations can greatly alter a map's representation of how a road either does or doesn't cross a particular parcel of land.

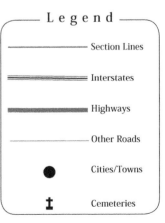

Legend

——— Section Lines

══════ Interstates

━━━━ Highways

——— Other Roads

● Cities/Towns

✝ Cemeteries

Scale: Section = 1 mile X 1 mile
(generally, with some exceptions)

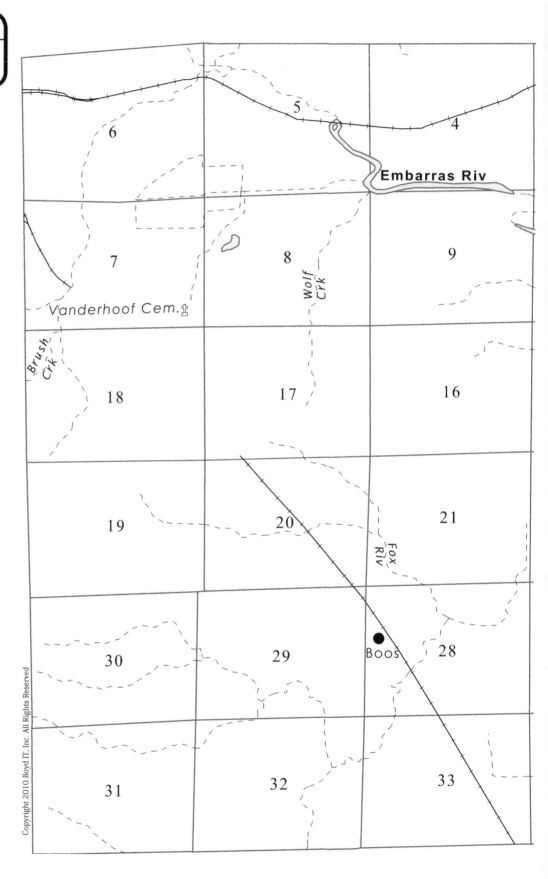

Historical Map

T6-N R10-E
3rd PM Meridian

Map Group 13

Cities & Towns
Boos

Cemeteries
Shiloh Cemetery
Vanderhoof Cemetery

6

5

4

Embarras Riv

7

8

9

Wolf Crk

Vanderhoof Cem.

Brush Crk

18

17

16

19

20

21

Fox Riv

30

29

Boos

28

31

32

33

Copyright 2010 Boyd IT, Inc. All Rights Reserved

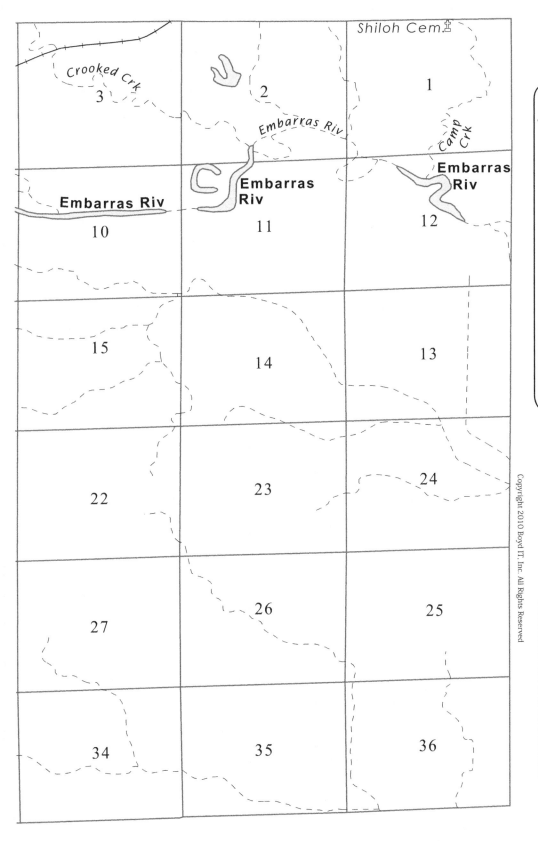

Shiloh Cem.✝

Crooked Crk

3

2

1

Embarras Riv

Camp Crk

Embarras Riv

Embarras Riv

10

Embarras Riv

11

Embarras Riv

12

15

14

13

22

23

24

27

26

25

34

35

36

Helpful Hints

1. This Map takes a different look at the same Congressional Township displayed in the preceding two maps. It presents features that can help you better envision the historical development of the area: a) Water-bodies (lakes & ponds), b) Water-courses (rivers, streams, etc.), c) Railroads, d) City/ town center-points (where they were oftentimes located when first settled), and e) Cemeteries.

2. Using this "Historical" map in tandem with this Township's Patent Map and Road Map, may lead you to some interesting discoveries. You will often find roads, towns, cemeteries, and waterways are named after nearby landowners: sometimes those names will be the ones you are researching. See how many of these research gems you can find here in Jasper County.

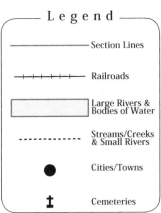

Legend ─────

─────── Section Lines

┼┼┼┼┼┼┼ Railroads

▭ Large Rivers & Bodies of Water

----------- Streams/Creeks & Small Rivers

● Cities/Towns

✝ Cemeteries

Scale: Section = 1 mile X 1 mile
(there are some exceptions)

Map Group 14: Index to Land Patents

Township 6-North Range 11-East (3rd PM)

After you locate an individual in this Index, take note of the Section and Section Part then proceed to the Land Patent map on the pages immediately following. You should have no difficulty locating the corresponding parcel of land.

The "For More Info" Column will lead you to more information about the underlying Patents. See the *Legend* at right, and the "How to Use this Book" chapter, for more information.

```
                    LEGEND
        "For More Info . . . " column
G = Group  (Multi-Patentee Patent, see Appendix "C")
R = Residence
S = Social Status

See Appendix A for list of abbreviations used by the
Illinois State Archives in describing the place and
nature of these land patents.

Note: if the Abbreviations contain "L", "BL", "LOT",
or "BLOCK", the exact whereabouts of the parcel within
the section is not known.
```

ID	Individual in Patent	Sec.	Sec. Part	Purchase Date	Sale Type	IL Aliquot Part	For More Info . . .
3953	ALLISON, Isaac	6	SESE	1840-06-15	FD	SESE	R:JASPER
3954	BAILEY, Jacob	6	NWSW	1848-03-08	FD	NWSW	R:JASPER
3948	DOTY, Daniel	6	S½NW	1849-01-27	FD	S2NW	R:JASPER
3958	DOTY, John	6	NENW	1849-12-15	FD	NENW	R:JASPER
3947	GOEPPNER, Charles	19	L3	1854-04-15	SC	LOT3N2S2N2SE	
3945	HARLEN, Aaron	6	NESW	1852-02-20	FD	NESW	R:JASPER
3946	HIGGINS, Adam	6	SWSE	1854-11-01	FD	SWSE	R:CRAWFORD
3951	HUFFMAN, Henry	19	L2	1854-04-15	SC	LOT2S2N2N2SE	G:38
3950	" "	19	L10	1854-04-15	SC	L10W2E2S2SE	G:38
3950	" "	19	L10	1854-04-15	SC	L11E2E2S2SE	G:38
3949	" "	19	L1	1854-04-15	SC	LOT1N2N2N2SE	G:38
3952	" "	19	L4	1854-04-15	SC	LOT4S2S2N2SE	G:38
3976	IRELAND, Richard G	7	SENE	1850-09-03	FD	SENE	R:JASPER
3977	LEFLER, Solomon	6	S½SW	1849-01-27	FD	S2SW	R:JASPER
3978	MIRES, William G	6	N½SE	1849-12-03	FD	N2SE	R:INDIANA
3962	PICQUET, Joseph	19	NE	1837-10-07	FD	NE	R:JASPER
3961	" "	18		1837-10-07	FD	SEC	R:JASPER
3970	" "	7	SE	1837-10-07	FD	SE	R:JASPER
3971	" "	7	SW	1837-10-07	FD	SW	R:JASPER
3963	" "	19	W½	1837-10-07	FD	W2	R:JASPER
3969	" "	7	NW	1837-10-07	FD	NW	R:JASPER
3968	" "	31		1837-10-07	FD	SEC	R:JASPER
3966	" "	30	S½	1837-10-07	FD	S2	R:JASPER
3964	" "	30	NENE	1837-10-07	FD	NENE	R:JASPER
3967	" "	30	SENE	1837-10-13	FD	SENE	R:JASPER
3965	" "	30	NW	1837-11-16	FD	NW	R:JASPER
3951	PICQUET, Xavia	19	L2	1854-04-15	SC	LOT2S2N2N2SE	G:38
3949	" "	19	L1	1854-04-15	SC	LOT1N2N2N2SE	G:38
3950	" "	19	L10	1854-04-15	SC	L11E2E2S2SE	G:38
3950	" "	19	L10	1854-04-15	SC	L10W2E2S2SE	G:38
3952	" "	19	L4	1854-04-15	SC	LOT4S2S2N2SE	G:38
3974	PIQUET, Joseph	19	L8	1854-04-15	SC	L8E2E2W2S2SE	
3972	" "	19	L5	1854-04-15	SC	L5W2W2W2S2SE	
3973	" "	19	L7	1854-04-15	SC	L7W2W2W2S2SE	
3979	PRICE, William	30	W½NE	1831-05-28	FD	W2NE	R:CRAWFORD
3955	RIDLEN, James B	6	NWNW	1849-04-18	FD	NWNW	R:INDIANA
3956	" "	7	SWNE	1849-09-27	FD	SWNE	R:INDIANA
3975	SCHIFFERSTEIN, Joseph	19	L6	1854-04-15	SC	L6E2W2W2S2SE	
3959	SHIRLEY, John	19	L9	1866-06-04	SC	L9W2W2SESE	
3960	SWOPE, John	6	NE	1849-05-28	FD	NE	
3957	TROBAUGH, James	19	L12	1854-04-15	SC	L12E2E2S2SE	

Map (Section Grid)

Section 6

RIDLEN James B 1849	DOTY John 1849	SWOPE John 1849
DOTY Daniel 1849		**6**
BAILEY Jacob 1848	HARLEN Aaron 1852	MIRES William G 1849
LEFLER Solomon 1849	HIGGINS Adam 1854	ALLISON Isaac 1840

Section 7

PICQUET Joseph 1837		
RIDLEN James B 1849	IRELAND Richard G 1850	**7**
PICQUET Joseph 1837	PICQUET Joseph 1837	

Section 18

18

PICQUET Joseph 1837

Section 19

PICQUET Joseph 1837	PICQUET Joseph 1837
19	

Lots-Sec. 19
L1 HUFFMAN, Henry [38] 1854
L2 HUFFMAN, Henry [38] 1854
L3 GOEPPNER, Charles 1854
L4 HUFFMAN, Henry [38] 1854
L5 PIQUET, Joseph 1854
L6 SCHIFFERSTEIN, Joseph 1854
L7 PIQUET, Joseph 1854
L8 PIQUET, Joseph 1854
L9 SHIRLEY, John 1866
L10 HUFFMAN, Henry [38] 1854
L12 TROBAUGH, James 1854

Section 30

PICQUET Joseph 1837	PRICE William 1831	PICQUET Joseph 1837
		PICQUET Joseph 1837

30

PICQUET Joseph 1837

Section 31

31

PICQUET Joseph 1837

Copyright 2010 Boyd IT, Inc. All Rights Reserved

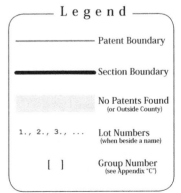

Patent Map

T6-N R11-E
3rd PM Meridian

Map Group 14

Township Statistics

Parcels Mapped	:	35
Number of Patents	:	1
Number of Individuals	:	20
Patentees Identified	:	19
Number of Surnames	:	18
Multi-Patentee Parcels	:	4
Oldest Patent Date	:	5/28/1831
Most Recent Patent	:	6/4/1866
Block/Lot Parcels	:	13
Cities and Towns	:	1
Cemeteries	:	2

Note: the area contained in this map amounts to far less than a full Township. Therefore, its contents are completely on this single page (instead of a "normal" 2-page spread).

Legend

—————— Patent Boundary

━━━━━━ Section Boundary

▨ No Patents Found (or Outside County)

1., 2., 3., ... Lot Numbers (when beside a name)

[ ] Group Number (see Appendix "C")

Scale: Section = 1 mile X 1 mile (generally, with some exceptions)

Road Map

T6-N R11-E
3rd PM Meridian

Map Group 14

Note: the area contained in this map amounts to far less than a full Township. Therefore, its contents are completely on this single page (instead of a "normal" 2-page spread).

Cities & Towns
Sainte Marie

Cemeteries
Assumption Cemetery
Sainte Marie City Cemetery

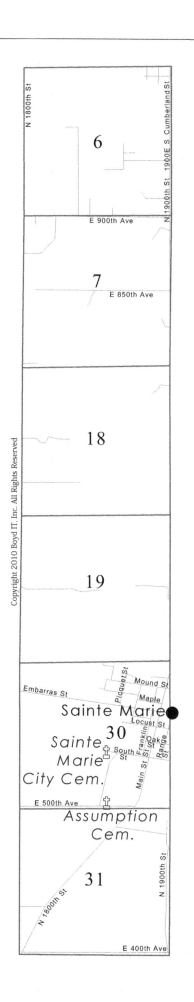

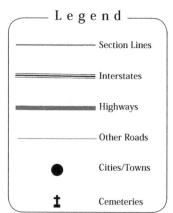

Legend

— Section Lines

═ Interstates

━ Highways

— Other Roads

● Cities/Towns

✝ Cemeteries

Scale: Section = 1 mile X 1 mile
(generally, with some exceptions)

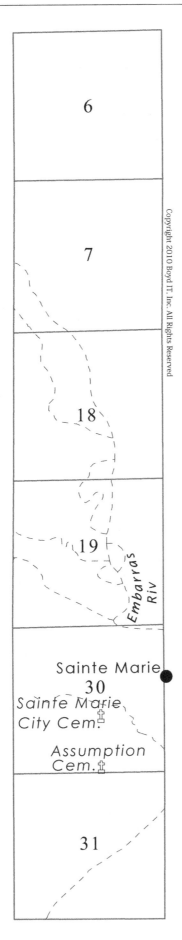

6

7

18

19

Embarras Riv

Sainte Marie
30
Sainte Marie
City Cem. ☩

Assumption
Cem. ☩

31

Historical Map

T6-N R11-E
3rd PM Meridian

Map Group 14

Note: the area contained in this map amounts to far less than a full Township. Therefore, its contents are completely on this single page (instead of a "normal" 2-page spread).

Cities & Towns
Sainte Marie

Cemeteries
Assumption Cemetery
Sainte Marie City Cemetery

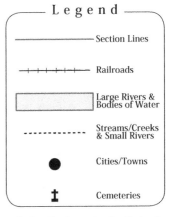

Scale: Section = 1 mile X 1 mile
(there are some exceptions)

Map Group 15: Index to Land Patents

Township 6-North Range 14-West (2nd PM)

After you locate an individual in this Index, take note of the Section and Section Part then proceed to the Land Patent map on the pages immediately following. You should have no difficulty locating the corresponding parcel of land.

The "For More Info" Column will lead you to more information about the underlying Patents. See the *Legend* at right, and the "How to Use this Book" chapter, for more information.

ID	Individual in Patent	Sec.	Sec. Part	Purchase Date	Sale Type	IL Aliquot Part	For More Info . . .
4068	ALLISON, Isaac	6	SESW	1838-03-29	FD	SESW	R:JASPER
4069	ALLISON, Isaac S	19	NWNW	1851-06-09	FD	NWNW	R:JASPER
4082	ALLISON, James	7	NWNE	1840-04-10	FD	NWNE	R:JASPER
4081	" "	6	E½SE	1849-12-05	FD	E2SE	R:JASPER
4080	" "	20	SENW	1849-12-05	FD	SENW	R:JASPER
4114	ALLISON, John	7	SENW	1851-10-21	FD	SENW	R:JASPER
4113	" "	17	SESW	1853-01-24	FD	SESW	R:JASPER
4205	ALLISON, Spear	6	SWSW	1840-06-22	FD	SWSW	R:JASPER
4206	ALLISON, Spear S	5	SESE	1852-09-14	FD	SESE	
4005	BACHMAN, Benjamin	9	E½SE	1839-08-29	FD	E2SE	R:JASPER
4213	BARRATT, Thomas	18	NE	1843-07-07	FD	NE	R:PENNSYLVANIA
4212	" "	17	NW	1843-07-07	FD	NW	R:PENNSYLVANIA
4181	BARRET, Michael	18	SESE	1844-06-06	FD	SESE	R:JASPER
4180	BLAKE, Marion	33	SWSW	1852-06-22	FD	SWSW	S:F
4074	BLASDEL, Jacob W	29	E½SE	1854-10-02	FD	E2SE	R:INDIANA
4075	" "	29	E½SW	1854-10-02	FD	E2SW	R:INDIANA
4076	" "	29	SWSE	1854-10-02	FD	SWSE	R:INDIANA
4077	" "	29	SWSW	1854-10-02	FD	SWSW	R:INDIANA
4078	" "	9	E½NW	1854-10-02	FD	E2NW	R:INDIANA
4006	BOGARD, Benjamin	34	SWNE	1853-11-22	FD	SWNE	R:CRAWFORD
4111	BOGARD, Jerushia	34	N½SE	1852-10-06	FD	N2SE	
4053	BOHAMAN, Greenup	19	NENW	1848-12-14	FD	NENW	
4047	" "	7	E½NE	1848-12-14	FD	E2NE	
4041	" "	18	E½SW	1848-12-14	FD	E2SW	
4042	" "	18	NWSW	1848-12-14	FD	NWSW	
4048	" "	8	W½NW	1848-12-14	FD	W2NW	
4052	" "	18	NWSW	1848-12-14	FD	NWSW	
4043	" "	19	NENW	1848-12-14	FD	NENW	
4044	" "	5	NESW	1848-12-18	FD	NESW	
4056	" "	5	SENW	1848-12-18	FD	SENW	
4045	" "	5	SENW	1848-12-18	FD	SENW	
4057	" "	5	W½NW	1848-12-18	FD	W2NW	
4054	" "	5	NESW	1848-12-18	FD	NESW	
4046	" "	5	W½NW	1848-12-18	FD	W2NW	
4043	BOHANNAN, Greenup	19	NENW	1849-01-31	FD	NENW	R:INDIANA
4044	" "	5	NESW	1849-01-31	FD	NESW	R:INDIANA
4042	" "	18	NWSW	1849-01-31	FD	NWSW	R:INDIANA
4046	" "	5	W½NW	1849-01-31	FD	W2NW	R:INDIANA
4051	" "	18		1849-01-31	FD	PTE2SW	R:INDIANA
4052	" "	18	NWSW	1849-01-31	FD	NWSW	R:INDIANA
4053	" "	19	NENW	1849-01-31	FD	NENW	R:INDIANA
4045	" "	5	SENW	1849-01-31	FD	SENW	R:INDIANA
4054	" "	5	NESW	1849-01-31	FD	NESW	R:INDIANA
4056	" "	5	SENW	1849-01-31	FD	SENW	R:INDIANA
4057	" "	5	W½NW	1849-01-31	FD	W2NW	R:INDIANA
4130	" "	18		1849-01-31	FD	PTE2SW	R:INDIANA

ID	Individual in Patent	Sec.	Sec. Part	Purchase Date	Sale Type	IL Aliquot Part	For More Info . . .
4055	BOHANNAN, Greenup (Cont'd)	5	NWSW	1852-09-01	FD	NWSW	
4050	" "	17	SWNE	1852-10-13	FD	SWNE	
4049	" "	16	L5	1854-06-03	SC	L5SWNW	
4176	BOLANDER, Lewis	19	SENW	1852-10-28	FD	SENW	R:JASPER
4062	CAMPBELL, Henry A	10	NENE	1852-12-17	FD	NENE	
4115	CARSON, John	19	SWNW	1852-06-29	FD	SWNW	R:JASPER
4230	CARTER, William	6	E½SW	1839-11-08	FD	E2SW	R:JASPER
4182	CASEY, Patrick	20	NWSW	1852-12-30	FD	NWSW	
4227	" "	20	NWSW	1852-12-30	FD	NWSW	
4231	DAVIS, William	32	NENE	1840-06-15	FD	NENE	R:JASPER
4087	DIXON, James	9	W½SE	1852-02-28	FD	W2SE	R:JASPER
4017	DOTY, Daniel	6	SENW	1839-11-06	FD	SENW	R:JASPER
3989	EATON, Absalom	7	W½SE	1831-06-07	FD	W2SE	R:CRAWFORD
3988	" "	7	SWNE	1837-10-10	FD	SWNE	R:JASPER
3985	" "	20	NWNW	1848-12-12	FD	NWNW	R:JASPER
3990	" "	8	W½SW	1848-12-12	FD	W2SW	
3987	" "	7	E½SE	1848-12-12	FD	E2SE	
3986	" "	6	SWSE	1848-12-14	FD	SWSE	R:JASPER
3991	EATON, Absolom	4	SWSE	1851-09-10	FD	SWSE	R:JASPER
3992	EATON, Absolum	16	L13	1854-06-03	SC	L13SWSW	
4007	EATON, Benjamin	6	NENW	1837-11-17	FD	NENW	R:JASPER
4008	" "	6	SENE	1837-11-17	FD	SENE	R:JASPER
4038	EUBANK, George	8	E½SE	1849-10-24	FD	E2SE	
4039	" "	9	W½SW	1849-10-24	FD	W2SW	
4037	" "	15	SWSW	1849-10-24	FD	SWSW	R:INDIANA
4089	FEESER, James	17	SWSE	1848-12-14	FD	SWSE	
4090	" "	20	NWNE	1848-12-14	FD	NWNE	
4088	" "	17	E½SE	1848-12-14	FD	E2SE	
4066	FORE, Hezekiah	18	SWSW	1848-04-17	FD	SWSW	R:JASPER
4000	FOWLER, Andrew W	33	SESE	1853-12-23	FD	SESE	R:CRAWFORD
4125	" "	33	SWSE	1854-01-09	FD	SWSE	R:CRAWFORD
4001	" "	33	SWSE	1854-01-09	FD	SWSE	R:CRAWFORD
4095	FOWLER, James M	34	SWNW	1853-12-23	FD	SWNW	R:CRAWFORD
4032	FULLER, Francis	31	NWSW	1852-10-13	FD	NWSW	R:JASPER
4178	GAULLOFF, Louis	19	SWSE	1852-11-11	FD	SWSE	R:JASPER
4021	GAYER, David A	10	W½NW	1850-02-01	FD	W2NW	
4022	" "	4	SESE	1850-02-01	FD	SESE	
4023	" "	9	NENE	1850-02-01	FD	NENE	
4109	GRIFFY, Jane C	9	NENW	1854-03-20	FD	NENW	R:INDIANA S:F
4120	GRUB, John	16	L4	1854-06-03	SC	L4NWNW	
4121	GRUBB, John	21	W½SW	1853-11-21	FD	W2SW	
4179	GUGUMUS, Louis	19	NWSE	1853-01-11	FD	NWSE	
4013	GUTHNICK, Charles	31	SWSW	1852-10-05	FD	SWSW	R:JASPER
4031	HALE, Ezekiel	10	SENW	1853-06-07	FD	SENW	R:IOWA
4214	HALSTED, Thomas	9	NWNW	1843-04-14	FD	NWNW	R:JASPER
3993	HAMIL, Amanda	34	W½SW	1853-12-17	FD	W2SW	S:F G:34
3993	HAMIL, John	34	W½SW	1853-12-17	FD	W2SW	S:F G:34
4216	HAMILTON, Thomas	5	NENW	1849-09-27	FD	NENW	R:INDIANA
4217	" "	9	SENW	1849-10-24	FD	SENW	R:INDIANA
4215	" "	5		1849-10-31	FD	NENWWA	R:INDIANA
4132	" "	5		1849-10-31	FD	NENWWA	R:INDIANA
4029	HARGIS, Elizabeth	3	NWSE	1853-01-26	FD	NWSE	R:JASPER S:F
4183	HARTMAN, Peter	27	E½NE	1853-09-29	FD	E2NE	
4211	HARTRICK, Theodore	30	NESE	1850-04-09	FD	NESE	R:JASPER
4012	HIGGINS, Cenith J	28	NWNW	1852-09-18	FD	NWNW	
4034	HOFMAN, Francis	28	SESE	1853-05-23	FD	SESE	R:JASPER
4033	" "	27	SWSW	1853-11-23	FD	SWSW	R:JASPER
4071	HUTSON, Jacob	22	E½SE	1853-09-07	FD	E2SE	
4086	IRELAND, James C	17	N½NE	1852-09-29	FD	N2NE	
4188	IRELAND, Richard G	8	SENW	1852-04-10	FD	SENW	R:JASPER
4187	" "	5	SWSW	1852-08-31	FD	SWSW	
4186	" "	20	NENE	1853-02-12	FD	NENE	
4067	JAMES, Horatio	15	NW	1839-09-04	FD	NW	R:OHIO
4189	JAMES, Richard	10	SENE	1852-01-05	FD	SENE	R:CRAWFORD
4237	JAMES, William	10	SW	1839-09-04	FD	SW	R:INDIANA
4238	" "	10	W½SE	1842-03-25	FD	W2SE	R:JASPER
4239	JOHNSON, William	16	L8	1858-11-16	SC	LOT08SENE	
4261	JOHNSTON, Wilson	34	SESW	1852-05-03	FD	SESW	R:CRAWFORD
4030	JONES, Erasmus	33	E½NW	1851-10-23	FD	E2NW	R:CRAWFORD
4124	KARR, John	9	SESW	1853-08-19	FD	SESW	R:INDIANA
4123	" "	18	NESE	1853-08-19	FD	NESE	R:INDIANA
4148	KENNEDY, Joseph	9	NWNE	1833-08-09	FD	NWNE	R:CRAWFORD
4061	KNIGHT, Hartwell	4	SWSW	1852-02-09	FD	SWSW	

ID	Individual in Patent	Sec.	Sec. Part	Purchase Date	Sale Type	IL Aliquot Part	For More Info . . .
4224	KRAUS, Valentine	33	NWNW	1841-04-26	FD	NWNW	R:JASPER
4225	" "	33	SWNW	1851-03-24	FD	SWNW	R:JASPER
4125	KROUS, John	33	SWSE	1853-10-20	FD	SWSE	R:JASPER
4001	" "	33	SWSE	1853-10-20	FD	SWSE	R:JASPER
4226	KROUSE, Valentine	32	SENE	1842-08-15	FD	SENE	R:JASPER
4020	LANCE, Daniel	3	W½SW	1850-02-01	FD	W2SW	R:INDIANA
4019	" "	3	S½NW	1850-02-01	FD	S2NW	R:INDIANA
4018	" "	3		1850-03-31	FD	PTW2SWWA	R:INDIANA
4236	LEE, William J	3	SESW	1853-09-14	FD	SESW	R:INDIANA
4207	LEGGITT, Stephens	16	L10	1905-02-18	SC	LOT10NWSE	
4182	LEINHART, Valentine	20	NWSW	1847-12-27	FD	NWSW	R:JASPER
4227	" "	20	NWSW	1847-12-27	FD	NWSW	R:JASPER
4228	" "	28	NESW	1849-05-28	FD	NESW	R:JASPER
4229	" "	31	SESW	1851-12-19	FD	SESW	R:JASPER
4198	LIGHTNER, Salathiel	29	NWSE	1852-01-22	FD	NWSE	R:JASPER
4199	"	29	NWSW	1852-04-09	FD	NWSW	R:JASPER
3984	LINDLEY, Abram S	7	NENW	1840-03-09	FD	NENW	R:CRAWFORD
4149	LITZELMANN, Joseph	30	NENE	1853-11-24	FD	NENE	R:JASPER
4150	LITZERMAN, Joseph	20	SWSW	1854-02-24	FD	SWSW	R:JASPER
4072	LORANCE, Jacob	30	SENE	1848-04-14	FD	SENE	R:JASPER
4096	MAHAN, James	34	NWNW	1853-08-24	FD	NWNW	R:INDIANA
4097	MANDLOVE, James	9	SENE	1853-05-15	FD	SENE	
4098	MCCARTY, James	3	NWNW	1851-12-22	FD	NWNW	R:INDIANA
4099	" "	3	SESE	1852-09-06	FD	SESE	R:JASPER
4240	MCDANIEL, William	9	NESW	1848-11-23	FD	NESW	R:JASPER
4064	MEESE, Henry	10	NWNE	1852-05-13	FD	NWNE	R:CRAWFORD
4190	MEESE, Robert	3	NESW	1854-01-11	FD	NESW	R:JASPER
4035	MERCERET, Francis	19	SESW	1853-01-05	FD	SESW	R:JASPER
4036	" "	30	W½NE	1853-01-05	FD	W2NE	R:JASPER
4011	MICKENBERGER, Morris	29	NE	1854-07-15	FD	NE	R:INDIANA G:48
4232	MIDKIFF, William E	33	SESW	1852-09-23	FD	SESW	
4112	MILLER, John	4	NESE	1852-11-17	FD	NESE	
4126	" "	4	NESE	1852-11-17	FD	NESE	
4204	MILLER, Samuel	4	NWSE	1837-10-10	FD	NWSE	R:JASPER
4202	" "	20	NENW	1848-12-14	FD	NENW	R:JASPER
4203	" "	4	E½SW	1849-10-27	FD	E2SW	R:JASPER
4220	MILLER, Thomas	3	SWSE	1850-02-01	FD	SWSE	R:JASPER
4219	" "	16	SWNE	1860-08-04	SC	SWNE	
4241	MILLER, William	17	SENE	1848-12-12	FD	SENE	R:JASPER
4243	" "	8	SESW	1849-10-29	FD	SESW	R:JASPER
4242	" "	18	NWSE	1849-11-05	FD	NWSE	R:JASPER
4233	MIRES, William E	6		1850-01-31	FD	N2SWWA	R:INDIANA
4234	MIRES, William G	6	N½SW	1849-12-03	FD	N2SW	R:INDIANA
4221	NEAL, Thomas	9	SWNW	1851-10-03	FD	SWNW	R:JASPER
4244	NEAL, William	16	L11	1860-08-04	SC	LOT11NESW	
4255	NEWBOULD, William R	22	W½SW	1854-02-06	FD	W2SW	R:INDIANA
4257	" "	28	SENE	1854-02-06	FD	SENE	R:INDIANA
4254	" "	22	W½SE	1854-02-06	FD	W2SE	R:INDIANA
4253	" "	22	SESW	1854-02-06	FD	SESW	R:INDIANA
4256	" "	28	NESE	1854-10-04	FD	NESE	R:INDIANA
4156	NICHOLAS, Joseph	34	NENW	1853-12-09	FD	NENW	R:INDIANA
4151	" "	27	E½SW	1853-12-09	FD	E2SW	R:INDIANA
4154	" "	27	SWNE	1853-12-09	FD	SWNE	R:INDIANA
4152	" "	27	NWSW	1853-12-09	FD	NWSW	R:INDIANA
4153	" "	27	SESE	1853-12-09	FD	SESE	R:INDIANA
4157	" "	34	NWNE	1853-12-09	FD	NWNE	R:INDIANA
4155	" "	27	W½SE	1853-12-09	FD	W2SE	R:INDIANA
4028	NICHOLS, Elijah	27	NESE	1850-10-14	FD	NESE	R:JASPER
4158	NICHOLS, Joseph	34	SWSE	1853-12-09	FD	SWSE	
4177	OST, Lewis	32	NESE	1853-12-13	FD	NESE	R:JASPER
4245	OWEN, William	29	NWNW	1852-01-22	FD	NWNW	R:JASPER
4100	PARKER, James	19	W½NE	1854-09-08	FD	W2NE	R:INDIANA
4246	PEYTON, William	4	E½NE	1850-03-23	FD	E2NE	R:INDIANA
3996	PHELPS, Amos	8	E½NE	1832-04-24	FD	E2NE	R:CRAWFORD
4101	PICQUET, James	30	SESE	1852-05-04	FD	SESE	R:JASPER
4167	PICQUET, Joseph	7	SW	1837-10-07	FD	SW	R:JASPER
4162	" "	31	E½NW	1837-10-07	FD	E2NW	R:JASPER
4161	" "	31	E½	1837-10-07	FD	E2	R:JASPER
4160	" "	30	W½	1837-10-07	FD	W2	R:JASPER
4159	" "	19	W½SW	1837-10-07	FD	W2SW	R:JASPER
4164	" "	32	W½	1837-10-07	FD	W2	R:JASPER
4165	" "	32	W½NE	1837-10-07	FD	W2NE	R:JASPER
4166	" "	32	W½SE	1837-10-07	FD	W2SE	R:JASPER

ID	Individual in Patent	Sec.	Sec. Part	Purchase Date	Sale Type	IL Aliquot Part	For More Info . . .
4163	PICQUET, Joseph (Cont'd)	31	W½NW	1840-04-04	FD	W2NW	R:JASPER
4103	PIECUIT, James	20	SWNE	1848-12-26	FD	SWNE	R:JASPER
4102	" "	20	NWSE	1848-12-26	FD	NWSE	R:JASPER
4104	PIEQUET, James	18	SWSE	1849-04-21	FD	SWSE	R:JASPER
4106	" "	29	SWNW	1850-08-20	FD	SWNW	R:JASPER
4105	" "	20	NESW	1850-08-26	FD	NESW	R:JASPER
4108	PIEQUET, James Sen	19	NENE	1849-11-20	FD	NENE	R:JASPER
3999	PING, Anderson S	3	SENE	1851-01-21	FD	SENE	R:JASPER
3998	" "	3	NWNE	1852-12-14	FD	NWNE	R:JASPER
3997	" "	3	NWNE	1852-12-14	FD	NWNE	R:JASPER
3998	" "	3	NWNE	1852-12-31	FD	NWNE	R:JASPER
3997	" "	3	NWNE	1852-12-31	FD	NWNE	R:JASPER
4004	PING, Asa	4	W½NE	1849-06-21	FD	W2NE	R:INDIANA
4003	" "	3	NENE	1851-01-21	FD	NENE	R:JASPER
4127	PING, John	10	SWNE	1849-12-08	FD	SWNE	R:JASPER
4191	PING, Robert	21	W½NE	1849-08-16	FD	W2NE	R:INDIANA
4193	" "	5	SENE	1849-09-24	FD	SENE	R:INDIANA
4192	" "	3	SWNE	1853-01-26	FD	SWNE	R:JASPER
4223	PING, Thomas	4	NWSW	1852-02-19	FD	NWSW	R:JASPER
4222	" "	3	NESE	1852-09-13	FD	NESE	R:JASPER
4247	PING, William	4	E½NW	1849-06-21	FD	E2NW	R:INDIANA
4248	" "	4	NWNW	1849-06-21	FD	NWNW	R:INDIANA
4249	" "	4	SWNW	1849-08-16	FD	SWNW	R:INDIANA
4251	" "	5	NWNE	1849-08-16	FD	NWNE	R:INDIANA
4250	" "	5	NENE	1849-12-08	FD	NENE	R:JASPER
4252	" "	9	SWNE	1852-02-19	FD	SWNE	R:JASPER
4107	PIQUET, James	30	W½SE	1848-02-12	FD	W2SE	R:JASPER
4014	PRESTON, Cyprian	8	NESW	1851-10-16	FD	NESW	
4016	" "	8	W½SE	1851-10-16	FD	W2SE	
4015	" "	8	SWNE	1851-10-16	FD	SWNE	
4218	PRICE, Thomas J	22	E½NE	1854-01-23	FD	E2NE	
4073	RAEF, Jacob	32	SESE	1853-12-07	FD	SESE	R:JASPER
4128	REPETTO, John	33	NWSW	1853-03-11	FD	NWSW	R:JASPER
3983	RIDLEN, Abraham	7	W½NW	1851-11-14	FD	W2NW	R:INDIANA
3982	" "	7	N½NE	1851-11-14	FD	N2NE	R:INDIANA
3980	" "	19	NESW	1852-12-08	FD	NESW	R:JASPER
3981	" "	19	NESW	1852-12-08	FD	NESW	R:JASPER
3981	" "	19	NESW	1852-12-31	FD	NESW	R:JASPER
3980	" "	19	NESW	1852-12-31	FD	NESW	R:JASPER
4083	RIDLON, James B	6	NENE	1848-10-20	FD	NENE	
4084	" "	6	NWSE	1848-10-20	FD	NWSE	
4085	" "	6	W½NE	1848-10-20	FD	W2NE	
4110	ROGERS, Jeremiah	27	NWNE	1853-12-28	FD	NWNE	R:INDIANA
4147	ROGERS, Jonah M	34	E½NE	1853-10-20	FD	E2NE	
4040	RUDDELL, George	27	NW	1853-11-25	FD	NW	
4195	RUTHERFORD, Robert	8	NWNE	1851-10-08	FD	NWNE	
4194	" "	8	NENW	1851-10-08	FD	NENW	
4235	RYAN, William G	3	NENW	1837-11-17	FD	NENW	R:JASPER
4173	SCHIFFERSTEIN, Joseph	16	L3	1854-06-03	SC	L3NENW	
4172	" "	16	L2	1854-06-03	SC	L2NWNE	
4168	" "	16	L1	1854-06-03	SC	L1NENE	
4169	" "	16	L12	1854-06-03	SC	L12NWSW	
4170	" "	16	L15	1854-06-03	SC	L15SWSE	
4175	" "	16	L9	1854-06-03	SC	L9NESE	
4171	" "	16	L16	1854-06-03	SC	L16SESE	
4174	" "	16	L6	1854-06-03	SC	L6SENW	
4208	SCHUFFENSTUN, Theodor	17	NESW	1849-10-11	FD	NESW	
4209	" "	17	NWSE	1849-10-11	FD	NWSE	
4210	" "	17	W½SW	1849-10-11	FD	W2SW	
4002	SCHWAGER, Anthony	31	NESW	1851-12-09	FD	NESW	R:JASPER
4009	SHAFER, Benjamin	5	NESE	1852-11-04	FD	NESE	
4024	SMITH, David	10	NENW	1853-09-07	FD	NENW	R:INDIANA
4094	STEEL, James H	22	NENW	1854-01-09	FD	NENW	R:CRAWFORD
4093	" "	15	W½SE	1854-01-09	FD	W2SE	R:CRAWFORD
4092	" "	15	SESW	1854-01-09	FD	SESW	R:CRAWFORD
4091	" "	15	E½SE	1854-01-09	FD	E2SE	R:CRAWFORD
4129	STEWARD, John	22	W½NE	1853-11-21	FD	W2NE	
4011	STUBNER, Carl	29	NE	1854-07-15	FD	NE	R:INDIANA G:48
3994	SUTTON, Amariah	33	E½SE	1853-09-21	FD	E2NE	R:INDIANA
3995	" "	33	N½SE	1853-09-21	FD	N2SE	R:INDIANA
4136	SWOPE, John	5	SWNE	1849-05-28	FD	SWNEVOID	
4137	" "	5	W½SE	1849-05-28	FD	W2SEVOID	
4135	" "	5	SWNE	1849-05-28	FD	SWNEVOID	

ID	Individual in Patent	Sec.	Sec. Part	Purchase Date	Sale Type	IL Aliquot Part	For More Info . . .
4134	SWOPE, John (Cont'd)	5	SESW	1849-05-28	FD	SESWVOID	
4133	" "	5	SESW	1849-05-28	FD	SESWVOID	
4138	" "	5	W½SE	1849-05-28	FD	W2SEVOID	
4131	" "	18	NW	1849-05-28	FD	NW	R:INDIANA
4215	" "	5		1849-06-30	FD	NESWWA	R:INDIANA
4051	" "	18		1849-06-30	FD	NWLWWA	R:INDIANA
4132	" "	5		1849-06-30	FD	NESWWA	R:INDIANA
4215	" "	5		1849-06-30	FD	W2SEWA	R:INDIANA
4130	" "	18		1849-06-30	FD	NWLWWA	R:INDIANA
4215	" "	5		1849-06-30	FD	SWNEWA	R:INDIANA
4132	" "	5		1849-06-30	FD	SWNEWA	R:INDIANA
4132	" "	5		1849-06-30	FD	W2SEWA	R:INDIANA
4134	" "	5	SESW	1851-12-08	FD	SESW	R:CLARK
4135	" "	5	SWNE	1851-12-08	FD	SWNE	R:CLARK
4137	" "	5	W½SE	1851-12-08	FD	W2SE	R:CLARK
4133	" "	5	SESW	1851-12-08	FD	SESW	R:CLARK
4138	" "	5	W½SE	1851-12-08	FD	W2SE	R:CLARK
4136	" "	5	SWNE	1851-12-08	FD	SWNE	R:CLARK
4122	TEDFORD, John H	10	E½SE	1853-12-17	FD	E2SE	
4142	TERREL, John	20	SWSE	1854-09-30	FD	SWSE	R:CRAWFORD
4139	" "	20	E½SE	1854-09-30	FD	E2SE	R:CRAWFORD
4140	" "	20	SENE	1854-09-30	FD	SENE	R:CRAWFORD
4141	" "	20	SESW	1854-10-05	FD	SESW	R:CRAWFORD
4196	TERREL, Robert	19	E½SE	1854-10-02	FD	E2SE	R:CRAWFORD
4197	" "	19	SENE	1854-10-05	FD	SENE	R:CRAWFORD
4143	THOMAS, John	21	E½NE	1849-10-24	FD	E2NE	
4144	" "	22	W½NW	1849-10-24	FD	W2NW	
4184	THOMAS, Reuben	20	SWNW	1849-10-24	FD	SWNW	R:INDIANA
4185	" "	21	NW	1849-10-24	FD	NW	
4010	TINGLEY, Benjamin	34	SESE	1851-10-23	FD	SESE	
4200	TODD, Samuel B	6	NWNW	1850-05-23	FD	NWNW	R:JASPER
4201	" "	6	SWNW	1851-09-09	FD	SWNW	R:JASPER
4145	VAN LUE, JOHN	21	SESW	1849-09-26	FD	SESW	R:INDIANA
4146	" "	21	SWSE	1849-09-26	FD	SWSE	R:INDIANA
4079	VANLIEU, James A	33	NESW	1853-08-23	FD	NESW	R:JASPER
4025	VANLUE, David	28	NENE	1849-09-26	FD	NENE	
4026	" "	28	NWSE	1849-09-26	FD	NWSE	
4027	" "	28	W½NE	1849-09-26	FD	W2NE	
4258	VANLUE, William	28	S½SW	1849-09-26	FD	S2SW	
4259	" "	28	SWSE	1849-09-26	FD	SWSE	
4260	" "	33	NWNE	1849-09-26	FD	NWNE	
4065	VANMETER, Henry	34	NESW	1852-03-30	FD	NESW	
4058	WADDLE, Harrison	21	E½SE	1849-09-26	FD	E2SE	
4059	" "	21	NESW	1849-09-26	FD	NESW	
4060	" "	21	NWSE	1849-09-26	FD	NWSE	
4070	WADDLE, Jackson	28	NW	1849-09-26	FD	NW	
4112	WILSON, Jesse G	4	NESE	1852-10-04	FD	NESE	R:INDIANA
4126	" "	4	NESE	1852-10-04	FD	NESE	R:INDIANA
4063	WRIGHT, Henry M	22	SENW	1851-03-24	FD	SENW	R:INDIANA
4117	WRIGHT, John F	15	NWSW	1846-10-17	FD	NWSW	R:CRAWFORD
4116	" "	15	NESW	1851-01-24	FD	NESW	R:CRAWFORD
4119	" "	34	SENW	1852-05-11	FD	SENW	
4118	" "	22	NESW	1852-12-16	FD	NESW	

Patent Map

T6-N R14-W
2nd PM Meridian

Map Group 15

Township Statistics

Parcels Mapped	:	282
Number of Patents	:	1
Number of Individuals	:	150
Patentees Identified	:	148
Number of Surnames	:	116
Multi-Patentee Parcels	:	2
Oldest Patent Date	:	6/7/1831
Most Recent Patent	:	2/18/1905
Block/Lot Parcels	:	14
Cities and Towns	:	0
Cemeteries	:	3

Copyright 2010 Boyd IT, Inc. All Rights Reserved

Section 6
TODD Samuel B 1850
EATON Benjamin 1837
RIDLON James B 1848
RIDLON James B 1848
BOHAMAN Greenup 1848
HAMILTON Thomas 1849 / HAMILTON Thomas 1849

TODD Samuel B 1851
DOTY Daniel 1839
EATON Benjamin 1837
BOHANNAN Greenup 1849

MIRES William G 1849
MIRES William E 1850
RIDLON James B 1848
BOHANNAN Greenup 1852
BOHAMAN Greenup 1848 / BOHANNAN John Greenup 1849

ALLISON Spear 1840
ALLISON Isaac CARTER William 1838/1839
EATON Absalom 1848
ALLISON James 1849
IRELAND Richard G 1852

Section 5
PING William 1849
PING William 1849
PING William 1849
SWOPE John 1851 / SWOPE John 1849
PING Robert 1849
PING William 1849
SHAFER Benjamin 1852
SWOPE John 1849
BOHANNAN Greenup 1848 / BOHANNAN Greenup 1849 / SWOPE John 1849
SWOPE John 1849
SWOPE John 1851
SWOPE John 1851 / SWOPE John 1849
SWOPE John 1851

Section 4
PING William 1849
PING Asa 1849
PEYTON William 1850
PING William 1849
MILLER Samuel 1837
MILLER John 1852 / WILSON Jesse G 1852
PING Thomas 1852
MILLER Samuel 1849
EATON Absalom 1851
GAYER David A 1850
ALLISON Spear S 1852
KNIGHT Hartwell 1852

Section 7
RIDLEN Abraham 1851
LINDLEY Abram S 1840
ALLISON James 1840
RIDLEN Abraham 1851
ALLISON John 1851
EATON Absalom 1837
BOHAMAN Greenup 1848
PICQUET Joseph 1837
EATON Absalom 1831
EATON Absalom 1848

Section 8
BOHAMAN Greenup 1848
RUTHERFORD Robert 1851
RUTHERFORD Robert 1851
PHELPS Amos 1832
IRELAND Richard G 1852
PRESTON Cyprian 1851
PRESTON Cyprian 1851
PRESTON Cyprian 1851
MILLER William 1849
EUBANK George 1849

Section 9
HALSTED Thomas 1843
GRIFFY Jane C 1854
KENNEDY Joseph 1833
GAYER David A 1850
NEAL Thomas 1851
BLASDEL Jacob W 1854
HAMILTON Thomas 1849
PING William 1852
MANDLOVE James 1853
MCDANIEL William 1848
DIXON James 1852
BACHMAN Benjamin 1839
EUBANK George 1849
KARR John 1853

Section 18
SWOPE John 1849
SWOPE John 1849
BARRATT Thomas 1843
BOHAMAN Greenup 1848 / BOHANNAN Greenup 1849
BOHAMAN Greenup 1848
MILLER William 1849
KARR John 1853
FORE Hezekiah 1848
BOHANNAN Greenup 1849
PIEQUET James 1849
BARRET Michael 1844

Section 17
BARRATT Thomas 1843
BOHANNAN Greenup 1852
MILLER William 1848
SCHUFFENSTUN Theodor 1849
SCHUFFENSTUN Theodor 1849
SCHUFFENSTUN Theodor 1849
ALLISON John 1853
FEESER James 1848
FEESER James 1848

Section 16
IRELAND James C 1852
IRELAND Richard G 1853

Lots-Sec. 16
L1 SCHIFFERSTEIN, Josep 1854
L2 SCHIFFERSTEIN, Josep 1854
L3 SCHIFFERSTEIN, Josep 1854
L4 GRUB, John 1854
L5 BOHANNAN, Greenup 1854
L6 SCHIFFERSTEIN, Josep 1854
L8 JOHNSON, William 1858
L9 SCHIFFERSTEIN, Josep 1854
L10 LEGGITT, Stephens 1905
L11 NEAL, William 1860
L12 SCHIFFERSTEIN, Josep 1854
L13 EATON, Absalom 1854
L14
L15 SCHIFFERSTEIN, Josep 1854
L16 SCHIFFERSTEIN, Josep 1854

MILLER Thomas 1860

Section 19
ALLISON Isaac S 1851
BOHAMAN Greenup 1848 / BOHANNAN Greenup 1849
PARKER James 1854
CARSON John 1852
BOLANDER Lewis 1852
RIDLEN Abraham 1852 / RIDLEN Abraham 1852
GUGUMUS Louis 1853
TERREL Robert 1854
PICQUET Joseph 1837
MERCERET Francis 1853
GAULLOFF Louis 1852

Section 20
PIEQUET James Sen 1849
EATON Absalom 1848
MILLER Samuel 1848
FEESER James 1848
TERREL Robert 1854
THOMAS Reuben 1849
ALLISON James 1849
PIECUIT James 1848
PIECUIT James 1848
TERREL John 1854
LEINHART Valentine 1847 / CASEY Patrick 1852
PIEQUET James 1850
TERREL John 1854
LITZERMAN Joseph 1854
TERREL John 1854
TERREL John 1854

Section 21
THOMAS Reuben 1849
PING Robert 1849
THOMAS John 1849
GRUB John 1853
WADDLE Harrison 1849
WADDLE Harrison 1849
WADDLE Harrison 1849
LUE John Van 1849
LUE John Van 1849

Section 30
PICQUET Joseph 1837
MERCERET Francis 1853
LITZELMANN Joseph 1853
LORANCE Jacob 1848
PIEQUET James 1850
HARTRICK Theodore 1850
PIQUET James 1848
LIGHTNER Salathiel 1852
PICQUET James 1852
BLASDEL Jacob W 1854

Section 29
OWEN William 1852
STUBNER [48] Carl 1854
LIGHTNER Salathiel 1852
BLASDEL Jacob W 1854
BLASDEL Jacob W 1854
BLASDEL Jacob W 1854

Section 28
HIGGINS Cenith J 1852
VANLUE David 1849
VANLUE David 1849
WADDLE Jackson 1849
NEWBOULD William R 1854
LEINHART Valentine 1849
VANLUE David 1849
NEWBOULD William R 1854
VANLUE William 1849
VANLUE William 1849
HOFMAN Francis 1853

Section 31
PICQUET Joseph 1840
PICQUET Joseph 1837
PICQUET Joseph 1837
FULLER Francis 1852
SCHWAGER Anthony 1851
GUTHNICK Charles 1852
LEINHART Valentine 1851

Section 32
PICQUET Joseph 1837
PICQUET Joseph 1837
PICQUET Joseph 1837

Section 33
DAVIS William 1840
KRAUS Valentine 1841
JONES Erasmus 1851
VANLUE William 1849
SUTTON Amariah 1853
KROUSE Valentine 1842
KRAUS Valentine 1851
OST Lewis 1853
REPETTO John 1853
VANLIEU James A 1853
SUTTON Amariah 1853
RAEF Jacob 1853
BLAKE Marion 1852
MIDKIFF William E 1852
KROUS John 1853 / FOWLER Andrew W 1854
FOWLER Andrew W 1853

MCCARTY James 1851	RYAN William G 1837	PING Anderson S 1852 PING Anderson S 1852	PING Asa 1851		
LANCE Daniel 1850		PING Robert 1853 3	PING Anderson S 1851	2	1
LANCE Daniel 1850	MEESE Robert 1854	HARGIS Elizabeth 1853	PING Thomas 1852		
LANCE Daniel 1850	LEE William J 1853	MILLER Thomas 1850	MCCARTY James 1852		

GAYER David A 1850	SMITH David 1853	MEESE Henry 1852	CAMPBELL Henry A 1852		
	HALE Ezekiel 1853 10	PING John 1849	JAMES Richard 1852	11	12
JAMES William 1839		JAMES William 1842	TEDFORD John H 1853		

JAMES Horatio 1839 15	*Jasper County*				13
WRIGHT John F 1846	WRIGHT John F 1851	STEEL James H 1854	STEEL James H 1854	14 *Crawford County*	
EUBANK George 1849	STEEL James H 1854				

THOMAS John 1849	STEEL James H 1854 22	STEWARD John 1853	PRICE Thomas J 1854	23	24
	WRIGHT Henry M 1851				
NEWBOULD William R 1854	WRIGHT John F 1852	NEWBOULD William R 1854	HUTSON Jacob 1853		
	NEWBOULD William R 1854				

RUDDELL George 1853 27	ROGERS Jeremiah 1853	HARTMAN Peter 1853		26	25
	NICHOLAS Joseph 1853				
NICHOLAS Joseph 1853	NICHOLAS Joseph 1853		NICHOLS Elijah 1850		
HOFMAN Francis 1853		NICHOLAS Joseph 1853	NICHOLAS Joseph 1853		

MAHAN James 1853	NICHOLAS Joseph 1853	NICHOLAS Joseph 1853	ROGERS Jonah M 1853	35	36
FOWLER James M 1853	WRIGHT John F 1852 34	BOGARD Benjamin 1853			
	VANMETER Henry 1852	BOGARD Jerushia 1852			
HAMIL [34] Amanda 1853	JOHNSTON Wilson 1852	NICHOLS Joseph 1853	TINGLEY Benjamin 1851		

Helpful Hints

1. This Map's INDEX can be found on the preceding pages.

2. Refer to Map "C" to see where this Township lies within Jasper County, Illinois.

3. Numbers within square brackets [ ] denote a multi-patentee land parcel (multi-owner). Refer to Appendix "C" for a full list of members in this group.

4. Areas that look to be crowded with Patentees usually indicate multiple sales of the same parcel (re-issues), cancellations or voided transactions (that we map, anyway) or overlapping parcels. We opt to show even these ambiguous parcels, which oftentimes lead to research avenues not yet taken.

Legend

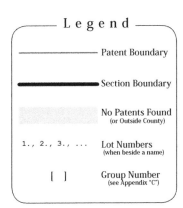

———— Patent Boundary

━━━━ Section Boundary

No Patents Found
(or Outside County)

1., 2., 3., ... Lot Numbers
(when beside a name)

[ ] Group Number
(see Appendix "C")

Scale: Section = 1 mile X 1 mile
(generally, with some exceptions)

Road Map

T6-N R14-W
2nd PM Meridian

Map Group 15

Cities & Towns
None

Cemeteries
Miller Cemetery
Sainte Valentine Cemetery
Yager Cemetery

| 3 | 2 | 1 |

E 900th Ave

| 10 | 11 | 12 |

N 2250th St
E 825th Ave

825N

| 15 | 14 | 13 |

N 2225th St
E 700th Ave

Crawford County

E 650th Ave

| 22 | 23 | 24 |

E 600th Ave

N 2300th St

| 27 | 26 | 25 |

Jasper County

N 2200th St

| 34 | 35 | 36 |

Helpful Hints

1. This road map has a number of uses, but primarily it is to help you: a) find the present location of land owned by your ancestors (at least the general area), b) find cemeteries and city-centers, and c) estimate the route/roads used by Census-takers & tax-assessors.

2. If you plan to travel to Jasper County to locate cemeteries or land parcels, please pick up a modern travel map for the area before you do. Mapping old land parcels on modern maps is not as exact a science as you might think. Just the slightest variations in public land survey coordinates, estimates of parcel boundaries, or road-map deviations can greatly alter a map's representation of how a road either does or doesn't cross a particular parcel of land.

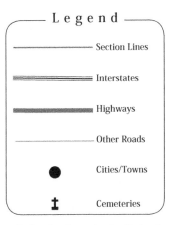

Legend

———————	Section Lines
═══════	Interstates
▬▬▬▬▬▬	Highways
———————	Other Roads
●	Cities/Towns
☦	Cemeteries

Scale: Section = 1 mile X 1 mile
(generally, with some exceptions)

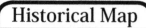

Historical Map

T6-N R14-W
2nd PM Meridian

Map Group 15

Cities & Towns
None

Cemeteries
Miller Cemetery
Sainte Valentine Cemetery
Yager Cemetery

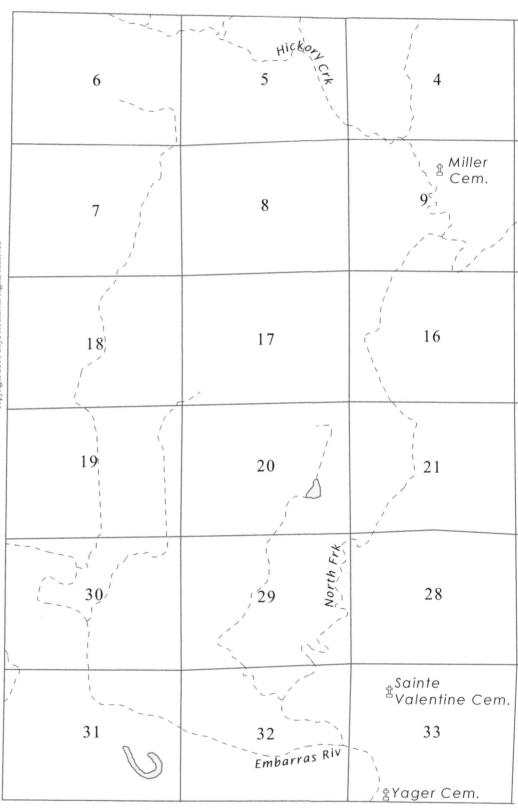

| 3 | 2 | 1 |

| 10 | 11 | 12 |

Jasper County

| 15 | 14 | 13 |

Crawford County

| 22 | 23 | 24 |

| 27 | 26 | 25 |

| 34 | 35 | 36 |

Copyright 2010 Boyd IT, Inc. All Rights Reserved

Helpful Hints

1. This Map takes a different look at the same Congressional Township displayed in the preceding two maps. It presents features that can help you better envision the historical development of the area: a) Water-bodies (lakes & ponds), b) Water-courses (rivers, streams, etc.), c) Railroads, d) City/ town center-points (where they were oftentimes located when first settled), and e) Cemeteries.

2. Using this "Historical" map in tandem with this Township's Patent Map and Road Map, may lead you to some interesting discoveries. You will often find roads, towns, cemeteries, and waterways are named after nearby landowners: sometimes those names will be the ones you are researching. See how many of these research gems you can find here in Jasper County.

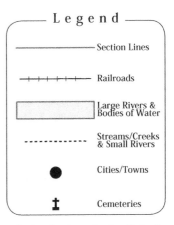

Legend

———————— Section Lines

+ + + + + + + Railroads

▭ Large Rivers & Bodies of Water

- - - - - - - Streams/Creeks & Small Rivers

● Cities/Towns

☨ Cemeteries

Scale: Section = 1 mile X 1 mile
(there are some exceptions)

223

Map Group 16: Index to Land Patents

Township 5-North Range 8-East (3rd PM)

After you locate an individual in this Index, take note of the Section and Section Part then proceed to the Land Patent map on the pages immediately following. You should have no difficulty locating the corresponding parcel of land.

The "For More Info" Column will lead you to more information about the underlying Patents. See the *Legend* at right, and the "How to Use this Book" chapter, for more information.

```
                        LEGEND
             "For More Info . . ." column
  G = Group   (Multi-Patentee Patent, see Appendix "C")
  R = Residence
  S = Social Status

  See Appendix A for list of abbreviations used by the
  Illinois State Archives in describing the place and
  nature of these land patents.

  Note: if the Abbreviations contain "L", "BL", "LOT",
  or "BLOCK", the exact whereabouts of the parcel within
  the section is not known.
```

ID	Individual in Patent	Sec.	Sec. Part	Purchase Date	Sale Type	IL Aliquot Part	For More Info . . .
4271	ADAMSON, Asa	6	NENE	1840-01-27	FD	NENEFR	R:CLAY
4286	BAKER, Daniel B	21	NENW	1853-10-20	FD	NENW	
4378	BAKER, Joseph T	8	W½SE	1853-02-28	FD	W2SE	
4423	BAKER, Samuel	23	SEN½	1853-10-22	FD	S2NE	R:OHIO
4422	" "	23	S½NW	1853-10-22	FD	S2NW	R:OHIO
4330	BALL, James	23	W½SE	1853-11-05	FD	W2SE	R:OHIO
4329	" "	23	NWSW	1853-11-10	FD	NWSW	R:OHIO
4369	BALL, Jonas	23	N½NW	1853-02-25	FD	N2NW	
4368	" "	23	N½NE	1853-02-25	FD	N2NE	
4367	" "	22	NENE	1853-02-26	FD	NENE	
4460	BARKER, William E	20	SENE	1853-10-10	FD	SENE	R:FAYETTE
4478	" "	20	SENE	1853-10-10	FD	SENE	R:FAYETTE
4486	BERRY, Wyatt L	24	SENE	1853-12-20	FD	SENE	R:FAYETTE
4491	BERRY, Wyatt S	20	NWNE	1853-08-02	FD	NWNE	R:FAYETTE
4447	" "	4	L2 (W½)	1853-08-19	FD	W2LOT2NW	R:FAYETTE
4494	" "	4	L2 (W½)	1853-08-19	FD	W2LOT2NW	R:FAYETTE
4489	" "	2	L1 (W½)	1853-10-21	FD	W2LOT1NW	R:FAYETTE
4321	" "	2	L2	1853-10-21	FD	LOT2NW	R:FAYETTE
4490	" "	2	L2	1853-10-21	FD	LOT2NW	R:FAYETTE
4493	" "	3	L2	1853-10-24	FD	LOT2NW	R:FAYETTE
4488	" "	15	W½NW	1853-12-01	FD	W2NW	R:FAYETTE
4487	" "	15	SENW	1853-12-01	FD	SENW	R:FAYETTE
4492	" "	24	E½SE	1853-12-27	FD	E2SE	R:FAYETTE
4446	" "	4	L2 (E½)	1854-01-05	FD	E2LOT2NW	R:FAYETTE
4495	" "	4	L2 (E½)	1854-01-05	FD	E2LOT2NW	R:FAYETTE
4450	BICKERS, William	1	E½SE	1853-05-13	FD	E2SE	
4451	" "	1	NWSE	1853-05-13	FD	NWSE	
4352	BLACK, John D	22	SESE	1853-06-21	FD	SESE	R:JASPER
4347	BODLE, John	1	L1 (W½)	1851-08-23	FD	W2LOT1NEFR	R:OHIO
4348	BOLDNEY, John	1	SW	1851-08-07	FD	SW	
4461	BONE, William E	17	NESW	1852-10-11	FD	NESW	R:INDIANA
4411	BOYD, Archibald	13	NWSE	1843-05-03	FD	NWSE	R:COLES
4270	" "	13	NWSE	1843-05-03	FD	NWSE	R:COLES
4272	BRACKET, Benjamin	16	L9	1855-02-18	SC	LOT09NESE	
4456	BROWN, William	9	W½SE	1853-03-03	FD	W2SE	
4455	" "	9	E½SW	1853-03-03	FD	E2SW	
4453	" "	4	L1 (E½)	1853-11-16	FD	E2LOT1NW	R:JASPER
4452	" "	21	NWNE	1853-11-16	FD	NWNE	R:JASPER
4454	" "	6	SW	1853-12-01	FD	SW	R:JASPER
4384	CARPENTER, Kernel A	24	NWSW	1853-11-24	FD	NWSW	R:JASPER
4351	CARTER, John	18	NENE	1853-07-30	FD	NENE	R:JASPER
4273	CHESNUT, Benjamin H	5	W½SE	1840-10-24	FD	W2SE	R:CLAY
4406	CHESNUT, Polly	5	NWNW	1845-08-08	FD	NWNW	R:JASPER S:F
4459	CHESTNUT, William	12	SWNE	1852-10-01	FD	SWNE	
4457	" "	12	E½NE	1852-10-01	FD	E2NE	
4458	" "	12	NESE	1852-10-01	FD	NESE	

ID	Individual in Patent	Sec.	Sec. Part	Purchase Date	Sale Type	IL Aliquot Part	For More Info . . .
4303	CLARK, Frederick A	4	SESW	1853-02-24	FD	SESW	R:INDIANA
4304	" "	9	E½NW	1853-03-02	FD	E2NW	
4385	COLBORN, Levi	19	E½SE	1853-01-28	FD	E2SE	
4386	" "	20	NWSW	1853-01-28	FD	NWSW	
4415	COLBOURN, Robert	7	SWSE	1839-11-14	FD	SWSE	R:CLAY
4414	" "	18	NWNE	1839-11-14	FD	NWNE	R:CLAY
4388	COLBURN, Levi	19	NW	1853-08-30	FD	NWFR	R:CLAY
4387	" "	18	N½NW	1853-09-06	FD	N2NW	R:CLAY
4480	COLLINS, Willis	1	LI (E½)	1853-04-29	FD	E2LOT1NE	
4263	CRAIG, Abigail	10	SWNE	1853-03-03	FD	SWNE	S:F
4345	CRAIG, Jimothy	11	NWSW	1853-06-27	FD	NWSW	
4442	CRAIG, Thomas	15	SENE	1853-04-13	FD	SENE	
4441	" "	15	NESE	1853-04-13	FD	NESEVOID	
4325	CRAVENS, Isaac R	14	N½SE	1855-10-29	FD	N2SE	R:JASPER
4462	" "	14	N½SE	1855-10-29	FD	N2SE	R:JASPER
4463	CRAVENS, William E	14	S½NE	1853-07-27	FD	S2NEVOID	
4325	" "	14	N½SE	1853-07-27	FD	N2SEVOID	
4462	" "	14	N½SE	1853-07-27	FD	N2SEVOID	
4464	" "	14	SEN½	1855-10-29	FD	S2NE	R:JASPER
4481	CRONER, Winston	24	N½NE	1852-09-28	FD	N2NE	
4482	" "	24	W½SE	1852-09-28	FD	W2SE	
4300	CROUSE, Eli	24	NENE	1853-11-01	FD	NENE	R:JASPER
4483	CROWS, Winston	24	NESW	1853-02-28	FD	NESW	
4485	" "	24	SENW	1853-02-28	FD	SENW	
4484	" "	24	S½SW	1853-03-01	FD	S2SW	
4269	DOWNER, Andrew N	15	NWSE	1861-04-11	FD	NWSE	R:COOK
4346	DRAKE, Joel	8	NENE	1853-01-28	FD	NENE	R:INDIANA
4359	DRAKE, John F	8	NWNE	1853-02-01	FD	NWNE	R:INDIANA
4358	" "	5	NESW	1853-02-01	FD	NESW	R:INDIANA
4366	DRAKE, John W	8	E½SW	1853-02-28	FD	E2SW	
4331	ELDER, James	1	SWSE	1852-12-09	FD	SWSE	
4477	ELDER, William M	2	SWSW	1853-01-04	FD	SWSW	
4475	" "	2	NESW	1853-01-05	FD	NESW	
4476	" "	2	NWSW	1853-01-07	FD	NWSW	
4267	ELSTON, Bluford	20	SWNW	1853-11-17	FD	SWNW	R:CLAY
4274	" "	20	SWNW	1853-11-17	FD	SWNW	R:CLAY
4336	ERVIN, James L	22	NWSW	1853-08-18	FD	NWSW	R:JASPER
4356	ESSEX, John	8	SEN½	1853-02-20	FD	S2NE	
4355	" "	8	S½NW	1853-02-20	FD	S2NW	
4357	" "	9	W½NW	1853-02-28	FD	W2NW	
4353	" "	7	W½NE	1853-02-28	FD	W2NE	
4354	" "	8	NENW	1853-02-28	FD	NENW	
4275	EVANS, Brison	5	SWSW	1840-06-03	FD	SWSW	R:JASPER
4277	EVANS, Caleb	9	NWSW	1853-04-08	FD	NWSW	
4276	" "	4	L1 (W½)	1853-06-07	FD	W2LOT1NW	
4381	EVANS, Joshua	5	SWNW	1843-11-06	FD	SWNW	R:JASPER
4433	EVANS, Stockley D	5	E½SE	1853-02-01	FD	E2SE	
4437	" "	6	SENE	1853-02-04	FD	SENE	
4436	" "	6	E½SE	1853-02-21	FD	E2SE	
4434	" "	5	NWSW	1853-02-21	FD	NWSW	
4438	" "	7	NENE	1853-02-21	FD	NENE	
4439	" "	8	NWNW	1853-02-21	FD	NWNW	
4435	" "	5	SESW	1853-02-28	FD	SESW	
4394	FORD, Moses	2	LI (E½)	1853-04-26	FD	E2LOTINW	
4393	" "	2	LI	1853-04-26	FD	W2LOTINE	
4376	FULTON, Joseph	21	W½SW	1853-10-20	FD	W2SW	
4375	" "	21	NESW	1853-10-20	FD	NESW	
4374	" "	20	SESE	1853-10-20	FD	SESE	
4389	FULTON, Lewis	21	SENW	1853-10-20	FD	SENW	
4264	GARDNER, Abner	17	NESE	1853-02-28	FD	NESE	
4278	GIBSON, Calvin	7	NW	1853-08-27	FD	NWFR	R:CLAY
4279	GIBSON, Calvin M	8	NWSW	1853-03-03	FD	NWSW	
4404	GOULD, Philander	20	E½NW	1853-03-04	FD	E2NW	
4401	" "	17	NWSE	1853-03-04	FD	NWSE	
4403	" "	17	SESW	1853-03-04	FD	SESW	
4405	" "	7	SENE	1853-03-04	FD	SENE	
4402	" "	17	S½SE	1853-03-04	FD	S2SE	
4292	GREGORY, Daniel	3	NWSW	1853-02-20	FD	NWSW	
4293	" "	4	NESE	1853-02-20	FD	NESE	
4291	" "	23	E½SW	1853-03-15	FD	E2SW	
4306	GROVE, George	1	N½NE	1849-06-13	FD	N2NE	R:JASPER
4319	GROVE, George W	3	N½SE	1853-03-21	FD	N2SE	
4320	" "	3	W½NE	1853-03-21	FD	W2NE	

ID	Individual in Patent	Sec.	Sec. Part	Purchase Date	Sale Type	IL Aliquot Part	For More Info . . .
4344	GROVE, Jesse	16	L8	1856-03-08	SC	LOT08SENE	
4324	HASTINGS, Hezekiah	22	E½SW	1853-02-25	FD	E2SW	
4323	" "	22	E½NW	1853-02-25	FD	E2NW	
4262	HILLBRANT, Aaron	5	NE	1852-10-18	FD	NE	
4377	HODGE, Joseph	17	NENW	1853-02-07	FD	NENW	
4310	HOUSTON, George	14	NW	1853-03-04	FD	NW	
4332	HURST, James	14	SWSW	1853-06-21	FD	SWSW	R:JASPER
4333	" "	23	SWSW	1855-11-10	FD	SWSW	R:JASPER
4281	JONES, Charles Floyd	19	N½NE	1854-02-14	FD	N2NE	
4360	JOSEPH, John	16	L14	1857-07-02	SC	LOT14SESW	
4490	KING, Granville	2	L2	1852-12-27	FD	LOT2NEVOID	
4321	" "	2	L2	1852-12-27	FD	LOT2NEVOID	
4305	KLEIN, Frederick W	4	W½SW	1852-09-09	FD	W2SW	R:INDIANA
4284	LANCASTER, Clement	1	E½NW	1853-02-25	FD	E2NW	
4301	LAY, Eliza	22	NESE	1853-02-28	FD	NESE	S:F G:42
4301	LAY, Martin	22	NESE	1853-02-28	FD	NESE	S:F G:42
4400	LEWELLYN, Peter	15	SWSE	1853-12-14	FD	SWSE	R:INDIANA
4399	" "	14	SESW	1853-12-14	FD	SESW	R:INDIANA
4285	LEWIS, Crawford P	6	SWNE	1842-06-09	FD	SWNE	R:CLAY
4392	LEWIS, Ludwin B	20	NWSE	1840-04-07	FD	NWSE	R:CLAY
4391	" "	18	SWNE	1854-02-14	FD	SWNE	
4445	LEWIS, Thomas Willis	6	NWNW	1839-03-26	FD	NWNWFR	R:CLAY
4465	LEWIS, William E	18	W½SE	1839-02-19	FD	W2SE	R:CLAY
4470	LEWIS, William H	18	SW	1852-11-10	FD	SWFR	R:JASPER
4467	" "	18	NESE	1852-11-10	FD	NESE	R:JASPER
4469	" "	18	SESE	1853-02-17	FD	SESE	R:JASPER
4466	" "	17	SWSW	1853-08-16	FD	SWSW	R:JASPER
4468	" "	18	S½NW	1853-08-16	FD	S2NW	R:JASPER
4290	LINN, Daniel C	2	N½SE	1853-05-23	FD	N2SE	
4337	LINN, James	2	S½SE	1853-05-23	FD	S2SE	
4338	" "	2	SESW	1853-05-23	FD	SESW	
4449	LINN, Westley E	2	L1 (E½)	1853-05-23	FD	E2LOT1NE	
4370	LISTER, Jonathan	17	NE	1852-09-28	FD	NE	
4302	LOLLAR, Ephraim	20	SWSE	1853-01-05	FD	SWSE	
4280	LOUGH, Charles B	12	S½SE	1853-02-28	FD	S2SE	
4282	MASON, Charles	20	NESW	1872-04-26	SW	NESW	
4283	" "	20	SWNE	1872-09-07	SW	SWNE	
4289	MCCOLLUM, Daniel B	12	W½SW	1851-08-23	FD	W2SW	R:OHIO G:46
4287	" "	12	NESW	1851-08-23	FD	NESW	R:OHIO G:46
4288	" "	12	NW	1851-08-23	FD	NW	R:OHIO G:46
4294	MCCOLLUM, Danil B	12	NWNE	1851-08-23	FD	NWNE	R:OHIO G:47
4288	MCCOLLUM, John W	12	NW	1851-08-23	FD	NW	R:OHIO G:46
4289	" "	12	W½SW	1851-08-23	FD	W2SW	R:OHIO G:46
4294	" "	12	NWNE	1851-08-23	FD	NWNE	R:OHIO G:47
4287	" "	12	NESW	1851-08-23	FD	NESW	R:OHIO G:46
4288	MCCOLLUM, Thomas D	12	NW	1851-08-23	FD	NW	R:OHIO G:46
4294	" "	12	NWNE	1851-08-23	FD	NWNE	R:OHIO G:47
4287	" "	12	NESW	1851-08-23	FD	NESW	R:OHIO G:46
4289	" "	12	W½SW	1851-08-23	FD	W2SW	R:OHIO G:46
4460	MCKEARBY, William	20	SENE	1853-04-26	FD	SENE	
4478	" "	20	SENE	1853-04-26	FD	SENE	
4339	MCPEAK, James	15	NENE	1853-11-05	FD	NENE	R:OHIO
4349	MCQUEEN, John C	19	SWSE	1853-12-07	FD	SWSE	R:JASPER
4350	" "	6	NW	1853-12-07	FD	NW	R:JASPER
4443	METZ, Thomas	22	SENE	1853-10-22	FD	SENE	R:OHIO
4444	" "	22	W½NE	1853-10-22	FD	W2NE	R:OHIO
4268	MULLENS, Allen T	7	SW	1852-10-08	FD	SWFR	R:INDIANA
4361	MULLINS, John	7	N½SE	1853-02-25	FD	N2SE	
4340	OCHELTREE, James	15	NENW	1840-05-18	FD	NENW	R:CLAY
4341	" "	15	W½NE	1840-05-18	FD	W2NE	R:CLAY
4390	OWEN, Lewis	16	L12	1858-03-09	SC	LOT12NWSW	
4395	PARKER, Napoleon B	10	W½SW	1853-02-19	FD	W2SW	
4396	" "	9	E½SE	1853-02-19	FD	E2SE	
4335	PARSHALL, James K	4	SESE	1853-06-29	FD	SESE	
4334	" "	10	NW	1853-06-29	FD	NW	
4265	PETERSON, Abner M	20	NESE	1853-12-27	FD	NESE	R:JASPER
4407	POMEROT, Ralph M	13	N½SW	1853-05-21	FD	N2SW	
4409	POMEROY, Ralph M	13	NW	1853-05-21	FD	NWVOID	
4410	" "	13	NW	1853-05-21	FD	NWVOID	
4413	" "	13	SWNE	1853-05-21	FD	SWNE	
4408	" "	12	NWSE	1853-06-29	FD	NWSE	
4270	" "	13	NWSE	1853-06-29	FD	NWSE	
4411	" "	13	NWSE	1853-06-29	FD	NWSE	

ID	Individual in Patent	Sec.	Sec. Part	Purchase Date	Sale Type	IL Aliquot Part	For More Info . . .
4412	POMEROY, Ralph M (Cont'd)	13	SENE	1853-06-29	FD	SENE	
4410	" "	13	NW	1854-05-03	FD	NW	
4409	" "	13	NW	1854-05-03	FD	NW	
4313	PRESTON, George R	13	E½SE	1853-09-05	FD	E2SE	
4311	" "	11	N½NE	1853-09-05	FD	N2NE	
4312	" "	11	N½NW	1853-09-05	FD	N2NW	
4315	" "	13	SWSE	1853-09-05	FD	SWSE	
4316	" "	13	SWSW	1853-09-05	FD	SWSW	
4317	" "	24	N½NW	1853-09-05	FD	N2NW	
4318	" "	24	SWNW	1853-09-05	FD	SWNW	
4314	" "	13	SESW	1853-09-05	FD	SESW	
4495	PRUET, Walter	4	L2 (E½)	1853-10-26	FD	E2LOT2NE	
4494	" "	4	L2 (W½)	1853-10-26	FD	W2LOT2NE	R:JASPER
4446	" "	4	L2 (E½)	1853-10-26	FD	E2LOT2NE	
4447	" "	4	L2 (W½)	1853-10-26	FD	W2LOT2NE	R:JASPER
4362	PULLIAM, John	6	W½SE	1853-02-08	FD	W2SE	
4474	REDMAN, William L	16	L15	1857-07-03	SC	LOT15SESE	
4473	" "	16	L13	1857-07-03	SC	LOT13SWSW	
4267	RIFE, Abraham	20	SWNW	1844-03-07	FD	SWNW	R:JASPER
4274	" "	20	SWNW	1844-03-07	FD	SWNW	R:JASPER
4266	" "	19	SWNE	1844-03-07	FD	SWNE	R:JASPER
4430	RIFE, Silas	17	NWNW	1853-02-17	FD	NWNW	R:JASPER
4432	" "	19	SENE	1853-02-17	FD	SENE	R:JASPER
4431	" "	19	NWSE	1853-02-23	FD	NWSE	R:JASPER
4419	ROBERTS, Zachary T	3	L2 (E½)	1853-09-08	FD	E2LOT2NE	R:JASPER
4496	" "	3	L2 (E½)	1853-09-08	FD	E2LOT2NE	R:JASPER
4429	ROWLAND, Sarah K	15	SW	1853-01-08	FD	SW	S:F
4416	SCOTT, Robert G	3	E½SW	1853-05-23	FD	E2SW	
4418	" "	3	L1 (W½)	1853-05-23	FD	W2LOT1NW	
4419	" "	3	L2 (E½)	1853-05-23	FD	E2LOT2NW	
4421	" "	4	L1	1853-05-23	FD	LOT1NE	
4496	" "	3	L2 (E½)	1853-05-23	FD	E2LOT2NW	
4420	" "	4	NWSE	1853-05-23	FD	NWSE	
4417	" "	3	SWSW	1853-05-23	FD	SWSW	
4424	SMALLWOOD, Samuel	10	NENE	1852-12-18	FD	NENE	
4427	" "	3	S½SE	1853-02-01	FD	S2SE	
4426	" "	10	SENE	1853-03-19	FD	SENE	
4425	" "	10	NWNE	1853-03-19	FD	NWNE	
4428	" "	3	SENE	1853-03-21	FD	SENE	
4342	STAPP, James T B	11	S½SE	1853-09-02	FD	S2SE	R:FAYETTE
4343	" "	14	N½NE	1853-09-02	FD	N2NE	R:FAYETTE
4373	STEWART, Jonathan	21	W½NW	1853-07-23	FD	W2NW	R:RICHLAND
4372	" "	21	E½SE	1853-07-23	FD	E2SE	R:RICHLAND
4371	" "	20	NENE	1853-07-23	FD	NENE	R:CLAY
4322	STIVERS, Harrison	15	E½SE	1853-02-01	FD	E2SE	
4363	STOUGHTON, John	4	NESW	1853-03-02	FD	NESW	
4327	SWARTZ, Jacob	9	NE	1851-09-25	FD	NE	
4299	TARR, Edwin S	21	SWSE	1853-01-05	FD	SWSE	
4472	TARR, William H	21	SESW	1853-01-05	FD	SESW	
4471	" "	21	NWSE	1853-01-10	FD	NWSE	
4479	TREXLER, William W	3	NESE	1853-11-22	FD	NESE	R:JASPER
4297	TUCKER, David M	10	SE	1853-03-04	FD	SE	
4296	" "	10	E½SW	1853-03-04	FD	E2SW	
4309	TUCKER, George H	14	N½SW	1853-03-04	FD	N2SW	
4308	" "	11	SEN½	1853-03-04	FD	S2NE	
4307	" "	11	N½SE	1853-03-04	FD	N2SE	
4295	VAUGHAN, David A	17	SENW	1852-10-11	FD	SENW	R:INDIANA
4383	VAUGHAN, Josiah	17	SWNW	1853-01-11	FD	SWNW	
4382	" "	17	NWSW	1853-01-11	FD	NWSW	
4364	VIXLER, John	12	SESW	1853-03-01	FD	SESW	
4365	" "	13	N½NE	1853-03-01	FD	N2NE	
4448	WARD, Washington H	20	S½SW	1853-11-22	FD	S2SW	R:JASPER
4379	WAYMAN, Joseph	7	SESE	1853-03-08	FD	SESE	
4380	" "	8	SWSW	1853-03-08	FD	SWSW	
4398	WEBSTER, Noah	16	L11	1856-10-16	SC	LOT11NESW	
4397	" "	16	L10	1856-10-16	SC	LOT10NWSE	
4298	WHITE, David S	23	E½SE	1853-01-05	FD	E2SE	
4326	WITSMAN, Isaac	21	E½NE	1853-02-28	FD	E2NE	
4328	WITSMAN, Jacob	21	SWNE	1853-01-10	FD	SWNE	
4440	WOOD, Susan	19	SW	1853-03-15	FD	SWFR	R:CLAY S:F

Patent Map

T5-N R8-E
3rd PM Meridian

Map Group 16

Township Statistics

Parcels Mapped	:	235
Number of Patents	:	1
Number of Individuals	:	131
Patentees Identified	:	128
Number of Surnames	:	98
Multi-Patentee Parcels	:	5
Oldest Patent Date	:	2/19/1839
Most Recent Patent	:	9/7/1872
Block/Lot Parcels	:	27
Cities and Towns	:	0
Cemeteries	:	5

Copyright 2010 Boyd IT, Inc. All Rights Reserved

Section 6
LEWIS Thomas Willis 1839
MCQUEEN John C 1853
LEWIS Crawford P 1842
ADAMSON Asa 1840
PULLIAM John 1853
EVANS Stockley D 1853
BROWN William 1853
EVANS Stockley D 1853

Section 5
CHESNUT Polly 1845
EVANS Joshua 1843
EVANS Stockley D 1853
DRAKE John F 1853
EVANS Brison 1840
EVANS Stockley D 1853
CHESNUT Benjamin H 1840
HILLBRANT Aaron 1852
EVANS Stockley D 1853

Lots-Sec. 4
L1 SCOTT, Robert G 1853
L1(E½) BROWN, William 1853
L1(W½) EVANS, Caleb 1853
L2(E½) BERRY, Wyatt S 1854
L2(E½) PRUET, Walter 1853
L2(W½) PRUET, Walter 1853
L2(W½) BERRY, Wyatt S 1853

KLEIN Frederick W 1852
STOUGHTON John 1853
SCOTT Robert G 1853
GREGORY Daniel 1853
CLARK Frederick A 1853
PARSHALL James K 1853

Section 7
GIBSON Calvin 1853
ESSEX John 1853
EVANS Stockley D 1853
GOULD Philander 1853
MULLINS John 1853
MULLENS Allen T 1852
COLBOURN Robert 1839
WAYMAN 1853

Section 8
EVANS Stockley D 1853
ESSEX John 1853
ESSEX John 1853
GIBSON Calvin M 1853
DRAKE John W 1853
WAYMAN Joseph 1853
ESSEX John 1853
DRAKE John F 1853
ESSEX John 1853
DRAKE Joel 1853
BAKER Joseph T 1853

Section 9
ESSEX John 1853
SWARTZ Jacob 1851
CLARK Frederick A 1853
EVANS Caleb 1853
BROWN William 1853
BROWN William 1853
PARKER Napoleon B 1853

Section 18
COLBURN Levi 1853
COLBURN Robert 1839
CARTER John 1853
LEWIS William H 1853
LEWIS Ludwin B 1854
LEWIS William H 1852
LEWIS William H 1839
LEWIS William E 1852
LEWIS William H 1853
RIFE Silas 1853
VAUGHAN Josiah 1853
VAUGHAN Josiah 1853
LEWIS William H 1853

Section 17
HODGE Joseph 1853
VAUGHAN David A 1852
BONE William E 1852
GOULD Philander 1853
LISTER Jonathan 1852
GOULD Philander 1853
GARDNER Abner 1853
GOULD Philander 1853

Lots-Sec. 16
L8 GROVE, Jesse 1856
L9 BRACKET, Benjamin 1855
L10 WEBSTER, Noah 1856
L11 WEBSTER, Noah 1856
L12 OWEN, Lewis 1858
L13 REDMAN, William L 1857
L14 JOSEPH, John 1857
L15 REDMAN, William L 1857

16
Jasper County

Section 19
COLBURN Levi 1853
JONES Charles Floyd 1854
RIFE Abraham 1844
RIFE Silas 1853
WOOD Susan 1853
RIFE Silas 1853
COLBORN Levi 1853
MCQUEEN John C 1853

Section 20
ELSTON Bluford 1853
RIFE Abraham 1844
GOULD Philander 1853
COLBORN Levi 1853
MASON Charles 1872
WARD Washington H 1853

Section 21
BERRY Wyatt S 1853
STEWART Jonathan 1853
MASON Charles 1872
BARKER William E 1853
MCKEARBY William 1853
LEWIS Ludwin B 1840
PETERSON Abner M 1853
LOLLAR Ephraim 1853
FULTON Joseph 1853
STEWART Jonathan 1853
BAKER Daniel B 1853
BROWN William 1853
FULTON Lewis 1853
WITSMAN Jacob 1853
WITSMAN Isaac 1853
FULTON Joseph 1853
FULTON Joseph 1853
TARR William H 1853
STEWART Jonathan 1853
TARR William H 1853
TARR Edwin S 1853

Clay County

30

29

28

31

32

33

Lots-Sec. 3
L1(W½) SCOTT, Robert G 1853
L2   BERRY, Wyatt S 1853
L2(E½) ROBERTS, Zachary T 1853
L2(E½) SCOTT, Robert G 1853

Lots-Sec. 2
L1(E½) LINN, Westley E   1853
L1(W½) BERRY, Wyatt S   1853
L2   BERRY, Wyatt S   1853
L2   KING, Granville   1852
LI   FORD, Moses   1853
LI(E½) FORD, Moses   1853

Lots-Sec. 1
L1(W½) BODLE, John 1851
LI(E½) COLLINS, Willis 1853

GROVE
George W
1853

SMALLWOOD
Samuel
1853

3

LANCASTER
Clement
1853

GROVE
George
1849

1

GREGORY
Daniel
1853

SCOTT
Robert G
1853

SCOTT
Robert G
1853

GROVE
George W
1853

TREXLER
William W
1853

SMALLWOOD
Samuel
1853

ELDER
William M
1853

ELDER
William M
1853

2

ELDER
William M
1853

LINN
James
1853

LINN
Daniel C
1853

LINN
James
1853

BICKERS
William
1853

BICKERS
William
1853

BOLDNEY
John
1851

ELDER
James
1852

PARSHALL
James K
1853

10

PARKER
Napoleon B
1853

SMALLWOOD
Samuel
1853

CRAIG
Abigail
1853

TUCKER
David M
1853

SMALLWOOD
Samuel
1852

SMALLWOOD
Samuel
1853

TUCKER
David M
1853

PRESTON
George R
1853

CRAIG
Jimothy
1853

11

PRESTON
George R
1853

TUCKER
George H
1853

TUCKER
George H
1853

STAPP
James T B
1853

MCCOLLUM [46]
Daniel B
1851

12

MCCOLLUM [47]
Danil B
1851

CHESTNUT
William
1852

CHESTNUT
William
1852

MCCOLLUM [46]
Daniel B
1851

POMEROY
Ralph M
1853

CHESTNUT
William
1852

MCCOLLUM [46]
Daniel B
1851

VIXLER
John
1853

LOUGH
Charles B
1853

OCHELTREE
James
1840

BERRY
Wyatt S
1853

15

ROWLAND
Sarah K
1853

OCHELTREE
James
1840

BERRY
Wyatt S
1853

DOWNER
Andrew N
1861

LEWELLYN
Peter
1853

MCPEAK
James
1853

CRAIG
Thomas
1853

CRAIG
Thomas
1853

STIVERS
Harrison
1853

HOUSTON
George
1853

14

TUCKER
George H
1853

HURST
James
1853

STAPP
James T B
1853

CRAVENS
William E
1853

CRAVENS
Isaac R
1855

LEWELLYN
Peter
1853

CRAVENS
William E
1855

CRAVENS
William E
1853

POMEROY
Ralph M
1853

POMEROY
Ralph M
1854

POMEROY
Ralph M
1853

PRESTON
George R
1853

POMEROY
Ralph M
1853

POMEROY
Ralph M
1853

BOYD
Archibald
1843

POMEROY
Ralph M
1853

13

VIXLER
John
1853

POMEROY
Ralph M
1853

PRESTON
George R
1853

PRESTON
George R
1853

PRESTON
George R
1853

HASTINGS
Hezekiah
1853

22

ERVIN
James L
1853

METZ
Thomas
1853

METZ
Thomas
1853

LAY [42]
Eliza
1853

BLACK
John D
1853

BALL
Jonas
1853

BAKER
Samuel
1853

BALL
James
1853

HURST
James
1855

HASTINGS
Hezekiah
1853

BALL
Jonas
1853

23

GREGORY
Daniel
1853

BAKER
Samuel
1853

BALL
Jonas
1853

BALL
James
1853

BAKER
Samuel
1853

WHITE
David S
1853

PRESTON
George R
1853

PRESTON
George R
1853

CARPENTER
Kernel A
1853

CROWS
Winston
1853

CROWS
Winston
1853

CROWS
Winston
1853

CRONER
Winston
1852

24

CRONER
Winston
1852

CROUSE
Eli
1853

BERRY
Wyatt L
1853

BERRY
Wyatt S
1853

27

26

25

34

35

36

Helpful Hints

1. This Map's INDEX can be found on the preceding pages.

2. Refer to Map "C" to see where this Township lies within Jasper County, Illinois.

3. Numbers within square brackets [ ] denote a multi-patentee land parcel (multi-owner). Refer to Appendix "C" for a full list of members in this group.

4. Areas that look to be crowded with Patentees usually indicate multiple sales of the same parcel (re-issues), cancellations or voided transactions (that we map, anyway) or overlapping parcels. We opt to show even these ambiguous parcels, which oftentimes lead to research avenues not yet taken.

Legend

———— Patent Boundary

▬▬▬▬ Section Boundary

░░░░ No Patents Found
(or Outside County)

1., 2., 3., ...   Lot Numbers
(when beside a name)

[ ]   Group Number
(see Appendix "C")

Scale: Section = 1 mile X 1 mile
(generally, with some exceptions)

Road Map

T5-N R8-E
3rd PM Meridian

Map Group 16

Cities & Towns
None

Cemeteries
Abbott Cemetery
Devore Cemetery
Fulks Cemetery
Pleasant Valley Cemetery
South Muddy Cemetery

Co Rd 2400 E

6

E 350th Ave
5

N 110th St

4

E 300th Ave

7

8

South Muddy Cem.
9 ✠ Abbott Cem.
Fulks Cem.

E 200th Ave

E 150th Ave
18

17

16

N 150th St

N 300th St

N 250th St

1775E

19

N 100th St

20

21

N 200th St

050 N

30

29

28

31

32

33

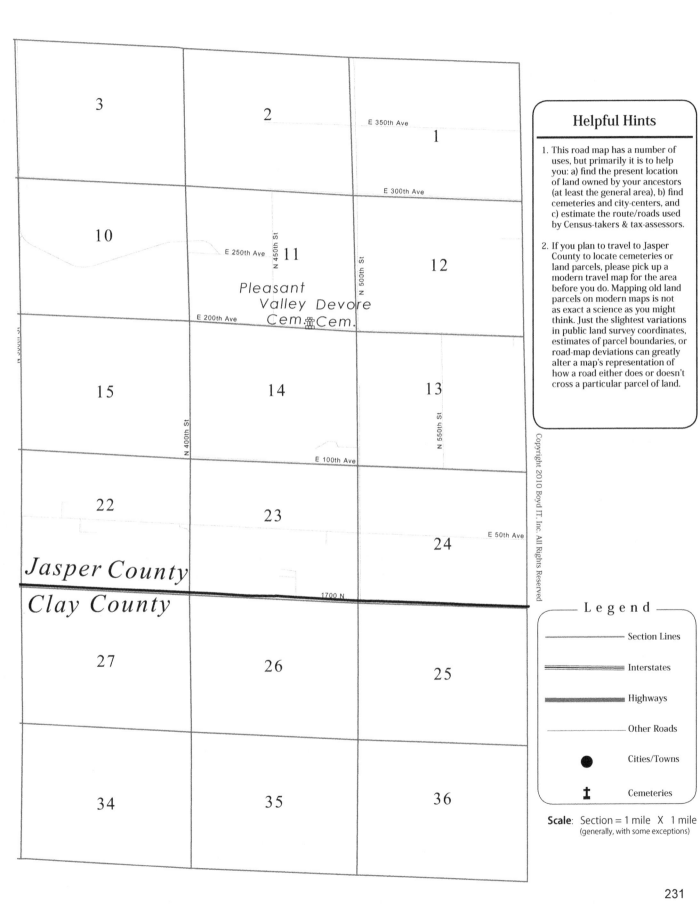

3

2

E 350th Ave

1

E 300th Ave

10

E 250th Ave   N 450th St   11

Pleasant
Valley Devore
E 200th Ave   Cem. Cem.

N 500th St

12

15

14

N 400th St

13

N 550th St

E 100th Ave

22

23

24

E 50th Ave

Jasper County

Clay County

1700 N

27

26

25

34

35

36

Helpful Hints

1. This road map has a number of uses, but primarily it is to help you: a) find the present location of land owned by your ancestors (at least the general area), b) find cemeteries and city-centers, and c) estimate the route/roads used by Census-takers & tax-assessors.

2. If you plan to travel to Jasper County to locate cemeteries or land parcels, please pick up a modern travel map for the area before you do. Mapping old land parcels on modern maps is not as exact a science as you might think. Just the slightest variations in public land survey coordinates, estimates of parcel boundaries, or road-map deviations can greatly alter a map's representation of how a road either does or doesn't cross a particular parcel of land.

Legend

—— Section Lines

══ Interstates

▬▬ Highways

—— Other Roads

● Cities/Towns

✝ Cemeteries

Scale: Section = 1 mile X 1 mile
(generally, with some exceptions)

Historical Map

T5-N R8-E
3rd PM Meridian

Map Group 16

Cities & Towns
None

Cemeteries
Abbott Cemetery
Devore Cemetery
Fulks Cemetery
Pleasant Valley Cemetery
South Muddy Cemetery

6	5	4
7	8	South Muddy Cem. 9 Abbott Cem. Fulks Cem.
18	Limestone Crk 17	16
19	20	21 Jasper County
30	29	Clay County 28
31	32	33

Big Muddy Crk

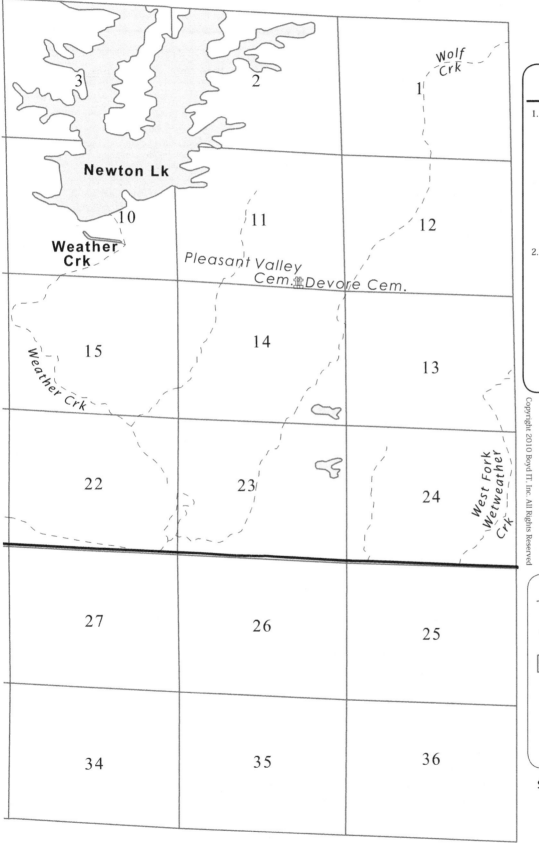

Helpful Hints

1. This Map takes a different look at the same Congressional Township displayed in the preceding two maps. It presents features that can help you better envision the historical development of the area: a) Water-bodies (lakes & ponds), b) Water-courses (rivers, streams, etc.), c) Railroads, d) City/town center-points (where they were oftentimes located when first settled), and e) Cemeteries.

2. Using this "Historical" map in tandem with this Township's Patent Map and Road Map, may lead you to some interesting discoveries. You will often find roads, towns, cemeteries, and waterways are named after nearby landowners: sometimes those names will be the ones you are researching. See how many of these research gems you can find here in Jasper County.

Legend

————————	Section Lines
+——+——+——+	Railroads
▭	Large Rivers & Bodies of Water
- - - - - - - -	Streams/Creeks & Small Rivers
●	Cities/Towns
⸸	Cemeteries

Scale: Section = 1 mile X 1 mile
(there are some exceptions)

Map Group 17: Index to Land Patents

Township 5-North Range 9-East (3rd PM)

After you locate an individual in this Index, take note of the Section and Section Part then proceed to the Land Patent map on the pages immediately following. You should have no difficulty locating the corresponding parcel of land.

The "For More Info" Column will lead you to more information about the underlying Patents. See the *Legend* at right, and the "How to Use this Book" chapter, for more information.

ID	Individual in Patent	Sec.	Sec. Part	Purchase Date	Sale Type	IL Aliquot Part	For More Info . . .
4498	AMES, Aaron H	7	SWNE	1852-06-02	FD	SWNE	
4497	" "	7	NWSE	1852-06-02	FD	NWSE	
4632	BALDREY, John	9	NWNW	1850-12-06	FD	NWNW	
4561	BEACH, Dennis	11	W½NW	1852-11-24	FD	W2NW	G:9
4562	" "	2	W½SW	1852-11-24	FD	W2SW	G:9
4562	BEACH, Spencer	2	W½SW	1852-11-24	FD	W2SW	G:9
4561	" "	11	W½NW	1852-11-24	FD	W2NW	G:9
4561	BEACH, Tamar	11	W½NW	1852-11-24	FD	W2NW	G:9
4562	" "	2	W½SW	1852-11-24	FD	W2SW	G:9
4729	BENNETT, William	10	NWNE	1873-04-08	RR	NWNE	
4730	BICKUS, William	6	E½NW	1853-05-06	FD	E2NW	
4731	" "	6	SWNW	1853-05-06	FD	SWNW	
4506	BLACK, Abner	8	SENW	1853-01-18	FD	SENW	
4505	" "	8	S½SW	1853-01-18	FD	S2SW	
4507	" "	8	SWSE	1853-02-01	FD	SWSE	
4558	BLACK, David A	14	NWNW	1851-06-02	FD	NWNW	R:JASPER
4557	" "	10	SWSE	1851-06-02	FD	SWSE	R:JASPER
4754	BLACK, William L	14	SENW	1851-10-28	FD	SENW	R:JASPER
4756	" "	3	NESW	1851-10-28	FD	NESW	R:JASPER
4753	" "	13	SWNW	1852-05-01	FD	SWNW	R:JASPER
4755	" "	16	L7	1853-11-14	SC	LOT7N2SENW	
4710	BLAIR, Thomas	16	L6	1853-11-14	SC	LOT6NESWNW	
4709	" "	16	L10	1853-11-14	SC	LOT10S2SENW	
4722	BLAIR, Thomas S	22	W½NW	1852-06-21	FD	W2NW	
4721	" "	21	E½NE	1852-06-21	FD	E2NE	
4525	BLANKENSHIP, Avery	16	L19	1853-11-14	SC	LOT19SESW	
4526	" "	16	L20	1853-11-14	SC	LOT20SWSW	
4634	BOOLE, John	6	SWNE	1851-08-25	FD	SWNE	R:INDIANA
4633	" "	6	E½NE	1851-08-25	FD	E2NE	R:INDIANA
4582	BOTOFF, George	20	E½NE	1851-04-03	FD	E2NE	R:JASPER
4583	" "	21	N½NW	1851-04-03	FD	N2NW	R:JASPER
4609	BRINDLEY, James	10	SWSW	1853-09-22	FD	SWSW	R:INDIANA
4610	" "	16	L1	1853-11-14	SC	LOT1NENE	
4611	" "	16	L2	1853-11-14	SC	LOT2NWNE	
4636	BRINDLEY, John	16	L14	1853-11-14	SC	LOT14NESW	
4659	" "	16	L13	1853-11-14	SC	LOT13NWSW	
4635	" "	16	L13	1853-11-14	SC	LOT13NWSW	
4518	BRISTOL, Andrew E	4	SWNE	1853-09-21	FD	SWNE	R:CRAWFORD
4643	BROWN, John	9	E½W½	1850-09-27	FD	E2W2	
4638	" "	17	NESE	1851-03-14	FD	NESE	R:INDIANA
4641	" "	20	NENW	1851-04-25	FD	NENW	R:INDIANA
4642	" "	4	SESW	1852-03-25	FD	SESW	R:JASPER
4640	" "	19	NWNE	1852-03-25	FD	NWNE	R:JASPER
4639	" "	18	SWSE	1852-03-25	FD	SWSE	R:JASPER
4637	" "	16	L12	1853-11-14	SC	LOT12SWSWNW	
4624	BYERS, James L	19	S½NW	1853-12-14	FD	S2NW	R:RICHLAND

ID	Individual in Patent	Sec.	Sec. Part	Purchase Date	Sale Type	IL Aliquot Part	For More Info . . .
4644	BYRN, John	22	E½NE	1852-02-17	FD	E2NE	R:INDIANA
4645	" "	22	NWNE	1852-04-12	FD	NWNE	R:JASPER
4711	BYRN, Thomas	15	S½NW	1853-08-08	FD	S2NW	
4612	CARTER, James	21	S½SW	1850-12-18	FD	S2SW	R:RICHLAND
4548	CHAMBERLAIN, Cyril	14	SWNW	1852-10-08	FD	SWNW	R:INDIANA
4547	" "	12	N½SW	1852-10-08	FD	N2SW	R:INDIANA
4546	" "	11	SESE	1852-10-08	FD	SESE	R:INDIANA
4524	COLLINS, Aquilla W	14	W½SE	1850-10-28	FD	W2SE	R:INDIANA
4732	COLLINS, William	14	E½SE	1852-06-29	FD	E2SE	
4500	CRAIG, Abigail	8	SWNW	1851-06-02	FD	SWNW	R:JASPER S:F
4499	" "	8	SENE	1851-06-02	FD	SENE	R:JASPER S:F
4613	CRAIG, James	7	NESE	1851-10-22	FD	NESE	
4614	" "	8	NWSW	1851-10-22	FD	NWSW	
4669	CRAVENS, Joseph	22	NENW	1849-11-03	FD	NENW	R:JASPER
4670	" "	22	NWSE	1851-05-21	FD	NWSE	R:JASPER
4714	" "	23	NWSW	1852-04-19	FD	NWSW	R:JASPER
4671	" "	23	NWSW	1852-04-19	FD	NWSW	R:JASPER
4733	CRAVENS, William	20	E½SW	1848-09-23	FD	E2SW	R:INDIANA
4735	" "	22	SENW	1848-09-23	FD	SENW	R:INDIANA
4712	" "	22	NESE	1852-04-12	FD	NESE	R:JASPER
4736	" "	22	SWNE	1852-04-12	FD	SWNE	R:JASPER
4734	" "	22	NESE	1852-04-12	FD	NESE	R:JASPER
4696	CROWLEY, Samuel B	13	NE	1853-05-04	FD	NE	
4536	CROWS, Calvin	7	SW	1853-03-02	FD	SW	R:RICHLAND
4535	" "	19	N½NW	1853-03-02	FD	N2NW	R:RICHLAND
4579	CURTIS, Eli	1	SESW	1853-03-12	FD	SESW	R:JASPER G:22
4580	" "	12	E½NW	1853-03-12	FD	E2NW	R:JASPER G:22
4581	EASTON, Eliphalet	20	S½SW	1853-07-09	FD	S2SW	
4617	EBLEN, James	19	SESE	1852-08-28	FD	SESE	R:INDIANA
4616	" "	19	S½SW	1852-08-28	FD	S2SWVOID	
4615	" "	19	S½SW	1852-08-28	FD	S2SWVOID	
4616	" "	19	S½SW	1859-07-28	FD	S2SW	
4615	" "	19	S½SW	1859-07-28	FD	S2SW	
4764	ELDER, William M	7	NWNE	1852-05-27	FD	NWNE	
4763	" "	6	SWSE	1852-05-27	FD	SWSE	
4762	" "	6	NWNE	1852-05-27	FD	NWNE	
4761	" "	5	SWSE	1852-05-27	FD	SWSE	
4760	" "	5	SENE	1852-05-27	FD	SENE	
4759	" "	5	NESE	1852-05-27	FD	NESE	
4757	" "	4	N½NW	1852-05-27	FD	N2NW	R:INDIANA
4758	" "	4	NWNE	1852-05-27	FD	NWNE	R:INDIANA
4627	FAGG, James M	10	SWNE	1853-09-07	FD	SWNE	R:JEFFERSON
4626	" "	10	NWSE	1853-09-07	FD	NWSE	R:JEFFERSON
4520	FISHER, Andrew	4	SWSE	1850-11-29	FD	SWSE	R:INDIANA
4522	" "	9	W½NE	1850-11-29	FD	W2NE	R:INDIANA
4519	" "	4	NWSE	1851-04-09	FD	NWSE	R:INDIANA
4521	" "	9	SENE	1851-04-09	FD	SENE	R:INDIANA
4508	FLEANER, Abraham	21	NESE	1852-10-18	FD	NESE	
4509	" "	21	SWSE	1852-10-18	FD	SWSE	
4511	FLEENER, Abraham	22	W½SW	1849-11-02	FD	W2SW	R:CLAY
4510	" "	21	SESE	1851-09-24	FD	SESE	R:JASPER
4685	GOODWIN, Nelson	9	SESE	1852-06-02	FD	SESE	
4683	" "	10	W½NW	1852-06-02	FD	W2NW	
4686	" "	9	SWSE	1852-06-02	FD	SWSE	
4684	" "	7	S½NW	1853-11-28	FD	S2NW	R:INDIANA
4655	GRAY, John M	19	SENE	1852-08-28	FD	SENE	R:INDIANA
4654	" "	19	N½SW	1852-08-28	FD	N2SW	R:INDIANA
4501	GRIMES, Abijah	16	L17	1853-11-14	SC	LOT17SESE	
4502	" "	16	L18	1853-11-14	SC	LOT18SWSE	
4584	GROVE, George	5	E½NW	1849-06-08	FD	E2NW	
4592	GROVE, George W	4	SWSW	1852-03-24	FD	SWSW	R:JASPER
4712	GRUBBS, Thomas	22	NESE	1852-09-10	FD	NESE	R:JASPER
4734	" "	22	NESE	1852-09-10	FD	NESE	R:JASPER
4713	" "	23	NWSE	1852-09-10	FD	NWSE	R:JASPER
4714	" "	23	NWSW	1852-09-10	FD	NWSW	R:JASPER
4671	" "	23	NWSW	1852-09-10	FD	NWSW	R:JASPER
4728	GRUBBS, Wesley	23	NESW	1851-12-19	FD	NESW	
4695	HALL, Richard	20	NWNE	1852-06-05	FD	NWNE	
4693	" "	16	L3	1853-11-14	SC	LOT3NENW	
4694	" "	16	L4	1853-11-14	SC	LOT4NWNW	
4563	HANDELY, Dennis	23	SESW	1851-01-03	FD	SESW	R:OHIO
4564	HANDLEY, Dennis	23	SWSE	1851-10-03	FD	SWSE	R:OHIO
4681	HANKINS, Moses	17	E½SW	1851-04-25	FD	E2SW	R:INDIANA

ID	Individual in Patent	Sec.	Sec. Part	Purchase Date	Sale Type	IL Aliquot Part	For More Info . . .
4682	HANKINS, Moses (Cont'd)	17	SWSE	1851-04-25	FD	SWSE	R:INDIANA
4646	HARRINGTON, John	17	NW	1851-11-13	FD	NW	
4706	HASTINGS, Stephen	5	SESE	1852-06-10	FD	SESE	R:INDIANA
4531	HEADY, Benjamin	17	NE	1851-03-20	FD	NE	
4533	" "	4	S½SW	1852-03-25	FD	S2SW	R:JASPER
4534	" "	9	NESE	1852-05-06	FD	NESE	R:JASPER
4532	" "	17	NWSE	1852-05-06	FD	NWSE	R:JASPER
4530	" "	16	L15	1853-11-14	SC	LOT15NWSE	
4676	HIGGINS, Martin	18	S½NW	1852-08-28	FD	S2NW	R:INDIANA
4675	" "	18	NE	1852-08-28	FD	NE	R:INDIANA
4673	" "	18	N½NW	1852-08-28	FD	N2NW	R:INDIANA
4674	" "	18	N½SW	1852-08-28	FD	N2SW	R:INDIANA
4677	" "	18	S½SW	1852-08-28	FD	S2SW	R:INDIANA
4657	HILL, John M L	13	E½SE	1853-03-09	FD	E2SE	
4658	" "	13	W½SE	1853-03-09	FD	W2SE	
4602	HOKE, Henry	17	SESE	1851-12-06	FD	SESE	
4544	HOOVER, Conrad	11	SWNE	1837-05-12	FD	SWNE	R:JASPER
4543	" "	11	NWNE	1851-03-29	FD	NWNE	R:JASPER
4545	" "	2	SESE	1853-02-01	FD	SESE	R:JASPER
4618	HOOVER, James	15	NENE	1851-03-29	FD	NENE	R:JASPER
4656	HOOVER, John M	2	SWSE	1850-11-11	FD	SWSE	R:JASPER
4715	HUGHES, Thomas	12	S½SW	1852-10-08	FD	S2SW	R:INDIANA
4718	" "	15	SENE	1852-10-08	FD	SENE	R:INDIANA
4717	" "	13	NENW	1852-10-08	FD	NENW	R:INDIANA
4716	" "	12	SE	1852-10-08	FD	SE	R:INDIANA
4742	HUMFREY, William	11	E½NE	1851-10-25	FD	E2NE	
4648	HUNTER, John	3	SESW	1852-12-06	FD	SESW	
4647	" "	10	NENW	1852-12-06	FD	NENW	
4619	HURST, James	11	NESE	1851-11-28	FD	NESE	R:JASPER
4651	JACKSON, John	6	E½SE	1849-11-16	FD	E2SE	
4652	" "	6	NWSE	1849-11-16	FD	NWSE	
4653	" "	7	NENE	1849-11-16	FD	NENE	
4649	" "	5	NWSW	1851-05-12	FD	NWSW	R:OHIO
4650	" "	5	W½NW	1851-05-12	FD	W2NW	R:OHIO
4745	JOHNSON, William K	2	W½NW	1853-05-04	FD	W2NW	R:OHIO
4744	" "	19	SWNE	1853-05-04	FD	SWNE	
4743	" "	19	NWSE	1853-05-04	FD	NWSE	
4746	" "	20	N½SW	1853-05-04	FD	N2SW	
4748	" "	3	E½SE	1853-05-04	FD	E2SE	
4747	" "	3	E½NE	1853-05-04	FD	E2NE	R:OHIO
4631	KELLAM, Jesse	13	SENW	1852-11-03	FD	SENW	
4662	KELLAM, John W	13	N½SW	1852-11-02	FD	N2SW	
4503	KETTLE, Abijah	1	SWSW	1853-03-03	FD	SWSW	G:41
4504	" "	12	W½NW	1853-03-03	FD	W2NW	G:41
4504	KETTLE, George	12	W½NW	1853-03-03	FD	W2NW	G:41
4503	" "	1	SWSW	1853-03-03	FD	SWSW	G:41
4504	KETTLE, Hulda A	12	W½NW	1853-03-03	FD	W2NW	G:41
4503	" "	1	SWSW	1853-03-03	FD	SWSW	G:41
4503	KETTLE, Josephine	1	SWSW	1853-03-03	FD	SWSW	G:41
4504	" "	12	W½NW	1853-03-03	FD	W2NW	G:41
4503	KETTLE, Silas	1	SWSW	1853-03-03	FD	SWSW	G:41
4504	" "	12	W½NW	1853-03-03	FD	W2NW	G:41
4504	KETTLE, Solomon	12	W½NW	1853-03-03	FD	W2NW	G:41
4503	" "	1	SWSW	1853-03-03	FD	SWSW	G:41
4749	KETTLE, William	15	E½SE	1851-10-25	FD	E2SE	
4750	" "	15	SESW	1851-10-25	FD	SESW	
4751	" "	15	SWSE	1851-10-25	FD	SWSE	
4503	KETTLE, William C	1	SWSW	1853-03-03	FD	SWSW	G:41
4504	" "	12	W½NW	1853-03-03	FD	W2NW	G:41
4700	KING, Samuel	19	NENE	1852-02-21	FD	NENE	R:INDIANA
4701	" "	21	E½NW	1853-02-01	FD	E2NW	
4608	KITCHELL, James A	24	SESW	1854-02-04	FD	SESW	R:CRAWFORD
4752	KITTLE, William	14	NENW	1852-05-01	FD	NENW	R:JASPER
4703	KOONS, Samuel	8	NWSE	1851-10-28	FD	NWSE	R:JASPER
4702	" "	8	NESW	1851-10-28	FD	NESW	R:JASPER
4541	LANCASTER, Clement	6	SW	1852-10-11	FD	SW	
4542	" "	7	N½NW	1852-10-11	FD	N2NW	
4523	LINN, Anna	3	NWNE	1853-09-17	FD	NWNE	R:JASPER S:F
4625	LINN, James	3	NWSE	1853-09-17	FD	NWSE	R:JASPER
4727	LINN, Wesley E	3	SWNE	1853-09-17	FD	SWNE	R:JASPER
4576	MCCARTY, Eijah	6	L3	1871-04-04	RR	LOT3NE	
4577	" "	6	L4 (E½)	1871-04-04	RR	E2LOT4NE	
4575	" "	6	L2 (S½)	1871-04-04	RR	S2LOT2NW	

ID	Individual in Patent	Sec.	Sec. Part	Purchase Date	Sale Type	IL Aliquot Part	For More Info . . .
4574	MCCARTY, Eijah (Cont'd)	6	L2 (N½)	1871-04-04	RR	N2LOT2NW	
4573	" "	6	L2	1871-04-04	RR	LOT2NE	
4572	" "	6	L1	1871-04-04	RR	LOT1NW	
4571	" "	6	W½SE	1871-04-04	RR	W2SE	
4570	" "	6	S½SW	1871-04-04	RR	S2SW	
4569	" "	6	NESE	1871-04-04	RR	NESE	
4568	" "	6	N½SW	1871-04-04	RR	N2SW	
4578	" "	6	L4 (W½)	1871-04-04	RR	W2LOT4NE	
4559	MCCULLOUGH, David	15	N½NW	1852-10-27	FD	N2NW	
4738	MCCULLOUGH, William D	10	SENW	1853-05-20	FD	SENW	
4737	" "	10	NWSW	1853-05-20	FD	NWSW	
4549	MCKAY, Daniel	15	NWNE	1853-09-22	FD	NWNE	R:INDIANA
4550	" "	16	L5	1853-11-14	SC	LOT5NWSWNW	
4552	" "	16	L9	1853-11-14	SC	LOT9SENE	
4551	" "	16	L8	1853-11-14	SC	LOT8SWNE	
4595	MEEK, Hamilton	1	SE	1853-05-04	FD	SE	
4601	" "	20	SWNE	1853-05-04	FD	SWNE	
4600	" "	20	SENW	1853-05-04	FD	SENW	
4599	" "	2	NESE	1853-05-04	FD	NESE	
4598	" "	2	E½NE	1853-05-04	FD	E2NE	
4596	" "	12	NE	1853-05-04	FD	NE	
4594	" "	1	NWSW	1853-05-04	FD	NWSW	
4593	" "	1	NESW	1853-05-04	FD	NESW	
4597	" "	19	SWSE	1853-05-04	FD	SWSE	
4692	METSKER, Philip	23	SWSW	1851-02-15	FD	SWSW	R:INDIANA
4704	MISNER, Sanford	18	NWSE	1853-11-28	FD	NWSE	R:INDIANA
4556	MONROE, Daniel P	24	W½SE	1853-03-04	FD	W2SE	
4554	" "	24	E½SE	1853-03-04	FD	E2SE	
4555	" "	24	W½NE	1853-03-04	FD	W2NE	
4553	" "	24	E½NE	1853-03-04	FD	E2NE	
4726	MUSER, Ulrick	23	NESE	1852-05-31	FD	NESE	
4687	NEEDHAM, Parkham S	8	NESE	1852-03-24	FD	NESE	R:KENTUCKY
4689	NEEDHAM, Philetus	3	SWSE	1852-12-06	FD	SWSE	
4690	NEEDHAM, Philetus S	10	N½NE	1851-06-02	FD	N2NE	R:JASPER
4691	" "	10	SENE	1852-03-24	FD	SENE	R:JASPER
4705	" "	10	SENE	1852-03-24	FD	SENE	R:JASPER
4769	NICELY, William S	24	SWSW	1852-05-31	FD	SWSW	
4767	" "	22	S½SE	1852-05-31	FD	S2SE	
4768	" "	23	SESE	1852-05-31	FD	SESE	
4635	NICHOLAS, John	16	L13	1857-09-22	SC	LOT13SWSW	
4659	" "	16	L13	1857-09-22	SC	LOT13SWSW	
4603	NOTINGHAM, Henry J	20	NWNW	1853-02-24	FD	NWNW	
4765	NOTINGHAM, William	20	SWNW	1852-10-12	FD	SWNW	
4680	PLANK, Mathew	14	NE	1850-10-28	FD	NE	R:INDIANA
4679	" "	13	NWNW	1850-10-28	FD	NWNW	R:INDIANA
4678	" "	11	SWSE	1850-10-28	FD	SWSE	R:INDIANA
4579	POWELL, John	1	SESW	1853-03-12	FD	SESW	R:JASPER G:22
4580	" "	12	E½NW	1853-03-12	FD	E2NW	R:JASPER G:22
4586	PRESTON, George R	21	W½NW	1853-08-13	FD	W2NW	
4585	PUTTROFF, George	16	L11	1853-11-14	SC	LOT11SESWNW	
4719	RAYLE, Thomas	11	NWSE	1851-10-25	FD	NWSE	
4529	" "	11	E½SW	1851-10-25	FD	E2SW	S:F G:50
4720	" "	11	SENW	1851-10-25	FD	SENW	
4591	REELHORN, George	24	NW	1852-05-13	FD	NW	
4590	" "	24	NW	1852-05-13	FD	NW	
4590	" "	24	NW	1852-05-31	FD	NW	
4589	" "	24	N½SW	1852-05-31	FD	N2SW	
4588	" "	13	SWSW	1852-05-31	FD	SWSW	
4587	" "	13	SESW	1852-05-31	FD	SESW	
4591	" "	24	NW	1852-05-31	FD	NW	
4707	RIDLEN, Stephen	17	W½SW	1851-08-23	FD	W2SW	
4708	" "	18	E½SE	1851-08-23	FD	E2SE	
4537	ROBERTS, Charles	6	NWNW	1850-08-27	FD	NWNW	R:INDIANA
4514	RUSING, Aguilla W	22	SWNW	1873-03-19	RR	SWNW	
4513	" "	20	SWSE	1873-03-31	RR	SWSE	
4766	RUSSEL, William	20	W½SE	1853-05-24	FD	W2SE	R:INDIANA
4623	SAMPSON, James J	15	W½SW	1852-06-29	FD	W2SW	
4622	" "	15	SWNE	1852-06-29	FD	SWNE	
4621	" "	15	NWSE	1852-06-29	FD	NWSE	
4620	" "	15	NESW	1852-08-23	FD	NESW	
4705	SANDS, Sarah	10	SENE	1873-01-27	RR	SENE	S:F
4691	" "	10	SENE	1873-01-27	RR	SENE	S:F
4607	SHORT, Isaac	7	S½SE	1852-06-02	FD	S2SE	

ID	Individual in Patent	Sec.	Sec. Part	Purchase Date	Sale Type	IL Aliquot Part	For More Info . . .
4660	SICKMEN, John	4	N½SW	1852-03-25	FD	N2SW	
4672	SMITH, Lewis N	21	W½NE	1853-02-14	FD	W2NE	
4629	STEWART, James	9	SWNW	1851-03-20	FD	SWNW	
4630	" "	9	W½SW	1851-03-20	FD	W2SW	
4628	" "	8	SESE	1851-03-20	FD	SESE	
4665	STEWART, Joseph A	4	E½NE	1851-04-09	FD	E2NE	R:INDIANA
4668	" "	9	NWSE	1851-04-09	FD	NWSE	R:INDIANA
4666	" "	6	NW	1851-04-09	FD	NW	R:INDIANA
4667	" "	7	SENE	1851-10-28	FD	SENE	R:JASPER
4661	TAYLOR, John	20	NESE	1853-09-03	FD	NESE	R:INDIANA
4527	THORNTON, Barbary A	11	NENW	1851-10-25	FD	NENW	S:F
4528	" "	2	NWSE	1851-10-25	FD	NWSE	S:F
4529	" "	11	E½SW	1851-10-25	FD	E2SW	S:F G:50
4699	TODD, Samuel B	5	W½NE	1851-07-25	FD	W2NE	
4697	" "	5	NENE	1851-07-25	FD	NENE	
4698	" "	5	NWSE	1851-07-25	FD	NWSE	
4515	TOLIVER, Allen	21	NWSE	1853-05-26	FD	NWSE	R:RICHLAND
4723	UNDERHILL, Thomas	11	W½SW	1843-01-24	FD	W2SW	R:JASPER
4560	VANWINKLE, David	3	L2 (S½)	1851-10-28	FD	S2LOT2SW	R:COLES
4538	WAKEFIELD, Charles	19	NESE	1852-04-20	FD	NESE	
4739	WATSON, William D	1	L4 (E½)	1852-08-28	FD	E2LOT4NE	R:COLES
4512	WEAVER, Abraham	16	L16	1853-11-14	SC	LOT16NESE	
4741	WHORTON, William H	1	NW	1853-05-20	FD	NW	R:INDIANA
4740	WHORTON, William H H	1		1853-05-20	FD	NERP	R:INDIANA
4604	WILLOUGHBY, Hiram	14	SW	1850-10-28	FD	SW	
4605	" "	23	NE	1850-10-28	FD	NE	
4606	" "	23	NW	1850-10-28	FD	NW	
4663	WOLF, John	18	NESW	1853-02-11	FD	NESW	R:RICHLAND
4565	WOOD, Dixon	5	SESW	1851-10-09	FD	SESW	R:JASPER
4664	WOOD, John	8	NENW	1851-10-21	FD	NENW	R:JASPER
4688	WOOD, Patrick E	8	NWNW	1852-02-16	FD	NWNW	R:INDIANA
4517	WOODFORD, Amasa D	4	E½SE	1837-11-06	FD	E2SE	R:CONNECTICUT
4516	" "	3	W½SW	1837-11-06	FD	W2SW	R:CONNECTICUT
4566	WOODS, Dixon	5	NESW	1852-06-26	FD	NESW	
4567	" "	5	SWSW	1852-11-05	FD	SWSW	
4539	WOOLLEY, Charles	2	E½NW	1852-11-24	FD	E2NW	R:INDIANA
4540	" "	2	W½NE	1852-11-24	FD	W2NE	R:INDIANA
4724	WORKS, Thomas	10	E½SE	1852-05-24	FD	E2SE	
4725	" "	10	E½SW	1852-05-24	FD	E2SW	

Patent Map

T5-N R9-E
3rd PM Meridian

Map Group 17

Township Statistics

Parcels Mapped	:	273
Number of Patents	:	1
Number of Individuals	:	137
Patentees Identified	:	129
Number of Surnames	:	105
Multi-Patentee Parcels	:	7
Oldest Patent Date	:	5/12/1837
Most Recent Patent	:	4/8/1873
Block/Lot Parcels	:	30
Cities and Towns	:	1
Cemeteries	:	3

Section 6
ROBERTS Charles 1850
STEWART Joseph A 1851
ELDER William M 1852
BOOLE John 1851
BICKUS William 1853
BICKUS William 1853
BOOLE John 1851
LANCASTER Clement 1852
MCCARTY Elijah 1871
MCCARTY Elijah 1871
JACKSON John 1849
MCCARTY Elijah 1871
Lots-Sec. 6
L1 MCCARTY, Elijah 1871
L2 MCCARTY, Elijah 1871
L2(N½) MCCARTY, Elijah 1871
L2(S½) MCCARTY, Elijah 1871
L3 MCCARTY, Elijah 1871
MCCARTY Elijah 1871
ELDER William M 1852
JACKSON John 1849
L4(E½) MCCARTY, Elijah 1871
L4(W½) MCCARTY, Elijah 1871

Section 5
JACKSON John 1851
GROVE George 1849
TODD Samuel B 1851
JACKSON John 1851
WOODS Dixon 1852
TODD Samuel B 1851
WOODS Dixon 1852
WOOD Dixon 1851
TODD Samuel B 1851
ELDER William M 1852
HASTINGS Stephen 1852

Section 4
ELDER William M 1852
ELDER William M 1852
STEWART Joseph A 1851
ELDER William M 1852
BRISTOL Andrew E 1853
SICKMEN John 1852
FISHER Andrew 1851
WOODFORD Amasa D 1837
GROVE George W 1852
HEADY Benjamin 1852
BROWN John 1852
FISHER Andrew 1850

Section 7
LANCASTER Clement 1852
ELDER William M 1852
JACKSON John 1849
GOODWIN Nelson 1853
AMES Aaron H 1852
STEWART Joseph A 1851
AMES Aaron H 1852
CRAIG James 1851
CROWS Calvin 1853
SHORT Isaac 1852

Section 8
WOOD Patrick E 1852
WOOD John 1851
CRAIG Abigail 1851
BLACK Abner 1853
CRAIG James 1851
CRAIG James 1851
KOONS Samuel 1851
BLACK Abner 1853
KOONS Samuel 1851
BLACK Abner 1853

Section 9
BALDREY John 1850
CRAIG Abigail 1851
STEWART James 1851
FISHER Andrew 1850
FISHER Andrew 1851
NEEDHAM Parkham S 1852
STEWART James 1851
STEWART Joseph A 1851
HEADY Benjamin 1852
STEWART James 1851
BROWN John 1850
GOODWIN Nelson 1852
GOODWIN Nelson 1852

Section 18
HIGGINS Martin 1852
HIGGINS Martin 1852
HIGGINS Martin 1852
HIGGINS Martin 1852
WOLF John 1853
MISNER Sanford 1853
RIDLEN Stephen 1851
HIGGINS Martin 1852
BROWN John 1852

Section 17
HARRINGTON John 1851
HEADY Benjamin 1851
RIDLEN Stephen 1851
HANKINS Moses 1851
HEADY Benjamin 1852
BROWN John 1851
HANKINS Moses 1851
HOKE Henry 1851

Section 16
Lots-Sec. 16
L1 BRINDLEY, James 1853
L2 BRINDLEY, James 1853
L3 HALL, Richard 1853
L4 HALL, Richard 1853
L5 MCKAY, Daniel 1853
L6 BLAIR, Thomas 1853
L7 BLACK, William L 1853
L8 MCKAY, Daniel 1853
L9 MCKAY, Daniel 1853
L10 BLAIR, Thomas 1853
L11 PUTTROFF, George 1853
L12 BROWN, John 1853
L13 BRINDLEY, John 1853
L13 NICHOLAS, John 1857
L14 BRINDLEY, John 1853
L15 HEADY, Benjamin 1853
L16 WEAVER, Abraham 1853
L17 GRIMES, Abijah 1853
L18 GRIMES, Abijah 1853
L19 BLANKENSHIP, Avery 1853
L20 BLANKENSHIP, Avery 1853

Section 19
CROWS Calvin 1853
BROWN John 1852
KING Samuel 1852
BYERS James L 1853
JOHNSON William K 1853
GRAY John M 1852
GRAY John M 1852
JOHNSON William K 1853
WAKEFIELD Charles 1852
EBLEN James 1852
EBLEN James 1859
MEEK Hamilton 1853

Section 20
NOTINGHAM Henry J 1853
BROWN John 1851
HALL Richard 1852
BOTOFF George 1851
NOTINGHAM William 1852
MEEK Hamilton 1853
MEEK Hamilton 1853
JOHNSON William K 1853
CRAVENS William 1848
RUSSEL William 1853
EBLEN James 1852
EASTON Eliphalet 1853
RUSING Aguilla W 1873

Section 21
BOTOFF George 1851
SMITH Lewis N 1853
PRESTON George R 1853
KING Samuel 1853
BLAIR Thomas S 1852
TAYLOR John 1853
TOLIVER Allen 1853
FLEANER Abraham 1852
CARTER James 1850
FLEANER Abraham 1852
FLEENER Abraham 1851

30 **29** **28**

31 **32** **33**

Section 3

Lots-Sec. 3
L2(S½) VANWINKLE, David 1851

LINN
Anna
1853

LINN
Wesley E
1853

JOHNSON
William K
1853

3

WOODFORD
Amasa D
1837

BLACK
William L
1851

LINN
James
1853

JOHNSON
William K
1853

HUNTER
John
1852

NEEDHAM
Philetus
1852

Section 2

JOHNSON
William K
1853

WOOLLEY
Charles
1852

WOOLLEY
Charles
1852

MEEK
Hamilton
1853

2

BEACH [9]
Dennis
1852

THORNTON
Barbary A
1851

MEEK
Hamilton
1853

HOOVER
John M
1850

HOOVER
Conrad
1853

Section 1

WHORTON
William H
1853

WHORTON
William H H
1853

1

MEEK
Hamilton
1853

MEEK
Hamilton
1853

MEEK
Hamilton
1853

KETTLE [41]
Abijah
1853

CURTIS [22]
Eli
1853

Lots-Sec. 1
L4(E½) WATSON, William D 1852

Section 10

GOODWIN
Nelson
1852

HUNTER
John
1852

BENNETT
William
1873

MCCULLOUGH
William D
1853

FAGG
James M
1853

NEEDHAM
Philetus S
1852

SANDS
Sarah
1873

10

MCCULLOUGH
William D
1853

WORKS
Thomas
1852

FAGG
James M
1853

BRINDLEY
James
1853

BLACK
David A
1851

Section 11

NEEDHAM
Philetus S
1851

BEACH [9]
Dennis
1852

THORNTON
Barbary A
1851

RAYLE
Thomas
1851

11

WORKS
Thomas
1852

UNDERHILL
Thomas
1843

THORNTON [50]
Barbary A
1851

HOOVER
Conrad
1851

HOOVER
Conrad
1837

RAYLE
Thomas
1851

PLANK
Mathew
1850

Section 12

HUMFREY
William
1851

HURST
James
1851

CHAMBERLAIN
Cyril
1852

KETTLE [41]
Abijah
1853

CURTIS [22]
Eli
1853

MEEK
Hamilton
1853

12

CHAMBERLAIN
Cyril
1852

HUGHES
Thomas
1852

HUGHES
Thomas
1852

Section 15

MCCULLOUGH
David
1852

MCKAY
Daniel
1853

HOOVER
James
1851

BYRN
Thomas
1853

SAMPSON
James J
1852

HUGHES
Thomas
1852

SAMPSON
James J
1852

SAMPSON
James J
1852

KETTLE
William
1851

15

SAMPSON
James J
1852

KETTLE
William
1851

KETTLE
William
1851

Section 14

BLACK
David A
1851

KITTLE
William
1852

CHAMBERLAIN
Cyril
1852

BLACK
William L
1851

WILLOUGHBY
Hiram
1850

14

PLANK
Mathew
1850

COLLINS
Aquilla W
1850

COLLINS
William
1852

Section 13

PLANK
Mathew
1850

HUGHES
Thomas
1852

BLACK
William L
1852

KELLAM
Jesse
1852

CROWLEY
Samuel B
1853

13

KELLAM
John W
1852

REELHORN
George
1852

REELHORN
George
1852

HILL
John M L
1853

HILL
John M L
1853

Section 22

BLAIR
Thomas S
1852

CRAVENS
Joseph
1849

BYRN
John
1852

RUSING
Aguilla W
1873

CRAVENS
William
1848

CRAVENS
William
1852

BYRN
John
1852

22

FLEENER
Abraham
1849

CRAVENS
Joseph
1851

CRAVENS
William
1852

GRUBBS
Thomas
1852

NICELY
William S
1852

Section 23

WILLOUGHBY
Hiram
1850

WILLOUGHBY
Hiram
1850

23

CRAVENS
Joseph
1852

GRUBBS
Thomas
1852

GRUBBS
Wesley
1851

GRUBBS
Thomas
1852

MUSER
Ulrick
1852

METSKER
Philip
1851

HANDELY
Dennis
1851

HANDLEY
Dennis
1851

NICELY
William S
1852

Section 24

REELHORN
George
1852

REELHORN
George
1852

REELHORN
George
1852

MONROE
Daniel P
1853

MONROE
Daniel P
1853

24

MONROE
Daniel P
1853

NICELY
William S
1852

KITCHELL
James A
1854

MONROE
Daniel P
1853

Jasper

Richland

Section 27

27

Section 26

26

Section 25

25

Section 34

34

Section 35

35

Section 36

36

Helpful Hints

1. This Map's INDEX can be found on the preceding pages.

2. Refer to Map "C" to see where this Township lies within Jasper County, Illinois.

3. Numbers within square brackets [ ] denote a multi-patentee land parcel (multi-owner). Refer to Appendix "C" for a full list of members in this group.

4. Areas that look to be crowded with Patentees usually indicate multiple sales of the same parcel (re-issues), cancellations or voided transactions (that we map, anyway) or overlapping parcels. We opt to show even these ambiguous parcels, which oftentimes lead to research avenues not yet taken.

Legend

——————— Patent Boundary

━━━━━━━ Section Boundary

▨▨▨▨▨▨▨ No Patents Found
(or Outside County)

1., 2., 3., ... Lot Numbers
(when beside a name)

[ ] Group Number
(see Appendix "C")

Scale: Section = 1 mile X 1 mile
(generally, with some exceptions)

Road Map

T5-N R9-E
3rd PM Meridian

Map Group 17

Cities & Towns
Shamrock

Cemeteries
Hankins Cemetery
Lancaster Cemetery
Woods Cemetery

6	5	4
7	8	9
18	17	16
19	20	21
30	29	28
31	32	33

N 725th St

Lancaster Cem.
E 300th Ave

Woods Cem.

N 700th St

N 600th St

N 800th St

N 875th St

E 200th Ave

N 750th St

Hankins Cem.

E 100th Ave

E Jasper Ln

Jasper

Richland

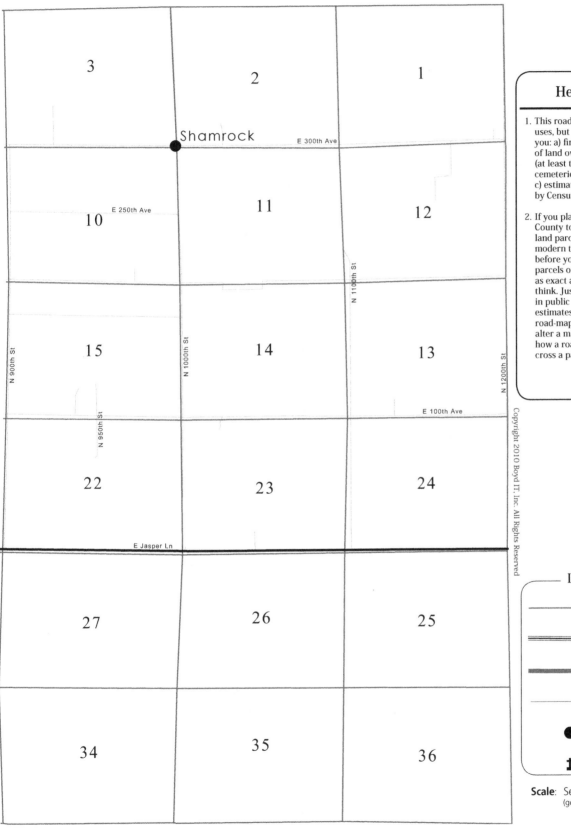

Helpful Hints

1. This road map has a number of uses, but primarily it is to help you: a) find the present location of land owned by your ancestors (at least the general area), b) find cemeteries and city-centers, and c) estimate the route/roads used by Census-takers & tax-assessors.

2. If you plan to travel to Jasper County to locate cemeteries or land parcels, please pick up a modern travel map for the area before you do. Mapping old land parcels on modern maps is not as exact a science as you might think. Just the slightest variations in public land survey coordinates, estimates of parcel boundaries, or road-map deviations can greatly alter a map's representation of how a road either does or doesn't cross a particular parcel of land.

Legend

———— Section Lines

═══════ Interstates

▬▬▬▬▬ Highways

———— Other Roads

● Cities/Towns

✝ Cemeteries

Scale: Section = 1 mile X 1 mile
(generally, with some exceptions)

Historical Map

T5-N R9-E
3rd PM Meridian

Map Group 17

Cities & Towns
Shamrock

Cemeteries
Hankins Cemetery
Lancaster Cemetery
Woods Cemetery

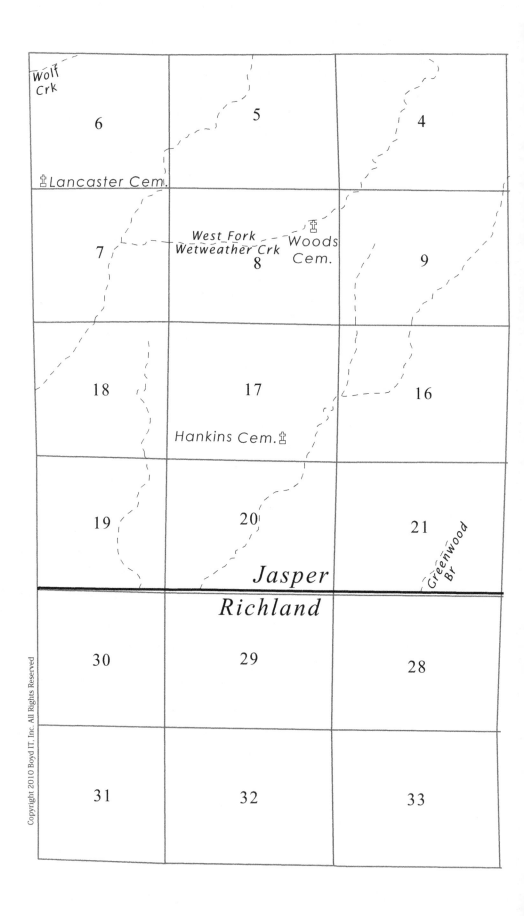

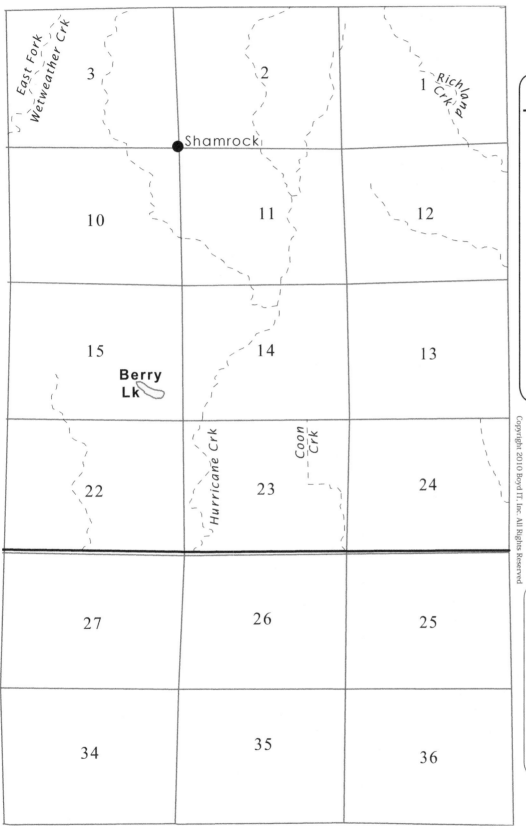

Helpful Hints

1. This Map takes a different look at the same Congressional Township displayed in the preceding two maps. It presents features that can help you better envision the historical development of the area: a) Water-bodies (lakes & ponds), b) Water-courses (rivers, streams, etc.), c) Railroads, d) City/town center-points (where they were oftentimes located when first settled), and e) Cemeteries.

2. Using this "Historical" map in tandem with this Township's Patent Map and Road Map, may lead you to some interesting discoveries. You will often find roads, towns, cemeteries, and waterways are named after nearby landowners: sometimes those names will be the ones you are researching. See how many of these research gems you can find here in Jasper County.

Legend

————————	Section Lines
+++++++++	Railroads
▭	Large Rivers & Bodies of Water
- - - - - - -	Streams/Creeks & Small Rivers
●	Cities/Towns
✝	Cemeteries

Scale: Section = 1 mile X 1 mile
(there are some exceptions)

Map Group 18: Index to Land Patents

Township 5-North Range 10-East (3rd PM)

After you locate an individual in this Index, take note of the Section and Section Part then proceed to the Land Patent map on the pages immediately following. You should have no difficulty locating the corresponding parcel of land.

The "For More Info" Column will lead you to more information about the underlying Patents. See the *Legend* at right, and the "How to Use this Book" chapter, for more information.

```
┌─────────────────────────────────────────────────────────────┐
│                       LEGEND                                  │
│         "For More Info . . . " column                         │
│  G = Group  (Multi-Patentee Patent, see Appendix "C")         │
│  R = Residence                                                │
│  S = Social Status                                            │
│                                                               │
│                                                               │
│  See Appendix A for list of abbreviations used by the         │
│  Illinois State Archives in describing the place and          │
│  nature of these land patents.                                │
│                                                               │
│  Note: if the Abbreviations contain "L", "BL", "LOT",         │
│  or "BLOCK", the exact whereabouts of the parcel within       │
│  the section is not known.                                    │
└─────────────────────────────────────────────────────────────┘
```

ID	Individual in Patent	Sec.	Sec. Part	Purchase Date	Sale Type	IL Aliquot Part	For More Info . . .
4869	ABELL, John S	22	NWSW	1852-09-08	FD	NWSW	
4867	" "	21	N½SE	1852-09-08	FD	N2SE	
4868	" "	21	SWNE	1852-09-08	FD	SWNE	
4853	ALLEN, John	16	L2	1853-05-14	SC	LOT2W2NE	
4852	" "	16	L1	1853-05-14	SC	LOT1NENE	
4954	BARTON, William H	22	W½NW	1852-08-11	FD	W2NW	
4953	" "	21	SWSW	1852-08-11	FD	SWSW	
4952	" "	21	E½NE	1852-08-11	FD	E2NE	
4904	BRICKENRIDGE, Magdale	6	S½SE	1853-02-14	FD	S2SE	
4942	BRUCE, William C	19	N½NW	1853-03-03	FD	N2NW	R:INDIANA
4944	" "	19	SWNW	1853-03-03	FD	SWNW	R:INDIANA
4943	" "	19	SENW	1853-03-04	FD	SENW	R:INDIANA
4770	BYERS, Alexander L	21	NENW	1853-12-14	FD	NENW	R:RICHLAND G:15
4771	" "	21	NWSW	1853-12-14	FD	NWSW	R:RICHLAND G:15
4770	BYERS, Robert	21	NENW	1853-12-14	FD	NENW	R:RICHLAND G:15
4771	" "	21	NWSW	1853-12-14	FD	NWSW	R:RICHLAND G:15
4828	BYRNE, Jacob	6	NENE	1852-09-07	FD	NENE	R:JASPER
4829	" "	6	NWNE	1853-10-20	FD	NWNE	R:JASPER
4945	CHERRY, William	14	SW	1853-02-25	FD	SW	
4937	CLARK, Samuel S	20	SESE	1852-09-03	FD	SESE	
4936	" "	20	NESW	1852-10-13	FD	NESW	
4814	CLUBB, Henry A	2	NW	1852-08-12	FD	NW	R:LAWRENCE
4905	CLUBB, Mary Jane	2	SW	1852-08-12	FD	SW	S:F
4786	COLEMAN, Daniel	18	SE	1853-02-25	FD	SE	
4788	" "	23	NW	1853-02-25	FD	NW	
4789	" "	23	NW	1853-02-25	FD	NW	
4787	" "	23	NESW	1853-02-25	FD	NESW	
4789	" "	23	NW	1857-02-04	FD	NW	
4788	" "	23	NW	1857-02-04	FD	NW	
4792	COLLINS, Elijah T	13	SESE	1852-09-03	FD	SESE	R:OHIO
4793	" "	24	NE	1852-09-03	FD	NE	
4794	" "	24	NW	1852-09-03	FD	NW	
4874	CROWLEY, Joseph B	7	N½NE	1853-05-04	FD	N2NE	
4931	CROWLEY, Samuel B	7	SW	1853-05-04	FD	SW	
4930	" "	7	NW	1853-05-04	FD	NW	
4920	CUMMINS, Robert	12	W½NE	1852-07-05	FD	W2NE	
4909	DOYLE, Michael	12	SENE	1850-07-26	FD	SENE	R:JASPER
4899	EARLY, Leeland	21	E½SW	1852-02-21	FD	E2SW	R:KENTUCKY
4898	" "	20	NESE	1852-02-21	FD	NESE	R:KENTUCKY
4951	ELIOT, William	16	L14	1853-05-14	SC	LOT14SESE	
4801	EYER, G Jacob	16	L9	1853-05-14	SC	LOT9NESW	
4800	" "	16	L3	1853-05-14	SC	LOT3E2NW	
4919	FERREE, Peter	12	W½SE	1852-06-12	FD	W2SE	
4918	" "	12	E½SW	1852-06-12	FD	E2SW	
4857	FOX, John	4	SENE	1852-11-27	FD	SENE	R:PENNSYLVANIA
4856	" "	4	N½NE	1852-11-27	FD	N2NE	R:PENNSYLVANIA

ID	Individual in Patent	Sec.	Sec. Part	Purchase Date	Sale Type	IL Aliquot Part	For More Info . . .
4855	FOX, John (Cont'd)	3	SWNW	1852-12-03	FD	SWNW	R: PENNSYLVANIA
4854	" "	3	SWNW	1852-12-03	FD	SWNW	R: PENNSYLVANIA
4854	" "	3	SWNW	1852-12-31	FD	SWNW	R: PENNSYLVANIA
4855	" "	3	SWNW	1852-12-31	FD	SWNW	R: PENNSYLVANIA
4783	GAINES, Benjamin	17	SWSE	1853-09-08	FD	SWSE	R: RICHLAND
4782	GAINS, Benjamin A	17	SESW	1853-02-17	FD	SESW	R: JASPER
4791	GARDINER, David M	19	NE	1852-11-06	FD	NE	
4858	GIBSON, John J	14	SEN½	1852-07-13	FD	S2NE	
4841	HALEY, James M	22	SWSW	1852-10-11	FD	SWSW	
4839	" "	21	SESE	1852-10-11	FD	SESE	
4840	" "	21	SWSE	1853-05-06	FD	SWSE	
4845	HALSEY, James S	12	NW	1852-06-14	FD	NW	
4846	" "	13	NENW	1852-07-13	FD	NENW	
4847	" "	13	NWNE	1852-07-13	FD	NWNE	
4848	" "	3	E½NE	1853-02-17	FD	E2NEVOID	
4851	" "	3	W½NE	1853-02-17	FD	W2NE	R: OHIO
4850	" "	3	E½NW	1853-02-17	FD	E2NW	R: OHIO
4849	" "	3	E½NE	1853-02-17	FD	E2NEVOID	
4848	" "	3	E½NE	1859-05-06	FD	E2NE	
4849	" "	3	E½NE	1859-05-06	FD	E2NE	
4917	HAMILTON, Pelatiah	19	W½SW	1853-03-07	FD	W2SW	R: OHIO
4915	" "	19	NESW	1853-03-07	FD	NESW	R: OHIO
4916	" "	19	SESW	1853-03-11	FD	SESW	R: OHIO
4838	HAY, James	6	SW	1853-05-04	FD	SW	
4837	" "	6	NW	1853-05-04	FD	NW	
4914	HINES, Patrick	9	NENE	1853-10-14	FD	NENE	R: INDIANA
4795	HINMAN, Fielding J	24	E½SW	1852-08-30	FD	E2SW	
4940	HINMAN, Titus M	24	W½SE	1852-07-09	FD	W2SE	
4941	" "	24	W½SW	1853-02-01	FD	W2SW	
4939	" "	16	L7	1853-05-14	SC	LOT7NESE	
4961	HOFFMAN, Willis	3	E½SE	1852-11-12	FD	E2SE	
4962	" "	3	W½SE	1852-11-12	FD	W2SE	
4921	HOUSTON, Robert	13	E½SW	1852-09-03	FD	E2SW	R: OHIO
4923	" "	13	SWNE	1852-09-03	FD	SWNE	R: OHIO
4924	" "	13	W½SE	1852-09-03	FD	W2SE	R: OHIO
4925	" "	13	W½SW	1852-09-03	FD	W2SW	R: OHIO
4922	" "	13	S½NW	1852-09-03	FD	S2NW	R: OHIO
4926	HUGHS, Robert	20	SENE	1851-10-15	FD	SENE	R: JASPER
4859	JACKSON, John	10	E½NE	1852-11-30	FD	E2NE	
4860	" "	10	NW	1852-11-30	FD	NW	
4862	" "	10	W½NE	1852-11-30	FD	W2NE	
4864	" "	11	W½NW	1852-11-30	FD	W2NW	
4863	" "	10	W½SE	1852-11-30	FD	W2SE	
4861	" "	10	SW	1852-11-30	FD	SW	
4785	KAUFFMANN, Cyriac	5	NENW	1852-02-16	FD	NENW	R: JASPER
4830	KENNERLY, Jacob	8	E½NW	1852-09-08	FD	E2NW	
4823	KING, Ira	22	S½SE	1852-07-12	FD	S2SE	
4824	" "	22	SESW	1852-07-12	FD	SESW	
4821	" "	18	SW	1853-03-11	FD	SW	R: CRAWFORD
4819	" "	18	NW	1853-03-11	FD	NW	R: CRAWFORD
4822	" "	22	NESW	1853-05-06	FD	NESW	
4825	" "	23	E½SE	1853-05-06	FD	E2SE	
4826	" "	23	NWSW	1853-05-06	FD	NWSW	
4827	" "	3	NWNW	1853-11-02	FD	NWNW	R: CRAWFORD
4820	" "	18	SENE	1853-11-02	FD	SENE	R: CRAWFORD
4784	LAGOW, Clark B	8	NWSW	1853-10-20	FD	NWSW	R: CRAWFORD
4878	LAWRENCE, Joseph	5	SW	1852-11-13	FD	SW	
4960	LAWRENCE, William	3	SW	1852-11-16	FD	SW	
4938	LILLY, Thomas W	21	NWNW	1852-12-23	FD	NWNW	
4790	LONG, David D	11	E½W½	1852-06-17	FD	E2W2	
4796	MATTINGLEY, Francis	18	SWNE	1852-08-23	FD	SWNE	
4802	MATTINGLEY, George	1	SWNE	1836-04-05	FD	SWNE	R: JASPER
4804	" "	9	SESE	1852-08-23	FD	SESE	
4803	" "	9	SENE	1852-08-23	FD	SENE	
4900	MATTINGLEY, Lewis	20	NENE	1847-02-17	FD	NENE	R: JASPER
4797	MATTINGLY, Francis	18	NENE	1852-02-21	FD	NENE	R: JASPER
4798	" "	18	NWNE	1852-06-25	FD	NWNE	
4799	" "	9	NESE	1853-03-09	FD	NESE	R: JASPER
4805	MATTINGLY, George	1	SENE	1839-09-26	FD	SENE	R: JASPER
4901	MATTINGLY, Lewis	20	E½NW	1852-11-02	FD	E2NW	
4902	" "	20	W½NE	1852-11-02	FD	W2NE	
4831	MAY, Jacob	16	L10	1853-05-14	SC	LOT10NWSW	
4818	MCCULLOUGH, Hiram	20	SWSE	1852-08-07	FD	SWSE	

ID	Individual in Patent	Sec.	Sec. Part	Purchase Date	Sale Type	IL Aliquot Part	For More Info . . .
4817	MCCULLOUGH, Hiram (Cont'd)	20	NWSE	1853-10-10	FD	NWSE	R:JASPER
4780	MCGAHEY, Allen	15	W½SW	1852-08-07	FD	W2SW	
4776	" "	15	E½SW	1852-08-07	FD	E2SW	
4775	" "	15	E½SE	1852-08-07	FD	E2SE	
4774	" "	15	E½NW	1852-08-07	FD	E2NW	
4777	" "	15	NE	1852-08-07	FD	NE	
4778	" "	15	W½NW	1852-08-07	FD	W2NW	
4779	" "	15	W½SE	1852-08-07	FD	W2SE	
4781	" "	16	L12	1853-05-14	SC	LOT12SESW	
4958	MCKINNEY, William J	13	NWNW	1852-06-17	FD	NWNW	
4959	" "	14	N½NE	1852-06-17	FD	N2NE	
4956	" "	11	SE	1852-06-17	FD	SE	
4955	" "	11	NE	1852-06-17	FD	NE	
4957	" "	12	SWSW	1852-06-17	FD	SWSW	
4927	MCKNIGHT, Robertson	22	E½NW	1852-10-21	FD	E2NW	
4928	" "	22	N½NE	1852-10-21	FD	N2NE	
4929	MCNIGHT, Robertson	16	L8	1853-05-14	SC	LOT8NWSE	
4932	MEDKIFF, Samuel	16	L13	1853-05-14	SC	LOT13SWSE	
4935	MIDKIFF, Samuel	24	E½SE	1852-06-11	FD	E2SE	
4934	" "	14	S½SE	1852-09-23	FD	S2SE	
4933	" "	14	N½SE	1853-02-12	FD	N2SE	
4947	MIDKIFF, William E	23	NENE	1852-09-23	FD	NENE	
4948	" "	23	NWNE	1852-09-23	FD	NWNE	
4949	" "	23	SEN½	1853-02-01	FD	S2NE	
4950	" "	23	W½SE	1853-02-12	FD	W2SE	
4946	" "	21	S½SW	1853-10-24	FD	S2SW	R:JASPER
4842	MINGS, James	7	N½SE	1852-09-08	FD	N2SE	
4843	" "	7	SEN½	1852-09-08	FD	S2NE	
4808	MORGAN, George	17	N½SE	1849-08-17	FD	N2SE	
4809	" "	17	N½SW	1849-08-17	FD	N2SW	
4810	" "	17	NWNW	1852-06-26	FD	NWNW	
4812	" "	7	S½SE	1852-06-26	FD	S2SE	
4813	" "	8	SWSW	1852-06-26	FD	SWSW	
4811	" "	17	SESE	1852-08-09	FD	SESE	
4807	" "	16	L5	1853-05-14	SC	LOT5SWNW	
4806	" "	16	L11	1853-05-14	SC	LOT11SWSW	
4772	MYERS, Alexander	6	N½SE	1852-09-10	FD	N2SE	R:KENTUCKY
4773	" "	6	SEN½	1852-09-10	FD	S2NE	R:KENTUCKY
4835	NICHOLS, James D	17	SWNW	1853-05-21	FD	SWNW	
4903	OST, Lewis	13	NENE	1852-08-04	FD	NENE	
4875	PAGE, Joseph C	19	SE	1852-08-12	FD	SE	
4877	" "	20	W½SW	1853-02-02	FD	W2SW	
4876	" "	20	SESW	1853-02-02	FD	SESW	
4844	PICQUET, James	1	SESE	1852-06-29	FD	SESE	
4890	PICQUET, Joseph	5	SENW	1837-10-07	FD	SENW	R:JASPER
4881	" "	1	W½	1837-10-07	FD	W2	R:JASPER
4884	" "	17	E½NW	1837-10-07	FD	E2NW	R:JASPER
4885	" "	17	NE	1837-10-07	FD	NE	R:JASPER
4886	" "	2	E½	1837-10-07	FD	E2	R:JASPER
4889	" "	5	E½	1837-10-07	FD	E2	R:JASPER
4896	" "	9	W½	1837-10-07	FD	W2	R:JASPER
4891	" "	5	W½NW	1837-10-07	FD	W2NW	R:JASPER
4892	" "	8	E½	1837-10-07	FD	E2	R:JASPER
4893	" "	8	E½SW	1837-10-07	FD	E2SW	R:JASPER
4888	" "	4	W½	1837-10-07	FD	W2	R:JASPER
4883	" "	12	E½SE	1839-04-10	FD	E2SE	R:JASPER
4880	" "	1	NWNE	1839-04-10	FD	NWNE	R:JASPER
4879	" "	1	NENE	1840-01-08	FD	NENE	R:JASPER
4887	" "	4	SE	1840-03-17	FD	SE	R:JASPER
4894	" "	9	NWNE	1840-04-04	FD	NWNE	R:JASPER
4895	" "	9	SWSE	1840-04-04	FD	SWSE	R:JASPER
4882	" "	1	W½SE	1841-02-09	FD	W2SE	R:JASPER
4865	POWELL, John	16	L4	1853-05-14	SC	LOT4NWNW	
4832	RAEF, Jacob	13	NESE	1853-03-09	FD	NESE	
4833	" "	13	SENE	1853-03-09	FD	SENE	
4866	RIPPETO, John	12	NWSW	1853-02-12	FD	NWSW	
4910	ROONEY, Michael	4	SWNE	1852-07-27	FD	SWNE	R:JASPER
4897	SCHELDBANER, Joseph	1	NESE	1848-04-26	FD	NESE	R:JASPER
4834	SHIPLEY, Jacob	10	E½SE	1852-10-19	FD	E2SE	
4836	STEEL, James H	8	NWNW	1853-10-20	FD	NWNW	R:CRAWFORD
4912	STONEBARGER, Nesbitt	22	SEN½	1852-08-03	FD	S2NE	
4913	" "	23	S½SW	1852-08-03	FD	S2SW	
4911	" "	22	N½SE	1852-08-03	FD	N2SE	

ID	Individual in Patent	Sec.	Sec. Part	Purchase Date	Sale Type	IL Aliquot Part	For More Info . . .
4908	TIPPIT, Mathew L	21	NWNE	1853-06-11	FD	NWNE	
4907	" "	20	W½NW	1853-06-11	FD	W2NW	
4906	" "	17	SWSW	1853-06-11	FD	SWSW	
4870	UNDERHILL, John	9	NWSE	1839-08-19	FD	NWSE	R:JASPER
4871	" "	9	SWNE	1839-09-05	FD	SWNE	R:JASPER
4872	WOLF, John	16	L6	1853-05-14	SC	LOT6SENE	
4816	ZELL, Henry	14	W½NW	1852-10-01	FD	W2NW	
4815	" "	11	W½SW	1852-10-19	FD	W2SW	
4873	ZELL, John	14	E½NW	1852-09-23	FD	E2NW	

Patent Map

T5-N R10-E
3rd PM Meridian

Map Group 18

Township Statistics

Parcels Mapped	:	193
Number of Patents	:	1
Number of Individuals	:	82
Patentees Identified	:	81
Number of Surnames	:	70
Multi-Patentee Parcels	:	2
Oldest Patent Date	:	4/5/1836
Most Recent Patent	:	5/6/1859
Block/Lot Parcels	:	14
Cities and Towns	:	1
Cemeteries	:	1

Section 6
- HAY James 1853
- HAY James 1853
- BYRNE Jacob 1853
- BYRNE Jacob 1852
- MYERS Alexander 1852
- MYERS Alexander 1852
- BRICKENRIDGE Magdale 1853

Section 5
- KAUFFMANN Cyriac 1852
- PICQUET Joseph 1837
- PICQUET Joseph 1837
- PICQUET Joseph 1837
- LAWRENCE Joseph 1852

Section 4
- PICQUET Joseph 1837
- FOX John 1852
- ROONEY Michael 1852
- FOX John 1852
- PICQUET Joseph 1840

Section 7
- CROWLEY Samuel B 1853
- CROWLEY Joseph B 1853
- CROWLEY Samuel B 1853
- MINGS James 1852
- MINGS James 1852
- MORGAN George 1852

Section 8
- STEEL James H 1853
- KENNERLY Jacob 1852
- LAGOW Clark B 1853
- PICQUET Joseph 1837
- PICQUET Joseph 1837
- MORGAN George 1852

Section 9
- PICQUET Joseph 1837
- PICQUET Joseph 1840
- HINES Patrick 1853
- UNDERHILL John 1839
- MATTINGLEY George 1852
- UNDERHILL John 1839
- MATTINGLEY Francis 1853
- PICQUET Joseph 1840
- MATTINGLEY George 1852

Section 18
- KING Ira 1853
- KING Ira 1853
- MATTINGLY Francis 1852
- MATTINGLY Francis 1852
- MATTINGLEY Francis 1852
- KING Ira 1853
- COLEMAN Daniel 1853

Section 17
- MORGAN George 1852
- PICQUET Joseph 1837
- NICHOLS James D 1853
- MORGAN George 1849
- PICQUET Joseph 1837
- MORGAN George 1849
- TIPPIT Mathew L 1853
- GAINS Benjamin A 1853
- GAINES Benjamin 1853
- MORGAN George 1852

Section 16
Lots-Sec. 16
L1	ALLEN, John	1853
L2	ALLEN, John	1853
L3	EYER, G Jacob	1853
L4	POWELL, John	1853
L5	MORGAN, George	1853
L6	WOLF, John	1853
L7	HINMAN, Titus M	1853
L8	MCNIGHT, Robertson	1853
L9	EYER, G Jacob	1853
L10	MAY, Jacob	1853
L11	MORGAN, George	1853
L12	MCGAHEY, Allen	1853
L13	MEDKIFF, Samuel	1853
L14	ELIOT, William	1853

Section 19
- BRUCE William C 1853
- BRUCE William C 1853
- BRUCE William C 1853
- GARDINER David M 1852
- HAMILTON Pelatiah 1853
- HAMILTON Pelatiah 1853
- HAMILTON Pelatiah 1853
- PAGE Joseph C 1852

Section 20
- TIPPIT Mathew L 1853
- MATTINGLY Lewis 1852
- MATTINGLY Lewis 1852
- MATTINGLY Lewis 1847
- HUGHS Robert 1851
- CLARK Samuel S 1852
- MCCULLOUGH Hiram 1853
- EARLY Leeland 1852
- PAGE Joseph C 1853
- PAGE Joseph C 1853
- MCCULLOUGH Hiram 1852
- CLARK Samuel S 1852

Section 21
- LILLY Thomas W 1852
- BYERS [15] Alexander L 1853
- TIPPIT Mathew L 1853
- ABELL John S 1852
- BARTON William H 1852
- BYERS [15] Alexander L 1853
- EARLY Leeland 1852
- ABELL John S 1852
- BARTON William H 1852
- MIDKIFF William E 1853
- HALEY James M 1853
- HALEY James M 1852

Section 30

Section 29

Section 28

Section 31

Section 32

Section 33

KING Ira 1853	HALSEY James S 1853	HALSEY James S 1853	HALSEY James S 1853 HALSEY James S 1859	CLUBB Henry A 1852	PICQUET Joseph 1837

3

2

1

PICQUET Joseph 1837

PICQUET Joseph 1839 | PICQUET Joseph 1840

MATTINGLEY George 1836 | MATTINGLY George 1839

SCHELDBANER Joseph 1848

FOX John 1852

LAWRENCE William 1852

HOFFMAN Willis 1852

HOFFMAN Willis 1852

CLUBB Mary Jane 1852

PICQUET Joseph 1841

PICQUET James 1852

10

JACKSON John 1852

JACKSON John 1852 | JACKSON John 1852 | JACKSON John 1852

LONG David D 1852

MCKINNEY William J 1852

HALSEY James S 1852

CUMMINS Robert 1852

12

DOYLE Michael 1850

JACKSON John 1852

JACKSON John 1852 | SHIPLEY Jacob 1852

ZELL Henry 1852

MCKINNEY William J 1852

RIPPETO John 1853

MCKINNEY William J 1852

FERREE Peter 1852

FERREE Peter 1852

PICQUET Joseph 1839

15

MCGAHEY Allen 1852

MCGAHEY Allen 1852

MCGAHEY Allen 1852

ZELL Henry 1852

ZELL John 1852

14

MCKINNEY William J 1852

GIBSON John J 1852

MCKINNEY William J 1852

HALSEY James S 1852

HALSEY James S 1852

OST Lewis 1852

HOUSTON Robert 1852

HOUSTON Robert 1852

RAEF Jacob 1853

13

MCGAHEY Allen 1852

MCGAHEY Allen 1852

MCGAHEY Allen 1852

MCGAHEY Allen 1852

CHERRY William 1853

MIDKIFF Samuel 1853

MIDKIFF Samuel 1852

HOUSTON Robert 1852

HOUSTON Robert 1852

HOUSTON Robert 1852

RAEF Jacob 1853

COLLINS Elijah T 1852

22

BARTON William H 1852

MCKNIGHT Robertson 1852

MCKNIGHT Robertson 1852

STONEBARGER Nesbitt 1852

COLEMAN Daniel 1853

COLEMAN Daniel 1857

MIDKIFF William E 1852 | MIDKIFF William E 1852

MIDKIFF William E 1853

COLLINS Elijah T 1852

COLLINS Elijah T 1852

24

ABELL John S 1852

KING Ira 1853

STONEBARGER Nesbitt 1852

KING Ira 1853

COLEMAN Daniel 1853

23

KING Ira 1853

MIDKIFF William E 1853

HINMAN Titus M 1853

HINMAN Fielding J 1852

HINMAN Titus M 1852

MIDKIFF Samuel 1852

HALEY James M 1852

KING Ira 1852

Jasper

KING Ira 1852

STONEBARGER Nesbitt 1852

Richland

27

26

25

34

35

36

Helpful Hints

1. This Map's INDEX can be found on the preceding pages.

2. Refer to Map "C" to see where this Township lies within Jasper County, Illinois.

3. Numbers within square brackets [ ] denote a multi-patentee land parcel (multi-owner). Refer to Appendix "C" for a full list of members in this group.

4. Areas that look to be crowded with Patentees usually indicate multiple sales of the same parcel (re-issues), cancellations or voided transactions (that we map, anyway) or overlapping parcels. We opt to show even these ambiguous parcels, which oftentimes lead to research avenues not yet taken.

L e g e n d

———— Patent Boundary

━━━━ Section Boundary

No Patents Found (or Outside County)

1., 2., 3., ... Lot Numbers (when beside a name)

[ ] Group Number (see Appendix "C")

Scale: Section = 1 mile X 1 mile (generally, with some exceptions)

Road Map

T5-N R10-E
3rd PM Meridian

Map Group 18

Cities & Towns
West Liberty

Cemeteries
Bethel Cemetery

| 6 | 5 | 4 |
E 330th Ave

E 300th Ave

| 7 | 8 E 250th Ave | 9 |

N 1400th St

E 200th Ave

| 18 | 17 | 16 |

Bethel Cem.

| 19 | 20 | 21 |

N 1450th St

E 25th Ave

N 1200th St

N 1300th St

N 1425th St

E Jasper Ln

State Rte 130

| 30 | 29 | 28 |

| 31 | 32 | 33 |

3

2

1

10

11

12

E 200th Ave

N 1700th St

15

14

13

N 1800th St

E 100th Ave

N 1600th St

22

Oson Ave

23

24

Oson

W Walnut St   Walnut St

N Elm St   N West St   N Silver St   N East St

E 25th Ave

West Liberty

Jasper

E Jasper Ln

E Richland Ave

Richland

27

26

25

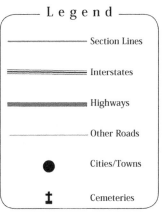

34

35

36

Scale: Section = 1 mile X 1 mile
(generally, with some exceptions)

Historical Map

T5-N R10-E
3rd PM Meridian

Map Group 18

Cities & Towns
West Liberty

Cemeteries
Bethel Cemetery

6	5	4
7	8	9
18	17	16
19	20	21
30	29	28
31	32	33

Richland Crk

Fox Riv

Bethel Cem.

Jasper

Richland

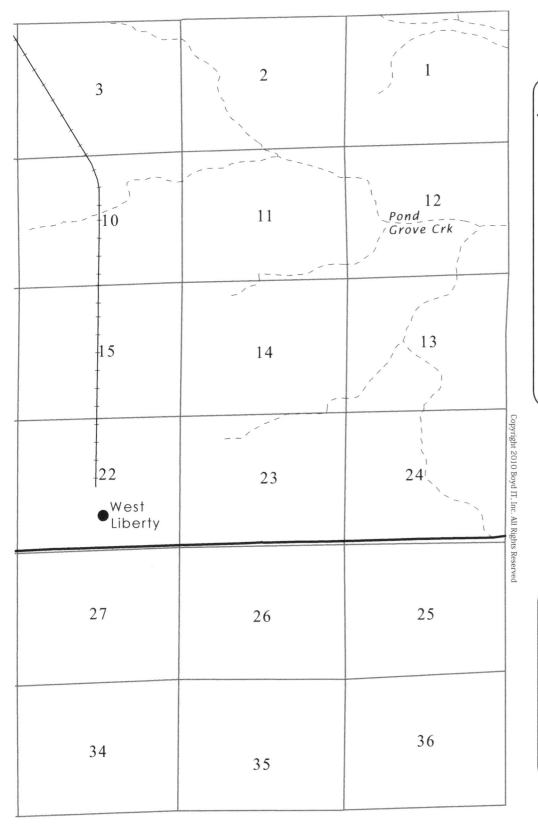

3

2

1

10

11

12
Pond
Grove Crk

15

14

13

22

23

24

●West
Liberty

27

26

25

34

35

36

Helpful Hints

1. This Map takes a different look at the same Congressional Township displayed in the preceding two maps. It presents features that can help you better envision the historical development of the area: a) Water-bodies (lakes & ponds), b) Water-courses (rivers, streams, etc.), c) Railroads, d) City/town center-points (where they were oftentimes located when first settled), and e) Cemeteries.

2. Using this "Historical" map in tandem with this Township's Patent Map and Road Map, may lead you to some interesting discoveries. You will often find roads, towns, cemeteries, and waterways are named after nearby landowners: sometimes those names will be the ones you are researching. See how many of these research gems you can find here in Jasper County.

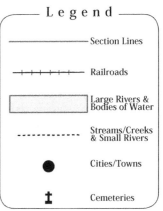

Legend

————————	Section Lines
+++++++	Railroads
▭	Large Rivers & Bodies of Water
- - - - - - - -	Streams/Creeks & Small Rivers
●	Cities/Towns
☨	Cemeteries

Scale: Section = 1 mile X 1 mile
(there are some exceptions)

Map Group 19: Index to Land Patents

Township 5-North Range 11-East (3rd PM)

After you locate an individual in this Index, take note of the Section and Section Part then proceed to the Land Patent map on the pages immediately following. You should have no difficulty locating the corresponding parcel of land.

The "For More Info" Column will lead you to more information about the underlying Patents. See the *Legend* at right, and the "How to Use this Book" chapter, for more information.

ID	Individual in Patent	Sec.	Sec. Part	Purchase Date	Sale Type	IL Aliquot Part	For More Info . . .
5002	BARRASIER, Thomas	19	NENE	1851-10-22	FD	NENE	R:JASPER
4991	BRAZIER, Julian	7	L6	1854-08-19	SC	LOT6E2SENE	
4969	BROWNFIELD, Felix	7	SWSE	1842-12-15	FD	SWSE	R:JASPER
4998	CASEY, Patrick	7	E½SE	1843-04-25	FD	E2SE	R:PENNSYLVANIA
4967	COLLINS, Elijah T	19	N½NW	1852-09-03	FD	N2NW	R:OHIO
4968	" "	19	NWNE	1852-09-03	FD	NWNE	R:OHIO
4966	" "	18	S½SW	1852-09-03	FD	S2SW	R:OHIO
4983	COOK, Joseph	18	E½SE	1852-07-20	FD	E2SE	
4992	DASHLER, Lewis	7	L3	1854-08-19	SC	L3W2SWSE	
4964	DOWNEY, Charles	7	NW	1843-04-22	FD	NW	R:PENNSYLVANIA
4984	FOOR, Joseph	7	L2	1854-08-19	SC	L2NWNE	
4985	FORE, Joseph	6	N½SW	1848-04-17	FD	N2SW	R:JASPER
4993	FRIEDLIEN, Lewis	6	SE	1843-01-12	FD	SE	R:JASPER
4974	MAY, Jacob	19	SESE	1851-12-29	FD	SESE	R:RICHLAND
4971	" "	19	NESE	1852-01-07	FD	NESE	
4973	" "	19	SENE	1852-01-07	FD	SENE	
4976	" "	19	SWNE	1852-06-23	FD	SWNE	R:CUMBERLAND
4975	" "	19	SW	1852-06-23	FD	SW	R:CUMBERLAND
4977	" "	19	W½SE	1852-06-23	FD	W2SE	R:CUMBERLAND
4972	" "	19	S½NW	1852-06-23	FD	S2NW	R:CUMBERLAND
4965	MURPHEY, Charles	7	SW	1843-04-22	FD	SW	R:PENNSYLVANIA
4994	OKEAN, Mortimer	6	NWNE	1853-12-08	FD	NWNE	R:JASPER
4995	" "	6	SENE	1853-12-08	FD	SENE	R:JASPER
4981	PICQUET, James	6	S½SW	1852-06-29	FD	S2SW	R:JASPER
4986	PICQUET, Joseph	6	NW	1837-10-07	FD	NW	R:JASPER
4978	RAEF, Jacob	18	NWSW	1853-03-09	FD	NWSW	R:JASPER
4979	" "	18	S½NW	1853-03-09	FD	S2NW	R:JASPER
4996	RAFE, Nicholas	18	E½NE	1840-06-10	FD	E2NE	R:JASPER
4997	" "	18	NWNE	1852-06-26	FD	NWNE	
5001	RAFE, Peter	18	W½SE	1853-05-24	FD	W2SE	R:JASPER
5000	" "	18	SWNE	1853-05-24	FD	SWNE	R:JASPER
4999	" "	18	NESW	1853-05-24	FD	NESW	R:JASPER
4988	SCHELDBANER, Joseph	6	SWNE	1848-04-11	FD	SWNE	R:JASPER
4987	" "	6	NENE	1848-04-26	FD	NENE	R:JASPER
4990	SCHIFFERSTEIN, Joseph	7	L5	1854-08-19	SC	L5W2SENE	
4989	" "	7	L1	1854-08-19	SC	L1NENE	
4980	SCHUHK, Jacob	7	NWSE	1853-12-30	FD	NWSE	R:JASPER
4963	SHUE, Andrew	18	N½NW	1852-08-06	FD	N2NW	R:JASPER
4982	SHUH, John B	7	L4	1854-08-19	SC	LOT4E2SWNE	
4970	STERCHY, Henry	6	SENW	1852-03-31	FD	SENW	R:RICHLAND

PICQUET Joseph 1837	OKEAN Mortimer 1853	SCHELDBANER Joseph 1848		
	STERCHY Henry 1852	SCHELDBANER Joseph 1848	OKEAN Mortimer 1853	

FORE Joseph 1848 **6**

FRIEDLIEN Lewis 1843

PICQUET James 1852

Lots-Sec. 7
L1 SCHIFFERSTEIN,Josep1854
L2 FOOR, Joseph   1854
L3 DASHLER, Lewis 1854
L4 SHUH, John B   1854
L5 SCHIFFERSTEIN,Josep1854
L6 BRAZIER, Julian1854

DOWNEY Charles 1843

7 SCHUHK Jacob 1853

MURPHEY Charles 1843

CASEY Patrick 1843

BROWNFIELD Felix 1842

SHUE Andrew 1852

RAFE Nicholas 1852

RAEF Jacob 1853

RAFE Peter 1853

RAFE Nicholas 1840

18

RAEF Jacob 1853

RAFE Peter 1853

RAFE Peter 1853

COOK Joseph 1852

COLLINS Elijah T 1852

COLLINS Elijah T 1852

COLLINS Elijah T 1852

BARRASIER Thomas 1851

MAY Jacob 1852

MAY Jacob 1852

MAY Jacob 1852

19

MAY Jacob 1852

MAY Jacob 1852

MAY Jacob 1852

MAY Jacob 1851

Jasper

Richland

30

31

Patent Map

T5-N R11-E
3rd PM Meridian

Map Group 19

Township Statistics

Parcels Mapped	:	40
Number of Patents	:	1
Number of Individuals	:	25
Patentees Identified	:	25
Number of Surnames	:	23
Multi-Patentee Parcels	:	0
Oldest Patent Date	:	10/7/1837
Most Recent Patent	:	8/19/1854
Block/Lot Parcels	:	6
Cities and Towns	:	0
Cemeteries	:	0

Note: the area contained in this map amounts to far less than a full Township. Therefore, its contents are completely on this single page (instead of a "normal" 2-page spread).

Legend

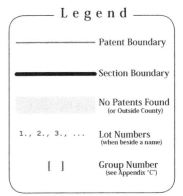

———— Patent Boundary

━━━━ Section Boundary

▨▨▨▨ No Patents Found (or Outside County)

1., 2., 3., ... Lot Numbers (when beside a name)

[ ] Group Number (see Appendix "C")

Scale: Section = 1 mile X 1 mile (generally, with some exceptions)

Road Map

T5-N R11-E
3rd PM Meridian

Map Group 19

Note: the area contained in this map amounts to far less than a full Township. Therefore, its contents are completely on this single page (instead of a "normal" 2-page spread).

Cities & Towns
None

Cemeteries
None

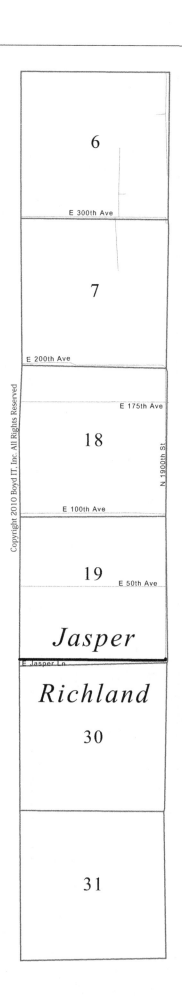

6

E 300th Ave

7

E 200th Ave

E 175th Ave

18

N 1900th St

E 100th Ave

19

E 50th Ave

Jasper

E Jasper Ln

Richland

30

31

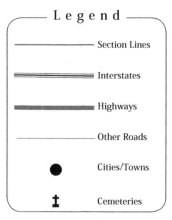

Legend

—————— Section Lines

═══════ Interstates

━━━━━━ Highways

—————— Other Roads

● Cities/Towns

✝ Cemeteries

Scale: Section = 1 mile X 1 mile
(generally, with some exceptions)

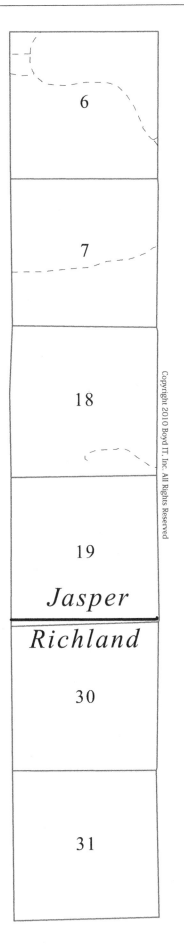

Historical Map

T5-N R11-E
3rd PM Meridian

Map Group 19

Note: the area contained in this map amounts to far less than a full Township. Therefore, its contents are completely on this single page (instead of a "normal" 2-page spread).

Cities & Towns
None

Cemeteries
None

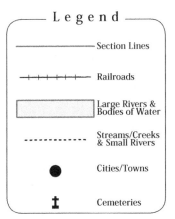

Legend

Section Lines

Railroads

Large Rivers & Bodies of Water

Streams/Creeks & Small Rivers

Cities/Towns

Cemeteries

Scale: Section = 1 mile X 1 mile
(there are some exceptions)

Map Group 20: Index to Land Patents

Township 5-North Range 14-West (2nd PM)

After you locate an individual in this Index, take note of the Section and Section Part then proceed to the Land Patent map on the pages immediately following. You should have no difficulty locating the corresponding parcel of land.

The "For More Info" Column will lead you to more information about the underlying Patents. See the *Legend* at right, and the "How to Use this Book" chapter, for more information.

```
                          LEGEND
              "For More Info . . . " column
G = Group   (Multi-Patentee Patent, see Appendix "C")
R = Residence
S = Social Status


See Appendix A for list of abbreviations used by the
Illinois State Archives in describing the place and
nature of these land patents.

Note: if the Abbreviations contain "L", "BL", "LOT",
or "BLOCK", the exact whereabouts of the parcel within
the section is not known.
```

ID	Individual in Patent	Sec.	Sec. Part	Purchase Date	Sale Type	IL Aliquot Part	For More Info . . .
5165	ADAMS, Waldo T	5	L1	1852-07-15	FD	LOT1NW	
5164	ALMAN, Von John	17	SESW	1852-07-07	FD	SESW	
5105	ANDREWS, Luther T	15	SESE	1865-05-09	SW	SESE	
5106	"	22	W½NE	1865-05-09	SW	W2NE	
5004	ANTHOFER, Andrew	6	SESE	1852-06-21	FD	SESE	
5011	BAUMAN, Christian	20	SWNE	1852-06-30	FD	SWNE	S:A
5009	BENNETT, Benjamin S	22	SENE	1865-05-19	SW	SENE	
5008	" "	22	NESE	1865-05-19	SW	NESE	
5077	BERLIN, John	21	NESE	1851-10-08	FD	NESE	
5035	BERRY, George	10	SWSE	1852-08-30	FD	SWSE	R:INDIANA
5020	BISHOP, Elisha	10	SESW	1854-01-10	FD	SESW	R:JASPER
5078	BLAKE, John	21	NESW	1843-08-02	FD	NESW	R:JASPER
5006	BOGARD, Benjamin	3	NE	1854-01-07	FD	NE	R:CRAWFORD
5103	BRASSIER, Julien	7	L3	1846-04-10	FD	LOT3NW	R:INDIANA
5021	" "	7	L3	1846-04-10	FD	LOT3NW	R:INDIANA
5023	BROWNFIELD, Felix	16	L9	1854-09-21	SC	LOT09NESE	
5044	BROWNFIELD, Jacob	21	NENE	1849-10-16	FD	NENE	R:JASPER
5169	BURNES, William	9	W½SE	1852-11-27	FD	W2SE	
5168	" "	9	SWNE	1852-11-27	FD	SWNE	
5167	" "	9	SENE	1853-02-26	FD	SENE	
5166	" "	8	NE	1853-02-26	FD	NE	
5170	CHERRY, William	17	NWNE	1853-02-25	FD	NWNE	
5126	CODER, Robert F	15	NESE	1865-05-09	SW	NESE	
5015	COLEMAN, Daniel	17	SEN½	1853-02-25	FD	S2NE	
5019	COLLINS, Elijah T	7	SWSE	1852-09-03	FD	SWSE	R:OHIO
5018	" "	6	L2 (S½)	1852-09-03	FD	S2LOT2SW	R:OHIO
5017	" "	5	S½SW	1852-09-03	FD	S2SW	R:OHIO
5064	CROSS, James L	15	SWSW	1865-05-09	SW	SWSW	
5065	" "	22	NENW	1865-05-09	SW	NENW	
5134	CROWLEY, Samuel B	4	SW	1852-11-26	FD	SW	
5136	" "	4	W½SE	1852-11-26	FD	W2SE	
5138	" "	9	N½NW	1852-11-26	FD	N2NW	
5141	" "	9	SWNW	1852-11-27	FD	SWNW	
5140	" "	9	NWSW	1852-11-27	FD	NWSW	
5139	" "	9	NWNE	1852-11-27	FD	NWNE	
5137	" "	8	SE	1853-02-26	FD	SE	
5135	" "	4	SWNE	1853-02-26	FD	SWNE	R:OHIO
5007	CRUZAN, Benjamin	21	SESW	1843-01-17	FD	SESW	R:JASPER
5010	CRUZAN, Catharine	15	SWNW	1843-08-09	FD	SWNW	R:JASPER S:F
5124	CUMMINS, Robert	7	L1 (N½)	1852-06-17	FD	N2LOT1NW	
5125	" "	7	L2 (N½)	1852-06-17	FD	N2LOT2NW	
5104	" "	7	L2 (N½)	1852-06-17	FD	N2LOT2NW	
5061	DAVIS, James	10	N½SW	1853-02-18	FD	N2SW	R:OHIO
5063	" "	10	NW	1853-02-18	FD	NW	R:OHIO
5062	" "	10	NE	1853-02-18	FD	NE	R:OHIO
5036	DERLER, George	17	SESE	1865-05-09	SW	SESE	

ID	Individual in Patent	Sec.	Sec. Part	Purchase Date	Sale Type	IL Aliquot Part	For More Info . . .
5012	DONNELL, Con O	19	NW	1843-04-12	FD	NW	R:JASPER
5046	" "	19	NW	1843-04-12	FD	NW	R:JASPER
5013	" "	7	SENE	1852-06-11	FD	SENE	
5091	EDWARDS, Joseph	6	L2	1852-06-04	FD	LOT2NE	
5090	" "	5	L2 (W½)	1852-06-04	FD	W2LOT2NW	
5119	FERREE, Peter	6	W½SE	1852-06-14	FD	W2SE	
5120	" "	6	L1	1852-06-14	FD	LOT1SW	
5114	FORE, Joseph	6	L1 (E½)	1852-06-21	FD	E2LOT1NE	
5109	" "	6	L1 (E½)	1852-06-21	FD	E2LOT1NE	
5092	" "	6	L1 (E½)	1852-06-21	FD	E2LOT1NE	
5079	FRIEDLEY, John	17	SWSE	1852-07-02	FD	SWSE	
5080	" "	20	NWNE	1852-07-02	FD	NWNE	
5038	FROST, George P	4	SENW	1861-02-01	FD	SENWLS	
5037	" "	21	NWSW	1861-02-01	FD	NWSWLS	
5003	GILLESPIE, Abraham	22	SESE	1865-05-18	SW	SESE	
5070	HALSEY, James S	7	L1	1852-07-13	FD	LOT1SW	
5067	" "	5	L1 (E½)	1852-09-15	FD	E2LOT1NE	R:CLARK
5107	" "	5	NWSE	1852-11-10	FD	NWSE	R:OHIO
5066	" "	5	NWSE	1852-11-10	FD	NWSE	R:OHIO
5069	" "	5	L2 (E½)	1853-07-05	FD	E2LOT2NW	R:CLARK
5068	" "	5	L1 (W½)	1853-07-05	FD	W2LOT1NE	R:CLARK
5174	HAY, William	15	N½NW	1850-01-23	FD	N2NW	R:JASPER
5173	" "	15	N½NE	1850-01-23	FD	N2NE	
5172	" "	15		1850-02-28	FD	PTN2N2WA	R:JASPER
5016	HEADY, Eli	9	NESW	1849-06-30	FD	NESW	R:JASPER
5024	HINMAN, Fielding	21	NENW	1852-08-30	FD	NENW	
5025	" "	21	NWNE	1852-08-30	FD	NWNE	
5153	HINMAN, Titus	16	L12	1854-09-21	SC	LOT12NWSW	
5152	" "	16	L11	1854-09-21	SC	LOT11NESW	
5154	" "	16	L16	1854-09-21	SC	LOT16SESE	
5155	" "	16	L4	1854-09-21	SC	LOT4NWNW	
5156	" "	16	L5	1854-09-21	SC	LOT5SWNW	
5157	" "	16	L8	1854-09-21	SC	LOT8SENE	
5151	" "	16	L1	1854-09-21	SC	LOT1NENE	
5159	HINMAN, Titus M	17	NWNW	1852-07-20	FD	NWNW	
5162	" "	20	SESW	1852-07-20	FD	SESW	
5163	" "	9	SWSW	1852-08-30	FD	SWSW	
5158	" "	17	E½NW	1853-02-01	FD	E2NW	
5161	" "	20	NWNW	1853-07-02	FD	NWNW	R:RICHLAND
5160	" "	17	W½SW	1853-08-27	FD	W2SW	R:RICHLAND
5127	HOUSTON, Robert	5	N½SW	1852-09-03	FD	N2SW	R:OHIO
5128	" "	6	L2 (N½)	1852-09-03	FD	N2LOT2SW	R:OHIO
5081	HUFFARD, John	8	SWNW	1852-06-17	FD	SWNW	
5089	HUGHS, Joseph C	10	SWSW	1853-03-11	FD	SWSW	R:OHIO
5178	JAMES, William	22	NWNW	1842-04-27	FD	NWNW	R:JASPER
5143	JENKINS, Samuel H	19	SESE	1840-11-30	FD	SESE	R:LAWRENCE
5144	" "	20	SWSW	1851-01-24	FD	SWSW	R:RICHLAND
5142	" "	17	NESW	1852-09-25	FD	NESW	
5180	JOHNSON, William K	4	L2 (E½)	1854-04-27	FD	E2LOT2NE	R:OHIO
5181	" "	4	L2 (W½)	1854-04-27	FD	W2LOT2NE	R:OHIO
5088	" "	4	L1 (E½)	1854-04-27	FD	E2LOT1NE	R:OHIO
5179	" "	4	L1 (E½)	1854-04-27	FD	E2LOT1NE	R:OHIO
5085	" "	4	L2 (W½)	1854-04-27	FD	W2LOT2NE	R:OHIO
5109	KELLER, Nicholas	6	L1 (E½)	1852-03-26	FD	E2LOT1NW	R:JASPER
5092	" "	6	L1 (E½)	1852-03-26	FD	E2LOT1NW	R:JASPER
5114	" "	6	L1 (E½)	1852-03-26	FD	E2LOT1NW	R:JASPER
5107	LANGLE, Mathias	5	NWSE	1865-05-10	SW	NWSE	
5066	" "	5	NWSE	1865-05-10	SW	NWSE	
5102	LEEMON, Josiah	9	SENW	1849-05-18	FD	SENW	R:JASPER
5082	LEMASTERS, John	3	SE	1852-11-05	FD	SE	
5182	LINDER, William	20	NESE	1852-06-26	FD	NESE	
5022	LOGAN, Erastus	5	W½SE	1851-08-25	FD	W2SE	
5047	MAY, Jacob	19	L1 (S½)	1851-01-23	FD	S2LOT1SW	R:RICHLAND
5048	" "	19	L2 (S½)	1851-01-23	FD	S2LOT2SW	R:RICHLAND
5045	" "	18	SE	1851-12-31	FD	SE	
5049	" "	19	L2 (N½)	1852-01-03	FD	N2LOT2SW	
5012	" "	19	NW	1852-01-07	FD	S2LOT3NW	
5046	" "	19	NW	1852-01-07	FD	S2LOT3NW	
5051	" "	7	SESE	1852-06-28	FD	SESE	
5052	" "	8	SW	1852-06-28	FD	SW	
5050	" "	19	L1 (N½)	1852-11-29	FD	N2LOT1SW	
5185	MCCLURE, Zachariah	21	SENW	1840-12-01	FD	SENW	R:INDIANA
5186	" "	21	SWNE	1840-12-01	FD	SWNE	R:INDIANA

ID	Individual in Patent	Sec.	Sec. Part	Purchase Date	Sale Type	IL Aliquot Part	For More Info . . .
5175	MCKINNEY, William J	7	NENE	1852-06-17	FD	NENE	
5176	" "	7	W½NE	1852-06-17	FD	W2NE	
5177	" "	8	NWNW	1852-06-17	FD	NWNW	
5129	MCRENLEY, Robert L	15	E½SW	1865-09-25	SW	E2SW	
5130	" "	15	SEN½	1865-09-25	SW	S2NE	
5131	" "	15	SENW	1865-09-25	SW	SENW	
5132	" "	15	W½SE	1865-09-25	SW	W2SE	
5027	MERCERET, Francis	6	L1 (W½)	1853-01-05	FD	W2LOT1NE	
5028	" "	6	L1 (W½)	1853-01-05	FD	W2LOT1NE	
5146	MIDKIFF, Samuel	18	W½NE	1852-06-11	FD	W2NE	
5116	" "	18	L1	1852-06-11	FD	LOT1NW	
5148	" "	9	SESW	1852-06-11	FD	SESW	
5147	" "	18	L1	1852-06-11	FD	LOT1NW	
5115	" "	18	L1	1852-06-11	FD	LOT1NW	
5145	" "	18	NENE	1852-06-21	FD	NENE	
5183	MIDKIFF, William	16	L13	1854-09-21	SC	LOT13SWSW	
5171	MIDKIFF, William E	17	SWNW	1853-10-13	FD	SWNW	R:JASPER
5108	MILLER, Mathias	6	NESE	1852-06-22	FD	NESE	
5071	MURPHY, James T	8	SENW	1860-12-15	FD	SENWLS	
5014	ODONNELL, Con	19	L3 (N½)	1852-03-06	FD	N2LOT3NW	R:JASPER
5076	ODOR, Jeremiah	3	NW	1853-03-11	FD	NW	R:OHIO
5113	PICQUET, Joseph	7	L2 (S½)	1865-05-10	SW	S2LOT2NW	
5094	" "	7	L2 (S½)	1865-05-10	SW	S2LOT2NW	
5093	" "	17	NENE	1865-05-10	SW	NENE	
5133	POLLIS, Robert	19	W½NE	1843-06-22	FD	W2NE	R:JASPER
5053	RAEF, Jacob	15	NWSW	1865-05-09	SW	NWSW	
5058	" "	21	W½NW	1865-05-09	SW	W2NW	
5057	" "	20	S½SE	1865-05-09	SW	S2SE	
5056	" "	20	NWSE	1865-05-09	SW	NWSE	
5059	" "	8	NENW	1865-05-09	SW	NENW	
5054	" "	20	E½NW	1865-05-09	SW	E2NW	
5055	" "	20	N½SW	1865-05-09	SW	N2SW	
5117	RAFE, Nicholas	18	L2	1840-11-12	FD	LOT2NWPRE	R:LAWRENCE
5110	" "	18	L2	1840-11-12	FD	LOT2NWPRE	R:LAWRENCE
5118	" "	18	L3	1843-02-02	FD	LOT3NW	R:JASPER
5111	" "	18	L3	1843-02-02	FD	LOT3NW	R:JASPER
5112	" "	7	N½SE	1852-06-11	FD	N2SE	
5094	" "	7	L2 (S½)	1852-06-17	FD	S2LOT2SW	
5113	" "	7	L2 (S½)	1852-06-17	FD	S2LOT2SW	
5095	REEGLE, Joseph	22	NESW	1865-06-19	SW	NESW	
5096	" "	22	SENW	1865-06-19	SW	SENW	
5097	" "	22	SESW	1865-06-19	SW	SESW	
5100	REIGLE, Joseph	22	W½SW	1865-05-09	SW	W2SW	
5098	" "	21	SESE	1865-05-09	SW	SESE	
5099	" "	22	SWNW	1865-05-09	SW	SWNW	
5116	REILEY, Patrick	18	L1	1844-08-30	FD	LOT1SW	R:DELAWARE
5115	" "	18	L1	1844-08-30	FD	LOT1SW	R:DELAWARE
5147	" "	18	L1	1844-08-30	FD	LOT1SW	R:DELAWARE
5116	REILLEY, Patrick	18	L1	1842-12-12	FD	LOT1SW	R:DELAWARE
5147	" "	18	L1	1842-12-12	FD	LOT1SW	R:DELAWARE
5115	" "	18	L1	1842-12-12	FD	LOT1SW	R:DELAWARE
5117	" "	18	L2	1843-02-08	FD	LOT2SW	R:DELAWARE
5110	" "	18	L2	1843-02-08	FD	LOT2SW	R:DELAWARE
5111	REILLY, Patrick	18	L3	1843-06-06	FD	LOT3SW	R:DELAWARE
5118	" "	18	L3	1843-06-06	FD	LOT3SW	R:DELAWARE
5083	REPETTO, John	7	L1 (S½)	1853-06-01	FD	S2LOT1NW	
5150	RIGGLE, Simon	9	E½SE	1852-09-03	FD	E2SE	R:OHIO
5084	RIPPETO, John	4	L1 (W½)	1853-02-12	FD	W2LOT1NW	R:JASPER
5085	" "	4	L2 (W½)	1853-02-12	FD	W2LOT2NW	R:JASPER
5181	" "	4	L2 (W½)	1853-02-12	FD	W2LOT2NW	R:JASPER
5101	SANDERS, Joseph	16	L15	1854-09-21	SC	LOT15SWSE	
5060	SHIPLEY, Jacob	20	SENE	1852-10-19	FD	SENE	
5109	SMITH, Nicholas	6	L1 (E½)	1852-06-03	FD	E2LOT1NW	R:JASPER
5092	" "	6	L1 (E½)	1852-06-03	FD	E2LOT1NW	R:JASPER
5114	" "	6	L1 (E½)	1852-06-03	FD	E2LOT1NW	R:JASPER
5027	SPITZER, Francis	6	L1 (W½)	1865-05-10	SW	W2LOT1NW	
5028	" "	6	L1 (W½)	1865-05-10	SW	W2LOT1NW	
5026	SPITZER, Francis J	6	L2 (W½)	1852-03-29	FD	W2LOT2NW	R:JASPER
5149	STANDISH, Samuel	22	NENE	1865-05-19	SW	NENE	
5043	TOTTEN, Israel	21	SWSW	1841-11-15	FD	SWSW	R:MARYLAND
5072	TRAINER, James	19	E½NE	1843-04-25	FD	E2NE	R:PENNSYLVANIA
5074	" "	19	W½SE	1843-04-25	FD	W2SE	R:PENNSYLVANIA
5075	" "	20	SWNW	1843-04-25	FD	SWNW	R:PENNSYLVANIA

ID	Individual in Patent	Sec.	Sec. Part	Purchase Date	Sale Type	IL Aliquot Part	For More Info . . .
5073	TRAINER, James (Cont'd)	19	NESE	1844-02-01	FD	NESE	R:JASPER
5123	TRAINER, Phillip	16	L7	1854-09-21	SC	LOT7SWNE	
5122	" "	16	L2	1854-09-21	SC	LOT2NWNE	
5121	" "	16	L10	1854-09-21	SC	LOT10NWSE	
5184	VANOLMAN, William	17	N½SE	1852-11-15	FD	N2SE	
5086	VON OLMAN, JOHN	18	SENE	1852-01-16	FD	SENE	R:RICHLAND
5125	WEISCOPF, Louis	7	L2 (N½)	1850-07-30	FD	N2LOT2SW	R:JASPER
5104	" "	7	L2 (N½)	1850-07-30	FD	N2LOT2SW	R:JASPER
5087	WHITENACK, John	10	E½SE	1852-11-05	FD	E2SE	R:INDIANA
5103	WILKERSON, Ephraim	7	L3	1842-12-19	FD	LOT3SW	R:JASPER
5021	" "	7	L3	1842-12-19	FD	LOT3SW	R:JASPER
5033	WILKERSON, Gary N	16	L14	1856-03-29	SC	LOT14SESW	
5034	WILKINSON, Gary	16	L6	1854-09-21	SC	LOT6SENW	
5005	WILSON, Anna	9	NENE	1852-11-05	FD	NENE	S:F
5029	WOLFE, Francis	21	SENE	1853-02-26	FD	SENE	
5032	" "	5	S½SE	1853-02-26	FD	S2SE	
5031	" "	5	NESE	1853-02-26	FD	NESE	
5030	" "	21	W½SE	1853-02-26	FD	W2SE	
5039	WOLFE, George	3	SW	1853-02-26	FD	SW	
5040	" "	4	E½SE	1853-02-26	FD	E2SE	
5041	" "	5	NENE	1853-02-26	FD	NENE	R:OHIO
5042	ZELL, Henry	20	NENE	1852-10-19	FD	NENE	
5088	ZELL, John	4	L1 (E½)	1852-09-23	FD	E2LOT1NW	R:INDIANA
5179	" "	4	L1 (E½)	1852-09-23	FD	E2LOT1NW	R:INDIANA

Patent Map

T5-N R14-W
2nd PM Meridian

Map Group 20

Township Statistics

Parcels Mapped	:	184
Number of Patents	:	1
Number of Individuals	:	96
Patentees Identified	:	96
Number of Surnames	:	85
Multi-Patentee Parcels	:	0
Oldest Patent Date	:	11/12/1840
Most Recent Patent	:	9/25/1865
Block/Lot Parcels	:	57
Cities and Towns	:	2
Cemeteries	:	1

Section 6

Lots-Sec. 6
L1   FERREE, Peter   1852
L1(E½) SMITH, Nicholas 1852
L1(E½) FORE, Joseph   1852
L1(E½) KELLER, Nicholas 1852
L1(W½) SPITZER, Francis 1865
L1(W½) MERCERET, Francis 1853
L2   EDWARDS, Joseph 1852
L2(N½) HOUSTON, Robert 1852
L2(S½) COLLINS, Elijah T 1852
L2(W½) SPITZER, Francis J 1852

MILLER Mathias 1852
FERREE Peter 1852
ANTHOFER Andrew 1852

Section 5

Lots-Sec. 5
L1   ADAMS, Waldo T   1852
L1(E½) HALSEY, James S 1852
L1(W½) HALSEY, James S 1853
L2(E½) HALSEY, James S 1853
L2(W½) EDWARDS, Joseph 1852

HOUSTON Robert 1852
COLLINS Elijah T 1852
LANGLE Mathias 1865
HALSEY James S 1852
LOGAN Erastus 1851
WOLFE Francis 1853
WOLFE Francis 1853

WOLFE George 1853

Section 4

FROST George P 1861
CROWLEY Samuel B 1853
CROWLEY Samuel B 1852
CROWLEY Samuel B 1852
WOLFE George 1853

Lots-Sec. 4
L1(E½) ZELL, John   1852
L1(E½) JOHNSON, William K 1854
L1(W½) RIPPETO, John   1853
L2(E½) JOHNSON, William K 1853
L2(W½) RIPPETO, John   1853
L2(W½) JOHNSON, William K 1854

Section 7

Lots-Sec. 7
L1   HALSEY, James S 1852
L1(N½) CUMMINS, Robert 1852
L1(N½) REPETTO, John   1853
L2(N½) CUMMINS, Robert 1852
L2(N½) WEISCOPF, Louis 1850
L2(S½) PICQUET, Joseph 1865
L2(S½) RAFE, Nicholas 1852
L3   BRASSIER, Julien 1846
L3   WILKERSON, Ephraim 1842

MCKINNEY William J 1852
DONNELL Con O 1852
RAFE Nicholas 1852
COLLINS Elijah T 1852
MAY Jacob 1852

Section 8

MCKINNEY William J 1852
MCKINNEY William J 1852
HUFFARD John 1852
RAEF Jacob 1865
MURPHY James T 1860
MAY Jacob 1852
BURNES William 1853
CROWLEY Samuel B 1853

Section 9

CROWLEY Samuel B 1852
CROWLEY Samuel B 1852
CROWLEY Samuel B 1852
LEEMON Josiah 1849
HEADY Eli 1849
WILSON Anna 1852
BURNES William 1852
BURNES William 1853
BURNES William 1852
RIGGLE Simon 1852

Section 18

Lots-Sec. 18
L1   REILLEY, Patrick 1842
L1   MIDKIFF, Samuel 1852
L1   REILEY, Patrick 1844
L2   REILLEY, Patrick 1843
L2   RAFE, Nicholas 1840
L3   RAFE, Nicholas 1843
L3   REILLY, Patrick 1843

MIDKIFF Samuel 1852
MIDKIFF Samuel 1852
OLMAN John Von 1852
MAY Jacob 1851

Section 17

HINMAN Titus M 1852
HINMAN Titus M 1853
MIDKIFF William E 1853
JENKINS Samuel H 1852
HINMAN Titus M 1853
CHERRY William 1853
PICQUET Joseph 1865
COLEMAN Daniel 1853
VANOLMAN William 1852
ALMAN Von John 1852
FRIEDLEY John 1852
DERLER George 1865

Section 16

Lots-Sec. 16
L1   HINMAN, Titus   1854
L2   TRAINER, Phillip 1854
L4   HINMAN, Titus   1854
L5   HINMAN, Titus   1854
L6   WILKINSON, Gary 1854
L7   TRAINER, Phillip 1854
L8   HINMAN, Titus   1854
L9   BROWNFIELD, Felix 1854
L10   TRAINER, Phillip 1854
L11   HINMAN, Titus   1854
L12   HINMAN, Titus   1854
L13   MIDKIFF, William 1854
L14   WILKERSON, Gary N 1856
L15   SANDERS, Joseph 1854
L16   HINMAN, Titus   1854

Jasper

Section 19

DONNELL Con O 1843
POLLIS Robert 1843
TRAINER James 1843

Lots-Sec. 19
L1(N½) MAY, Jacob   1852
L1(S½) MAY, Jacob   1851
L2(N½) MAY, Jacob   1852
L2(S½) MAY, Jacob   1851
L3(N½) ODONNELL, Con 1852

TRAINER James 1843
TRAINER James 1844
JENKINS Samuel H 1840

Section 20

HINMAN Titus M 1853
TRAINER James 1843
JENKINS Samuel H 1851
RAEF Jacob 1865
HINMAN Titus M 1852
FRIEDLEY John 1852
BAUMAN Christian 1852
ZELL Henry 1852
SHIPLEY Jacob 1852
RAEF Jacob 1865
RAEF Jacob 1865
LINDER William 1852

Section 21

RAEF Jacob 1865
HINMAN Fielding 1852
MCCLURE Zachariah 1840
FROST George P 1861
HINMAN Fielding 1852
MCCLURE Zachariah 1840
BLAKE John 1843
WOLFE Francis 1853
TOTTEN Israel 1841
CRUZAN Benjamin 1843
BROWNFIELD Jacob 1849
WOLFE Francis 1853
BERLIN John 1851
REIGLE Joseph 1865

Richland

30	29	28
31	32	33

ODOR Jeremiah 1853 / BOGARD Benjamin 1854 **3** WOLFE George 1853 / LEMASTERS John 1852	**2**	**1**
DAVIS James 1853 / DAVIS James 1853 **10** DAVIS James 1853 HUGHS Joseph C 1853 / BISHOP Elisha 1854 / BERRY George 1852 / WHITENACK John 1852	**11**	**12**
HAY William / HAY William 1850 / HAY William 1850 CRUZAN Catharine 1843 / MCRENLEY Robert L 1865 / **15** / MCRENLEY Robert L 1865 RAEF Jacob 1865 / MCRENLEY Robert L 1865 / CODER Robert F 1865 CROSS James L 1865 / ANDREWS Luther T 1865	*Crawford* **14**	**13**
JAMES William 1842 / CROSS James L 1865 / ANDREWS Luther T 1865 / STANDISH Samuel 1865 REIGLE Joseph 1865 / REEGLE Joseph 1865 / **22** / BENNETT Benjamin S 1865 REIGLE Joseph 1865 / REEGLE Joseph 1865 / BENNETT Benjamin S 1865 REEGLE Joseph 1865 / GILLESPIE Abraham 1865	**23**	**24**
27	**26**	**25**
34	**35**	**36**

Helpful Hints

1. This Map's INDEX can be found on the preceding pages.

2. Refer to Map "C" to see where this Township lies within Jasper County, Illinois.

3. Numbers within square brackets [ ] denote a multi-patentee land parcel (multi-owner). Refer to Appendix "C" for a full list of members in this group.

4. Areas that look to be crowded with Patentees usually indicate multiple sales of the same parcel (re-issues), cancellations or voided transactions (that we map, anyway) or overlapping parcels. We opt to show even these ambiguous parcels, which oftentimes lead to research avenues not yet taken.

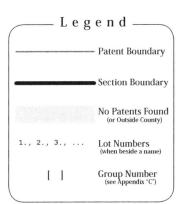

Legend

———————— Patent Boundary

━━━━━━━━ Section Boundary

▨▨▨▨ No Patents Found
(or Outside County)

1., 2., 3., ... Lot Numbers
(when beside a name)

[ ] Group Number
(see Appendix "C")

Scale: Section = 1 mile X 1 mile
(generally, with some exceptions)

Road Map

T5-N R14-W
2nd PM Meridian

Map Group 20

Cities & Towns
Raeftown

Cemeteries
Dark Bend Cemetery

6	5	4
7	8	9
18	17	16
19	20	21 Dark Bend Cem.
30	29	28
31	32	33

N 1975th St · N 2125th St · E 350th Ave · E 325th Ave · E 300th Ave · E 200th Ave · N 2150th St · E 100th Ave · 2050 Ave · Raeftown · E 50th Ave · E Jasper Ln

3	2	1
10	11	12
Crawford 15	14	13
Jasper 22	23	24
Richland 27	26	25
34	35	36

N 2225th St

N 2300th St

E 250th Ave

N 2200th St

1900E

Helpful Hints

1. This road map has a number of uses, but primarily it is to help you: a) find the present location of land owned by your ancestors (at least the general area), b) find cemeteries and city-centers, and c) estimate the route/roads used by Census-takers & tax-assessors.

2. If you plan to travel to Jasper County to locate cemeteries or land parcels, please pick up a modern travel map for the area before you do. Mapping old land parcels on modern maps is not as exact a science as you might think. Just the slightest variations in public land survey coordinates, estimates of parcel boundaries, or road-map deviations can greatly alter a map's representation of how a road either does or doesn't cross a particular parcel of land.

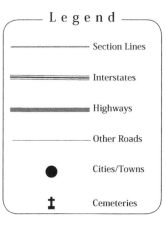

Legend

———————	Section Lines
═══════	Interstates
▬▬▬▬▬▬▬	Highways
———————	Other Roads
●	Cities/Towns
✝	Cemeteries

Scale: Section = 1 mile X 1 mile
(generally, with some exceptions)

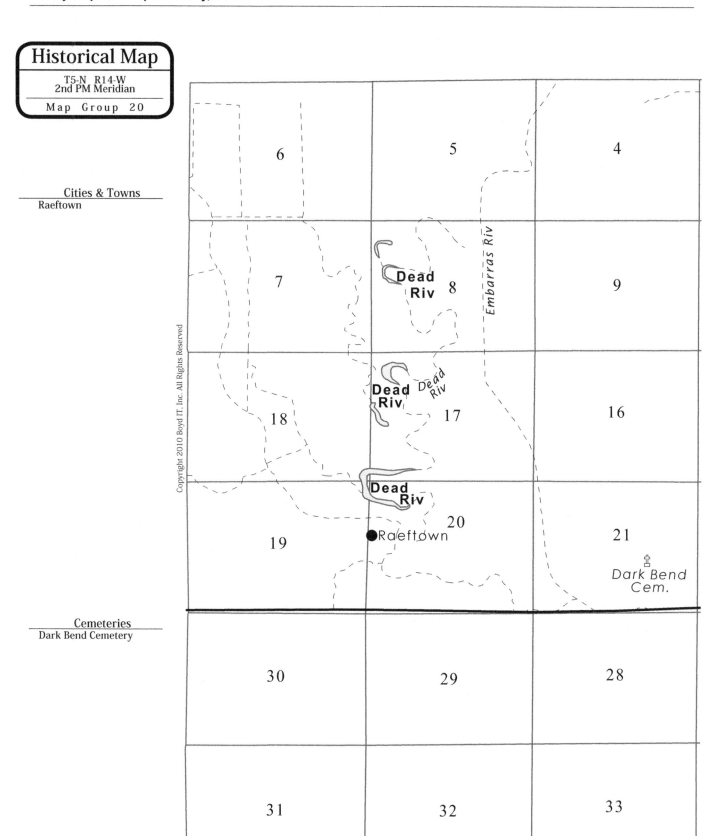

Historical Map

T5-N R14-W
2nd PM Meridian

Map Group 20

Cities & Towns
Raeftown

Cemeteries
Dark Bend Cemetery

6

5

4

7

Dead
Riv

8

9

Embarras Riv

18

Dead
Riv

Dead
Riv

17

16

19

Dead
Riv

20

●Raeftown

21

Dark Bend
Cem.

30

29

28

31

32

33

3	2	1
10	11	12
15	14	13
22 *Jasper*	*Crawford* 23	24
Richland 27	26	25
34	35	36

Helpful Hints

1. This Map takes a different look at the same Congressional Township displayed in the preceding two maps. It presents features that can help you better envision the historical development of the area: a) Water-bodies (lakes & ponds), b) Water-courses (rivers, streams, etc.), c) Railroads, d) City/town center-points (where they were oftentimes located when first settled), and e) Cemeteries.

2. Using this "Historical" map in tandem with this Township's Patent Map and Road Map, may lead you to some interesting discoveries. You will often find roads, towns, cemeteries, and waterways are named after nearby landowners: sometimes those names will be the ones you are researching. See how many of these research gems you can find here in Jasper County.

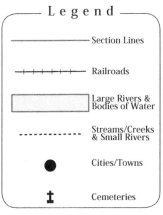

L e g e n d

———————— Section Lines

+‑+‑+‑+‑+‑+ Railroads

Large Rivers & Bodies of Water

‑ ‑ ‑ ‑ ‑ ‑ Streams/Creeks & Small Rivers

● Cities/Towns

✝ Cemeteries

Scale: Section = 1 mile X 1 mile
(there are some exceptions)

Appendices

Appendix A - Illinois Archives Abbreviations

The following abbreviations are used by the Illinois State Archives in describing the nature and locations of the land-patents in their "Tract Indexes" at www.cyberdriveillinois.com. Most line-items in the Patent Indexes in this volume will contain one or more of these abbreviations. When multiple abbreviations are used, no space will be found between each (and that can sometimes be confusing). Many of these are fairly easy to decipher, but many ambiguities exist. Only after reviewing a copy of the original land-patent can one be certain of the meaning of any given abbreviations.

Abbrev.	Description		Abbrev.	Description
A	assumed		COM	Commission(er)(s)
AA	acres assumed		COR	corner
AB	Alton & Shelbyville Railroad		CP	captive
AC	act		CPE	cape
AD	addition		CR	corner
AG	Agricultural College		CT	cattle
AI	alias		CY	city
AL	others		D	deceased veteran of War of 1812
AM	Alton & Mt. Carmel Railroad		DANE CNTY	Dane County
AN	Administrator		DD	date-of-deed
APR	Apple River		DE	date
AR	Army		DESR	Des Plaines River
ART	artillery		DG	DuPage
AS	assignee		DH	detached
ASC	associate		DI	description
ASM	assemble		DIIO	description incomplete
ASS	association		DINT	description notation
AT	attorney (lawyer)		DIV	division
AW	Alton & Shawneetown Railroad		DO	donation
B	block, outblock, inblock, bank		DP	date-of-purchase
BAP	Baptist		DPT	detached part
BET	between		DQ	DuQuoin
BL	block, outblock, inblock, boundary line		DR	doctor
BMR	Big Muddy River		DS	discount
BNK	bank		DT	district
BO	board		DU	Dutch
BR	British		E	East
BRO	brothers		E2	East half
BT	Baptist		EC	excess
BUXTON ISL	Buxton Island		EDGE	Edgewood
C	claim		EL	Eldena
CA	Catholic		EMP	emporium
CALR	Calumet River		END	end
CARB	carbon		EP	Episcopal
CE	center		ES	estate
CEM	cemetery		ET	and
CEN	central		ET AL	and others
CENT	Centralia		ETG	unknown symbol meaning
CFT	counterfeit		EV	Evangelical
CG	Congregation(al)		EX	executor
CH	Church		EXCPT	except
CHI	Chicago		F	feet
CHR	Christian		FD	federal
CI	Centralia		FEED	feeder
CK	creek		FEL	Fellons
CL	college		FFR	forfeited land redeemed
CM	Commerce Street, County Microfilm		FK	Franklin Street
CN	canal		FL	float
CNTY	county		FNB	First National Bank
CO	company		FO	forgery

Abbrev.	Description	Abbrev.	Description
FOR	Forrestor	MA	money assumed
FR	fractional	MAIN	main
FS	forfeited land stock	MANT	Manteno
FT	first	MANUF	manufacture(r)(s)(ing)
FUL	Fulton	MARS	Marshal(l)
FV	Fox River	MATT	Matthiessen
FX	Fox River	ME	Methodist
GAL	Galena	MID	middle
GD	guard	MIN	mining
GEN	General	MISSR	Mississippi River
GER	German	MLK	Milwaukee
GIR	Girardeau	MNLD	mainland
GLD	gold	MO	Missouri
GN	guardian	MT	military tract
GR	grand	MU	Minuscule
GT	Gratiot Street	N	North
H	heir of deceased veteran of War of 1812	N2	North half
HEG	Hegeler	NAT	national
HO	house	NE	Northeast
HR	heir or heirs	NEG	Negro
HS	Homestead	NM	name
I	initials	NMA	name assumed
IBL	Indian boundary line	NO	number
IC	included	NR	Nora
IL	inlot	NT	note
ILL	Illinois	NW	Northwest
ILLR	Illinois River	OA	Ottawa
IM	improvement	OD	Odin
IN	Indian	OF	office
INST	institute	OL	outlot
IO	incomplete	OT	original town
IR	Iroquois River	P	[unknown currency]
ISL	island	PA	paper
JL	Joliet	PE	Presbyterian
JOHNS ISL	Johns Island	PECK	Pecatonica River
JR	Junior	PEN	Pennsylvannia
KA	Kankakee	PET	petroleum
KANKR	Kankakee River	PLK	plank
KNOX CNTY	Knox County	PM	[unknown currency]
KP	Kappa	PNT	patent
KSRR	Kaskaskia River	PR	Plum River
L	lot, outlot, inlot, line	PRA	prairie
LA	Loda	PRE	pre-emption
LD	land	PRES	president
LG	lodge	PT	part
LI	listed	PY	payment
LIB	liberal	R	river
LK	Lake	RAILRD	railroad
LL	little	RC	recorded
LNT	Lieutenant	RD	railroad
LO	lot, outlot, inlot	RE	reservation
LOC	locust	REL	real
LOCK	lock	REV	ecclesiastical title, Reverend, Bishop, etc.
LP	Lockport		
LS	(military) land scrip or LaSalle	RI	reinstated
LT	left	RIC	Richview
LU	Lutheran	RIP	ripple
LUT	Lutheran	RL	release
M	money	RM	redeemed

Abbrev.	Description
RO	Roman
RP	receipt
RQ	relinquished
RR	Rock River or railroad
RS	residence
RT	right
RTW	right of way
RV	reserved
S	South
S2	South half
SA	saline
SAND	Sandoval
SANGR	Sangamon River
SC	section or school
SD	side
SE	Southeast
SECT	section (640 acres)
SEN	senior
SH	Shawneetown
SIDE	side
SIL	silver
SK	stock
SL	saline, slough or sublot
SM	seminary
SN	senior
SOC	society
SPR	Spoon River
SR	Sugar River
ST	state
STC	St. Charles
STCK	Stillman Creek
STIS	St. Isadore (Church)
STP	St. Paul
STPET	St. Peter
SUBD	subdivision
SUP	Superintendent
SURV	survey
SW	Southwest or swamp
SX	settlement
SY	sale
TAB	tabernacle
TB	timber
TE	treaty
TF	transferred
TIMLT	timberlot
TN	town
TOL	Tolono
TOW	tower
TR	trustees
TRA	transportation
TS	township
TT	tract
TX	tax
TY	treasury
UN	Unitarian
UNKWN	Unknown
V	void, canceled, etc.
VC	Vincennes
VI	village

Abbrev.	Description
VO	void, canceled, etc.
VOID	void, canceled, etc.
W	West
W2	West half
WA	warrant
WAR CNTY	Warren County
WB	Wabash
WP	Wapella
WT	Water Street
X	exclusive

Appendix B - Section Parts (Aliquot Parts)

The following represent the various abbreviations we have found thus far in describing the parts of a Public Land Section. Some of these are very obscure and rarely used, but we wanted to list them for just that reason. A full section is 1 square mile or 640 acres.

Section Part	Description	Acres
\<none\>	Full Acre (if no Section Part is listed, presumed a full Section)	640
\<1-??\>	A number represents a Lot Number and can be of various sizes	?
E½	East Half-Section	320
E½E½	East Half of East Half-Section	160
E½E½SE	East Half of East Half of Southeast Quarter-Section	40
E½N½	East Half of North Half-Section	160
E½NE	East Half of Northeast Quarter-Section	80
E½NENE	East Half of Northeast Quarter of Northeast Quarter-Section	20
E½NENW	East Half of Northeast Quarter of Northwest Quarter-Section	20
E½NESE	East Half of Northeast Quarter of Southeast Quarter-Section	20
E½NESW	East Half of Northeast Quarter of Southwest Quarter-Section	20
E½NW	East Half of Northwest Quarter-Section	80
E½NWNE	East Half of Northwest Quarter of Northeast Quarter-Section	20
E½NWNW	East Half of Northwest Quarter of Northwest Quarter-Section	20
E½NWSE	East Half of Northwest Quarter of Southeast Quarter-Section	20
E½NWSW	East Half of Northwest Quarter of Southwest Quarter-Section	20
E½S½	East Half of South Half-Section	160
E½SE	East Half of Southeast Quarter-Section	80
E½SENE	East Half of Southeast Quarter of Northeast Quarter-Section	20
E½SENW	East Half of Southeast Quarter of Northwest Quarter-Section	20
E½SESE	East Half of Southeast Quarter of Southeast Quarter-Section	20
E½SESW	East Half of Southeast Quarter of Southwest Quarter-Section	20
E½SW	East Half of Southwest Quarter-Section	80
E½SWNE	East Half of Southwest Quarter of Northeast Quarter-Section	20
E½SWNW	East Half of Southwest Quarter of Northwest Quarter-Section	20
E½SWSE	East Half of Southwest Quarter of Southeast Quarter-Section	20
E½SWSW	East Half of Southwest Quarter of Southwest Quarter-Section	20
E½W½	East Half of West Half-Section	160
N½	North Half-Section	320
N½E½NE	North Half of East Half of Northeast Quarter-Section	40
N½E½NW	North Half of East Half of Northwest Quarter-Section	40
N½E½SE	North Half of East Half of Southeast Quarter-Section	40
N½E½SW	North Half of East Half of Southwest Quarter-Section	40
N½N½	North Half of North Half-Section	160
N½NE	North Half of Northeast Quarter-Section	80
N½NENE	North Half of Northeast Quarter of Northeast Quarter-Section	20
N½NENW	North Half of Northeast Quarter of Northwest Quarter-Section	20
N½NESE	North Half of Northeast Quarter of Southeast Quarter-Section	20
N½NESW	North Half of Northeast Quarter of Southwest Quarter-Section	20
N½NW	North Half of Northwest Quarter-Section	80
N½NWNE	North Half of Northwest Quarter of Northeast Quarter-Section	20
N½NWNW	North Half of Northwest Quarter of Northwest Quarter-Section	20
N½NWSE	North Half of Northwest Quarter of Southeast Quarter-Section	20
N½NWSW	North Half of Northwest Quarter of Southwest Quarter-Section	20
N½S½	North Half of South Half-Section	160
N½SE	North Half of Southeast Quarter-Section	80
N½SENE	North Half of Southeast Quarter of Northeast Quarter-Section	20
N½SENW	North Half of Southeast Quarter of Northwest Quarter-Section	20
N½SESE	North Half of Southeast Quarter of Southeast Quarter-Section	20

Section Part	Description	Acres
N½SESW	North Half of Southeast Quarter of Southwest Quarter-Section	20
N½SESW	North Half of Southeast Quarter of Southwest Quarter-Section	20
N½SW	North Half of Southwest Quarter-Section	80
N½SWNE	North Half of Southwest Quarter of Northeast Quarter-Section	20
N½SWNW	North Half of Southwest Quarter of Northwest Quarter-Section	20
N½SWSE	North Half of Southwest Quarter of Southeast Quarter-Section	20
N½SWSE	North Half of Southwest Quarter of Southeast Quarter-Section	20
N½SWSW	North Half of Southwest Quarter of Southwest Quarter-Section	20
N½W½NW	North Half of West Half of Northwest Quarter-Section	40
N½W½SE	North Half of West Half of Southeast Quarter-Section	40
N½W½SW	North Half of West Half of Southwest Quarter-Section	40
NE	Northeast Quarter-Section	160
NEN½	Northeast Quarter of North Half-Section	80
NENE	Northeast Quarter of Northeast Quarter-Section	40
NENENE	Northeast Quarter of Northeast Quarter of Northeast Quarter	10
NENENW	Northeast Quarter of Northeast Quarter of Northwest Quarter	10
NENESE	Northeast Quarter of Northeast Quarter of Southeast Quarter	10
NENESW	Northeast Quarter of Northeast Quarter of Southwest Quarter	10
NENW	Northeast Quarter of Northwest Quarter-Section	40
NENWNE	Northeast Quarter of Northwest Quarter of Northeast Quarter	10
NENWNW	Northeast Quarter of Northwest Quarter of Northwest Quarter	10
NENWSE	Northeast Quarter of Northwest Quarter of Southeast Quarter	10
NENWSW	Northeast Quarter of Northwest Quarter of Southwest Quarter	10
NESE	Northeast Quarter of Southeast Quarter-Section	40
NESENE	Northeast Quarter of Southeast Quarter of Northeast Quarter	10
NESENW	Northeast Quarter of Southeast Quarter of Northwest Quarter	10
NESESE	Northeast Quarter of Southeast Quarter of Southeast Quarter	10
NESESW	Northeast Quarter of Southeast Quarter of Southwest Quarter	10
NESW	Northeast Quarter of Southwest Quarter-Section	40
NESWNE	Northeast Quarter of Southwest Quarter of Northeast Quarter	10
NESWNW	Northeast Quarter of Southwest Quarter of Northwest Quarter	10
NESWSE	Northeast Quarter of Southwest Quarter of Southeast Quarter	10
NESWSW	Northeast Quarter of Southwest Quarter of Southwest Quarter	10
NW	Northwest Quarter-Section	160
NWE½	Northwest Quarter of Eastern Half-Section	80
NWN½	Northwest Quarter of North Half-Section	80
NWNE	Northwest Quarter of Northeast Quarter-Section	40
NWNENE	Northwest Quarter of Northeast Quarter of Northeast Quarter	10
NWNENW	Northwest Quarter of Northeast Quarter of Northwest Quarter	10
NWNESE	Northwest Quarter of Northeast Quarter of Southeast Quarter	10
NWNESW	Northwest Quarter of Northeast Quarter of Southwest Quarter	10
NWNW	Northwest Quarter of Northwest Quarter-Section	40
NWNWNE	Northwest Quarter of Northwest Quarter of Northeast Quarter	10
NWNWNW	Northwest Quarter of Northwest Quarter of Northwest Quarter	10
NWNWSE	Northwest Quarter of Northwest Quarter of Southeast Quarter	10
NWNWSW	Northwest Quarter of Northwest Quarter of Southwest Quarter	10
NWSE	Northwest Quarter of Southeast Quarter-Section	40
NWSENE	Northwest Quarter of Southeast Quarter of Northeast Quarter	10
NWSENW	Northwest Quarter of Southeast Quarter of Northwest Quarter	10
NWSESE	Northwest Quarter of Southeast Quarter of Southeast Quarter	10
NWSESW	Northwest Quarter of Southeast Quarter of Southwest Quarter	10
NWSW	Northwest Quarter of Southwest Quarter-Section	40
NWSWNE	Northwest Quarter of Southwest Quarter of Northeast Quarter	10
NWSWNW	Northwest Quarter of Southwest Quarter of Northwest Quarter	10
NWSWSE	Northwest Quarter of Southwest Quarter of Southeast Quarter	10
NWSWSW	Northwest Quarter of Southwest Quarter of Southwest Quarter	10
S½	South Half-Section	320
S½E½NE	South Half of East Half of Northeast Quarter-Section	40
S½E½NW	South Half of East Half of Northwest Quarter-Section	40
S½E½SE	South Half of East Half of Southeast Quarter-Section	40

Section Part	Description	Acres
S½E½SW	South Half of East Half of Southwest Quarter-Section	40
S½N½	South Half of North Half-Section	160
S½NE	South Half of Northeast Quarter-Section	80
S½NENE	South Half of Northeast Quarter of Northeast Quarter-Section	20
S½NENW	South Half of Northeast Quarter of Northwest Quarter-Section	20
S½NESE	South Half of Northeast Quarter of Southeast Quarter-Section	20
S½NESW	South Half of Northeast Quarter of Southwest Quarter-Section	20
S½NW	South Half of Northwest Quarter-Section	80
S½NWNE	South Half of Northwest Quarter of Northeast Quarter-Section	20
S½NWNW	South Half of Northwest Quarter of Northwest Quarter-Section	20
S½NWSE	South Half of Northwest Quarter of Southeast Quarter-Section	20
S½NWSW	South Half of Northwest Quarter of Southwest Quarter-Section	20
S½S½	South Half of South Half-Section	160
S½SE	South Half of Southeast Quarter-Section	80
S½SENE	South Half of Southeast Quarter of Northeast Quarter-Section	20
S½SENW	South Half of Southeast Quarter of Northwest Quarter-Section	20
S½SESE	South Half of Southeast Quarter of Southeast Quarter-Section	20
S½SESW	South Half of Southeast Quarter of Southwest Quarter-Section	20
S½SESW	South Half of Southeast Quarter of Southwest Quarter-Section	20
S½SW	South Half of Southwest Quarter-Section	80
S½SWNE	South Half of Southwest Quarter of Northeast Quarter-Section	20
S½SWNW	South Half of Southwest Quarter of Northwest Quarter-Section	20
S½SWSE	South Half of Southwest Quarter of Southeast Quarter-Section	20
S½SWSE	South Half of Southwest Quarter of Southeast Quarter-Section	20
S½SWSW	South Half of Southwest Quarter of Southwest Quarter-Section	20
S½W½NE	South Half of West Half of Northeast Quarter-Section	40
S½W½NW	South Half of West Half of Northwest Quarter-Section	40
S½W½SE	South Half of West Half of Southeast Quarter-Section	40
S½W½SW	South Half of West Half of Southwest Quarter-Section	40
SE	Southeast Quarter Section	160
SEN½	Southeast Quarter of North Half-Section	80
SENE	Southeast Quarter of Northeast Quarter-Section	40
SENENE	Southeast Quarter of Northeast Quarter of Northeast Quarter	10
SENENW	Southeast Quarter of Northeast Quarter of Northwest Quarter	10
SENESE	Southeast Quarter of Northeast Quarter of Southeast Quarter	10
SENESW	Southeast Quarter of Northeast Quarter of Southwest Quarter	10
SENW	Southeast Quarter of Northwest Quarter-Section	40
SENWNE	Southeast Quarter of Northwest Quarter of Northeast Quarter	10
SENWNW	Southeast Quarter of Northwest Quarter of Northwest Quarter	10
SENWSE	Souteast Quarter of Northwest Quarter of Southeast Quarter	10
SENWSW	Southeast Quarter of Northwest Quarter of Southwest Quarter	10
SESE	Southeast Quarter of Southeast Quarter-Section	40
SESENE	SoutheastQuarter of Southeast Quarter of Northeast Quarter	10
SESENW	Southeast Quarter of Southeast Quarter of Northwest Quarter	10
SESESE	Southeast Quarter of Southeast Quarter of Southeast Quarter	10
SESESW	Southeast Quarter of Southeast Quarter of Southwest Quarter	10
SESW	Southeast Quarter of Southwest Quarter-Section	40
SESWNE	Southeast Quarter of Southwest Quarter of Northeast Quarter	10
SESWNW	Southeast Quarter of Southwest Quarter of Northwest Quarter	10
SESWSE	Southeast Quarter of Southwest Quarter of Southeast Quarter	10
SESWSW	Southeast Quarter of Southwest Quarter of Southwest Quarter	10
SW	Southwest Quarter-Section	160
SWNE	Southwest Quarter of Northeast Quarter-Section	40
SWNENE	Southwest Quarter of Northeast Quarter of Northeast Quarter	10
SWNENW	Southwest Quarter of Northeast Quarter of Northwest Quarter	10
SWNESE	Southwest Quarter of Northeast Quarter of Southeast Quarter	10
SWNESW	Southwest Quarter of Northeast Quarter of Southwest Quarter	10
SWNW	Southwest Quarter of Northwest Quarter-Section	40
SWNWNE	Southwest Quarter of Northwest Quarter of Northeast Quarter	10
SWNWNW	Southwest Quarter of Northwest Quarter of Northwest Quarter	10

Section Part	Description	Acres
SWNWSE	Southwest Quarter of Northwest Quarter of Southeast Quarter	10
SWNWSW	Southwest Quarter of Northwest Quarter of Southwest Quarter	10
SWSE	Southwest Quarter of Southeast Quarter-Section	40
SWSENE	Southwest Quarter of Southeast Quarter of Northeast Quarter	10
SWSENW	Southwest Quarter of Southeast Quarter of Northwest Quarter	10
SWSESE	Southwest Quarter of Southeast Quarter of Southeast Quarter	10
SWSESW	Southwest Quarter of Southeast Quarter of Southwest Quarter	10
SWSW	Southwest Quarter of Southwest Quarter-Section	40
SWSWNE	Southwest Quarter of Southwest Quarter of Northeast Quarter	10
SWSWNW	Southwest Quarter of Southwest Quarter of Northwest Quarter	10
SWSWSE	Southwest Quarter of Southwest Quarter of Southeast Quarter	10
SWSWSW	Southwest Quarter of Southwest Quarter of Southwest Quarter	10
W½	West Half-Section	320
W½E½	West Half of East Half-Section	160
W½N½	West Half of North Half-Section (same as NW)	160
W½NE	West Half of Northeast Quarter	80
W½NENE	West Half of Northeast Quarter of Northeast Quarter-Section	20
W½NENW	West Half of Northeast Quarter of Northwest Quarter-Section	20
W½NESE	West Half of Northeast Quarter of Southeast Quarter-Section	20
W½NESW	West Half of Northeast Quarter of Southwest Quarter-Section	20
W½NW	West Half of Northwest Quarter-Section	80
W½NWNE	West Half of Northwest Quarter of Northeast Quarter-Section	20
W½NWNW	West Half of Northwest Quarter of Northwest Quarter-Section	20
W½NWSE	West Half of Northwest Quarter of Southeast Quarter-Section	20
W½NWSW	West Half of Northwest Quarter of Southwest Quarter-Section	20
W½S½	West Half of South Half-Section	160
W½SE	West Half of Southeast Quarter-Section	80
W½SENE	West Half of Southeast Quarter of Northeast Quarter-Section	20
W½SENW	West Half of Southeast Quarter of Northwest Quarter-Section	20
W½SESE	West Half of Southeast Quarter of Southeast Quarter-Section	20
W½SESW	West Half of Southeast Quarter of Southwest Quarter-Section	20
W½SW	West Half of Southwest Quarter-Section	80
W½SWNE	West Half of Southwest Quarter of Northeast Quarter-Section	20
W½SWNW	West Half of Southwest Quarter of Northwest Quarter-Section	20
W½SWSE	West Half of Southwest Quarter of Southeast Quarter-Section	20
W½SWSW	West Half of Southwest Quarter of Southwest Quarter-Section	20
W½W½	West Half of West Half-Section	160

Appendix C - Multi-Patentee Groups

The following index presents groups of people who jointly received patents in Jasper County, Illinois. The Group Numbers are used in the Patent Maps and their Indexes so that you may then turn to this Appendix in order to identify all the members of the each buying group.

Group Number 1
ALEXANDER, Joshua H; AVERY, John H

Group Number 2
ALEXANDER, Joshua H; GREELY, Carlos S

Group Number 3
ALEXANDER, Joshua H; GRRELY, Carlos S

Group Number 4
ALEXANDER, Joshua H; RENICK, Robert M

Group Number 5
ALLEN, James C; KITCHELL, James A

Group Number 6
ANDERSON, Jacob; STEPHENSON, William H

Group Number 7
BAKER, Peter; HUME, Benjamin

Group Number 8
BARTLEY, David; BARTLEY, John P

Group Number 9
BEACH, Dennis; BEACH, Spencer; BEACH, Tamar

Group Number 10
BERRY, Myatt; BERRY, Wyatt S

Group Number 11
BOOTH, Beeber; CURTIS, Van Ranseler

Group Number 12
BOYD, Robert; HARMON, John

Group Number 13
BRISTOL, Andrew E; BRISTOL, Orla H

Group Number 14
BUSH, George F; BUSH, Margaret

Group Number 15
BYERS, Alexander L; BYERS, Robert

Group Number 16
CALDWELL, Albert G; CALDWELL, Robert J

Group Number 17
CARTER, Francis; HARRIS, Benjamin

Group Number 18
CLAWSON, Ephraim; CLAWSON, Josiah

Group Number 19
COMSTOCK, Norman; MCCUBBINS, Jack H

Group Number 20
COURE, George W; COURE, William

Group Number 21
CURTIS, Eli W; POWELL, John

Group Number 22
CURTIS, Eli; POWELL, John

Group Number 23
CURTISS, Eli; POWELL, John

Group Number 24
DAVIS, Precilla; MATHEWS, David W; MATHEWS, James; MATHEWS, Joseph; MATHEWS, Rebecca; MATHEWS, Sarah; MATHEWS, Thomas

Group Number 25
DE GAEGER, THEODORE; THADDAUS, John Juda

Group Number 26
DELOTT, Jonah F; DELOTT, Nancy Jane

Group Number 27
DIXON, James H; SELBY, Laban

Group Number 28
FLINT, Abigail; FLINT, John; FLINT, Sarah

Group Number 29
FOUST, Benjamin; FOUST, Charles

Group Number 30
GARDNER, William; GLOVER, Andrew J

Group Number 31
GORE, Esteline; GORE, James W; GORE, John A

Group Number 32
GORE, John A; GORE, Silas M

Group Number 33
GREEN, Abner C; GREEN, Jeremiah

Group Number 34
HAMIL, Amanda; HAMIL, John

Group Number 35
HARMON, John; WADE, Hiram; WADE, Lorenzo D

Group Number 36
HARRIS, Benjamin F; HARRIS, Bushrod W; HARRIS, William C

Group Number 37
HARRIS, Benjamin; HERRON, John

Group Number 38
HUFFMAN, Henry; PICQUET, Xavia

Group Number 39
HUME, John; MONRONEY, George

Group Number 40
KECK, Enoch; KECK, Frederick

Group Number 41
KETTLE, Abijah; KETTLE, George; KETTLE, Hulda A; KETTLE, Josephine; KETTLE, Silas; KETTLE, Solomon; KETTLE, William C

Group Number 42
LAY, Eliza; LAY, Martin

Group Number 43
LEACH, Elizabeth; LEACH, Joseph N; LEACH, Mary Ann; LEACH, Nancy N; LEACH, Nathaniel; LEACH, Richard; LEACH, Thomas; LEACH, Walter

Group Number 44
MATTINGLY, Edward; MATTINGLY, James; MATTINGLY, Jane; MATTINGLY, John

Group Number 45
MCCALL, Christley; MCCALL, William P; SELLERS, Mary

Group Number 46
MCCOLLUM, Daniel B; MCCOLLUM, John W; MCCOLLUM, Thomas D

Group Number 47
MCCOLLUM, Danil B; MCCOLLUM, John W; MCCOLLUM, Thomas D

Group Number 48
MICKENBERGER, Morris; STUBNER, Carl

Group Number 49
MYERS, John; THOMAS, John

Group Number 50
RAYLE, Thomas; THORNTON, Barbary A

Group Number 51
RILEY, John; RILEY, Owen

Group Number 52
RYAN, William G; TINDAL, Robert

Group Number 53
SEGELER, John B; WELDAM, Joseph

Group Number 54
SIGLER, Johann B; SIGLER, Johann H

Group Number 55
SNIDER, Henry P; SNYDER, Henry P

Group Number 56
SPEARS, Charles; SPEARS, William M

Group Number 57
SUTTON, Chapman; SUTTON, Hester E; SUTTON, Isaiah; SUTTON, Nancy; SUTTON, Susan E

Group Number 58
VANDERHOFF, Richard; VANDERHOOF, Richard

Group Number 59
WHIGHT, Eva; WHIGHT, William R

Group Number 60
WOHLTMANN, Carston; WOHLTMANN, Johann

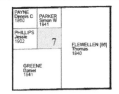

Extra! Extra! (about our Indexes)

We purposefully do not have an all-name index in the back of this volume so that our readers do not miss one of the best uses of this book: finding misspelled names among more specialized indexes.

Without repeating the text of our "How-to" chapter, we have nonetheless tried to assist our more anxious researchers by delivering a short-cut to the two county-wide Surname Indexes, the second of which will lead you to all-name indexes for each Congressional Township mapped in this volume :

For your convenience, the "How To Use this Book" Chart on page 2 is repeated on the reverse of this page.

We should be releasing new titles every week for the foreseeable future. We urge you to write, fax, call, or email us any time for a current list of titles. Of course, our web-page will always have the most current information about current and upcoming books.

Arphax Publishing Co.
2210 Research Park Blvd.
Norman, Oklahoma 73069
(800) 681-5298 toll-free
(405) 366-6181 local
(405) 366-8184 fax
info@arphax.com

www.arphax.com

How to Use This Book - A Graphical Summary

Part I
"The Big Picture"

Map A ▸ *Counties in the State*

Map B ▸ *Surrounding Counties*

Map C ▸ *Congressional Townships (Map Groups) in the County*

Map D ▸ *Cities & Towns in the County*

Map E ▸ *Cemeteries in the County*

Surnames in the County ▸ *Number of Land-Parcels for Each Surname*

Surname/Township Index ▸ *Directs you to Township Map Groups in Part II*

The <u>Surname/Township Index</u> can direct you to any number of **Township Map Groups**

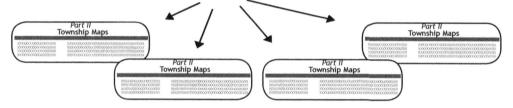

Part II
Township Map Groups
(1 for each Township in the County)

Each Township Map Group contains all four of of the following tools . . .

Land Patent Index ▸ *Every-name Index of Patents Mapped in this Township*

Land Patent Map ▸ *Map of Patents as listed in above Index*

Road Map ▸ *Map of Roads, City-centers, and Cemeteries in the Township*

Historical Map ▸ *Map of Railroads, Lakes, Rivers, Creeks, City-Centers, and Cemeteries*

Appendices

Appendix A ▸ *Illinois State Archives Abbreviations*

Appendix B ▸ *Section-Parts / Aliquot Parts (a comprehensive list)*

Appendix C ▸ *Multi-patentee Groups (Individuals within Buying Groups)*

Made in the USA
Las Vegas, NV
10 October 2021

32093167R00162